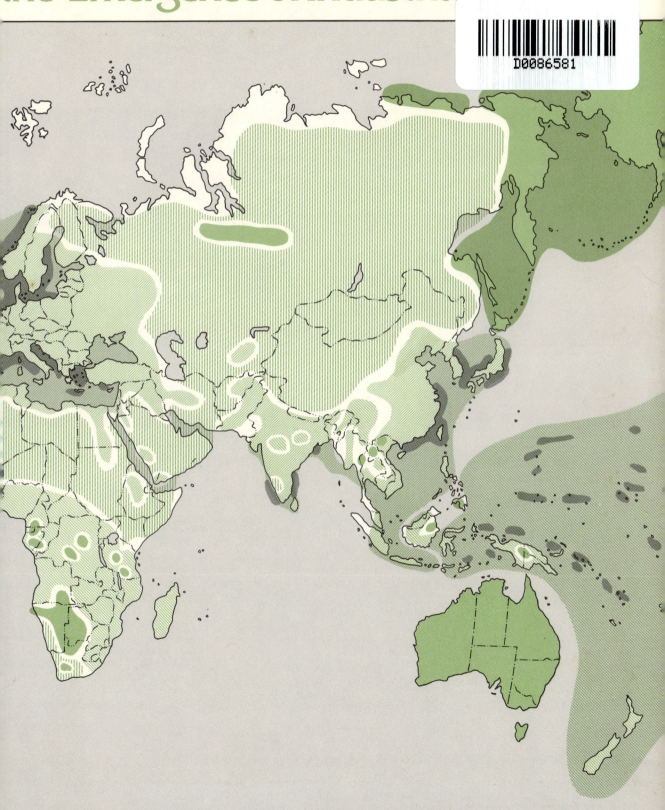

Introduction
to Anthropology

ROGER PEARSON

Introduction
to
Anthropology

5AO

HOLT, RINEHART AND WINSTON, INC.
New York   Chicago   San Francisco   Atlanta
Dallas   Montreal   Toronto   London   Sydney

Library of Congress Cataloging in Publication Data

Pearson, Roger.
Introduction to anthropology.

Includes bibliographies.
1. Anthropology. I. Title.
GN24.P34   301.2   73-8654
ISBN 0-03-091517-1

To My Family

Preface

During the brief history of anthropology there have been many different theoretical schools, each advancing its own distinctive integrative principles around which explanations of human behavior might be organized. Among these various theoretical schemes we have seen Social Darwinism, Boasian Particularism, Rivers' and Smith's Diffusionism, Schmidt's *Kulturkreise,* Radcliffe-Brown's Structural Functionalism, Malinowski's Psychological Functionalism, and the currently fashionable Cultural Materialism. All have made valuable contributions to the understanding of society, but none has yet been accepted as the essential foundation stone on which a comprehensive theory of human social behavior can be based. Most introductory textbooks in anthropology seek just such an integrative approach, attempting to coordinate the seemingly bewildering array of cultural alternatives. Their task is no less than to try to explain what men are, in all their variety, and how they became this way. Basic orienting concepts and theories are necessary in order to make this attempt at integration at all possible. This text takes the concepts of evolution and ecological adaptation as starting points for the analysis of long-term change in human life and the explanation of diversity in contemporary cultural forms.

The critical observer of our contemporary world will note that although men believe that they are directing the great technological and sociological changes that characterize our age, this is not the case. The history of men, as both biological and cultural beings, is the product of evolutionary forces. Men do not live as their earliest ancestors did. They have gone a long way from the level of the primordial protozoan and the early Pleistocene scavenger to become the wanton destroyers of their own animal kin and of the rich world of nature in whose bosom they were nourished. This pattern of evolutionary change, whatever its results, arises from the continuing efforts by all life forms to survive in the environment in which they find themselves.

The concept of ecological adjustment provides a foundation stone around which all other anthropological structures may be built. Biological, social, and cultural evolution are all moulded around the principles of ecological adaptation. This new ecological-evolutionary approach should not be confused with the intellectually immature evolutionary thought of the nineteenth century that saw mankind as the apple of God's eye, preordained for triumph and glory, a species that could do no wrong. Instead, the new evolutionists see men as members of a total ecological system that they may damage but cannot destroy, for the system is balanced in such a way that it would destroy them before they could destroy it. Modern evolutionary anthropologists see men as an integral part of a total life system which cannot be carelessly disrupted except at their own peril; indeed, they see the whole history of human evolution as having taken place within this ecological system, as a result of interacting biological and cultural adaptations which serve to promote the continuing survival of the species in a constantly changing environment.

Unfortunately, men have acquired immense powers to manipulate and modify their environment so recently that they have not yet had time in which to learn how to use these new powers with safety. Knowledge about human biological and cultural behavior can help teach us how to use these powers in accord with the vast ecological reality that constitutes our universe. This textbook is dedicated as a small contribution to this end. It is intended for the introductory course in anthropology in which both the biological and cultural processes of hominid evolutionary adaptation in time and space are examined. The time dimension begins with an account of life forms long before the appearance of "intelligent man" and is continued up to the present. The spatial dimension includes all of the major geographic areas of the world. A wide variety of cultural forms is considered, and some attention is given to the emergence of European culture, a subject often neglected in contemporary anthropological textbooks. In particular, an effort has been made to provide the beginning student with a total overview of the entire panorama of human cultural history, as conceptualized within the framework of ecological-evolutionary theory—an exposition which has been further reinforced by the linguistic survey contained in the postscript, and by the many maps and pictures inserted throughout the text.

R. P.

Acknowledgments

Although the preparation of a comprehensive text of this nature can be a great pleasure for the author, it is a pleasure earned at the expense of those around him whom he loves and whose lives are disrupted thereby. I would therefore like to thank my family for their encouragement during the many months that I have been involved in this project, and especially my wife for long hours of reading and discussion. I am also eager to thank David P. Boynton, a publisher of creative imagination and great intellectual strength. Similarly I have an immense debt of gratitude to editors George and Louise Spindler for their constant advice and invaluable criticisms, which have contributed heavily to the overall planning and scope of the text as well as to details. Such faults as the text contains, however, are wholly mine, and not theirs. Also at Holt, Rinehart and Winston, I wish to express my gratitude for the generous and very expert assistance of editor Ruth Stark.

I am further indebted to those several anthropological colleagues who read the text with care, and added to it with many valuable corrections and always useful criticisms, and in particular, to my colleague Dietrich Luth, whose abilities as a painstaking and reliable researcher have contributed heavily to the final revision of the pages that follow. I must also add my thanks to Frederick W. Brewer, who gave me the benefit of an anthropology graduate student's reactions to all that the text contains. Finally, but by no means least, one very large vote of thanks to secretaries Roberta Harrison and especially Mary Hill, who have labored over the manuscript for long hours and by now must know it as well as any student is ever likely to.

R. P.

Contents

Preface   vii

Acknowledgments   ix

PART II Ethnological Analysis 159

PART III Ecological Adaptation 299

Introduction
to Anthropology

INTRODUCTION

The Scope of Anthropology

ANTHROPOLOGY has been aptly called "the science of man." Combined from the Greek words *anthropos,* meaning "man," and *logos,* meaning "study," the term *anthropologia* was first used by the Greek philosopher Aristotle to convey the sense of a lofty, far-seeing view of mankind, in contrast to the more narrow, unimaginative, and self-oriented outlook of everyday life. Modern anthropology continues this tradition. Seeking to study all men and all societies—comparing one society with another and relating past societies to those of the present in an evolutionary sequence—the anthropologist endeavors to synthesize a comprehensive science of man and his behavior from all those more specialized fields of inquiry which are in any way concerned with the study of man and his works.

Not that anthropology is in itself an ancient science; it is actually one of the youngest. In the sixteenth century Magnus Hundt was still using the term *anthropologium* in the more restricted meaning of "anatomy," and in the seventeenth century the term *anthropologie* was used to refer to a supposedly inherent "human nature," organically rooted in the human mind and body. Thus, nineteenth-century scholars inherited the term *anthropology* in a sense analogous with what we today call PHYSICAL ANTHROPOLOGY—the study of human biology—and with the advent of Darwin, anthropology became even more closely associated with the study of fossil remains and the question of their relationship to living men.

Meanwhile the nineteenth century saw the rise of another academic discipline concerned with the study of man—SOCIOLOGY. A Frenchman named Auguste Comte, in particular, pioneered sociology, intending it to become a new "science of man" which would study human society systematically to find out how it worked, in order that the information so gained could be employed to rebuild society on a more "efficient" basis. At first Comte and other early sociologists such as Herbert Spencer cast their net widely and tried to found their new science of man on a broad base of empirical knowledge. In the course of time, however, the preoccupation of many of these sociologists with the search for tools with which to reform society, and to heal its "social ills," led them to concentrate their attention more upon contemporary Western society and its pressing problems to the exclusion of the debate concerning the origin of man and his different styles of life. Their pragmatic interest in the affairs of their own societies caused them to ignore the many reports that were beginning to reach Western scholars from explorers, colonial administrators, and missionaries concerning the strange ways of life of "primitive" peoples in other parts of the world.

It was at this point that anthropology began to supplant sociology as the overall synthesizing science of man. As anthropologists worked closely with archeologists in the study of the fossil remains of early human and protohuman societies, they could not but become interested in the various stone tools and pieces of pottery which were found in association with such early remains, for these seemed to indicate the course of migration and admixture of prehistoric societies. But when it became apparent that many of the tools used in extinct prehistoric societies closely resembled those being used by societies still surviving in the more remote corners of the contemporary world, anthropologists began to link the information derived from archeology to the reports coming in from explorers, missionaries, and colonial administrators. Adding information derived from historical sources, they now began to compile a broad and comprehensive picture of the total history of man and society, while sociologists by contrast increasingly narrowed their field of interest to the study of contemporary complex societies.

Nevertheless, in recent years it has become increasingly obvious that anthropology and sociology are both studying the same phenomena —man and his works—and that logically the two disciplines should never have become separated. It is impossible to understand contemporary Western society unless we have a clear and broad view of the origins and nature of man, and can see human society in an unlimited temporal and spacial perspective. Sociologists made the mistake of losing themselves in the present, even though the early pioneers tried to maintain a broader perspective, and ignored the evidence of extinct societies and what seemed to be exotic and irrelevant living "primitives." Anthropologists saw the vital relevance of the past and of the living primitive societies and so made anthropology the far-seeing "science of man" that Auguste Comte had originally intended sociology to be. Indeed, sociology can today be logically regarded as a specialized subdivision of anthropology, and although few sociologists may be prepared to concede this claim, most will agree that modern anthropology may advance legitimate claims to be regarded as a widely synthesizing discipline concerned with all information that in any way relates to the origin and evolution of the living varieties of men, their different life styles, and their manifold technical and artistic creations.

If he accepts this role as synthesizer, the anthropologist must attempt to keep abreast of the latest views in each of the many diverse fields of research that concern the study of man and his works, although he will usually tend to specialize in either physical anthropology or cultural anthropology. Thus PHYSICAL ANTHROPOLOGY—the study of the origin, evolution, and diversity of men as living organisms—is related to the study of ANATOMY, the physical structure of the human body; PALEONTOLOGY, the study of extinct forms of life in general; PALEOANTHROPOLOGY, the study of all extinct species that were in any way ancestral to living men; and GENETICS, the science of heredity.

Research in these areas suggests that man is a "social animal," in that his forebears were living in social groups and probably even possessed a kind of family system, long before they ever evolved to the level of *Homo sapiens,* or "intelligent man," as we so flatteringly call ourselves. No true understanding of human behavior can be acquired, therefore, without some knowledge of ZOOLOGY, the study of animal life in general; of ANIMAL ETHOLOGY, the study of animal behavior; and of PRIMATOLOGY, the study of apes and monkeys.

But the anthropologist must do still more than this. Man has developed certain peculiarities which are not shared by other animals to any marked degree. One of these characteristics is *speech,* the power of verbal communication; and the other is *culture,* the accumulation of ideas, experiences, information, misinformation, likes, dislikes, and attitudes that men share with each other and pass on from generation to generation as a result of living in groups and being able to communicate with other members of their group. Because of the steady accumulation of culture, men no longer respond directly with "uncultured" or instinctive biological reflexes to the events that impinge upon their lives. Instead human behavior is conditioned by the accumulation of ideas and attitudes which we acquire from other members of society, thus causing us to act in very "unnatural" ways. CULTURAL ANTHROPOLOGY is therefore concerned with the study of all aspects of learned behavior, including more instinctive biological behavior that has been partially modified by learning. Cultural anthropology embraces the study of human technology and man-made artifacts as well as the narrower field of social relations implied by the older term SOCIAL ANTHROPOLOGY, which is mainly concerned with the analysis of social organization *per se.*

Cultural anthropologists are interested in the origin and evolution of culture and society as well as with the description and function of different societies. ARCHEOLOGY aids the cultural anthropologist by providing him with information about past societies through the study of their material creations, and HISTORY provides valuable data with respect to those literate societies that left written documents and records. ETHNOGRAPHY, as the description of both living and extinct societies, is a vital area of cultural anthropology, and ETHNOLOGY, the comparative analysis of contrasting societies and cultures, attempts a scientific analysis of the collected data, seeking to reveal general principles of a scientific character.

In related fields, psychology, the science of individual human behavior, is obviously relevant to cultural anthropology and more especially to social psychology, which concentrates on studying the relationship between human behavior and the social setting, helping us to see how men behave differently in different cultures. At the same time, since culture is transmitted by communication, linguistics, the study of human language and languages, is relevant to any attempt to master the pattern of cultural evolution. Economics, the science which deals with the production, distribution, and consumption of goods and services is intimately linked to the social structure and the ideologies of a society, and the literature of a society is nothing more than a reflection of the overall culture. Even philosophy is the product of the society and culture in which the philosophers lived, so that a study of their ideas helps to contribute to a better understanding of their life and times. Nor does political science escape the anthropologists' net, for the political institutions of any society are an integral part of the culture and social structure of that society, existing only as a result of the interplay of social and cultural forces operating in history.

Seeing human society and human behavior as something which is not static, but which is instead a dynamic and constantly evolving "action system," clearly we must not allow ourselves to assume that our interest in the present and future makes it desirable to ignore the "past." One of our great problems is our tendency to categorize time into the "past," the "present," and the "future." Nothing can be

And comparing their imitations, speech and visages, I doubt many of them haue no better Predecessors then Monkeys: which I haue seene there of great stature.

The women giue their Infants sucke as they hang at their backes, the vberous dugge stretched ouer her shoulder.

And though these Sauages be treacherous, yet doubtlesse they esteeme more of an Englishman then of *Portugall* or *Flemming*.

This is sufficient to speake of the Inhabitants. I will adde one line of the Bay, and so goe on.

Anthropology had its origins in the accounts given by early European travelers and explorers about the various peoples with whom they came into contact. Unscientific and exaggerated though these sometimes were, many still provide valuable source material for anthropologists who want to know how the various indigenous people lived before their pattern of life was altered by contact with Western civilization. Illustrated here is a page from Sir Thomas Herbert's *Travalle into Afrique and Asia*, which was published in 1634 and contained one of the earliest known commentaries on the Hottentots of South Africa. (Courtesy of the South African Information Service.)

more misleading, for the present is an anachronism, an illusion arising from our failure to see the continuing thread of causality which operates in all things. The present is no sooner mentioned than it has gone. We are living not in the "present" but in "time"; we are moving constantly along that seemingly endless thread which runs from what we call the past into what we call the future. All human behavior takes place in time, and culture and society are things that "happen"; they comprise a continuous series of actions—of people doing things. A photograph taken of a group of people tells us something about them in a static sort of way, as they were at the moment the camera lens was opened, but it does not explain their relations with each other. The picture does not tell us how they came to be together, nor what they did after the picture was taken. To understand human behavior we must see it as a series of events, as a continuing causal nexus which runs unbroken from the past into the future without ever stopping for the "present." Like a man wandering in the desert, only if we turn our heads and spy out our earlier footsteps in the sand, can we know whether we are walking in a straight line or whether we are simply wandering helplessly in circles. It follows that whatever happens today has its roots in the past, and will affect the events of tomorrow; indeed, the acts and deeds of yesterday contain in embryo form the events of tomorrow. Anthropology must consequently be approached from a time-oriented, "longitudinal" or "case study" approach. Like the analysis of a rope, we must follow the strands as they intertwine with each other through time.

However, this does not mean to say that we cannot also sharpen our understanding by making descriptive "pictures" of particular societies at particular moments in time. Indeed, this is essential. If we cut across the "rope" of causality at intervals and look at the way the fibers are related to each other in cross section—how they stand in relation to each other at any one particular point along the continuum—we will have a better idea how society functions, and how all its parts relate to each other, than if we restrict ourselves to a purely historical or time-oriented study.

In preparing a textbook on anthropology, therefore, our problem is to describe something that operates in four dimensions—three in space and one in time—in a printed book, in which the flow of words runs in one dimension only. To solve this problem we have divided our text into three sections, the first of which we have entitled *The Evolutionary Background*. In this part we seek to describe not only man's biological origins, but something of the basic principles of evolution which govern all life forms, and which must be understood clearly if we are to be able to comprehend the nature of man and his relationship to the other animals. Evolution is essentially concerned with one thing only: the question of existence, or what is sometimes called *survival*. Existence is synonymous with survival and all biological change is subject to the one tautologous law of evolution, "that which does not survive, ceases to exist."

In Part II we carry our inquiry beyond the biological world into the "cultural" world, the world of learned behavior. Social life evolved among those species to whom group life enhanced the chances of survival; without group life the young of certain species might have failed to survive to maturity, to reproduce themselves, and so to perpetuate the species. But in group life there is the opportunity for learning, and CULTURE—the intergenerational accumulation of learned behavior—develops to reinforce the survival chances of the species.

Man's culture is one of the tools that help to keep him alive, and cultural behavior may be seen as an evolutionary function promoting survival in the ecological niche that the more complex life forms have built for themselves. Any attempt to study man and his behavior without a clear grasp of the fact that survival is dependent upon biological and cultural adaptation, and that any biological or cultural system which does not promote survival must inevitably become extinct, is not only futile but may actually reinforce unrealistic patterns of behavior that may endanger man's future chances of survival in a rapidly changing ecological system.

Since human social behavior is consequently subject to the same evolutionary principles that govern survival in the biological world—the need to adjust satisfactorily to changing environmental conditions—Part II of our text, entitled *Ethnological Analysis,* likewise approaches the analysis of the structural components of social and cultural behavior from an evolutionary viewpoint. Essentially it represents a projection of the evolutionary principle, as exemplified in Part I, into the area of social and cultural behavior, tracing the trend from the relatively homogeneous cultural systems of the Paleolithic to the cultural heterogeneity of Neolithic and Metal Age societies, and from the simplicity of early band-type communities to the almost overwhelming complexity of modern industrial societies. Culture is behavior, or at least it manifests itself in actions, and we have consequently sought to discuss the traditional, functionally oriented aspects of human behavior, such as kinship and economic, religious and political systems, in a time-oriented evolutionary or developmental sequence.

Part III is organized to reflect the ecological emphasis in current anthropological thought. This is based upon the realization that all aspects of human behavior are not only time-oriented in an evolutionary sequence, but that all cultural change like biological change must in the long run be adaptive. Societies that do not adapt to ecological change must eventually become outdated and disappear. There has consequently been an all important evolutionary trend in the history of mankind in which primordial hunting and gathering societies have yielded to horticultural, fishing, and herding cultures, and these have tended to give way to agriculture wherever the environment permitted. Agricultural societies in turn are in the process of becoming industrialized in our present world, and with each of these "advances" in man's methods of subsistence, his basic adaptation to the problem of survival in his ecological environment, his style of life, his beliefs, and his outlooks have also changed.

For this reason, Part III of our text, suggestively entitled *Ecological Adaptation,* attempts to survey the entire panorama of human history in a series of ethnographic pen-pictures of various societies at different levels of ecological adaptation. It seeks to synthesize the principle of behavioral "adaptation" as ultimately ecological adaptation, in an evolutionary setting, influenced by the cumulative growth of human culture.

Unfortunately for our peace of mind, we can no longer sit back in comfort and contemplate the history of evolution with unadulterated and complacent satisfaction as did the scientists of the nineteenth century. We cannot point to a steady record of "progress" from the "primitive" methods of primordial subsistence to the security of more "advanced" systems. All is not well with our contemporary world. In abandoning the "primitive," man has abandoned patterns of behavior that may offend our modern humanitarian susceptibilities but which possessed proven effectiveness from the point of view of long-term survival. Modern industrialization, which is discussed in the concluding chapter of Part III, is by no means the final and ultimate stage of the ecological-evolutionary process; it is by no means the final goal of human history, as so many assume it to be. From a survival point of view it poses many questions from which simpler levels of adaptation were free. Thus modern industrial man suffers from psychological and social tensions unknown in earlier tribal and kinship-dominated societies; far worse, modern industrial man also faces the possibility of ecological disaster—and even of genetic disaster as a result of the relaxation of natural selection—precisely as a result of his technological accomplishments.

Anthropologists, more than anyone else, tend to be aware of the fact that modern industrial society, both democratic and totalitarian, is in many ways far out on a cultural limb, way beyond the ecological niche in which man originally evolved as an intrinsic member of a balanced ecological community. All agree that it is human technology that brought man into this predicament, but few can agree on the solution. Some cry "onward"; some others even seek to cry "back." Maybe our cries are futile and the causal forces at work are not subject to human decision making, for it can be argued that we have no free will and that even the decisions we appear to make may be but a part of the total cosmic causal process. But whatever may be the case, there can be no denying that we are privileged to live at a moment of crucial significance in solar time, when the biological organisms we call men—the product of 3.7 billion years of evolutionary development—have acquired unparalleled control over their environment and are now in a position to manipulate this environment in an almost limitless variety of ways. Possessing these unaccustomed powers, and violently disagreeing on how they may be used, what men do to their environment and to their own cultural and biological heritage during the lifetime of the reader may well make the difference between the ultimate survival or the extinction of the human species.

For Further Reading

Harris, M., 1968, *The Rise of Anthropological Theory*. New York: Thomas Y. Crowell Company.

Hays, H. R., 1958, *From Ape to Angel: An Informal History of Social Anthropology*. New York: Alfred A. Knopf.

Lowie, R. H., 1937, *The History of Ethnological Theory*. New York: Holt, Rinehart and Winston, Inc.

Penniman, T. K., 1965, *A Hundred Years of Anthropology*. New York: Humanities Press, Inc.

Wendt, H., 1956, *In Search of Adam*. Boston: Houghton Mifflin Company.

PART I

The Evolutionary Background

CHAPTER 1

In the Beginning...

Science has not yet provided us with any final statement regarding the nature of time, matter, and the universe, and even though we know that our earth is approximately 4.5 billion years old, we are still not sure how it was first formed. On the basis of the available evidence, however, it seems probable that our solar system originated in a cloud of dust and gases located in an empty part of the Milky Way, and that through eons of time this mass of cosmic matter was slowly compressed by the force of energy derived from starlight. Eventually, gravitation began to accelerate the accumulation process, but because of turbulence within the cloud the final pattern of coagulation was by no means uniform, and the end result was the separate condensation of matter into a central sun—emitting light and heat much as at present—and a number of smaller bodies, one of which was to become our earth and another the moon.[1]

[1] For other theories concerning the origin of the earth consult J. A. Coleman, *Modern Theories of the Universe* (New York: New American Library of World Literature, 1963).

The Emergence of Life

For something like a billion years our planet was virtually lifeless; but all through this time chemicals reacted with chemicals, and physicochemical forces caused vast movements of matter so that the earth and its accompanying atmosphere were by no means still. At first the atmosphere which enveloped the more solid material comprised mainly nitrogen, hydrogen, water vapor, and methane, but a fall in temperature would have caused much of the water vapor to condense and to be drawn by gravity to collect as oceans in the deeper depressions which scored the uneven surface of the earth. Although there was no life, the basic elements required for life—*hydrogen, nitrogen, carbon, and oxygen*—are among the commonest in the universe, and the earth was a particularly suitable place in which these elements could combine to create organic living matter, for it was large enough to hold all four elements by the force of gravity, and it was just far enough from the sun to maintain a temperature at which water, an essential for life, could exist in liquid form.

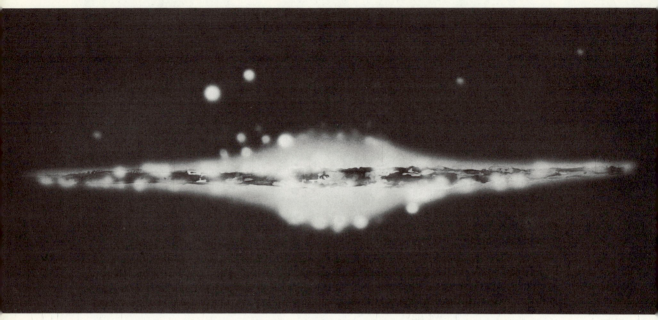

A galaxy of stars (viewed from an edge-on position) held together by mutual attraction. Our own solar system is but a minor element of one such galaxy, which is itself dwarfed by the vast distances of space that separate it from other galaxies. (Courtesy of the American Museum of Natural History.)

Although it is customary to think of life as uniquely distinct from nonliving matter, in essence both living material and nonliving material are subject to the same physical and chemical laws. Living, organic material is more complex in structure than inorganic material, but it is not easy, scientifically, to say exactly at what point in the transition from molecular simplicity to molecular complexity nonliving matter ends and living matter begins. Vital and continuing reactions may take place among nonliving organic materials which almost rival the activity of organic living matter in their complexity. Fire, for example, maintains itself, and may even be regarded as capable of reproducing itself in a certain sense. In fact, many of our ancestors worshiped it as a supernatural being, believing it to have life and a spiritual existence in its own right.[2] Yet fire differs essentially from life in that life is the product of organic catalysts, while fire contains no such catalysts.

Life is customarily described as an open system of organic reactions catalyzed by specific enzymes, for life is a process rather than a thing. This chain of reactions hinges upon the storage and release of energy in an operation known as *metabolism*. In plant life the metabolic process is known as *photosynthesis,* and involves extraction of energy from light and its storage in organic form. Among animals, by contrast, metabolism is directed toward the release of the energy stored in organic material, utilizing oxygen in a process which

---

[2] Although fire may be classified as distinctly nonliving by strict scientific criteria, a greater problem exists in the case of viruses. These contain amino acids but are unable to reproduce without the aid of biological host organisms. Whether viruses may be regarded as "living" organisms is seriously questioned by David J. Merrell, *Evolution and Genetics* (New York: Holt, Rinehart and Winston, 1962), p. 150.

we call *respiration.* In both cases the process of synthesis is achieved by minute protein particles constructed of *amino acids* of extreme molecular complexity, a single protein particle comprising literally tens of thousands of atoms. But what is unique about living organisms is that in addition to conducting complex chemical activities of this kind, they are self-duplicating, capable of both growth and replication, and also of initiating responses to environmental stimuli.

The analysis of a meteorite which landed in Australia in 1968—estimated to be of roughly the same age as the earth itself—revealed traces of no less than 5 of the 20 major amino acids present in life on this earth![3] This information is significant in two ways. In the first place it provides us with our first definite evidence of suspected chemical evolution in other parts of the universe, suggesting that, as we have long imagined, there may be life elsewhere in the universe. In the second place it implies that the long process of inorganic evolution which led ultimately to the spontaneous appearance of life may have begun even before the earth was born. Since even the simplest of primeval life forms represented the pinnacle of an extremely lengthy process of chemical evolution, the possible existence of amino acids at the time of the formation of the earth would help to explain the relatively early appearance of living matter.

The earliest simple organic material that was to evolve into life probably originated on the surface of the oceans, beneath the atmosphere of nitrogen, as minute chains of linked amino acid molecules which combined with nitrogenous bases, sugar, and phosphates to evolve into floating blobs of polymer jelly. The earliest metabolic process was photosynthesis, extracting and storing energy from light and releasing free oxygen into the atmosphere in the process, thus creating the oxygen in the atmosphere on which land animals are today dependent. At no time was the physicochemical evolution of the earth static, anymore than it is static today. It is, indeed, a sobering thought that life is no longer being spontaneously created on our planet, as the conditions under which it first arose 3.7 billion years ago no longer pertain. The life process has so changed the chemical environment that it has destroyed the conditions under which life originally arose and the spontaneous creation of new life came to an end long ago. All life that exists today is 3 billion years old. Once destroyed, that would be the end of it!

Biological Imperatives

Since life is nothing more than physicochemical metabolism when reduced to its simplest form, then it follows that there are certain BIOLOGICAL IMPERATIVES without which it cannot survive. These biological imperatives have controlled and shaped life since its earliest inception, and still continue to control the shape and behavior of all living things. They are natural laws that are immutable. The story of biological EVOLUTION—of the continuous genetic adaptation of organisms to their environment—is that of the search for successful responses to these imperative demands.[4]

Because metabolism is indeed a physicochemical process, the first biological imperative requires that for metabolism to take place

---

[3] Amino acids combine basic amino (NH_2) with acidic carboxyl (COOH) groups. Most, such as those contained in vitamins, are obtained from the environment, but others can be synthesized by living organisms. Twenty amino acids occur commonly in proteins, but several additional rare amino acids have also been identified.

[4] The use of the term *search* must not be taken as implying the existence of any teleological or directional guiding force operating behind evolution. The French philosopher Henri Bergson posited an *élan vital* or dynamic guiding force directing the course of evolution "upwards" and "forwards," but no scientific evidence for such a force has ever been revealed. In fact all evidence would indicate that the contrary is the case, and that evolution is shaped simply and solely by the criterion of short-term survival.

the chemicals concerned must be kept at an *appropriate temperature*. Chemical reactions occur only within certain temperature ranges, outside of which the properties of the chemicals may be so altered as to impede the metabolic process or even to set in motion undesired and destructive reactions. Thus metabolism cannot take place at temperatures that are too low, and indeed can be stopped for all time by extreme scorching heat. This was one of the many reasons why life first evolved in the oceans, for the great water masses maintain a fairly constant temperature all year round, whereas life on land faces more serious problems because of the wider temperature range.

But the right temperature is not the only biological imperative. Since the metabolic process essentially involves the extraction of energy from light in the case of plants and from organic materials in the case of animals, these and other resources utilized in this process, such as light or water or oxygen, must also be available. No life form can function for long without adequate supplies of whatever raw materials it requires for the metabolic process. For animals, *food, oxygen,* and *water* are biological imperatives, partial deprivation of which can result in a slowing down of activity, total deprivation bringing death. At the same time, contact with chemicals which might initiate *harmful chemical reactions* is also clearly undesirable, as for example contact between living tissues and nitric acid. All "poisons" must be avoided if life is to function effectively. Indeed, since we are dealing with physical realities and since especially the more advanced life forms constitute highly refined and delicately adjusted physical structures, *freedom from physical destruction* is another imperative for the survival of life.

This list of imperatives could be refined yet further by bringing in concepts such as radiation, but the nature of the problem is already clear. The survival of living organisms depends upon their ability to meet the challenge of their environment. There is nothing moral or immoral in this statement; it is simply an amoral fact. Nevertheless, if there is any yardstick against which we can hope to judge the behavior of living organisms it is surely this one invariable law. In the Domesday Book of Nature, behavior which is not conducive to the survival of the species brings with it its own inevitable nemesis—extinction.

Such is the nature of life that once the metabolic process has been set in motion there seems to be no reason why it should ever terminate, providing the biological imperatives are met. Life itself may have the capacity for immortality, yet the first life forms would probably have been eliminated soon after they emerged had not one of them stumbled upon an invention of the greatest biological magnitude—one which we all too often take for granted—the process of reproduction. Although no individual organism has yet succeeded in avoiding death, the road to immortality was opened by way of reproduction. REPRODUCTION is usually defined as the process by which new living organisms are generated, but in reality the metabolic life process is continuous between generations and is not broken by the act of reproduction. When an individual living organism dies, that is an end to it. But if it has been able to divide into two or more parts prior to its demise, then there is a very good chance that one at least of those parts may survive to reproduce itself in like fashion, and thus to perpetuate life and propagate the species onward into the future.[5]

---

[5] Evidence that evolution is only concerned with the survival of the species, not with the survival of the individual, is to be found in the fact that after successful reproduction individual organisms begin to lose their efficiency and eventually die of "old age." If individual longevity had any evolutionary value, natural selection would work to give us a much longer life span than we currently enjoy. The fact is that once mammals have produced their offspring and protected these to the age that they too can successfully perpetuate the lineage, the older generation has no further useful function, and natural selection ignores the progressive breakdown of the mental and physical capacities that constitutes the aging process.

The Living Cell

The basic unit of life is known as a CELL, a microscopic but clearly definable organism which is itself a complex aggregate of subunits comprising fats, carbohydrates, ash, nucleic acids, and proteins. Structurally the cell consists of a *nucleus* surrounded by a jellylike material known as *cytoplasm,* the whole of which is enclosed in an external membrane. Within the limits of this membrane the life process manifests itself in constant chemical activity, most of which is submicroscopic, but some of which can be actually discerned under magnification. In the case of plants this activity is primarily devoted to the synthesizing and storage of energy from light, while with animals, by contrast, metabolism releases energy from organic energy storing materials. Though it is the protein particles that are responsible for synthesis, the overall pattern of activity in the cell is directed by the nucleic acids, and in particular by *ribonucleic acid,* commonly known as RNA, which is transfused from the nucleus to the cytoplasm and carries with it the coded directions that control the metabolic process.

Within the nucleus is another nucleic acid known as DNA, or *deoxyribonucleic acid,* that is the basic component of the genetic mechanism conventionally called genes. GENES were formerly regarded as discrete particles and as the basic units of heredity. Today we know that genes as such do not exist, for recent advances in biochemistry have shown that the DNA molecule comprises a pair of equidistant but entwined *helices* or spirals which are connected by chemical bases of sugar and phosphate. The genetic message is conveyed in *codons,* combinations of these paired bases, which in a complex living organism such as man may number up to 5 million.[6] Since these

Man in his environment—the universe. Organic life may seem microscopic in proportion to the mass of inorganic material distributed throughout the vastness of the universe, but evolution has endowed man with a seemingly unique heritage of intellectual and behavioral versatility. The key to long-term survival may well depend on man's ability to evolve from being a mere passenger on "space ship earth," wantonly consuming the available resources, to becoming a rational crewman, husbanding the supplies of fuel and other raw materials. (Courtesy of the American Museum of Natural History.)

base pairs operate in ordered sequences, the variety of the genetic message is virtually as infinite as the number of different statements that can be made in the English language through the rearrangement of letters and

[6] Genetic science earlier assumed a total of around 20,000 genes in man. Research into the chemistry of the DNA molecule has therefore revealed a far greater potential for genetic variability in man than was formerly realized. For a brief explanation of modern genetic theory read F. H. C. Crick, "The Genetic Code III," *Scientific American* 215:55–62 (1966).

words, a virtually incalculable variety of combinations. However, research into the chemistry of the gene is still at an early stage, and it is still customary to use the established concept of the "gene" when discussing genetics, since this term does effectively help to conceptualize the genetic process.

It is consequently the DNA that bears the primary responsibility for storing and transmitting structural and behavioral directions from generation to generation, thus ensuring that succeeding generations will generally resemble their predecessors in both structure and function. In order to permit precise replication of the daughter cells at the time of reproduction, this DNA is carried within the nucleus of a cell in threadlike bodies known as *chromosomes*. Storing the metabolic instructions within the DNA and being responsible for generating the RNA which carries these instructions to the cytoplasm, the nucleus may therefore be regarded as the operations center for the entire cell.

Growth and Replication

The very earliest forms of life comprised nothing more than single cells, known as *protista*, not all exactly the same but all basically as we have just described. For protista, reproduction is relatively simple. Using the older terminology of the gene and chromosome, we may say that the genetic message is encoded within the "genes," which are arranged in lineal order along the threadlike chromosome within the nucleus. In reproduction the chromosomes duplicate themselves into two equal sets, each carrying in its array of genes a complete copy of the genetic message. When this is done, the two sets of chromosomes move to opposite ends of the nucleus and the nucleus divides. The separation of the two parts of the nucleus, a process known as *mitosis*, is followed by a corresponding division of the surrounding cytoplasm, and when the parent organism

finally splits into two equal parts, the resultant daughter cells will be complete and fully adult in every way. They will also be identical twins carrying identical genetic messages in their respective nuclei.

This type of reproduction involves nothing more than a division of a single parent cell. It is the universal pattern of reproduction for unicellular plants and animals, and is also the process by which the living cells in our own body replicate themselves in growth and in the replacement of worn-out tissue. Cancer, it is interesting to note in passing, results from an unplanned, runaway replication of cells which in a highly complex and delicately refined organism can obstruct the proper working of the total system to the point that it may prove fatal.

Although the process of replication by mitosis is normally extremely precise, errors can sometimes occur in the division of the chromosomes, so that the two parts will not be precisely equal and will not carry identical messages. In addition, sudden variations can arise in the atomic structure of the DNA contained within the genes due to exposure to certain kinds of radiation and other causes not yet fully identified that result in arbitrary changes in the genetic message known as *mutations*. Following either chromosome error or mutation, the genetic character of subsequent offspring inheriting the mutant condition will also be affected, and all future offspring will be liable to inherit the new structural and behavioral formula.

With the possible exception of ultramicroscopic viruses that penetrate and reproduce within living cells, unicellular protista were the only type of life that appears to have existed from 3.7 to 1.2 billion years ago—two thirds of the total span of life on this earth. At this level most organisms were completely autonomous, totally individual and independent, even reproducing without the cooperation of other organisms. However, because of mutations and

FIG. 1   EVOLUTIONARY TIME CHART

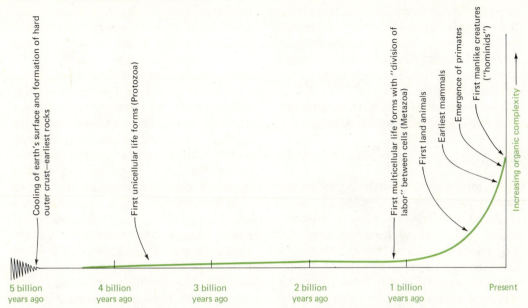

errors in chromosome division, protista did develop in many different directions and today there are no less than 70,000 different varieties of unicellular organisms in our world. Directly relevant to the history of man, however, is the fact that certain of these mutations led to the eventual appearance, around 1.2 billion years ago, of multicellular life forms—larger organisms comprising an aggregate of specialized cells—which we know collectively as metazoa.

Metazoa presumably resulted from a genetic irregularity affecting the reproductive process which caused the two daughter cells to remain attached to each other after division of the parent cell instead of separating in the usual fashion. The new instructions would have been transmitted to the subsequent generations of the mutant organism, so that new multicellular life forms arose which were actually colonies of daughter cells that had failed to separate after division. At first such multicellular life forms were merely an accumulation of identical cells, each seeking its own raw materials

and continuing its own metabolic process in the manner of sponges. Later on, however, further mutations were to result in a diversification of the function of the various cells in such a colony, and so the evolutionary process continued until mutually cooperating and highly specialized masses of cells appeared which were controlled by a central nervous system, thus providing the basis for further evolution leading eventually to those higher forms of life from which man himself evolved.

Although individual cells can replicate themselves simply by mitosis, multicellular life forms are faced with many new problems, and a more sophisticated system of SEXUAL REPRODUCTION became common, involving a specialization of individual organisms in male and female roles. Sexual reproduction is effected when a specialized reproductive cell leaves the male organism to unite with a similarly specialized reproductive cell within or on the surface of the female organism. As a result of a process known as *meiosis,* the offspring receive only half of their genetic heritage from each respective parent organism, and thus will not replicate either parent precisely. The changes that arise from mutations and chromosomal error, and the more limited variability derived from sexual reproduction, have played a significant role in the history of life, for if all offspring were exact replicas of their parents, there could have been no evolution.

Evolution and Genetics

It is easy to see that mutations play an especially important role in introducing the structural and functional variability which makes evolution possible, but this is only one part of the evolutionary process. Not all variability is desirable; in fact, the greater part of it is undesirable. EVOLUTION may be defined as the process of organic change by which new forms are constantly arising and replacing others less suited to survive in a state of competition. But random change itself achieves nothing, and most mutant forms may be expected to detract from efficiency rather than the reverse, especially in the case of highly sophisticated and intricately refined complex organisms. In many such cases mutations prevent pregnancy or else result in miscarriage. In other cases the mutant offspring are so handicapped by their lowered efficiency that they are eliminated before they can reproduce themselves. Fortunately, all organisms tend to produce more offspring than the environment can accommodate and in the resulting competition for the available resources, a substantial proportion die off before they can reproduce themselves. When mutations and other genetic variations create disparities within a population, those individuals which are less well equipped to survive in the prevailing environment are more likely to be eliminated than those better equipped to meet the challenge of survival.

NATURAL SELECTION, the elimination of those genes least favored to promote survival in the prevailing environment by selective forces which prevent the carriers of such genes from reproducing, thereby bringing about a reduction in the frequency of such genes in the succeeding generations, is an essential concomitant to evolution. Without it there can be no biological progress from simpler unicellular life forms toward more complex life forms capable of more varied responses to different stimuli, and therefore capable of surviving considerable changes in the environment. In fact, if the pruning effect of natural selection is temporarily relaxed, genetic deterioration sets in. Mutations are a constant factor in all populations and unless mutant forms which are inimical to the survival of an organism in its particular environment are weeded out, a GENETIC LOAD of undesirable genes will build up, promising eventual disaster.[7] Natural selection may be temporarily relaxed, but in the long run its ruthless impact cannot be evaded.

The selective process is complicated by the fact that every sexually reproducing organism possesses in its *genotype*, or complete genetic message, two genes for each inherited quality. However, in its own physical makeup—in its own *phenotype*—it is frequently shaped by only one of these two genes. Thus an organism may pass on either gene to its offspring, but will usually be shaped phenotypically by only one. When two disparate genes are paired in the genotype, one of these genes may be

[7] The concept of "genetic load" is one of the more fiercely debated areas in contemporary human genetics. Some authors such as Bruce Wallace, *Genetic Load; Its Biological and Conceptual Aspects* (Englewood Cliffs, N.J.: Prentice-Hall, Inc., 1970), believe that the situation will not necessarily become critical in the near future. Others such as H. J. Müller, "Our Load of Mutations," *American Journal of Human Genetics* 2:111–176 (1950), and J. Marvin Weller, *The Course of Evolution* (New York: McGraw-Hill Book Co., 1969), p. 654, stress the opinion that the "relaxation of natural selection" in modern societies must inevitably result in a buildup of genetic load in contemporary human populations.

dominant and the other may be *recessive*. Dominant genes are so named because when combined in the genotype with recessive genes, it is the dominant gene which will shape the phenotype or actual structure of the organism. Recessive genes only shape the phenotype when the organism inherits a pair of matching recessive genes.

Let us assume that an adverse mutation causes genetic "damage" in an animal population—resulting, in an "unhealthy" or disadvantageous gene that will cause offspring to be born without arms and legs. If the disadvantageous gene is dominant it will be quickly eliminated by natural selection, for any offspring that inherit this gene will themselves (phenotypically) be armless and legless, and in a natural state will be unlikely to live to pass this gene on to a third generation. In the case of recessive genes, however, natural selection works more slowly, for the recessive gene can be passed on to successive generations, dormant in the genotype, as a part of the genetic load of disadvantageous genes which all populations carry. It will only reveal itself in the phenotype when two of these disadvantageous recessive genes come together in the genotype. When the breeding population or total *gene pool* is small, as was commonly the case prior to the coming of industrialization, close inbreeding brings such recessive genes together and produces defectives (the "village idiots" of popular tradition being an example of the process).[8] Since these defectives are less likely to reproduce, the stock is thereby "pruned" of deleterious genes continuously. Outbreeding, by introducing new and possibly more healthy genes into a weak lineage, can save the weak lineage—but only at the cost of infecting the healthy line. Deleterious genes can only be eliminated by the failure of the carrying individual to reproduce. Close inbreeding, which is the rule among most higher life forms living in a natural environment, facilitates the natural selection process by which disadvantageous recessive genes are kept to a tolerable level in a feral population.[9]

The Evolutionary Process

Although mutations and other alterations in the genetic material, such as "crossing-over" (the disruption of existing gene linkages), appear to occur at random without meaningful direction, natural selection has imposed a definite pattern upon evolution, so that three distinct trends, tendencies, or directions may be discerned in the evolutionary process. These are: adaptation, diversification, and increasing complexity.

Adaptation expresses itself in the tendency for all life forms to become anatomically and

[8] See H. Eldon Sutton, *An Introduction to Human Genetics* (New York: Holt, Rinehart and Winston, Inc., 1965), pp. 242-243, on the effects of inbreeding combined with rigorous natural selection. As Ernst Mayr, *Animal Species and Evolution* (Cambridge, Mass.: Harvard University Press, 1963), expresses it, outbreeding merely "postpones the day of reckoning."

[9] If each phenotypical characteristic were controlled by a single gene operating independently, the genetic process behind natural selection would be simple. However, the fact is that not all genes reveal a straightforward dominant-recessive relationship to each other. Evolution has tended to produce cooperating groups of genes, operatively linked together. Any disruption of these *supergenes* can produce physiological disharmonies, especially in complex organisms. Furthermore the same gene may have several different phenotypical effects, some deleterious and some advantageous to survival. In such cases, the elimination of the gene by the death of carriers who inherit it in pure or homozygous form may be counterbalanced by the superior survival potential of those who inherit it in the heterozygous form, and we are confronted with the concept of a *balanced polymorphism*, discussed in Chapter 11. In such cases natural selection prevents the deleterious gene from dominating the total gene pool but never eliminates it, because of its beneficial effect on the phenotype when inherited in combination with a disparate gene. (See L. N. Morris, *Human Populations, Genetic Variation and Evolution*. (San Francisco: Chandler Publishing Company, 1971), pp. 202-220.

FIG. 2   HOW NATURAL SELECTION OPERATES ON THE PHENOTYPE

Natural Selection can operate only on characteristics which manifest themselves in the phenotype. Deleterious *dominant* genes are rapidly weeded out of the gene pool when natural selection operates freely, but deleterious *recessive* genes (which show themselves in the phenotype only when combined in a homozygous condition) are most effectively eliminated in relatively small, inbreeding populations. Deleterious recessive genes can never be completely eliminated from the gene pool, but under conditions of natural selection their incidence is kept down to a relatively low level.

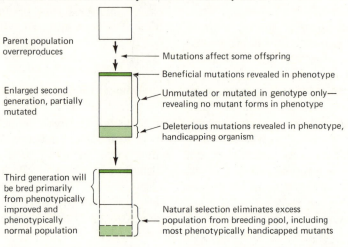

Parent population overreproduces

Mutations affect some offspring

Beneficial mutations revealed in phenotype

Enlarged second generation, partially mutated

Unmutated or mutated in genotype only— revealing no mutant forms in phenotype

Deleterious mutations revealed in phenotype, handicapping organism

Third generation will be bred primarily from phenotypically improved and phenotypically normal population

Natural selection eliminates excess population from breeding pool, including most phenotypically handicapped mutants

Elimination of Disadvantageous Dominant Genes

Elimination of Disadvantageous Recessive Genes

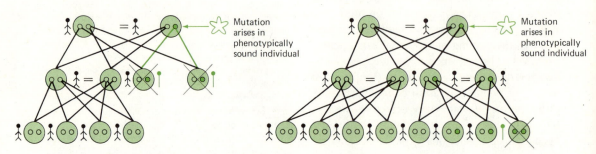

Mutation arises in phenotypically sound individual

Mutation arises in phenotypically sound individual

In this diagram it is supposed that a mutation causing the birth of armless and legless offspring arises in a dominant genetic form. Any offspring inheriting this mutant gene will be phenotypically armless and legless. Natural selection prevents these individuals from contributing to the gene pool of the succeeding generations and the disadvantageous gene is consequently speedily eliminated from the gene pool.

When disadvantageous genes are recessive, outbreeding with "healthy" stock will ensure that the gene does not occur in a homozygous condition in the second generation, which will comprise phenotypically "healthy" individuals. But the disadvantageous recessive genes remain in the gene pool. Only when brought together by close inbreeding, can such recessive genes be eliminated by natural selection.

physiologically adjusted to their environment when subjected to a constant pattern of natural selection over a succession of generations. When constant and unchanging selective forces repeatedly weed out all mutant forms less suited to survive in that environment, and consistently favor a particular combination of characteristics, a new variety of organisms will evolve which are "adapted" to that environment. Once this process of adaptation is complete, if there are no further essential changes in the environment, the organism may thereafter remain remarkably stable; crocodiles, for example, have hardly changed over the past 70 million years. Any deviant forms will necessarily represent less efficient variations from the more successful model and will be less competitive than the phenotypically standard organisms which in such cases may be regarded as having reached a stage of *genetic equilibrium*.

Evolution also implies a second trend. The process of evolutionary change leads to *diversification* as new life forms emerge. As a result of the pressure to adapt to local environmental conditions evolution has produced many different answers to the problem of survival and *adaptive radiation* has occurred in a multitude of different directions. If members of the same population are separated into noninterbreeding groups occupying different environments, diversification becomes inevitable. Diversification is a constant element in the process of evolution, and whenever a single population becomes divided into two or more noninterbreeding groups, each will surely develop its own distinctive biological characteristics. We have already noted the large number of protista that have evolved as a result of differentiation among the unicellular organisms, but this is a small total when set against the grand total of 1.6 million different living species which biologists have so far identified on this planet. This figure, which may be short of the actual total by a million, is all the more impressive when we reflect that this spectacular

panorama of living organisms may have evolved from a single homogeneous, undifferentiated, unicellular prototype.

But complete adaptation to any one environment is not always beneficial in the long run, for it can make an organism totally dependent upon the continuity of that environment. Climate and other environmental conditions can change abruptly, and overadaptation can lead to extinction. Survival sometimes necessitates constant readaptation to changing and uncertain environmental conditions, which can result in the evolution of originally simple life forms into new organisms of *increasing complexity*. This third evolutionary tendency has the effect of facilitating variable responses to diverse environmental stimuli. Locomotion, for example, makes an organism less dependent upon external conditions, for it can move in search of required resources, instead of being obliged to wait until these chance to come its way. Mobility also makes it possible to move away from undesirable extremes of heat and

FIG. 3   THE EVOLUTIONARY PROCESS

Two trends result from speciation: (a) the trend from uniformity to diversity and (b) the trend from organic simplicity to complexity. Today hundreds of thousands of different species of bacteria and protozoa reflect great diversity without corresponding complexity. On the other hand, some species have tended to become increasingly complex due to more sensory and nervous equipment which enables them to make diverse responses to a wider variety of changing environments.

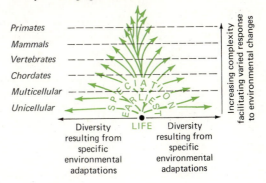

cold, or away from dangerous chemical and physical contact—and even to search for a suitable mate, in the case of organisms that reproduce sexually. In order to achieve these more elaborate responses to external stimuli, many organisms therefore tend to grow more complex as the generations go by.

With this in mind, the evolutionary ladder has been likened to the staircase in a very tall house. On each floor open doors invite the climber to enter and take rest in cozy bedchambers instead of continuing the steep upward climb. Those life forms which leave the staircase and accept a comfortable niche in the unchanging environment of these comfortable rooms go to sleep, cease to evolve, and become utterly dependent for survival upon the continuity of their environment. But those which are forced for one reason or another to remain on the staircase are constantly subjected to new environmental challenges and to fierce selective forces, and therefore continue to proceed upwards as they develop a greater flexibility which may enable them to cope with a wider range of environmental challenges. Not that more complex forms will always survive where simpler forms die out—the mammoth became extinct while the more "primitive" opossum has survived, or an atomic war might seriously challenge the survival of all "higher" or more complex life forms while leaving bacteria unharmed. However, more complex life forms, generally speaking, do have a greater ability to vary their responses to a greater range of diverse environmental stimuli than do simpler life forms. Intelligence, after all, is simply the ability to analyze environmental situations more efficiently, thereby facilitating the production of more effective survival-oriented responses to external stimuli.

For Further Reading

Altman, J., 1965, *Organic Foundations of Animal Behavior*. New York: Holt, Rinehart and Winston, Inc.

Beerbower, J. R., 1968, *Search for the Past: An Introduction to Paleontology*. Englewood Cliffs, N.J.: Prentice-Hall, Inc.

Bernal, J. D., 1951, *The Physical Basis of Life*. London: Routledge & Kegan Paul.

Cannon, H. G., 1958, *The Evolution of Living Things*. Manchester, England: Manchester University Press.

Hardin, G., 1959, *Nature and Man's Fate*. New York: Holt, Rinehart and Winston, Inc.

Hockett, C. F., 1973, *Man's Place in Nature*. New York: McGraw-Hill, Inc.

Huxley, T. H., 1959, *Man's Place in Nature*. Ann Arbor: University of Michigan Press.

Moore, J. A., 1963, *Heredity and Development*. New York: Oxford University Press.

Munson, R., 1971, *Man and Nature: Philosophical Issues in Biology*. New York: Dell Publishing Co.

Oparin, A. I., 1964, *The Chemical Origin of Life*. Springfield, Ill.: Charles C Thomas, Publisher.

Ponnamperuma, C., 1967, *On the Origin of Life,* in A. Cockburn, ed., *Infectious Diseases: Their Evolution and Eradication*. Springfield, Ill.: Charles C Thomas, Publisher.

Simpson, G. G., 1964, *This View of Life*. New York: Harcourt Brace Jovanovich, Inc.

Young, L. B., 1970, *Evolution of Man*. New York: Oxford University Press.

CHAPTER 2

Ecology and Adaptation

Despite the fact that competition is one of the basic laws of evolution, the 1.6 million different species of life on this earth are bound together in an intricate network of interdependence. Plants extract energy from light by the process of photosynthesis and store this energy in organic material, without which animals could not exist. Animals, in turn, break down organic material to release carbon dioxide, and so help to maintain the chemical balance which is essential for the survival of plant life. The oxygen we breathe at this moment may have been manufactured by plankton as far away as Lake Baikal, where, as in Lake Michigan and so many other inland waters close to industrial centers, they may now be in danger of extinction as a result of industrial pollutants. All life on this planet may therefore be said to be a part of a single global ecological system—an ultimately interrelated collation of living organisms, sharing a single habitat, and united by an extremely complex network of symbiotic ties.

Within the framework of this larger global symbiosis, smaller natural regions reveal their own particular subpatterns of plant and animal life which are normally referred to as ECOLOGICAL COMMUNITIES. These, too, are semiindependent population systems, and indeed the most significant factor relating to ecological communities is that the level of population of any one species is intimately bound up with the population level of other species sharing the same habitat. For this reason, the main principle of ecology is that no one species will ever, under normal circumstances, overeat its food supply.

Control Mechanisms

The reasons why overeating of resources does not occur are quite simple. In the first place there is a *supply and demand factor*. In the case of predators, for example, when prey is plentiful, killing is easy and the number of predators will increase. When they increase, they will reduce the quantity of prey as a result of their heavier depredation, and killing will become more difficult so that the number of predators must fall off again. What is more, the particularly heavy selection that the predators exert upon their prey will mean that only the better equipped of the prey will survive to reproduce. The next generation of prey will therefore be more difficult to kill than the previous generation.

If the slower antelopes, for example, are eliminated, the next generation will be descended from the more fleet-footed survivors. This in turn will tend to slow down the rate of predation, and it will be the less efficient predators that are squeezed out, so that the next generation of predators will tend to be more efficient.[1] Thus the evolutionary process will serve to maintain a moving balance between predators and their prey. This is not to say that a population could never be preyed upon until it was totally eliminated, but before that happens, the predatory population will generally fall off sufficiently to allow recovery of the prey, or else switch its attentions to an alternative source of food supply, thus taking some of the pressure off the more heavily depleted species.

A second mechanism also appears to come into operation if ecological imbalance persists. It is an axiom of modern zoology that there is an *optimum density* for all animal populations in a natural or feral condition and the ecological community will be in balance when each species maintains its appropriate optimum density. During the long evolutionary history of any complex life form, the entire glandular

and neurochemical basis of behavior becomes adjusted to operate with maximum efficiency at the level of optimum population density. The secretion of adrenalin, for example, will vary according to the distance that separates individuals from each other, and patterns of behavior will arise which will be adjusted to a given density of population and will have survival value at that density. A change of density, however, may trigger different glandular and chemical responses and can result in behavioral patterns which may be detrimental to survival. Thus an increase in population density far in excess of the normal optimum for that species may result in a state of stress. This condition may modify behavior to the point that some elements of the population set off in search of a less crowded environment. By this process a population that is locally successful and increases its numbers within its own territory may send out emigrants to invade and colonize neighboring territories. On the other hand, if the species is unable to do this—because it inhabits an island or because the neighboring territories are securely held by their present proprietors, or even because the neighboring territories do not provide the type of resources that this species needs—then as stress builds up so will deviant behavior.

In experiments with Norwegian wild rats, J. B. Calhoun[2] demonstrated that a variety of abnormal behavior patterns may develop when a population increases above its optimum density, each of which will have negative survival value and will therefore tend to reduce the population until it returns to the level of optimum density. Working with some six different populations of rats, Calhoun discovered that Norwegian rats have an optimum density under feral or natural conditions of 150 to a quarter acre. When the density of the rat population was increased to double this figure,

---

[1] This explanation of the evolutionary process has been challenged by some who argue that if it were true antelopes would eventually move with the speed of light. The fact is that antelopes of today move far more rapidly than the first amphibians were capable of moving on land, and that this development has occurred in a surprisingly short evolutionary period. Furthermore, the survival of the antelope does not depend purely on speed. Other physiological needs have also to be taken into consideration which would render overadaptation in the direction of speed impracticable from a selective viewpoint long before the speed of light could be reached.

[2] J. B. Calhoun, "Population Density and Social Pathology," *Scientific American* 206, 2:139 ff. (1962).

various patterns of aberrant behavior developed, each of which was antithetical to reproduction or survival. The main patterns of aberrant behavior observed may be summarized as follows:

1. Some rats in these overcrowded communities appeared to develop hypersocial tendencies, seemingly obtaining accentuated satisfaction from close social contacts, refusing to eat except in the company of their companions.
2. Other rats became socially isolated and disorientated, although these rats retained a better physical condition than those which became hypersocial.
3. Many of the females began to reject the advances of the males.
4. Hypersexuality developed among some males, estrus females being pursued by packs of hypersexual males. This resulted in a high mortality rate among the females unable to escape the attentions of the males, and even attempts by the females to escape to burrows did not always discourage the efforts of the males to reach them.
5. Many females in the overcrowded community were unable to carry their pregnancies, successful reproduction becoming increasingly difficult for them.
6. After the birth of offspring, many females refused to feed their infants or else failed to fulfill other maternal functions.
7. Homosexuality appeared in some male groups.
8. Cannibalism became quite common among the males, newborn infants being the object of their attacks.

Calhoun's observations have been reinforced by parallel research with other animal communities. The obvious implication is that a substantial increase in population density far above the optimum, if not checked by other forces, will result in behavior that has negative survival value which in due course will tend to rectify the ecological imbalance. Some social scientists have suggested possible parallels in contemporary human society with antisocial,

hypersexual, hypersocial, and homosexual tendencies especially marked in crowded urban communities. This speculation remains unsubstantiated at the present time. What is of significant interest is that most of these aberrant behavior patterns can be matched with the behavior of caged animals, so that there is the strong suggestion that any drastic interference with feral behavior may disturb animal behavior patterns in a more or less predictable manner.

Genetic factors may also operate to maintain a balance of population in ecological communities, and the French zoologist François Bourlière[3] recorded the history of a population of deer occupying a plateau in Arizona in an ecological balance with a population of wolves, coyote, and puma. Their optimum density seemed to be around 4000 when the predators kept the population well pruned of all malformed animals, effectively eliminating those suffering from the effects of undesirable mutations, such as constantly arise in all populations. Then early in this century man began to hunt down the predators, and as a result the balance of the ecological community was upset. The deer population began to shoot upward, and by 1920 it had reached 60,000; but this higher population level was not maintained. The population eventually declined until it numbered 10,000. Genetic deterioration, because of the absence of any selective mechanism to weed out mutations, was believed to have contributed to this collapse, which served to reduce the deer population to a figure more closely approximating its ecological optimum.

Territoriality

Implicit in the concept of ecological communities, at least in so far as mammals are concerned, is the concept of TERRITORIALITY, one of the most significant contributions made

[3] For similar arguments see François Bourlière, *The Natural History of Mammals* (New York: Alfred A. Knopf, Inc., 1954).

Urban dwellers are frequently impressed by the apparent openness of the "world of nature." However, despite the absence of fences and visible boundaries, even the expanses of the Transkei in Southeast Africa, pictured above, are actually divided into local territories by the various birds, mammals, and other higher life forms that live therein. (Courtesy of the South African Information Service.)

by zoologists to the study of anthropology during this century. The theory of territoriality assumes that more advanced living organisms will seek a regular and assured food supply, and that in the case of the higher animals, these resources can be most conveniently secured when individuals or groups of individuals adopt a roughly defined territory for their own regular use. Under normal circumstances the proprietors of such areas tend to live out their lives contentedly within the general limits of their own "homeland," and will seldom enter neighboring territories except under special provocation such as drought, famine, or an internal population increase.[4] The territorial

impulse is easy to understand. Animals born and bred in a particular locality become accustomed to finding their food there and will avoid other areas except under compelling reasons.

As members of an ecological community, territorial animals will, of course, share their territory with members of other species that are not dependent upon the same source of food. There is no tension within any ecological community providing the member species are not dependent upon identical resources, but many proprietors respond to a *territorial imperative* to resist invasions by members of their own or closely related species because such animals would be competitors for their food supply. When alien animals enter the territory but do not compete as rivals for the available food

---

[4] Many cases have been recorded in which mammals have died from the effects of drought rather than leave their own territories.

supply, there will be no reaction, but the appearance of a rival for the same food will provoke a defensive reaction. It has been repeatedly observed that many animals which do not show any strongly aggressive behavioral tendencies outside their own territory will become very aggressive inside their own territory when confronted by a rival for their own private food resources. It is almost as though the territory has become associated, in a Pavlovian way, with food. The appearance of possible food rivals in this territory sets up, maybe in a slightly milder way, something of the same aggressive reaction that would occur if the rival were to attempt to seize food from under the occupant's very nose.

Not all animals that are territorial in habit and customarily restrict their movements to their home ranges reveal a clear territorial imperative to defend their living space with tooth and claw.[5] Few of the more placid herbivores do this; but carnivores are often aggressive in the protection of their territories. Not only do many carnivores openly threaten intruders who enter their territories, but it has been pointed out that in some instances they may possess advantages which aid them in repelling such invaders—if, in fact, the invaders have the temerity to press their intrusion. The defenders will know the layout of their homeland better than the strangers, and if the defenders should have young offspring at the time of the intrusion, then in most higher species this too will intensify the ferocity with which they will challenge the advance of the invaders. To the extent that an inborn pro-

pensity toward the defense of the territory may exist in some species, the territorial imperative would have been favored by selection. Those animals which lacked this propensity would have been deprived of their living area and so would have been unable to raise progeny.

While no one would deny that the ancestors of living men may have been largely territorial in the sense that they probably kept to separate but possibly overlapping homelands, the extent to which they may have possessed an imperative territorial urge to defend these homelands is debatable. Possibly the answer is linked to the extent to which such early protohumans were herbivorous or had become carnivorous (see Chap. 8).

Territoriality, in the simpler sense of local residence, with or without aggressiveness, serves an ecological purpose because it contributes to the demographic balance of communities by stabilizing populations at the optimum density.[6] The mating practices of some animals clearly reveal a territorial basis, as in the case of African ungulates such as waterbuck, gazelles, and springbok. The female Uganda kob (genus *Adenota*), for example, will not mate with any male that does not possess its own territory, and surplus males who are unable to obtain territories are left to congregate in all-male herds, in which they fail to reproduce.

At any one time there will normally be a surplus of animals that have been unable to secure territories of their own. Most survive only provided they can secure a territory on the death of its proprietor or possibly by outright annexation. The wastage of lion cubs, for example, is around 50 percent, and only the healthier and better equipped usually survive to adulthood to take their place in the ecological community. It therefore follows that if

---

[5] Robert Ardrey's *The Territorial Imperative* (New York: Atheneum Press, 1966) is challenging but inadequate. In particular, the role of aggression in territorial behavior is overemphasized, and the concept of territoriality should not be equated exclusively with defensive behavior. Many species reveal close ties with particular territories, but do not attempt to defend their living space against immigrants competing for the same resources. In such cases the outcome depends on victory in the competition for scarce resources.

[6] The "optimum population" of any species in a given locality must not be regarded as rigid. If it were rigid, evolution would never take place. Instead the "optimum population" represents a center of moving equilibrium.

animals are allowed to retain an adequate living area, reasonable depredations by hunters will not endanger their survival. Unless too severely pressed, their population will continue to expand up to the optimum density as determined by the available niches, but the reverse also holds true, for we may effectively exterminate a species by depriving it of its living area without actually killing any of the animals.

It is thus no accident that territoriality has developed among those animals—mammals and birds in particular—that possess the greatest potential for mobility. If whole populations of dominant animals were to wander unpredictably backward and forward in all directions, such behavior would disrupt the ecological order. The development of territoriality among the more mobile animals has helped to facilitate local ecological harmony as well as to prevent excessive intraspecies conflict for food. At the same time, local competition for food resources still exists under territorial conditions, and the necessary forces of natural selection still prevail. While territoriality does permit a degree of conflict, necessary for selection, in practice it tends to prevent the contest between members of the same species from becoming unbearable.

Territoriality thus plays a vital role in the evolutionary process in that it promotes demographic stability and thus prevents conditions in the ecological community from becoming chaotic. Life in the wild is not the disorderly "jungle" we often picture in our minds; there is a pattern of ordered relations that permeates the entire symbiotic fabric of organic interdependence. If any living organism has brought disorder into the organic world, it is man, not the feral predator. Man is destroying the ecological balance in his efforts to free himself from ecological controls, whereas the depredations of the wild carnivores take place strictly within the ecological system and serve to maintain, not to disrupt it.

Speciation

But territoriality also aids evolution in another way: it facilitates that continuous process known as SPECIATION by which existing populations subdivide and evolve into new species. Speciation occurs whenever a population becomes divided into two or more genetically separate breeding isolates.

Evolution arises as a result of a continuous process of adaptation taking place in phylogenetic continua—in breeding populations, species, subspecies, races, and lineages. This process of continuous change has resulted in the formation of widely diverse SPECIES, populations whose members resemble each other but differ significantly from other populations and who can breed among each other but who have lost the ability to breed successfully with other living organisms.

Species should not be thought of as fixed and unchanging realities. Genetic systems are essentially "action" systems, constantly subject to modification, and even if rigidly segregated from all genetic admixture with other species or subspecies, no population will retain precisely the same genes through the generations. Mutations, natural selection, and genetic drift will inevitably bring about modifications, even though the rate of change may be so slow as to be hardly noticeable over hundreds of millions of years, as is the case with so many surviving unicellular organisms which have evolved only slightly during the entire span of life on this earth.

When a population spreads over a wide geographical area, it follows that the organisms at one end of the region may have to contend with very different geographical, climatic, and ecological conditions from those which prevail at the other end. A single genetically homogeneous animal population, for example, may expand slowly up a long valley until the vanguard eventually finds itself in an alpine environment quite different from that of the

FIG. 4   HOW NATURAL SELECTION LEADS TO SPECIATION

a. Migrant population settles new territory in which there is a wide range of environmental conditions, becoming widely dispersed over the entire habitable area.

b. After hundreds or even thousands of generations of mutation, natural selection, and local inbreeding, the resultant populations will become adapted to local survival conditions. If the population settlement area is continuous, the two extremes will be linked by intervening *racial clines,* even though they may reflect marked differences in both genotype and phenotype.

c. Should any barrier prevent gene flow, as when a rise in the sea level submerges the intervening land areas, then a clear-cut contrast will become apparent between the two now isolated populations. In short, the interracial cline that formerly linked the two extreme variants now no longer exists and the two separate subspecies or races are on their way to becoming separate species. If isolated under different selective influences, even the races of living men would tend to evolve into mutually infertile species.

parent population remaining at the lower end of the valley in semitropical conditions. Here the settlers may be free from many of the problems of life in the tropics, but will be exposed to the effects of a higher altitude and much stronger solar radiation. While the parent population remains in the original luxuriant, semitropical lowlands where rich foods are available, but the sunshine is filtered by the thick foliage of the forests, and where myriads of tropical pests and diseases confront them, the migrant population has to contend with an entirely different set of survival conditions.

In such cases, the forces of natural selection which will work upon the migrant element in the population will be very different from those which continue to develop and shape the original parent population in the lowlands. If the individual members were to retain an excessive mobility, moving backward and forward and freely interbreeding with all segments of the population, clearly there would be no possibility of local specialization, since genetic migration within the total population would tend to counterbalance the effect of local genetic adaptation as quickly as this took place. But a sense of territoriality restricts excessive migration and results in the formation of local DEMES or mainly inbreeding local groups, each with its own more or less separate GENE POOL or distinctive reservoir of genes.[7]

Where the demes are entirely inbreeding, because of geographical or social isolation, local diversification will be rapid, and each deme will soon become a *microrace*, a small but distinct subspecies, in its own right. But where limited interbreeding exists between neighboring demes, each deme will tend to develop its own characteristic phenotype—its own distinctive, genetically based physiological form—which will represent an equilibrium

between the force of local selection and the impact of genetic migration between the deme and its neighbors. When this occurs, the total population will retain the general characteristics of a single species, but will reveal what is called a *racial cline*, a genetic gradient stretching from one major environmental area to the other.[8] In this case the frequency with which specific genes evidence themselves will steadily change as we move from the area of original settlement up the valley to the new environment. At no point will there be any sharp break in the genetic gradient linking the two extremes of this continuous population, but the colonial population at the extreme end of the racial cline will eventually develop a markedly different phenotype from the older-type population which remained in the original homeland and consequently retained the original phenotypical character.

Should an environmental barrier, such as the flooding of a low valley or the incursion of a rival species, sever the population into two genetically isolated parts, then the gene flow between the two wings will be totally halted, and the two populations will henceforth develop quite separately into two distinct subspecies. Even without the divisive effect of territoriality, speciation will result whenever a genetic barrier arises to prevent the migration of genes throughout the total population; that is, whenever the total population ceases to comprise a single gene pool. Once the flow of genes is disrupted, natural selection will be able to operate more effectively to select for survival in the different environments, free from the negating effects of genetic migration. The separate populations will then evolve into

[7] Consult G. W. Lasker, *Physical Anthropology* (New York: Holt, Rinehart and Winston, Inc., 1973), pp. 79 ff., on the relevance of local "demes," or gene pools, in evolutionary genetics.

[8] A clear distinction between interracial and intraracial clines is drawn by Harvard anthropologist Carleton S. Coon in *The Living Races of Man* (New York: Alfred A. Knopf, Inc., 1969). Ironically Coon's theories of human racial origins have been justly criticized for failing to acknowledge the full extent of prehistoric migration. Yet both interracial and intraracial clines result from the fact of migration.

new and distinct subspecies and these may continue to diversify in the course of time until they become entirely separate SPECIES in their own right, populations whose members resemble each other and can breed with each other but who have lost the ability to breed successfully with other types of organisms. This lineage, constantly evolving through time, is called a PHYLOGENETIC CONTINUUM. The evolutionary changes in such intergenerational racial units can be so great that if the living and the ancestral forms were to be placed side by side, taxonomists would classify them as separate species.

Even when a population becomes separated in two environments which are not basically dissimilar, genetic isolation will usually lead to

FIG. 5   THE PHYLOGENETIC CONTINUUM

Species continually tend to divide into separate subspecies, which in turn evolve into separate species. The reality is the phylogenetic or racial continuum, persisting through time, subdividing, and occasionally becoming extinct. The species and subspecies identified by taxonomists represent the state of affairs that exists at one moment in time only.

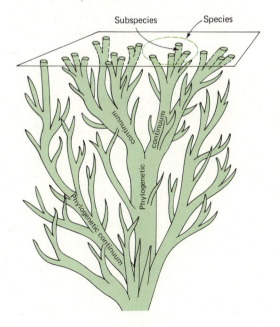

Subspecies   Species

Phylogenetic continuum

Phylogenetic continuum

speciation as a result of a phenomenon known as GENETIC DRIFT. This is the name given to random changes which occur in the genetic content of inbreeding, isolated populations and are not due to and do not serve to adapt the organism to any particular set of environmental conditions. The random destruction caused by a flood, for example, may eliminate some part of a population, and in so doing cause a slight change in the average phenotype of that population, even though the change may be meaningless in terms of survival and natural selection.

Such changes in the genetic character of a population which arise from chance variation rather than from natural selection are more common among *nonadaptive traits,* characteristics which do not have any immediate survival value and which are therefore not subject to natural selection.[9] They are also more likely to be significant in small rather than in large populations. When a gambler throws just one or two dice, the chances that a given number may fail to come up are quite high. But when a thousand dice are thrown, the law of averages will ensure a more or less equal frequency for each number. By the laws of probability, therefore, the genetic constitution of a small isolated population will be likely to drift in one direction or the other due to chance alone, but larger breeding populations will not be so easily modified by random inequalities of reproduction or by the accidental death of a few members.

Genetic Homogenization

When speciation occurs, not all the genetic characteristics of these two populations will necessarily come to differ. Changes will only take place in those genetic qualities that respond to the particular needs of the new environment. The "Mongolian Spot," a dark blue patch that commonly appears on the skin of

[9]See p. 20.

Mongolian infants at the base of the spine, seems to have no survival value and is therefore apparently unaffected by most environmental circumstances, so that we say that it is a nonadaptive characteristic.[10]

Physical anthropologists formerly believed that a large number of inherited characteristics were nonadaptive; that is, that they were not subject to the forces of environmental selection. However, this view is no longer held because the power of environment, in which we must include disease, is now known to be far more extensive than we previously imagined. In consequence, the continuous elimination of particular genes in genetically isolated populations, localized in a constant environment, will tend to promote a high degree of phenotypical uniformity when inbreeding takes place over a long period. This is not to say that its members would ever become identical because not all genes will be adaptive to the prevailing selective forces and in any case mutations constantly tend to recreate a degree of diversity. Completely "pure" races therefore exist only as a hypothetical concept, and would have to be made up of identical siblings produced by mitosis or cell division of the fertilized egg, but all isolated inbreeding populations do tend toward a high degree of uniformity where adaptive characteristics are concerned, thus undergoing progressive GENETIC HOMOGENIZATION.

Thus territoriality plays an important role in preventing hybridization and thereby facili-

tating speciation among potentially mobile populations. If the members of these remained free to wander all over large areas, a constant remingling or recombination of genes would frustrate the tendency toward local adaptive specialization. Plants, of course, are rooted where they are, and most varieties can only interbreed with their immediate neighbors, so that they possess a natural territoriality. Territoriality, implying the tendency to "stay put" in a home territory, only becomes an evolutionary necessity, from the point of view of promoting speciation, in the case of birds, mammals, and according to Konrad Lorenz,[11] some fishes. While territoriality does not rule out the possibility of invasions or seasonal migrations, it helps to localize the population so that environmental adaptations are able to accumulate through the generations. But for territoriality, evolution among the higher animals would have proceeded much more slowly, with possibly far less speciation than actually arose.

Feral Constraints

Although geographical and territorial boundaries both serve to isolate populations genetically, there are other forces at work which facilitate that genetic segregation which is an essential prerequisite to speciation. Obviously, evolution would have been impossible if every evolutionary experiment had been cancelled out by crossbreeding or by reabsorption of the diverging population in parental or sibling stocks. For successful speciation it is necessary that subspecies remain genetically isolated until all possibility of genetic admixture has disappeared. To achieve this, all higher animals living under natural or feral conditions reveal a marked unwillingness amounting usually to

---

[10] Some authorities today maintain that there are no physical traits that are *not* adaptive. They claim that all physiological characteristics are in one way or another subject to selective forces, even though the rate of selection may be very slow in some cases. It is hard to see, however, how the possession of the "Mongolian Spot"—to cite one potentially "nonadaptive" characteristic—could affect the reproductive chances of the individual. Logically it could be true that all physiological characteristics are in the long term "adaptive," but the selective value of some traits must be so minimal that to all intents and purposes they may be regarded as "nonadaptive."

[11] Konrad Lorenz stresses the fact that the older distinction between "innate" and "learned" behavior is overrigid. See Konrad Lorenz, *Evolution and Modification of Behavior* (Chicago: University of Chicago Press, 1967).

positive refusal to interbreed with members of other subspecies. Animals in a wild condition do not even attempt to mate with other species, since they are subject to FERAL CONSTRAINTS which prevent such wasted biological activity.

Zoologists identify two types of constraint: *built-in constraints,* based on physical "sign stimuli," and *acquired constraints* or "prejudices." *Built-in constraints* or sign stimuli operate as a positive stimulus to engage in reproductive behavior, and these take the form of movements, colors, smells, and combinations thereof, common to animals of the same subspecies but absent in other populations. When the right signs are there, mating is attempted; conversely, the wrong indications discourage mating. When the stimuli serve as a warning to other subspecies not to attempt sexual relations, they act like a sign that reads: "Danger, a new biological experiment is in progress here. Do not approach." Species-specific sign stimuli are like the yellow flag flown by a ship entering a harbor, when quarantining itself because of infectious disease on board. All who are not already on board are warned to keep well away.

In addition to built-in sign constraints, the distinguished zoologist Peter Klopfer[12] believes that acquired constraints or prejudices also come into action. These may arise because of behavioral *imprinting* and habituation. Imprinting takes place during the first few days of life, while *habituation* to the parent-type occurs during the more prolonged relationship that links immature mammalian offspring to their mothers. Both work to ensure that when sexual maturity is attained, mating will only be attempted with those forms that resemble the parent or siblings.

Both imprinting and habituation supplement built-in constraints in a feral state, thus making speciation possible and preventing genetic ad-

[12] See Peter M. Klopfer, "Imprinting: A Reassessment," *Science* 47:302–303 (1965); also *Behavioral Ecology* (Belmont, Calif.: Dickenson Publishing Co., 1970).

mixture even when two closely related subspecies may find themselves in contact. But in conditions of domestication or captivity the story is very different, and in the case of man, culture has created a nonferal environment which, particularly where the sense of territoriality has become weak, has resulted in the near-abandonment of constraints against crossbreeding. However, as we shall observe later, culturally motivated prejudices still do operate among men in forms which are basically similar, in principle at least, to the acquired constraints that are universal among feral animals.

Intraspecies Competition

When geographical isolation, territoriality, or simply feral constraints create a genetically isolated population, evolution can take either of two routes. The adaptations that take place may be of purely local survival value, favoring qualities which assist the organism to survive in that particular environment, but which have no added survival value in other environments. Protective skin coloration, for example, is valuable in tropical climate zones, but may be actually undesirable in more extreme latitudes where the sun's rays are weaker and the skin needs to be able to absorb all the vitamin D it can obtain from sunshine. On the other hand, diversification may be the result of evolutionary developments which, by enhancing the organism's ability to vary its response to a variety of different stimuli, have survival value in a wide variety of conditions. The temperature control system of mammals and the heightened intelligence of primates both represent steps up the evolutionary ladder which are of value in many different circumstances and do not make the organism a prisoner of its particular environment. This type of evolutionary advance usually occurs when the selective forces are particularly fierce and environmental changes succeed each other with considerable rapidity. Such was probably the case during the Devonian period when the first terrestrial vertebrates slithered in the mud left by the drying lakes and again during the ice ages of the Pleistocene when the size of the brain among our ancestors tripled in less than 2 million years.

As population increases, the stress caused by overpopulation may cause surplus animals to attempt to move away from their own territory in search of more thinly populated areas. In most cases this situation will mean that they will be obliged to invade neighboring territories which are already occupied and that a struggle will result between the invaders and proprietors for the available resources. If the proprietors are better adapted to the local conditions than the invaders, they may succeed in defending their territory successfully. On the other hand, if the invaders come from a more competitive subspecies, they may be expected to succeed in ousting the older, less sophisticated breed, and another scene in the evolutionary drama will have been enacted. In this manner we may expect the new and more evolved subspecies to increase in number and expand first over one territory then another, annihilating all less advanced competitors in their path by expropriation of living area, if not by actual physical violence.

In many cases the proprietors of such territories may be a less evolved variety of the invader's own species, and since the food requirements of such populations will be the most nearly similar, a bitter conflict will result. Unless the older, less evolved variety is protected by some natural barrier, as were the animals of Australia and the Americas following the isolation of these continents by continental drift, it may be eliminated, leaving the more modern variety or subspecies as the sole surviving representative of the species. Only when subspecies have become sufficiently distinctive in their character to have evolved into separate species with nonconflicting food habits will they stop competing with each other and become capable of living amicably within the same ecological community.

Natural selection operates, therefore, not only in competition for survival between the individual members of any one population but also through competition between closely related species for control of the available resources. Among the higher animals this takes the form of both intraspecies and interspecies competition for territorial control, since territory implies access to resources and to reproductive privileges. Just as the gray squirrel, introduced to England from North America some decades ago, has ever since been systematically expropriating the indigenous English red squirrels from their territories by harassment, so the history of evolution may be analyzed in terms of expansionist pressure by the more competitive species and subspecies resulting in the expropriation and extinction of the less competitive by their own close relatives.

For Further Reading

Calhoun, J. B., 1962, "Population Density and Social Pathology," *Scientific American* 206, 2:139 ff.

Caspari, E. W., and A. W. Ravin, 1969, *Genetic Organization: A Comprehensive Treatise.* New York: Academic Press, Inc.

Dubos, R., 1965, *Man Adapting.* New Haven, Conn.: Yale University Press.

Ehrlich, P. R., 1971, *Man and the Ecosphere.* San Francisco: W. H. Freeman and Company.

Esser, A. H., 1971, *Behavior and Environment.* New York: Plenum Press.

Fisher, R. A., 1958, *The Genetical Theory of Natural Selection.* New York: Dover Publications, Inc.

Hinde, R. A., 1959, "Behavior and Speciation in Birds and Lower Vertebrae," *Biological Reviews* 34:85–128.

Klopfer, P., 1965, "Imprinting: A Reassessment," *Science* 147:302–303.

————, 1970, *Behavioral Ecology*. Belmont, Calif.: Dickenson Publishing Co., Inc.

————, and J. P. Hailman, 1967, *Introduction to Animal Behavior: Ethology's First Century*. Englewood Cliffs, N.J.: Prentice-Hall, Inc.

Lasker, G. W., 1946, "Migration and Physical Differentiation" *American Journal of Physical Anthropology* 43:273–300.

Lerner, I. M., 1968, *Heredity, Evolution and Society*. San Francisco: W. H. Freeman and Company.

Lorenz, K., 1952, *King Solomon's Ring*. New York: Thomas Y. Crowell Company.

Mayr, E., 1963, *Animal Species and Evolution*. Cambridge, Mass: Harvard University Press.

Merrell, D. J., 1962, *Evolution and Genetics*. New York: Holt, Rinehart and Winston, Inc.

Morris, L. N., 1971, *Human Populations, Genetic Variation and Evolution*. San Francisco: Chandler Publishing Company.

Odum, E. P., 1959, *Fundamentals of Ecology*. Philadelphia: W. B. Saunders Company.

Simpson, G. G., 1949, *The Meaning of Evolution*. New York: Oxford University Press.

Sutton, H. E., 1965, *An Introduction to Human Genetics*. New York: Holt, Rinehart and Winston, Inc.

Wright, S., 1968–1969, *Evolution and the Genetics of Populations,* Vols. 1 and 2. Chicago: University of Chicago Press.

CHAPTER 3

The Fish That Crawled

Knowledge of the evolutionary story, of the morphological history of the many species that have inhabited this world, is obtained through PALEONTOLOGY, the study of extinct life forms. Paleontologists search for and compare *fossils,* those parts of dead organisms that have been preserved in recognizable form. In many cases fossils have survived only through impregnation of the dead organisms by minerals which seep in solution into organic remains as they lie in the ground. Although the organic material may subsequently decay, the minerals which have calcified persist, preserving the shape of the decayed organism. In cases of more recent origin, actual bones and teeth may survive. On occasion paleontologists have the good fortune to discover complete organisms which have been preserved through freezing in extreme latitudes or mummification in peat, and these are of course of particular value in that they preserve the soft parts of the body intact. Needless to say, only a very few organisms normally become fossilized. While the chalk downs of England constitute the remains

of incalculable numbers of fossilized protozoa, once at the bottom of the sea, and coal is made from fossil vegetation that lived in the distant Carboniferous period, reading the record of the rocks has not been so easy as it might otherwise sound. Only occasionally have paleontologists stumbled across such rich sources of information as the California tar pits, oily swamps which trapped many large mammals during the Cenozoic. Often they have to be content with a few incomplete bones or simply the mold or cast of a leaf impressed in the rocks before the leaf itself decayed.

Dating Techniques

If we are to be able to read the story that the fossils have to tell us, it is important that we should be able to arrange them chronologically. Formerly the paleontologists had to rely primarily upon reference to the geological strata in which the fossils were found, but in recent years the problem of dating has been greatly eased by new methods and the paleontological time chart is today far more precise than formerly.

The new dating techniques hinge mainly upon the measurement of radioactivity emanating from fossil remains.[1] CARBON-14, for example, provides us with fairly accurate estimates of age up to 30,000 years, and can still be used to date fossils up to 60,000 years in age, but beyond that the results are very unreliable. The method used is quite simply explained. All living organisms tend to absorb the radioactive isotope carbon-14, which arises as a result of the action of cosmic rays in the upper atmosphere. When the organism dies, the remains cease to absorb carbon-14, but that which has already been absorbed breaks down at a regular rate. Carbon-14 is known to have a "half-life" of around 5740 years. This means that in 5740 years the intensity of radioactivity emitted by it will be reduced to one half, and in a similar further period of time, the remaining level of radioactivity will be reduced by half again. As a result, measurement of the intensity of radioactivity will indicate the date at which the organism died. In addition to being used to date fossil remains, any organic material used by early man, including charcoal from wood fires, may be dated by the carbon-14 process.

For much older geological periods, URANIUM dating can be used. Radioactive uranium changes as it disintegrates until it finally leaves a residue of lead, but since it breaks down very slowly, measurement is only accurate in terms of millions of years. Uranium testing is therefore of no value in attempting to date the remains of life forms which lived during the last few million years.

To some extent the gap left between carbon-14, which cannot be used effectively much beyond 60,000 years, and uranium, which is only accurate to the nearest million years, is

[1] For further information on dating methods, see K. P. Oakley, *Frameworks for Dating Fossil Man* (Chicago: Aldine Publishing Co., 1964).

filled by the POTASSIUM-ARGON dating technique. Radioactive potassium-40 has a half-life of 1.4 billion years. This method does not permit the accuracy of the carbon-14 process, but does provide a means by which dates can be estimated for the important period between 3 million and 60,000 years ago.

Another dating technique which can be employed in certain circumstances measures the FLUORINE content of fossil bones and teeth. There is fluorine in all water in the ground, and fluorine consequently penetrates any fossil remains found in the earth. Unfortunately, the concentration of fluorine varies from area to area, but all fossils located in the same immediate locality will reveal a similar fluorine impregnation if they date from the same age. Fluorine testing revealed the famous Piltdown hoax which had perplexed eminent anthropologists for some forty years. The case goes back to 1912, when an amateur geologist, Charles Dawson of Sussex, England, produced some discolored fragments of a human cranium, complete with part of a jawbone, which he said had been found by a workman in a local quarry, in association with several flint tools. Although "Piltdown Man" was accepted into the pantheon of significant fossil remains, it created many problems. As Sir Arthur Keith, one of Britain's leading physical anthropologists successfully demonstrated, the incomplete cranium was equivalent in size and shape to that of a modern Englishman, but the jawbone was positively apelike. How could such a disparate combination of characteristics be explained? It was not until 1953 that fluorine-testing finally uncovered the hoax. Professors J. S. Weiner, W. E. Le Gros Clark, and K. P. Oakley proved by fluorine testing that the "fossil" bones were by no means as old as the ferruginous gravel in which they were reported to have been found.[2] Charles Dawson, who had meanwhile died content in the private knowl-

[2] See J. S. Weiner, *The Piltdown Forgery* (New York: Oxford University Press, 1955).

edge that his practical joke had not yet been discovered, had artificially discolored fragments from a relatively modern human skull and hidden these in the quarry along with the flint tools and the jawbone of an orangutan.

GEOLOGICAL ERAS

As a result of dating and classifying the multitude of fossils which have been examined, paleontologists have divided the history of life on the earth into a number of *eras*. The first of these eras, beginning with the formation of the earth's crust some 4.5 to 5 billion years ago and lasting down to 3.6 billion years ago, is usually known as the AZOIC era because in that early period the earth was "without life." The next era, which runs for a full two thirds of the total history of life on the earth, extends from 3.6 billion down to 1.2 billion years ago, and is labelled the ARCHAEOZOIC, or age of "primitive life." During this time only unicellular life forms existed.

When we begin to find traces of multicellular life forms, such as metazoa, paleontologists speak of the PROTEROZOIC, the age of "earlier life," which is believed to have lasted another 625 million years until the commencement of the geological Cambrian strata some 575 million years ago.

It was during the PALEOZOIC era, the age of "ancient life," which is associated with many different geological strata beginning with the Cambrian and ending with the Permian, that evolutionary progress began to accelerate. Paleontologists trace the appearance first of *chordates*—marine animals with a central nervous system but without vertebrae—followed by true fishes, with vertebrae and an elementary brain which began to develop at one end of the central nervous cord. It was during the Paleozoic also that both plants and animals began to spread over the surface of dry land, and by the beginning of the rich Carboniferous geological period, some 345 million years ago,

fishlike amphibians crawled among huge forests of giant ferns and mosses.

The Paleozoic lasted 350 million years, and was followed by a shorter era of around 160 million years called the MESOZOIC. This was the era of "intermediate life," popularly known as "the age of reptiles," associated with the fossil-bearing rocks of the Triassic, Jurassic, and Cretaceous geological periods. Early reptiles known as archosaurs gave way to giant dinosaurs, and more significantly, the first birds and mammals appeared. Then, around 65 million years ago, the Mesozoic faded into the CENOZOIC, divided into a *Tertiary* period, extending down to 3 million years ago, and a *Quaternary* period, from 3 million years to the present. It was during this last 65 million years that our early primate forebears became differentiated into monkeys, apes, and eventually hominid or manlike creatures.

The Tertiary period of the Cenozoic is identified with the epochs known as the Paleocene, Eocene, Oligocene, Miocene, Pliocene, and the Quaternary is usually divided into Pleistocene and Holocene. The Pleistocene was formerly applied to the last million years, but is now extended back as far as the past 3 million years while the Holocene includes only the last 12,000 years before the present. It is the Quaternary that concerns anthropologists most deeply, for it was during this last 3 million years that manlike creatures who walked erect were evolving to the level of modern *Homo sapiens*.[3] During this past 3 million years, also, these manlike creatures were developing the power of speech, and accumulating ideas and information about themselves and their environment.

Archaeozoic Era

When the first traces of life are found in the Archaeozoic era, there is no sharp division between plants and animals. If we regard

[3] For further discussion on the concept of "the first man" see Chapter 7

plants as synthesizing *autotrophs,* extracting energy from light and storing it in organic form, and the animals as predatory *allotrophs,* consuming organic material in order to secure energy, we find some unicellular *protista* which are simultaneously both autotrophs and allotrophs. In these unicellular organisms, the oxygen required for metabolism diffused into the cell generally through the membrane, and carbon dioxide and other forms of metabolic waste diffused back through the membrane into the surrounding water.

In the course of time, more precisely specialized protista appear. Those which specialize in extracting energy from light, such as the *algae,* become plants. Others that obtain energy by consuming organic material become animals, such as the minute unicellular *protozoa.* Many of these early protozoa, such as the amoeba, still survive today only slightly evolved from their early Archaeozoic prototypes,[4] but others developed refinements such as flagellae—thin extensions used to propel the cell through the water—or pseudopods, used for propulsion, ingesting food, or anchoring the cell to a more stable body such as a rock. Other protista developed *tropisms,* elementary responses to simple stimuli such as gravity, salinity, or even differences in temperature.

Proterozoic Era

It is impossible to draw a sharp dividing line between the Archaeozoic and the Proterozoic eras, and evolution in the direction of multicellular life forms may well be said to have begun in the Archaeozoic. The transitional step is illustrated by COLONIAL PROTOZOA. These comprise a number of similar cells, linked together, but each engaged in their own independent metabolic process. Then in other organisms such as *porifera,* we find colonies in which some differentiation of purpose has

[4] There is probably no life form that has survived unchanged since the Archeozoic. Even living protozoa are much more complex than the earlier ancestral forms.

begun to develop, so that the cells at one end are more concerned with locomotion while others assume the task of reproduction.

The main line of evolution in the direction of more advanced multicellular animals may well have been through porifera, for some species show the development of a system of canals, so that the colony becomes hollow inside, and by a beating of the flagella, water is drawn into the central canal and driven out at an open end. All food-gathering, respiratory, and excretory functions become concentrated in the cells that line this canal and undertake the vital metabolic process while the cells outside become primarily protective in function. Our modern sponges are descended from the porifera, and seem to have achieved such a satisfactory answer to the problem of survival in their comfortable marine environment that little further adaptation has been necessary.

In another direction, probably ancestral to man, paleontology identifies METAZOA or multicellular animals which reveal a distinctive differentiation of function between the cells,

One of the world's simplest living animals, the microscopic unicellular amoeba resembles an irregular mass of living jelly, which moves about by extending fingerlike projections of its substance and flowing into them. (Courtesy of the American Museum of Natural History.)

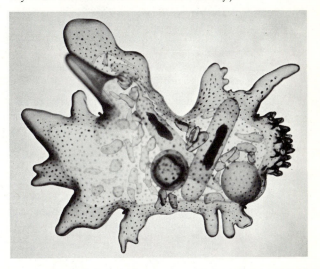

FIG. 6   PROTOZOAN, METAZOAN, INVERTEBRATE CHORDATES, AND VERTEBRATES

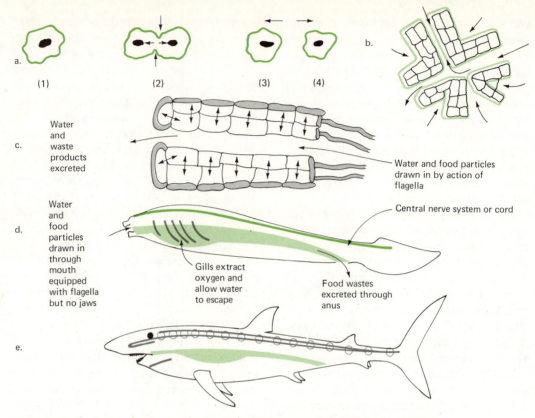

a.

(1)   (2)   (3)   (4)

b.

c. Water and waste products excreted

Water and food particles drawn in by action of flagella

Central nerve system or cord

d. Water and food particles drawn in through mouth equipped with flagella but no jaws

Gills extract oxygen and allow water to escape

Food wastes excreted through anus

e.

a. Protozoan or unicellular life forms are fully developed and self-supporting from the moment of division. Unlike more complex mammalian life forms, there is no period of immaturity or dependence upon adults.

b. In the case of colonial protozoan the individual cells may remain connected after division, but these larger masses of undivided unicellular organisms, each carrying out its own life functions independently, are possible only because of canals that enable every cell to obtain water and nutrients.

c. Metazoan or multicellular life forms appear when a division of labor develops between the cells. In this example, the work of digestion has devolved entirely upon the inner cells, while the outer cells have developed a protective function. The external cells at one end have also developed flagellae which wave water and food particles through the hollow center of the organism—the prototype of our alimentary canal. The organism illustrated is a simplified tunicate.

d. Chordates embody a number of refinements on the basic plan of diagram c. above. Activity is coordinated by a central nervous cord—the prototype of our own spinal cord. Gill slits have developed, comprising cells specialized in the extraction of oxygen from water, while other cells carry out the functions of our intestines and our liver. The organism illustrated is *Amphioxus*. It is symmetrical and has the appearance of a translucent fish, but has no bones, no brain, and no specialized sense organs.

e. Fishes evolve by degrees from marine invertebrate chordates. The developed fish possesses a skeleton, with jaws to control the mouth opening, an elementary brain (arising at the front end of the central cord), and specialized sense organs, including eyes. These comprise cells which have specialized in identifying differences in lightness and darkness until such areas become clearly distinguished from each other.

and these are the true achievement of the Proterozoic period. The earlier metazoa, such as *coelenterata,* were at first little more than floating mouths around which an array of tentacles helped to wave food-bearing water into a central cavity.

Some coelenterata affixed themselves to rocks or other stable matter by their base, but others were free swimming, and it is from the more mobile variety that the main line of animal evolution is to be traced. It is also at this level of multicellular life that the first meiosis and the complex pattern of sexual reproduction arose. This served to accelerate the evolutionary process by reshuffling the genes and dealing a freshly assorted hand with each generation. Such reshuffling exposes weak genes to the forces of selection and so hastens phylogenetic improvement.[5]

The Early Paleozoic

As history moves into the Paleozoic era, primitive *Arthropoda,* namely *Trilobita,* begin to evolve. The Arthropoda phylum is today one of the largest in the animal kingdom, including insects, spiders, centipedes, and crabs, but it was the trilobites that pioneered the way to the appearance of the more advanced Arthropoda of today and probably also to all higher forms of life. The trilobites are now extinct as a class, but were abundant in the Cambrian and Silurian phases of the Paleozoic era. Somewhat resembling living woodlice, they were small marine creatures which reveal the development of a variety of primitive organs, including an elementary eye, that at first was merely capable of distinguishing different intensities of light. They also developed a central nervous cord, which controlled the overall behavior of the organism.

Following the appearance of the trilobites

[5] The concept of the "phylogenetic continuum" is essential if we are to break away from the static concept of "unchanging species."

A hydrozoa of the phylum *Coelenterata.* Hydrozoa reveal little differentiation of tissues or cell function, and are essentially primitive metazoa, only slightly evolved beyond the level of colonial protozoa. (Courtesy of the American Museum of Natural History.)

a series of marine INVERTEBRATE CHORDATES, protofish, emerge. These take in water through a jawless mouth and pass it through an internal passage wherein food is extracted and diffused through the blood to the cells. In the cells the molecules of organic tissues which constitute the food are broken down to release energy using free oxygen that has been carried by the blood from the gills. The waste produced by the cells in the metabolic process then diffuses back through the cell walls to the blood and is finally let out into the surrounding water.

The total organism is able to maneuver and pursue food, and also avoid dangers, as a result of impulses relayed from the spinal ganglia to cells which are specialized to operate as muscles. Not that such invertebrate chordates were active swimmers, but in their day they represented the elite of the living world.

Most marine invertebrate chordates of this time were essentially long, streamlined organisms, with a muscular tail to aid propulsion, a mouth at one end, an anus at the other (situated just in front of the tail), and a central nervous system or spinal cord running the entire length. This cigar-shaped, symmetrical body, with eyes and other external organs balanced on each side, was to become the standard shape for all higher forms of animal life.

Although man has lost the tail, he is still basically cigar-shaped and symmetrical, the end product of an evolutionary line which, commencing with the chordates, retained its early symmetry, but which, after evolving beyond the level of fishes, steadily lost its streamlined effect. Thus in fishes the jaws are tucked away behind a long streamlined snout, but reptiles lose this snout and leave the jaws to protrude well in advance of the brain and eyes. With mammals the jaw is usually less pronounced than in reptiles, and although monkeys and apes are both still *prognathous* (possessing protruding jaws), the facial angle is relatively flat. The evolution of man in particular records a progressive decline in the size of the jaws and a corresponding increase in the size of the brain case, until with the appearance of *Homo sapiens sapiens* (see Chap. 10) we find that the jaws have receded completely beneath the prominent nose and forehead, leaving a sharp protrusion beneath the jaws which we call the chin.

The first appearance of an elementary brain dates from the Paleozoic. This takes the form of a *cerebellum,* which is at first little more than a swelling at the front end of the spinal cord. While the spinal cord remains the center of ordinary reflex actions, the cerebellum helps the body to maintain balance and muscle tone, and the *medulla,* which connects it to the spinal cord, controls the movements of the heart, gills, fins, and other more or less automatic functions. The cerebellum is first found among MARINE VERTEBRATES, or fishes. These also possess a skeletal structure that provides greater rigidity which also facilitates fast and effective movement.

But all this increasing complexity means that the organism is going to take longer to grow to maturity, in contrast with the protozoa which is virtually adult from the moment of division. Fishes therefore lay eggs which contain a yolk or supply of nutrients for the developing fetus. The female fish lays hundreds of thousands or even millions of small eggs. In many cases these are simply deposited by the female in the surrounding water to be fertilized by a male, who later covers the eggs with sperm. The male and female have no "social" contact whatsoever in the act of reproduction, and the eggs, fertilized or unfertilized, are usually left without any protection. Large numbers are likely to be consumed by predators or otherwise destroyed, and they do not even have the protection of a shell, hence the need to spawn so many offspring.

The Devonian Period

Until some 325 million years ago all major life forms were still restricted to the oceans and similar deposits of water. When next you visit the seashore, reflect for a while that for nine tenths of our ancestral history the sea was our homeland! Our ancestors inhabited the ocean and lakes for over 3 billion years, and for most of this time very little in the way of life existed outside of the water—indeed for hundreds of millions of years the atmosphere could not have contained sufficient oxygen to make terrestrial animal life practicable. However, plants did succeed in making the transition to dry land long before animals, and when the first fishes learned to crawl in the mud, the swamps and plains were already covered with a wide variety of plant life.

Paleontologists do not try to put an exact date on the event, because the transition to terrestrial living must have been a very slow process, as all evolution has been, but the records of the Devonian geological strata indicate a number of dramatic changes in climate which substantially affected many varieties of living

FIG. 7   THE VERTEBRATE FAMILY TREE

(After A. S. Romer, *The Vertebrate Story.* © 1959 by The University of Chicago. By permission.)

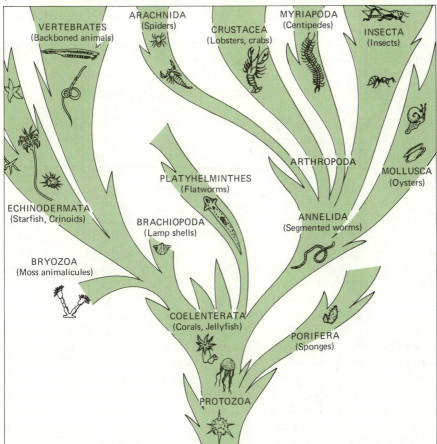

organisms. In all, there appears to have been a long and slow transition to dryness during which the lakes dried up and the ocean levels receded. This transition took millions of years and involved cycles of dryness and wetness, but in the long run the dry seasons became steadily drier. As a result of these changes, many aquatic life forms must have been stranded temporarily during periods of dryness, sometimes just for a few days, and those that failed to survive deprivation of the oxygen and food-bearing water for these short periods would be eliminated, so that the ensuing generations would be born from those that survived.[6] Under these circumstances the population of an isolated lake which showed an increasingly frequent tendency to dry up for days or even weeks at a time would be under rapid selective pressure and might eventually breed a new type of amphibious organism capable of withstanding long periods of drought.

The first of these amphibians must still have depended essentially on a water environment,

[6] For an outline of the evolution of amphibians, read I. I. Schmalhausen, *The Origin of Terrestrial Vertebrates* (New York: Academic Press, 1968).

even though they had developed the ability to survive without water-borne oxygen and food for extended periods of time. Eventually, however, true land animals appeared, and by 280 million years ago were leaving their remains for paleontologists to find.

The earliest terrestrial life forms were but small in size, and terrestrial plants and animals had to face entirely new problems. In the first place, oxygen had to be extracted from the atmosphere where it had been building up, thanks to the activity of plankton in the sea. This required new biological devices, and in addition the air was subject to much more violent temperature changes than was the ocean. Being lighter, it was more readily disturbed, and it also absorbed and lost heat more readily. Furthermore, the animals that lived on land also had to learn how to cope with the force of gravity without the aid of water. While life forms in the sea had long ago become efficiently adapted to the problems that faced them, those life forms that found themselves on the land were subjected to very new selective processes. The prime focus of evolutionary activity was therefore now transferred to the land.

Our own ancestors were not among the first creatures to emerge from the waters, since these appear to have been nonvertebrate. As a technique for adapting to the periodic droughts, some Arthropoda developed a hard external covering known as an *exoskeleton*, which had the advantage of preventing excess evaporation from the surface of the body during the periods that they would be stranded by a drying-up of the lakes or marshes. In due course, gills were replaced by an internal respiratory system and fins by legs, and later some of the Arthropoda developed wings and evolved into insects, becoming the main source of food supply for man's insectivorous ancestors.

The first TERRESTRIAL VERTEBRATES, the class from which man is descended, retained a strongly fishlike appearance complete with fishlike tails. These must have wallowed in the mud, pushing themselves along on their fins, until the more successful found themselves back in the life-giving water. Eventually the fins of such species became increasingly adapted by fierce selection to serve as legs. The first legs were splayed out to each side of the animal, and could not be drawn up underneath the body until pelvic and pectoral girdles, capable of taking the total weight of the organism, eventually developed.[7] Lungs evolved, as indicated by the disappearance of gills from the fossil evidence, and it is to be assumed that the flood plains and swamps became happier hunting grounds for such creatures after they developed powerful jaws and lost their fishlike snouts.

The first true REPTILES found in the early Permian, 280 million years ago, were *Archosauria*, with legs that were now located underneath the body for greater effectiveness, instead of sprawling clumsily beside the heavy body. Some archosaurs developed wings and took to gliding, to become the ancestors of the toothy *Archaeopteryx*. Later descendants of these "lizard birds" developed wings and feathers, lost their tails and their teeth, learned to fly properly, and evolved into birds.

A mammallike reptile (*Lycaenops*), or Therapsid, from the late Permian. All primates, including man, were probably descended from some species of reptilian ancestors of this kind, by way of insectivores. (From E. H. Colbert, 1969, *Evolution of the Vertebrates.* By permission of John Wiley & Sons, Inc.)

[7] See A. S. Romer, *The Vertebrate Body* (Philadelphia: W. B. Saunders Company, 1970).

Reptiles were already well established by the end of the eventful Paleozoic era, and embrace a very significant number of physiological innovations. It is in reptiles that teeth became common, though these were suitable for tearing only, and reptiles are known as *homodonts,* because they do not possess any grinding teeth, and are obliged to ingest their food in solid, unmasticated form, in much the same manner as among fishes and even trilobites. The teeth of crocodiles, nevertheless, undoubtedly aid the food-securing process, especially facilitating attacks on larger animals which are veritable treasure houses of organic material if only they can be caught. But perhaps the most significant contribution of the reptiles to the evolutionary record is in their greatly developed brains, where an entirely new unit evolves: the *cerebral cortex,* which is associated in reptiles and all animals descended from reptiles with that higher mental activity which we call intelligence.[8]

Complicated innovations in the brain necessitate a still longer period of infant development, and the offspring of reptiles need more time in which to mature. Fish, we have seen, reproduce effectively by laying large numbers of eggs in the water and leaving it more or less to chance that some will be fertilized and will survive to hatch out into fully independent and self-sufficient young fishes without any assistance or protection from their parents. But for the young reptile the period of growth is

[8] Read Chapter 8 in Ruth Moore, *Evolution* (New York: Time-Life Books, 1969), for an elementary exposition of cerebral evolution in primates.

too extended for such simple methods. The developing embryo needs substantial supplies of food, while developing to the point that it can break out of the egg; thus reptilian eggs contain a much larger yolk. With the evolutionary process operating as it does, it did not take more than a few million years before other animals came to realize that reptiles' eggs, containing a large yolk, offered a good source of food supply, and eggs to this day are on the preferred diet of many predators besides human beings.

The reptilian response to this was not entirely satisfactory, but it helped a little. This response was the *amniote egg,* coated with a hard rubbery protective covering of soft but thick shell, which still allowed air to permeate through to the interior. With this improvement, the embryo was protected from death through excessive evaporation and consequent dehydration, and the egg could consequently be laid in places safely removed from the usual haunts of the more likely predators. But this in turn, created a further problem. Eggs contained in hard rubbery shells cannot be fertilized externally by a passing male, so another innovation was called for. That innovation was prefertilization of the egg while still inside the female. Male and female were brought into personal contact for the purpose of reproducing. All subsequent varieties of life descended from reptiles have continued this process down to the present—the best part of 300 million years of internal fertilization. An event had occurred which was to have a very large bearing on the social life of modern man.

For Further Reading

Beerbower, J. R., 1968, *Search for the Past: An Introduction to Paleontology.* New York: Prentice-Hall, Inc.

Matthews, W. H., 1962, *Fossils: An Introduction to Prehistoric Life.* New York: Barnes & Noble, Inc.

Moore, R., 1964, *Evolution.* New York: Time-Life Books.

Oakley, K. P., 1964, *Frameworks for Dating Fossil Man.* Chicago: Aldine Publishing Company.

Romer, A. A., 1966, *Vertebrate Paleontology.* Chicago: University of Chicago Press.

Shaw, A. B., 1964, *Time in Stratigraphy.* New York: McGraw-Hill, Inc.

CHAPTER 4

Mammals Supplant Reptiles

Reptiles headed the evolutionary hierarchy at the beginning of the Mesozoic and our ancestors at that time must have been reptilian. However reptiles were not very adequately adapted to the climatic problems and were obliged to remain within tropical or semi-tropical areas, to take refuge in the seas during the colder periods, or else to hibernate if the external temperature fell below the optimum for metabolism. The Mesozoic generally was a period of humid warmth, and temperature at first may have presented no real problems, but ultimately forms of temperature control did develop, some reptiles developing in the direction of birds, with others becoming modified in the direction of mammals.

Both birds and mammals are known as *homotherms,* since they have developed an organic thermostat in the region of the thalamus which, with the aid of additional devices such as feathers or hair, or sweating and shivering, enables them to maintain the temperatures of their bodies well within the range at which optimum metabolism began to take place, re-

gardless of limited changes in the external temperature of their environment.

The invention of internal heat-controlling devices enabled both mammals and birds to spread out widely over the total surface of the globe, and it is interesting to note that around this time some plants also adapted to the problem of temperature. Although plants did not attempt to maintain their organism at an appropriate temperature for metabolism, deciduous plants evolved, adapted for life in temperate climates. These were hyperactive during the warmer season but shed their leaves and passed into a period of rest and comparative inactivity during winter.

Temperature control was by no means the only innovation to be found in mammals. The circulatory system is much more efficient and complex in mammals than among lower animals and this supplies more oxygen to meet the needs of a greatly enlarged brain. There are also substantial evolutionary developments in the process of respiration. The body metabolism of snakes and reptiles is relatively low

FIG. 8   THE MAMMALIAN FAMILY TREE

The evolutionary or "family tree" of the eutherian (placental) mammals, showing their evolution from reptilian ancestors by way of insectivores. (After A. S. Romer, 1970, *The Vertebrate Body*, pp. 69 and 71, Figs. 43 and 44. By permission.)

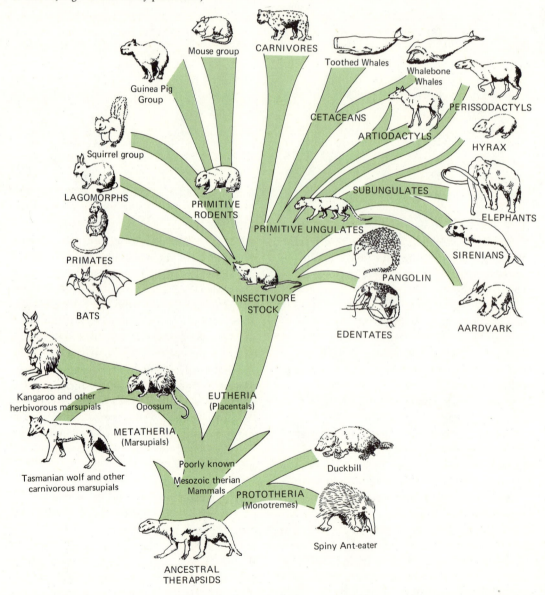

Mouse group

CARNIVORES

Toothed Whales

Whalebone Whales

Guinea Pig Group

CETACEANS

PERISSODACTYLS

ARTIODACTYLS

HYRAX

Squirrel group

SUBUNGULATES

LAGOMORPHS

PRIMITIVE RODENTS

ELEPHANTS

PRIMITIVE UNGULATES

SIRENIANS

PRIMATES

PANGOLIN

BATS

INSECTIVORE STOCK

AARDVARK

EDENTATES

Kangaroo and other herbivorous marsupials

Opossum

EUTHERIA (Placentals)

METATHERIA (Marsupials)

Duckbill

Tasmanian wolf and other carnivorous marsupials

Poorly known Mesozoic therian Mammals

PROTOTHERIA (Monotremes)

Spiny Ant-eater

ANCESTRAL THERAPSIDS

and a small amount of oxygen suffices. But for mammals the metabolic rate is much higher because of the need for energy to meet their more advanced pattern of activity. In reptiles it sufficed, therefore, for the nostrils to open directly into the mouth, but with food in the mouth, breathing could not be efficient. Mammals consequently developed a modification by which the air is taken in through the nostrils but is kept out of the mouth by a second palate, and is conducted separately to the lungs. The respiratory system is thus separated from the digestive, and mammals can chew their food before swallowing, which aids digestion and prevents undue incapacitation while digestion is taking place.

To facilitate mastication, there are substantial innovations in the mammalian teeth. Specialized incisors for biting and cutting, canines for piercing, and premolars and molars for grinding replace the unspecialized teeth of the homodonts. Hearing, too, is improved, and whereas the ear is external in reptiles, the hearing mechanism of mammals is located safely inside the head, with an external flap to guide and concentrate the sound waves. But all these developments take time to manufacture, and necessitate a lengthy period of growth by the offspring; equally significant innovations became necessary in the process of reproduction.

Protomammals

As far back as the Permian period, even before the appearance of dinosaurs, certain small reptiles appeared to have been developing mammalian characteristics such as larger brains, and by the Triassic period, 160 million years ago, there were *theriodonts* which had teeth like those of mammals, complete with canines, molars, and incisors. Some theriodonts also had second palates, and from them mammalian ancestry is traced through *Therapsida*. These creatures were probably pre-dominantly insect-eating and somewhat resembled living lizards, but our ancestors continued to evolve until definite protomammals may be identified by the end of the Mesozoic.

Because Australia and New Guinea were separated from Southeast Asia at an early date by a marine gulf known as the Wallace Line,[1] which runs east of Borneo and the Celebes, these territories, especially Australia, have been a refuge for many of the Mesozoic and early Cenozoic species which were eliminated on the Asian and African mainlands by competition from the more highly evolved species that appeared during the later Cenozoic period. In Australia, therefore, where evolution never proceeded to the level of true mammals, the platypus and the spiny anteater still survive to illustrate the evolutionary transition from reptiles to mammals. These remarkably archaic creatures are known to zoologists as PROTOTHERIA. They are classed as mammals because they share with other mammals the development of an internal heat-control system which maintains the blood temperature at a fairly constant level, appropriate to maximum metabolic activity. This mammalian thermostatic device is supplemented by a furry covering in the platypus, and by a coat of spines in the anteater. Unlike other mammals, however, they are toothless and they lay eggs.

Complicated developments like this thermostatic device prolong still further the requisite growth period of the offspring, and unprotected over long periods, eggs stand very little chance of survival. This is the problem that must have faced the giant dinosaur. The dinosaur did not become extinct because of his unwieldy size—a suggestion that conjures up

[1] The Wallace Line, named after the renowned naturalist who was both a contemporary of Darwin and a co-founder of the theory of organic evolution, is a theoretical line running east and west through the Flores Islands, separating the placental Asian mammals (found north of this line) from the marsupials of Australia.

FIG. 9   PALEOANTHROPOLOGICAL TIME CHART

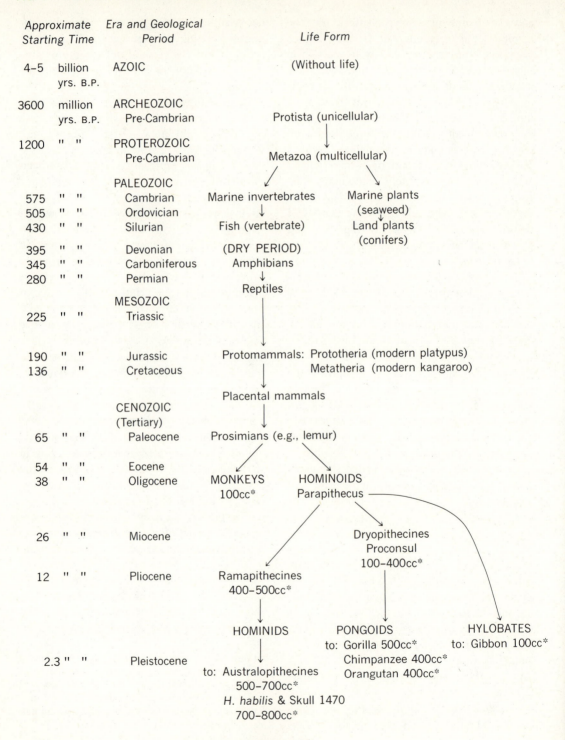

Approximate Starting Time	Era and Geological Period	Life Form
4–5 billion yrs. B.P.	AZOIC	(Without life)
3600 million yrs. B.P.	ARCHEOZOIC Pre-Cambrian	Protista (unicellular)
1200 " "	PROTEROZOIC Pre-Cambrian	Metazoa (multicellular)
	PALEOZOIC	
575 " "	Cambrian	Marine invertebrates — Marine plants (seaweed)
505 " "	Ordovician	
430 " "	Silurian	Fish (vertebrate) — Land plants (conifers)
395 " "	Devonian	(DRY PERIOD)
345 " "	Carboniferous	Amphibians
280 " "	Permian	Reptiles
	MESOZOIC	
225 " "	Triassic	
190 " "	Jurassic	Protomammals: Prototheria (modern platypus)
136 " "	Cretaceous	Metatheria (modern kangaroo)
		Placental mammals
	CENOZOIC (Tertiary)	
65 " "	Paleocene	Prosimians (e.g., lemur)
54 " "	Eocene	MONKEYS HOMINOIDS
38 " "	Oligocene	100cc* Parapithecus
26 " "	Miocene	Dryopithecines Proconsul 100–400cc*
12 " "	Pliocene	Ramapithecines 400–500cc*
2.3 " "	Pleistocene	HOMINIDS PONGOIDS HYLOBATES

MONKEYS 100cc*

HOMINIDS
to: Australopithecines
500–700cc*
H. habilis & Skull 1470
700–800cc*

PONGOIDS
to: Gorilla 500cc*
Chimpanzee 400cc*
Orangutan 400cc*

HYLOBATES
to: Gibbon 100cc*

* Estimated cranial capacity indicated in cubic centimeters (cc).

50

A spiny anteater (*Echidna Tachyglossus aculeatus*)—one of the few surviving Prototheria or primitive mammals. The spiny anteater is warmblooded but lays eggs. (Courtesy of Ron Garrison, San Diego Zoo.)

pictures of lithe smaller animals attacking the great dinosaur and tearing it to pieces. In all probability the immediate demise of the dinosaur was due to climatic changes which affected the entire ecological structure and brought extinction to many other species as well. Nevertheless, it has been suggested that dinosaur eggs must have represented a veritable treasure house of organic food for any egg-eating animal. Taking much longer to hatch out—and being, we assume, unprotected as are most reptilian eggs—it would take only a small animal similar to our own ancestors of this period to be responsible for eating the last dinosaur egg and thereby effectively exterminating the species without giving it a chance to adjust to climatic changes as other reptiles did.

The fact is that at the end of the Mesozoic a vast multitude of reptiles became extinct whereas our ancestors prospered. These had also developed a complex body mechanism, and their eggs must have taken quite as long if not longer than those of the dinosaur to hatch out. But if the example of the spiny anteater is any guide to early protomammals of that period, they were wiser than the reptiles and stayed around to protect their eggs.

Although Prototheria do not possess mammary glands which are as refined as those of true mammals, their breastlike glands deliver a milklike food substance.[2] For the first time in the history of living organisms, a species had evolved which nurtured the offspring

[2] The mammary glands of the Prototheria are distributed over a general area, producing a milklike substance when this area is licked by the offspring. They therefore contrast with the mammary glands of placental mammals, which are concentrated in protruding teats, yielding milk when sucked.

Tasmanian gray kangaroo (*Macropus gigantea tasmaniensis*). Isolated by continental drift, the marsupials of Australia and Tasmania occupied the pinnacle of the hierarchy of life in the Australasian continent until the arrival of man and other placental mammals. (Courtesy of the San Diego Zoo.)

after birth to the extent of providing them with easily digested food. Increasing care of the offspring is indeed one of the most significant of all trends that may be determined in the course of evolution. In the higher forms of life, nature cannot leave it to chance to ensure the survival of these relatively helpless offspring while they undergo the long path of individual growth to maturity. Instead, since the lineage is the all-important evolutionary reality, ever-improving methods are developed for the protection of the offspring until self-sufficiency.

Closer to true mammals are the METATHERIA, several species of which are also found in Australia—the kangaroos, wallabies, wombats, and koala bears—but others such as the lowly opossum still survive in other parts of the world. Metatheria are more advanced than Prototheria in that they not only possess het-

erodont teeth and elementary mammary glands with teats, but under the pressure of further increases in the brain and other organs, have revolutionized the whole process of reproduction.

In the Metatheria the fetus still develops, as with all earlier forms of life from the reptiles onwards, in a prefertilized egg. But the Metatheria do not simply lay these eggs where predators can get at them. Instead, they retain the egg, complete with a small yolk, inside the female body, giving birth after a brief pregnancy to very small and immature offspring. To provide additional after-birth care, the Metatheria carry the infant in a pouch on the mother's body, secure and warm, with ready access to the milk-bearing teats, which eject milk at intervals as the result of a direct reflex when approached by the offspring. Of these remarkable protomammals the koala bear is of particular interest in that it appears to have been a carnivorous animal which for some reason reverted to a herbivorous diet, probably after taking to an arboreal existence. Other Metatheria, such as the kangaroo and wallaby, remained firmly on the ground, and though originally descended from insect eaters, became and remained essentially herbivorous.

Placental Mammals

From the protomammals of the sophistication of the Metatheria, it is perhaps not such a long way to full mammals, and these are already identifiable by the beginning of the Tertiary period of the Cenozoic, during the geological epoch known as the Paleocene, some 65 million years ago.

True mammals retain heat when the external temperature falls, not merely through the circulation of the blood but by the contraction of blood vessels to conserve the needed heat. When the temperature rises in excess of the optimum metabolic level, the dilation of the blood vessels, aided by sweating, will serve to dispose of the surplus heat absorbed by the body.

Along with the control of heat, true mammals also reveal improved senses of hearing, sight, and touch—the ability to feel through the skin as a result of advanced nerve mechanisms just below the epidermis. In the brain, as well, there is a marked enhancement in the efficiency of the cerebral cortex and therefore, we may assume, in reasoning power, deep folds appearing in the cerebral lobes as though an enlarged cerebral cortex is now compressed into a space too small for it. In order to provide for the still more extended period of infant growth, a further reproductive innovation marks off true mammals from protomammals and leads them to be known as EUTHERIAN or PLACENTAL MAMMALS.

Though giving considerable protection to their offspring by keeping the egg within the female body until all the food in the yolk had been consumed, the Metatheria were still severely limited in the length of time that such protection could be afforded by the natural limitations on the size of the yolk that could be conveniently provided to nourish the fetus. Eutherian or placental mammals overcame this problem by dispensing with the idea of the yolk altogether and instead feeding the fetus directly from the female's own body. Joining the fetus to the mother by way of a membrane, the mother's blood may even mingle to some extent with that of the fetus, and this too tends to provide a degree of immunity against diseases for which the mother has already built up a resistance.

With the aid of such new biological devices true mammals were able to spread out over much wider areas than the reptiles. Although the first mammalian fossils are found little more than 100 million years ago, mammals have achieved a high degree of diversity precisely because their sophisticated organic equipment enabled them to disperse into widely different ecological niches. There are today some 3200 different mammalian species as a result of fierce and varied environmental selection. Following the example of the birds, some mammals, such as bats, took to the air; others returned to the sea, evolving into the whales, sea lions, and dolphins of today, and yet others went underground, becoming the ancestors of the moles. Most, however, stayed on the surface of the earth and evolved separately according to the nature of their habitat and their approach to the problem of survival in their own particular ecological niche.

Only the process of continental drift stopped placental mammals from settling every corner of the earth. No placental mammals reached the New World until the Paleocene, while placental carnivores did not find their way into the Americas until as late as the Pliocene. Because Australasia was cut off by continental

FIG. 10   CONTINENTAL DRIFT

The survival of protomammals and of prosimians in places such as Australia and Madagascar is explained by *continental drift*. This diagram illustrates the possible geological forces at work approximately 65 million years ago at the end of the Cretaceous period.

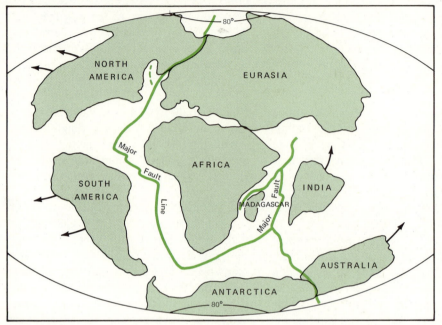

drift from contact with other major continental masses before placental mammals evolved, the marsupial protomammals were able to retain their control of Australia, New Zealand, and associated land masses free of competition from more advanced species until man arrived in the late Pleistocene. These men brought with them another carnivorous mammal, the dog, to assist them in harassing the Australian marsupials. Although the protomammals and various archaic birds of New Zealand escaped more advanced competition until just a few centuries ago, it likewise did not take the Polynesian Maoris long to exterminate the archaic Moa after their canoes eventually brought them to the remote shores of that southern paradise.

For Further Reading

Matthews, W. H., 1962, *Fossils: An Introduction to Prehistoric Life.* New York: Barnes & Noble, Inc.

Morris, R., and D. Morris, 1968, *Men and Apes.* New York: Bantam Books.

Romer, A. S., 1966, *Vertebrate Paleontology.* Chicago: University of Chicago Press.

Simpson, G. G., 1945, The Principles of Classification and a Classification of Mammals," *Bulletin of the American Museum of Natural History* 85:1–450.

Young, J. Z., 1957, *The Life of Mammals.* New York: Oxford University Press.

CHAPTER 5

Into the Trees

Man's ancestors must be sought in a small group of mammals that must have resisted the temptation to return to the sea, to go underground, or to take to the air, but still did not remain purely terrestrial or land-bound. While most mammals adapted themselves to life on the plains, becoming efficient four-legged running animals, some apparently found refuge in the forest fringes, in the necks of woodland alongside the rivers, or possibly where trees were interspersed with rocks along a cliff front. With a diet of insects, eggs, and leaves, they would have made regular incursions into these trees and also found that the trees provided a place of refuge from the larger carnivorous mammals on the ground.

Prosimians and Primates

Slowly becoming more arboreal, these creatures spent their lives walking with careful steps along the branches, grasping boughs to pull themselves upward, hanging upright from the forelimbs, and eventually, in the case of certain primates, swinging from the branches in a motion known as *brachiation.*[1] Millions of years of climbing, hanging, and swinging in an erect position brought about a number of physiological adjustments. In order to clutch the branches effectively, the forefeet evolved into prehensile, or grasping, hands, an adaptation that was later to be very useful to man in enabling him to grasp and handle tools. The swinging motion adopted by apes when brachiating led to greater flexibility of the shoulder blade until the arm could be swung in almost every direction, while a substantial modification of the forearm and wrist made it possible to rotate the hand in a full circle.

Since the body was carried upright during many of these arboreal movements, especially brachiation, the head became balanced on the shoulders instead of hanging forward, thus facilitating the later growth of the brain, the weight of which is more easily carried when balanced on the shoulders. More important,

[1] Not all primates brachiate; many, like the baboon, are phylogenetically incapable of brachiation.

As a prosimian, the common tree shrew (*Tupaia glis*) is one of the simplest of the primates. (Courtesy of the San Diego Zoo.)

though, with the head being carried erect, the eyes began to move round to the front of the face, making stereoscopic vision possible. Being relatively safe in the trees from terrestrial predators, these creatures gradually lost the sense of smell which is so valuable to terrestrial mammals, both carnivorous and herbivorous. But this loss was more than compensated for by improvements in eyesight. Acute vision is of the utmost importance when jumping from branch to branch, and a shortsighted monkey does not live to reproduce. Primates —that order of mammals which includes tree shrews, tarsiers, lemurs, monkeys, apes, and men—consequently learned to judge distances accurately, and most developed both stereoscopic and color vision.

As we move on into the Cenozoic, some 70 million years ago, fossil remains reveal the first protoprimates: PROSIMII or PROSIMIANS as they are generally called. In Madagascar and the Philippines, both island reservations in which a number of less evolved species have managed to survive free from the fiercer competition that raged on the mainlands of Africa and Asia,[2] prosimians are still to be found, Madagascar having no monkeys at all. In the Philippines the little *tree shrew*—with five digits on each foot, separate "thumbs," and a clear differentiation of function and shape of the forelimbs from the hindlimbs—survives as an

[2] Marginal areas, far removed from the major centers of competition, generally harbor older and less competitive forms of life long after the corresponding life forms have been annihilated in the more central areas or have evolved under the fierce selection into new subspecies or species.

example of a prosimian which is distinctly ancestral in type to true primates, even though it has an extremely long snout by primate standards.

A better known prosimian is the *lemur* of Madagascar. Lemurs are small arboreal animals which congregate in groups and exist on insects, leaves, bugs, and birds' eggs. They have a shorter snout than the tree shrew and are less ratlike and more simian or monkeylike in appearance. In addition, they boast well developed, rotating forearms and prehensile hands and feet, but still retain an unsimian, refined sense of smell, while their brains are poorly developed and it is unlikely that they possess either color or stereoscopic vision. Also unlike true primates they are nocturnal in their habits. Lemurs have survived in Madagascar only because this large island was separated from other continents before the evolution of carnivorous mammals and monkeys, so that they have no rivals in their habitat. By contrast, those of their relatives that remained on the mainland were eliminated in competition with more rapidly evolving members of the same prosimian assemblage, except for the nocturnal bushbaby and galago.

A third living prosimian is the *tarsier*, which has survived in Indonesia. The tarsier is the least prognathous of the prosimians, and may possess stereoscopic but not color vision.[3] Although its brain is not highly convoluted, the important cerebrum or forward region is particularly well evolved, and it has fully prehensile hands and rotating forearms. Instead of claws like the tree shrew, the tarsier's fingers are equipped with nails. However, it has developed disclike pads on the tips of the fingers for a better grip when climbing, giving the hands, which would otherwise look quite human, a ghoulish appearance.

Tarsiers live mainly on insects and have

[3] Color vision in the tarsier is not postulated because the retina lacks cones, being comprised solely of rods. See J. R. Napier and P. H. Napier, *Handbook of Living Primates* (New York: Academic Press, Inc., 1967), p. 325.

large, well developed eyes because they live by jumping and catching the insects that fly at dusk and by night. They produce only one offspring at a time, and the females have a menstrual cycle similar to that of the primates. If tree shrews may be said to be intermediate between insectivores and prosimians, so tarsiers may be said to be intermediate between prosimians and true primates.

Anthropoids

Paleontology has revealed that the first marsupials appeared in the Cretaceous period of the Mesozoic, sometime after 136 million years ago. By the beginning of the Paleocene, 70 million years ago, lemurs, tarsiers, and other prosimians lived in abundance throughout the warmer parts of Africa, Asia, and North America, and it is in the Paleocene, which appears to have been a very warm and humid period, that the primates evolved. Vast tropical forests then spread over the areas today known as Europe, Africa, and South Asia. Although it is difficult to reconstruct the geography of the world at that time, continental drift must have begun, for it was at some time during the Paleocene that the Old and New Worlds were severed from each other. The actual separation probably took place shortly before the appearance of true primates, as New World monkeys appear to have evolved from prosimian stock independently of, but largely parallel to, the evolution of Old World monkeys.

There are ample fossil remains of early anthropoids of the Catarrhine type in the Old World at all levels of evolution. Primate evolution from earlier prosimian ancestors seems to have been by way of a creation known as *Parapithecus,* found in Africa, which is midway between a tarsier and a true primate. An early type of true anthropoid, found in Burma and named *Amphipithecus,* has three submolars, but all later Old World anthropoids from the Oligocene and Miocene reveal only the modern standard formula of two premolars, and by the Pliocene some of the modern varieties of monkeys had come into existence.

With the land bridge to North America still open in the Oligocene, some advanced prosimians migrated to the New World. Becoming isolated by continental drift and climatic changes, they evolved in a parallel direction to their cousins in the Old World, but more slowly perhaps because of the relative absence of competition in their more isolated environment. A basic division therefore exists between the flat-nosed *Platyrrhini* or New World monkeys and the long-nosed *Catarrhini* or Old World monkeys, both of which belong to the primate suborder ANTHROPOIDEA.

There are two divisions of the New World or Platyrrhini monkeys, the smaller of which are known as *Callithricidae* (the marmosets), and the larger as *Cebidae*. Their brains are larger and more convoluted than those of tarsiers, and they have stereoscopic vision. Although some can brachiate, many are still nocturnal like the tarsiers. Their thumbs are not so fully opposable to the fingers as are those of the Catarrhini, and the New World spider monkeys have specialized in brachiation to the extent of losing their thumbs altogether. On the other hand, the tail of the spider monkey can grasp a branch, rather like an extra hand. These tails have hairless patches at the end, just as our hands are hairless, and the skin on these patches has even developed *dermatoglyphic markings* or "fingerprints" for better grasping power.

Teeth provide an example of lagging evolution among the New World *Callithricidae* and *Cebidae*. The jaws of primates are growing smaller in the course of evolution, as the face becomes flatter, hands take over many of the functions of the teeth, and there is a decline in the number of teeth. The original mammalian dental formula was 3-1-4-3, which means three incisors, one canine, four submolars, and three molars. The New World monkeys became modified to 2-1-3-3, but did

not evolve beyond this point. The Old World monkeys, and with them apes and men, lost another submolar and have a dental formula of 2-1-2-3. Among men the wisdom tooth now survives with little use, and among some of the flatter-faced peoples of Europe, one child in six never develops wisdom teeth at all, indicating a further trend towards a future formula of 2-1-2-2.

The Cebidae live in large groups like the monkeys of the Old World and resist the approach of alien troops with much screaming and other signs of hostility. Within the group, however, there is little mutual aggressiveness. The insectivorous marmosets live in much smaller groups, and are remarkable in that they produce twin offspring, as distinct from other Anthropoidea which normally produce one offspring at a time.

In general, Catarrhini or Old World monkeys do not brachiate, but run along the branches on all fours, jumping from one branch to another with dexterity. Although they are capable of reaching up from their hind legs and using their hands to pluck food, they seldom carry objects in their hands. Old World monkeys are mostly territorial, but as herbivores they do not always make a very strong attempt to defend their territories against alien incursions.[4]

Although the New World monkeys have been isolated so long that even the lice that live on their coats have become diversified into quite separate species, either the lower intensity of competition in the New World or the absence of the appropriate ecological opportunity or perhaps a combination of both factors meant that they never evolved beyond the level

[4]S. L. Washburn and D. A. Hamburg claim that the aggressiveness of Old World monkeys in defense of their territories has been underestimated in the past. See S. L. Washburn and D. A. Hamburg, "Aggressive Behavior in Old World Monkeys and Apes," in Phyllis Dolhinow (ed.), *Primate Patterns* (New York: Holt, Rinehart and Winston, Inc. 1973), p. 287.

The forests that house the orangutan of Borneo (*Pongo pygmaeus*) are steadily disappearing at the hands of man, with the primate now facing extinction—a common fate for animals which fail to compete with their more successful relatives for living space. (Courtesy of the American Museum of Natural History.)

of the Cebidae, and no apes or apelike fossils have ever been found in the Americas. In fact the brachiating spider and howler monkeys represent the nearest New World equivalent to the Old World apes.

The Emergence of Hominoids

Unfortunately, the fossil record from the Paleocene and the Eocene, covering the important period from 70 million to 38 million years ago, is very sparse. The first really plentiful evidence which we have of early primates comes to us from Egypt. Here in an area known as the Fayum Depression, only 60 miles southwest of Cairo, the dry desert sands have preserved a rich variety of primate fossil remains from the Oligocene. During this period, it would appear that the Mediterranean coastline extended up to the Fayum Depression and that 38 million to 30 million years ago the Fayum area[5] was covered with rich tropical forests well watered by one or more rivers draining from Africa into the Mediterranean.

One of the oldest fossils found at Fayum is called *Oligopithecus,* after the Oligocene. This was an early primate which appears to be ancestral to the Old World monkeys, having only 32 teeth instead of 34. But a study of other Fayum fossils provides us with evidence that during the Oligocene the primates were already beginning to divide into monkeylike and hominoidlike varieties—HOMINOIDEA being simply definable as that taxonomic superfamily which includes both apes and men. Thus while the Old World or Catarrhini monkeys have molar teeth with four cusps or protrusions on the grinding edge arranged in what is known as a *bilophodont* pattern—two pairs of cusps joined by short ridges—hominoids are distinguished by possessing five cusps on their lower molars. *Propliopithecus,* also found at Fayum, is generally regarded as the first known hominoid, because its lower molars have evolved five cusps.[6]

Apes resemble men in that they do not have tails but remain closer to monkeys in that the sexual skin of the female swells periodically

[5] For a list of the Fayum fossil remains see C. Arambourg, "Continental Vertebrate Faunas of the Tertiary of North Africa," in F. C. Howell and F. Bourlière (eds.), *African Ecology and Human Evolution* (Chicago: Aldine Publishing Co., 1966), pp. 58–59.

[6] Dental characteristics play an important role in paleoanthropology because portions of the jawbone and teeth are among the commonest surviving fossil remains.

The evolutionary history of bipedal locomotion among the primates is illustrated by a study of the primate foot. Lemurs and monkeys have feet well adapted to grasping branches, but the big toe of the chimpanzee reveals that this creature spends much of its time on the ground, since the foot is largely adapted for walking. By contrast, the human foot has become even more thoroughly specialized for rapid locomotion in an upright posture, and in humans the big toe is no longer opposible to the other toes. (Courtesy of the American Museum of Natural History.)

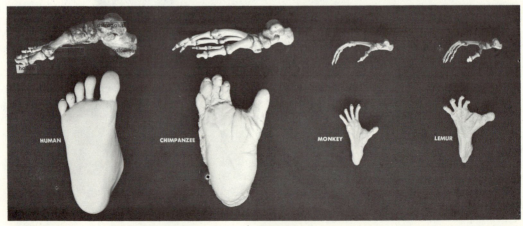

like that of the female monkey. In general, it may be said that all apes have arms which are longer than their legs, and the gibbon can touch the ground with his fingertips even when standing erect. Like men, apes can walk erect on their lower limbs, but only for shorter periods of time.

Ease of BIPEDALISM, or the art of walking on the two hind legs, depends to some extent on a low center of gravity.[7] In men the center of gravity is situated around the top of the pelvis, whereas in the gibbon it is located as high as the chest. In consequence the gibbons have to wave their long arms for balance when trying to walk erect.

Propliopithecus, a snoutlike creature that wandered in Europe and Africa, is generally regarded as a possible ancestor of the gibbon, and is dated around 30 million years ago. If we may regard *Propliopithecus* as a hominoid, then the anthropoid family had begun to divide into monkeys and hominoids. This separation is more certain when we come to the large variety of *Dryopithecines,* with whom *Proconsul* is usually associated, which date from 25 million years ago and are found in Europe, Africa, and India. Dryopithecines are distinctly apelike and reveal a larger cranium than that of either living or fossil monkeys. Whereas monkeys do not usually exceed 100 cubic centimeters in cranial capacity (which is indicative of the overall size of the brain, but not of the development of specific areas), these earlier hominoids reveal increasing cranial capacity of up to 400 cubic centimeters.[8] The Dryopithe-

cines in particular are believed to be ancestral to the *Pongidae*—the gorillas, chimpanzees, and orangutans—while the *Hylobates* or gibbons may have begun to evolve separately from the Pongidae at the *Propliopithecus* level.

Gibbons are usually distinguished from the other three apes, the Pongidae, because they are much smaller, usually not exceeding 3 feet in height, and have a lower cranial capacity which seldom exceeds 100 cubic centimeters. With their enormously long arms, more than twice as long as their body, gibbons have retained great skill in brachiating. Their habitat is Southeast Asia, their nearest ape relative being the orangutan which is found in Borneo and Sumatra. More characteristically apelike, orangutans stand around 5 feet in height and weigh up to 200 pounds. Their cranial capacity is around 400 cubic centimeters, but they are still primarily arboreal, although not so obviously as the gibbon. Neither the gibbon nor the orangutan is regarded as being as closely related to man as the chimpanzee and the gorilla, both found in what may be man's old homeland, Africa.

Gorilla males have been known to reach over 6 feet in height and may weigh up to 600 pounds in captivity, although those in the wild seem to keep themselves in better shape and seldom exceed 300 to 400 pounds. Their cranial capacity ranges up to around 500 cubic centimeters, but the ratio of brain size to body size is certainly not as impressive as in the case of the chimpanzee, and weight of brain alone, under these circumstances, would not be meaningful were it not for the fact that the gorilla brain reveals relatively well convoluted cerebral lobes.[9]

---

[7] See B. G. Campbell, *Human Evolution* (Chicago: Aldine Publishing Co., 1968), Chap. 11, for the evolution of bipedalism.

[8] Differences in cranial capacity do not directly imply differences in intelligence. Within the same species larger animals tend to have larger brains. What is more significant is the differential development of the relative areas of the brain. However, it is generally agreed that when tracing the overall evolution of the hominids as a series of phylogenetic continua, the evolution of the various areas of the brain—particularly of the highly convoluted

cerebral cortex and the important frontal lobes—has resulted in an increase in the overall size of the cranium. In such a context, comparative cranial capacity within the hominid lineage possesses definite evolutionary significance.

[9] For further discussion of the evolutionary significance of the cerebral cortex, see Campbell, Chaps. 8 and 9.

Competition has eliminated many of the more advanced primate species leaving the chimpanzee (*Pan troglodytes*) as the most intelligent surviving relative of *Homo sapiens*. Note that the chimpanzee walks on bent knuckles, not on the extended fingers, which are adapted to prehensile functions. (Courtesy of the San Diego Zoo.)

Gorillas often sleep in the trees for protection, but the day is spent almost entirely on the ground. Much of this time is spent sitting or walking erect, allowing the arms to dangle by their sides, but when alarmed, they usually flee on all fours for greater speed, resting their weight on the knuckles of the hands rather than on the extended fingers which are now too specialized to be used like toes.

Unlike the gorilla, the chimpanzee can brachiate well but spends much time on the ground and shows some preference for traveling on the ground, on all fours, instead of through the trees. The chimpanzee is perhaps the most intelligent of all nonhuman animals, standing approximately 5 feet high but weighing only 100 to 120 pounds. With this smaller body, it is significant that the cranial capacity still averages around 400 cubic centimeters. Chimpanzees have been taught to ride bicycles, to use knives and forks while eating, and even to understand several hundred English words.

Possibly the most amusing test of learning ability among domesticated chimpanzees was carried out with the aid of a slot machine which dispensed food. Not only did the chimpanzee soon discover how to use the slot machine to obtain food, but he also learned how to earn coins with which to purchase his meals. When different foods were made available at various prices in several machines, the chimpanzee learned to select which he preferred.[10] Probably the most human response occurred when the price of the food was raised, the machine being altered so that it required more coins to effect the same supply. The chimpanzee protested violently, lying on its back kicking and screaming, but—like humans—eventually learned to accept the hard fact of inflation!

[10] Other examples of learned behavior and social relations among captive chimpanzees are described in R. M. Yerkes and Ada W. Yerkes, *The Great Apes* (New Haven, Conn.: Yale University Press, 1929).

For Further Reading

Alland, A., Jr., 1967, *Evolution and Human Behavior.* Garden City, N.Y.: Natural History Press.

Buettner-Janusch, J., 1966, *Origins of Man.* New York: John Wiley & Sons, Inc.

Chiarelli, B., ed., 1968, *Taxonomy and Phylogeny of Old World Primates with References to the Origin of Man.* Torino, Italy: Rosenberg and Sellier.

Eimerl, S., and I. DeVore, 1965, *The Primates.* New York: Time-Life Books.

Jolly, A., 1972, *The Evolution of Primate Behavior.* New York: The Macmillan Company.

Lasker, G. W., 1961, *The Evolution of Man.* New York: Holt, Rinehart and Winston, Inc.

Le Gros Clark, W. E., 1970, *A History of the Primates.* London: British Museum (Natural History).

McCown, T. D., and K. A. R. Kennedy, 1972, *Climbing Man's Family Tree.* Englewood Cliffs, N.J.: Prentice-Hall, Inc.

Napier, J. R., and P. H. Napier, 1967, *A Handbook of Living Primates: Morphology, Ecology and Behaviour of Nonhuman Primates.* New York: Academic Press, Inc.

Poirier, F. E., 1973, *Fossil Man: An Evolutionary Journey.* St. Louis, Mo.: The C. V. Mosby Co.

CHAPTER 6

Mammalian Social Life

The fact that all primates live in groups is not without significance for anthropology and before we take up the search for man's earliest human ancestors, let us tarry for a while to look at the structures of these groups. Indeed, to appreciate the evolutionary significance of primate social behavior, we must examine this in the wider setting of mammalian social life.

Both prenatal and postnatal care of infants become biological imperatives at the mammalian level of evolution because of the enormous gap that separates the newly conceived fetus from the physiological complexity of the mature organism—in particular the helplessness of the offspring at birth. Something new and essentially cultural now emerges which characterizes all mammalian behavior: a mother-child relationship which generates strong emotional ties.

With mammals, therefore, we are definitely on the threshold of human society and human-type communication and culture. Man is the only animal that has evolved the power of speech, but rudimentary forms of communication exist throughout mammalian society, as well as among other advanced life forms such as birds and insects, and not all mammalian behavior is directly unlearned or "instinctive." We shall discuss the growth of communication and the accumulation of culture among men in a later chapter, but for the present let us simply observe that speech and culture were not invented overnight. There is nothing miraculous about either, nothing superorganic nor supernatural; both have a long evolutionary history which antedates the advent of *Homo sapiens,* or "intelligent man," as we choose to call ourselves.

Evolutionary Value of Society

The same is true, even more patently, of the concept of society. Some of the eighteenth-century encyclopedist philosophers, whose ideas still influence many people today, were prone to argue that society was a human invention which arose as a result of an intentional, rational decision made by early men to collaborate with their fellows. But Aristotle, 2000 years earlier, was nearer to the truth when he described man as a "social animal." Our subhuman ancestors were already social animals, living a group life, long before they evolved even the power of speech. Society and culture are both older than *H. sapiens* and are part of the evolutionary order, a natural and presumably inevitable product of the law of natural selection and the survival of the fittest. Society appeared because it helped to ensure survival; society evolved at the mammalian level because it provided protection for the helpless mammalian offspring during their increasingly long infancy and improved the chances of survival to adulthood and hence parenthood.[1] Those of our ancestors who were inherent "loners" were eliminated by predators, and only those that tended to congregate in groups produced offspring which in turn survived long enough to attain parenthood.

Taking a wider view, the mammalian mother-child relationship has evolutionary value not only in that it meets the immediate biological need of providing nourishment and direct physical protection to the child during the period of helplessness, but also in that it facilitates the imprinting of the attitudes and behavior pattern of the mother on the infant. This imprinting process provides the first elementary basis for the transmission of acquired skills and the rudimentary foundation of culture. At higher levels of mammalian life, where the offspring spend even longer with their parent or parents, the transmission of more sophisticated acquired skills becomes possible, and the education process is further enhanced as improved means of communication develop. Among many predators, quite complex hunting skills are conveyed from generation to

generation simply by example and imitation. It has also been demonstrated that among birds, which have evolved many social patterns of behavior surprisingly parallel to those of mammals, the young learn the route by which they should migrate by imitation and example, and young birds which have been separated from the adult community do not know which way to migrate even though the urge to migrate seems to be inborn.[2]

Mother-child groups

Zoologists have distinguished some four different patterns of social relationship among mammals, which are undoubtedly of significance to us if we wish to see human behavior in an overall evolutionary perspective. At the lower level of mammalian life—and we may include protomammals such as the platypus in this category—society does not extend beyond a mother-infant relationship. Male and female squirrels, for example, nest separately, and only come together for a brief mating contact. The female squirrel produces the offspring in her own nest, and provides them with protection and food until they are sufficiently matured to attempt an independent existence. The male plays no part in the upbringing of the offspring; all necessary care and protection is afforded solely by the female and no question of any male-female pair relationship exists.

Herds

Herd animals practice a considerably more sophisticated type of relationship. Herds comprise a number of females and their offspring who associate together for mutual protection.

---

[1] See also J. S. Dimond, *The Social Behavior of Animals* (New York: Harper & Row Publishers, 1970).

[2] For entertaining but informative reading concerning behavior in animals, the reader would enjoy Konrad Lorenz, *King Solomon's Ring* (New York: Thomas Y. Crowell Company, 1961).

In such groups each infant learns to identify its mother by a process of psychological imprinting immediately following birth, and the mothers tend their own offspring, rejecting all advances by other offspring. Among some species the females and their offspring are attended for either part of the year or permanently by a dominant male who acts as leader, but in others the males may live alone or else congregate in all-male herds separately from the females, who then raise their offspring without male assistance.

Permanent male-female troops

In a third category, which includes most monkeys, we find groups of females and their offspring who have succeeded in winning the permanent protection of the males, so that permanent societies of males, females, and offspring are the rule. This category is known as the permanent male-female troop and is typically simian. Young primates take so long to grow to self-sufficiency that the females—most of whom come into estrus monthly and

A troop of baboons roam amicably alongside a herd of zebra at a waterhole in an East African game reserve. (Courtesy of Sherwood Washburn.)

unlike other mammals remain capable of breeding all year round—are burdened with dependent children throughout the greater part of their adult life. In fact, virtually the entire adult life of female monkeys is spent in pregnancy and in the care of young children. Under these circumstances it is obvious that year-round protection by the males has definite survival value. Intersexual relations within these permanent male-female groups are essentially promiscuous and the social system is primarily rooted in the straightforward dominance of the larger and tougher animals over the weaker, modified only by the tendency to form small cohorts or groups whose members support each other in intratroop conflicts.

Although men, apes, and monkeys have evolved in separate directions over the past 40 to 15 million years, it is generally assumed that man's early arboreal ancestors may well have lived in permanent male-female groups, since their environmental problems must have been similar to those of contemporary monkeys. Too much should not be read into speculations of this kind, which are at best intelligent and informed conjecture, but keeping this warning in mind, let us take a look at the major features of baboon social organization, illustrating as it does this third class of mammalian social organization.

Baboon Troops

Baboons are probably one of the most intelligent of the monkey species. Those which live on the edge of the woodlands spend much time on the ground, but being very nervous of snakes as well as of carnivorous mammals, they prefer to sleep in the security of trees. During the day they may trek on foot across quite substantial stretches of open country, but they always take care to arrive at a clump of trees before nightfall and remain in their aerial retreats until well after dawn.

Role of Males   Like all other monkeys, savannah baboons are highly gregarious creatures,

living in troops ranging from 10 to 100 or even 150 individuals, and never roaming more than a few yards from the companionship of the troop all their lives. Group life undoubtedly serves the needs of each in protecting them individually from predators, and is of particular evolutionary value in affording greater protection to the mothers and infants, for the survival of a species is not at stake when an aging adult dies, but it is endangered by depredations which affect the young. The prime evolutionary value of the baboon troop consequently seems to rest in the fact that it provides year-round protection for the females and infants. Without such protection it is doubtful how many baboon infants would survive to reach parenthood.

The role of the males in providing protection for the females and infants is apparent at all times. When the troop is feeding, there are always several males on guard duty who bark warnings at the appearance of a predator. On the approach of danger the males will invariably adopt a position in front of the females and infants unless tree refuges are available, where the entire troop can take to safety. Similarly, when baboon troops are on the move, the females and infants are placed in the safe company of the dominant males in the middle of the line while the van, the rear, and the flanks are protected by subordinate males.[3]

The Absence of Food Sharing   Unlike most other monkeys the baboons are not strict herbivores. Their diet comprises flowers, seeds, bulbs, grass, fruit, leaves, and insects, but they are also known to eat small monkeys and even young gazelles on occasion. However, readiness to supplement their diet with meat, although suggestive of the ease with which our own ancestors may have adapted to a meat diet,

[3] For further reading on baboons consult K. R. L. Hall and I. DeVore, "Baboon Social Behavior," in Phyllis Dolhinow (ed.), *Primate Patterns* (New York: Holt, Rinehart and Winston, Inc., 1972).

FIG. 11   TERRITORIALITY AMONG PRIMATES

Baboon territories in the Nairobi Game Park, East Africa. The six territories illustrated below overlap, but each troop has its own core area in which are located its customary sleeping trees. Penetration of the core areas is likely to result in markedly aggressive reactions, while marginal areas are entered and used by the neighboring troops without fear. (After Irven DeVore, 1965, *Primate Behavior*, p. 36, Fig. 2-7. By permission.)

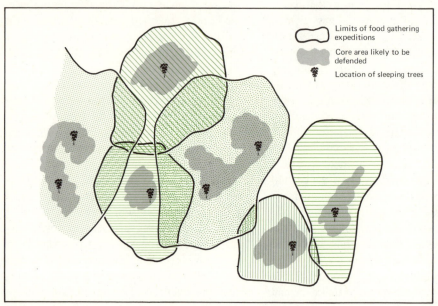

Limits of food gathering expeditions

Core area likely to be defended

Location of sleeping trees

has not materially affected their pattern of life or social organization. As food gatherers, feeding mainly upon an ample supply of grass, fruit, and insects, supplemented with birds' eggs and even crocodile eggs where available, the females are perfectly able to find their own food alongside the males, and there is no food sharing except between mother and young, nor therefore any division of labor, except in matters of defense and care of infants. Not only is there no food sharing, but there is no assistance, either, for wounded or sick members of the troop. Should a baboon break a leg, fall ill, or just become weak from old age, the others make no attempt to assist it, and falling behind when the troop is on the move, that member will soon become a prey for predators. Only the young are given the benefit of positive aid and assistance.

As may be expected, the savannah baboons are essentially territorial animals in that they tend to keep to their own familiar homeland.[4] Each group ranges a territory which may extend from 3 to 6 square miles, with little or no contact between troops occupying neighboring territories, even though these may have originated in the subdivision of a single original troop at some earlier time. Each troop is therefore intensely inbred over the generations—a circumstance which promotes rapid evolutionary change. Some inquisitiveness may

[4] It should be noted that the carnivorous tendencies of the East African savannah-dwelling baboons have developed as an evolutionary response to the problem of survival under the prevailing ecological conditions. The forest-dwelling baboons of Central Africa have no difficulty in finding sustenance on a more purely frugivorous diet, eating meat much less frequently than the savannah variety.

be observed when two troops meet at a water hole regarded as neutral territory, but there is neither animosity nor fraternization. By contrast, definite aggressive postures are adopted should an alien troop penetrate deeply into the home territory. Actual combat is rare, but perhaps only because aggressive poses are usually sufficient to drive intruders away.

Dominance-Submission Within baboon troops, however, the general law of dominance and submission seems to prevail. Certain animals dominate others, and these become centers of attraction and of popularity around whom the weaker eagerly gather. Regular cliques develop among the males which become, in effect, political groups, and in the course of time a pattern of hierarchy develops between cliques, with the toughest *and most cohesive* group dominating the others and the dominant male in that group emerging as the leader of the entire troop.[5] Once a pattern of hierarchical leadership has been established, the dominant male and his lieutenants will maintain order among the subordinate members of the troop, scolding and even slapping adults and infants who may squabble too seriously or who may challenge their authority.

Mating Behavior Like human females, female baboons ovulate approximately once a month but unlike human females, are receptive to male contacts for only a few days. During the early stage of estrus the female will approach the younger and less dominant males, consorting with these, and only later when fully receptive will she present herself to the dominant males. Since each dominant male usually de-

[5] S. L. Washburn, P. C. Jay, and Jane B. Lancaster, "Field Studies of Old World Monkeys and Apes" in Dolhinow, pp. 246-260, have suggested that the baboon grooming clique is generally comprised of siblings. If this is demonstrated to be the case, then the patterns of kinship that are a characteristic of human societies have a far older evolutionary history than has hitherto been supposed—protokinship bonds being present at even the nonhuman primate level.

mands privacy in the area immediately around him, allowing in only regular friends for grooming purposes, she may first have to accept a certain amount of physical punishment before being permitted to trespass close enough to be able to win his attentions.

At this stage there will be a temporary pairing off of a male and the estrus female for a few hours or even for so long as a few days, during which time all other social ties and loyalties are modified. Male and female may move to the edge of the troop, avoiding other social contacts during this period. Such temporary social relations may be interrupted, however, by another male who will harass the other until one admits submission, and the female is then passed to or remains with the more dominant. At birth the neonate becomes temporarily the center of attraction for the entire troop, but thereafter the infant develops special emotional links with the mother and with her other offspring—who are in effect his siblings. The identity of the father is not known, and therefore no father-infant relationship exists. Baboon societies consequently bear no resemblance to the human family system, the closest parallel to the baboon troops known in human experience being the concept of the commune.

Gorilla Troops

Because of the obvious biological relationship of apes to men, many writers have implied close parallels between ape and human societies. While monkeys as a whole tend to give the impression of being excitable extroverts, chattering, squealing, and exhibiting a rather "childish" attitude of curiosity to all that takes place around them, the behavior of gorillas seems more ideally restrained. The gorilla especially impresses humans as being the "strong and silent type," dignified and aloof.

Contrary to the native legends recounted by early explorers, gorillas are not fierce and aggressive monsters, but are actually somewhat

Strong, relatively silent, and frequently silent, and frequently aloof, the lowland gorilla (*Gorilla gorilla*) has always commanded respect from his more excitable and physically diminutive relative, *Homo sapiens*. However, the gorilla is by no means as aggressive as legend and folklore suppose, and like other noncarnivores is actually a retiring animal. (Courtesy of the San Diego Zoo.)

shy, retiring, and peaceful creatures as one would expect herbivores to be. They spend most of their time on the ground and can stand and walk erect, although when alarmed they flee on all fours. At night they make nests of broken branches either on the ground or more often in trees. Because of their physical size and strength they have few enemies other than leopards and men, and are far too large to brachiate. Unlike the ungulates they are not obliged to spend the entire day endlessly gathering food, and much of their life is spent in indolent ease, with feeding restricted to a morning breakfast which is followed by a midday siesta and an afternoon meal before the evening rest.

The Gorilla "Patriarch" Gorilla troops vary in size, but 5 to 20 is the more common number, and they are not known to exceed a maximum of 25 to 30. Each troop possesses its own territory, anywhere between 10 or 15 square miles in size and is invariably dominated by an adult male, usually a "silver-back," so named because in the prime of life (from 10 years of age) the hair down the back of a gorilla turns gray. This dominant male, generally the largest, is unlikely to retain leadership into old age, for the basis of gorilla society, like that of baboons, is one of dominance and submission.[6] The gorilla troop is not divided into cliques even though there are usually two or three younger, black-backed males, some half a dozen females, and probably the same number of dependent infants. The sex ratio of gorillas is not known for certain, but female births appear to outnumber male births, although not so heavily as with monkeys, so that in gorilla troops the ratio of females to males is usually 2:1 or 3:2. As with the baboon, infants are born singly, but despite the long period of gorilla pregnancy, adult females are almost permanently pregnant or feeding young infants, and there is a surplus of offspring, out of which natural selection takes its toll, thus keeping the genetic pool well pruned.

In contrast with baboon troops in which all males cooperate in defending the group, the defense of the gorilla troop rests almost entirely upon the patriarch, and should danger threaten, it is the dominant male alone who will normally come forward to meet the challenge, beating his chest in the popular fashion as if to offer single combat. But in addition to offering protection, the silver-back shows considerable interest in the infants, and when in a tolerant mood, will even allow them to play around and over him. Mothers are also extremely protective and affectionate, and have been known to carry dead children for several days before finally discarding the corpse.

Observers have been able to acquire considerable knowledge of gorilla gestures or sign language. To stare a dominant gorilla in the eyes is the height of rudeness; in fact, it is a challenge to his authority, and human observers have learned that they too, if confronted by a dominant male, must turn their eyes away or risk the threat of attack. A broad grin indicates friendship. Smacking the lips, in imitation of the peaceable sounds and motions made by an anthropoid as it eats the lice it has taken from the coat of the animal it is grooming, denotes peaceable intentions. Nodding the head indicates compliance, while apologies are conveyed by shaking the head.

An Unsolved Question It has not yet been possible to determine whether a gorilla troop involves a permanent pair relationship between specific males and females. The evidence suggests that fairly permanent male-female relations exist, and the gorilla troop essentially represents a dominant male in more or less permanent association with a number of females, their offspring, and several younger males.

Unfortunately, observers have been able to witness only a few matings, for although the female ovulates once a month, the long period of pregnancy, from 250 to 300 days, followed by lactation, means that they are in estrus only infrequently. The matings that have been observed have not always involved the dominant male. In every case it was the female who approached the male, and in one case at least, the dominant male has been observed to permit relationships between the females and a younger male without interest. Consequently, gorilla troops may be contrasted to baboon troops by their small size, by the absence of competing grooming cliques, and by the consequent dominance of a single "patriarchal"

---

[6]This should not be interpreted as implying conflict. Conflict may occur, but patterns of dominance and submission, once established, appear to persist for very considerable periods of time.

male. In addition, whereas baboon troops are seemingly inbreeding and genetically isolated, the small gorilla troop seems to maintain friendly relations with at least some of the neighboring troops, and since gorilla territories often overlap, neighboring troops will sometimes nest side by side for the night. On the other hand, suspicion and antagonism have been observed when two strange troops meet, and gorillas do appear to be much more at ease with familiar faces. Consequently it has been suggested by some observers that since young males sometimes break away from the parent troop, and drawing females from other troops, establish their own troops, known instances of gorilla familiarity between neighboring troops could indicate the remembrance of earlier associations. However further observation would be necessary to determine whether this hypothesis is valid.

Family communities

In the absence of food sharing, the gorilla troop must be regarded as a permanent male-female troop and cannot be included in our fourth and last category of mammalian society, the *family community*. Rooted in permanent or at least semipermanent, male-female "pair-bonds," and more common among carnivores than herbivores, it is under the family category of mammalian social organization that we class human societies.

Most of the great carnivores of Africa and Asia form family groups, but it is the pack-hunters whose social system bears the closest similarity to that of man. It may come as a surprise to those who are acquainted with the promiscuous behavior of our domesticated canines to learn that in their natural state wolves form permanent male-female pair relationships, and that wolf packs are in fact *extended families*.

Wolf packs have now been recognized as family or kinship units that hunt cooperatively. They grow up around a pair of adult wolves and their offspring. Adult males pair off with adult females, establishing a permanent or semipermanent pair-bond, each pair possessing their own "den" in which, as a nuclear family, they raise their own litter. Since the females have to care for offspring during the "denning" season, hunting becomes the responsibility of the male at this time, and food sharing develops on a family basis because of a basic dichotomy of role—a basic division of labor—between the paired male and female. At times when the female is unable to join the chase, the male, on his return from a successful hunt, will regurgitate sufficient food for her sustenance. On occasion, adults leave the parental pack to set up their own pack. Having a permanent family-type society, wolves take a great interest in their offspring, extending much care not only to the nourishment and protection but also to the socialization and education of their young. Wolf fathers share their consorts' interest in the litter and appear to educate the cubs in the techniques of hunting.[7]

Just as earlier writers suggested that the small gorilla troop constituted an emergent family-type community because of the relative smallness of the group and the clear dominance of a single male, later writers have suggested that there are other primates that live in family groups—notably the gibbon and the South American marmoset. In both these cases one male seems to form a more or less permanent bond with a single female, and the gibbon and marmoset social group comprises a single adult male and adult female, living in their territory and raising their own offspring. However, at this point the analogy with the family concept breaks down. There is no division of labor between males and females, and there is no

[7] The extent to which the cubs merely copy the hunting activities of the parents can be debated, but most observers agree that the wolf parents deliberately strive to educate their young.

food sharing. The small social groups of the gibbon and marmoset remain permanent male-female groups in these essential qualities, and though the absence of other adult males and females precludes promiscuity, these units by no means fulfill the evolutionary functions of the family group.

It is not difficult to see why pair-bonding would become reinforced by food sharing and a basic sexual division of labor among carnivorous species dependent on pack hunting operations to create a family-type society. While the pregnant or lactating herbivore female can feed herself without difficulty, the female wolf is quite unable to participate in the chase without leaving her cubs unprotected. Those which failed to gain the assistance of a male partner might be more likely to lose their young, either through miscarriage while hunting, or more likely the young might be lost after birth while the mother was obliged to absent herself on hunting expeditions. Successive generations would therefore tend to be bred from those male and female wolves that developed the

family system and its implied correlate—food sharing. The pair-bond, reinforced by food sharing, is the basic quality of the family, for the members of a family face the challenge of survival as a joint unit, with male and female developing reciprocal, specialized roles to promote not only their own survival but particularly the survival of their genes, embodied in their living offspring.

It seems to have been no accident, therefore, that the ancestors of man, who unlike the other primates became carnivorous predators, developed pair-bonding and a family-type social system, and that their social evolution was intimately linked to their ecological and biological needs. Since the basic roots of human society are therefore evolutionary and ecological, let us now turn our attention to the identification of man's early apelike ancestors and try to piece together their changing way of life as evolutionary forces caused them to become increasingly dependent upon hunting to supplement the simpler food gathering practices of their more simian forebears.

For Further Reading

Bastock, M., 1967, *Courtship: An Ethological Study*. Chicago: Aldine Publishing Company.

Chance, M. R. A., and C. J. Jolly, 1970, *Social Groups of Monkeys, Apes and Men*. New York: E. P. Dutton.

DeVore, I., 1965, *Primate Behaviour*. New York: Holt, Rinehart and Winston, Inc.

Dolhinow, P. J., and J. Goodall, 1968, *Primates: Studies in Adaptation and Variability*. New York: Holt, Rinehart and Winston, Inc.

Dimond, S. J., 1970, *The Social Behavior of Animals*. New York: Harper & Row, Publishers.

Kummer, H., 1971, *Primate Societies*. Chicago: Aldine Publishing Company.

Morris, D., 1969, *Primate Ethology*. New York: Doubleday & Company, Inc.

Sahlins, M. D., 1959, "Social Life of Monkeys, Apes and Primitive Man," *Human Biology* 31:1.

Schaller, G. B., 1963, *The Mountain Gorilla*. Chicago: University of Chicago Press.

Scott, J. P., 1963, *Animal Behavior*. New York: Doubleday & Company, Inc.

Southwick, C. H., 1963, *Primate Social Behavior*. Princeton, N.J.: D. Van Nostrand Company, Inc.

Tiger, L., 1969, *Men in Groups*. New York: Random House, Inc.

CHAPTER 7

In Search of the Missing Link

It has been suggested that man's ancestors may have lived like the savannah baboon, gorilla, and chimpanzee, only on the fringes of the more heavily wooded areas. But there can be no doubt that the flexibility of man's shoulders and forearms, his prehensile grip, and so many other primate characteristics, could only have been developed in the trees, and that man's ancestors, like those of the baboon, chimpanzee, and gorilla, must at one time have led an arboreal existence.

Why did man's ancestors leave the trees? During the Miocene the forests that formerly spread from Africa to Southeast Asia began to break up, giving rise to extensive sections of savannah-type grasslands. As the world became cooler towards the end of the Tertiary period, man's ancestors must at some time have found themselves isolated in a neck of woodlands, which steadily shrank in size until it was reduced to an isolated island of forest around which there was only open grassland. As the trees slowly continued to recede over thousands of years, these prehuman ancestors were

forced progressively to adapt to life on the open grasslands. Man therefore did not so much come down from the trees as find himself increasingly stranded without trees. Like chimpanzees and baboons he was probably not averse to supplementing his diet of insects and fruit with a little meat where available, and with the declining availability of fruit, nuts, and berries he became increasingly a carnivore.

Evidence of Human Evolution

Although it is no longer necessary to debate what used to be called "Darwin's theory" of the evolution of man, some of the evidence which has been assembled in corroboration of the fact of human evolution makes instructive reading.

The earliest evidence of human evolution produced by Darwin was based primarily on COMPARATIVE MORPHOLOGY. The primary resemblances between related species may be demonstrated by exposing the similarities of their skeletal, organic, and muscular structures and functions. Although in the course of evolution the great majority of skeletal and organic elements become modified and rearranged—and where modification is substantial, some organs may even be lost altogether—the process of natural selection works slowly, and many VESTIGIAL REMAINS may survive for long periods of time after they have lost their usefulness, before finally being eliminated.

Thus it can be readily demonstrated that the human skeleton corresponds in all of its parts to that of the ape, except that in man the thirteenth rib, which is still present among apes, is missing. Both apes and men have lost their tails but nevertheless preserve the vestigial remains of a tail—a small stump on the base of the spine which is known as the *coccyx*. Although this coccyx does not normally show externally, in a few cases of genetic irregularity it does protrude slightly, and the human young are sometimes born with a small external tail.

Another instance of a vestigial survival which all of us possess is to be found in the unnecessary length of our intestines. Our early primate ancestors were vegetarians, who needed long intestines to enable them to digest the large quantities of food which they were obliged to eat for sustenance. Today, obtaining much of our food in concentrated form, either as meat or in highly nutritious milk, fats, and rich vegetables, men no longer need the lengthy intestines that they have inherited. Yet another vestigial survival that plagues us is the appendix which serves little or no useful function in man but is still an integral part of the gorilla's digestive system.

Further evidence of the reality of evolution is provided by the study of EMBRYONIC DEVELOPMENT. This involves two concepts known as phylogeny and ontogeny. *Ontogeny* is a biological term which refers to the life history of the individual organism. *Phylogeny* describes the evolutionary history of the species. Significantly, ontogeny has been said to recapitulate

phylogeny. Although this is something of an exaggeration, there can be no doubt that while in the fetal stage an organism tends to recapitulate the history of the species. Thus the human embryo begins as a single fertilized cell rather like the protozoan. By a process of cell division and increasing specialization, it becomes analogous to the metazoan. At a later stage of development it reveals many of the characteristics of the chordates, and embryonic gill formations may be observed. Even new born infants may reflect ancestral traits. This principle operates so regularly that since young lions are frequently born with spots, this has been taken as evidence that the ancestors of our living lions may at one time have been spotted like leopards.

Phylogenetic relationships can also be demonstrated by BIOCHEMICAL ANALYSIS. The quantitative comparison of protein structures indicates the close relationship between men and apes, but probably the most dramatic evidence of man's kinship with the primates is to be found in *serology,* the study of the qualities of human and animal blood. Ever since our ancestors in early Europe believed that genetic characteristics were conveyed in the blood and that we acquired our distinctive hereditary traits as a result of the mingling of the blood of our two parents, we have been prone to talk of "blood relationship," and indeed there is hardly a human society which does not attach some mystical significance to blood in its own right. It is therefore not inappropriate that man's relationship to the primates may be demonstrated by blood similarities. The evidence is revealed with the use of *vaccines,* which are prepared from *serum,* the thin fluid that separates from the blood when it coagulates, by injecting a toxin or virus into an animal's blood, which reacts to produce *antibodies* to destroy the toxin. Thus if we inject the blood of a dog into a rabbit, antibodies will develop in the blood of the rabbit to reject and destroy the alien qualities in the dog's blood, and we will be able to extract what may be called an "antidog" serum. When this antidog serum is mixed in a test tube with the blood of a dog, a white precipitate is formed.

When experimenting with the antidog serum, it will be further found that if the serum is mixed with the blood of a wolf a precipitate is formed but that this will not be quite as thick as was the case with the precipitate formed in the dog's blood. Furthermore, when the antidog serum is mixed with the blood of a fox, a still weaker precipitate is formed, although this is still strong enough to demonstrate that the blood of the fox is related to that of the dog. Because the precipitate is less thick than in the case of the wolf's blood, it may be assumed that the dog is more closely related to the wolf than it is to the fox. No precipitate is formed when an antidog serum is mixed with the blood of cats or other noncanines.

A similar "anticat" serum can be obtained by injecting the blood of a cat into a rabbit, and this may be used to demonstrate the closeness of the relationship between cats, leopards, tigers, and other feline species. But the test of human evolution comes when an "antiman" serum is formed by injecting the blood of man into a rabbit. Tests using this serum reveal a close relationship between men and apes. Strong precipitations are formed when the antiman serum is mixed with the blood of a gorilla or chimpanzee, while weaker precipitations are obtained when the antiman serum is mixed with the blood of an orangutan or gibbon. A very slight precipitation is formed when antiman serum is mixed with the blood of a lemur or tarsier.[1]

Primate Predecessors

One other objection that used to be raised to "Darwin's theory" was based on the fact that in Darwin's time the only evidence discovered

[1] Successful tranfusions of human blood have been given to apes of the same ABO blood group.

by paleontology of protohuman fossils was restricted to a few broken portions of Neanderthal skulls found in Europe, which were not simian in type and which are today actually classified as *Homo sapiens* (see Chap. 10). Members of the Christian faith, having been reared in an oriental revelation religion which claimed that the world had been miraculously created by an all-powerful god within the space of seven days and that all the existing plant and animal species had been divinely created in the exact forms that they retain today, objected to the evolutionary origin of man on the grounds that no one could produce the "missing link," fossil evidence of a "subhuman" intermediate in physical character between the living apes and living men. The idea of the missing link captured popular imagination to such an extent that although a continuous chain of missing links has since been uncovered linking living men and apes to a common ancestral species, laymen still talk about *the* missing link as though "it" may never be found. In this chapter let us therefore examine some of the missing links which enable us to chart the story of human evolution with considerable precision, and also endeavor to speculate on their possible manner of subsistence.

The main problem which faces the anthropologist in his search for our protohuman ancestors is the simple fact that we really do not know what they looked like. All that we can be really sure of is what *we* look like. Nevertheless, if we first classify the living higher primates into New and Old World forms and then divide the Old World higher primates into monkeys, apes, and men, we are able to obtain some valuable clues. Thus we are able to distinguish between the more monkeylike, the more apelike, and the more manlike of the fossil remains which the paleoanthropologist, whose task it is to search for evidence of extinct protohuman species, may succeed in uncovering.

Hominidae

The largest of the Fayum fossil primates, called *Aegyptopithecus* in honor of Egypt, was actually no larger than a large monkey. Although still arboreal, it reveals a considerably larger forebrain and several other structural changes which seem to indicate that it may be definitely ancestral to the later hominoids. Another fossil discovery from the Fayum area suggests that by the Pliocene, 10 million years later, protogibbons may already have been evolving separately from the other hominoids. Known as *Pliopithecus,* this animal also possessed molar teeth with five cusps; its skeleton indicates free-swinging arms, a semiupright stance, and a flat apelike face, and the face, jaws, and teeth, in particular, resemble living gibbons.[2]

It is not until the Miocene, which lasted from 26 to 12 million years B.C., that it becomes possible to trace a distinct diversification between HOMINIDAE or manlike hominoids, also called "hominids," and those fossils more clearly ancestral to the living PONGIDAE—the gorilla, chimpanzee, and orangutan. The first fossil evidence of such a separation comes to us from East Africa where we find *Dryopithecus africanus,* otherwise known as *Proconsul*—named with a touch of humor after a popular zoo ape of the day known as "Consul"—which appears to have lived in open parkland and must have spent a certain amount of time on the ground. But although Proconsul reveals a larger brain case than the earlier fossils of the Oligocene, the shape of the cranium suggests a closer correspondence to the anatomical pattern of the modern great apes than to that of living hominids.

The Proconsul fossil remains are given an age of around 25 million years and are succeeded by an increasing variety of protoape fossils, some of which are as large as a modern gorilla. These appear throughout the Miocene and the ensuing Pliocene, and from Proconsul onward are known collectively as *Dryopithecines,* some revealing a cranial capacity of 300 to 400 cubic centimeters, almost in the range of living pongoids whose cranial capacity varies between 400 and 500 cubic centimeters. Like *Propliopithecus,* and *Pliopithecus,* the Dryopithecines have five cusps on their molars instead of four like the Old World monkeys. Yet still at this time there are no fossil remains which can be distinguished as distinctly manlike.

Then in the late Miocene and early Pliocene, between 15 million and 10 million years ago, we find fossil remains of a hominoid known as *Oreopithecus.* The first *Oreopithecus* remains were excavated in Italy, but numerous others have now been discovered in other European countries. *Oreopithecus* stood around 4 feet high and must have weighed as much as a heavy dog. He was certainly a brachiating creature, for his arms were longer than his legs, as is the case with living apes, but what is particularly interesting is that his pelvis shows certain anatomical developments which resemble those of living hominids, and paleoanthropologists are sure that he was capable of maintaining an upright position for considerable periods of time. An examination of his foot bones further indicates that he was able to walk on his hind legs in an imperfect bipedal gait, and some authorities have therefore claimed him as an early hominid. These point out that the *Oreopithecus* remains have been found in coal deposits, thus suggesting that he lived in swampy areas. While no living apes live in swamps, men frequently prosper on the edges of swampy areas where they gather roots, water lily seeds, and other types of swamp food.

Although the majority of authorities prefer to classify *Oreopithecus* as a hominoid whose line became extinct, and therefore exclude him

[2] Hylobates separated from the monkeys much earlier than did the Pongidae and although classified as apes, they are sharply differentiated from the Pongidae.

FIG. 12   DISTRIBUTION OF OLD WORLD PRIMATES AND RAMAPITHECINE FOSSIL SITES

The regional flora and climatic conditions shown below are contemporary. Although these are relevant to the distribution of living primates, it must be remembered that climatic and geographical conditions would have been substantially different when the Ramapithecines were alive.

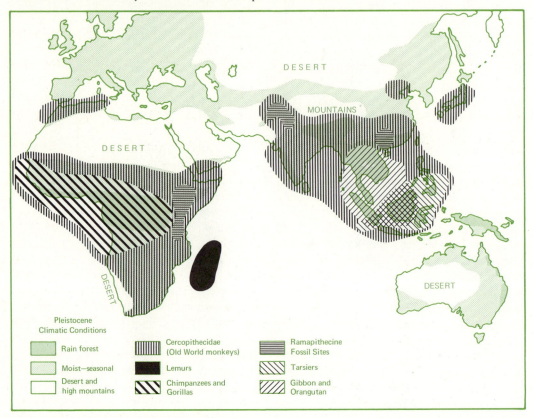

Pleistocene Climatic Conditions

- Rain forest
- Moist—seasonal
- Desert and high mountains
- Cercopithecidae (Old World monkeys)
- Lemurs
- Chimpanzees and Gorillas
- Ramapithecine Fossil Sites
- Tarsiers
- Gibbon and Orangutan

from the human lineage, one of his slightly younger contemporaries is universally accepted as ancestral to man. This is *Ramapithecus,* a genus which includes a variety of fossil remains found in the late Miocene and early Pliocene.

The Ramapithecine Assemblage

The first *Ramapithecus* remains were found in northern India and were consequently named after an Indian god, Rama. Subsequent

fossils found in East Africa by Louis S. B. Leakey and labeled *Kenyapithecus* are also classified in the *Ramapithecus* genus. *Kenyapithecus wickeri* from Fort Ternan has been dated at 14 million years while some jaw fragments of even greater antiquity found in Ethiopia have likewise been classified as Ramapithecines, thus giving the genus a possible antiquity of as much as 20 million years. Such fossils are identified by their small canine teeth, and a general dental equipment which is closely similar to that of living men. This

Part of the right lower jaw of a Ramapithecine that roamed the grasslands of northern India before its death some 13 million years ago. Notice the massive bone structure of a jaw that possessed much greater crushing power than that of modern man. (Courtesy of the American Museum of Natural History.)

suggests a small creature which used its hands for feeding rather than relying upon its jaws to tear and break its food. Further evidence suggests that the Ramapithecines were by no means confined to forested areas, thus implying that they may have been capable of walking erect. Unfortunately, however, we lack the skeletal evidence which would provide positive evidence of this ability, and it is from the dental equipment, so markedly parallel to that of living men, that Ramapithecines are usually recognized as the first true HOMINIDS or man-like creatures, clearly distinguishable from apes.

If the hominids first separated from the general hominoid assemblage during the Miocene, they appear to have continued to evolve in a manlike direction through the Pliocene, which lasted from 12 million to 3 million years ago. Their remains extend from eastern Africa to India, with some evidence suggesting that they may also have lived in Europe and possibly as far east as southern China.

An Analogy with Chimpanzees

In attempting to reconstruct the Ramapithecine way of life, it seems reasonable to believe that this may not have been so very different from that of the modern chimpanzees of East Africa. In the previous chapter we described the pattern of social life among baboons and gorillas. However, many primatologists believe that the chimpanzee resembles man more closely than do any of the other primates. The brain of the chimpanzee is nearly twice as large as that of the baboon and almost as large as that of the gorilla; in fact when we compare the size of the chimpanzee and the gorilla, it becomes obvious that the brain of the chimpanzee, proportionate to overall body size, is larger than that of the gorilla.

What is of particular interest is the fact that the chimpanzees of Tanzania live in thinly forested and partially open savannah country, somewhat similar to that which man's earlier hominid ancestors are believed to have inhabited. It is believed that in brain size and in stature the chimpanzees also compare closely with the Ramapithecine level of hominid evolution, and although it would be unscientific to attempt to read too much into these basic analogies, a brief description of chimpanzee life in the less densely forested areas of East Africa is by no means out of place here.[3]

[3] This description of East African savannah-dwelling chimpanzees is taken largely from the reports by Jane van Lawick-Goodall on chimpanzees.

Chimpanzees live in small but very loosely structured male-female groups, in which the largest males tend to be dominant. Aggression within a chimpanzee band is rare, and displays of dominance and submission are not so obvious as among baboons. However, like baboons, chimpanzees have neither family nor harem types of relationship, and when the female chimpanzee comes into estrus, six or seven males may patiently wait their turn to associate with her without revealing any overt signs of rivalry or antagonism. In most cases the sexual approach is made by the female, although in some instances contact is initiated by the male. Occasionally the female appears to resent male contact, but since the males are considerably larger than the females, the will of the male usually prevails.

The members of a chimpanzee band sleep in trees at night, each making a separate nest of sticks and leaves. The chimpanzee mother usually suckles her infant until it is two or three years of age, and the baby rides on its mother's back during the daytime and sleeps in her nest at night. During this period the infant is seldom allowed out of the mother's sight, and much learning takes place, although evidence of deliberate instruction by the mother has not been observed. Not surprisingly, chimpanzees reveal predictably strong mother-infant bonds, and status patterns seem to be even more strongly dependent on the mother's status than in the case of baboons. In short, emergent kinship ties are now clearly supplanting individual status based on dominance and submission as the basis of group organization. Some element of an incest taboo may also be emerging, since no adult male chimpanzee has yet been observed to attempt sexual relations with its own mother.

During the day chimpanzee bands roam around a very loosely defined home range, gathering fruit and also depending to a very large extent on a diet of insects—including the insects which males and females find on each others bodies. Termites, especially, are eaten in large quantities. A chimpanzee will pick up a stick, break it to a convenient length, wet it with his lips, and dip it into a termite's hill, using it much like a spoon to convey the termites to his mouth. Another effective tool is the sponge, made from a handful of leaves, which is used to soak up the water that collects during heavy rain in the crotch of a tree. In other parts of Africa chimpanzees have been seen to use stones to break open the hard outer casing of nuts. Chimpanzees have also learned to use their hands for carrying objects and to walk in a semierect position when they have their hands full. Indeed, they spend a considerable amount of time in an erect position, frequently walking short distances between trees on their hind legs.

But the chimpanzee is by no means averse to varying his diet with eggs and animal flesh when either is available, and the East African chimpanzees are not only food gatherers but hunters. When moving on the ground, they frequently rear up on their hind legs in order to peer over the top of the tall grass, since like all primates their sense of smell and hearing is inferior to their sight. This is particularly interesting data, since it tallies closely with our conjectures regarding *Ramapithecus.* Because we believe that Ramapithecines also lived in open country and that they similarly depend on eye sight rather than on hearing or smell, we may also assume that they pursued their quarry by sight rather than by other senses, and would therefore spend more time erect, running with their heads above the grass, until they came to develop a habitual bipedal gait.

Animals which become hunters but lack the physical equipment of more traditional carnivores will be obliged to rely heavily upon cunning. If the Ramapithecines were driven by their savannah environment to supplement the more restricted supplies of fruit by captured meat, there would be a strong tendency for natural selection to operate in favor of the more intelligent and the more cooperative of the species. Intelligent hunting would lead to group or pack hunting, which definitely played an important role in the emergence of distinctly hominid behavior.

As *Ramapithecus* may have done, the chimpanzee hunter depends more upon cunning and stealth than upon tooth and claw—and indeed as a primate he has no claws, only flat nails. When creeping up upon a young monkey in a tree, two or more chimpanzees may cooperate in an organized hunting pattern. One approaches just close enough to attract and hold the victim's attention without behaving in such a way as to cause it to flee, and the other stealthily advances on the victim from behind, to grab the unsuspecting animal by the neck, while its attention is still held by the decoy, and strangle it to death.

Chimpanzees appear to derive great excitement from killing animals, and attracted by the sounds of conflict, the entire band gathers to run backward and forward, screaming loudly and hugging each other. This activity resembles a communal celebration, and such dance patterns amount almost to a ceremonial ritual during thunderstorms, when the excitement of the noise, the flashes of light, and the downpour of heavy tropical rain causes the adult males to dance and scream for as long as two or three hours at a time, watched with rapt attention by an audience of females and infants. Such communal excitement is not just an involuntary reaction to the sight and sound of a thunderstorm but has a distinctly social meaning, as is confirmed by the fact that similar celebrations often take place when two bands meet. It is easy to visualize the origins of hominid ceremonial dances in a steady elaboration of Ramapithecine group dances over the millions of years of slow evolution that separates earlier hominoids from the manlike hominids of more recent times.

Like the chimpanzees the Ramapithecines may have used simple tools, but unlike men they did not use tools to make tools. It is totally improbable that they could have developed articulate speech; similarly, it is unlikely that they could spend long periods of time erect with comfort. Although they represent a true "missing link," we do not experience any feeling of sympathy or understanding when we study their fossil remains or attempt to reconstruct their life, such as undoubtedly assails us when we study the next level of evolving hominids, the Australopithecines of Africa.

For Further Reading

Buettner-Janusch, J., 1966, *Origins of Man.* New York: John Wiley & Sons, Inc.

Coon, C. S., 1967, *The Origin of Races.* New York: Alfred A. Knopf.

Craig, D., 1959, *Adventures with the Missing Link.* New York: The Viking Press, Inc.

Howell, F. C., and F. Bourlière, 1963, *African Ecology and Human Evolution.* Chicago: Aldine Publishing Company.

Howells, W., 1967, *Ideas on Human Evolution: Selected Essays 1949–1961.* New York: Atheneum Publishers.

Kortlandt, A., and M. Kooj, 1963, *Protohominid Behavior in Primates.* Zoological Society of London, Vol. 10.

Lasker, G. W., 1973, *Physical Anthropology.* New York: Holt, Rinehart and Winston, Inc.

Le Gros Clark, W., 1967, *Fossil Evidence for Human Evolution.* Chicago: University of Chicago Press.

Poirier, F. E., 1973, *Fossil Man: An Evolutionary Journey.* St. Louis: C. V. Mosby Company.

Reynolds, V., 1967, *The Apes.* New York: Harper & Row, Publishers.

von Koenigswald, G. H. R., 1966, *The Evolution of Man.* Ann Arbor: University of Michigan Press.

Washburn S. L., 1961, *Social Life of Early Man.* Chicago: Aldine Publishing Company.

——, 1963, *Classification and Human Evolution.* Chicago: Aldine Publishing Company.

Weidenreich, F., 1946, *Apes, Giants and Man.* Chicago: University of Chicago Press.

CHAPTER 8

An African Eden?

Despite the fact that the map of the world is constantly changing, it is interesting to note that Charles Darwin advised that Africa was the continent in which we should search for the "missing link," basing his judgment on the fact that tropical Africa was the home of man's two closest surviving relatives, the gorilla and the chimpanzee. Darwin did not know it, but Africa also has the distinction of having preserved a tropical climate during periods of climatic fluctuation which would have rendered many other parts of the world uninhabitable to primates. While we cannot claim that Africa was the exclusive cradle of man, for Ramapithecines inhabited Asia as well as Africa, it is Africa that has provided us with the major source of fossil remains from another level of hominid evolution: the *Australopithecine assemblage.*

Although we have no evidence of pair-bonding or of social behavior among the early hominids, discoveries from the Pleistocene, which began around 3 million years ago, provide us with ample evidence of more manlike hominids living in Africa. These had evolved brains that were larger than any living ape. All must have been tool users and manufacturers like the chimpanzee, while some of them had begun to make tools from stone.[1]

"Southern Apes"

The discovery of these more advanced hominids was made by a professor of anatomy at a South African university. In 1924, Professor Raymond A. Dart identified pieces of a manlike skull case from a quarry not far from Johannesburg in the high veldt known as the Transvaal. This proved to be part of the cranium of a child, probably aged only five or six years at death. Since it was found at Taung it is sometimes called the "Taung skull" and sometimes, more facetiously, "Dart's baby." However, because anthropologists of the early

[1] There is still some debate as to whether *Australopithecus africanus* or *Homo habilis* manufactured these stone tools, but there can be no doubt that both used a variety of tools, possibly of a less durable nature.

twentieth century believed that man had evolved in Asia, as a result of discoveries in China and Java, Dart's epic work was largely ignored.[2] The attention of the scientific world was not finally secured until Robert Broom subsequently discovered a number of other hominidlike fossils in the same South African area, namely at Sterkfontein and Swartkrans, and until Dr. L. S. B. Leakey, excavating in the rich fossil area of the Olduvai Gorge in what is today called Tanzania, discovered a number of other hominidlike remains.

Since then an increasing number of early African hominid fossil remains have been uncovered, all of which have been classed as Australopithecines. The name *Australopithecus* was originally chosen by Dart for his Taung skull. The choice was perhaps unfortunate in that it means "Southern Ape," for although the South African discoveries belong to the Southern Hemisphere, some of the more recent East African discoveries fall north of the equator and furthermore, the Australopithecines are no longer regarded as apes but are recognized as definite hominids. Modern dating techniques confirm that the Australopithecines lived in the early Pleistocene period, known as the Villafranchian, between 3.5 million and 1 million years ago. The renowned *Zinjanthropus,* discovered by Mary D. Leakey at Olduvai Gorge in Kenya, has been dated at only 1.7 million years,[3] but Australopithecine-like remains found in the Omo Valley in Ethiopia have been estimated to date from the Pliocene.

The resemblance of the Australopithecines to modern man is based not on the slight advance in the size of their brain cases, which range between 450 and 650 cubic centimeters in cranial capacity, but upon a number of other anatomical characteristics. Perhaps the most important of these is the shape of the pelvis which indicates without doubt that they normally walked erect, although perhaps in a slightly stooping posture and without the litheness of living men. Proof of their bipedal gait is also provided by the shape of the foot bones, which are quite distinct from those of the pongoids and Dryopithecines, and are distinctly manlike. Their large toe could no longer be used for grasping, as it can among apes, but instead the foot bones indicate an animal which was capable of running with some speed. Indeed, *Australopithecus* has been described as man from the waist down, and ape—except for dentition—from the waist up.

However, although the shape of the *foramen magnum* indicates that the head was carried in a rather forward position, as is also confirmed by the indication of heavy neck muscles, the development of the mastoid process, the small bony protrusion behind the ear, indicates that they were able to swing their heads from side

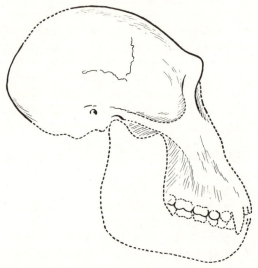

An outline restoration of the skull of an *Australopithecus robustus.* (Courtesy of the American Museum of Natural History.)

[2] Most physical anthropologists at first refused to accept Professor Dart's interpretation of the *Australopithecus* fossils in South Africa, just as they had earlier rejected Dubois' reports on *Homo erectus.*

[3] Zinjanthropus, or *Australopithecus boisei,* was found in Bed 1 at Olduvai. Classed as *A. robustus,* Zinjanthropus was characterized by extremely massive jaws.

to side with considerable ease.[4] Believed to have been around 4 feet tall, the Australopithecines would have stood only a few inches shorter than the modern Pygmy. In brief, a study of the considerable quantity of Australopithecine fossil remains that are available today indicates that during the long period of the Miocene and Pliocene, the Ramapithecines had evolved a very long way to the new level indicated by the Australopithecines.

Some authors have spent a great deal of time debating the issue: which was the first man? This is a rather ridiculous question, partly because it is like asking which came first, the chicken or the egg, and partly because the selection of the characteristics which would distinguish "men" or living hominids from "prehuman" hominids is a purely arbitrary matter, with no scientific validity. Certainly it would be ridiculous to suggest that a Ramapithecine mother ever gave birth to an Australopithecine child or that a protohuman parent produced a *Homo sapiens* or "human" offspring. What we are dealing with is a slow and constant process of genetic change which continues like the thread of a rope through the millions of years of hominid evolution. There is no point at which we can say that the parent generation was only a protoman. The sharp division which today separates the living hominids from other living hominoids exists only because competition and other evolutionary forces have eliminated all the intermediate hominid varieties. But as we go back along the course of a phylogenetic continuum, the transition from living to ancestral species is achieved imperceptibly, without sudden changes or abrupt distinctions.

Although for convenience we usually group the fossil remains of our various hominid ancestors under labels which imply that they represented separate species, the concept of a species applies only to distinct, noninterbreeding populations which live contemporaneously, and cannot be applied to different generations within the same continuum. Thus, the differences that separate living men from living gorillas are sufficiently sharp to allow us to categorize each with different taxonomic labels, but although living men differ just as much from *Aegyptopithecus* of the Oligocene as they do from the living gorillas, any attempt to arrange the intermediate generations in distinct species and subspecies must be artifical. Similarly, any attempt to claim the Australopithecines as the first "men" and to disown the Ramapithecines as protomen smacks of an anthropocentric preoccupation with an outdated concept of "man" as the unique, unchanging goal of an evolutionary process now complete. No doubt if the Australopithecines and Ramapithecines were still alive, we would have to decide whether they were entitled to share in such discriminatory and anthropocentric privileges as the "Rights of Man," which we deny to animals. Fortunately for our political philosophers they no longer exist, and we are spared such agonizing decisions.[5]

Robustus and africanus

Another interesting debate is the relationship between two physically different types of Australopithecines which are known to have inhabited southern and eastern Africa during the Villafranchian era. These are *Australopithecus robustus* and *Australopithecus africanus*. *A. robustus* was somewhat larger than *A. africanus* but may have been less ferocious,

[4]The mastoid process is a protrusion of the temporal bone, behind the ear, to which the muscles responsible for revolving the head are fixed.

[5]It is a fundamental principle of both anthropology and modern "humanism" that men make their own "rights," and are not born with these as the eighteenth-century American Declaration of Rights implied. Being man-made, such "rights" naturally tend to be anthropocentric, but at best we may hope that the day will come when men recognize the "right" of posterity to enjoy the wide variety of animal life that still enriches the world at the present time.

since the teeth suggest a more obviously vege-tarian diet. The *A. robustus* cranium also re-vealed a sagittal crest similar to that found on gorillas. No evidence of tools or tool making has been found in association with *A. robustus* remains, and although he may have possessed an *osteodontokeratic* technology—which means that he would have used teeth, bones, horn, and sinews as tools—it seems probable that *A. robustus* had not learned how to make stone tools.

In contrast with the *A. robustus* species, *A. africanus* had smaller molars. Both *A. africanus* and *A. robustus* had small canines similar to those of modern man, in contrast to Ramapithecus whose canine teeth still pro-truded slightly like those of the mythical vam-pire.[6] But while *A. robustus* probably only occasionally ate meat, *A. africanus* is believed to have been more heavily carnivorous. His remains are frequently associated with the bro-ken bones of a variety of small animals, and there has been occasional evidence that even large animals played a part in his diet. Al-though it is customary to regard *A. robustus* as a more primitive species, which was possibly driven into extinction by *A. africanus,* the fact that both were quite definitely contemporaries has led a few paleoanthropologists to assert that both belonged to the same species, though whether or not they belonged to the same genetic species (that is to say, whether they were capable of interbreeding to produce fer-tile offspring) we may never know.[7]

Australopithecine Technology

But the most significant distinction between *A. robustus* and *A. africanus* is the fact that

the remains of *A. africanus* are frequently as-sociated with elementary stone implements. These have sometimes been called EOLITHS, where it is not possible to say whether they were simply rough stones conveniently frac-tured by nature which were picked up and used by the early hominids, or whether they were the crude products of the earliest attempt at stoneworking. Recent excavations at the Olduvai Gorge, however, have also assembled a number of primitive *pebble tools,* usually called *choppers,* which reveal evidence of a regular technique of stoneworking which would have been transmitted from generation to generation as a part of the developing cul-tural tradition (see Fig. 13).

These Olduvai choppers comprised a rounded pebble which could be conveniently held in the hand, but which had been delib-erately fractured at one end as to provide a sharp cutting edge.[8] Not only would they have been useful for cutting sticks of wood, but they could also be used to kill and butcher an ani-mal, breaking its limbs apart, and cracking open the bone to allow the marrow to be ex-tracted. Like modern men, *A. africanus* clearly lacked the massive canines which would enable him to tear large chunks of meat apart, and may have made good use of his stone tools in this respect. Such chopper tools could also be used to skin the hide from a dead animal, thus raising the possibility that the hides may have been used as clothes or handbags.

There is no doubt that if *A. africanus* possessed stone chopping tools, he must have also possessed a variety of wooden and bone tools. Contemporary primitive people use a short stick for digging up edible roots, and it is likely that possessing stone tools, *A. africanus* would have learned how to sharpen the ends of such sticks to make stab-bing spears. It is also probable that he may have used a heavier stick as a club and may even have thrown sticks as offensive projec-

[6] Much of "civilized" behavior seems to be rooted in man's desire to prove how "unanimal" he is, hence the feeling of revulsion at the idea of a human being with protruding canine teeth.

[7] For further discussion of the concept of "species," refer to Ernst Mayr, *Animal Species and Evolution* (Cambridge, Mass.: Harvard University Press), Chap. 2.

[8] Chopper tools were held in the hand, *not* fixed to a shaft.

FIG. 13   PEBBLE TOOL CULTURES AND AUSTRALOPITHECINE/SKULL 1470 FOSSIL SITES

The oblique shading denotes the areas in which evidence of ancient pebble tool cultures has been found. The vertical shading over Australia and New Guinea indicates that the pebble cultures of these areas are not of such great antiquity as those of Eurasia and Africa.

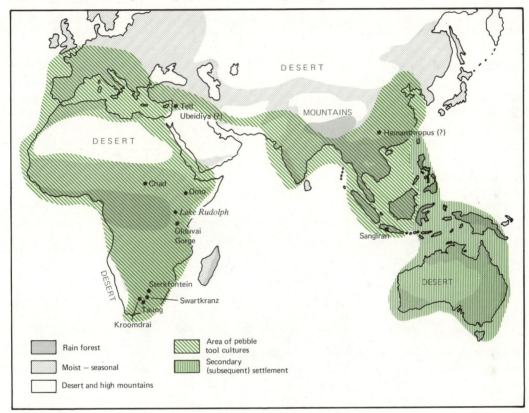

tiles, like the throwing sticks of the Australian aboriginals. Although no proof exists that either *A. robustus* or *A. africanus* knew the use of fire, there is evidence of outdoor camps whose occupants deliberately built a wall of loose stones either as a windbreak or as protection against lions and leopards, probably reinforcing this with sticks and pieces of thorn bush as African villagers still do today.

A study of the various bones found at the *A. africanus* camp indicates a wide diet, ranging from large animals like rhinoceros and giraffe (which must have been killed by being driven over a precipice or into some form of trap, or scavenged from the kill of biologically specialized predators) to small animals such as tortoises, and to birds and birds' eggs. *A. africanus* also appears to have been fond of baboon meat, and there is some evidence that he may have even been a cannibal.[9]

Homo habilis and Skull 1470

Meanwhile there is now clearcut fossil evidence that hominids belonging to a much

[9] It could be possible that the animals slaughtered at the "kill site" were slain not by Australopithecines but by the more advanced *Homo habilis* and Skull 1470 populations.

higher level of human evolution already walked the earth long before either *A. robustus* or *A. africanus* had become extinct. In 1960 Dr. Louis S. B. Leakey found the remains of yet a third type of hominid at Olduvai Gorge in Tanzania, which he called *Homo habilis* because the evidence showed that this subspecies definitely used tools regularly. These remains were reliably dated at 1.8 million years of age, making them contemporary with both varieties of Australopithecines. But although contemporary to the Australopithecines, *H. habilis* had a larger and altogether more modern cranium than even *A. africanus*. Unwilling to see the former neat picture of a generalized hominid evolution disturbed, some

authorities preferred to minimize these differences, treating *H. habilis* as simply an advanced *Australopithecus*, but Leakey insisted that it was the representative of an entirely discrete species that must have been evolving separately and far more rapidly than the Australopithecines for a very long period of time.[10]

But *H. habilis* is by no means the end of the story. It is doubtful whether he is even the beginning. In 1972 Leakey's son Richard E. Leakey identified the remains of a fairly com-

[10] For a brief, relatively up-to-date summary of *Homo habilis,* consult G. W. Lasker, *Physical Anthropology* (New York: Holt, Rinehart and Winston, Inc., 1973), pp. 264 ff., bearing in mind that this was written prior to the more recent of the Skull 1470 discoveries.

Richard Leakey displaying the 2.7 million-year-old Skull 1470. Note the high forehead and relatively unobtrusive brow ridges in contrast with those of the Australopithecine skull on page 84 and of the much later *Homo erectus* skull on page 96. (Courtesy of Bob Campbell and the National Geographic Society.)

plete hominid cranium, found east of Kenya's vast Lake Rudolf in deposits which have been effectively dated as over 2.8 million years of age. Since then parts of a further skull belonging to a five or six year old child of the same species have been found, as well as the femur of a hominid even more completely adapted to an upright stance than the Australopithecines. Until such time as it may be possible to interpret these new finds more fully, no new labels have yet been assigned to them, and Richard Leakey simply refers to "Skull 1470," that being the official registration number given to the first specimen by the Kenya National Museum.[11]

These fossil remains indicate an entirely new variety of hominid which was astonishingly modern in type when compared to the Australopithecines, and more modern, even, than the *H. habilis* fossil from Olduvai. The adult cranium was probably 800 cubic centimeters in capacity, compared with 650 cubic centimeters in the larger Australopithecines and a range of between 1275 and 1475 for normal male crania among the living races of hominids. More important than cranial size, however, was the essential modernity of the crania, which reveal moderately high foreheads, small brow ridges, and reduced prognathism. In many respects the Skull 1470 hominids seem more modern in type than many fossil species that survived in parts of Africa and Asia until as late as 300,000 years ago.

Genetic Competition

What happened to the Australopithecines? Presumably like all other life forms they were subjected to evolutionary competition. Some probably died out; the remainder survived in more out of the way corners of the inhabited world and perhaps even continued to evolve

[11]R. Leakey's first published report on the originality of Skull 1470 appeared in the *National Geographic Magazine* 143, 6:818–829 (June 1973).

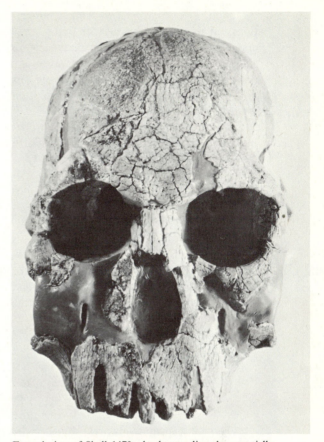

Frontal view of Skull 1470, clearly revealing the essentially modern shape of the skull. Richard Leakey's continuing search for further fossils east of Lake Rudolf, Kenya, is sponsored by the National Geographic Society. (Courtesy of Bob Campbell and the National Geographic Society.)

further until they too were eliminated as competition for living space became more acute. The *H. habilis,* Skull 1470, and Australopithecine populations must have been very sparse, probably much less than one adult per square mile in density, and the evidence suggests they lived in small bands of not more than one or two dozen individuals. During a period of hundreds of thousands of years, genetic inbreeding must have been very considerable, thus facilitating rapid local adaptation and creating an extremely favorable potential for rapid evolution.[12] By analogy with primate populations and also to some extent with living hunters and gatherers, it would be reasonable to suppose that not more than 50 percent of any one generation survived to reproduce, and this high death rate would promote rapid evolution when selective pressures were fierce.[13]

Spread over large areas of Africa and probably Asia, these various populations must also have developed very considerable genetic variation. Separate subspecies or local races, not necessarily sharply different from their neighbors, must have vied with each other for unconscious genetic leadership and possibly for territorial control. Those populations such as *H. habilis* and Skull 1470 which acquired favorable genetic adaptations, especially in the area of intelligence, would tend to multiply and their genes would spread outward from the more favored area.

The tentative evidence of cannibalism and the fact that these distinct populations were not always geographically isolated imply that actual territorial conflict may have taken place. The answer to our question—"What happened to the Australopithecines?"—therefore already seems apparent. It was probably the *H. habilis* and Skull 1470 populations that were to become the ancestors of modern man. But the Australopithecines may not have become extinct immediately. The evidence of two mandibles from Java (which was attached to the mainland of Asia during much of the Pleistocene) suggests that *A. robustus* may have survived in that area until a mere half million years ago,[14] long after becoming extinct in Africa. This would be quite in keeping with zoological evidence which shows that older populations tend to survive longest in peripheral areas. Even though *A. robustus* was a vegetarian, this may not have protected him totally from the competition of more carnivorous hominids,[15] any more than the frugivorous habits of the orangutan of Southeast Asia have protected this more distant relative of man from fast approaching extinction at the hands of his contemporary human relatives. Australopithecines may have survived and continued to evolve in some parts of the world for a considerable period of time, and may even have contributed some of their genes to later hominid populations in these marginal areas, before finally disappearing from the fossil record as a distinct and recognizable type.

Sexual Division of Labor

In the light of the available evidence, it seems reasonable to suppose that *A. africanus, H. habilis,* and the Skull 1470 populations may have been pack hunters. If this were the case, the females would have been incapacitated by pregnancy and the need to care for their slowly maturing offspring, and we may therefore assume that it would have been the males who would have made up the larger part of the hunting pack. While the women, burdened by slow-growing infants, gathered roots, herbs, fungi, and insects in the immediate neighborhood of the camp, the males roamed over

[12] For further reading consult D. J. Merrell, *Evolution and Genetics* (New York: Holt, Rinehart and Winston, Inc., 1970).

[13] H. V. Vallois, "The Social Life of Early Man: The Evidence of Skeletons," in S. L. Washburn (ed.), *The Social Life of Early Man* (Chicago: Aldine Publishing Co., 1961), pp. 214–235. Evidence is produced to show that upward of 50 percent of fossil human populations were eliminated by selection before they could contribute to the continuing gene pool.

[14] F. S. Hulse, *The Human Species* (New York: Random House, Inc., 1971), p. 207.

[15] J. B. Birdsell strongly advances the view that intergroup conflict was one of the forces contributing to rapid hominid evolution. Apart from the evidence of cannibalism, he suggests that technological achievements, such as the spear and the subsequent spearthrower, helped the later Cro-Magnons to eliminate the Neanderthals. See J. B. Birdsell, *Human Evolution* (Chicago: Rand McNally and Company, 1972), p. 329.

much larger distances, unhampered by the presence of small infants, in pursuit of fresh meat "on the hoof."

By becoming carnivorous, the hominids of these varieties would thus develop a division of labor between the sexes, such as is found among contemporary bands of human hunters and gatherers, but which is never found among nonhuman primates. With the emergence of a division of labor between man the hunter and woman the food gatherer and child tender, these hominids would have also developed that most important of all social bonds: *food sharing*. This marks another important step in the social evolution of man away from the characteristic pattern of primate societies in which the nonhuman primate females have to find their own food even when pregnant or caring for their young. Although in some primitive hunting and gathering societies of today it has been reported that the males do not always trouble to share the fruits of the chase with the females, in general it seems fair to surmise that, in common with other pack hunting carnivores, pack hunting habits led to a sexual division of labor and to the introduction of food sharing at the hominid level.

Food Sharing and Cooperation

The importance of food sharing from a social viewpoint cannot be overstressed. No adult animals, except those which have a family pattern, regularly share food. The struggle to secure a maximum share of the available food is one of the natural forces of selection which operate at the individual level in such species. The general pattern of dominance and submission will cause the weaker to wait until the stronger have had their fill, and in times of shortage this means that the weaker will starve to death. Even among some carnivores who have developed a family-type society, the pattern of dominance and submission remains

strong; for example, when lions feed, the male takes preference over the females, and the cubs eat only after the adults have gorged themselves. The weaker lion cubs are always edged away from the carcass by the stronger, and seldom live to reach maturity. The sharing of food between the members of a group is a social achievement which leads to a decline in the significance of dominance and submission and to its ultimate replacement by a new pattern of social cooperation. The principle of *achievement*, or personal self-seeking, gives way to the principle of *ascription*, the cooperative division of resources according to some prearranged entitlement, and the pattern of dominance and submission tends to be replaced by the reciprocal obligations of kinship (see Chap. 14).

But food sharing has deeper psychological implications. All early human and protohuman life still revolved, as it does among animals, around the procurement and consumption of food. For primitive men, as for animals, the meal is not something to be taken hurriedly during a reluctant 15 minute break from the more important business of the day; it is the prime object of the day's activities. In food sharing societies, those individuals with whom a man peacefully shares the day's food—the members of his own band—are drawn together by the common meal into an intense emotional interdependence and cohesion. Food sharing to the primitive man is the symbol of fellowship and trust. Even to this day we indicate sentiments of goodwill and comradeship by an offer to share a carcass with a friend. Businessmen who wish to promote a spirit of personal goodwill do so by eating together. British army officers, like the Spartans of old, eat at long tables, not at small private tables, because of the symbolic significance of eating together. Sharing food is still the most symbolic gesture of friendship that predatory modern man can make, but it is the act of a pack-hunting carnivore, not the act of a herbivorous ape.

Physiological Adaptations

There is a particularly significant physiological development which distinguishes living men from the nonhuman primates. Although we can gather little evidence from skeletal remains concerning the evolution of the glandular system, the fact remains that sometime during the period of hominid evolution our ancestors developed the habit of pair-bonding between males and females, and hominid females became genetically modified in a unique and peculiar manner that facilitates the success of such pair-bonds. Since the female needs the support of one or more males during the period of pregnancy and child rearing—which in effect means the greater part of her adult life—a protracted pair-bond between a particular male and a female will tend to guarantee this attention. Most nonhuman primate females are attractive to males only when in estrus—which is only infrequently, since they are either pregnant or lactating for much of their adult lives. If hominid females were similarly oriented toward temporary and brief sexual activity, it is less likely that they would be able to retain the permanent attention of a single male. In consequence, a process of Darwinian selection favored those hominid females who were receptive to male advances even when not in estrus, since these had a better chance of raising their offspring successfully than those which attracted male attention only at the height of estrus. In consequence, hominid females became sexually receptive to males on a year-round basis, while at the same time losing the emotionally disruptive impact of estrus—both brought about by natural selection to facilitate effective pair-bonding.

One other physiological characteristic of the modern hominids is also worthy of note. While baboons and other monkeys that live in large male-female groups customarily produce a much higher proportion of female than male offspring and while even gorillas and chimpanzees produce more female than male offspring, in the case of living hominids male and female babies are born in a more or less one-to-one ratio. This ensures the availability of a male for the protection and assistance of every female in the group. Although human societies are subject to a multitude of cultural variations—and monogamy is by no means universal—the biological fact of the one-to-one ratio of male-female births, found only in those few primate societies (such as the gibbon of Southeast Asia and the marmoset of South America) which live in small monogamous permanent male/female groups, cannot be without implications for human social behavior.

How far these biological and cultural adaptations had progressed by the time of *A. africanus,* we do not know, but the evidence for tool making and meat hunting would suggest that at least some of these distinctively hominid social patterns may have evolved in the case of the *A. africanus, H. habilis,* and Skull 1470 populations while *A. robustus,* the vegetarian, may still have lived in looser male-female groups after the fashion of the East African chimpanzee. Although we must not break our own rule by proclaiming *A. africanus, H. habilis, or* Skull 1470 to represent "the first men," there is general agreement that all lived the life of hunters and food gatherers; and except for a poverty of language and culture, still probably only very lightly developed, their material existence may not have been so radically different from that of many of the more primitive hunters and food gatherers of recent times.

For Further Reading

Ardrey, R., 1961, *African Genesis*. New York: Atheneum Publishers.

Brace, C. L., H. Nelson, and N. Korn., 1971, *Atlas of Fossil Man*. New York: Holt, Rinehart and Winston, Inc.

Braidwood, R. J., 1967, *Prehistoric Men*. Glenview, Ill.: Scott, Foresman and Company.

Chard, C. S., 1969, *Man in Prehistory*. New York: McGraw-Hill, Inc.

Dart, R., 1957, "The Makapansgat Australopithecine Osteodontokeratic Culture," *Proceedings of the Third Pan-African Congress on Prehistory,* 161–171.

Etkin, W., 1963, "Social Behavorial Factors in the Emergence of Man," *Human Biology* 35:299–310.

Howell, F. C., 1965, *Early Man*. New York: Time-Life Books.

——, and F. Bourlière, eds., 1966, *African Ecology and Human Evolution*. Chicago: Aldine Publishing Co.

Hulse, F. S., 1971, *The Human Species*. New York: Random House, Inc.

Le Gros Clark, W. E., 1967, *Man-Apes or Ape-Man*. New York: Holt, Rinehart and Winston, Inc.

——, and L. S. B. Leakey, 1951, *The Miocene Hominoidea of East Africa*. London: British Museum (Natural History).

Oakley, K. P., and B. G. Campbell, 1967, *Catalogue of Fossil Hominids, Part I: Africa*. London: British Museum (Natural History).

Pilbeam, David, 1972, *The Ascent of Man*. New York: The Macmillan Company.

Sahlins, M. D., 1960, "The Origin of Society," *The Scientific American* 203(3):76–86.

CHAPTER 9

The Man Who Walked Erect

As the long Villafranchian period of the Pleistocene came to an end, the world climate gradually became cooler, and the earth moved into a series of four major glacial epochs which have been named Günz, Mindel, Riss, and Würm. It should be explained that the term Pleistocene was formerly used to refer only to the last 1 million years during which these four major glaciations were believed to have extended over northern Europe, linking the Alps to the Arctic under a continuous sheet of snow and ice. However, geologists today prefer to extend the Pleistocene back to include the last 3 million years, thus covering the entire Villafranchian period and the earlier Donau glaciation of the Villafranchian.

The Pleistocene

The names of these major glacial periods were taken from valleys in Europe where glaciers from the respective periods had deposited rocks, boulders, and other debris from the mountains. However, the successive glacial epochs represent a vast simplification of the actual pattern of climatic variation, since each constituted a complex series of successive hot and cold periods, resulting in many temporary advances and recessions, rather than a single "ice age" that advanced or receded at a regular pace.

These glaciations only covered the northern parts of Europe and America, while the rest of the world remained free of ice, but as temperatures were lower everywhere, the area of tropical vegetation shrank substantially with each glacial epoch. Furthermore, as the heavy polar ice caps formed, they absorbed so much water that the level of the sea fell substantially during each glacial period, and the geography of the world therefore changed continuously.

The development of tool making skills among *A. africanus, H. habilis,* and Skull 1470 populations must have helped to make it possible for them or their descendants to spread more widely over the face of the earth by very slow, unconscious stages. Technology became to some extent a substitute for genetic adaptation, but by spreading into new ecological environments the "migrant" populations would become subject to new forces of genetic selection. Although those that remained in the equatorial areas may not have found their lives drastically affected by the successive glaciations, others that eventually settled outside the strictly tropical areas may have been subjected to increased selective forces as a result of the Donau glaciation, which is dated approximately 1.8 million to 1.3 million years ago, and by the Günz glaciation, which was effective between 1.3 million and 1.1 million years ago.

During these periods of climatic and ecological change, any hominids that lived in the affected areas would find their tropical environment slowly changing. As the older plant and animal populations became more sparse and new varieties evolved, some changes would have become necessary among the hominids also if they were to survive. The heaviest premium would be placed upon man's prime evolutionary achievement: intelligence. Undoubtedly some corresponding adaptive physical changes may have arisen to modify the human physiology to nontropical conditions, and a loss of pigmentation may have occurred in some areas. Although it is not possible to document all the changes taking place in the fleshy parts of the body among these diverse populations, it seems certain that throughout the Pleistocene the world hominid populations comprised a variety of relatively isolated and certainly widely dispersed subspecies. These must have come into contact occasionally—when there would have been either avoidance, conflict, or genetic admixture.[1]

Unfortunately the repeated glaciations of

Europe destroyed almost all the archeological records of the evolving hominid populations which may have inhabited the European mainland during the interglacial periods. But well before the time of the Mindel glaciation, between 800,000 and 700,000 years ago, many hominids may have evolved considerably further in the direction of modern man, and it is from the age of the Mindel glaciation and the Mindel-Riss interglacial period that we find fossil remains of a much more highly evolved variety, which are customarily labeled *Homo erectus*. Although the fossil record is by no means complete, the examples which have been discovered mark the course of human evolution as surely as wooden poles standing out of winter snowdrifts trace the course of the road that lies below the surface of the snow.

Java Man

The first discovery of *Homo erectus*, "the man who walked erect," was actually made as early as the end of the nineteenth century by a young Dutchman named Eugene Dubois. Dubois was an enthusiastic anatomist who came to the conclusion that the Dutch East Indies might be the best place in which to find fossil evidence with which to substantiate the theory of evolution. Unable to finance the cost of an expedition, he signed up as a medical doctor with the Dutch colonial service in order to be able to live and work in the Dutch East Indies, where he eventually uncovered evidence of *Homo erectus* on a terrace of the Solo River in Java.[2] Being ignorant of the existence of Australopithecine and *H. habilis* fossil remains representing earlier species of hominid which had also walked erect, he called his Southeast Asian discovery, *Pithecantropus erectus*, which may be literally translated as

[1] Some estimates suggest that 5 to 15 percent of the modern European gene pool is of Neanderthal origin, acquired by genetic admixture. J. B. Birdsell, *Human Evolution* (Chicago: Rand McNally and Company), p. 329. In other areas of Cro-Magnon colonization the adoption of Neanderthal genes was probably much larger.

[2] Franz Weidenreich, *Apes, Giants and Man* (Chicago: University of Chicago Press, 1946), p. 26.

Skull and restored head of Java Man (*Pithecanthropus erectus*). Although relatively accurate reconstructions can be made of the fleshy parts of the body, the reconstruction of the hair is totally conjectural. (Courtesy of the American Museum of Natural History.)

"erect ape man," believing it to represent the missing link that he had set out to find.

Peking Man

Some 30 years after these discoveries, Professor Davidson Black, an anatomist teaching at Western Medical College in Peking, was given a large fossil tooth to inspect, and formed the opinion that although it was human, it belonged to a species now extinct.[3] Making inquiries, he discovered that it had been found in a cave at Choukoutien, not far from Peking. For centuries the local villagers had been digging up the fossil bones of ancient men and extinct animals from these cave deposits to sell them to the Chinese apothecaries who ground them down into powder to make

[3]Weidenreich, p. 27.

magical potions. Obtaining a grant for research, Black secured permission to excavate the deposits and soon found additional fossil remains. After his death, his work was carried on by the renowned Franz Weidenreich, and a new name *Sinanthropus pekinensis* was awarded to the range of hominid fossils discovered. Subsequently, however, it was realized that the finds in Java and those in Choukoutien both belonged to a single genus, and accordingly both were named *Homo erectus,* the Chinese fossils being known as *Homo erectus pekinensis.*

Subsequent fossil evidence of *H. erectus* from Europe and Africa indicates that by as early as 900,000 B.C., some of the descendants of the earlier hominids had evolved to a level which is distinctly classed as *Homo.* The cranial capacity of these first so-called "men"

Work in progress during Franz Weidenreich's excavations at Choukoutien, near Peking in northern China, where *Sinanthropus pekinensis* fossils were found. (Courtesy of the American Museum of Natural History.)

ranged from 850 to 1100 cubic centimeters, and although they may have walked with a very slight stoop at the knees and carried their heads a little further forward than do their present-day descendants, their skeletal development was essentially on a par with that of modern man. It was primarily in the shape and size of the cranium and in the shape of the head generally that *H. erectus* differed too widely from living men for us to be able to classify him as *Homo sapiens*.

There are certain skeletal and dental charac-

teristics of *H. erectus*, who frequented the Choukoutien caves over a period of a hundred thousand years or more, which are still found among the men of eastern Asia today, but which are very rare or even nonexistent among other living races. Probably the most distinctive of these is what is called the *shovel-shaped incisor*.[4] The upper incisor teeth of Peking man were hollowed or scooped out at the back to

[4] See A. Hrdlička, "Shovel-shaped teeth," *American Journal of Physical Anthropology* 3:429–463 (1920).

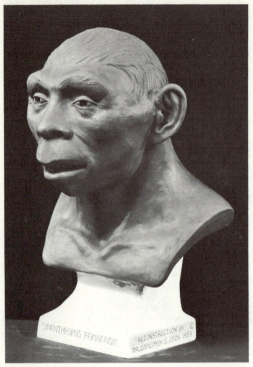

Reconstructed head of *Sinanthropus pekinensis* (*Homo erectus*) from fossil evidence recovered at Choukoutien. (Courtesy of the University Museum, Harvard.)

a bone that contributes to the lower orbit of the eye. This projected forward, as among living Chinese, creating the "high cheekbone" appearance which is so well known. Yet again, the Choukoutien fossils exhibited what is called an "Inca bone," an extra bone within the uppermost part of the occipital area, a physical trait which is still common among living Mongoloids. Although any suggestion that the *H. erectus* facial features were already developing in the direction of the living Mongoloids is regarded as an overstatement, there is sufficient evidence to suggest that the living Mongoloids must have inherited at least some of their genes from these early "erect men" who lived in northern China half a million years ago.

The various fossil finds from Java, which are also classified as *H. erectus,* do not exhibit the distinctively Mongoloid characteristics of those from China. Subsequent discoveries of other members of the *H. erectus* assemblage, sometimes known as Pithecanthropines, have been identified in Africa, and Heidelberg man, found at Mauer near Heidelberg in Germany and dated nearly 900,000 years ago by the long Pleistocene chronology,[5] as well as fossil remains from Gibraltar and nearby Ternifine in North Africa, are also often included in this genus. Since the various *H. erectus* fossils which have been discovered in these widely scattered locations lived at different times over a span of 750,000 years, it would be dangerous to read too much into the differences that distinguish them from each other, but it would seem reasonable to say that local selective forces had already resulted in the development of distinct local varieties of *H. erectus*. Since *H. erectus* populations could not have been

give them an unusual shovel shape which appears to be a genetic peculiarity that has no certain evolutionary or survival value and which may therefore be "nonadaptive." What is more interesting is that subsequent fossil remains from much more recent archeological sites in northern China also possess this shovel-shaped incisor tooth, while over 90 percent of the living population of northern China still reveal the same remarkable genetic trait. The incidence of shovel-shaped incisors decreases the further we travel from northern China, and the trait is distinctly linked to what is called the Mongoloid race, being extremely rare in Europe and completely absent from Africa.

Another distinctive characteristic of *Homo erectus pekinensis* was the shape of the *malar,*

[5] The dating of the Pleistocene periods is difficult due to the inadequacies of scientific dating methods between 50,000 and 3,000,000 years ago, already previously mentioned. However, the general trend is to push the Pleistocene further back to the dates indicated in our chronological chart (rear inside cover).

highly mobile, the existence of separate races would not be at all surprising.[6]

Ecology and Life Style

While the climate of Java during the Mindel-Riss interglacial must have been tropical, that of Peking is believed to have been considerably colder than it is at the present time, and sufficient evidence exists for us to be able to say that *H. e. pekinensis* knew the use of fire. The evidence of frequent hearth fires also tends to suggest that he used the caves, in which his bones were found, almost continuously over very long periods of time.

While it is certain that *H. erectus* used fire,[7] it seems probable that he may not have known how to make it and may merely have captured it from wild fires. The obvious value of fire is great: not only would it give warmth to *H. e. pekinensis* in northern China, but it would also give him protection against wild animals. What is more, the camp fire acts as a center of social life in the long dark evenings and serves to bond the emerging family-type groups together with greater solidarity. The cooking of food makes it possible for men to broaden their diet effectively and also in some cases to preserve food for a slightly longer period of time. In addition, fire can be used as a tool, not only to sharpen spear points, which may be charred until they become sharp and hard, but also to burn out the center of logs and the base from a tree far more quickly than the logs or trees could be cut with primitive hand tools. Fire can even be used as a hunting weapon to terrorize animals into galloping over the edge of a cliff, into prepared pitfalls, or simply into the spears of hunters waiting in ambush.

H. erectus undoubtedly remained essentially a hunter and scavenger, subordinate to the forces of nature, one of a number of living organisms in an ecological community. Nevertheless, he had surely become the dominant animal in this community. Excavations of a bog at Ambrona in Spain[8] suggest that *H. erectus* successfully drove herds of huge tusked elephants into the deep mud where they would be left to struggle helplessly until they were sufficiently weak to be dispatched with primitive spears. Although *H. erectus* would be unable to move the complete carcass of an elephant, it could be dismembered with hand choppers on the spot where it fell, the meat being carried away to be cooked and eaten over the camp fire.

H. erectus was also a cannibal, for the Peking caves were littered with the broken bones of a wide variety of animals, including a sufficient variety of the broken bones of *H. erectus* to indicate cannibalism—and a particular fondness for human marrow.

Technology

A. africanus, H. habilis, the Skull 1470 populations, and *H. erectus* all lived in what has been called the Lower Paleolithic. The term *Paleolithic* simply means the Old Stone Age, and was invented when the study of the stone tools was the prime guide to the record of human evolution. The adjective "Lower" was added to Paleolithic to refer to the lower and deeper strata in which these earlier finds were discovered, since an excavator has generally to dig deeper and lower into the ground to uncover older material.

Unfortunately we have little knowledge of the technology or style of life of *H. e. javanen-*

---

[6] M. Boule and H. V. Vallois, *Fossil Men* (New York: The Dryden Press Inc., 1957), subdivide Neanderthals and Cro-Magnons into different races.

[7] See K. P. Oakley, "On Man's Use of Fire," in S. L. Washburn (ed.), *Social Life of Early Man* (Chicago: Aldine Publishing Co., 1961).

[8] See E. White and Dale Brown, *The First Men* (New York: Little, Brown and Company, 1973).

sis, as Java man is today called, but comparable sites in the Soan River valley in India and at Kota Tampan in Malaya reveal a primitive pebble tool culture of the kind similar to that of the earlier hominids of Africa, and pebble tools found in Hungary and in Europe may have been used by Heidelberg man, who is classified as *H. erectus.* In eastern Asia, *H. e. pekinensis* undoubtedly continued the old pebble tradition of the Australopithecines. In other words he merely hammered a few chips of stone from a suitable pebble, so that the *core* which remained could be used for chopping, cutting, or scraping. Tools of this type arise continuously in the Lower and early Middle Pleistocene deposits all over the warmer parts of the Old World which were occupied by Australopithecines and early *H. erectus* populations.

However something new emerged among the populations of southern Europe, the Middle East, India, and eastern and southern Africa during the Middle Pleistocene. Around 900,000 years ago Western "erect men" developed the art of *secondary flaking* over both sides of the core of the stone on which they were working. This produced a more effective tool, sometimes known as a BIFACED CORE TOOL or hand axe, and at other times labeled *Abbevillian* after the French site where examples were first identified, which has been dated as early as 650,000 years ago.[9] In Africa at Bed II of Olduvai, similar tools called *Chellean* are found in association with other *H. erectus* remains, but, it is significant that this improved method of tool making penetrated from western Eurasia through the Middle East into southern India, yet never reached China or Southeast Asia. Additionally, it was the old chopper tool technology of eastern Asia that was carried into Australia by the very first settlers of that continent.

[9] See J. M. Coles and E. S. Higgs, *The Archeology of Early Man.* (New York: Frederick A. Praeger, Inc., 1969), p. 62.

The Problem of Pleistocene Migration

At this time northern and eastern Europe and northern and central Asia appear to have remained uninhabited. The only possible route for cultural and genetic contact between eastern Asia and western Asia, Europe, and Africa therefore lay through India. Since the bifacial hand axe, representing a superior technology, never penetrated further east than India, it has been suggested that a division known as Movius' Line separated India from Burma, Southeast Asia, and China, following a geographical mountain boundary that constituted a very real cultural and genetic barrier separating the *H. erectus* of eastern and southeastern Asia from the populations of western Eurasia and Africa for a period of some 500,000 years.[10] Similarly there is no evidence that bearers of the bifacial core technique ever penetrated the dense equatorial forests of the Congo or along the West African coast.

The whole question of the diffusion of technology in the prehistoric period is one of considerable interest to anthropologists. Since there were no printed books, no radios, and no artificial communication, ideas could be conveyed only as a result of face-to-face contact. When we find a diffusion of technology in prehistoric times, we may also be fairly sure that there was a genetic diffusion as well. In some cases a people with more advanced technology may have experienced an increase in population, and in the zoological tradition of the animal world some of them would have invaded and colonized adjacent territories at the expense of neighbors who were equipped with only a more primitive technology. Such competition would not necessarily involve actual conflict because many primitive peoples at this level of development tend to migrate

[10] See H. L. Movius, Jr., "Old World Prehistory: Paleolithic," in A. L. Kroeber (ed.), *Anthropology Today* (Chicago: University of Chicago Press, 1953), pp. 163–192.

FIG. 14   BIFACE CORE TOOLS AND *HOMO ERECTUS* FOSSIL SITES

Biface core tools have never been found east of Movius' Line, dividing western from eastern Asia. Possibly heavy rain forests in eastern India prevented the eastward migration of savannah-adapted *Homo erectus* populations from the west. Nevertheless, hominids of the *Homo erectus* level of physical evolution lived in Java and China, having presumably evolved separately from earlier pebble-tool-using populations.

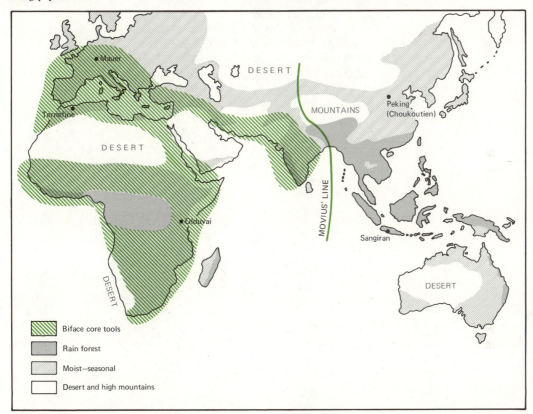

Biface core tools

Rain forest

Moist—seasonal

Desert and high mountains

away from invading competitors rather than risk conflict. When hominid behavior becomes more "modern" in type, there is the possibility of an admixture of genes, as the more successful slay the men and keep the women. However, the fact that, like the Australopithecines, *H. erectus* was a cannibal does imply the possibility that he chose the simpler course and ate his way to world supremacy over the less evolved hominid subspecies.

For Further Reading

Braidwood, R. J., 1967, *Prehistoric Man*. Glenview, Ill.: Scott, Foresman and Company.

Boule, M., and H. V. Vallois, 1957, *Fossil Men*. New York: The Dryden Press Inc.

Butzer, K. W., 1964, *Environment and Archeology: An Introduction to the Pleistocene*. New York: McGraw-Hill, Inc.

Clark, G., 1970, *Aspects of Prehistory*. Berkeley: University of California Press.

Coles, J. M., and E. S. Higgs, 1970, *The Archaeology of Early Man.* New York: Frederick A. Praeger, Inc.

Day, M. H., 1968, *Guide to Fossil Man: A Handbook of Human Paleontology.* Cleveland, Ohio: The World Publishing Company.

Hole, F., and R. F. Heizer, 1973, *An Introduction to Prehistoric Archeology.* New York: Holt, Rinehart and Winston, Inc.

Howells, W., 1959, *Mankind in the Making.* New York: Doubleday & Company, Inc.

Leakey, L. S. B., 1953, *Adam's Ancestors.* New York: Harper & Row, Publishers.

Oakley, K. P., B. G. Campbell, and T. I. Molleson, 1971, *Catalogue of Fossil Hominids, Part II: Europe.* London: British Museum (Natural History).

Pfeiffer, J. E., 1969, *The Emergence of Man.* New York: Harper & Row, Publishers.

von Koenigswald, G. H. R., 1956, *Meeting Prehistoric Man.* London: Thames and Hudson.

Washburn, S. L., 1961, *The Social Life of Early Men.* New York: The Viking Press, Inc.

Weidenreich, F., 1946, *Apes, Giants and Men.* Chicago: University of Chicago Press.

CHAPTER 10

The Coming of Homo sapiens

As early as the later peak of the Mindel Alpine glaciation (around 700,000 years ago) a new technique of working stone appeared at Vértesszöllös in Hungary. This is associated with a fossil occipital bone which is distinctly modern in type—more modern than those of the *H. erectus* populations that were contemporary to it in other parts of the world. This Vértesszöllös species, now known as *Homo sapiens paleohungaricus,* had a brain of hitherto unprecedented size, certainly not less than 1475 cubic centimeters.[1]

Homo sapiens steinheimensis

The excavations at Vértesszöllös revealed chopper tools made from pebbles and also flake tools made not from the core of the stone but from flakes that had been struck off the core. Some two hundred thousand years later similar FLAKE TOOLS appeared in other parts of Europe,

North Africa, and Southwest Asia.[2] These were similarly produced by striking small chips off the core, not for the sake of shaping the core as hitherto, but to produce sharp flakes which could be used as tools by themselves. The object of the new flake tradition was to retain and use the flakes, not the core from which they were chipped. Needless to say, the flake tradition is quite sophisticated in its conception because it involves preparing the core stone in order that the flake will be struck from it in the desired form, ready for use.

This tradition first appears, in its more developed form, at Clacton-on-Sea in England, where it is called *Clactonian.* This site dates from around 500,000 years ago, during the Mindel-Riss interglacial period of warmth, if we accept the older or longer estimate of Pleistocene chronology. Similar but even more evolved flake tools have also been found at many later sites, these being called *Levalloisian*

[1] J. B. Birdsell, *Human Evolution* (Chicago: Rand McNally & Company, 1972), p. 316.

[2] J. M. Coles and E. S. Higgs, *The Archeology of Early Man* (New York: Frederick A. Praeger, Inc., 1969), p. 269.

from the site in France where they were first discovered.[3] Levalloisian tools are associated with *tortoise cores,* so named because the core of stone from which the flake was struck was first carefully prepared to ensure that the flake was of the desired size and shape. After the flake had been struck from it, the remaining core which was discarded had the shape of a tortoise.

A third new technique of stoneworking, known as *Acheulian,* after another site in France, also appeared around 500,000 years ago,[4] and it is found in association with remarkably modern looking fossils. At Steinheim in Germany and at Swanscombe in England two incomplete skulls dating from the same period reveal the existence of a modern type of man with a large cranial capacity, the actual extent of which remains uncertain since neither of the crania are complete. Of these, the Swanscombe skull was unquestionably associated with the improved Acheulian core tradition.[5] Unfortunately the soil of Northern Europe was so completely disturbed by subsequent glaciations that most fossil remains from this period were probably destroyed. This period of advanced technological progress, represented by the Levalloisian flake tradition and the Swanscombe and Acheulian biface core traditions may be referred to as the *Advanced Lower Paleolithic.*

At first many anthropologists classified the Swanscombe and Steinheim fossils into a separate genus which they called *Homo modernus.* More recently, however, the generic term *Homo sapiens steinheimensis* has been used and fossil discoveries at Fontéchevade (dated around 200,000 years ago)[6] have been included

in this genus. Whether Swanscombe, Steinheim, and Fontéchevade men were descendants of the "intelligent man of Hungary," we do not know. To ask whether Vértesszöllös, Swanscombe, Steinheim, and Fontéchevade men were all descended directly from the Skull 1470 or *H. habilis* populations, rather than from *H. erectus* stock, is also speculative and unanswerable at the present time. Nevertheless, the facts of Skull 1470 and *H. habilis* in Africa, and of Vértesszöllös and Fontéchevade in Europe—none of which fit into *Australopithecus* → *H. erectus* → Neanderthal formula—make it clear that we can no longer see hominid evolution in terms of a vague, general worldwide advance, but must think instead in terms of the coexistence of much more modern hominids contemporaneously with survivors of more primitive lineages. For convenience some anthropologists have classified the members of the *H. steinheimensis* genus as early Neanderthals, in the same way that they first attempted to classify *H. habilis* as an Australopithecine. But this was simply a short cut to taxonomic tidiness, which is not supported by the fossil evidence.

What happened to Vértesszöllös, Swanscombe, Steinheim, and Fontéchevade men? The evidence and date of their remains are indisputable. Sufficient pieces of the crania survive to give us a reasonable impression of what they looked like, and their age, between 700,000 and 200,000 years, is not disputed. But who these men were, where they came from, and what happened to them are questions that cannot be answered at the present time. All we know is that these modern types disappeared in Europe around 200,000 years ago, and Classic Neanderthal men appeared, with marked brow ridges and marked prognathism, and a distinctive technology. If further fossil remains could be found to bridge the time gap which separates the Swanscombe, Steinheim, and Fontéchevade fossils from living men, the picture would be clear. This genus mysteri-

[3]Coles and Higgs, pp. 145, 163.

[4]Coles and Higgs, pp. 206–214.

[5]K. P. Oakley, *et al., Catalogue of Fossil Hominids, Part II, Europe* (London: British Museum (Natural History), 1971), p. 40.

[6]M. Boule and H. V. Vallois, *Fossil Men* (New York: The Dryden Press Inc., 1957), pp. 148–150.

ously disappears and we find no further fossils of such modern appearance during the entire length of the Neanderthal occupation of Europe.

Homo sapiens neanderthalensis

By 120,000 years ago, following the last Riss glacial peak, new stoneworking techniques appear in Europe, and we stop talking about the Lower Paleolithic and refer instead to the Middle Paleolithic. This new *Mousterian* culture seems to have combined both the Acheulian and the Levalloisian techniques.[7] It was accompanied by the appearance of a wide variety of geometrical flake tools, and there is evidence to show that during the Mousterian period Levalloisian stone points were fixed to the end of sticks, possibly with the aid of leather thongs, to produce stone-pointed spears.

Everywhere in Europe the Mousterian culture is associated with the remains of NEAN-DERTHAL man. Named after the Neander River in Germany where the first Neanderthal fossil remains were found, the European Neanderthal (also spelled "Neandertal") possessed such relatively primitive features that the first skull to be discovered in the Neander Valley was taken to be that of an idiot—a very inaccurate impression. The jaws were prognathous, the forehead was sloping, and there was a bony *occipital bun* or protrusion on the back of the skull.[8] The evidence of the backbone and sacrum suggests that the Neanderthals did not carry themselves quite as erect as modern man, but this is disputed. Although they stood a little over 5 feet in height, their chests were somewhat barrel-shaped. We know little about the fleshy parts of the body, but the skeletal evidence indicates that their noses were broad

and rather flat, and that they possessed strong brow ridges over the eyes. From the imprints which they left in caves, we know that their fingers were short and stubby, and their feet were broad and low arched. Possibly they were descended from Heidelberg man, because they reflect several of his peculiar characteristics, including massive jaw bones and *taurodontism,* extremely large pulp cavities in the teeth.[9] Like all hominids who lived in northern climates for a long period of time, we may assume that the European Neanderthals were probably fair-skinned, but the older idea that they must have been very hairy people has no scientific foundation.

The Neanderthal Life Style

Knowledge that the Neanderthals made gougers of stone which would have been suita-

[9] Birdsell, p. 328.

An artist's impression of the European Neanderthal. This much maligned *Homo sapiens* could almost mingle unnoticed with living hominids. (From C. S. Coon, *Races of Europe* (New York: The Macmillan Company, 1939), p. 24. By permission of the author.

[7] J. Jelínek, *Das grosse Bilderlexikon des Menschen in der Vorzeit* (Gütersloh: Bertelsmann Lexikon-Verlag, 1972), pp. 138–139.

[8] Jelínek, p. 93.

ble for making holes in skins and that they also possessed small stone burins capable of gouging a slender needle out of a piece of ivory or bone is regarded as evidence that they probably made clothes from animal hides. Indeed they appear to have been great hunters, pursuing the mammoth and the woolly rhinoceros, an animal related to the tropical rhinoceros of today, but adapted for the arctic conditions which prevailed in Europe during the Würm glaciation. Even the bones of cave bears are found among their refuse. With Neanderthal man we discover improvements in technology which are testimony to his highly evolved mental capacity, many of his tools being superior to those still in use among living primitives at the beginning of this century. Their cranial capacity was large, ranging from 1400 to 1600 cubic centimeters, larger than that of many living peoples, while they were no more prognathous than many living peoples of today. Indeed, most of their physical characteristics can be matched among many peoples living in the marginal areas of the modern world.[10] Not surprisingly, therefore, Neanderthals are today called *Homo sapiens neanderthalensis* being classed as *H. sapiens,* or "intelligent man," along with all living hominids.

The Neanderthals have been portrayed as brutish, but they have left us with ample evidence of very human virtues. Skeletal remains indicate that some who received permanent injuries so severe that they would have had difficulty in fending for themselves, nevertheless lived to die of ripe old age. In addition, Neanderthal men carefully buried their dead, usually·in shallow graves among the refuse that covered the floors of their caves. Not only did they bury their dead, but in many cases they placed the tools and possessions of the dead man with his body. In the Shanidar Cave of Iraq, one man was even buried on a bed made from flowers of hyacinths, hollyhocks, and

ragwort, which is believed to further indicate the beginnings of religious ritual.[11]

However, the Balkan site at Krapina reveals broken and charred human bones which are strong evidence of cannibalism; in another case, in Italy a Neanderthal male had been killed by a violent blow on the head, and an opening had been made in the foramen magnum through which the brains could have been extracted, presumably to be eaten for the sake of the magical qualities they might contain—a practice well known among Melanesian headhunters in recent times.[12] In this case, after the brain had been extracted, the skull was placed in a special chamber in the cave, where it was carefully surrounded by a circle of small stones in what can only have been some kind of magicoreligious ritual.

Evidence of Migrations

It is interesting to observe that the Levalloisian-Mousterian culture of Neanderthal man corresponded in geographical distribution very closely to the locations in which Neanderthal remains have been found. This includes the southern half of Europe from southern England, France, Switzerland, Austria, and the Balkans to the Crimea, as well as the mountains of Iraq and the Palestinean area, with one North African site in Libya. However there appears to have been some expansion of the Levalloisian-Mousterian culture into Africa, and parts of India also show tools which appear to be of Levalloisian-Mousterian origin.[13] This would suggest—though it by no means proves—that some Neanderthals may have migrated into Africa and India. Evidence of

[10]G. Constable, *The Neanderthals* (Boston: Little, Brown and Company, 1973), p. 27.

[11]Constable, p. 101.

[12]A. C. Blanc, "Some Evidence for the Ideologies of Early Man," in S. L. Washburn (ed.), *Social Life of Early Man* (Chicago: Aldine Publishing Co., 1961), p. 127.

[13]H. L. Movius, Jr., "Old World Prehistory: Paleolithic," in A. L. Kroeber (ed.), *Anthropology Today* (Chicago: University of Chicago Press, 1953), p. 183.

Levalloisian-Mousterian influence in Africa is found in the Aterian, Fauresmith, and Still Bay sites, but there is no evidence of any corresponding cultural influence in the region of the equatorial rain forests. However, the evidence of Broken Hill in Zambia reveals the survival of primitive Neanderthaloids (so primitive as to be classified as *H. erectus* by some authorities[14]) down to 38,000 B.C. This fossil has been called *Rhodesian Man,* and their right to the classification Neanderthal is supported by the circumstantial evidence that they used elementary Still Bay tools.[15] Evidence of a similar population has also been revealed by fossil remains uncovered at *Saldanha* in Southern Africa.

Although the presence of prehistoric technological influence does not constitute conclusive proof of any hominid migration, the evidence of prehistoric technology could be transmitted only on a face-to-face basis, meaning that technological diffusion raises the possibility of substantial genetic dispersion and probably actual migration of the culture-bearing stock. The location of Neanderthal-type fossil remains in Asia—the oldest hominid remains to be found in the steppelands and Central Asian region—suggests that the Central Asian route from Europe to China, north of Afghanistan and Tibet but south of the Siberian wastes, may have been opened by the Neanderthals with their superior technology.

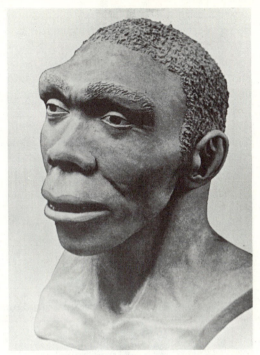

Rhodesian Man, otherwise known as *Homo rhodesiensis.* This reconstruction was made on the basis of the fossil remains found at Broken Hill in Zambia, estimated at 30,000 years B.P. (Courtesy of the University Museum, Pennsylvania.)

Thus Neanderthal-type remains are found at Mt. Carmel, Skhūl, and Shanidar in the Middle East,[16] at Teshik in Uzbekistan (more evidence of cannibalism),[17] at Ordos in Mongolia,[18] and at Ting-ts'un in China.[19] Those remains cannot be taken as prima facie evidence of a Neanderthal migration from one side of Asia to another because the more advanced tools of western Eurasia do not reach eastern Asia at this time, and the Ting-ts'un *Neanderthal*-type fossils reflect a somewhat

[14] The debate over the classification of Rhodesian Man hinged on the fact that as C. S. Coon, *The Origin of Races* (New York: Alfred A. Knopf, Inc., 1967), pointed out, the facial features match those of *H. erectus,* while the cranial capacity although low for a Neanderthal is considerably larger than that of any other *H. erectus.*
[15] In appearance the Still Bay tools could represent an early but arrested stage in the development of Acheulian techniques, but in view of their late date they are more likely to be a degenerate form acquired by diffusion from a more highly evolved center. See F. C. Howell and J. D. Clark, "Acheulian Hunter-Gatherers of Sub-Saharan Africa," in F. C. Howell and F. Bourlière (eds.), *African Ecology and Human Evolution* (Chicago: Aldine Publishing Co., 1966), pp. 474–476.

[16] See T. McCown and Sir Arthur Keith, *The Stone Age of Mt. Carmel* (London: Oxford University Press, 1939).
[17] A. L. Mongait, *Archeology in the USSR* (London: Penguin Books, 1961), pp. 83–85.
[18] K. C. Chang, *The Archeology of Ancient China* (New Haven, Conn.: Yale University Press, 1971), pp. 59–63.
[19] Chang, pp. 57–58.

different eastern Asian type, very dissimilar to that of western Eurasia.[20] But the salient fact is undeniable: *H. sapiens* populations have now settled much if not all of the steppeland corridor that links eastern and western Asia, north of the Himalayas, for the first time in hominid history.

One fact that may not be without significance is that the ample fossil remains of Classic Neanderthal in Europe indicate a marked de-

gree of homogeneity,[21] suggesting that there were few if any Neanderthal migrations into Europe from Asia or Africa and that a necessarily small European Neanderthal population was therefore substantially inbred over a very long period of time. By contrast, Neanderthal-type fossils found at *Omo* in Abyssinia are much more heterogeneous, at least one suggesting the Swanscombe-Skhūl features, possibly from the Middle East, a second reflecting the more primitive features of Rhodesian

[20] Both the Ordos and the Ting-ts'un fossils differ from those of western Asia Neanderthals in the possession of shovel-shaped incisors.

[21] Birdsell, p. 325.

FIG. 15   FACET FLAKE AND DERIVED FACET FLAKE CULTURES SHOWING LOCATION OF NEANDERTHAL FOSSIL SITES

The most highly developed facet flake cultures were centered in Europe, western Asia, and North Africa, but peripheral facet flake cultures penetrated parts of Africa and India.

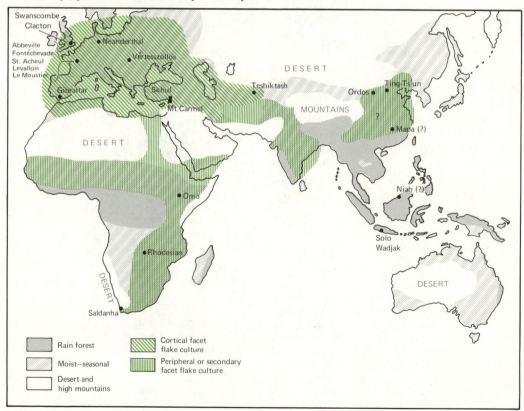

man (which were perhaps characteristic of all sub-Saharan Neanderthals of this time) and another an intermediate type.[22] Such variability would be extremely unlikely in an inbred population,[23] and we are left with the possibility that the heterogeneity of the Omo Neanderthals resulted from contact between the widely disparate Rhodesian-type Neanderthals of sub-Saharan Africa and the more progressive population of the Middle East.

Similar heterogeneity is found among the later Choukoutien fossils in China,[24] again suggesting an element of outbreeding, possibly of an immigrant population with older local stocks. But while the possibility of a migration of Middle Eastern Neanderthals into Africa is supported by the evidence of technological diffusion, there is at present no evidence of technological diffusion between East and West Asia to support the possibility of genetic contact between East Asian and West Asian Neanderthals at this time.

Neanderthal remains disappear in Europe quite suddenly, around 40,000 years ago, although a solitary Libyan site has been dated at 38,000 B.C., and one very late Neanderthal site in France has been dated at 33,000 B.C.

In their place, somewhere between 40,000 and 33,000 B.C., just as the Würm glaciation began a temporary retreat, a new and entirely modern people appear fully evolved in Europe. These are the CRO-MAGNONS who seem to be directly ancestral to the living Europeans. To distinguish them from their *Homo sapiens neanderthalensis* predecessors, they have been called *Homo sapiens sapiens.*[25]

Cro-Magnon Man

With the appearance of Cro-Magnons in Europe and West Asia we identify an entirely new cultural period known as the UPPER PALEOLITHIC. Although technically the Cro-Magnons still lived in what we call the Old Stone Age, there was a complete revolution in the character of human life, and in many ways we find ourselves in essentially modern times.

The Classic Neanderthals of Europe were uniform in type, although those of areas outside Europe varied considerably, and the Cro-Magnons who now took over western Eurasia were also generally uniform. Only one Upper Paleolithic population located in the Mediterranean area, labeled Grimaldi man, was not Cro-Magnon in type. This possessed long limbs and facial features suggestive of modern Negroes, and their taxonomic position awaits clarification.[26]

Contemporary East European anthropologists have classified Cro-Magnon fossil remains into three subraces, which they believe may be ancestral to the major subraces of modern Europe, but such attempts to divide Cro-Magnon men into subraces have not been

[22] See R. E. F. Leakey, "Early *Homo sapiens* Remains from the Omo River Region of Southwest Ethiopia," *Nature* 222:1132–1134 (1969).

[23] As pointed out by G. A. Harrison, J. S. Weiner, J. M. Tanner, and N. A. Barnicot in *Human Biology* (New York: Oxford University Press, 1964), p. 162, natural selection operating on an inbreeding population tends to produce a high degree of racial uniformity or "homozygousness." This principle has been confirmed by A. Montagu and T. Dobzhansky, and is applied by F. E. Poirier to the Mt. Carmel remains. See F. E. Poirier, *Fossil Man* (St. Louis: C. V. Mosby Co., 1973), p. 180. Even populations that are historically known to have been the product of hybridization can through inbreeding and selection achieve a degree of homogeneity equivalent to those of an "unmixed race," according to J. C. Trevor in *Race Crossing in Men: the Analysis of Material Characters* (London: Cambridge University Press, Eugenics Lab. Mem. N. 36. 1953).

[24] Poirier, p. 200.

[25] G. W. Lasker, *Physical Anthropology* (New York: Holt, Rinehart and Winston, Inc., 1973), p. 312.

[26] The "Grimaldi" group of fossils found in a cave on the Italian Riviera revealed prognathous jaws and a skull shape similar to living Negroes. Many writers now accept the argument that these skulls were simply deformed by the way they were buried, but this view is not yet universally accepted.

accepted by Western anthropologists. Indeed the lack of contact between the anthropologists of the West and those of the East European nations has proved to be a barrier to the exchange of ideas and information.

Some early fossils from Skhūl in Palestine, dated around 36,000 years ago suggest an intermediate Neanderthal–Cro-Magnon type, which could possibly indicate the evolution of Cro-Magnons from Neanderthals. They could also represent the hybrid offspring of miscegenation between the two *H. sapiens* varieties, a possibility that is heightened by their obvious heterogeneity.[27] Except for a few intermediate Middle Eastern fossils such as Skhūl, the contrast between the plentiful Cro-Magnon remains which we have found and those of Neanderthal is generally extremely sharp.[28] Furthermore the Cro-Magnons of Europe lacked the taurodont teeth of the Neanderthals they supplanted, although taurodontism is found among Wadjak and other Neanderthal fossils outside Europe and is still common among living South African Bushmen, Eskimoes, and American Indians.[29] It is therefore by no means sure that Cro-Magnon men evolved from Neanderthal ancestors, and some

anthropologists especially in Europe, argue in favor of a separate evolution of Cro-Magnon from *H. steinheimensis* forebears.[30] But it lacks adequate corroborating fossil evidence, because, as already observed, the last Würm glaciation destroyed much of the archeological evidence of former human habitation north of the Alps. The southeast European and western

[30] H. V. Vallois has been one of the leading exponents of the derivation of Cro-Magnons from *H. steinheimensis,* a view which has been generally contested by American physical anthropologists who prefer the tidier solution that assumes the evolution of Cro-Magnons from Middle Eastern Neanderthals.

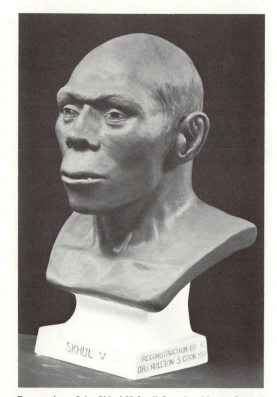

Restoration of the Skhūl V fossil found at Mount Carmel in Palestine, dated *c.* 36,000 B.P. This individual may represent an evolutionary stage intermediate between Neanderthal and Cro-Magnon or could be a hybrid resulting from an admixture of these two hominid varieties. (Courtesy of the University Museum, Pennsylvania.)

[27] The earlier Skhūl fossils are distinctly Neanderthal, but later remains reveal what is essentially a Cro-Magnon type possessing certain Neanderthal traits. The variability of individual types within the later cave suggests recent hybridization. Those who prefer the hybridization theory point out that the time factor would require exceptionally rapid evolution if we are to regard Skhūl as evidence of evolution from Neanderthal to Cro-Magnon, and suggest the Russian steppes as the probable location in which the Cro-Magnons may have evolved from *H. steinheimensis* ancestors.

[28] Although many writers declare that there is no evidence of Neanderthal hybridization with Cro-Magnons in Europe, J. B. Birdsell believes that some hybridization occurred even in Europe, and that Neanderthal genes survive in certain living European populations to as much as 5 percent or even 15 percent of the contemporary gene pool. Birdsell, p. 329.

[29] For a brief discussion of taurodontism among Heidelberg and Neanderthal populations, see Birdsell, p. 328.

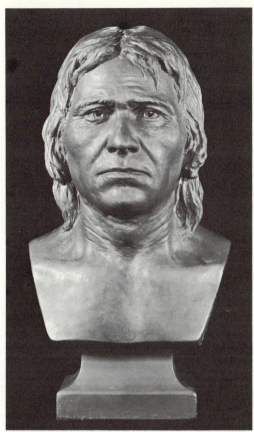

Reconstruction of Cro-Magnon skull, revealing its characteristically modern European features. With the exception of a group of non-Cro-Magnon skulls found at Grimaldi in Southern France, Upper Paleolithic European fossils were generally uniform in type, though frequently slightly narrower in face than the fossil portrayed above. (Courtesy of the American Museum of Natural History.)

Asian areas, which remained habitable to man during the Würm III glaciation and could have been the homeland of a distinctive and rapidly evolving proto–Cro-Magnon population, have not yet been extensively excavated.

The Cro-Magnons had large brains, revealing a cranial capacity varying between 1500 and 1800 cubic centimeters, which is actually larger than that of living North Europeans of today, whose average is between 1450 to 1500

cubic centimeters. Most Cro-Magnons were long-headed, although a few had somewhat broader heads, and their skulls indicate long straight noses like most living Europeans. They revealed no trace of prognathism, and their crania show high, almost vertical foreheads, although occasionally traces of brow ridge are to be found. Even more than the Neanderthals, the Cro-Magnons possessed very pronounced, protruding chins. Altogether their general skeletal build was similar to that of living Europeans, and since they were tall in general stature, well proportioned, and athletic, some admirers have seen Cro-Magnon man as a kind of Adonis—a supercreation of evolution with ourselves as his degenerate survivors.[31]

However, whether we look upon the Cro-Magnons with admiration or envy, we must admit the superiority of their culture over everything which preceded it.

The Upper Paleolithic Revolution

The new Upper Paleolithic technology, employing percussion or punch techniques, produced a distinctive variety of knives, projectile points, scrapers, and burins used for working bone, antlers, and ivory, as well as distinctive engravings. It first appeared in the Middle East and Europe around 30,000 to 40,000 years ago, but subsequently spread into northern Europe as the Würm glaciation finally receded, so that Upper Paleolithic settlements are found in Russia as far as 55 degrees north. Upper Paleolithic technology, and with it we may presume a number of Cro-Magnon genes, then migrates east of the Ural Mountains across the steppelands of Asia to enter Japan and northeastern Siberia, where it is found in association with older Mousterian traditions, implying an admixture of traditions

[31] R. C. Andrews, *Meet Your Ancestors* (London: John Long Ltd. (n.d.) p. 108.

and perhaps people.[32] From there it crossed the Bering Strait into the New World with the migrants who settle the Americas. Interestingly enough, the first migration of Upper Paleolithic culture does not seem to have penetrated China or Southeast Asia, these areas having to wait until a subsequent wave of the derivative MESOLITHIC culture transported them directly from the Paleolithic to the Mesolithic, without their ever experiencing a Middle Paleolithic or Upper Paleolithic tradition, in the same way that most of sub-Saharan Africa also passed directly from Lower Paleolithic to a Mesolithic tradition.

While the European Neanderthals appear to have lived in caves and other hominids at this level of evolution who lived in more favorable climates may have camped in the open, some *H. s. sapiens* built semisubterranean *pit houses.* Making a shallow hollow in the ground, which gave coolness in summer and warmth in winter, they raised a small mound of earth around the outside of this pit and, sticking branches or even mammoth bones in the ground to serve as a frame, covered the upper part of the house with hides and skins and possibly an outer covering of mud. Some of the more sophisticated houses reveal a device which prevented the warm air on the inside from escaping when they entered or left the chamber. This was done by constructing a short semisubterranean entry tunnel, which at its lowest point descended below the level of the floor of the hut and so served as an air lock, preventing the warm air from escaping. This device was to be carried, along with many other aspects of the European Upper Paleolithic culture so admirably designed to combat the prevailing subarctic conditions, right across Asia, as the Würm glaciation retreated, to survive among the Eskimos who continued to live in subarctic and even arctic conditions on the North American continent into our own age.

Although the later Cro-Magnons built relatively solid houses in winter, it seems that in summer many may have used lightweight tents, made of sticks and covered with hides, rather like an Indian wigwam, and there is archeological evidence to suggest that such tents may have been pitched in regular rows.

Not only did the Cro-Magnons live in houses instead of caves—though some of the earlier Cro-Magnons built these houses in the safety of a cave mouth—but they also appear to have been excellent housekeepers, gathering up their refuse and throwing it onto an exterior rubbish dump, in strict contrast to the Neanderthals who let their refuse lie where it fell.[33] In addition, the Cro-Magnons were talented artists who not only improved the quality of workmanship of their tools but exerted considerable effort to ensure a balanced esthetic symmetry, far greater than was required for technological efficiency. They also began to carve bone and ivory tools and weapons into esthetically pleasing and ornamental animal shapes.

Cro-Magnons also added with considerable ingenuity to the variety and character of their weapons and tools. Not only did they produce fine new elegant stone blades, but they also learned how to fit wooden handles to stone axes and designed the spearthrower which is a small piece of wood with a hook at one end that acts as an extension of the arm and enables men to throw a spear with greater force and accuracy than is possible with the bare hand. Later Cro-Magnons invented the bow and arrow so that projectile weapons became an important part of their hunting and, we also understand from cave pictures, their military equipment.

---

[32] For a more detailed exposition of the spread of Upper Paleolithic technology from Europe across Asia, see R. F. D'Amare, "El Antropogeno de Siberia y el Hombre Americano," *Investigaciones: Instituto Nacional de Antropologia e Historia* No. 8, (1965).

[33] H. L. Movius, Jr., "The Chatelperronian in French Archaeology," *Antiquity* 43:111–123 (1969) p. 122.

Reconstructed Cro-Magnon tent. Although Cro-Magnon men also built permanent huts, many used skin-covered tents for temporary quarters, arranging them in rows in orderly campsites. These were closely similar in type to the North American wigwam, which is probably a cultural survival from the Upper Paleolithic. (Courtesy of Landesmuseum, Schloss Gottorp).

The Cro-Magnon Life Style

Some of the cave paintings also show scenes of combats between rival Cro-Magnon groups. The fact that these indicate as many as 20 archers on each side of the battle suggests that the Cro-Magnon social organization had become quite complex and that they were no longer living in very small unrelated bands.

The earliest Cro-Magnon cultures in Europe are known as *Perigordian* and the *Aurignacian*, both of which began about 35,000 years ago and appear to have existed side by side. It was during this Aurignacian period that the spearthrower was invented, and we find evidence of Cro-Magnon men and women adorning themselves, possibly for the first time in hominid history, with necklaces made from rhythmic patterns of bones and shells.

Indeed it is in the field of art that the Aurignacians have most astonished the modern world. In the cave paintings near Les Eyzies in France they have painted a large variety of animals in most vigorous and pleasing styles, many in color.

The purpose of most cave paintings seems to have been magical or religious. The many scenes of the hunt suggest a ritual intended to enhance the hunters' prowess, while other paintings may have been designed as a backdrop for religious ceremonies intended to enhance the fertility of the animals hunted. In yet other rituals a skeleton of a bear seems to have played a central role in a mystical bear cult similar to that which was still practiced in recent times by the Ainu of the northern Japanese islands.[34]

In the ensuing *Solutrean* phase which ap-

[34]Evidence of a bear cult is widespread in Europe, and also across Asia to include the Ainu in historical times. Traces of a similar cult are also found among North American Indians.

Reindeer shoulder blades perforated by holes believed to have been made by the spears of Cro-Magnon men. A bone harpoon of the Upper Paleolithic period is shown piercing one of the shoulder blades. Found at Stellmoor near Hamburg. (Courtesy of Landesmuseum, Schloss Gottorp.)

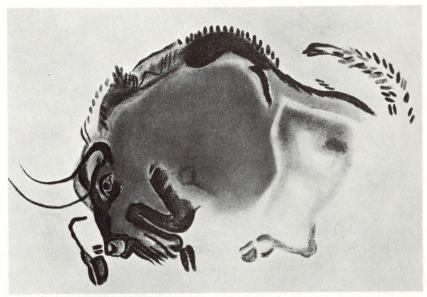

(*Right*) Renowned painting of a bison, executed by a Cro-Magnon artist on the wall of a cave in Altamira, Spain, circa 28,000 B.P. (Courtesy of the American Museum of Natural History.) (*Bottom*) Bushman cave drawings from South Africa, not more than a few centuries old, which echo the Upper Paleolithic cave paintings of Old Europe. (Courtesy of the South African Information Service.)

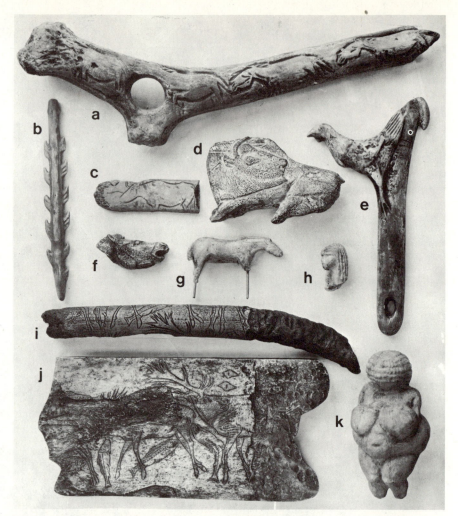

The European Upper Paleolithic provides us with the first evidence of esthetic sensitivity in man. More remarkably, this evidence reveals a highly developed art tradition. Illustrated above: (a) A Magdalenian tool made from reindeer antler ornamented with wild horses. (b) A Magdalenian harpoon carved in bone. (c) A Magdalenian drawing of a wild ox incised on bone. (d) A carved bone reproduction of a bison looking over its left shoulder, also from the Magdalenian culture. (e) An exquisitely carved dart thrower made from reindeer antler; Magdalenian. (f) The head of a horse, carved in ivory from the tusk of a mammoth; probably Aurignacian. (g) A horse carved in mammoth ivory; Magdalenian. (h) An Aurignacian carving of a female head, executed in ivory (notice the elaborate headdress). (i) Drawings of deer and fish carved on a piece of reindeer antler; Magdalenian. (j) A flat cast made from (i) above. (k) The renowned "Venus of Willendorf" from Austria, carved in stone. The Upper Paleolithic provided numerous images of heavily rounded figurines, possibly indicative of a female in pregnancy, and similar images have been found in later Mesolithic and Neolithic sites (see illustration in Chap. 20). It is believed that such images may be associated with the worship of a fertility goddess antecedent to the religion of the Great Mother which survived in the Mediterranean into historical times. (Courtesy of the American Museum of Natural History.)

peared around 20,000 years ago, there seems to be evidence of a new and militaristic Cro-Magnon culture which is noted for its beautifully worked willow-leaf spear points and stone tools. But the Solutrean period did not last long before the final Upper Paleolithic culture, the *Magdalenian*, came in around 17,000 years ago, continuing to around 10,000 B.C. It is in the Magdalenian period that the bow and arrow was invented and that the very finest cave paintings were executed at Altamira in Spain. During the Magdalenian, also, many extremely small stone tools, called MICROLITHS, sometimes only a quarter of an inch in size, were manufactured. These facilitated extremely fine working of bone, ivory, and leather.

While Neanderthal men may have made some form of clothing out of skins, Cro-Magnon men regularly dressed themselves in leather, and we have every reason to believe that they were expert tailors. They possessed an excellent range of tools for leatherwork and were probably quite as skilled in this art as the average leatherworker of today.

In death, especially, the Cro-Magnon attitudes reveal a new dimension. Whereas the Neanderthals buried their dead but seemed to have regarded the departed spirit with feelings of fear, there is substantial evidence of ancestor worship among the Cro-Magnons who seems to have shown a respect and reverence for the dead rather than a vague fear of that which was not understood. Cro-Magnons thus initiated the custom of painting the remains of the dead with red ochre, probably believed to have life-giving qualities.[35] They also buried amulets with the body, which we believe were intended to assist in the revitalization of the body as a home for the soul in the afterlife. Both these practices survived in eastern Europe into Neolithic times.

The Mesolithic

Although it is customary to close out the Upper Paleolithic with the end of the Magdalenian culture around 10,000 B.C., in actual fact the *Azilian* culture which ensued is really only an extension of the Upper Paleolithic. It is customary to identify the Azilian as a Mesolithic culture, distinguished by the wide range of small geometrical stone tools which were produced and which are evidence of a very advanced technical level of craftsmanship. The Mesolithic has also been renowned for the painted pebbles of the Azilian era, and now that evidence of an early form of writing has been identified in the Balkan cultures as early as 6000 B.C., it seems quite possible that these late Cro-Magnons may have pioneered the world's first written script. Certainly the first pottery was made (without the benefit of the potter's wheel) in the Balkans during the Mesolithic, and it was the descendants of Cro-Magnon men who first domesticated man's oldest animals friend, the dog, on the shores of the Baltic.

Recent excavations in the Lower Danube have revealed the existence of a high civilization in that area, which grew out of the Mesolithic, extending from 7000 B.C., to 3500 B.C., when it was overrun by invading pastoralists from the Pontic Steppes. Although interpretative work is still in progress, it seems highly probable that the Mesolithic culture of Europe was directly ancestral to the known civilizations of the Etruscans and the Cretans, and Mesolithic inscriptions[36] may prove to be

---

[35] The evidence of living peoples suggests that a) red ochre may be applied to the bodies before burial; b) the body may be exposed until only the bones are left and these can be stained with red ochre before burial; or c) the bones may be exhumed after burial, the flesh having decayed, painted with red ochre, and buried again. In each case the red coloring is believed to imply life-giving properties.

[36] M. Gimbutas, "Old Europe, 7000-3500 B.C.," *Journal of Indo-European Studies* 1, 1:1-20 (1973).

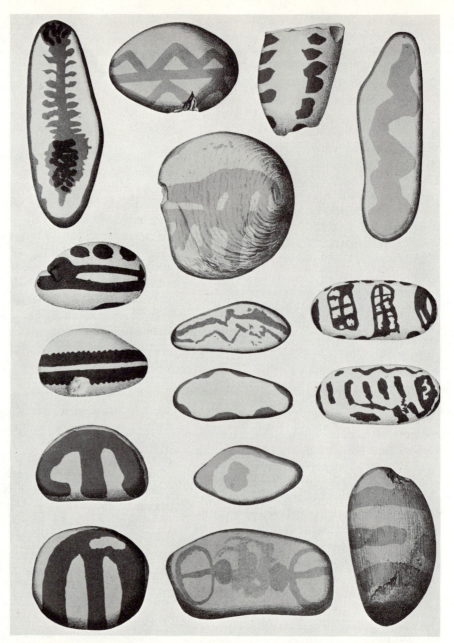

Painted pebbles from the Azilian culture of the European Mesolithic. These are painted with pictographic symbols possibly representing ancestral spirits. Like the churinga of living Australian aboriginals and the ancestor pebbles of East Africa, they may have been regarded as places of residence for the spirits of the dead forefathers. (Courtesy of the American Museum of Natural History.)

FIG. 16   THE UPPER PALEOLITHIC AND SUBSEQUENT MESOLITHIC EXPANSION

The Upper Paleolithic never expanded beyond the area shown in the map below. It was in the Mesolithic—essentially a late stage of the Paleolithic—that this high culture diffused outward to most parts of the world (see arrows).

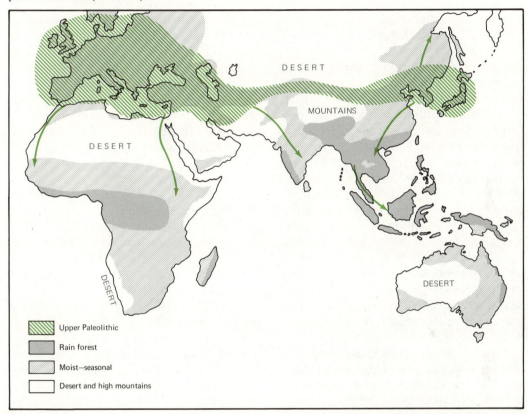

Upper Paleolithic

Rain forest

Moist—seasonal

Desert and high mountains

the source of the earliest written script to be used by man.

Beyond Europe

Following the advent of the Mesolithic era, characterized by numerous and varied minute microliths and various forms of slotted haft weapons and tools, there was a virtually worldwide cultural migration from Europe and southwestern Asia into almost every part of Africa, across southern Asia into southeastern Asia, as well as into northern China by way of the Asian steppes. This migration took the bow and arrow, the spearthrower, the dog, and an entire range of tools and symbols to almost every continent, leaving only a few more remote peoples without the benefit of Mesolithic inventions.[37]

While these events were taking place in western Eurasia, it would be wrong to assume that no evolutionary changes had occurred in other parts of the world. Genetic change and genetic migration are likely to occur even where ecological changes are not severe. Al-

[37] See G. Clark, *Aspects of Prehistory* (Berkeley: University of California Press, 1970).

though the physical history of the more recent hominids in Africa is still somewhat obscure, we find remains at the Olduvai Gorge of a modern type of man, somewhat similar to the modern South African Bushman, around 20,000 B.C., while other Bushman-type remains have been found at Boskop in the Transvaal. These and other fossil remains from East Africa, dating around 10,000 years ago, are not particularly Negroid in type, and may be related to the European Cro-Magnon. Certainly on the North African Mediterranean coast, Cro-Magnon skulls are found at Afalou, dating from around 10,000 years ago. Of the ancestors of the Negroes we can find few traces, since the rain forests of the Congo have not so far provided us with a single hominid fossil and probably have not preserved any such remains. On the other hand, the fossil remains of Rhodesian man, found at Broken Hill in Rhodesia, represent a late *H. erectus* or early Neanderthal with prognathous jaws and heavy brow ridges, which apparently survived in Africa until 38,000 years ago. Indeed some claim that the genes of Rhodesian man still survive among living Bushmen.

The few human remains found in the Middle East which date from this period correspond to the Cro-Magnons of Europe, but there is a complete dearth of fossil remains around this time in India and Southeast Asia. Only at the Niah cave in northern Borneo, do we find the skull cap of a boy, uncertainly dated at around 39,000 B.C., in association with pebble tools of the older Southeast Asian tradition, as begun by Australopithecines and developed by *H. erectus*. This fragment is Neanderthaloid or *H. sapiens* in character—and is in many ways suggestive of the modern Australian aboriginal—but in the absence of the facial bones it is impossible to make a proper classification, and the facial characteristics could well have been too primitive to allow the Niah boy to be classified as *H. sapiens*.

Similar finds at Wadjak in Java, dating from around 12,000 years ago, also reveal the same heavy brow ridges, receding forehead, prognathism, and long skull shape that characterize the Australian aboriginal people of today and are undeniably *H. sapiens* in character, being generally classified as an advanced Neanderthal. Indeed, pebble tools were still in fashion in Southeast Asia when Australia was first settled from the general area of Java, by just a few small bands of hunters and gatherers. It was only later that elements of the Mesolithic tradition diffused into the Southeast Asian and Australian area.

Clearly, we shall have to wait until we have found more fossil remains in Africa and Asia before we can hope to piece together the origins of the living races of man. Unfortunately, a frank discussion of the subject is also frequently clouded by prepossessions and prejudices, and no objective conclusion can be reached unless we are prepared to put aside value judgments and attempt to look at the available evidence scientifically and dispassionately. Let us therefore examine the techniques of modern physical anthropology in the next chapter.

For Further Reading

Birdsell, J. B., 1972, *Human Evolution: An Introduction to the New Physical Anthropology.* Chicago: Rand McNally.

Brace, C. L., H. Nelson, and N. Korn, 1971, *Atlas of Fossil Man.* New York: Holt, Rinehart and Winston, Inc.

Bordes, F., 1961, "Mousterian Cultures in France," *Science* 134(3482):803–809.

Boule, M., and H. V. Vallois, 1957, *Fossil Men.* New York: The Dryden Press Inc.

Clark, G., 1970, *Aspects of Prehistory.* Berkeley: University of California Press.

Coon, C. S., 1967, *The Origin of Races.* New York: Alfred A. Knopf.

Deetz, J. F., 1971, *Man's Imprint from the Past.* Boston: Little, Brown & Company.

Graziosi, P., 1960, *Palaeolithic Art.* London: Faber & Faber, Ltd.

Hulse, F. S., 1971, *The Human Species: An Introduction to Physical Anthropology.* New York: Random House, Inc.

Jelínek, J., 1972, *Das Grosse Bilderlexikon des Menschen in der Vorzeit.* Gütersloh, Germany: Bertelsmann Lexikon Verlag.

Kraus, B. S., 1964, *The Basis of Human Evolution.* New York: Harper & Row, Publishers.

Leakey, R. E., 1973, "Skull 1470," *National Geographic Magazine.* 143(6):818–829.

Le Gros Clark, W., 1967, *Fossil Evidence for Human Evolution.* Chicago: University of Chicago Press.

Leroi-Gourhan, A., 1957, *Prehistoric Man.* New York: Philosophical Library, Inc.

Marshack, A., 1972, *The Roots of Civilization.* New York: McGraw-Hill, Inc.

Oakley, K. P., B. G. Campbell, and T. I. Molleson, 1971, *Catalogue of Fossil Hominids, Part II: Europe.* London: British Museum (Natural History).

Pfeiffer, J. E., 1969, The Emergence of Man. New York: Harper & Row, Publishers.

Poirier, F. E., 1973, *Fossil Man: An Evolutionary Journey.* St. Louis: C. V. Mosby Company.

Vallois, H., 1954, *Neanderthals and Presapiens.* Journal of the Royal Anthropological Institute, 84:11.

CHAPTER **11**

From Calipers to Biochemical Markers: Physical Anthropology Comes of Age

After tracing the general course of hominid evolution into recent prehistoric times, the physical anthropologist now faces the problem of relating the living hominid populations of the world to those of prehistory. The present state of knowledge in this area is unfortunately very unsatisfactory since the variety of hypotheses seems to far exceed the amount of evidence available. Africa and Asia have, in general, been but poorly excavated, and where fossil evidence has been uncovered, the skeletal remains are frequently incomplete, comprising usually a skull, a jawbone, or maybe parts of a skeleton. On the other hand, there is a plethora of material available for study in the case of modern man—for here we are dealing with live flesh and blood organisms—and ultimately it is the living parts of the body that are important from an evolutionary point of view, rather than the bone tissues which become fossilized. But before we examine the living races, and speculate on their origin, let us first look at the techniques available to the physical anthropologists of today.

TRADITIONAL ANTHROPOMETRY

Traditional methods of physical anthropology relied heavily on the external measurement and description of the human body and, in particular, upon the skeleton.[1] Such measurements were useful in that they could be applied to the analysis and classification of fossil remains, as well as to the study of living populations. Although it may be objected that the skeleton is merely a frame for the living parts of the body, the skeletal framework of any living organism becomes adapted, in the course of evolution, to the functional requirements of the living parts, and therefore provides us with valuable evidence regarding the all-important functional abilities of the organism as a whole.

[1] The classic source for traditional anthropometry was R. Martin, *Lehrbuch der Anthropologie* (Stuttgart: Gustav Fischer Verlag). A summary of such traditional techniques is contained in G. Olivier, *Practical Anthropology* (Springfield, Ill.: Charles C Thomas, Publisher, 1969).

The Cranium

In particular the earlier physical anthropologists concentrated their attention on the study of the human cranium. All hominids since *Homo erectus* appear to have walked erect without difficulty, and as we have already observed there has been relatively little evolution of the human skeleton over the past million years other than primarily local adaptations. On the other hand, there have been very substantial developments in the human cranium during the period of time which separates *H. erectus* from the living hominids. In consequence, measurements of the cranium provide valuable information which can be used as the basis for comparisons not only between living races or subspecies but also between the various fossils which reveal the course of evolution leading to the modern varieties of man.

The human cranium can be measured in many ways. We have frequently referred to the cubic capacity of the brain case of both hominoids and hominids. This is known as the *cranial capacity* and is usually measured in cubic centimeters. Large-headed populations are described as *macrocephalic;* small-headed peoples as *microcephalic.* When compared to the overall size of the body, cranial capacity provides a general indication of the growth of the brain at different levels of hominid evolution. In a broad sense such gross measurements have undoubted significance, but human cultural achievement is actually dependent on the evolution of particular areas of the brain, such as the cerebral cortex, associated with intelligence, and the frontal lobes, associated with purposeful behavior. Thus an elephant has a larger brain than any man due more to the size of the lower brain centers concerned with the control of its vast body, than to the development of the elephant's cerebral cortex and frontal lobes.

The position of the *foramen magnum,* the opening through which the spinal cord enters the cranium, is another important indicator of hominid evolution because it indicates the position in which the head is carried. This will reflect the extent to which the evolving hominids have abandoned their protosapiens slouch in favor of an upright carriage, with the head balanced centrally on the shoulders. Again, the size of the *mastoid process,* the bony protrusion behind the ear to which the muscles that rotate the head from side to side are fixed, is important as an indicator of hominid evolution. Physical anthropologists also note the size of the brow ridge, for prominent brow ridges are a primitive trait, not characteristic of *Homo sapiens sapiens,* although Australoids and some other varieties of living men still reveal fairly strong brow ridges. Yet possibly the most characteristic of *H. s. sapiens* traits is the existence of a chin. This is partly associated with the decline in *prognathism,* the degree of projection of the maxillary portion of the face. Man is the least prognathous of all the mam-

This 2000 year old skull, complete with hair still tied in a "Suebian knot," was preserved in a peat bog near Osterby in Schleswig Holstein. (Courtesy of Landesmuseum, Schloss Gottorp.)

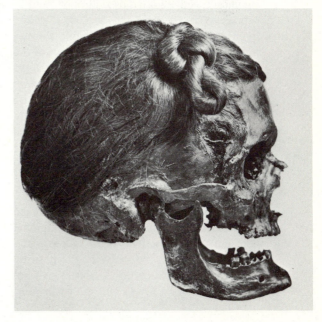

mals, but prognathism still survives in some living hominid populations.

Statistical measurements relating to the overall shape of the skull play an important role in anthropometry as a means of identifying specific populations. These are recorded by measurements known as *cranial indices,* the most important of which is the *cephalic index,* which measures the maximum head breadth divided by the maximum head length, the index being determined by multiplying the resultant fraction by 100. Some populations, including most Negroes, are *dolichocephalic* or long-headed, while others, such as the Alpines of Bavaria, the Armenians, and the Lapps, are *brachycephalic* or broad-headed. Where the cephalic index is 75.9 or less, a population or individual is said to be dolichocephalic; where it falls between 76 and 80.9, they are described as *mesocephalic;* and where it exceeds 81 they are said to be brachycephalic.

Facial Features

The general shape and length of the nose and other fleshy parts of the body are also significant, and are often used as popular indications of racial variation. Indeed, it is the living parts of the body rather than the skeleton (which only serves the requirements of the soft parts) that are primarily subject to evolutionary selection. The nose is actually quite useful for classificatory purposes because its shape seems to be determined by relatively simple genetic factors. Where a particular nose shape is linked to a single dominant gene, a single lineage may acquire a characteristic "family nose" which will reoccur constantly through a large number of generations.

The most common nasal measurement is the *nasal index,* which may be related to regional climatic differences. The nasal index is obtained by dividing the width of the nose by its height and multiplying the resultant fraction by 100. Most Causasoids are *leptorrhine,*

having long and narrow noses, with an index of 69.9 or less, or *mesorrhine* with a nasal index between 70 and 84.9. On the other hand, Bantu-speaking Negroes and Bushmen, as well as the Australoids of Australia, are *platyrrhine,* with broad noses and a nasal index of 85 or more.

To describe the shape of the nose accurately, it is also necessary to observe the nasal depression, indicating whether this is shallow or deep or even nonexistent; the bridge of the nose, which may be straight, concave, or convex; and also the slope of the tip, which may be sharp or bulbous. Even the septum may be seen to slope either upward or downward when observed from the side. In addition, the nares or nose openings may be high and narrow, giving the pinched-in appearance characteristic of the noses of most Englishmen; medium and relatively broad, as among most East Asian peoples; or else broad and flaring as among Negroes and Negritoes.

The shape of the lips, which may be either thin and narrow, or thick and everted, is another of the living, fleshy characteristics which are particularly important in that they vary so distinctively between differing varieties of living hominids. Like the color of the skin, lips tend to be readily noticed by the untrained laymen and therefore play an important part in stimulating racial consciousness and promoting social distance between the members of different populations. The lips are nothing more than a portion of the mucus-covered inside lining of the mouth which protrudes externally and provides protection for the surrounding skin against the action of saliva.

The reason for these different lip shapes, which can be very marked, has not yet been determined. Thick and everted lips are more common among the more prognathous races, but no general rule can be laid down; for example, nonhuman primates are far more prognathous than any living hominid, but have narrow and lightly developed lips like nonprognathous Caucasoids.

Other Morphological Differences

In the field of morphology, *skin color* is perhaps one of the most obvious of racial differences and one which is of considerable sociological importance for its role in determining social distance between the members of different populations. The color of the skin derives primarily from the presence of *pigmentation,* but partially from other factors such as different skin thicknesses. Heavy pigmentation consequently has survival value in tropical environments, where a light-skinned person can suffer tissue damage from the impact of solar radiation sufficient to cause cancer of the skin. On the other hand, in more temperate northerly climates the rays of the sun are heavily filtered by the greater depth of atmosphere through which they have to penetrate when striking the earth at an acute angle. In such environments pigmentation has a negative survival value in that it prevents the skin from absorbing sufficient sunshine to be able to manufacture the vitamins necessary for protection against rickets. It is only to be expected, therefore, that after a few hundred generations of selection a darker-skinned subspecies which had migrated into a northerly latitude will tend to lose its pigmentation as a result of a process of natural selection, while those which live in a tropical environment will retain their protective pigmentation.

The founder of physical anthropology Pierre Broca developed a scale of 34 chromatic tones for measuring skin color which is still used. These comprised 10 shades of each of the three basic skin colors—white, yellow, black—which he found in different types of human skin. According to this chromatic scale, Bantu Negroes are black-skinned, Melanesians are brownish black, Australoids are chocolate brown, American Indians are warm yellow, and Chinese are pale yellow. Since Broca,[2]

[2] For further information consult G. A. Harrison, *et al., Human Biology* (New York: Oxford University Press, 1964).

other authorities have identified as many as 358 recognizably distinct shades of human skin coloring, and even more recently reflectometers have been introduced for greater precision and objectivity in the measurement of light reflectance. Because the genetic determinants of skin color are actually very complex, populations of mixed racial descent customarily reveal a wide variety of skin colors, with even brothers and sisters inheriting quite different coloring.

Albinism, the absence of pigmentation, is not a racial characteristic in the conventional sense of the term, being more appropriately classified as a genetic defect, but it nevertheless tends to be concentrated more heavily in some populations than in others. Thus, the American Indians of the Panama area reveal approximately 138 albinos in 20,000 individuals, an incidence around 50 times higher than that of any other population.

Skin also serves to insulate the body from the external environment, and again Negroes receive better protection than most other races from the rays of the sun because they possess much thicker skin than Caucasoids. Other physiological differences exist and some black nationalists have recently complained that white physicians in America have failed to study the differences between the Negro skin and Caucasoid skin, and consequently persist in attempting to treat Negroes for skin infections with chemicals which, although successful with whites, cause irritation on the Negro skin.

Differences in the color of hair and eyes are another obvious racial characteristic. Light eye coloring is almost entirely concentrated among populations which originated in northern and western Europe where only the pigmentary membrane exhibits granulation and the eye consequently appears to be blue or grey. Where medium pigmentation is present, a green or light brown color eye may result, but in the overwhelming majority of the world's inhabitants, the eye color is dark brown.

Light-colored hair also tends to be concentrated in northern Europe, decreasing in incidence as we travel eastward or southward. Thus the population of Scandinavia today, notwithstanding admixture with other populations in recent times, still reveals 65 to 83 percent blondness while in England the proportion is down to between 45 and 68 percent, and among Armenians blondness is as low as 5 percent. No blond hair is found among indigenous populations of the Far East, Oceania, America, or sub-Saharan Africa. Among Australian aboriginals blondness occasionally occurs in infancy but disappears with approaching adulthood.

Human hair also varies considerably in its shape. Mongoloids have characteristically straight hair which is described as *lissotricous*. This tends to be round in cross-section, and grows out of the skin at a vertical angle. On the other hand, Negroes and many Negritoes usually have frizzy or peppercorn hair, described as *ulotricious*, which has a pronounced oval shape in cross-section, and a curved follicle. Among Bushmen and Pygmies the follicle grows in tight clusters separated by bald spaces. Such hair tends to matt easily. Caucasoids have finer hair than the Mongoloids, with a much greater number of hairs per square centimeter. Their hair is usually either straight or wavy, and in cross-section is intermediate between the oval hair of the Negroes and the round hair of the Mongoloids.

The Human Body

When attempting to classify the fossil remains of hominid subspecies, comparisons may also be made concerning the overall shape, proportion, and dimensions of the skeleton. *Height* is one of the most obvious skeletal characteristics and subspecies which have long been domiciled in savannah-type country will usually be taller than those which are located in forested regions. Thus Pygmies from the Congo Forest average 4 feet 6 inches in height, while the Watutsi from the Sudan Grasslands average 6 feet 6 inches. But although height is primarily an inherited quality, the height of individual generations within the same lineage can vary according to environmental factors such as diet and exposure to disease. Thus, an examination of the skeletons found in cemeteries in Iceland (which was settled in the eleventh century A.D. and experienced very little immigration after that date) shows that the original Icelanders of the eleventh century commonly stood 5 feet 10 inches to 6 feet in height, but that during the Middle Ages, disease and food shortages brought the average height down to 5 feet 6 inches. Since then, the descendants of these same people have again largely regained the stature of their earlier ancestors, and the average height of an adult male Icelander is today around 5 feet 10 inches.

However, most other physical characteristics are less responsive to diet and other environmental factors. The shape of the pelvis is of particular importance in tracing the evolution of the hominids, since it indicates by its shape the extent to which erect posture has become habitual. Among the living races of man, there are no significant variations in this respect, but compared to the height, the *pelvic index,* the breadth of the pelvis, varies substantially. Among Caucasoids and Negroes considerable *sexual dichotomy*—the inherent differences between the sexes—exists in the pelvic index, the pelvic index of women contrasting sharply with that of men. But among other peoples, such as the Melanesians of Oceania, such sexual differences are only slight. *Steatopygia,* a pronounced protrusion of the buttocks characteristic of the South African Bushman population, is also more marked among females than males.

The relative *length of the limbs* also tends to vary between different subspecies. The length of the arm, for example, measured from acromion or lateral bony protrusion of the shoulder to the radiale or elbow joint, is customarily compared to the total stature and expressed by the formula

$$\frac{\text{upper extremity} \times 100}{\text{stature}}$$

Populations will be found to differ considerably in these statistics. Subspecies which are localized in open savannah country commonly reveal longer limbs and with longer legs are usually able to spring faster than those which, like the Pygmy, have evolved over long periods of time in a forest environment. Although differences in the length of the arm are not as obvious between human subspecies as between primate species—the hands of the gibbon, for example, touch the ground even when he is standing erect—marked differences do exist between human populations. Long arms (com-

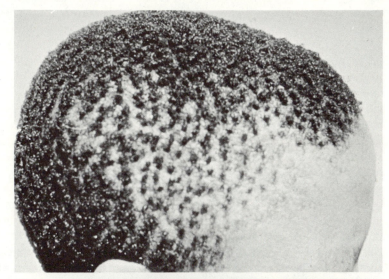

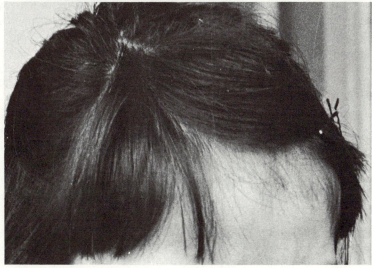

Two extreme variants in hair form. On the top is portrayed the "peppercorn" hair characteristic of South African Bushman populations. This type of hair grows in tightly curled clumps and is oblong in cross-section. By contrast, the bottom picture portrays the stiff straight hair characteristic of eastern Asia, which is round in cross-section. (Courtesy of Hans W. Jürgens.)

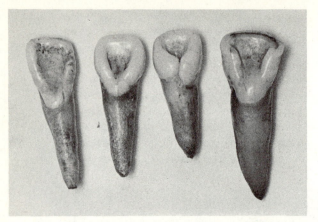

Shovel-shaped incisor teeth, characteristic of East Asian, Eskimo, and American Indian peoples. (Courtesy of Peabody Museum, Cambridge, Mass.)

mon in sub-Saharan Africa) are described as macrobrachion when they reveal an average index of 47 and above; those whose index falls between 45 and 46.9, metriobrachion; and those whose index falls below 44.9 and who are therefore relatively short-armed, brachybrachion.

As early as the end of the nineteenth century, police laboratories classifying fingerprints had developed the science of *dermatoglyphics* and had revealed that there are substantial racial differences in the inheritance of fingerprint patterns. Pygmies reveal a high percentage of arches, whereas Caucasoid fingertips usually have loop patterns, and Mongolian populations reveal a higher percentage of whorls than do Negroes or Caucasoid peoples.[3]

In addition to general variations as described above many populations reveal uniquely distinctive traits. The Mongoloid peoples of eastern Asia display two distinctive physical traits that are virtually absent among populations which have no history of genetic connection with the Mongoloids. One of these is the classic "shovel shaped" lingual surface of the front

incisor teeth, which is found in most East Asian fossils since *Homo erectus pekinensis,* and is still dominant in northern China. The other is the Mongolian spot, a small black or blue mark which appears on the lower part of the back during the first few years of life but disappears before adulthood. Ninety-eight percent of the northern Chinese inherit the Mongolian spot, and the fact that 3.7 percent of the Turks reveal the same characteristic may possibly be accounted for by the fact that the Turks originally lived in Central Asia, adjacent to a Mongoloid population.

BIOCHEMICAL ANTHROPOLOGY

The traditional methods of anthropometry are today supplemented by more sophisticated biochemical techniques. Since the differences in the physical makeup of populations are not simply skin deep, there are innumerable methods by which biochemical techniques of classification and analysis may be developed, tracing what are known as *biochemical markers.* BIOCHEMICAL TAXONOMY deals not with set anatomical measurements but with the dynamics of living tissues and glandular secretions. Thus there are racial differences in the mineralization of bone, Negro skeletal material being more dense and stronger than that of Caucasoids, while most Asiatics tend to have lighter, less compact skeletons than Caucasoids. The children of mixed Chinese-Caucasian ancestry reveal intermediate degrees of bone compactness, suggesting genetic determinants, although the relative role of diet has not been fully determined.[4] Another biochemical variant of undoubted genetic character is that class of proteins known as *transferrins.* Transferrin C reveals a higher degree of mobility in an electrical field than transferrin D.

[3] The implications of fingerprinting for physical anthropology were first realized by Sir Francis Galton in *Finger Prints* (London: Macmillan, Ltd., 1893).

[4] See M. Trotter, G. E. Broman, and R. R. Peterson, "Densities of Bones of White and Negro Skeletons," *Journal of Bone and Joint Surgery* 42A:50 (1960).

Caucasoids are believed to be around 99 percent homozygous for transferrin C, but among the Negro and Asian races the incidence of genes for transferrin D averages 5 to 10 percent in a heterozygous condition; Australian aborigines reveal 22 to 41 percent transferrin D in a heterozygous condition, and Venezuelan Yupa Indians record 42 percent heterozygous and an additional 16 percent homozygous for transferrin D.[5]

Body odor varies chemically; it is a factor which probably plays an important role in keeping mammalian subspecies separate in a feral environment but which has less significance where men are concerned because of the poorer human sense of smell and because human behavior is heavily modified by culture. However, resistance to heat and cold also differs to suit the regional needs under which the different peoples have evolved.[6] Races which have been adapted to humid conditions can usually work better in torrid climates than those adapted for other climates. Even earwax can differ, for Negroes and Caucasoids customarily have sticky earwax, while Mongoloids normally have dry and crumbly wax.[7]

Another biochemical distinction which has attracted considerable attention—because it is easily measured—is the ability to taste PTC or phenyl-thio-carbamide. Only 2 percent of Navaho Indians are unable to taste this substance but 40 percent of the Eskimoes tested lacked this biological ability.[8] Biochemical

studies annually increase the list of genetically based variations of this kind.

Although some of those variations do not seem to have any apparent survival value, local physiological adaptations of obvious adaptive value may also be observed. Eskimoes have a better blood circulation in the extremity of their limbs than do the members of races which evolved in tropical climates, thus enabling them to resist the attacks of frostbite better, while Peruvian Indians who have been domiciled at high altitudes in the Andes have experienced selective adaptations to their circulatory system.

The Spanish wives who accompanied their husbands to Peru after the Spanish Conquest of the Inca empire were unable to produce live offspring at the high altitudes of Cuzco because of their inability to supply the fetus with adequate oxygen. Negro slaves brought in to work the old Inca mines had the same problem, but the *mestizos*—mixed descendants of Spanish men and Indian women—were usually able to produce live offspring, while the local Peruvians, of course, experience no difficulty in reproducing at even the highest altitudes. The reason for this phenomenon was that the constitution of the Peruvians had become genetically adapted by selection over thousands of years to life at high altitudes.[9] Their chests, lungs, and hearts are proportionately larger, and their bodies contain around seven quarts of blood in contrast to the five quarts common to most races adapted to low altitudes. Furthermore, their blood contains a greater concentration of red corpuscles than other races, as a further adaptation to the problem of survival at high altitudes. The larger quantity of blood and the greater density of red corpuscles have the effect of facilitating the carriage of oxygen to all parts of the body, thus enabling an ade-

[5] Transferrins have iron-binding properties, transporting iron to and from the marrow and other storage areas.

[6] G. A. Harrison, *et al.*, *Human Biology* (New York: Oxford University Press, 1964), p. 449.

[7] Differences in earwax are discussed by E. Matsunaga in "Polymorphism in Ear Wax Types and its Anthropological Significance," *Zinruikagu Zassi* 67, 722:171–184 (1959).

[8] Variations in the ability to taste PTC have attracted attention because they are so susceptible to simple testing methods and appear to have little adaptive value. See I. Schwidetzky, *Die Neue Rassenkunde* (Stuttgart: Gustav Fischer Verlag, 1962).

[9] For further details see C. Monge, *Acclimatization in the Andes* (Baltimore: The Johns Hopkins Press 1948), and M. T. Newman, "Mankind and the Heights," *Natural History* 67, 1:9–19 (1958).

quate supply of oxygen to be maintained despite the thinner density of the mountain air.

SEROANTHROPOLOGY

Associated closely with biochemical anthropology is seroanthropology, which is concerned with the analysis and classification of variations in the character and content of human blood.

During World War I, Allied medical officers at the Gallipoli front in Turkey attempted to give blood transfusions to wounded soldiers who had suffered heavy losses of blood. In some cases these transfusions produced satisfactory results, but in others patients who should have recovered died shortly after the transfusion. Attempts to discover the reason for such deaths revealed that not all human blood is identical and that death resulted when the donated blood proved to be incompatible with the patient's blood. Further study of the problem led to a new science dealing with the classification of blood according to its properties and activities, which is known as SEROLOGY.

Blood, which carries oxygen and nutrients to the tissues of the body and carries away waste products produced by metabolism, comprises a liquid known as *plasma* which contains various clotting agents that cause scabs to form over wounds, thus helping to prevent excessive loss of blood after injuries. Large numbers of red blood cells known as *erythrocytes* float in this plasma, and it is these that carry the oxygen. However, there are also white blood cells, or *leukocytes,* whose function it is to combat bacteria and other alien bodies.

The red blood cells carry blood group substances known as *antigens* on their surface. These are large protein molecules with various sugar molecules attached, whose duty it is to produce the *antibodies* which react against any foreign substances that enter the bloodstream.

However, not all antigens are alike, and some produce antibodies which will react against alien red cells bearing a different type of antigen. Thus, it is possible to give a man a transfusion of blood containing antigens which will produce antibodies that will attack the antigens of the host blood, with serious and possibly even fatal results. Some of the transfusions of blood given on the beaches of Gallipoli must have involved two incompatible types of antigens.

Blood Group Systems

Many different types of antibody-producing antigens have been identified, and serologists have classified these into BLOOD GROUP SYSTEMS. Possibly the best known of these is the ABO system, which is concerned with the antigens which have been labeled A and B. Both A and B antigens may exist independently, or in the combined form known as AB, or may be absent altogether, in which case we class the blood plasma as O. Since A and B antigens produce anti-B and anti-A antibodies respectively, a person with type A blood can receive a blood transfusion of type A blood or even a transfusion of type O (which contains neither A nor B antigens), but he cannot receive a transfusion from a person with type B blood because this will produce anti-A antibodies. Similarly a person with type B blood cannot receive a transfusion from a person with type A blood, but may receive transfusions from a person with type B or type O blood. Persons with type O can safely give blood to A, B, or AB, but cannot receive a transfusion from A, B, or AB donors. Persons with AB blood can receive transfusions from any of the other categories.

Since an error in identifying the ABO pattern can lead to a fatal transfusion in a hospital, all blood used for medical purposes is classified on the basis of the ABO system. Hospital records consequently provide us with substantial information about the distribution of ABO phenotypes throughout most parts of the world. The information so provided reveals that although each of types A, B, AB, and O is found in most parts of the world, there are substantial variations in the frequency with which these phenotypes occur in different populations, since they are inherited on a directly Mendelian genetic basis (see Fig. 17).

While the ABO system in itself does not tell us too much about human evolution, there are many other blood group systems, and some of the more rare varieties, especially, are more revealing. However, since the ABO and Rh systems are the only ones which pose a serious threat to life when admixed, no attempt is usually made to identify the other blood group categories when giving transfusions, even though the policy is to use blood from a close relative, when this is possible, in order to reduce the possibility of adverse reactions due to incompatibility of blood types. Since little money is available for the study of blood group systems which do not have an immediate relevance to medical problems, only inadequate efforts have so far been made to chart the distribution of the remaining 30 or more different systems identified to date throughout the human populations of the world.

Of the remaining groups, the best known is the Rh system, since like the ABO the results of an admixture can be fatal. All human blood can be classified as either Rh positive or Rh negative. Most people are Rh positive, but in some parts of the world, mainly in western Europe, there is a fairly substantial proportion of the Rh negative trait. The Rh negative condition stimulates the production of anti-Rh positive antibodies, and if the child of an Rh positive father and an Rh negative mother inherits the Rh positive blood group from the father, this may cause anti-Rh positive antibodies to be created in the mother's blood. Some of these will enter the fetal circulation and attack and destroy the red cells in the blood of the fetus, causing the death of the fetus.

It would appear probable that the Rh negative gene, which is fairly common in western Europe, may be inherited from an Old European population, still represented by the Basque population of today, since the Basques show an especially high proportion of Rh negative genes. When the Indo-European speaking Celts and Teutons arrived, they presumably mixed with the Old European population and absorbed a substantial proportion of the Rh negative genes, with consequent complications whenever an Rh positive bearer takes an Rh negative partner.[10]

Sickle Cell Trait

Blood may also differ in a number of ways distinct from antigen differences, and since these other differences are also hereditarily controlled, they have a bearing on racial classification. The sickle cell trait is one such hereditary variant.

Hemoglobin is a protein contained in the erythrocytes or red blood cells. It comprises *globin,* a protein made up of the main amino acids, and *heme,* a large organic molecule containing an atom of iron which serves an important role in fixing oxygen or carbon dioxide so that it can be carried in the blood. When the amount of hemoglobin in the blood falls below the level necessary to transport adequate oxygen, we say that a person is suffering from anemia. Anemia may be caused by an inherited abnormality known as the sickle cell trait, so called because the red cells shrink and take on a sickle shape in an oxygen-free atmosphere. An individual who is *homozygous* for the sickle cell trait—someone who has inherited the sickle cell trait from both of his parents—will

[10] One of the highest frequencies of Rh negative is found in western Europe, concentrated in that area between Spain and France where the Basque language is still spoken.

suffer from severe anemia, which is usually fatal.[11] But individuals who are *heterozygous* for the sickle cell—inheriting one sickle cell-determining gene from one parent and one normal gene from the other parent—are unlikely to die from anemia, but under stress their body tissues may be unable to metabolize effectively for lack of oxygen, and they are liable to experience mild anemia. Since they may fall sick in aircraft flying at high altitudes, such individuals are seldom recruited for aircrew duties.

However, the sickle cell trait possesses selective advantages in a malarial climate, when present in a heterozygous condition, for in this condition it provides a marked degree of resistance to malaria. In consequence, the sickle cell trait has become part of the genetic equipment of those populations which have been domiciled for long periods of time in central Africa and certain other malarial areas.

Balanced Polymorphism

Since the sickle cell has a deleterious effect on health in a heterozygous condition and a fatal effect when homozygous, it is unlikely to survive indefinitely in areas in which it has no positive survival value. Under a process of natural selection, the sickle cell trait will tend to be eliminated from populations in nonmalarial areas, should it arise as a result of mutations or from the importation of the sickle cell gene through admixture with carrier populations.

Yet even in areas in which malaria is common, it is impossible for the sickle cell to become universal to the exclusion of the normal genes. Even in malarial areas, individuals who are homozygous for the sickle cell will die of anemia. Thus in malarial climates, persons heterozygous for the sickle cell trait have superior survival chances over all others. Consequently, whenever a particular genetic trait is deleterious to survival when homozygous but, like the sickle cell, has positive survival value when heterozygous, it can never become universal throughout the entire breeding population, nor can it be eliminated by selection. Instead, the gene pool will come to contain a balanced proportion of normal genes and specific genes. This is known as a BALANCED POLYMORPHISM. A balanced polymorphism will emerge whenever individuals who are heterozygous for a particular pair of genes have a better chance of surviving than individuals who are homozygous for either of the alternate genes.[12]

Blood Groups and Taxonomy

Despite the absence of adequate statistics concerning the distribution of the majority of blood group systems throughout the world and despite the fact that hospital statistics provide only gross data which are not classified according to the ethnic background of the donor, W. C. Boyd[13] has suggested a tentative racial classification based on blood group gene frequencies. This corresponds surprisingly close to the traditional grouping based upon anthropometry.

The first of Boyd's groupings is a hypothetical Early European race, with a high proportion of Rh negative and probably no group B. This Early European group is now extinct, although the Basques represent a hybrid vestige of the original group. Their place was taken by a European (or Caucasoid) group. According to Boyd, the other living races identifiable by blood groups are an African or

[11] See Stephen L. Wiesenfeld, "Sickle-Cell Trait in Human Biological and Cultural Evolution," *Science* 157:1134–1140 (1967).

[12] For further details see Sewall Wright, *Evolution and the Genetics of Populations,* Vol. 2: *The Theory of Gene Frequencies* (Chicago: The University of Chicago Press, 1969) pp. 54–56.

[13] See W. C. Boyd, *Genetics and the Races of Man* (Boston: Little, Brown and Company, 1953).

FIG. 17   DISTRIBUTION OF BLOOD GROUP GENE B IN THE ABORIGINAL POPULATIONS OF THE WORLD

The study of blood groups provides objective measurable data regarding qualities which are inherited on directly Mendelian lines. Unfortunately, although over 30 different blood groups have been identified among human populations, research into many of these has been incomplete due to lack of funds.

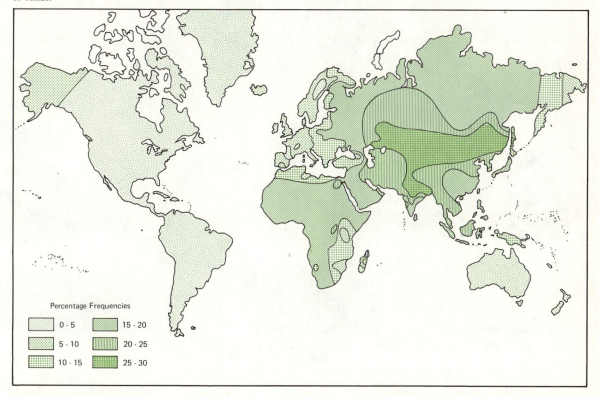

Negroid race, an Asiatic or Mongoloid race, an Australoid race, and an American Indian race. Studying the Malayo-Polynesian speakers of the Pacific, Boyd noted a confusing variety of genes, which is what we would expect to find if the Malayo-Polynesians represent an admixture of Caucasoid, Mongoloids, Negritoes, and Australoid genes, and he therefore excludes the Oceanic peoples from his scheme of classification.

Quite obviously, a single blood group statistic of the ABO type does not tell us much about the phylogenetic background of an individual, for blood groups only have anthropological significance when expressed in a statistical form. Like heme data blood group statistics make statements about gene pools. Nevertheless, some very interesting observations have already been made on the basis of such data which help us to unravel the prehistory of living populations. For example, the sickle cell, so characteristic of the Negroid people of Africa, is virtually absent from the Bushman population of southern Africa, whose relationship to the Negroes has always been disputed. At the same time, the sickle cell is

This photograph of a group of village girls from Hungary reveals the close similarity of physical features common in populations which have been closely inbred over many generations. (Courtesy of Musée de l'Homme, Paris.)

quite common among certain of the aboriginal peoples of central and southern India who are classified as Negrito or partially Negrito. This suggests an original connection or common heritage shared by both Negroes and Negritoes. Again, the blood group B is rare in western Europe, but becomes increasingly frequent as we travel eastward through Russia into central Asia, and it achieves its highest incidence among the Mongoloids of eastern Asia, thus suggesting that blood group B may have arisen in Europe as a result of the historically known Mongoloid incursions.

In some cases it has even been possible to classify the blood of long dead individuals, such as the Egyptian pharaohs, within the ABO system by the examination of dried mummified tissues and bones. But although a comprehensive study of blood group patterns among aboriginal or autochthonous populations around the world would prove of inestimable value in our attempt to trace the pattern of historic and prehistoric migrations, some of the early hopes and aspirations which caused the discovery of blood groups to be hailed as a new and statistically valid means of classifying mankind have waned. This original enthusiasm was based on the belief that different blood groups had no selective advantage in the struggle for survival, and would therefore have remained unaltered by natural selection through thousands of generations. But this opinion is no longer held. Blood groups have been shown to be intimately related to susceptibility and resistance to disease. Type A may be linked to stomach cancer, type O to susceptibility to the bubonic plague, and several diseases are related to abnormal hemoglobins. That being the case, we must assume that the distribution of blood groups will be subject to the variety of forces of natural selection at work in different environments, and blood patterns may therefore have been no more constant through the ages than any of the more obvious physical characteristics measured by traditional methods of anthropometry. This does not mean that further study in the area of serology will not materially advance our knowledge concerning the pattern of human evolution. It simply means that—as we already know—evolution is concerned with dynamic life processes, not with static or unchanging phenomena.

For Further Reading

Boyd, W. C., 1953, *Genetics and the Races of Man.* Boston: Little, Brown & Company.

Coon, C. S., and E. E. Hunt, Jr., 1963, *Anthropology: A to Z.* New York: Grosset and Dunlap, Inc.

Emery, A. E. H., 1968, *Heredity, Disease and Man: Genetics in Medicine.* Berkeley: University of California Press.

Galton, D. A. G., and K. L. G. Goldsmith, 1961, *Haematology and Blood Groups.* Chicago: University of Chicago Press.

Goodman, M., 1963, "Serological Analysis of the Phyletic Relationships of Recent Hominoids," *Human Biology* 35:377–436.

Handler, P., 1970, *Biology and the Future of Man.* New York: Oxford University Press.

Harrison, G. A., J. S. Weiner, J. M. Tanner, and N. A. Barnicot, 1964, *Human Biology: An Introduction to Human Evolution, Variation and Growth.* New York: Oxford University Press.

Kelso, J., and G. Ewing, 1962, *Introduction to Physical Anthropology Laboratory Manual.* Boulder, Col.: Pruett Press, Inc.

Kuttner, R. E., ed., 1969, *Race and Modern Science.* New York: Social Science Press.

Lasker, G. W., 1952, "Mixture and Genetic Drift," *American Anthropologist* 54:433–436.

———, 1973, *Physical Anthropology.* New York: Holt, Rinehart and Winston, Inc.

Livingstone, F. B., 1967, *Abnormal Hemoglobins in Human Populations: A Summary and Interpretation.* Chicago: Aldine Publishing Company.

Martin, R., 1957, *Lehrbuch der Anthropologie,* 3d ed. Stuttgart, Germany: Gustav Fischer Verlag.

Olivier, G., 1969, *Practical Anthropology.* Springfield, Ill.: Charles C Thomas, Publisher.

Race, R. R., and R. Sanger, 1968, *Blood Groups in Man.* Philadelphia: F. A. Davis Company.

Rhine, S., 1971, *The Beginnings of Mankind: A Laboratory Notebook.* Fort Collins, Col. Robinson-Warfield Company.

Sheldon, W. H., 1954, *Atlas of Man.* New York: Gramercy Publishing Co.

Wallace, B., 1970, *Genetic Load: Its Biological and Conceptual Aspects.* Englewood Cliffs, N.J.: Prentice-Hall, Inc.

CHAPTER 12

Classifying the Living Hominids

Despite the recent advances in biochemical and serological anthropology, an effective analysis of the interrelationship, diversity, and evolutionary history of the living hominids runs into two problems. First, most students bring preconceived notions about race into class with them, notions which are usually highly charged with emotional content, and not even authors are totally free from such value biases. Secondly, because men do not live in complete genetic isolation and hominid populations have been moving around the world and intermingling for we know not how long, the genetic picture is by no means as clear as it would be if we were studying less mobile animals in a feral condition. Let us therefore begin this chapter by asking such questions as: What are "races"? What is their relationship to the concept of "subspecies"? Do "pure" races exist?

Many definitions of the term RACE have been offered, but today it is generally agreed that a race is a breeding population whose members share a number of distinctive genetic characteristics which distinguish them from the members of other breeding populations. In theory, a race is a subspecies—an evolutionary experiment—a population which has developed a high degree of genetic exclusiveness and which, in a natural state, might be expected to evolve into a new and distinct species, losing the ability to interbreed with other races. Unfortunately the reality is not as simple as that.

A race which had been totally isolated from contact with other groups, either by geographical or even by social barriers, would certainly constitute a separate subspecies. But few living hominid populations have enjoyed long periods of genetic isolation. Technological progress has changed man's pattern of life, making him more mobile, and has also tended to break down the various restraints on interbreeding which generally prevent the admixture of mammalian subspecies in a natural or feral state. Consequently when we study the living hominids in most cases we are not dealing with populations or gene pools which have been totally isolated for long periods of time.

Any classification of living men into discrete

physical and distinct racial varieties must therefore be attempted with very restrained and cautious terminology. Possibly the safest approach is to distinguish between the old major GEOGRAPHICAL RACES, which do admittedly reflect certain very obvious genetic differences, and which owe their loose and very ill-defined existence to geographical barriers such as deserts, oceans, and mountains; LOCAL RACES, which represent smaller breeding populations set apart by political and cultural as well as geographical boundaries, and MICRORACES, closely inbred populations sharing a distinctive gene pool and living in relative genetic segregation within the limits of a larger society.[1] The Indian caste group is an excellent illustration of the microrace. Although the Indian subcontinent contains a wide variety of racial types, most Indians marry their own cousins, preserving the primordial tradition of close inbreeding generally typical of kinship societies around the world and consequently India comprises a vast number of remarkably homogeneous microraces which cannot be effectively charted on a map because several microraces may live in the same area for generations without ever admixing their genes.

In the world of modern man the racial reality is often the microrace rather than the geographical race. The hominid racial pattern is so blurred in some areas that it is possible to speak only of *genetic clines,* which trace statistical differences in the distribution of diverse physical characteristics such as skin color and shape of hair. Nevertheless, to the extent that all men and women in the world do not freely intermarry—even when they inhabit the same geographical area—separate *gene pools* with distinctive combinations of genes do exist and will doubtless persist far into the future. To this extent it is still valid to speak of different races ranging in magnitude from geographical races to microraces. The Hindu caste group, whose members have been effectively inbreeding over literally hundreds of generations, represents a very real microrace. Hindus of caste status, who consistently marry cousins from within their own caste, create the impression that brother is marrying sister, so similar are husband and wife in their physical appearance. Whatever may be the fate of the geographical races and the local races, in a world in which transportation is becoming easier every year, the microraces will be with mankind for as far into the future as it is possible to see, not only among the upper levels of society where powerful social and political elites tend to marry only among themselves, but also as ethnic groups in the lower strata.

The Evolution of the Living Races

Essentially, all theories of modern hominid evolution can be grouped under one or other of three rival theories.

The first of these is the theory of separate but parallel evolution from pre-*sapiens* ancestors. Some physical anthropologists, notably Franz Weidenreich and Carleton S. Coon, have suggested that the major stocks of mankind evolved separately under a substantial degree of genetic isolation from originally separate *Homo erectus* ancestors.[2] According to

[1] See S. M. Garn, *Human Races* (Springfield, Ill.: Charles C Thomas, Publisher, 1971).

[2] See C. S. Coon, *The Origin of Races* (New York: Alfred A. Knopf, Inc., 1967) for the full development of this view. But Coon tends to ignore the effects of prehistoric migration. This obliges Coon to lump together numerous relic populations from the Congo in Africa and from southeast Asia, the Philippines, and New Guinea; populations that (if they are related at all) are less closely related than are the few European races recognized by these authors.

Those who take the extreme opposite view and see Cro-Magnon man as totally replacing all earlier populations also show the same tendency to oversimplify by lumping together too many diverse populations. Thus, as recently as 1973, T. Prideaux, *Cro-Magnon Man* (New York: Time-Life Books), pp. 38–39, asserts that "Cro-Magnon man spread to every continent and overspread every environment on earth," and proceeds to classify even such widely disparate fossils as Nelson Bay men in South Africa and the Niah Cave boy of Borneo as "Cro-Magnon."

FIG. 18   THREE THEORIES OF HOMINID EVOLUTION*

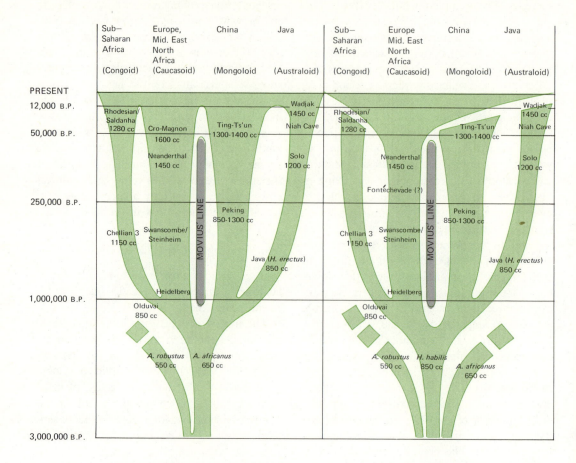

a. Discarded Theory of Multilineal Evolution of Races in Geographical Isolation. Originally developed by Franz Weidenreich and refined by Carleton S. Coon, this theory assumes the separate evolution of the living hominid races from distinct *Homo erectus* ancestors. It is based on the persistence of local regional traits, such as shovel-shaped incisor teeth, implying the absence of any significant migrations until recent times. According to this theory contemporary racial differences were of pre-*sapiens* antiquity.

b. Discarded Theory of Unilineal Evolution of Living Races. The logical alternative to multilineal evolution is found in the assumption that all living hominids are descended from a single modern *Homo sapiens* stock, which spread over the entire earth, supplanting and extinguishing the older Neanderthal varieties. This *sapiens* stock was then believed to have acquired its contemporary physical differences as a result of dispersal under diverse selective conditions.

*Estimated cranial capacity has been quoted in cubic centimeters where a generally acceptable figure is available. However, cranial capacity must not be regarded as an absolute indicator of evolutionary advancement or of intelligence. It is significant only when considered in conjunction with other physiological factors.

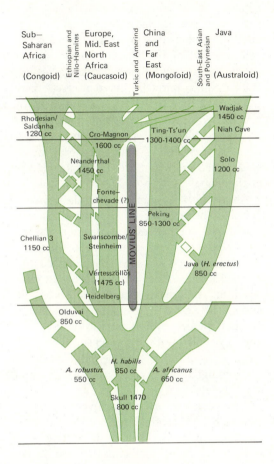

this theory, those hominids which were isolated in sub-Saharan Africa became *Capoids* and *Negroes;* those isolated north of the Sahara and in Europe evolved into *Caucasoids;* those isolated in eastern Asia became *Mongoloids;* while those isolated in different parts of the Southeast Asian/Australian region became *Australoids* and *Negritoes.* These populations preserved a substantial degree of genetic isolation, because of their sparse density of settlement and their relative territorial immobility, and consequently evolved in relative isolation from separate *Homo erectus* ancestors, through the Neanderthal level, to become the separate races of the modern world (see Fig. 18a). In relatively recent times, suggests Coon, some of the populations evolved more rapidly than others and gaining greater control over their environment, increased in number and began to expand territorially. Colonizing new lands, they mingled genetically with the aboriginal populations, just as the Malayo-Polynesians of Oceania probably arose as a result of an admixture between Mongoloids, Australoids, and Caucasoids. Powerful evidence for this theory can be found in the survival of specifically local physical traits such as the shovel-shaped incisor of the Mongoloids in separate geographical regions over hundreds of thousands of years. However, the theory has been criticized on the grounds that it underestimates the likelihood of Pleistocene migrations.

At the other extreme of the forum, many of those who reject the idea of the separate but more or less parallel evolution of the living races of man distinct from *H. erectus* ancestors have tried to claim that all living races are but local varieties of a single *H. s. sapiens* genetic stock. According to this theory, it is assumed that most *H. erectus* varieties became extinct, possibly as a result of the expansion of one or more Neanderthaloid varieties of hominids, and that in turn the various Neanderthaloid populations eventually disappeared before a

c. Contemporary Multilineal Theory of Hominid Evolution. Today there are few supporters for the theory of multilineal racial evolution demonstrated in (a), and none for (b). Indeed the truth appears to lie somewhere between these two theories. It would seem that living races do reflect ancient regional lineages, but in a pattern much modified by periodic amalgamation between immigrant populations and the older indigenous stocks.

single *H. s. sapiens* populations which colonized the entire world (see Fig. 18b).

Unfortunately for this theory, the heavy pigmentation and spiral hair of the Negroes of Africa and the Negritoes of Asia represent a useful adaptation to equatorial latitudes that must have taken very many generations to develop. Since the earliest known *H. s. sapiens* fossil remains are only 40,000 years old, insufficient time has elapsed for such distinctive differences in pigmentation and hair form which distinguish Negroes and Negritoes from Caucasoids and Mongoloids to have evolved separately within a common *H. s. sapiens* population. Indeed, American Indians are believed to have been domiciled in the Americas for probably 20,000 years, but the difference in pigmentation between those that live in tropical areas and those who live in the Arctic areas is minimal, and differences in hair form are virtually nonexistent. Furthermore, such a theory does not satisfactorily explain differences of a developmental kind, such as disparities in prognathousness, prominence of brow ridges, and tooth size.

Quite clearly, if we do not accept the idea of a separate evolution of the modern races from geographically distinct *H. erectus* populations, and are yet able to demonstrate convincingly that the modern races of the world could not have evolved from a single *H. s. sapiens* population living only 40,000 years ago, then only one alternative remains: separate evolution from distinct Neanderthal populations, with local differences becoming substantially modified by intermittent migration and admixture. Indeed, this is the generally accepted view today, and such a theory does not exclude the survival of some local traits from even older *H. erectus* populations (see Fig. 18c).

While sharp genetic barriers were probably rare in most phases of hominid evolution, local inequalities in the rate of natural selection and evolution can be demonstrated to have existed at all times; indeed, without geographical segregation, in different environments, separate varieties could not have evolved. But where one population develops superior survival ability ahead of the others, competition for survival must result. Since all animals, including hominids, normally overreproduce, there would have been slow but persistent competition for living space throughout hominid history, in just the same way that there is competition between all life forms. The more evolved stock would spread out over the habitable areas of the globe.

Although it is probable that there would normally be little or no gene flow between early hominid populations dispersed over wide areas, as men developed culture so their patterns of feral behavior became modified and at some time or other genetic flow must have occurred. *H. erectus* was a cannibal, but there undoubtedly came a time when the colonizing hominid victors stopped annihilating the conquered populations, and though still killing the men, began to keep the women, thereby effectively mingling the genes of two formerly separate populations.[3]

It is difficult to say at what level of hominid evolution hybridization developed, but at some time or other it did emerge. From that time onward colonizing populations may well have begun to mingle their genes with the older populations, thus acquiring local adaptive traits—such as skin coloring—which had taken thousands of generations to develop among the older populations.

Whenever it was that this situation developed, by historical times we have sufficient evidence to show that where an aboriginal population is not eliminated, considerable genetic admixture usually takes place between the colonizers and the indigenous peoples.

[3] Thus F. E. Poirier suggests that Cro-Magnons appropriated the Neanderthal females for procreation purposes. F. E. Poirier, *Fossil Man* (St. Louis: C. V. Mosby Company, 1973), p. 187.

**FIG. 19   CONJECTURAL RECONSTRUCTION OF *HOMO SAPIENS*
MIGRATIONS DURING THE LATE PLEISTOCENE**

The theory has been advanced the Negroes and Negritoes resemble each other because both are adapted to life in rain forests. Capoids originally adapted to moist African savannah, while Australoids evolved in similar conditions in India and southern China. Mongoloids evolved in the temperate climate of northern China, Mongolia, and Manchuria, while Caucasoids evolved in temperate western Eurasia, later colonizing North Africa, India, and much of Central Asia. (After David J. de Laubenfels, "Australoids, Negroids and Negroes: A Suggested Explanation for Their Disjunct Distributions," *Annals of the Association of American Geographers* 58, 2:42–50 (1968). By permission.)

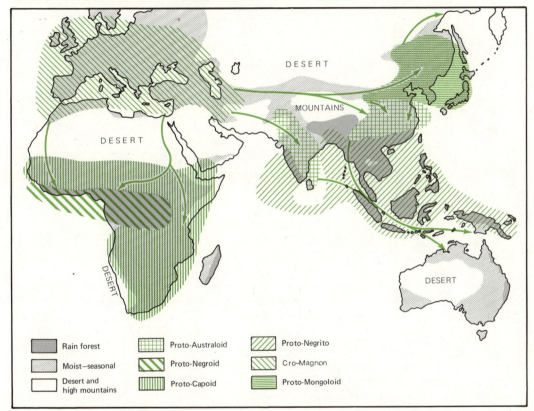

Thus we know that the Tasmanian aboriginals became extinct in "pure" form after the arrival of Caucasoids, but left a genetic legacy among the White colonists by virtue of racial admixture. Similarly American Indian genes have entered the population of the Caucasoid settlers of the Americas, particularly in areas like Oklahoma. When a hybrid population is formed in this way, it is a simple principle of Mendelian genetics that the offspring of such interracial crosses will be very varied in their genetic heritage. In tropical areas the darker hybrid offspring of a cross between light and dark-skinned peoples would have a better chance of survival than the lighter colored offspring—especially in a preindustrial society lacking clothing and air conditioners. Consequently long-established local adaptations

FIG. 20   RACIAL DISTRIBUTION PRIOR TO THE EXPANSION OF THE EUROPEAN PEOPLES IN RECENT CENTURIES

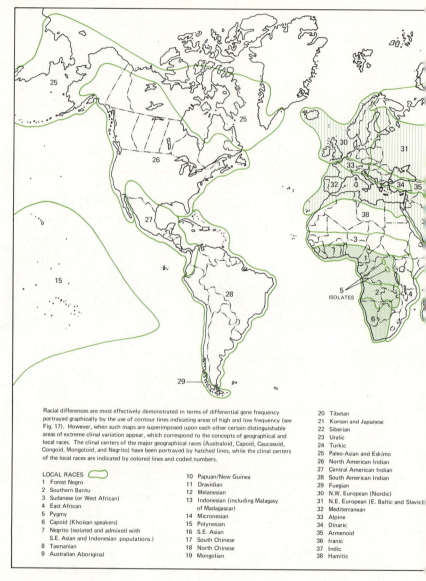

Racial differences are most effectively demonstrated in terms of differential gene frequency portrayed graphically by the use of contour lines indicating areas of high and low frequency (see Fig. 17). However, when such maps are superimposed upon each other certain distinguishable areas of extreme clinal variation appear, which correspond to the concepts of geographical and local races. The clinal centers of the major geographical races (Australoid, Capoid, Caucasoid, Congoid, Mongoloid, and Negrito) have been portrayed by hatched lines, while the clinal centers of the local races are indicated by colored lines and coded numbers.

LOCAL RACES

1 Forest Negro	20 Tibetan
2 Southern Bantu	21 Korean and Japanese
3 Sudanese (or West African)	22 Siberian
4 East African	23 Uralic
5 Pygmy	24 Turkic
6 Capoid (Khoisan speakers)	25 Paleo-Asian and Eskimo
7 Negrito (isolated and admixed with	26 North American Indian
S.E. Asian and Indonesian populations.)	27 Central American Indian
8 Tasmanian	28 South American Indian
9 Australian Aboriginal	29 Fuegian
10 Papuan/New Guinea	30 N.W. European (Nordic)
11 Dravidian	31 N.E. European (E. Baltic and Slavic)
12 Melanesian	32 Mediterranean
13 Indonesian (including Malagasy	33 Alpine
of Madagascar)	34 Dinaric
14 Micronesian	35 Armenoid
15 Polynesian	36 Iranic
16 S.E. Asian	37 Indic
17 South Chinese	38 Hamitic
18 North Chinese	
19 Mongolian	

which possessed survival value would persist in a genetic admixture and even become dominant in the ensuing generations. Many local genes, such as those responsible for the shovel-shaped incisor of Peking man, might survive any genetic admixture arising from the immigration of a newer population. In all cases of admixture following immigration, the resultant hybrid population would undergo rigorous natural selection in favor of those qualities inherent in either ancestral line which had local survival value. In the course of hundreds

GEOGRAPHICAL RACES

- Clinal center of Australoid geographical race
- Clinal center of Capoid geographical race
- Clinal center of Caucasoid geographical race
- Clinal center of Congoid geographical race
- Clinal center of Mongoloid geographical race
- Negrito isolates in S.E. Asia and Indonesian area

The Living Races

The so-called geographical races of the present day therefore seem to owe their differences to the survival of specific local adaptations, such as degrees of skin pigmentation, developed over very long periods of time. These races apparently owe their basic similarities to the fact of repeated expansion and colonization by the culturally and biologically more advanced populations, who then admix with the older and locally more specialized populations—without which admixture the unity of mankind would have been lost, and several distinct and mutually infertile hominid species may have come into existence by today. Let us therefore look briefly at the major geographical races that have been identified, remembering that these are best conceived in terms of clinal extremes, rather than as clearly defined and absolute realities.

Australoids

The Australoids of Australia and the largely Australoid population of New Guinea appear to represent one of the most archaic of living populations showing close affinities to the Wadjak fossils. Indeed it has been said that the Niah cave boy of 40,000 years ago could be easily lost among the living peoples of the highlands of New Guinea.[4] They reveal surprisingly large brow ridges, receding foreheads, and jaws which are markedly prognathous and are equipped with large teeth. Their noses are broad, with a depressed nasal root, but the lips are not particularly everted. Skin color varies from a light chocolate to dark brown color. Their skulls are generally doli-

of generations a new and relatively homogeneous local variety would evolve, preserving those local qualities best suited to promote survival in the prevailing ecological-environmental conditions.

[4] J. B. Birdsell states that Niah is definitely not *H. erectus*, but "could be lost in some of the living populations of the rain forest of northeastern Australia, and in almost any of the populations of hybrid New Guinea." J. B. Birdsell, *Human Evolution* (Chicago: Rand McNally & Company, 1972), p. 320.

(*Above*) Reconstruction of Wadjak Man (courtesy of Wayland Minot), a Neanderthaloid variety from Java, believed to have been ancestral to the living Australoids represented (*left*) by an Australian aboriginal woman (courtesy of Musée de l'Homme, Paris).

and a number of living peoples, such as the Yumbri of Laos, reveal indications of at least a partial Australoid heritage.[6]

Capoids

Another major geographical race found in Africa, which formerly occupied very large areas of the grass-covered uplands (before these were taken over by the expanding Negroes in historical times) are the Capoids, today mainly confined to the Bushmen and Hottentots in Southwest Africa. The physical anthropology of the Capoid, who has been described as the polar opposite of the Australian aboriginal, differs sharply from that of the Negro. Adapted to life on the African

chocephalic, and unlike Negroes, Negritoes, and Capoids, they grow very plentiful facial and body hair. Because of the close degree of similarity between the Wadjak fossil remains and the skeletal characteristics of living Australoids, some authorities suggest that the Australoid population resulted from an admixture of immigrants from the Asian mainland with the older Wadjak peoples.[5]

One fact of great interest is that India, southern China, and Southeast Asia were also once settled by an Australoid-type population,

[5] W. Howells, *Mankind in the Making* (New York: Doubleday & Company Inc., 1967), p. 244.

[6] B. Lundman, *Geographische Anthropologie* (Stuttgart: Gustav Fischer Verlag, 1967), pp. 143–147.

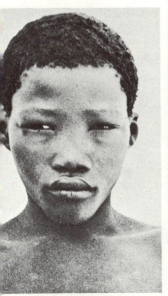

Capoids from Southern Africa. (*Right*) Two Bushman women revealing the characteristic steatopygia or protrusion of the buttocks. (Courtesy of the South African Information Service.) (*Left*) Frontal view of a Bushman youth. (Courtesy of Hans W. Jürgens.)

savannah this lineage can be traced to Boskop man, who lived in the grasslands of the South African Transvaal.[7] Although they are dolichocephalic, their skin color is lighter, being a yellow-brown. In some facial details, particularly the epicanthic eyefold, a piece of skin which stretches across the upper lid creating a slanting appearance, they reflect the Mon-

goloid race, although no historical connection existed prior to the arrival of Malayo-Polynesian settlers on the East Coast of Africa long after the Capoids had come into existence as a distinct people. While still exhibiting broad noses, their lips are seldom as everted as those of the Forest Negroes of the Congo, their foreheads are more bulbous, and their jaws less prognathous. Steatopygia, a pronounced protrusion of the buttocks, is very common among Capoids, and the modified steatopygia often

[7]C. S. Coon, *The Origin of Races* (New York: Alfred A. Knopf, Inc., 1967), pp. 637-638.

found among the Bantu Negroes may be due to genetic admixture with Capoids. From a serological point of view, the Capoids differ substantially from the Negro and contrast particularly with Asian blood types.

Caucasoids

The peoples of Europe and western Asia seem to have belonged to the Caucasoid race since Upper Paleolithic times, with only occasional minor intrusions of Mongoloids from central Asia—if we disregard the more sub-stantial immigrations from Africa and Asia which have followed in the wake of the breakup of White colonial domination of those continents in this century. The peoples of North Africa and India are also generally classed as Caucasoid; although living on the fringes of the Caucasoid world, they reveal considerable genetic admixture with neighboring populations as well as clinal variations based upon the effect of local climatic and geographical selection.

Caucasoids are generally fair-skinned and tend to be light-eyed and light-haired in the more northerly regions, where this type is

(*Left*) Caucasoid from Northwestern Europe. (Courtesy of La Documentation Française, Paris.) (*Right*) An Arab from the Lebanon, of the Mediterranean local race. (Courtesy of National Council of Tourism in Lebanon [CNT/Magnin].)

(*Left*) Caucasoid from Afghanistan of Iranian type. (Courtesy of Musée de l'Homme, Paris.) (*Right*) Caucasoid of Indic type from Himachal Pradesh, India. (Courtesy of Press Information Bureau, Government of India.)

divided between the Nordic or Northwest Europeans and the broader-headed East Baltic or Northeast Europeans. The hair form is oval in cross-section and hangs either straight or in waves. High-bridged noses and sharp features are characteristic of northern Europe and the Mediterranean where dolichocephalic skulls also prevail but hair and eye coloring tends to be dark. However, there is a broad belt of brachycephaly running from Belgium through the Alps and reappearing strongly in Armenia, which is often associated with a heaviness of the fleshy part of the face and less aquiline features. In general there are few sharp genetic breaks anywhere in the area of Caucasoid settlement, and with the exclusion of certain areas such as Scandinavia, the valleys of the Caucasus, and other pockets, substantial prehis-

Caucasoids from Africa: (*Top*) Haile Selassie, Emperor of Ethiopia. (Courtesy of Ministry of Information, Addis Ababa.) (*Bottom*) A Moor from Timbuktoo in the Republic of Mali. (Courtesy of La Documentation Française, Paris.)

toric and historical migrations have tended to reduce local physical variations which may have been more evident in earlier times.

Mongoloids

The Mongoloids of Southeast Asia are usually brachycephalic or broad-headed, broad-faced, and relatively short in stature. Hair coloring is black, and the hair form is straight and coarse. They have very little if any facial or body hair, and their eyes are marked by the epicanthic fold. Prognathism is present only among those Mongoloid populations which may have acquired some Australoid or Negrito genes. Although it is widely believed that the Mongoloid characteristics represent the effects of adaptation to an Arctic climate,[8] it would appear that 4000 years ago the Mongoloids were largely restricted to northern China and eastern Siberia. Continual expansion and migration in a southerly direction has since caused them to settle the entire area of China and Japan quite thoroughly, while also populating most of Southeast Asia in a series of migrations continuing into historic times.

Southeast Asians, however, although usually classified as Mongoloids, generally reveal admixture with older Australoid and Negrito populations. Indonesians, Malays, and Polynesians probably represent a relatively recent Mongoloid-Caucasoid admixture with strong Negrito elements present among the Melanesians. The Japanese, by contrast, are similar to the northern Chinese, except that they tend to be more dolichocephalic, and their narrow foreheads give them a slightly more Caucasoid appearance. There is also evidence of Ainu or Paleo-Asian admixture in the northern portion of Japan.

[8] The various geographical and climatic adaptations of the human races are discussed in C. S. Coon, S. M. Garn, and J. B. Birdsell, *Races: A Study of the Problems of Race Formation in Man* (Springfield, Ill.: Charles C Thomas, Publisher, 1950).

Two females of Mongoloid type. (*Top*) Yakut woman from Siberia. (Courtesy of the U.S.S.R. Embassy, Washington, D.C.) (*Bottom*) Woman From Thailand. (Courtesy of Musée de l'Homme, Paris.)

Northeastern Siberia contains a number of *Paleo-Asians,* related to the Ainu of Japan, who are noted for their profuse body and facial hair. Although occasionally classified as Mongoloids, they usually lack the epicanthic eyefold of the Mongoloid. Their heavy brow ridges and broad noses suggest a Neanderthal type which survived in eastern Asia in admixture, to varying degrees, with immigrant Mongoloid populations. Paleo-Asians may have contributed largely to the predominantly Mongoloid settlement of the Americas, and hence to the ancestry of the contemporary American Indians.

Negroids

Another obvious geographical race is the Negroid of sub-Saharan Africa. Negroes are characterized by heavily pigmented dark brown or black skin, dark eyes, spiral head hair (which like the body hair is black), lightly developed calf muscles, and relatively long forearms and lower legs. The pelvis is usually narrow; the forehead rounded, the face is usually short, and the head shape generally dolichocephalic. The jaws reveal varying degrees of prognathism, the nose is likely to be low bridged with flaring nostrils, and the lips are always everted. This latter is a distinctive evolutionary trait.

The clinal center of the Negroid stock is typified by the Forest Negro of the Congo and the West African coast. Indeed, the population appears to reveal a high degree of adaptation to the conditions of life in equatorial rain forests, indicating a long period of evolutionary residence in such an environment. Fossils from Kanjera in East Africa, dating between 30,000 and 100,000 years of age and living in a period when that area was heavily forested, closely resemble contemporary Negroids.[9] The influence of Rhodesian and Saldanha man may

[9] Birdsell, *Human Evolution,* p. 321.

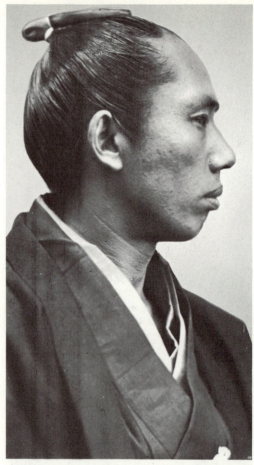

(*Above*) Japanese nobleman. (Courtesy of Musée de l'Homme, Paris.) (*Left*) Eskimo (Courtesy of the late A. M. Sharp.)

also be present possibly as a result of admixture with a Kanjera-type ancestor of the Negroids. The first completely contemporary Negro skeleton dates from only 4000 B.C. and was found at Asselar in Mali.

The Pygmies who also live in the interior of the African rain forests under climatic conditions similar to those of the Forest Negroes resemble the Negroids in many outward characteristics, but differ from them primarily in their reduced height and much greater prognathism. However, the list of minor morphological differences is so considerable that many physical anthropologists prefer to regard Pygmies as having a separate origin.

There are a number of other features in addition to height which distinguish the Pygmies from their neighbors, the Forest Negroes. While the average Pygmy adult stands under $4\frac{1}{2}$ feet in height, the legs of the Pygmy are disproportionately short, and since the head is no smaller than that of the Negro, the disproportion between the size of the head and the body creates a strikingly unusual impression of imbalance. Although the Pygmy resembles the Forest Negro in being prognathous and loose-jointed, and possessing large eyeballs and a broad flat nose, the Pygmies are often even more prognathous than the Negroes, and in some cases the Pygmy nose is almost as broad as the mouth beneath it. Like that of the Negro, the Pygmy hair grows in peppercorn tufts, but some Pygmies are extremely hirsute, having a covering of hair over the entire body, while the Forest Negro seldom grows much body or facial hair.

In blood analysis also, the Pygmies differ from the Negroes. Pygmies possess an unusually high incidence of the sickle cell trait, which has a definite survival value in the malarial forests of central Africa. This evidence serves to reinforce the belief that they have been domiciled in the Congo forests for many thousands of years. It is possible that the Negroes may have acquired the sickle cell trait in some degree from admixture with the Pygmies, since it is known that for a substantial number of generations there has been a constant flow of Pygmy genes into the adjacent Negro tribes. This occurs because Pygmy women frequently enter Negro villages as con-

(*Right*) Melanesian male from New Caledonia, wearing traditional sheath. (Courtesy of Musée de l'Homme, Paris.) (*Above*) Polynesian beauty from Raiatea, wearing a flower behind her ear. (Courtesy of Ministére de la France d'Outre-Mer.)

(*Left*) Dogrib Indian from northwest Canada. (Courtesy of Musée de l'Homme, Paris.) (*Right*) Xavante Indian from San Domingos, South America. (Courtesy of A. G. de Díaz Ungría.)

cubines or second wives, bringing Pygmy genes into the Negro gene pool; however, there is no reverse genetic flow of Negro genes into the Pygmy stock, for no Negro man or woman ever joins a Pygmy band.

Negritoes

Often likened to the Negroes of Africa are the Negritoes who have survived as hunters and gatherers in various parts of Southeast Asia, particularly in Indonesia, the Philippines, and the Andaman Islands situated in the Bay of Bengal. Negritoes are dark-skinned and moderately prognathous, with tight curly or woolly hair, so that their general appearance resembles that of Negroes in a superficial way.

However, no migration of either Negro or Negrito people between Africa and Southeast Asia has taken place, and both Negroes and Negritoes seem to derive their distinctive genetic qualities as a legacy from older populations, each long established in their own respective tropical areas.

Certainly the Negritoes derive much of their genetic character from an older population of Paleolithic hunters and gatherers that survived only in the most remote forested regions or islands after an immigrant population of Malayo-Polynesian horticulturalists seized control of their more attractive hunting lands. The continued flow of genes between the Negrito and Malayo-Polynesian populations in historic times indicates that prehistoric racial admixture probably had already substantially modified the differences which may once have distinguished the immigrant Malayo-Polynesians much more sharply from the ancestors of the aboriginal Negritoes.

Although the precise relationship of the Negritoes to the Negroes of Africa has not yet been satisfactorily determined, it is therefore probable that the similarities between the two races may represent the survival of genetic elements from ancient populations, both adapted to tropical conditions, rather than to a single population that migrated from Africa to Asia, or vice versa, in recent times.

Contemporary Attitudes toward Race

As we have already observed, attitudes toward the study of human physical variation have been highly colored by political and ideo-

(*Left*) Forest Negro from the Republic of Gabon. M. Leonard Badinga, member of the Government of Gabon. (Courtesy of Service Information République Gabonaise.) (*Right*) A southern Bantu woman from South Africa. (Courtesy of the South African Information Service.)

(*Left*) Sudanese Negro from the Republic of Central Africa (Mobaye tribe). (Courtesy of La Documentation Française, Paris.) (*Right*) Sudanese woman from West Africa; a Peuhl from the Republic of Guinea. (Courtesy of La Documentation Française, Paris.)

logical considerations as well as by popular bias. Nowhere does this reveal itself more obviously than in the debates about intelligence and race which have been further heightened in recent years by Arthur R. Jensen's studies of the relationship between genetics and educability[10] and H. J. Eysenck's book, *The IQ Argument*.[11] These and other writers, mostly psychologists or geneticists, see intelligence primarily as a genetically determined capacity that varies from one race to another. This view has been strongly opposed by C. Loring Brace and others who argue that intelligence tests make inadequate allowance for cultural differences.[12] In fact, some commentators have argued that further examination of this question should be halted because of racist implications, while others even claim that the very word *race* is so loaded with political connotations that it would be better to avoid the term altogether and talk only about "human variations." Such a policy would lead away from

[10] A. R. Jensen, *Genetics and Education* (New York: Harper & Row, Publishers, 1972).

[11] H. J. Eysenck, *The I.Q. Argument* (New York: Library Press, Ltd, 1971).

[12] C. L. Brace, *et al., Race and Intelligence* (Washington, D. C.: American Anthropological Association, 1971).

(*Left*) Young Pygmy mother and child. (*Below*) Older Pygmy woman. (Courtesy of Hans W. Jürgens.)

the concept of the "ideal type," and instead emphasize genetic gradients and interracial clines.

In biological reality a race is essentially a phylogenetic continuum, and it is the total gene pool that is important. The underlying fact is the genotype not the phenotype. The consensus of opinion consequently emphasizes the advantages of approaching the study of human differences from a quantitative, statistical point of view. There is also agreement that although it was geographical segregation that originally produced different races, the contemporary mobility of human populations has decreased the relationship between race and geography. In many areas, such as the United States, race survives because of socially determined genetic segregation rather than the geographical isolation of the separate gene pools.

Consequently, as increasing geographical mobility makes it more difficult to chart human variation on a geographical or clinal basis, race persists because of the social awareness of phenotypical differences and readily observable typological distinctions. In short, despite the separate geographical origins of the major races, modern breeding patterns are dependent largely on social attitudes. Whatever the significance of the physical differences between the races may be, social attitudes toward race have become increasingly more important. Let us therefore now leave the arena of physical anthropology and turn instead to the study of culture and learned behavior.

Semang Negritoes from Malaya. Small pockets of Negritoes survive in many parts of Southeast Asia. (Courtesy of Musée de l'Homme, Paris.)

For Further Reading

Barnicot, N. A., 1957, "Human Pigmentation," *Man* 144:1-7.

Beddoe, J., 1972, *The Races of Britain: A Contribution to the Anthropology of Western Europe.* London: Hutchinson's University Library.

Birdsell, J. B., 1972, *Human Evolution.* Chicago: Rand McNally and Company.

Brace, C. L. *et al,* 1971, *Race and Intelligence.* Washington, D.C.: American Anthropological Association.

Coon, C. S., 1965, *The Living Races of Man.* New York: Alfred A. Knopf.

——, 1972, *The Races of Europe.* Westport, Conn.: Greenwood Press, Publishers.

Eysenck, H. J., 1971, *The IQ Argument.* New York: Library Press, Ltd.

Garn, S. M., 1963, "Culture and the Direction of Human Evolution," *Human Biology* 35:221-236.

———, 1971, *Human Races.* Springfield, Ill.: Charles C Thomas, Publisher.

Jensen, A. R., 1972, *Genetics and Education.* New York: Harper & Row, Publishers.

Laubenfels, D. J., 1968, "Australoids, Negroids and Negroes," *Annals of the Association of American Geographers* 58(2):42-50.

Poirier, F. E., 1973, *Fossil Man: An Evolutionary Journey.* St. Louis: The C. V. Mosby Co.

Sonneborn, T. M., 1967, *The Control of Human Heredity and Evolution.* New York: The Macmillan Company.

PART **II**

Ethnological
Analysis

CHAPTER 13

Culture and Society

In tracing the evolutionary history of our own living bodies from the first blobs of polymer jelly floating in water billions of years ago to the disparate varieties of living men who keep us company on earth today, we have also tried to identify the evolution of society. As we said in our introduction, society is older than man, and social life is not something which our hominid species invented after they had attained the level we so proudly call *Homo sapiens*.

The Concept of Culture

Nevertheless hominids differ from their earlier protohominid ancestors in the extent to which their behavior becomes modified by *learning*. All complex living organisms learn to some extent from their environment; all develop patterns of modified behavior which promote the chances of survival under varying conditions. In the absence of any ability to communicate what they have learned to other members of their species, the learned informa-tion dies with the individual. However, animals which live in social groups tend to influence each other's behavior, and where such behavior has survival value, it may become perpetuated in the group. Since there is a continuous contact between successive generations in a kinship group, learned behavior patterns also tend to be communicated from generation to generation. This intergenerational copying process is further facilitated in mammalian societies by the prolonged dependency of the infant offspring, who learn by imitating their mother's behavior. When regular patterns of activity are copied from generation to generation, it is possible to say that a system of cultural or learned behavior has evolved.[1]

The concept of CULTURE was originally defined by the pioneer British anthropologist, Sir Edward Tylor, as that complex whole which

---

[1] Konrad Lorenz stresses the biological difficulties in distinguishing between the idea of strictly "innate" and "learned" behavior. K. Lorenz, *Evolution and Modification of Behavior* (Chicago: University of Chicago Press, 1967).

161

includes knowledge, belief, art, morals, law, and custom, and any other capabilities acquired by man as a member of society.[2] But is man the only animal that possesses culture?

In Tylor's day it was customary to distinguish rigidly between men and animals. Men were believed to be intelligent rational beings capable of communicating and learning from each other, while animals were regarded as primarily instinctive in their behavior in that they responded to stimuli in a purely biologically determined fashion. In short, men possessed culture but animals had no culture. This

[2] Edward B. Tylor, *Primitive Culture: Research into the Development of Mythology, Philosophy, Religion, Language, Art and Custom* (London: John Murray, (Publishers) Ltd., 1871), p. 1.

distinction was based on the old biblical tradition that men were created separately from animals, and that a creator God had in fact given man dominion over "beasts." In opposition to this now outdated prejudice, continued research in animal behavior has revealed that animals, like men, are capable of considerably complex patterns of learned behavior and that no mammals behave in a purely predetermined biological fashion. As with men, their biological impulses are channeled by learning into patterns of behavior which may normally be expected to have survival value. Thus we know that birds which migrate annually have to learn the direction in which to migrate from the older generation and that a young bird separated from its companions may feel the

It is a fallacy to imagine, as did many eighteenth century philosophers, that there is such a being as the totally "feral" or uncultured man. Culture evolved along with man, and although preurban populations enjoy many freedoms that we lack, they are by no means without stringent cultural regulations of their own. (Courtesy of La Documentation Française, Paris.)

urge to migrate when the season is right, but will not know in which direction to migrate if it has never had the chance to follow other members of its species. Even migratory behavior to a certain extent is learned behavior, and may in a sense be regarded as a form of *protoculture*.

In an attempt to preserve the idea that there is an essential qualitative difference between men and animals, some writers have suggested that since human beings are capable of a refined pattern of verbal communication, human societies are qualitatively different from animal societies, in which members merely copy each other's behavior. However, even this contention may be questioned. The study of animal behavior indicates that animals can and do interpret each other's actions, gestures, and cries. Anger, threats, and warnings are customarily conveyed by expressions and signs. Among baboons one short bark uttered by a male baboon on guard duty indicates the presence of danger, whereas several barks indicates an immediate threat. Japanese monkeys are capable of making a greater variety of distinct vocal sounds than lie within the human range, each of which is believed to convey a specific meaning. The cries of birds indicate their presence to other birds and also contain information regarding territorial claims or even mating possibilities. Furthermore, verbal communication is by no means the only form of communication that can exist among living organisms. Insects have a multitude of ways of communicating messages and instructions. The famous bee dance, in which a worker bee wobbles its abdomen and moves its body in circles to indicate the direction and distance in which honey may be found, is a well known illustration of the transmission of information by nonverbal means.

In the face of the accumulated evidence of communication among animals, those who seek to distinguish qualitatively between humans and animals fall back on the suggestion that human communication is intentional while social animals communicate only unintentionally, merely observing each other's behavior and interpreting this in accordance with their previous experiences. Clearly the key word here is *intention*. What, the psychologist may ask, is intentional behavior? At what point of evolution did hominid behavior stop being unintentional and become intentional? Is it possible to deny that a baboon acts intentionally when he communicates his desire to have his back scratched by tapping his grooming partner on the arm and presenting the appropriate portion of his anatomy to be groomed?

The basic facts are undeniable. Most higher animals and all mammals possess learned traditions that may be called protoculture if not culture, and communicate this to each other. Where men differ from other animals is in the sense that men have developed a means of communicating complex ideas and experiences by a sophisticated system of oral communication which we call SPEECH. This permits the communication of *abstract* ideas so that a far greater quantity of information, highly refined and symbolic in character, can be readily shared between the members of a human social group.[3] Since men are social animals, any improvements in the means of communication facilitate still further the exchange of information and stimulate the buildup of that accumulation of information and misinformation which we call culture.

Material and Normative Culture

Some authors have debated whether culture is really an accumulation of information, misinformation, ideas, and attitudes arising out of the ability to communicate, or whether it should not be regarded as *behavior*. After all,

[3] The physical problems involved in the evolution of human speech are discussed in E. H. Lenneberg, *Biological Foundations of Language* (New York: John Wiley & Sons, Inc., 1967).

society is made up of people doing things; life takes place in time, and people "act out" their cultures. The concept of culture can perhaps best be understood if we regard it as a form of behavioral programming—as a form of "know-how" that ideally has evolutionary survival value, but can sometimes be based upon inaccurate information or erroneous reasoning, in which case it can become a hindrance rather than an aid to survival.

Culture as behavioral know-how can be divided into two distinct categories. In the first place there is purely technical know-how, which represents material skills with obvious survival value, such as the ability to identify poisonous plants, to fashion a stone spearhead, to manufacture a boomerang, or for that matter, to drive an automobile. This type of culture is usually known as *material culture,* but some writers also refer to it as "technological culture" and others as "existential culture." Material or technological culture arises simply and directly as an evolutionary adaptation to the environment.

But there is another kind of culture, which may be called *normative culture,* that is not always transmitted from one group to another. This refers to the *norms,* values, and total ideational culture of a society. Some writers refer to all of this as "social know-how," since successful social life depends to a large extent on the predictability of the behavior of the other members of the group. It would be impossible to live in the company of other men and women if one never knew from one day to the next whether one was likely to be treated with kindness or to be submitted to violent physical abuse. A man can relax only in the company of others whose behavior he can anticipate and predict. Because uncertainty and friction within a group hinders cooperation and negates the purpose of social life, it is essential that newcomers to a social group should learn the likes and dislikes, the views and attitudes, indeed, the total value system of the group they

are joining. An understanding of, and reasonable degree of compliance with, the normative culture of the group is essential for smooth cooperation in the pursuit of agreed goals, and consequently for the survival of the group.

Culture as a Compelling Force

There can be no doubt that as a social animal living in a group, an individual man is under strong pressure to accept the attitude of his group. Consequently the value elements in a culture, that part of the social know-how which every individual must learn if he is to be able to get along with the other members of his society, were classified by the pioneer American anthropologist, William Graham Sumner, into two categories: *folkways* and *mores.*[4] These terms unfortunately imply a rigid dichotomy which is not intended, but the conceptual basis for such a dichotomy is valid and since both terms frequently reoccur in popular literature, the student should be acquainted with their meaning.

According to Sumner, folkways and mores differ from each other according to the degree of insistence with which society demands compliance to the approved pattern of cultural behavior. Those patterns of behavior which are obligatory upon all members of society, because they are intimately linked to the approved goals of a society, were called mores from the Latin word *custom,* due to the fact that the Romans placed such emphasis upon strict compliance with the customs of their forefathers. Thus in our society a man who ill-treats a child, strikes a woman, or murders another man may be said to be breaking the mores of his society. In short, mores were described as group practices which are enforced upon the individual by the culture of his group, any violation of which is likely to

---

[4] W. G. Sumner, *Folkways* (New York: Mentor Books, 1940).

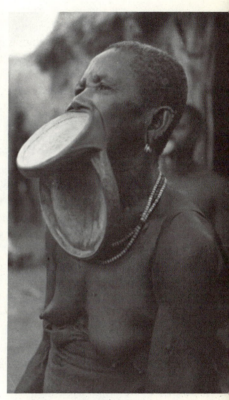

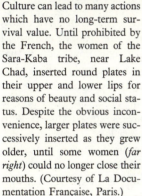

Culture can lead to many actions which have no long-term survival value. Until prohibited by the French, the women of the Sara-Kaba tribe, near Lake Chad, inserted round plates in their upper and lower lips for reasons of beauty and social status. Despite the obvious inconvenience, larger plates were successively inserted as they grew older, until some women (*far right*) could no longer close their mouths. (Courtesy of La Documentation Française, Paris.)

be followed by emotional revulsion and possibly even violence on the part of the group.

But not all of the values which we acquire as a member of society require us to follow the standard practices with such emphatic concern. There are many less important standards of behavior, adherence to which is positively enjoined by our society. These certainly form a part of the social know-how, but may be broken, should we choose, with considerable impunity. Such minor customs as the correct way to hold one's knife and fork at the table were called folkways. Any characteristic pattern of behavior occurring in a given situation which is positively approved by the members of a group but which is not insisted upon with emotional intensity was considered a custom or folkway. Folkways exist for a sensible and pragmatic reason. While it is possible to break many of the lesser customs of the group without challenging the basic values, the very fact that we deliberately adopt such folkways implied by the way we eat, the way we dress, or the way we talk is a token of our willing identification with the group and its values. Our adherence to these petty conventions is our way of showing people that we are loyal members of the group, that we positively identify with the group and its values, that our behavior is safely predictable, and that we may be expected to conform to the group values.

Thus, when convention required the members of a society to wear their hair short, as was the case in America a generation ago, the man or youth who wore his hair long was not necessarily challenging the basic values of the society, but he was deliberately flaunting his individualism and his willingness to oppose at least some of the patterns of behavior conventional in his group. A person who is prepared deliberately to challenge the group culture on small issues may also challenge it on more important issues, and even minor breaches of the folkways tend to be interpreted to mean that the violator is either an outsider or else a potentially unreliable member of the group. The deliberate decision of many young men to wear their hair long when the folkways demanded short hair consequently created feelings of uneasiness, suspicion, and even resentment among those who still conformed to the older convention. However, few people are truly individual, and most seek to identify with one group or another. Even the "hippie" subculture has its own folkways which come to be accepted as a badge of membership and as a symbol of revolt against the traditional cultural values. Clearly there is nothing intrinsically wrong with either long or short hair. If Western society should choose to return to the aristocratic long-haired tradition of the Middle Ages, it would then be the short-cropped people, still following the archaic Roman tradition, who would be regarded with suspicion as potentially dangerous obstructionists.

Culture and Biology

Earlier writers on the subject of culture were prone to suggest that there was something superorganic or nonmaterial about culture. But culture does not exist without people; essentially it exists in the minds of people as a manifestation of biological and physicochemical functions. Culture is a part of us in that it expresses itself in behavior. When we acquire a culture, we do not leave the biological world behind us and enter a new cultural world. We remain biological organisms just as we always were; the only thing that changes is that our patterns of behavior become modified by the patterns of learned behavior which constitute our culture. When a child grows up in a particular culture, he acquires a ready-made, integrated, and cohesive pattern of behavioral reactions which will shape his reactions to future stimuli.

Possibly the best analogy to illustrate the relationship between culture and biology is to see man as a piece of machinery, more complex than the most advanced computer yet made, the potentials of which are clearly determined by the way the machine is constructed, that is to say, by biology and heredity. However, just as a machine may be programmed to behave in a variety of different ways so the human machine may be programmed with different cultural materials to behave in a very wide variety of patterns. The early hominids, evolving in "natural" or feral conditions and unprogrammed by sophisticated cultural systems, were shaped by evolution to respond to environmental stimuli in a manner that was conducive to survival under those conditions. A man born into a human society may be programmed by the culture which he acquires to respond in quite "unnatural" ways to the environment in which he lives.

Although all cultured behavior is to some extent "unnatural" behavior, the individual whose cultural training channels his impulses into a socially approved pattern of behavior will be applauded by his group for this "unnatural" behavior. In cultured societies he learns to control his impulses and to express these only in patterns of behavior condoned by his culture. Should the cultural program-

FIG. 21   BIOLOGY, CULTURE, AND ENVIRONMENT

The biocultural triangle illustrates the mutual interaction of biology, environment, and culture. Both biology and culture modify the environment, and themselves undergo modification as they adjust to their environment.

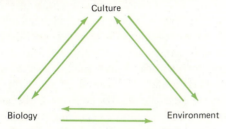

ming break down so that he fails to control his natural impulses, he is likely to be severely criticized and possibly even punished by the members of his group. Alternatively, should the cultural programming be faulty so that he learns to channel his impulses into an artificial pattern of behavior which is *not* approved by his society, then such behavior will be de-scribed as a perversion. Thus, homosexuality is culturally conditioned behavior which is certainly not "natural," and in those societies which do not recognize homosexuality as a socially approved pattern of culturally determined sexual behavior it is conceived to be a "perversion."

Cultural Transmission

Since culture as a pattern of programming cannot exist separately from the biological organism, culture must be transmitted, otherwise it dies with the culture bearer. Consequently it is customary to speak of ENCULTURATION or SOCIALIZATION when we refer to the process of learning by which a child or other new member of a social group or society acquires the culture of that society. However, culture can also be transmitted from the members of one group to another when two different societies come into contact with each other, and this process is known as ACCULTURATION, a process of

The process by which a society passes on its culture to successive generations is known as *enculturation.* In more complex societies the need for effective enculturation has led to the rise of organized schooling. Picture shows a class of school children in India. (Courtesy of Government of India Press Bureau, New Delhi.)

learning and adjustment whereby an individual or a society accepts some or all of the cultural values of another people. When an individual leaves one group to join another, it is of course necessary for him to acquire the culture of the new group. If he adopts the new culture to the point that he rejects any conflicting attitudes or beliefs acquired from his former culture, then he is said to have undergone ASSIMILATION into the new culture.

When culture is transmitted from one generation to another within the same society, we talk about a process of SOCIAL HEREDITY. But when culture is transmitted from the members of one group to another, or from the members of one society to another, we customarily use the term CULTURAL DIFFUSION.

Material know-how is usually readily borrowed, and most hunters and gatherers, for example, will be happy to replace their bows and arrows by rifles and shotguns and to accept any other technological innovation which will be useful in helping them to achieve their goals. But normative culture, or social know-how, is not so readily transmitted from one society to another. Attitudes and values are so closely associated, through habit, with our emotional system that attempts to impose new values upon an adult who has been enculturated in a different value system can even cause severe emotional and psychological disorders. It follows, therefore, that when two societies come into contact, each may readily borrow from the other's resources of material and technological know-how—in the same way that Europeans borrowed the potato and tobacco from the American Indians and the American Indians acquired the horse, cow, and sheep from the Europeans—but each may strongly resent the introduction of different ideologies from the alien culture. In brief, the Arabian sheikh who visits America with oil royalties to spend may purchase a fleet of Cadillacs to replace the traditional camels of his own culture, but will not necessarily accept conversion to monogamy and resolve to give up his harem on his return to Arabia.

While most ideas seem to be transmitted via social heredity or by diffusion from one culture to another, there are occasions in history when new ways of doing things are actually "invented," and in such cases we speak of CULTURAL INNOVATION. On those occasions when two different societies both independently invent the same *cultural trait*—by which we mean any identifiable unit of culture—the term PARALLEL INVENTION is used. It seems probable, for example, that the cultivation of plants was a parallel invention, occurring quite independently in both the Old World and the New World, though not at the same time in history.

Culture and Evolution

Culture clearly has survival value for man, or has had survival value up to the present, otherwise man would not have survived to inherit the vast accumulation of culture which now dominates so much of his behavior. Yet not all the information that individuals acquire and communicate to each other is necessarily accurate, and a great deal of the culture of any human society is more correctly labeled "misinformation" than information. Misinformation seldom has any survival value, and can even handicap the ability of members of a group to respond satisfactorily to their environment by causing them to misinterpret stimuli and consequently to produce inadequate or inappropriate responses to such stimuli. The same principle applies to inappropriate value systems that have negative survival value to those who adhere to them.

In the course of time, societies must consequently weed out the unsuitable or inappropriate elements in their culture, or else find themselves so handicapped by the accumulation of misinformation and inappropriate value systems that they cease to be competitive as members of the total ecological community. In

Two instances of "acculturation": (*Above*) Two North American Indians, photographed at the end of the nineteenth century, who have adopted the costumes popular in Victorian England, even to the point of dressing the boy in an English "sailor" costume. (Courtesy of British Columbia Provincial Museum, Victoria, Canada.) (*Right*) Attired in western European costume, General J. A. Ankrah, of the Republic of Ghana, supports himself against a Classic Greek pedestal. (Courtesy of the Ghana Information Services.)

short, even culture is subject to the test of survival, and in the long run inefficient cultures will be eliminated when they come into conflict with more survival-oriented cultures. Thus, at the hominid level, survival ceases to be a directly biological matter, and the survival of a group or society comes to depend largely on the culture that it possesses. Let us now look to the nature of these social groups, since the social group is the essential culture-bearing unit, the ultimate receptacle of culture.

Social Systems as Cultural Systems

Since we are social animals and since the simple fact of proximity causes some men to live in close contact with each other, while having less contact or no contact with the members of other groups, it follows that some men will share a fairly extensive communication of ideas, while other men scarcely ever communicate. Our primordial ancestors lived in small, intimate and personal social units

An extreme example of crosscultural contacts. Japanese film producer Yoshishige Yoshida (clad in formal western attire) marrying Japanese actress Mariko Okada (wearing a traditional Japanese kimono) at Aschau in Germany. The Japanese wedding ceremony was dramatized by an "alphorn" salute, sounded by Germans in Bavarian national costume. (Courtesy of German Information Center, Bonn.)

which we call PRIMARY GROUPS. Today the family still preserves some of this ancient primary group character, its members living in close face to face contact and exchanging ideas freely on a wide range of subjects. Since the members of the family meet regularly on an intimate and frequent basis, communicating extensively, they tend to possess a common set of ideas and a common way of doing many things—a common culture. But because the modern family exists in a complex setting, its members individually experiencing a variety of outside contacts that the primordial family member could never have, this culture is not so homogeneous and perfectly integrated. The modern American family consequently experiences many intrafamily conflicts of a kind unknown to family members in simpler societies.

Complex societies also produce less intimate social groups, which have looser ties and which share a more restricted quantity of culture, and these are called SECONDARY GROUPS. Thus the members of a SODALITY, an association of people linked in pursuit of a common purpose—such as a service organization made up of businessmen who dine together once a week and pursue certain common goals—would constitute a secondary group. Nevertheless, like primary groups, these secondary groups also have their own subculture, their own distinct set of shared ideas which the members of the group hold in common and which tend to distinguish them from persons who are not members of the group. This subculture will distinguish them, if only slightly, from the total culture of the community in which they live.[5]

Among our earlier hominid ancestors the community was no more than a large family group occupying its own territory—a single primary group in which every member lived in regular face-to-face contact with each other and therefore shared common ideas and knew each other's personality intimately. In such simple societies the family/band was not only a primary group but also the total COMMUNITY; that is to say, it represented an interdependent geographical grouping of people. Where the community was socially isolated from other communities, this primary group also constituted the total SOCIETY—the sum total of persons who share a distinctive set of cultural values and who maintain an organized pattern of interaction with each other. To the earliest hominids, the primary group was therefore at one and the same time the total community and also the total society.

However, as technology improves and the density of population increases, larger com-

munities emerge, comprising not a single large family but several families, and a clear distinction develops between family and community. Similarly, a further growth will lead to the appearance of societies which embrace a number of different communities, and a distinction arises between community and society. Only in the very simplest of human social systems is it possible to say that the primary group coincides with the community and with the total society, as it does with the gibbons and marmosets. Most human societies comprise several different communities which in turn can be subdivided into small primary or family groups, and the patterns of human social and cultural interaction consequently tend to be highly complex.

Group Consciousness

Because men are essentially social animals and experience strong impulses which lead them to live in groups, they undoubtedly seek to *identify* with those other individuals to whose behavior patterns they have become adjusted. Improved interpersonal communication reinforces the pressure upon the individual to accept and identify with the prevailing value systems of his group; consequently it tends to reinforce even further the identification of the individual with his own primary group and to a lesser extent with his own community. Such close identification has survival value to the extent that the survival of an individual is largely dependent on the survival of the group or community to which he belongs, for competition exists not only between individuals but between human groups, communities, and societies. A self-conscious group, community, or society which reveals a strong "team spirit" is more likely to win the competition for survival than the social unit that lacks social cohesion and effective cooperation between its members.

Consequent upon communication, therefore, the members of a social group normally tend

[5] The concept of primary and secondary groups, which is of considerable anthropological importance, was actually developed by sociologist Charles H. Cooley in *Social Organization* (New York: Charles Scribners' Sons, 1915) on the basis of Ferdinand Tönnies, *Community and Society: Gemeinschaft und Gesellschaft* originally published in 1887 (available from New York: Harper & Row, 1963, in a translation by C. P. Loomis).

to identify themselves not only with their group but with its values. Group, community, and societal patriotism emerges because it has survival value; this patriotism in turn leads to the phenomenon known as ETHNOCENTRISM, the tendency of individuals and groups to judge the behavior of the members of other groups and societies on the basis of their own value systems. Quite obviously, it is impossible to identify with the culture and values of our own society without coming to regard these as the "best." If one's own ideals were not the "best" ideals, one would change them. Ethnocentrism is thus essentially a quality which is complementary to GROUP IDENTIFICATION, by which we mean positive recognition that one is a member of a group and that there are responsibilities to such membership. However, as scientists attempting to understand the workings of other human societies, we must not allow ethnocentricism to blind us to a proper understanding and appreciation of why other people act as they do and believe as they do; nor should it encourage us to condemn their behavior out of context. Even if we wish to be an effective member of our own group or society, an attachment to its values should not cause us to prejudge the cultures of other societies. It is probable that no one can be an effective and cooperating member of a group or a society unless he identifies with its values, but to the extent that ethnocentrism implies a tendency to prejudge, and consequently misinterpret, the value systems of other societies, it can and will invalidate any scientific appreciation of their nature.

Culture Shock

An individual who has grown up in one culture but subsequently finds himself living in another culture will at first have difficulty in understanding how to behave in the new culture; that is, he will find himself ignorant of the social know-how of his new society. In his ignorance of the culture of the people with whom he is now mixing, he will have difficulty in interacting effectively with them because his way of doing things will in many cases contravene the customs of the new culture, and may even lead to his being rejected. At the same time the patterns of behavior of the people around him will conflict with his own standards and values, and the result is that he will experience CULTURE SHOCK, a strong feeling of confusion and frustration at his own inability to be effective in this new setting.[6] However, if the individual concerned is obliged to remain in the guest society for a substantial period of time, it is probable that he will become acculturated to the new ways of doing things. As he learns more about the culture of the new society and acquires a degree of social know-how, he will begin to find himself more effective and will feel more at home. What is happening, of course, is that he is becoming acculturated, and even partially assimilated, into the new cultural system. If this happens when he returns to his own society, he may find that his own value systems have changed so substantially that he experiences a fresh wave of reverse culture shock, and may have considerable difficulty in settling down in his own country again.

Culture Conflict

In simpler societies, where we find a relatively close face-to-face type of relationship, the overall cultural system of the entire society is usually quite well *integrated,* by which we mean that there is a high degree of cohesion and agreement on cultural values. However, in larger and more complex societies, as in contemporary America, the substantial division of labor, the sheer size of society, and the extensive area over which its members are dispersed,

[6] For a discussion of "culture shock" see G. M. Foster, *Traditional Cultures and the Impact of Technological Change* (New York: Harper & Row, Publishers, 1962), pp. 187–194.

According to the principle of "cultural relativity," individuals derive their standards of conduct from the society in which they live. Two contrasting concepts of "correct" female clothing are illustrated here, each reflecting the distinctive life style of the community to which the wearer belongs. (*Left*) Zulu costume, from South Africa. (Courtesy of Musée de l'Homme, Paris.) (*Right*) Traditional costume from the Allgäu, West Germany. (Courtesy of German Information Center, Bonn.)

all lead to the rise of many different subcultures reflecting diverse occupational, class, or regional groups. Indeed modern societies may even include different racial or ETHNIC GROUPS, the term used to refer to groups which share a common national, linguistic, racial, and cultural heritage that sets them apart from other elements in society. To the extent that each of these separate groups possesses a distinctive subculture of its own, there will be considerable possibility of CULTURE CONFLICT, since

the moral systems and behavior patterns will not match.

When the members of two different subcultures or even of two different societies become aware of their cultural differences, it is customary to say that a SOCIAL DISTANCE exists between them. This distance is not a spatial measurement, but refers to the feeling of separation between individuals or groups, arising from cultural incompatibility. Since such cultural differences usually have values attached to them, social distance also normally implies a feeling of superiority or inferiority on the part of those involved.

Cultural Relativity

The fact that each society possesses its own particular cultural traditions and in particular its own values and ideals has important implications which ethnographers and anthropologists in general have always to bear in mind. The culture of a society can make any action right or any action wrong for its members. A youth who has been thoroughly enculturated into the culture of his own society will accept cannibalism as one of the necessary and desirable rituals of his society if the culture so decrees. A man can judge his own actions only in the light of the ideas and values that he has learned during his own life experience, and according to the principle of CULTURAL RELATIVISM, all actions must be judged in relation to the cultural setting in which they occur. This important principle teaches us the problems inherent in attempts to impose "international" standards upon diverse peoples with different cultural traditions. It has raised serious disputes among anthropologists regarding the validity of attempts by the victors in war to bring the leaders of a defeated nation "to justice."

For Further Reading

Beals, A. R., G. Spindler, and L. Spindler, 1973, *Culture in Process*. New York: Holt, Rinehart and Winston, Inc.

Beattie, J., 1964, *Other Cultures*. New York: The Free Press.

Chapple, E. D., 1970, *Culture and Biological Man*. New York: Holt, Rinehart and Winston, Inc.

Evans-Pritchard, E. E., 1956, *The Institutions of Primitive Society*. Oxford: Blackwell Scientific Publications Ltd.

Hall, E. T., 1969, *The Silent Language*. New York: Fawcett World Library.

Huxley, T. H., 1959, *Man's Place in Nature*. Ann Arbor: University of Michigan Press.

McGaugh, J. L., and others, 1967, *Psychobiology*. San Francisco: W. H. Freeman and Company.

Schwartz, B. M., and R. H. Ewald, 1968, *Culture and Society*. New York: The Ronald Press Company.

Sumner, W. G., 1940, *Folkways*. New York: Mentor Books.

Tyler, E. B., 1899, *Anthropology: An Introduction to the Study of Man and Civilization*. New York: Appleton-Century-Crofts.

————, 1958, *Primitive Culture*. New York: Harper Torchbooks.

CHAPTER 14

Band, Tribe, and Nation

While nonhuman primates tend to respond to sexual stimuli with very direct and largely unrestrained biological responses, human societies heavily restrict sexual behavior according to elaborate conventions, and it has been suggested that under these circumstances much of the emotional energy associated with sex tends to be sublimated into other activities. But the practice of pair-bonding leads among humans to something even more important than this. It leads to the institutionalization of the FAMILY, a social group comprising the original pair-bonded adults plus their offspring.

Anthropologists and sociologists still debate the ideal definition of the term *family,* but all agree that in some way the idea of the family combines the idea of pair-bonding with the concept of the *household,* a cooperating economic unit. The evolutionary history of the family as a social institution makes this clear. The pair-bond is a form of cooperation which developed because it promoted the survival chances of the offspring. The essence of the family is rooted in the formation of a pair-bond between adult males and females who cooperate to ensure not only their own survival but more particularly the survival of their offspring—to ensure, in broader evolutionary terms, the genetic survival of the lineage. The family may therefore best be defined as a social group comprising one or more males linked by a socially recognized set of mutual obligations and privileges to one or more females, together with their offspring, who face the problem of survival as a joint enterprise.

The human family is itself but the basic unit in a more complex network of community ties. As memory developed among our hominid forebears, so the pattern of behavior learned in infancy tended to be preserved into adulthood. Baboon infants lose their special relations with their mother as they grow into adulthood; and of course they know no father. On the other hand, chimpanzees, which we have equated with a Ramapithecine level of behavior, may reveal a partial extension of infant patterns of behavior into adulthood in the apparent development of *incest prohibitions* that prevent the adult male from attempting sexual relations with his own mother. The further development of memory among our own hominid ancestors resulted in a still greater projection of attitudes learned during childhood into adulthood.

The slow but significant evolution of speech among hominids would also tend to promote the conventionalization of patterns of learned behavior, not only through the exchange of ideas but also by the invention of fixed labels for particular individuals. Labels such as "mother," "father," "sister," and "brother" which are learned in infancy continue to be

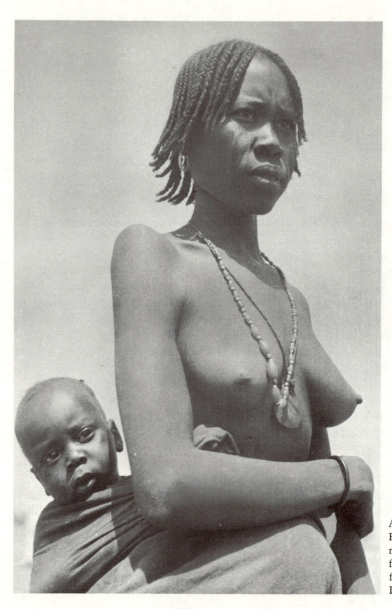

A mother and child from the Republic of Chad. The mammalian mother-child bond is the fundamental basis of the human family group. (Courtesy of La Documentation Française, Paris.)

used in adulthood, and thus perpetuate into adulthood the patterns of affection, trust, and mutual obligation acquired during infancy. As adults, human males and females continue to be guided by the social rules learned in infancy. In contrast to most nonhuman primate societies, in which old age incapacitates individuals in the struggle for dominance and submission, the human father may retain the loyalty of his children even in sickness and senility.

Patterns of affection and obligation develop between siblings as well as between parents and children, and as brothers and sisters grow up to marry and establish their own families, so eventually the entire community will tend to become interlaced by a pattern of learned roles, attitudes, and statuses. Thus a man's brother becomes, in the course of time, an uncle to his children, and his brother's children become his own sons' cousins. In this way not only did pair-bonding produce the family, but at the human level it also produced the concept of KINSHIP. It effectively replaced intragroup conflict by intragroup cooperation substituting patterns of mutual obligations for dominance and submission as the basis of social order. Henceforth every hominid born into the group acquired at birth a set of privileges and obligations, a recognized niche in an integrated social system. Kinship had evolutionary value in that it replaced the principle of dominance, rooted in conflict, with an ascriptive system in which social order was ensured by a pattern of learned behavior—the rules and obligations implicit in kinship ties—acquired at birth; thereby transforming the hominid band into a more efficient team of cooperating individuals who faced the problem of survival as a joint venture. Kinship was a cultural innovation that had survival value, and those groups which first developed efficient kinship systems had superior survival chances over those that lagged in this respect.

Held together by a network of kinship privileges and obligations, earlier human societies saw kinship not as we see it. In kinship based societies kinship is not just another category of social behavior in the sense of political, religious, or economic relations. In such societies kinship implies almost every other kind of relationship known to society. It embraces them all. In such societies kinship is the bond that holds all the members of the society together, and defines their behavior and relationships completely. Traditional kinship obligations and privileges define the limits of all possible relationships between the members of the community.

Only when society becomes larger do we begin to find distinctive political institutions that are not an integral part of the kinship system. POLITICAL INSTITUTIONS may be described as socially approved processes for defining the norms of acceptable conduct, for allocating offices of leadership, for settling disputes, and for organizing group defense. In earlier human societies the kinship system took care of all this. Only at a higher level of social complexity do distinctive nonkinship political institutions begin to emerge. Government consequently emerges unheralded as local groups begin to grow in complexity, initially through an elaboration of the kinship system, and only later by the inauguration of political institutions separate from the kinship structure.

Band Societies

Thus the analogy of primate society, the evidence of archeology, and the study of surviving hunting and gathering societies all suggest that man's primordial hominid ancestors lived in small territorially based communities long before they had evolved to *Homo sapiens* status. These early hominid territorial groups are known as BANDS, to distinguish them from the nonhuman primate *troop* from which they probably evolved and from which they differ because the hominid habit of pair-bonding and the resultant family pattern of social organization involves food sharing and a division of labor between the sexes.

At the simplest level these small human bands[1] each represented a distinct Mendelian population, being primarily inbreeding and hence largely isolated from a genetic point of view, like nonhuman primate troops. Such predominantly inbreeding hominid territorial groups are known as ENDOGAMOUS BANDS.

Each endogamous band is autonomous in its own territory, and roams around this territory more or less continuously in search of food. Although divided into families, each individual is linked to every other individual by ties of kinship and the bonds of close companionship. The principle of *incest* normally operates to

prevent sexual relations between members of the same family unit, but the simple fact of distance causes the members of these bands to find a mate from another family within the band.

Band type societies are described as *acephalous*.[2] They generally lack headmen or leaders. A person who shows particular talent may be listened to with respect, but each adult male, as the head of his own nuclear family, is essentially a free agent in his own right, bound only by the cultural traditions which oblige him to show loyalty and diffidence to his fellows, particularly to those who are senior to him in the kinship system. There is no sense of authoritative power in a band type of society in the sense that authority implies coercive power vested in any individual by the members of the group.

[1] Band type societies are further discussed in Elman R. Service, *Primitive Social Organization* (New York: Random House, Inc., 1971).

[2] See Morton H. Fried, *The Evolution of Political Society* (New York: Random House, Inc., 1967), on "equalitarian societies."

FIG. 22   NONHUMAN PRIMATE TROOPS AND ENDOGAMOUS HUMAN BANDS

a. The nonhuman primate troop occupies its own distinctive territory. Order is maintained primarily through dominance and submission. There is no food sharing.

b. The endogamous human band occupies its own territory but is distinguished by pair-bonding relationships which involve food sharing. Order is maintained principally by kinship ties arising out of family units.

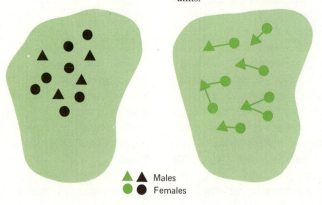

▲ ▲ Males
● ● Females

Truly endogamous band-type societies are rare in the contemporary world, although several peoples, such as the Yahgan (see Chap. 23) are predominantly endogamous, only occasionally intermarrying with neighboring groups. But since nonhuman primate troops generally inbreed, it seems justifiable to suppose that at some earlier stage in the history of hominid social evolution predominantly endogamous bands were the rule rather than the exception.

Exogamous Bands

We have noted that baboon troops sometimes increase in numbers to the extent that they are forced to divide into two distinct troops, sending off a colony to occupy a neighboring territory. Human bands may also become too large for the territory they occupy and send off a colony to settle a new territory. But after baboon troops divide, they lose contact with each other, and even if the two troops subsequently meet at a common waterhole, they show no evidence of particular friendship or recognition. Gorillas and chimpanzees, by contrast, show signs of recognizing former associates; and at the human level, kinsmen and kinship ties are definitely remembered. Consequently when a human band sends off a detachment to colonize a neighboring territory the kinship ties may be preserved, and the two groups may retain any preexisting attitudes of sympathy and kinship. When the members of the two groups meet again, they will then do so with confidence, because they are meeting cousins and kinsmen who share a common language and a common folk tradition with them.

In such cases there will be no barrier to the exchange of young women as wives for each other's sons, and should interband marriages take place, these reinforce the mutual ties between the bands for yet another generation. The exchange of womenfolk as wives serves to prevent the bands from drifting apart genetically, linguistically, and culturally, and intermarriage keeps them united in every way except economically. As the principle of incest operates, it may even become the rule to find a wife from a related and friendly neighboring group rather than from within one's own group, thereby reducing the possibility of tension and conflict arising out of rivalry over women within each separate territorial band. As among the Arunta of Australia, described in Chapter 23, the result is a group of local bands each independent and autonomous in its own territory, but all held together by a common language, a common culture, and even by a common gene pool. Although the members of these bands may know nothing about genetics, they will know that they look alike, that they share descent from common ancestors, that they share common folk-memories or traditions, and that they are recognizably different from the members of alien bands speaking alien languages, whom they will treat with suspicion.

Interbreeding exogamous bands feel a sympathy for each other, not only because of the bonds of intermittent companionship, language, and culture that unite them, but also because regular intermarriage binds them tightly with kinship ties. In consequence, the members of a group of exogamous bands may sometimes unite to aid each other, as when under the pressure of an expanding population the territory of a related band is subjected to infiltration by newcomers. The members of band-type societies do not always fight to defend their territories. An Eskimo band whose territory is invaded by rival hunters usually pack their belongings and move on to a less crowded area rather than attempt to dispute against a more formidable group. But if the new territory is marginal land, providing less food, a bad year may eliminate the band that was ousted from the better territory. Because a group of cooperating exogamous bands con-

FIG. 23   EVOLUTION OF EXOGAMOUS BANDS AND CLAN-TYPE TRIBAL SOCIETIES

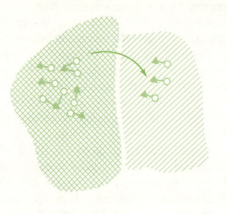

a.

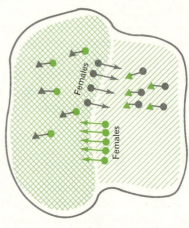

b.

a. Formerly Endogamous Band Colonizes Neighboring Territory. Overpopulation or similar circumstances cause an emigrant group to colonize the neighboring territory, establishing a separate, autonomous band.

b. Two Intermarrying Exogamous Bands Formed. Exogamy develops, possibly as an extension of the incest principle, and the marital arrangements continue to reinforce the cultural, linguistic, and genetic unity of the total society generation after generation. This diagram illustrates the relationship between two exogamous bands, each politically autonomous in its own territory.

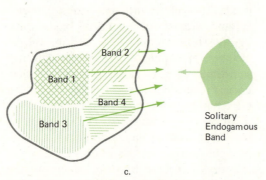

c.

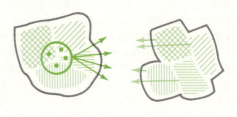

d.

c. Cooperating Exogamous Bands. Exogamous bands have a greater survival potential than endogamous bands in the event of conflict over territorial occupancy. The consciousness of cultural and genetic unity is likely to cause the exogamous bands to cooperate when threatened by alien intrusion.

d. (*Left*) Tribal Society with Central Coordinating Authority. (*Right*) Exogamous Bands Relying on Spontaneous Cooperation without Central Political Body. Tribal societies, with tribal councils, chieftains, or other coordinating personnel, also have a greater survival potential than groups of exogamous bands, which, though willing to cooperate with each other for mutual survival, lack an efficient coordinating mechanism.

stitutes a considerably more formidable body than a single endogamous band, the latter inevitably give way to exogamous bands. Only a few endogamous band-type societies have survived into this century, and these are mostly located, like the Yahgan, in the more remote corners of the earth.

Clans

In the course of time exogamous bands tend to emphasize kinship rather than the concept of contiguity. Territoriality is the main principle behind the band, even though internal cooperation is ensured by kinship, but the regularization of interband marriages will emphasize the role of kinship to the point that the concept of kinship eventually replaces that of territoriality in social significance. When this happens the members of an exogamous band will think of themselves as the members of a specific and identifiable kinship group, such as a clan.

By definition, a CLAN is a group of people who believe themselves to be bound to each other by reciprocal privileges and obligations by virtue of descent from a common ancestor, real or imaginary. Clans always have distinguishing names, and this may be the name of a patriarchal hero-founder. Thus, if a man called Donald were to lead his family to settle a new territory, it is possible that—as in the Highlands of Scotland—the descendants of this hero-father called Donald may call themselves "MacDonalds," for *Mac* means simply "grandson of," a term which also by implication includes great-grandsons and all subsequent descendants. The Irish *O'* has the same meaning, an "O'Reilly" being a "grandson" (or descendant) of the great clanfounder, the hero-leader Reilly. All subsequent members of the band might then call themselves "MacDonalds" or "O'Reillys" as the case may be.

In the course of time the MacDonalds may be successful in their new location and proliferate, sending off a new colony to settle fresh land adjacent to the parent territory. Only one or two families may be involved, and if the leader of this colony is named "Millan," the succeeding generations may call themselves "MacMillans." Because the MacMillans and the MacDonalds share the same heritage of folklore, language, and culture, and because they will remember that they are related to each other, they will feel safe with each other when they meet on the border, and probably negotiate exogamously, MacDonald men marrying MacMillan women and vice versa. Many variations on this hypothetical pattern of naming and clan organization may arise, such as the totemistic system described in the following chapter, but the principle is the same.

Tribes

The concept of the tribe is one of the most disputed subjects in anthropology.[3] Some writers accept a group of intermarrying exogamous bands as a tribe, provided that the members think of themselves as a kin-related group and share a common language, culture, and contiguous set of territories. They stress that a band is essentially a territorial unit, whereas the principle of the tribe is rooted in the principle of kinship rather than that of territory. It would seem reasonable, however, to distinguish between bands and tribes more clearly than this, by enquiring to what extent a degree of political integration may exist. Bands are essentially autonomous units; but in a political sense a tribe always has some established formula for coordinating the relationship between the member clans or other kinship units. When territorially segregated clans that cooperate regularly establish a clan council to exercise some kind of cohesive unity between the different territories or clans, they become a tribe. Such a council of clan or tribal

---

[3] Fried, pp. 154 f.

With increasing social complexity some form of authoritative community leadership becomes necessary. In a kinship based society the community "headmen" will normally be appointed from one of the more respected families, possibly on an hereditary basis. Portrayed above are village headmen from the Tauran District of North Borneo. (Courtesy of the North Borneo Information Service.)

elders may or may not elect a permanent chieftain, and may not necessarily have any coercive power; but even if it functions in a consultative sense only, once some kind of supraband coordinating mechanism exists, we have a politically cohesive tribal society.

The earliest tribal councils were still rooted in the concept of kinship. Thus among the Bantu tribes of Rhodesia, all government is essentially familistic at the village level. When an issue is to be decided, the male heads of families will meet to discuss the matter under

the "chairmanship" of the village headman, a position which is usually hereditary, being equivalent to a clan or lineage chief. All decisions are taken unanimously. The idea of a majority group dominating a sulking minority is objectionable in a tight kin group. Such debates may take several days, but in the end, as the mood of the meeting becomes more clear, the minority will eventually withdraw any objections they may have had and agree with the majority element, putting on as good a face as possible. In such debates, however,

FIG. 24   THE TRIBAL COUNCIL

Political organization in a kinship-based society frequently takes the form of a council of family heads or clan elders, status positions being ascribed by birth and marriage.

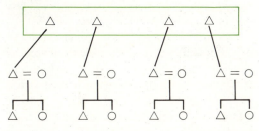

the more senior, experienced, and respected family heads may wield more influence than the younger ones, and the better orators often have considerable influence. When a unanimous village opinion has been reached, the headman and several other villagers will attend a similar meeting of village representatives at the home of the district chief, and the process is repeated. Eventually the district chiefs attend a meeting at the residence of the tribal chieftain, when a final and binding resolution is passed.

Tribal societies can be classified according to two major principles. The obvious way in which a tribe can come into existence is by an increase in population, with a resultant expansion in area of settlement, which causes a single band to grow into a number of exogamous bands. As these become separate intermarrying clans, linked by a tribal council of clan chiefs and possibly by a tribal chieftain, we have what has been called a *classical segmentary tribe*—one that has come into existence in a classical pattern of expansion in numbers and territory, resulting in a segmentation of the original group into a number of intermarrying clans.

Such classical segmentary tribes are often reasonably equalitarian because all members share common ancestors, but tribes can also

result from an amalgamation of different peoples. A population may expand and seize neighboring territories without eliminating the indigenous population. If the victorious tribe subordinates the defeated peoples, treating them as slaves or inferiors and refusing to intermarry with them, a new situation will develop. While admitting the conquered people as inferior clans under their political hegemony, the victors may still keep the descendants of the conquered clans in subjugation. Such units, comprising a politically unequal agglomeration of various nonintermarrying clans of diverse origins and diverse status, differ markedly from classical segmentary tribes, and may be described as *composite tribal societies.*

Nations

Such is the pressure of populations on resources and territories, that not only have band type societies given way to tribes, but some tribes have multiplied and expanded at the expense of others, absorbing or dispersing the remnants of the less powerful peoples. In such cases the enlarged and more widely dispersed population may itself become subdivided into a number of related and cooperating tribal units. Where external pressures reinforce the internal bonds of loyalty to ensure cooperation under the prestige of a common kinship leader, the term *nation* may be applied.

The relationship between the nation and the tribe is apparent even etymologically, for our word *tribe* comes to us from the Latin *tribus,* indicating a third part of a nation. Nations reflect the kinship ideal at its maximum political and territorial extension. Although effective government may become bureaucratic rather than hereditary in principle and the nation may be held together by a variety of economic, political, and social forms, in the thoughts of its nationals a nation is still essentially a large kinship grouping, representing a particular ethnic type with a distinct gene pool, and regarding all its members as kinsmen who speak the same language and share a common cultural, historical, and linguistic heritage.

Thus national government in early historic Europe mostly had its roots in the collective village settlement, originally comprising a related group of families, the members of which owned the land communally. The town of Hastings in England, for example, was originally called *Haest-inga* meaning simply the *inga* or descendants of Haest. The heads of families in each village were regarded as equals, but a village chief was normally chosen for life from among the eligible members of one family which was regarded as senior to the others. The heads of families then assembled after work every day to discuss the day's events, under the chairmanship of the village headman. When a tribal decision had to be made, the headman from each village would attend a tribal council where he represented his kinsmen under the chairmanship of a tribal chieftain.[4] In the course of time, as larger political units came into being, this elementary system of kinship representation became transformed into a three-tier political structure comprising a hereditary national leader or *King;* a *Council of Nobles* representing the local clan or tribal chieftains who met periodically with the king as an advisory body, and a *General Assembly* of all the adult freemen who, being heads of households, were entitled to be consulted on important matters. This ancient system is still reflected in the British system of a King; a House of Lords, comprising the hereditary nobles; and a House of Commons, representing the freemen. Only in the last century was political representation in Britain extended to women and other adults who were not heads of households.

It is significant that the English word *king* derives from the Anglo-Saxon *cyning,* literally meaning a "man of the kin," in the sense of the purest descendant from the original tribal founder and therefore the "father" of the living family of descendants. When an hereditary nobility and royalty emerge we talk of a *ritually stratified society,*[5] for hereditary positions of leadership always tend to be reinforced by ritual ceremonial and frequently also by magicoreligious sanctions. Kings will be crowned with solemn ceremony and sacrifices may be offered to royal ancestors. The existence of such ritual stratification in a tribal society does not necessarily mean that the hereditary officeholders exercise arbitrary authority. Kings are not necessarily "people who order other people around," as an American schoolchild once told the author. On the contrary, traditional kings *reigned* rather than *ruled.* As symbols of tribal and national blood unity, the authority of kings is generally heavily circumscribed by custom. While kinship remains the basis of society, no king may impose any decision on his kinsmen that may be regarded as unjust according to tradition and the dictates of the national culture. Prior to the coming of feudalism, kings were customarily loved and revered as symbols of the unity of the nation-family, the people feeling that the kings belonged to them, rather than the reverse.

The Principle of Coercive Power

In the various social systems which we have so far described, ranging from bands to tribal and national organizations, kinship has been the dominant principle around which social relations are organized. Because of the relative simplicity of the societies which we have described, the individual band, clan, or tribal member is able to play a fairly significant role

[4] See also Paul Kirchoff, "The Principles of Clanship in Human Society," in M. F. Fried (ed.), *Readings in Anthropology,* Vol. II (New York: Thomas Y. Crowell Company, 1968).

[5] See J. G. Frazer, *The Magical Origin of Kings* (London: Dawson of Pall Mall, 1968), for further reading on the origins of kingship.

Even large industrial societies may preserve the unifying concept of "nationhood," for so long as the members believe themselves to be linked together by common bonds of language, culture, and kinship. The resultant sentiments of unity and willing cooperation can be a source of considerable political power, as witnessed in this century in the case of Germany. View of Berliners on the Kurfürstendamm, West Germany. (Courtesy of the German Information Center, Bonn.)

in his community, and habit and custom govern the course of behavior. Decision making is rigidly controlled within traditional limits and the concept of law making, or law giving, in the sense that this implies the deliberate creation of new principles of behavior, is generally unknown.

But as societies become larger and more complex, rivalries may develop between kinship groups that threaten to disrupt the community. A village headman or clan chief who is obliged to rely for authority on custom and the willingness of disputants to obey custom

may be unable to prevent an internecine struggle from breaking out, something that would seldom if ever occur in a community comprising only 20 or 30 individuals. It follows inevitably that such leaders tend to acquire, through common consent, a degree of authoritative power. This means that when moral persuasion fails, they may use other forms of restraint, including possibly physical intervention to halt a dispute, with the full weight of public consent behind them.

In the earliest *Homo sapiens* societies, and for most of human history, society revolved around the traditionally *ascribed* responsibilities of kinship cooperation. Only as such societies become more complex and kinship structures began to break down did the old primate principle of dominance and submission, today known as competitive *achievement,* begin to undermine the principle of ascription by which roles are determined by the order of birth. As new political institutions steadily replace kinship ties, men begin to eulogize intragroup and even individual competitiveness. Participating eagerly in the scramble to win a presidential election or to secure a seat on the politburo in competition with their fellows, they abandon the age-old principle of kinship ascription in favor of a pattern of competitive social mobility and party politics oddly reminiscent of the baboon troop.

Centralized Chieftainships

Accordingly, there comes a time when positions of political and administrative responsibility are reinforced by the right to coerce —which in turn may be reinforced by the *means* to coerce, in the form of a body of armed retainers. In such cases, high office becomes in effect a prize for the successful competitor.[6] In place of kinship leaders who exercise authority restricted by custom on the basis of the consent of the members of society, we find men who regard public offices as spoils to be secured for the sake of the personal rewards that they can bring. Regarding authority as their personal property, they may even seek to maintain their position by coercion or by the deliberate manipulation of public opinion. In such societies kinship may still remain an important element in primary, face-to-face loyalties, and the facade of the old clan and tribal chieftainships may survive. But in reality the tribal kinship structure has been replaced by a competitive power system, and the principles of coercion and manipulation have re-

placed the principles of ascription and custom. All subordinate offices—earldoms, chancellorships, and even the position of the village headman—come to be allocated to those who support the successful candidate for supreme office, as one of the rewards of individual loyalty.

When substantial centralized coercive power is vested in the leaders of a society, we speak of *centralized chieftainships.* While the leaders of Yahgan, Arunta, Pygmy, and Nuer societies have only advisory power, and the Kazak khan, who comes from a White Bone family,[7] also has little or no coercive authority, a centralized chieftain such as the Baganda king "rules" rather than "reigns." All power is vested in the person of one man whose will, however arbitrary, will prevail.

In a sense, this development represents the beginning of bureaucracy; and the centralization of power in the hands of a single leader has a certain organizational superiority over the older pattern of village headmen, elected or hereditary clan chieftains, and representative tribal councils. Decisions can be made incisively and enforced ruthlessly. Since by the nature of the power structure, the supreme officeholder is likely to be a man skilled in political reality, the chances that he will make a reasonably effective leader are moderately high. In consequence, centralized chieftainships, in which a single individual or family effectively controls appointments to subordinate positions, arise as an evolutionary necessity wherever they have a greater survival value than the traditional clan and tribal systems which delegate only limited powers to their leaders. The most favorable condition for such a development is likely to be a society troubled by constant warfare, which may be forced to accept a strongly centralized system of social control in order to survive.

Many quite large and complex societies that are not exposed to the threat of war have re-

[6] Service, pp. 133 f.

[7] C. Daryll Forde, *Habitat, Economy and Society* (New York: E. P. Dutton & Co., Inc., 1963), p. 332.

vealed the ability to live contentedly under clan councils and clan chieftains without ever appointing any full-time authoritative officers. In this way, the Saxons of ancient Europe lived without kings until they were finally conquered by the renowned "central chieftain" Charlemagne. But whenever there is a degree of political turbulence, with pressure being exerted from outside groups, or whenever migration and war require an effective coordinating system, social power tends to become authoritatively vested in a single individual or lineage. Although in tribal societies the kingship may remain elective within the royal family, centralized chieftainships usually become strictly hereditary in the mode of succession. Indeed the principle of PRIMOGENITURE—the inheritance of an office by the eldest son or daughter —may often arise as a device intended to avoid internecine dispute following the death of the previous officeholder.

Centralized chieftainships are in effect pyramidal or cone-shaped hierarchical structures, in which the ruler occupies the key position with the power to direct the life of the community in an arbitrary fashion, although in reality such power is frequently limited by traditional moral restraints or by the existence of subordinate pressure groups. In this sense they differ from contemporary totalitarian regimes only by the fact that the administration remains essentially personal because of the smaller scale of society. The problems involved in supervising a large and rambling empire are considerable, and history records many examples of chieftainships which rose and fell in the lifetime of a single individual leader because of an overextension of the state beyond the limits that a single ruler can effectively control.

Feudalism

FEUDALISM represents the principle of the centralized chieftainship at its most highly organized but still personal and prebureaucratic level. In a feudal society the centralized chieftain no longer depends for his authority purely upon tribal ties of kinship with the persons over whom he rules. Indeed, the feudal king no longer "reigns" but now "rules" with largely arbitrary authority. Claiming ownership of the land and all who are born upon it, he allocates the control of geographical districts to subordinate officers who remain solely responsible to his authority.

The contrast between a kinship or tribal society and a feudal society is amply illustrated in the history of Europe. Prior to the rise of feudalism, northern Europe remained essentially tribal, each people having its own king or kin-father, who was designated as the *King*

Feudalism combines the authoritative power of a centralized chieftainship with a bureaucratic system of subordinate chieftains or territorial, overlords. The castle of Almourol in Portugal stands as an impressive reminder of the responsibility for defense that attached to feudal office. (Courtesy of the Director-General of Information, Portugal.)

of the English, the *King of the Francs,* or the *King of the Saxons.* Feudalism introduced the idea of land and territory as the unifying principle, substituting territoriality for the principle of kinship. After the introduction of feudalism these kings became the *King of England,* the *King of France,* and the *King of Saxony,* claiming ownership of the land and of the people born on that land. The common people ceased to be "tribesmen" and became "subjects." In a sense our contemporary nationality laws still reflect the feudal concept of the *subject* who belongs to the king or to the government of the land on which he is born. A man or woman born in the land of Britain is today "British" no matter what nationality his parents were, and the same is the case in America. The child "belongs" to the governing authority of Britain or America regardless of the kinship status or race of his parents. Such principles for determining *nationality* would be impossible in a tribal society—or even in ancient Greece or Republican Rome—where membership of the city-state was based on kinship, not on the accident of being born within the limits of the territory.

"State" versus "Nation"

As power and control over land and people replaces the principle of kinship in feudal societies, the institutions of government become identifiably separate from the rest of the social structure. In the feudal Ashanti kingdom of West Africa we may identify all the main offices found in a modern bureaucracy, including an administrative machinery with regular revenue-collecting personnel, law courts, army, and exchequer, each operating as separate facets of a single central government which was legitimized by the symbol of the sacred "stool," in which the soul of the royal ancestors was supposed to reside.

Feudalism consequently introduced the idea of the *political state* as a separate legal entity divorced from kinship. The state is essentially a political and economic unit, not a kinship group. It represents a governing political clique who are essentially distinct from the people, hence the antagonism felt by the peasantry against the government and its tax collectors, who are seen as exploiting aliens, external to the local kindreds. While central chieftains and successful feudal lords may still surround themselves with an aura of legitimacy derived from genealogical claims, the idea of the political state is more difficult to reconcile with the idea of the "people." Indeed, a new polarization of concepts develops, portraying the state as being in opposition to the individual. Government becomes so depersonalized that it is often seen as a tool of oppression, and not infrequently those who control the government may wage war against the older kinship groupings or even against the very institution of the family, seeing these as rivals for the loyalty and control of the citizen.

The concept of the state is thus subtly different from that of the nation. The term *state* implies authoritative political institutions, while the concept of *nation* implies a society in which the members conceive of themselves as being linked by the common possession of a shared cultural, linguistic, and genetic heritage. Nations still, consequently, comprise a distinct *people,* bound together more by a sense of ethnic identity than by subordination to a single political ruler or system. By contrast, the subjects or citizens of a state may even speak different languages, as did the citizens of the Austro-Hungarian empire, or belong to different races, as do the citizens of the United States of America.

Because of their frequent reliance upon military power to maintain their autocratic position, centralized chieftains may find themselves in possession of a powerful war machine and may be tempted to establish CONQUEST STATES by the subordination of less organized neighbors. Such agglomerations of diverse ethnic origins are also called PRIMITIVE STATES, the label "primitive" being applied since government is still personalized, not bureaucratic. The Zulu kings of Africa ruled over a large primitive state, and effectively made "Zulus" out of the people they conquered. The Aztecs, by contrast, did not attempt to assimilate their subject tribes but maintained their hegemony over a multinational or multiethnic state. But such primitive states are usually limited in size and often highly unstable when controlled by the personal abilities of a single centralized chieftain and his henchmen. Long-lasting primitive states consequently tend to develop more complex and professionalized bureaucratic systems of government, capable of perpetuating themselves independently of the life span or genius of the ruler. In such fullfledged BUREAUCRATIC STATES as Ancient Egypt, Ancient China, or the Austro-Hungarian empire, the bureaucracy usually succeeds in subordinating the central chieftain to the system, and we find ourselves studying the type of centralized bureaucratic state system with which we are so familiar in the contemporary Western world.

The Need for Legitimacy

Although the possession of coercive power is the attribute of government officials from the centralized chieftain to the bureaucratic officials who direct the modern state, social power which is rooted solely in the use of force is costly in terms of effort and always raises the possibility of reaction and rebellion. Government actions which contravene old established norms will certainly provoke hostility among those who are ruled. Those who hold power in such societies will constantly strive to reduce their dependence upon coercive power by seeking to *constitutionalize* their position and so gain the willing cooperation of their subjects. Essential in this process is the need to create an impression of LEGITIMACY.[8]

A "legitimate" officeholder, in the final analysis, is simply one who holds his position with the approval of the members of his society. Kinship certainly provides legitimacy, and a chieftain who annexes a neighboring land by

[8] Gerhard Lenski, *Power and Privilege* (New York: McGraw-Hill, Inc., 1966), pp. 59 f.

The conquest of one people by another frequently leads to the formation of multiethnic "conquest states" where peoples of diverse ethnic, cultural, and linguistic backgrounds are subordinated under a single government and are held together by political, and sometimes military, means rather than by shared traditions, values, and attitudes. This mosaic wall depicts a scene of conflict during Moorish domination of the Iberian Peninsula in Europe. (Courtesy of the Portuguese Director-General of Information.)

force may marry the heiress to the throne of that country so that his heirs will be legitimate heirs in the eyes of the people. Furthermore, the careful ruler will maintain law and order, suppress criminals, and uphold the traditional mores of the society so as to win public approval. Successful international ventures, which raise the nation's self-esteem, will also win public support, and so serve to legitimize the ruler's position.

But there are less constitutional ways in which a ruler or ruling clique can secure its position. *Economic control* is more subtle than outright military coercion. When the ruling group can monopolize control over the major economic activities, it will be in a position to offer economic rewards for collaboration and penalize noncollaborators by denying them access to the more profitable fields of enterprise. Even more insidious is the attempt at *mind control*. In simpler societies the norms and attitudes of society are transmitted through custom, folklore, and tradition by word of mouth from generation to generation, but in more complex societies, sentiments and attitudes are largely disseminated through mass media and by way of formal education. Since the control of mass media and education falls within a series of structured and bureaucratic systems, it is highly susceptible to manipulation. In totalitarian societies both the mass media and the educational system are usually government-owned and therefore under direct political control. Through them, even basic norms, values, and judgments can be substantially remodeled to suit the requirements of the dominant group. It is one of the characteristics of the multiethnic and culturally diverse modern political state that the government, frequently representing the interests of one section of society only, will resort to mind control in the attempt to educate all members of society to accept the values and goals of the dominant element—which need not necessarily be the majority element.

For Further Reading

Eisenstadt, S. N., 1959, "Primitive Political Systems," *American Anthropologist* 61:200–219.

Evans-Pritchard, E. E., 1940, *The Political System of the Anuak of the Anglo-Egyptian Sudan.* London: London School of Economics, Monographs on Social Anthropology, 4.

———, 1948, *The Divine Kingship of the Shilluk of the Nilotic Sudan.* New York: Cambridge University Press.

Fortes, M., and E. E. Evans-Pritchard, 1961, *African Political Systems.* Oxford: International African Institute.

Fried, M. R., 1967, *The Evolution of Political Society.* New York: Random House, Inc.

Krader, L., 1968, *The Formation of the State.* Englewood Cliffs, N.J.: Prentice-Hall, Inc.

Leach, E. R., 1971, *Political Systems of Highland Burma.* New York: Humanities Press, Inc.

Lowie, R. H., 1927, *The Origin of the State.* New York: Russell and Russell.

Mair, L., 1962, *Primitive Government.* Baltimore: Penguin Books, Inc.

Ratzenhofer, G., 1893, *Wesen und Zweck der Politik,* 3 vols. Leipzig: F. A. Brockhaus Verlag.

Schapera, I., 1956, *Government and Politics in Tribal Societies.* London: C. A. Watts & Co., Ltd.

Service, E. R., 1971, *Primitive Social Organization.* New York: Random House, Inc.

CHAPTER 15

Marriage and Kinship

The evolution of pair-bonding among men implies the concept of MARRIAGE. Baboons mate with each other, but human beings do more than mate, they marry. Marriage is institutionalized when the members of a society adopt a set of customs or mores which recognize the habit of pair-bonding, and lay down rules governing the pattern of relationship between individuals who enter into such a pair-bond, and also the behavior of other members of society toward them. Since different societies can lay down different rules governing pair-bonding and the raising of children, anthropologists consequently identify many different types of family in human societies.[1]

The simplest type of family group is known as the NUCLEAR FAMILY, a term used to refer to an individual set of parents and their offspring.[2] But in many societies groups of

[1] J. Goody, *Kinship* (Baltimore: Penguin Books, Inc., 1971), may be regarded as an authoritative work on the subject of marital and kinship relations.

[2] The term nuclear family is also frequently used to refer to the smaller husband-wife-children units within larger extended and joint families, as well as to independent nuclear families.

related families may cooperate to work the same patch of land or tend the same herd of animals. When fathers keep their sons with them even after the sons have married, the resultant grouping, comprising two or more generations of the same family who share economic interests in common under the guidance of a recognized family head, is known as an EXTENDED FAMILY. Sometimes the different nuclear families that make up such extended families live in separate houses and comprise a small village, as in Anglo-Saxon England, but in other cases they may live together in a single large house, enjoying close psychological interaction, in which case we talk of a JOINT FAMILY. Joint families usually share all property among their members, this still being the preferred pattern in many societies, such as modern Hindu India.

Marital Systems

The formation of a new pair-bond, which represents to men the founding of a new family unit, is celebrated by the kinsmen of the prin-

Not only is the nuclear family, comprising parents and their immediate children, the basic element in the extended family system, but it may also exist as an independent social unit. The members of this German family from Bavaria have established their own household separately from the households of both sets of parents. The custom of separate or *neolocal* nuclear families also remains dominant in countries such as the United States and Canada which were originally colonized from North Europe. (Courtesy of the German Information Center, Bonn.)

cipals at a ritual ceremony known as a WED-DING. After the wedding, the married couple has to live somewhere. The wife may join the husband at his place of domicile, in which case we speak of *patrilocal residence*. However, it is also possible that the husband may go to live with the wife's family, and then we speak of *matrilocal residence*. In societies that live in nuclear family households as is customary in America today—with neither joint nor extended families—the newly married couple must establish its own home independently, in which case we talk of *neolocal residence*.

In any family one or the other marital part-

Afro-Asiatic and particularly Moslem societies are usually patriarchal. Among the Azougni pastoralists of Mauritania in North Africa, the men ride while the women walk. (Courtesy of La Documentation Française, Paris.)

ners is likely to assume a dominant or leadership role, and most societies will tend to emphasize the right of either the male or the female to be dominant. *Patriarchal* societies place the leadership officially with the male; *matriarchal* societies give this position to the female. Other societies may ideally assume an *equalitarian* marital arrangement, in which neither husband nor wife is supposedly dominant.[3]

No instances of fully promiscuous human societies have ever been recorded; in all, some form or other of sexual regulation exists. But although we speak in zoological terms of pair-bonding, and although MONOGAMY, the marriage of one male to one female, prevails in most human societies it is by no means universal. Many societies practice POLYGYNY in which a man may have several wives especially where—as among the Baganda of Africa—there is a heavy male fatality rate. Polygyny is also found among the upper classes in many societies, where it is regarded as a luxury and a status symbol. Thus the Islamic culture permits men to have as many as four wives if they can afford to support this number, and the Inca nobility were permitted plural wives as a reward for holding high office.

[3] The terms *patriarchal* and *matriarchal*, although still widely used, are actually subject to serious questioning. In many so-called "matriarchal" societies, such as the Hopi, the position of the men is not always so directly subordinate to that of the women as the term would imply.

POLYANDRY, in which several husbands share one wife, is much more rare, being normally found in the more impoverished societies such as the Todas of India, among whom women were considered a luxury and polyandry was regarded as an effective way of husbanding economic resources, the surplus females being killed off at birth. The term POLYGAMY is sometimes used to refer to any type of plural marriage, whether polygynous or polyandrous.

In one or two cases, polyandry has given way to a form of GROUP MARRIAGE wherein a number of women are collectively married to a number of men. Thus the polyandrous Toda society in India was faced with the problem of a surplus of marriageable females when British colonial rule prohibited the killing of female infants. Rather than adopt monogamy, however, the Todas remained true to their polyandrous tradition and solved the problem by allowing groups of brothers to take multiple wives. Among the Polynesians of the Marquesas Islands, Oceania, a form of group marriage also developed out of polyandry. Here a chief traditionally sought to recruit young fighting men of noble rank to join his household. Since only the eldest son of a chief could inherit his father's title and property, it was found that the best way of recruiting young warriors from other chiefly households was by introducing polyandry and sharing all possessions, including wives, with the warrior-companions, who in effect became cohusbands. The more wealthy chieftains soon found that

This polygynous Melanesian from New Caledonia has three wives. (Courtesy of La Documentation Française, Paris.)

they could further enlarge the size of their bodyguard by taking several wives and sharing these with an even larger number of secondary husbands or warriors. This also resulted in a situation which virtually corresponded to the concept of group marriage.[4]

Marriage Arrangements

Once kinship has become the basis of social organization, the marriage of two individuals is, in effect, an alliance between two descent groups. In consequence, kinsmen invariably take keen interest in the choice of the bride and bridegroom, and not infrequently make the selection without consulting the principals involved. Indeed, in many tribal societies, patterns of PREFERENTIAL MATING grow up as a recognized formula. Thus the Arunta have a complicated system of marital arrangements which ensures a pattern of marriages that, generation after generation, serves to tie all members of society together in a closely woven fabric of mutual interdependence.

In those societies which practice unilineal descent, cousin marriage is the most commonly approved pattern of preferential marriage. Cross cousin marriage is a very widespread

[4] The idea of "group marriage" was formerly widespread until rejected by Edward Westermarck in *The History of Human Marriage* (New York: The Macmillan Company 1894).

This African village, situated on the Ivory Coast, is by no means a casual jumble of residences as the uninformed observer might suppose. Instead the entire social life, including the location of the huts, follows an orderly pattern rooted in kinship. (Courtesy of Service Information de la Côte-d'Ivoire.)

phenomenon, the Chinese preferring cross cousins for spouses. In a CROSS COUSIN MARRIAGE a man will marry either the daughter of his father's sister or the daughter of his mother's brother. In those few cases in which PARALLEL COUSIN MARRIAGE is preferred, a man usually marries his father's brother's daughter. Needless to say, in a cross cousin marriage the spouse necessarily belongs to a different clan from that of her cousin, since (in the case of a patriclan) a man's father's sister will have married outside the patriclan, and her children will belong to her husband's clan. On the other hand, parallel cousin marriage usually results in very close inbreeding. This system is popular among the Bedouin Arabs of Arabia, where each camel herding band tends to be endogamous, continuously inbreeding within its own narrow confines generation after generation.

Not all societies deprive individuals of the right to choose their own marriage partners. The Polynesians, as we shall see, permit considerable premarital sexual experimentation among the lower classes, as also do the Hopi. Both allow individuals to select their own marriage partners. But *romantic love* usually flourishes only where sexual relations are somewhat restricted, thus the Polynesians tend to be matter-of-fact about their sexual relations, regarding the idea of romantic love as childish and immature.[5]

Marriage negotiations frequently involve an exchange of gifts and in some cases the payment of a substantial amount of wealth. In many societies in which it is considered a moral duty for a father to provide a husband for his daughter a system of dowry has developed. A DOWRY is essentially a portion of the family property which passes out of the family with a daughter at the time of her marriage. In most cases the dowry remains the wife's property after marriage, and should she divorce her husband or should she be left a

[5] See Margaret Mead, *Coming of Age in Samoa* (New York: William Morrow and Company, Inc., 1928).

widow, the dowry that she brought with her serves to guarantee her economic well-being. In reality, however, the dowry can become a bribe offered to the bridegroom, for a large dowry may be an incentive for a young man of high social status to accept a wife of lower status. Where marriages take place between ruling dynastic families, a large dowry, representing an entire province or even a nation, may be offered with the bride in order to secure a marital alliance with a powerful ruling family. Thus in the seventeenth century, when England was a world power and Portugal was declining in its ability to protect its vast overseas empire, Charles II of England was persuaded to take as his wife Princess Catherine of Braganza, a member of the Portuguese ruling house. She brought with her a dowry that included the strategic cities of Bombay and Tangiers as well as a large sum of money—and Britain has ever since been Portugal's traditional ally.

In other cases it may be customary for the family of the bidegroom to pay a BRIDE PRICE to the family of the bride. In its crudest form, this has been represented as a payment to the bride's family to compensate them for the cost of rearing a daughter. In cases where emphasis is placed on human stock-breeding, families with a proud genealogy may openly demand a high price from the prospective bridegroom on the understood principle that he is acquiring a valuable piece of breeding stock.

Among the Bantu of Africa, the bride price is frequently known as a *lobolo,* this taking the form of a payment of cattle, goats, or cowrie shells to the relatives of the bride, the exact extent of which will be the result of protracted negotiating and bargaining, for the bride price is an indicator of family status. Weddings will seldom take place until the bride price has been paid in full, although the Kazaks do permit some sexual liberties after the first installment has been paid. When bride price is paid, a wife who proves to be infertile may usually be returned to her relatives, who are then expected to refund the amount paid. Similarly, if a woman is ill-treated, she is entitled to return to her relatives. However, since they will be responsible for repaying the bride price that they received at the time of her marriage, she is likely to be under considerable pressure to tolerate her husband's behavior, especially if the payment received has already been passed on to yet another family as part of the bride price paid to obtain a wife for one of her brothers.

Where a man cannot raise the full amount of the bride price, he may be permitted in some societies to perform BRIDE SERVICE.[6] In other words, he may agree to work for his wife's family for a period of time as an alternative to making a payment in animals or cash. In a sense, the corn grinding carried out by the Hopi bride for her future mother-in-law represents a form of "bridegroom service," which has become traditional in the Hopi matriarchal society.

Divorce

Most human societies disapprove of divorce, since divorce implies the break-up of a family group and by its very occurrence tends to threaten the integrity of the pair-bond principle. Nevertheless virtually all human societies permit divorce under certain specific circumstances, which vary considerably from culture to culture. Among the Arunta of Australia and the Baganda of East Africa a husband may divorce his wife virtually at will, whereas a wife may only divorce her husband in case of severe mistreatment. In Moslem societies a man may divorce his wife by simply repeating the words "I divorce you" three times in front of a witness. Among the Hopi, both husband

[6]Bride service is relatively rare but is practiced among others by the Ekoi and Igbira of Southern Nigeria. See G. P. Murdock, *Africa: Its Peoples and their Culture History* (New York: McGraw Hill, Inc., 1959), p. 246.

and wife may divorce each other with very little formality, and in many other societies the rights of husband and wife are more or less equal where divorce is concerned. But even where a divorce may be easily obtained, the status of divorced people is often low because their action seems to represent a challenge to the stability of marital institutions in general. Virtually all societies regard marriage as ideally a permanent union even if in practice many individuals fail to achieve this ideal.

Levirate and Sororate

When a man dies, there is always the problem of providing protection for his widow and her children. In many patriarchal societies this is solved by requiring the widow to marry one of her deceased husband's surviving brothers. If he is already married, the widow acquires the status of a second wife, as is the case among the Kazaks. The purpose of this custom, known as the LEVIRATE, is to provide support and protection for the widow and her offspring. Nevertheless, in some societies there is a custom known as the *anticipatory levirate,* by which a man's brothers enjoy sexual privileges with his wife, on the principle that all brothers should be prepared to share all possessions freely with each other. Elements of this custom are found among the Haida, and the principle has been extended among the Todas to the point that it becomes polyandry, where the wife is regularly shared by a number of brothers.

When it is the wife who dies, leaving her husband a widower, remarriage is common, and in many North American Indian societies the widower is bound by a system known as the SORORATE, whereby his deceased wife's sister is entitled to claim him as her husband. Nevertheless, there have been other societies, such as the Hindu and Scythian, which hold firm convictions regarding the immortality of the soul and consequently believe that mar-

Kinship-regulated societies almost invariably make careful provisions for the relative role of the aged kinsmen, though not always in the same household as their younger kinfolk. Pictured above is a Bontok hangout for old men, in the Phillipines. (Courtesy of the Phillipine Information Services.)

riage continues after death. In such societies remarriage may be strictly prohibited, and in recent times the widow of an Indian Brahman was expected to commit *suttee,* or suicide, in order that she might be immediately reunited with her deceased husband.[7]

Infanticide

Since pair-bonding and the family appear to have arisen for the evolutionary purpose of promoting the survival of the offspring, it may at first sight appear anachronistic that most kinship-based human societies practice IN-FANTICIDE, the deliberate, but usually selective, killing of babies and young infants.

In a few instances, such as *female infanticide,* the motivation appears to be a partisan custom aimed at keeping the ratio of females to males artifically low. Female infanticide is therefore associated with polyandry among the Todas of India. In other cases, such as *ritual infanticide,* the motivation is religious. Thus the Baganda formerly killed the first child if it were male, since they believed that a first born male child presaged the early death of the father. Many Australian aboriginals also killed one of a pair of twins, believing that twins were unnatural and a bad omen. Such practices illustrate our earlier statement that not all culture is beneficial and that much of the information content of many cultural systems, including our own, is actually *misinformation.*

Where infanticide has persisted into more complex societies, however, it usually takes the form of *eugenic infanticide.*[8] To the extent that

[7]S. V. McCasland, *et al., Religions of the World* (New York: Random House, 1969), p. 364 f.

[8]Ralph Linton, *The Tree of Culture* (New York: Alfred A. Knopf, Inc., 1972), p. 587.

cooperation in human society reduces the immediate impact of natural selection, bringing about what geneticists call a *relaxation of natural selection,* there must necessarily be an increase in genetic load, in the number of disadvantageous genes carried in the gene pool. Since children are being produced in abundance, many human societies therefore practice eugenic infanticide, killing off grossly malformed or mentally retarded offspring soon after birth rather than be faced with the burden of supporting such severely handicapped infants who will never be able to enter functionally into the reciprocal pattern of mutual duties and obligations that kinship implies. Needless to say, the decision to practice infanticide will usually be made before the infant is formally accepted as a member of the kinship group, for once accepted as a kinsman, infanticide would become fratricide, the ultimate of all evils in a kinship-based culture.

Lineages, Clans, and Totemism

By far the greater part of human history has been spent in social systems in which the concept of kinship is dominant, and all human societies from the band level to the tribal level reveal rules defining the respective obligations of an individual to his many relatives and marital connections. Since an individual may be related to other individuals many times over—his aunt may become his wife or his cousin may become his brother-in-law—the main purpose of kinship principles is to restrict and systematize the patterns of mutual expectation and obligation, which govern every aspect of human behavior. This is achieved by grouping individuals into DESCENT GROUPS, comprising people who are regarded as being related according to the cultural convention of the group. Such conventions may or may not attempt to take cognizance of the actual degree of genetic identity.

Kinship obligations are thus reflected in regular systems of kinship labels or *nomenclature,* which serve to identify the descent group to which an individual belongs. As shown in the preceding chapter, this frequently results in the use of a *surname* or sire name, derived from an EPONYMOUS ANCESTOR—an earlier patriarch from whom all the later descendants take their name. A group of related individuals who believe themselves to be bonded together by special responsibilities because of common descent from a known ancestor is called a LINEAGE. In cases where this original ancestor died so long ago that the actual genealogical connection may be forgotten, but his descendants still recognize a kinship with each other because they share a common name, we speak of a CLAN.

So powerful is the concept of kinship in some societies that it is regarded as incorrect to address an individual by his personal name. Instead in a custom known as TEKNONYMY, all members are addressed by the appropriate kinship term indicating their relationship to the individual who is speaking, such as "father," "mother," "cousin," "my father's brother."[9]

Because membership of lineage and clan determines role and status in society, most kinship societies maintain elaborate genealogies, particularly where a degree of social inequality has developed, and some clans and lineages are more highly respected than others, as among the Kazaks, the Polynesians, the Homeric Greeks, and the Chinese. Such genealogies may be faithfully kept over hundreds of years. One of the prime objectives of the Red Guard in the Chinese "Cultural Revolution" of the last decade was the destruction of all tablets recording the genealogies of the elite families, with the object of destroying the basis of their pride.

Among many primitive peoples, however, the original progenitor of the descent group may be forgotten, and vague myths and leg-

[9]John J. Honigmann, *The World of Man* (New York: Harper & Row, Publishers), p. 406.

ends confused with magicoreligious traditions may imply that the original ancestor was an animal which possessed supernatural powers. Such a belief is known as TOTEMISM. As among the Australian aboriginals and the old Peruvian villagers, the members of a totemic descent group will usually refrain from killing or eating their totemic animal, except on special ritual occasions when certain members of the lineage group (usually the adult males) may gather together to consume the flesh of this animal as a magicoreligious ritual. Such totemic descent groups usually have badges representing the totemic ancestor. The totem poles raised outside a Haida dwelling house consist of carved and painted representations of the totemic animals symbolic of the lineage to which the family occupying the house belongs. It is also probable that the animal crests worn by medieval European nobles on their

shields and helmets derived from a forgotten tradition of totemic clan symbols of the greatest antiquity.

In essence, totemism is a form of primitive ancestor worship in which a symbolic animal progenitor is revered. *Ancestor worship,* based on reverence for the dead forefathers, will be discussed in Chapter 20, but is mentioned here because it can be a powerful force binding the members of a clan, tribe, or nation together in a community of worship. As Tacitus tells us,[10] the German peoples formerly believed themselves to be descended from an ancient, eponymous semidivine hero named *Mannus,* and consequently called themselves "men" by virtue of belonging to the descent group named "man," so-named after their eponymous ancestor. No more impressive example of intellectual ethnocentrism could be found than the process by which the tribal name "man" has come to be extended in popular usage to apply to hominids throughout the world, regardless of their own separate tribal, national, or racial background.

Totem poles from British Columbia, in Canada, portraying the totemic animals of ancestral clans and lineages. (Courtesy of the University of British Columbia.)

Unilineal Descent Groups

Persons who are believed to be related to each other by birth are known as CONSANGUINE, *agnatic,* or *blood* relatives. But men and women may also have some responsibilities to the relatives of the person they marry, and these "in-laws" are called AFFINAL, *marital,* or *cognatic* relatives. It is difficult to take a marriage partner, with all the obligations that this involves, and ignore the ties that this partner has with his or her parents and siblings.

One of the most common principles by which a society may be organized is known as the UNILINEAL DESCENT GROUP. As shown in Figure 25 (p. 203) the unilineal principle means that an individual will be grouped to

[10] Tacitus, *Germania,* trans. by M. Hutton (Cambridge, Mass.: Harvard University Press, 1970), p. 131.

all his consanguineal relatives in the male line, in which case we talk of a PATRILINEAL descent group, or in the female line, a MATRILINEAL descent group. In a unilineal descent system every individual belongs to a patrilineage or matrilineage, depending upon the society in which he lives, and will be obligated to lend aid and assistance to all other members of this kinship group.

Clans can sometimes become so large that they split apart and become divided into a cluster of clans which still remember they share a common ancestry. Such clans constitute what is known as a PHRATRY. One other kinship grouping must be identified. This is the MOIETY. Many tribal peoples, like the Todas of India, divide the larger tribal society into two separate divisions, each made up by a number of clans. Moieties may be exogamous, but not necessarily so. Among the Todas the two moieties are unequal in status, and members of the socially superior moiety never marry those from the inferior moiety.

Nevertheless, there is always a limit beyond which men are not to be permitted to search for wives. In simpler societies this limit is usually enforced by simple geographical considerations, but in more sophisticated societies, patterns of culture, custom, and language tend to define the limits in which *connubium*, the right to marry, is permitted.[11] Consequently a tribe comes into being, which represents the sum total of interbreeding descent groups. The tribe is usually an endogamous group within which all marriages take place. Tribes, therefore, not clans or phratries, usually represent the effective gene pools in kinship-dominated human societies. Since the giving and taking of wives serves to link the member descent groups both genetically and culturally, a tribe may often be distinguished from its neighbors by distinctive physical similarities as well as by a distinctive dialect and folk tradition.

[11] See N. D. Fustel de Coulanges, *The Ancient City* (New York: Doubleday & Company, Inc., 1955).

Double Descent Groups

Variations on the patrilineal descent group include not only the matrilineal descent group, but a much more distinctive system known as double descent. DUOLINEAL or DOUBLE DESCENT SYSTEMS, common in many parts of West Africa,[12] differ from unilineal descent in that the individual does not disown his mother's relatives but considers himself a member of two descent groups, one traced patrilineally through his father and one traced matrilineally through his mother (see Fig. 25). The only persons who share the same pattern of kinship obligations in a double descent system will be siblings.

This is quite an important distinction, for whereas all the members in a unilineal descent group share an identical pattern of kinship responsibilities, in the double descent system only brothers and sisters will share the same pattern of matrilineal and patrilineal obligations. Double descent systems therefore tend to place more emphasis upon the individuality of each member of society. Thus among the Ibo of eastern Nigeria, where double descent prevails, all the members of a village belong to the same patriclan and all village matters fall under the direction of this patriclan. However, men also belong to matrilineal clans through their mothers' lineage, and there will therefore be a number of matriclans in each village. Although village affairs are handled by the patriclans, the matriclans are rigidly exogamous, and a man is strongly obligated to avenge members of either his patriclan or his matriclan. Eighty-five percent of the land is owned by the matriclans, each of which has a clan chief who is a man but who inherits his office through his mother's lineage. Thus the

[12] See A. R. Radcliffe-Brown, *African Systems of Kinship and Marriage.* (New York: Oxford University Press, 1950). Also Simon Ottenberg, *Double Descent in an African Society: The Afikpo Village-Group* (Seattle: University of Washington Press, 1968).

FIG. 25   UNILINEAL, BILATERAL, AND DOUBLE DESCENT SYSTEMS OF KINSHIP

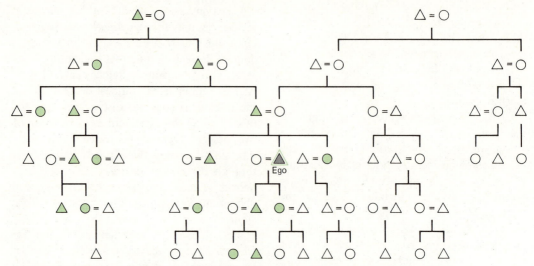

a. Kinship in a Patrilineal Clan System. Individuals indicated in solid color belong to same clan as Ego.

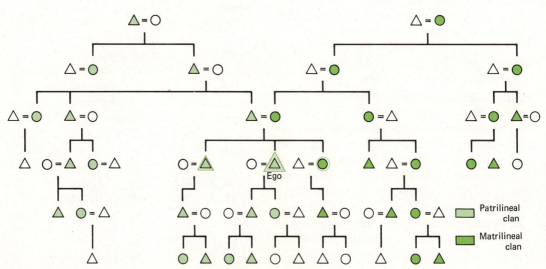

b. Bilineal Kinship. Ego belongs to two clan systems, one patrilineal and one matrilineal, each controlling distinct and separate areas of social obligation.

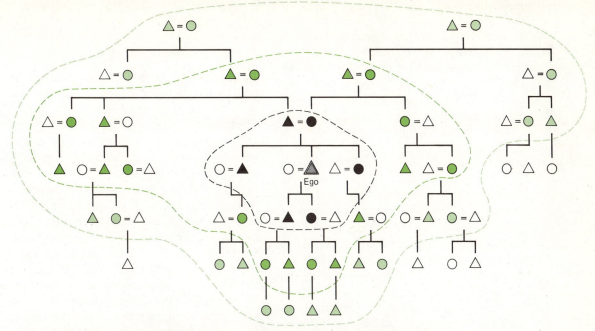

c. The "Kindred" in a Bilateral Kinship System. Ego is related to kinsmen through both male and female lines, but the degree of affinity becomes weaker as the number of kinship degrees separating the two kinsmen increases. Most bilateral systems have a definite "cut-off" point (for example, sixth or ninth degree of kinship) beyond which kin ties carry no special obligations beyond the responsibilities owed to any member of the tribe or nation.

pattern of Ibo life is organized around two types of descent group—the *matriclan* and the *patriclan*—but there is a natural division of function between the two, so that they are complementary and do not conflict with each other.

Bilateral Descent Groups

The trend toward individualism is even more heavily stressed by the genetically-oriented system of bilateral descent, which was characteristic of the North European peoples and is the type of kinship system which still predominates among most Euro-Americans. The BILATERAL DESCENT SYSTEM takes full recognition of the mother's as well as the father's relatives, regardless of whether they are male or female, and is most common where constant periods of turbulence or migration prevent unilineal clans from developing or else cause families to break away from the traditional clan

structure to pioneer new areas of settlement.

Since the bilateral descent groups recognize cognates or marital relatives, tracing descent through the mother's family as well as through the father's family, the area of kinship responsibility tends to be limited to individuals not more than two to three generations distant.[13] Without some such limitation, ultimately the whole of society would be included within every descent group! Thus, unlike unilineal and double descent systems the bilateral descent system does not emphasize lineages. Instead, the responsible kinship group is known as a KINDRED, and usually includes parents and grandparents, cousins and second cousins, sons, grandsons, and nephews on both sides of the family. The bilateral descent system is also still common in India where Hindu families

[13] See Paul Bohannan and John Middleton (eds.), *Kinship and Social Organizations*, Vol. IV, *Bilateral Systems and the Kindred* (New York: Natural History Press, 1968), pp. 233–272.

are customarily grouped in kindreds known as *sapiṇḍa,* comprising people who are descended from the same ancestor three generations removed, and *samanodaka* comprising all who are descended from the same ancestor six generations removed.

The kindred in a bilateral system is a constantly changing group, sometimes referred to as the *shifting kindred,* and bilateral descent groups consequently do not possess distinctive *patronymic* or lineage names. Thus in Iceland, as in ancient Scandinavia and England, there were formerly no surnames—no lineage names. A man was known as "the son of so and so." Indeed, in Iceland to this day, the son of a man called Hrothgar will be known perhaps as Edwin Hrothgarsson, while his sister, Sigrid, would be known as Sigrid Hrothgarsdotter (*dotter,* or "daughter"). Furthermore, since there are no clans in Iceland, a woman cannot join her husband's clan when she marries. She therefore keeps her own name, so that a man and wife may introduce themselves as Mr. Hrothgar Edwinsson and Mrs. Emma Hrothgarsdotter! Only when Christianity came to northern Europe did patronymics come to be introduced, in accordance with the Roman tradition, and names like Johnson and Peterson came to be retained permanently from generation to generation, in imitation of the clan patronymic honoring an eponymous forebear.

In order to trace their genealogies, the English and Scandinavian peoples formerly demonstrated kinship by a complex, interlocking pattern of rings instead of by the "family tree" tradition appropriate to unilineal descent groups such as the Romans possessed. Although the Roman system of recording genealogies has become universal in the Western world, it is clearly unsuitable for bilateral systems, and many anthropologists today prefer the idea of KINSHIP SETS, which can be used to portray any system.

Systems of Nomenclature

A key to the pattern of kinship relations that holds a society together may consequently be found in the system of nomenclature used.[14] These fall primarily into two main categories. DESCRIPTIVE NOMENCLATURE SYSTEMS designate each particular relative with a specific term, identifying his genetic connection to the speaker. The European and Euro-American systems tend in this direction, distinguishing first and second cousins from brothers and sisters, and nephews from sons and daughters. On the other hand, the Hawaiians and Eskimoes have CLASSIFICATORY NOMENCLATURE SYSTEMS which lump together all the members of a particular generation of relatives under the same term, so that a man addresses his father, his father's brother, and all his father's male cousins by the one term "father." A man's mother, her sisters, and all her female cousins are addressed as "mother," and similarly, no distinction is made between nephews and sons, nor between nieces and daughters.

Certain traditional terms are sometimes used to categorize the main types of kinship systems which customarily arise out of combinations of the above variables. These originated in the works of the nineteenth-century American pioneer anthropologist, Lewis H. Morgan.[15] Unfortunately his choice of labels was unscientific from a taxonomic point of view, since he chose these at random from various societies which exemplified the principle he wished to identify, and they therefore have no causal or taxonomic significance whatsoever.

According to these traditional labels, a bilateral system which merges all relatives at a

[14] See E. L. Schusky, *Manual of Kinship Analysis* (New York: Holt, Rinehart Winston, Inc., 1965).
[15] See Lewis H. Morgan, *Systems of Consanguinity and Affinity of the Human Family.* (Washington, D.C.: Smithsonian Contributions to Knowledge, 1875).

given generational level is called a *Hawaiian* system because it is found in Hawaii, among other places. Similarly, a bilateral system which views the direct ascendant and descendant relatives (parents and grandparents, sons and daughters, and so on) as distinct from the collateral relatives (brothers and cousins) is often called *Eskimo*.

A matrilineal system which merges the father's brothers with the father from the point of view of terminology, while distinguishing both from the mother's brothers (a practice called BIFURCATE MERGING), is customarily labelled *Crow*, after the Crow Indians of North America, while a patrilineal system which does the same thing is labelled *Omaha* after the Omaha Indians.

One other category of note is the *Sudanese*, which is distinctive in that in contrast to the Hawaiian system it uses separate descriptive terms for all relatives, thus emphasizing the individuality of each kinsman.

Fictive Kinship

In societies which are totally organized around a kinship system, a man therefore has no status nor any legal rights except as a member of a kinship descent group. For this reason many societies have invented systems of FICTIVE KINSHIP or "blood brotherhood." Traders entering a territory from foreign lands would have no security unless they could gain the protection of the local descent groups by a system of fictive kinship. Usually fictive kinship involves ritual ceremonies such as that followed by the Gypsies who cut the veins to allow the blood of the two persons to mingle. Thus trade frequently developed out of the fiction of an exchange of gifts between "blood brothers," before the idea of selling goods for profit was accepted as a morally valid activity.

We also find fictive *godparents* in Euro-American culture, who have no genetic rela-

tions, but who are expected to assume certain social obligations to their godchildren. A similar system, which appears to have been introduced by the Spaniards and has become widely adopted in Central and South America, is the *compadrazgo* or coparenthood system.[16] The Latin American *compadres* or godparents become responsible for the care and upbringing of a child in the event of the death of the parents, and also have obligations to supervise the moral and religious training of their fictive sons and daughters.

Kinship and Genetics

Although in our own society we tend to think of kinship as being essentially a matter of genetic relationship, it is incorrect to assume that in simpler societies, in which even the biological fact of paternity may be unknown, the idea of kinship always has genetic implications. Indeed, in most simpler societies kinship is determined by traditional social conventions which have little to do with actual genetic relationship. In such societies kinship is a matter of who lives with whom and who has social, political, and economic obligations to whom. Thus in societies in which wife lending is a widespread practice, a child who is born to a man's wife usually "belongs" to that man and is regarded as his son. In other cases, where descent is through the female line, it may be of no importance who the child's father is, because the child will belong to the mother's clan—and everyone knows who the child's mother is.

The concept of genetic relationship normally only becomes significant as social inequality begins to develop in a society and as the members of the upper social strata seek to assure themselves that their lineage has not been tainted by socially or racially "inferior"

16Honigmann, p. 438.

genes. Especially in societies which are patrilineal, the problem of determining legitimacy then becomes acute. Thus we shall see that the Baganda of East Africa carry out tests for legitimacy by dropping the natal cord into a pot of beer to see whether it floats or sinks. In patriarchal Republican Rome no child could be admitted to a *gens,* or clan-type descent group, until the father had picked the infant up in his arms as a token of his acceptance of the child's legitimacy. This was done publicly in front of the assembled kinsmen in a solemn ceremony known as *Levana,* "the uplifting." Similarly, in the classical period in ancient Athens nobody possessed citizenship unless his father had been a member of one of the free phratries and had appeared before the phratry to affirm that the child was his own legitimate offspring and that the child's mother had also been born into one of the free Greek phratries. Citizenship in the ancient Greek city or *polis* was a tribal right rooted in kinship, not a political privilege, and was granted exclusively to those who could claim it as a birthright.

For Further Reading

Beattie, J., 1964, "Kinship and Social Anthropology," *Man* 64:101–103.

Bender, D. R., 1967, "A Refinement of the Concept of Household: Families, Co-residence and Domestic Functions," *American Anthropologist* 69:493–504.

Buchler, I. R., and H. A. Selby, 1968, *Kinship and Social Organization: An Introduction to Theory and Methods.* New York: The Macmillan Company.

Elkin, A. P., 1964, *The Australian Aborigines.* Garden City, N. Y.: Natural History Press.

Evans-Pritchard, E. E., 1951, *Kinship and Marriage among the Nuer.* New York: Oxford University Press.

Fortes, M., 1969, *Kinship and the Social Order.* Chicago: Aldine Publishing Company.

Fox, R., 1967, *Kinship and Marriage.* Baltimore: Penguin Books, Inc.

Ghurye, G. S., 1962, *Family and Kin.* New York: Humanities Press, Inc.

Goody, Jack, 1971, *Kinship.* Baltimore: Penguin Books, Inc.

Günther, H. F. K., 1951, *Formen and Urgeschichte der Ehe.* Göttingen: "Musterschmidt" Wissenschaftlicher Verlag.

Lancaster, L., 1958, "Kinship in Anglo-Saxon Society," *British Journal of Sociology* 9:230–250.

Lévi-Strauss, C., 1963, *Totemism.* Boston: The Beacon Press.

———, 1967, *Les structures élémentaires de la parenté.* New York: Humanities Press, Inc.

Murdock, G. P., 1965, *Social Structure.* New York: The Free Press.

Radcliffe-Brown, A. R., 1950, *African Systems of Kinship and Marriage.* New York: Oxford University Press.

Schusky, E. L., 1965, *Manual of Kinship Analysis.* New York: Holt, Rinehart and Winston, Inc.

CHAPTER 16

Custom and Law

In nonhuman primate societies, social order is maintained primarily by the threat of physical coercion. Mothers chide and on occasion smack their infants, and dominant males rely on the threat of violence to control the behavior of subordinate males and females. It is rare that a dominant male baboon or gorilla will be obliged to resort to actual conflict in order to enforce discipline. Once a pattern of dominance has been asserted, it is usually only necessary for the leader of the group to raise his eyes and stare at the peacebreaker to bring the offender to order. If staring does not suffice, the leader may growl or even raise himself in readiness to charge the offender. But though the threat of force is normally adequate, the principle of physical coercion remains.

Primatologists recognize elemental mores in primate societies, and coercion is not necessarily enforced arbitrarily.[1] Undoubtedly there is a drive to maintain a basic harmony of thought and behavior in such societies, and

[1] P. Dolhinow, *Primate Patterns* (New York: Holt, Rinehart and Winston, Inc., 1972), pp. 369 ff.

once a particular group of males has achieved dominance, they suppress serious squabbling or fighting between members of the group. Social order and group unity are enforced because no society can afford constant conflict between its members.

In early human societies, however, kinship replaces the threat of conflict as the basis of social order. In small face-to-face societies, such as those of the Yahgan and Pygmies, children are so thoroughly socialized into the traditional patterns of kinship obligation that what we call *formal social controls*—coercion and the threat of physical force—are generally unnecessary. Instead, *informal social controls*, resting upon expressions of shame, ridicule, horror, and revulsion, on the one hand, and of approval and admiration on the other, are sufficient to establish a warning atmosphere of *social distance* between the guilty individual and his kinsmen. Since band membership is for life, few members are prepared to face the hostility and criticism of their kinsmen, and the erring member of a small human band will normally voluntarily correct his or her behavior in order to regain the approval and goodwill of the group.

In such band-type societies a high degree of social cohesion is inevitable. Lacking deliberately framed laws, the individual roles and statuses—transmitted as custom—are inculcated in the minds of all members during the early days of their childhood and are often heavily reinforced by magicoreligious precepts.

Through the intensely personal nature of their interaction, individuals tend to accept their roles in the group without question. Having few ideas or desires other than those which have been transmitted to them in the highly homogeneous culture of the group, they experience little sense of frustration or of freedom-denied. Each individual is permitted to act in whatever ways the culture has taught him to desire, and in the absence of any ideological

Eskimo bands, scattered widely over large expanses of land, are governed only by custom, not by law. Mild disputes are sometimes settled by song contests, in which the disputants vilify and ridicule each other in verse; but more serious disputes between nonkinsmen frequently end in death. (Courtesy of the late R. M. Sharp.)

schisms in his society, the individual seldom conceives of any course of action which his society will not approve. There is consequently relatively little sense of alienation, deprivation, or repression in primitive hunting and gathering communities. When disputes arise between individuals, these can generally be handled by informal social controls. Because of the smallness of the group, psychological pressures will generally be effective, and there are seldom any procedures for applying formal social controls. Only occasionally, when informal pressure fails to control a psychopathic member, do some groups resort to spontaneous murder. But such action is rare because of the development of kinship concepts, and outlawry or expulsion from the group is more common.

Public Contests

In most simple kinship societies there is thus no provision for any formal enforcement of custom, and the simpler human bands have no chiefs authorized to apply force in any form. However, peaceful and cooperative relations are a matter of concern to all members, and when a dispute arises, it is possible that an informal public hearing may be held at which the two opposing individuals publicly state their complaints. Such public hearings can hardly be regarded as trials, since the dispute is regarded essentially as a matter personal to the two contestants and there is no provision for enforcing a decision, even if a judgment were made, except by the power of unanimous social disapproval. Instead, the main function of such hearings is to enable the contestants to verbalize their complaints against each other publicly so as to get the dispute "off their chests."

Thus the Eskimoes, like the Icelanders of old, are often invited to settle a dispute in a public song contest, at which each complainant abuses and vilifies the other in verse.[2] The PUBLIC CONTEST does not purport to solve the dispute with justice, for the participant who insults the other with the greatest dexterity is judged the winner, but there is always the chance that the contest will serve to ease the tensions between the two disputants. The Arunta of Australia similarly encourage public contests between disputants. In their case, the contestants throw spears at each other, in what is normally a harmless ritual performed before the assembled relatives. Blood is seldom drawn, since it is easy to dodge a spear when one knows it is coming, but the contest serves to release tension. In one sense, the custom of the duel, which still persisted in Europe into this century, was another survival—though more deadly—of the ancient tradition of public contest.

Collective Responsibility

At more complex levels of kinship organization, the principle of COLLECTIVE RESPONSIBILITY usually applies. In such cases the individual is not left to defend himself, for since society is now larger and organized into clans or other kinship groupings, all kinsmen are collectively responsible for the protection and good behavior of their relatives. But in addition to protecting their kinsmen, the group will also seek to exact vengeance for injuries. This principle of collective responsibility is therefore often linked to the BLOOD FEUD,[3] a widespread institution among tribal peoples, involving the biblical maxim, "an eye for an eye and a tooth for a tooth." The members of each descent group are expected to revenge any

[2] Rockwell Kent, *N by E* (New York: Brewer and Warren, (1930), p. 250.

[3] For a penetrating historical analysis of the blood feud in ancient Europe, see J. T. Rosenthal, "Marriage and the Blood Feud in Heroic Europe," *British Journal of Sociology* 17:133–143 (1966).

injury done to one of their group, and feuds can develop which continue through the generations as sons revenge the deaths of their fathers.

There is a very good reason for the kinsman of an injured or murdered man to demand vengeance. In a society in which no man owes any obligation to those who are not his kinsmen, the only bar to widespread murder and pillage is the fear of retaliation. The members of a kin group who do not retaliate when one of their number is victimized will soon get a reputation for being easy victims, and will be ambushed and robbed by rival or alien kin groups with impunity, losing their women and their possessions if not their lives. In such conditions annihilation is the fate of the group which does not retaliate and take vengeance; a reputation for group loyalty and swift vengeance has positive survival value in the absence of any system of law enforcement.

But kinship-based societies do not always live in a cauldron of blood feuds. Wherever the blood feud is found, there is usually also a system of traditional composition payments or fines, by payment of which the danger of a blood feud may be avoided. Where physical assault is involved, such composition payments are usually referred to by anthropologists as WERGILD. Collective responsibility combined with the principle of the blood feud therefore means that when a man is injured, his relatives will unite to demand wergild from the relatives of the aggressor, according to a traditional scale of compensation which has evolved through time and precedent. The offender may be unable to raise the full amount of such wergild himself, but this does not matter, for under collective responsibility all the members of his descent group are obliged to contribute to the payment. In short, the conflict is not between two individuals, but between two descent groups; all of the aggressor's relatives must contribute toward raising the amount of

the wergild, which is then shared among all the relatives of the injured man.

The system of collective responsibility makes each man his brother's keeper, and rather than become responsible for paying wergild, the members of a descent group usually keep their more unruly members under tight control. Similarly, because the relatives of the injured man will share in the benefits derived from any compensation, bonus, or wergild they are able to collect, they have a direct and personal interest in standing by the rights of all their members. An actual feud only develops when the relatives of the accused refuse to pay the wergild, but this rarely happens, for few people desire to be faced with a blood feud if this can be evaded by a payment which is relatively light when shared by all the offender's relatives.

Determining Guilt

The main problem faced by societies which pay wergild is that of determining the guilt of the accused. In some cases, this may be achieved by reference to a mediator, such as the Leopard Skin Chief of the Nuer. In other cases, a tribal council or chieftain may arbitrate, since it is a matter of importance to the entire society that internal disputes between clans or other descent groups should be effectively resolved, lest an enemy take advantage of the prevailing state of dissension to stage an attack. Such arbiters may be selected because they are deemed to possess divine insights which enable them to detect the truth more accurately than lesser mortals, or else they may represent the leaders of the other clans.

Among the Homeric Greeks, disputes were argued before a council comprising the chiefs of the 12 clans of the tribe—a practice which was widespread among the Indo-Europeans and which leaves a vestigial trait in the English and American legal systems in the 12 members who still serve on a jury. In Homeric Greece, old Germany, and many parts of Europe, these 12 chiefs heard the evidence of "oath takers" or witnesses who were expected to swear to the innocence or guilt of the accused.[4] The duty of the *jury* was to check the validity of the evidence and to count the number of valid witnesses for each side, the decision going in favor of the group that produced the largest number of acceptable witnesses. But the jury never decided the penalty or the amount of the compensation; this was determined by precedent or custom. The function of the jury, as today, was limited to deciding the fact of guilt or innocence, and the king or presiding chieftain then pronounced the established and customary compensation. In later years in Europe, as the size of societies increased beyond the tribal system, the jury came to be composed of 12 local dignitaries, and the kings delegated their role as court chairmen to judges.

Although the jury system was common to many Indo-European societies, in other societies decisions regarding the innocence or guilt of the accused might be based on magical divination. The Baganda, for example, use magical oracles to determine the identity of the offender, as described in Chapter 28. Similarly, with the coming of Christianity to Europe, the Christian Church opposed the ancient custom of trial by jury and secured the right for Christians to opt for trial by a church court in which the decision concerning their guilt was arrived at by magicoreligious ordeals. Such trials, relying upon God to indicate by signs the guilt or innocence of the accused, proved popular with those who had reason to believe that they could not prove their innocence in front of witnesses and a jury.

[4] Judicial councils throughout tribal Europe usually numbered twelve members, see "Government in the Heroic Age," in H. M. Chadwick, *The Heroic Age* (London: Cambridge University Press, 1967), Chap. 18.

Private Law

In tribal societies based upon the principles of kinship, the maintenance of social order is essentially a matter of PRIVATE LAW. All disputes are regarded as disputes between kinship groups, and there is no authoritative state officer who is entitled to make arbitrary decisions. Even where the clan leaders sit as a jury, they are seldom authorized to enforce their decisions, and should the losing descent group refuse to pay the traditional wergild, a blood feud may result.

Should a dispute arise within a clan or a kindred, the kinship leader or possibly a kinship council may intervene, but since it is considered morally wrong to lay hands upon a kinsman, OUTLAWRY is the only penalty which can be imposed in such cases. An outlaw has in effect been placed outside the protection of society or in a tribal system outside the protection of his own kin group. He cannot possess property, and may even find his life in danger, for without the protection of kinsmen there is always someone ready to appropriate his possessions and slay him if he resists. Thus an outlaw was not someone who had voluntarily put himself outside the laws of his society, but was more usually someone who had been expelled from that society—a man unprotected by "law." The system is surprisingly effective, and costs nothing. It has even been suggested that outlawry might be an effective and economical way of punishing the more gross wrongdoers in our own society.

Outlawry usually follows FRATRICIDE, the killing of a kinsman or brother. The killing of a kinsman amounts to sacrilege in a kinship-based society but seldom attracts legal proceedings, since the offense concerns only his own descent group. Since the murderer is a kinsman, he cannot be slain because his blood is also sacred, so expulsion from the kinship group is the usual solution.

Public Law

When we reach the level of centralized chieftainships, in which the leader of society is able to exercise coercive power over his subjects, the concept of PUBLIC or CRIMINAL LAW appears. Whereas in private law the state or its representatives cannot intervene to enforce decisions, and compensation payments go to the injured individual and his kinsmen, under criminal law all offenses are regarded as offenses against the chieftain, king, or other representative of the state, and offenders will be prosecuted by the state and will be subjected to punishment by the state.

It is at this stage in the evolution of social order that the idea of punishment as a deterrent begins to supplant the idea of wergild as compensation, and formal social controls become institutionalized under the direction of the co-ordinating authorities. Thus, a king or chieftain may assume responsibility for enforcing law and order, but since the king will be obliged to maintain some kind of law enforcement agency, using his personal bodyguard perhaps for the apprehension of offenders, he must have some means of supporting these helpers. Eventually the customs change and instead of the full compensation being paid by the relatives of the offender to the relatives of the injured, half of this—and eventually the whole amount—may be paid to the king to compensate for his expenses in apprehending fugitives and enforcing justice.

When feudalism came into Europe and replaced the older tribal-type nations, private law came to be supplemented, though not entirely replaced, by criminal law. Indeed it was the kings of the Franks who first began to prosecute offenders, collecting the fine or wergild for the state treasury rather than allowing it to be paid to the relatives of the injured man. As a result of this development, today in Britain and America an individual who suffers as a result of a criminal action may receive no compensation from the criminal, although the criminal may be fined or otherwise punished by the state.

Once the king or state becomes responsible for maintaining social order and bringing offenders to trial, there is an inevitable tendency for the concept of punishment to replace the principle of compensation. The king or chieftain will not wish to be troubled by habitual offenders, who pay compensation only when forced to do so. In such cases the traditional compensation payments become converted into *fines,* intended as a deterrent to wrongdoers who flout the law, and an effort will be made to make an example of offenders. *Physical punishment* may be introduced as a supplement or substitute for the fine. Among the Baganda, offenders were cruelly punished, and in modern Libya and Arabia thieves are still punished by amputation of the offending hand. *Imprisonment* may also become common, on the principle that it is more convenient to keep habitual offenders locked up than to have the trouble of hunting them down each time they commit a new offense. The *death penalty* is an even cheaper and more spectacular way of dealing with serious offenders, especially when execution is performed publicly as among the Ashanti or in Medieval Europe.

Needless to say, the advantage of criminal law is that the state can afford to maintain a permanent police force to enforce law and to apprehend offenders. Where the police force is run efficiently, the law breaker is in a less happy position than under a system of private law. Also there can be no doubt that under the system of private law, blood feuds did sometimes get out of hand. In the eleventh century we find one Swedish king complaining that the constant blood feuds among his people were killing off all their best fighting men, so that he had difficulty in raising a strong army to protect the nation from its external enemies. State intervention in the matter of social order was perhaps inevitable, but even then the principle of collective responsibility did not die at once. The Hittite kings, for example, prosecuted justice but held all the relatives of a wrongdoer punishable for his crimes, extirpating an entire clan if just one of its members turned traitor. The Old Testament of the Bible states that a man's sins shall be visited on his children, and the Incas held village chiefs responsible for the actions of their villagers.

With the coming of centralized chieftains and the invention of criminal law, the opportunity for deliberate LEGISLATION or lawmaking also appears. Rooted in the principle of kinship, most tribal societies tend to regard LAW as being simply codified custom, but centralized chieftains abrogate to the state the right to modify old customs to suit their needs. Centralized chieftains are therefore often great "law givers," like Hammurabi of Mesopotamia and Asoka of India, who collect the old customs together, edit them, and publish them as "laws." Thus the concept of lawmaking becomes accepted. To this day, the English legal system still distinguishes between *common law,* based upon legal precedent and the idea of custom, and *statute law,* representing deliberately innovative laws enacted by the King in Parliament.

Law and Individual Freedom

With the old principle of private law steadily giving way to the idea of statute law, powerful rulers substitute state law for private law and custom, as Napoleon did with his Napoleonic Code. But statute law suffers from the fact that deliberate, man-made innovative laws may often conflict with the traditional customs and mores. While in a tribal society both laws and mores are essentially a part of the culture into which every individual is socialized, and are therefore accepted freely as a part of the content of socialization, in complex modern societies many laws come to be enacted which

offend against the values that an individual may have acquired in the course of his lifetime. In modern societies, therefore, deliberate man-made laws frequently seem to be repressive.

Because the problem of cultural divergency creates animosity and rebellion in multiethnic and multicultural modern states, many ruling political cliques have attempted to reimpose a state of cultural homogeneity upon all the members of culturally diverse states, in an effort to recreate the conditions of simpler, happier, traditional, culturally integrated societies. Thus many contemporary states employ government-appointed censors and seek to decide what may or may not be taught in schools and universities. Radio, television, and newspapers may be manipulated in such a way as to persuade the members of society to adopt a single coherent and homogeneous set of cultural values. The Incas effectively integrated all the members of their conquest state into a single cultural system, centered on the worship of the Sun God and his Incan descendants, by requiring children of conquered tribal leaders to attend school in Cuzco and then sending them back when adequately indoctrinated to rule their tribes as officials of the divine Inca king.[5] Similarly, modern totalitarian states— and even a number of those states which purport to be free societies—seek to suppress cultural variety by making attendance at government schools obligatory and then manipulating the educational curriculum.

There can be no doubt that where a homogeneous set of cultural values exists, into which all the members of society have been adequately socialized, there will be a substantial reduction in the number of offenses against the law, providing the law accurately reflects these cultural values. But the spontaneity of cultural homogeneity in small face-to-face societies cannot be recreated in complex societies,

[5]P. de Cieza de León, *The Incas,* trans. by H. de Onis (Norman: University of Oklahoma Press, 1959), Chap. 47.

for the division of labor and other factors tend constantly to create cultural variety. Attempts at deliberate thought control often cause individuals, enculturated into different subcultures, to react against the attack upon their own particular values.

Anthropology consequently reveals the inaccuracy of philosophical theories which portray the state as the product of a deliberate "social contract," entered into by intelligent men who were living alone but who desired to collaborate. Society is older than man, and men never agreed to renounce their freedom. In a primordial band which provides a virtually complete homogeneity of cultural experience, petty squabbles may develop, but ideological differences are nonexistent, and a man can seldom conceive of any course of action other than that to which he has become habituated since childhood. That which is done according to *tradition* in a primitive society therefore contravenes no one's freedom; only that which is done in opposition to tradition and custom can represent a violation of traditional "rights." But in the cultural complexity of industrial societies, much invention, innovation, and personal creativeness arises from the interaction of diverse subcultures. Attempts to suppress these subcultures and to blend all the diverse components of a complex society into a single mold can easily be interpreted as political oppression. There is no simple solution to the problem of maintaining order in complex societies without resorting to laws which may seem too oppressive to some and too lax to others.

For Further Reading

Fustel de Coulanges, N. D., 1970, *The Ancient City*. New York: Doubleday & Company, Inc.

Hartland, E. S., 1971, *Primitive Law*. Port Washington, N.Y.: Kennikat Press.

Hoebel, E. A., 1940, *The Political Organization and Law Ways of the Comanche Indians*. Washington, D.C.: American Anthropological Association, Memoir 54.

————, 1954, *The Law of Primitive Man: A Study in Comparative Legal Dynamics*. Cambridge, Mass.: Harvard University Press.

Hogbin, I., 1934, *Law and Order in Polynesia*. London: Bailey Bros.

Maine, Sir Henry, 1906, *Ancient Law*. New York: Henry Holt and Company, Inc.

Mair, Lucy, 1962, *Primitive Government*. Baltimore: Penguin Books, Inc.

Malinowski, B., 1926, *Crime and Custom in Savage Society*. London: Routledge and Kegan Paul, Ltd.

Puhvel, J., (ed.), 1970, *Myth and Law among the Indo-Europeans*. Berkeley: University of California Press.

Radcliffe-Brown, A. R., 1965, *Structure and Function in Primitive Society*. New York: The Free Press.

Rosenthal, J., 1966, "Marriage and the Blood Feud in Heroic Europe," *British Journal of Sociology* 17:133–144.

CHAPTER 17

Economic Organization

Economics is concerned with the problem of organizing the production, distribution, and consumption of material goods which are in short supply. Biological needs that are not in short supply—such as air and, in most societies, water—do not involve economic decisions; and where food is also plentifully available, it could be argued that simple human bands exist without ever being obliged to make a conscious economic decision. However, we may safely predict that sooner or later in all societies a shortage of food or other material necessities will arise, and an economic decision will have to be made. Even the simplest cultures must consequently decide what immediately consumable wealth such as food or more durable objects such as tools and furs shall be procured, who shall procure this wealth, and if a cooperative effort is required, who shall direct the effort. Furthermore, once these goods have been secured, a further economic decision is required to determine what proportion of the goods shall be distributed to partic-

ular individuals, and some regulation may even apply regarding the use to which these goods shall be put by the recipient.

Survival as a Group Activity

It is at this point that the significance of the pair-bond and kinship becomes apparent. Pair-bonding and food sharing develop simultaneously, and the family is a unit whose members face the problem of survival cooperatively. Kinship groupings represent units that are larger than the family, but whose members are linked by ascriptive obligations to assist each other in the struggle for survival.

In effect, all the members of a band-type society will be related by kinship. In band societies the economic system is therefore only another facet of the kinship system. Economic rights and obligations are seen as kinship rights and obligations, adjusted to a basic division of labor which reflects the biological functions of

215

the sexes and the different capacities of the young, the mature, and the aged. Thus among the Bushmen of the Kalahari Desert it is the men who hunt antelope and other game, while the women, assisted by the children and hindered by the very young, gather what food they can closer to the camp. While the men may sometimes glut themselves from a recent kill without waiting to return to camp, tradition requires that none of the band shall be allowed to starve. Among the Arunta of Australia the customs governing the distribution of food are even more elaborate, separate parts of the slaughtered animal being reserved for the men, the womenfolk, and the children.

At the hunting and gathering level of human society, the survival of the group thus tends to take precedence over the interests of the individual. The reward for the more efficient hunter is not greater wealth nor a more satisfied stomach, but the approval of his kinsmen and higher status among his fellows. What is produced is produced for the band. The lazy individual or the poor hunter does not necessarily lose his claim to share in the food caught by others, but by contributing to the economy of the band, the individual demonstrates himself to be a loyal member of the group, and his social life will be pleasanter as he bathes in the approval of his fellows.

The Concept of Property

In our society the concept of *property* is so intimately bound up with the idea of *economic wealth*—goods which are in short supply and have "value in exchange"—that many writers, including even anthropologists, assume that property is necessarily equivalent to economic wealth, resulting in the frequent misinterpretation of the nature of economic life in simpler societies. The plain fact is that people living in simpler societies have radically different ideas as to the nature of property

from those generally held in our own society.[1]

In simple hunting and gathering societies, the idea of private property is generally associated with psychological, magical, and religious concepts rather than with economics. Private property, in the sense of individual ownership of land or the means of production, does not exist because survival is a group activity, and the hunting lands or territory belong to the group as a whole. Since survival is primarily a group function, land that provides food for the group belongs to the group, and few peoples who hunt for a living have any notions of individual landownership. All things that have survival utility are essentially communal property, in the sense that the welfare of the economic band, held together by kinship ties and mutual responsibilities, is a communal and not an individual affair. All the productive resources of the group must, when necessary, be shared with other members of the group; for example, tools and weapons necessary for survival are freely loaned by Eskimoes from one member of the band to another and are not always returned.

Yet this is not to say that there is no concept of personal property. Men become emotionally involved with the things that they habitually wear on their bodies, or carry with them in their hands. The things that become closely associated with an individual come to be regarded as his "property," containing some of his personality, and in this sense the concept of personal property is present in even the simplest human societies. The evidence of burial among hunters and gatherers from Neanderthal societies onward indicates that those things which a man creates and habitually uses are believed to acquire something of his personality, and for this reason they are frequently destroyed at his death or else buried

[1] See M. J. Herskovitz, *Economic Anthropology* (New York: Alfred A. Knopf, Inc., 1960), Chap. 14. Also Max Weber, *General Economic History* (New York: The Free Press, 1950), Chap. 1.

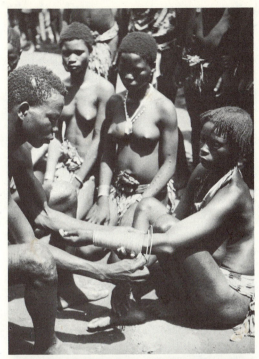

with him. Just as the human child develops close emotional bonds with particular toys—a sense of property which is psychological rather than based on market value—so property in simple human societies has its roots in psychological and magicoreligious forces rather than in economic exploitation. Some social theorists have advocated the abolition of private property, stressing the fact that primitive human societies take economic cooperation for granted, but their arguments overlook the psychological quality of property, underlying the most ancient cultural traditions of mankind. Early man probably never knew private property in the modern sense of economic wealth, but there is considerable evidence of strong psychic ties linking individuals to specific material objects.

In closed kinship societies, private property consequently consists of those very personal artifacts which, because of their close association with the human body of their owner, acquire some of his magical powers and become imbued with some of the qualities of the person who customarily uses them. Charms, talismans, and magical amulets, such as the G-string which the Australian aboriginal makes from the hair of his dead father, are quite definitely private property.[2] Indeed, none but the legitimate heir to the dead man's magic would consider wearing an Arunta G-string. Primitive societies have the concept of "property in use," but the idea of owning something which is not intimately associated with the owner because of "value in exchange" does not

[2] The magical properties are effective only for persons entitled by kinship to wear these tassels. Thus they may be regarded as private property in that they have "value in use" only for the wearer.

In societies which have not yet developed a market economy wealth has little value except as a status symbol. (*Top*) Women of the Republic of Chad being fitted with ornamental armbands. (*Bottom*) Married woman from the Republic of the Congo wearing-displaying her wealth of neck and arm ornaments. (Courtesy of La Documentation Française, Paris.)

exist. There is no trade or barter within the group, and all material assets which contribute toward the survival of the band, such as land, are shared as need be. Early men never thought to exploit their kinsmen in order to increase their own share of economic wealth, even though the idea of personal property—in the sense of physical objects to which man becomes emotionally attached—appears to be one of the basic cultural traits that distinguish human from animal societies.

The Growth of the "Household"

In more complex societies in which the total size of the community is larger and the production of material wealth is greater, the pattern of interpersonal relationships must necessarily be more complex than in smaller groups, allowing greater variety of potential social relationships to develop. In such cases, the personal bonds linking all individuals as a group will be less intimate, and material objects, even of a utilitarian type, will come to be more closely identified with the family that habitually uses them. Land and animals may cease to be communally owned by the total society, the right to the "possession" or use of particular land and animals becoming particularized in HOUSEHOLDS representing separate families or lineages.

As knowledge of methods of cultivation and the domestication of animals increases productivity, human settlements expand in size, leading to a more distinct separation of interest between the individual family and the enlarged society. Although the bonds of overall community interest are not lost, the family preserves the communal ethos more strongly than does society as a whole. Every member of the family has a right to be fed, housed, and, if the culture requires it, clothed. Differences in status may arise within the family, but in general food and other essential commodities are

shared as a matter of obligatory right, and no one in the family will be permitted to starve. The custom of *inheritance* of property arises out of the recognition of the family or lineage as a property-owning unit—with a permanent right, for example, as among the Haida Indians of British Columbia, to a specific house site. The successive generations of family members inherit the family property for the very reason that the property belongs to the family as a unit, not to individuals. In short, the ancient concept of communal primary groups has not disappeared. The concepts of family and community are now more distinct, but as the basic primary group, the family preserves the spirit of "shared destiny" that characterized the smaller family band of earlier times. The individual has no "testatory" or proprietorial rights over any property which is essential to the survival of the lineage. As a family member he enjoys the family property during his life, but cannot dispose of this property outside of the family either during his life or on his death bed.[3]

Reciprocity

Despite the individualization of economic wealth among families and lineages at this level of economic evolution, men still desire to prove their loyalty to the total group and to their fellow members of society. The most effective way of showing goodwill is by making a contribution to the welfare of the individual concerned, and the gift of a tool or a furskin rug conveys such a message of friendship. But the man who receives proof of another's good intentions toward him will also normally wish to make a similar gift in return, in order to prove his own good intentions. This situation can lead to a tradition of *reciprocal*

[3] But even when movable property has become particularized in separate families, land may remain the property of the entire village community.

Heavy ankle bracelets worn by Tchikoumbi women of the Peoples' Republic of the Congo. (Courtesy of La Documentation Française, Paris.)

gift giving, by which wealth passes back and forth between the different families in the total community in a series of gift-giving exchanges. Such gifts usually comprise food—either in a storable form or else as an invitation to participate in a feast—furskin pelts, or ornaments and ritual objects. But when the gift contains something of the magical aura of the giver's body, the symbolism is even higher, for the gift then serves to bind the giver and receiver together in a mystical union, and henceforth they will be united by shared supernatural forces, not merely by the fact of having exchanged usable wealth.

It is probable that the idea of making gifts at the time of marriage also originated out of this concept of reciprocal gift giving. Since the bride's family is giving one of its members to the bridegroom's family, some reciprocal gift should be made in return to prove goodwill. In a simple way the Pygmies make the reciprocal gift of a bride in return for the provision of a bride for one of their group. It is easy to see how this may develop into the idea of a gift of wealth in return for a bride, and how

in due course such a gift can become an actual payment or *bride price,* the subject of protracted negotiations and haggling.[4]

Reciprocal gift giving is in no way to be confused with the trading that takes place in a market economy. It occurs only between kinsmen, but it can lead to inequalities of status. Thus, among the Haida Indians, who have more wealth than they can consume, the habit of reciprocal gift giving as an honor-earning activity has developed to elaborate levels, culminating in the gift-giving ceremony known as the *potlatch,* described in Chapter 25. Even though the Haida cannot themselves consume all the pelts and elaborately carved ritual objects they accumulate, the fact that a family can earn honor, prestige, and status by giving away such wealth means that differences in rank arise, and those families that accumulate most wealth achieve higher status by outdoing the others in the extent of their generosity. Since this gift giving is essentially reciprocal, however, those who give wealth away in due

[4] Herskovitz, pp. 381 ff.

Gift-giving plays an important part in the lives of most kinship-oriented societies. In the Fiji Islands any event of importance is preceded by massive gift distribution. The above scene depicts a spokesman, attired formally in modern Western clothing, presenting a giant sea turtle and a mound of *taro*—one of the basic Fijian foods—on behalf of the group seated in the background. (Courtesy of the Public Relations Office, Fiji Government.)

course become the recipients of reciprocal gifts, possibly even more munificent in their proportions. In this way there arises a class of noble families who are able to make huge property gifts to each other, while those families that cannot afford to participate in their gift-giving round of potlatch parties become regarded as inferior "commoners."

In Melanesia also, reciprocal gift giving ceremonies have led to the rise of a similar superior class, the heads of the more respected families becoming known as "Big Men."[5] An

[5] M. Mead, *Cooperation and Competition among Primitive Peoples* (New York: McGraw-Hill, Inc., 1937), Chap. 1.

entire Arapesh kinship group, occupying its own village, works to breed and feed pigs which are then slaughtered and given by the "Big Man" or leader as gifts to another "Big Man" representing a neighboring clan group, who has to provide a similar gift in return. As with the Haida, the occasion is an opportunity for ceremonial feasting and religious ritual.

Redistribution

In many cases the idea of communal ownership of the means of subsistence may survive into advanced horticultural and even agrarian societies. Thus the Slavic *zadruga*, described in Chapter 24, continued to own all land communally, retaining only the character of an extended family.[6] Even though larger social groupings develop, the ownership of land and animals will remain for a time within clans, as among the reindeer-herding Tungus and the cattle-herding Kazaks, who brand the animals with separate clan crests and among whom each clan has a separate territory.[7] Eventually, however, the ownership of land and animals may also become particularized in separate families. When this happens the seniormost adult male may be regarded as the representative of his own family grouping and so may be regarded nominally, at least, as the "householder." While the total territory held by the community usually remains the communal property of the entire clan or village, particular plots of land may be allocated to families for cultivation in the case of horticulturalists or agriculturalists, or for herding animals in the case of pastoralists. This allocation is usually made directly to families or households, for the household now becomes a clearly distinct economic unit—the basic element of the economy.

Once this happens, the respective households usually retain the food which their labors produce on the land allocated to them, and very real inequalities of economic wealth can begin to appear. In order to prevent gross disparities from arising, rules may exist requiring the periodic redistribution of land or even animals. Thus, in Anglo-Saxon England each family in a village received a new allocation of land each year to ensure that no one

family had a monopoly of the best land. Among extended families a periodic redistribution per capita may be made, as with the ancient Irish *fine* or extended family group, to ensure that a family with more sons is not left with less land per capita than the family with only one son.[8] Similarily, as C. Daryll Forde has recorded, Tungus clans regard their reindeer as the property of individual families, but should one family lose its herd in a disaster, it can obtain fresh animals from other families. No family is allowed to starve.

Yet redistributive systems of exchange do not always lead to equality. The complexity of the societies that we are now discussing necessitates a coordinating or ruling class of clan leaders, village chieftains, and even of tribal monarchs, who devote much of their time to the management of the cooperative affairs. To support them while they devote themselves to the commonweal, gifts may be made to them by their fellow tribesmen or villagers. In the course of time custom may conventionalize these gifts into a tribute or *corvée*, a form of traditionally determined taxation.[9] As with the reindeer that are reassigned to a luckless Tungus family facing starvation, this transfer of wealth is not a reciprocal affair; it is a one way transaction, hence the term *redistribution.*

Like the Central American *cacique*, or clan chief, who received gifts of food and labor from his clansmen, the chieftain who accepts such gifts is not necessarily exploiting his community. In many cases he will devote his life to the welfare of his community with considerable integrity, believing his duties to be a sacred obligation. The gifts are made in order that he shall be free to devote himself to wise thoughts, brave deeds, and the correct obser-

[6] Philip E. Mosely, "The Zadruga," in C. F. Ware (ed.), *The Cultural Approach to History* (New York: Gordon Press, 1940), pp. 95–108.

[7] Among the Kazaks only the winter quarters are regarded as the property of separate clans. In summer the grazing lands are more than ample to satisfy the needs of all and are not particularized between clans. See C. Daryll Forde, *Habitat, Economy, and Society* (New York: E. P. Dutton & Co. Inc., 1963), p. 333.

[8] See T. G. E. Powell, *The Celts* (New York: Frederick A. Praeger, Inc., 1958), for further discussion of Irish property ownership.

[9] P. Boissonnade, *Life and Work in Medieval Europe* (New York: Alfred A. Knopf, Inc., 1937), pp. 92 ff.

vance of the religious rituals that may also devolve upon him as the official leader of the total community. But of course the opportunities for exploitation increase as the size of the community increases, especially if a philosophy of individualism replaces the old kinship ties.

Slavery

In more advanced societies one of the main factors which contributes to social stratification and to the abandonment of the principle of the communality of property is the invention of slavery. In particular, in cultivating societies slavery leads rapidly to the destruction of the idea of the common ownership of land. Slavery is indeed a very ancient institution, arising quite early after the invention of cultivation and pastoralism. While it is not possible to make use of a slave in the hunting field—for it is seldom wise to give a slave a spear or other weapon and then trust him to follow his owner through the brush—slaves can always be used to till fields or tend herds. The slave with a hoe can do the back-breaking work of cultivation, and is no challenge to the man with a spear.

Since most societies at this stage of evolution have surplus land available for cultivation or for the herding of larger flocks, a slave-owning family can take in the extra land and put it to use with the aid of their slaves. Thus noble families, descended from those whose prowess in war led them to accumulate slaves, find themselves regularly cultivating more land than the other members of their community, or else herding larger flocks than their fellows. In Europe especially, a distinction arose between the *folkland* still held communally by the villagers and the *bookland* granted by the king to noble warrior families, which was cultivated by their slaves or serfs. Bookland was so-called because a written record was kept of the land grant; while the folkland of the vil-

lages was held through tradition and was not redistributed but was the permanent property of the family which cultivated it. Our modern *freehold* land is the direct descendant of medieval bookland.[10]

Slavery is also found in some fishing societies, and we see an example of slavery in a fishing society when we study the Haida. A man whose life is spared in war is expected to work for his "benefactor" in return for the debt of his life. Although the Haida could use slaves only for menial tasks, for a slave could not be sent out in a fishing boat in which he might escape, the cultivator or the pastoralist can make ready use of the slave's labors to help him cultivate more land or herd more sheep and cattle than his own wives, sons, and daughters could manage unaided by slave labor.

The variety of reciprocal and contractual relations which may link one man to another is actually so great that slavery cannot be defined in purely economic terms. Among the South American Chaco Indians, for example, the only way to make an unruly slave obey his master was for the master to threaten to take away the horse and other equipment which he had been supplied, and to refuse him work and protection. In such a case, some might suggest that the relationship was that of employee and employer rather than slave and master, but the crucial fact was that in the eyes of society the slave was not a kinsman, but a nonperson who could not own property and possessed no rights to the use of the communal property.

In kinship-based societies, a SLAVE is a man, woman, or child who is not a member of the kin group and who therefore has no rights except as the property of someone who is a kinsman. However, in urban civilizations the concept of property tends to supplant the principle of kinship significance, and slavery becomes more closely associated with economic

[10] F. M. Stanton, *Anglo-Saxon England* (London: Oxford University Press, 1955), pp. 305-308.

factors. Thus in ancient Sumeria and among the Aztecs a free citizen might enter into a condition of slavery as a penalty for crime, or in order to work off a debt—and at the end of an agreed period of satisfactory service he might achieve his freedom again. Such arrangements are close to the system of indentured or contract labor. Is the modern American football player a slave to the team with which he is contracted? No, for his society does not regard him as being private property and protects his rights in an infinite variety of ways, even though he can be forced to work in accordance with his agreement, and in this sense can be "sold" from one club to another.

The Rise of Commerce

Even in hunting and gathering societies which are partially segregated from each other, some trade may be found between communities, although the idea of exchanging goods for a profit *within* the community would be rare. Thus the Pygmies trade forest produce with the neighboring Negro tribes, receiving horticultural produce in exchange. At the Neolithic level few communities are entirely isolated economically, and in agricultural societies there is always a constant exchange of surplus specialist produce with neighboring communities.

At first, this exchange of surplus produce is achieved by BARTER, which is an exchange of goods for the purpose of self-benefit without the use of money or any other symbol of value. The idea of *profit* is overtly present where barter is concerned, and that is why barter first emerges between unrelated communities, not within a community where the fiction of exchanging gifts is kept up rather than admit to attempting to make a profit out of a fellow villager and kinsman.[11]

[11] For discussion concerning rise of capitalism, see also Max Weber, *The Theory of Social and Economic Organization,* trans. by A. M. Henderson and Talcott Parsons (New York. The Free Press, 1956), pp. 279–280.

Slavery was the common basis of urban civilization in preindustrial societies. The Romans enslaved whole populations of defeated towns, including even members of the educated aristocracy, using Greek slave philosophers to tutor their children. Portrayed above are Philonicus and Demetrius, two "freedmen" whose slave status had been manumitted by their Roman owner, Publius Licinius, for loyal service. (Courtesy of the British Museum, London.)

In Neolithic societies certain families, lineages, and clans may become specialized as traders and begin to travel widely, establishing regular trading relations with particular host customers. Thus in early agricultural Europe, and even earlier in the Mesolithic, amber from the Baltic was traded by these itinerant merchants for pottery from the Mediterranean and many other specialist products, often over distances of hundreds of miles. Under the stimulus of a regular export trade, entire villages, still usually representing a single lineage, began to concentrate on the mining of flint and salt, and on the manufacture of spearheads, bows and arrows, and silver ornaments. Barter for profit developed as an international or intercommunity trade before it intervened in the life of the local settlements, which still remained largely communal in their concept of property. The itinerant craftsmen and merchants who still visit the village of Gopalpur in South India are an example of professional traveling specialists who operate for a profit, while the specialists who live in the village are still supposed to receive traditional fees or gifts for their services without any element of debate or negotiation. For so long as lineal settlements survived, in which all men and women were regarded as being close kinsmen, the idea of barter or trade within the community remained inhibited. Only with multilineal communities are the barriers against trading and bartering within the community removed, and individualism and the profit motive begin to replace the older communalism.

However, the mistrust that exists between all people who are not kinsmen has to be overcome before barter can develop between communities. In some cases, to avoid personal contact, goods may simply be left in a forest clearing or other recognized exchange place, as is customary in some instances such as trade between Negroes and Pygmies. After one trading partner has left his wares, the other will come along to the clearing and place against each object on display the items which he is prepared to offer in exchange. After his departure the first party will return, and where the exchange is acceptable, the goods will be removed, but when the offer is unacceptable, the proferred goods will be allowed to remain where they lie.

Such a system does not in itself overcome the psychological barrier to more efficient trading relations. In most societies in which barter is known, the answer is to extend blood

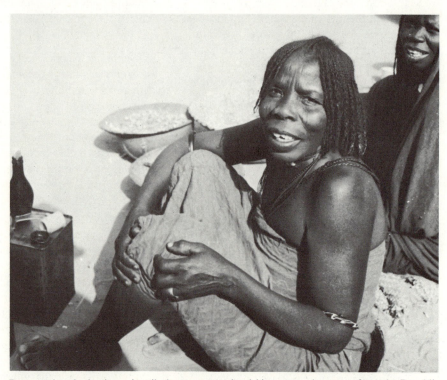

Barter and trade develop primarily between nonrelated kin groups. A woman from the Republic of the Chad, waiting to trade her wares at a local trading center. (Courtesy of La Documentation Française, Paris.)

brotherhood to the trading partner, and then the trade is treated as though it were an exchange of gifts between kinsmen. Thus the Haida trade only with recognized trading partners among other Indian tribes along the coast, visiting these annually to exchange goods.

In the South Pacific a very famous trading system, known as the Kula Ring, developed on the same principle. Among the Melanesians living on a group of islands off the east coast of New Guinea, long and dangerous voyages are attempted ostensibly for the purpose of exchanging armbands and necklaces of white and red shells. The white shell armbands called *mwali* are taken from one island to the next in a counterclockwise direction, where they are exchanged with the residents for red shell necklaces called *soulava*. These residents then take them on to the next group of islands to effect similar exchanges. Thus the *mwali* and *soulava* continually travel in their respective counterclockwise and clockwise directions around the group of islands in the Kula Ring in a series of voyages accompanied by feasting, dancing, and much ceremonial show of friendship.[12]

At first sight this would appear to represent an absurd expenditure of energy—and a considerable hazard because of the long sea voyages undertaken in small outrigger craft—simply to maintain ties of friendship between people who really have no need to meet. But the reality is that the exchange of these symbolic gifts acts as a ceremonial and symbolic cover for the real business, which is the barter of other articles not available in all the islands which are linked by this method. After the symbolic gift giving is over, and all the courtesies have been completed, the voyagers return to their homes with more than the *mwali* or *soulava* which they have been given.

[12] See B. Malinowski, *Argonauts of the Western Pacific* (New York: E. P. Dutton & Co., Inc., 1922), and "Kula: The Circulating Exchanges of Valuables in the Archipelagos of Eastern New Guinea," by the same author, in *Man* 20:97–105 (1920).

The invention of money as a token of value greatly facilitated the development of a market economy. The first tokens to be stamped with a crest as evidence of their value appeared in Sumeria. Pictured above are early Greek coins. (Courtesy of the British Museum, London.)

FIG. 26   THE KULA RING

Map showing some of the major islands linked by the Kula trade. The Soulava goes counterclockwise, and the Mwali goes clockwise. Islands included in the Kula Ring are in italics.

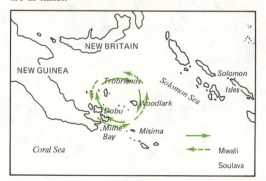

Under feudalism the resources of a society can be readily canalized into selected social projects, among which religious activities normally play a prominent role. Elaborate altar piece sculpted in stone in a medieval Catholic cathedral, Portugal. (Courtesy of the Director-General of Information, Portugal.)

Economic Implications of Feudalism

Feudalism represents a combination of the family-household principle with the idea of a division of labor and a hierarchical system of centralized control. While it preserves the ancient idea of society as an economically integrated whole whose members labor together to produce wealth for the common good, it introduces an elaborate division of labor and an almost bureaucratic control system which works to replace clan and tribal rights and substitutes property for the idea of kinship as the basis of social organization. Furthermore, although tribal society seldom loses sight of the ancient belief in the ultimate equality of all free-born kinsmen, feudalism asserts the right of different role players to different economic rewards, according to the importance of their role.

Feudalism preserves the idea that the land belongs to the total community, but the title to the land becomes vested in the central chieftain who holds this land, theoretically at least, for the community as a whole. The chieftain is then responsible for the allocation of land to subordinate chiefs and subchiefs, who in turn allocate it out to individual family or household heads. The whole fabric is held together not by bonds of kinship but by the emphasis on contracted obligations inherent in the acceptance of a grant of land, and on the reciprocal obligations of every role player to the total society, as personified by the ultimate dispenser of land, the king or chieftain.

From an economic point of view, feudalism represents a very logical development. Full-time professional specialists skilled in the manipulation of the supernatural or in the art of war must be supported by the agriculturalists and the craftsmen, who now produce more goods than they and their families can consume. In return for their services as producers of food, clothing, and metalwork, or whatever their speciality may be, the workers receive the benefit of being administered by the chieftain and his officials, of having their disputes settled by professional judges and lawyers, and of being protected from the ravages of rival armies by professional soldiers and from the wrath of their gods by the intercession of professional clergy.

While it is true that some feudal societies were technologically simple and socially barbaric, as was the case with the Baganda; others were to produce some of the most rapid cultural advances that the world has ever seen in the fields of art, science, literature, and other human attainments, under the patronage of cultured aristocrats. But in both cases feudalism represents a stage in the evolution of more modern economic systems in that it effectively combines the idea of a community of welfare, of functional interdependence of society, with a hierarchical and virtually bureaucratic division of labor which is in many ways intensely modern.

Property as Wealth in Exchange

It is with the rise to importance of the merchants that the foundations of capitalism and individualism are laid, both deriving from the concept of a MARKET ECONOMY—an economic situation in which production is for exchange rather than for subsistence, and the emphasis is upon exchanging the surplus to the maximum advantage of the individual making the exchange. Although in a market economy some remnants of community consciousness and of tribal and national consciousness may survive, these sentiments may be the strongest among

Market day in a contemporary Uganda market village. (Courtesy of the Uganda Government Ministry of Information.)

those who are least successful in a pattern of life which is rooted in the personal profit motive. The benefit that may be won from additional time spent on production may be small compared to that which may be lost or won in a successful exchange of commodities. But the profit made from an exchange of commodities is to a large extent obtained at the expense of the person with whom the exchange has been negotiated. Although both parties may benefit from an exchange of surplus produce, there is no economic law that says both parties shall benefit equally.

Consequently it is the merchants who first rebel against the older tradition of a society as a functional whole and demand economic freedom. Merchants may apply to kings for special privileges exempting them or the cities in which they live from the pattern of national obligations and national interdependence. In a feudal society the kings, nobles, chieftains, and subchiefs were intimately tied to the welfare of the community as a whole, for their prosperity was the outcome of a prosperous society. The merchant, however, has a constant temptation to maximize his own returns at the expense of other members of his community, and if he can make a better profit by trading with other societies, he may turn his back upon his own people. Commerce also leads to a new emphasis upon property in the form of *capital.* Anything that has value and can be traded or used to produce further wealth is converted into private property, even though the owner may never see it nor have any direct emotional or personal relationship with it. While the clan chief and even the feudal baron felt a loyalty and attachment to "his" land and to "his"

people, the successful merchant believes nothing has value except in exchange. All values become economic values. The goodness of a thing comes to be measured by its utility to produce further wealth in exchange. Even land, traditionally bound to the kinship group by the primordial relationship between "blood" and "soil," ceases to be regarded as a birthright of the group, ceases to be seen as the homeland of the people, and becomes instead just another item to be traded for a profit.

As a result of this change in the concept of property, which now sees property not as something personally and intimately associated with the owner and his kinsmen but instead as something that can be bought or sold, society becomes profoundly changed. Communities and nations become conglomerates of individuals, each individual engaged in a kind of economic war against the other, each individual seeking to maximize his own profit at the expense of his own countrymen. The wealth which once belonged to the kin group is now exchanged as economic wealth in a series of bitterly contested bargains. Tribal and national loyalties decline. Even within the family an attempt may be made to divide what is owned between man and wife as individuals, each jealous of their separate "bank accounts," thus negating the ancient tradition of the family as a cooperating group facing the problem of survival as a joint endeavor. Indeed, the voyage of mankind has brought us, at the industrial level, to a discouraging and dangerous position, midway between the friendless Scylla of excessive individualism and the impersonal Charybdis of the totally planned, bureaucratic, state-controlled economy.

For Further Reading

Belshaw, C. S., 1949, *In Search of Wealth.* Washington, D. C.: American Anthropological Association, Memoir 80.

Dalton, G., 1972, "Primitive Money," in J. D. Jennings and E. A. Hoebel, eds., *Readings in Anthropology.* New York: McGraw-Hill, Inc.

Firth, R., 1959, *Economics of the New Zealand Maori,* 2d ed. New York: Humanities Press, Inc.

Forde, C. D., 1937, *Habitat, Economy and Society.* New York: E. P. Dutton & Co., Inc.

Gabel, C., 1967, *Analysis of Prehistoric Economic Patterns.* New York: Holt, Rinehart and Winston, Inc.

Herskovits, M. J., 1960, *Economic Anthropology. A Study in Comparative Economics.* New York: Alfred A. Knopf.

Le Clair, E. E. Jr., and H. K. Schneider, 1968, *Economic Anthropology: Readings in Theory and Analysis.* New York: Holt, Rinehart and Winston, Inc.

Mauss, M., 1967, *The Gift.* New York: W. W. Norton & Co.

Pospisil, L., 1963, *The Kapauku Papuans of West New Guinea.* New York: Holt, Rinehart and Winston, Inc.

Weber, M., 1947, *The Theory of Social and Economic Organization.* New York: The Free Press.

———, 1950, *General Economic Theory.* New York: The Free Press.

CHAPTER 18

Social Stratification

Man is essentially a discriminating animal in that he is able to assess and interpret situations in which he finds himself, and then vary his conduct in order to adjust his behavior to the circumstances. Men discriminate between those situations and choices of action that seem to promise favorable responses to their needs and desires and those which seem less favorable. We can readily see how this leads to value judgments in regard to different aspects of the material environment. It does not take a great deal of reflection to come to the realization that such patterns of selective discrimination and prejudgment may also affect the individual's evaluation of social situations involving other men and women.

Since men are social animals and find most of their satisfaction in a group setting, all men tend to seek situations which will place them in a favorable relationship with their fellows. The member of society who is respected or appreciated by his fellow beings enjoys several benefits. His anxiety concerning his future survival will be assuaged and even replaced by a feeling of assured confidence. He can be secure in the knowledge that he may expect the support and cooperation from the fellow members of his group in times of need and that he has no need to fear expulsion from the group. Since so much depends upon successful group participation, a consciousness of the approval of society thus carries immediate psychological rewards.

Status

In consequence there is a universal tendency for men living in groups to seek the approval or respect of their fellows; in other words, to seek status. A man's STATUS reflects the extent to which he possesses those properties most highly valued in the culture of the group.

Social stratification may be said to exist when there is a general and conscious ranking of individuals on a scale of status superiority or inferiority. Such status judgments are made by individuals, but since they are rooted in the cultural system of the society, we may expect

FIG. 27   SOCIAL STATUS: DETERMINANTS OF STATUS IN THREE DIFFERENT KINDS OF SOCIETY

Status in an Equalitarian Society
(Most hunting and food gathering bands)

    Prestige
    (personal qualities) ⟶ Status

Status in a Rank Society
(Elementary horticulturalists and simple pastoralists)

    Prestige
    (personal qualities)
              ⟶ Status
    Authoritative Power
    (elected or inherited office)

Status in a Stratified Society
(Advanced horticulturalist, advanced pastoralist, fishing, agrarian, and industrial)

    Prestige
    (personal qualities)
    Authoritative Power
    (elected or inherited office) ⟶ Status
    Wealth
    (economic power—income and capital)

to find a fairly uniform consensus of opinion in any one community as to the relative status or social rank of each member. *Social status,* the position that an individual or a group occupies in the hierarchy of status, is rooted in a myriad of unconscious subjective judgments made by each individual member of the community in answer to the unspoken question: "Would I like to be in that man's position?"

There are three main components of status (see Fig. 27). These are prestige, power, and wealth.[1] The first of these, *prestige,* is based

[1] See Max Weber, "Social Stratification and Class Structure," in Talcott Parsons *et al.* (eds.), *Theories of Society* (New York: The Free Press, 1965).

upon a man's personal qualities—the extent to which he reflects in his personality and behavior the ideals of the culture. An individual who is not loyal to a group and its culture will be deemed unreliable and a potential traitor. A person who is loyal to the group and contributes to the survival of the group and its ideals will be treated with respect and admiration.

In simpler societies, in which food tends to be shared among all members, the efficient hunter enjoys greater prestige because of his superior contribution to group welfare and group survival. Extreme readiness to sacrifice individual interests to the well-being and survival of the group brings additional prestige. Bravery in war and generosity in feast-giving are qualities which attract prestige. Aggressiveness on behalf of the group is normally praised, whereas aggressiveness against other members of the group may be condemned, because its divisive effect endangers group harmony and consequently group survival. The sagacious and experienced leader who places his wisdom at the service of the group also enjoys prestige because he helps to perpetuate the security of the group. Similarly, a witch doctor or other expert in the supernatural acquires prestige to the extent that he is believed to possess the power to manipulate or propitiate supernatural forces in the interest of the group and its members. And in ancestor-worshiping societies which have hereditary chieftains, the chief and the members of his family are generally awarded prestige because of their supposedly close kinship connection to the revered progenitor of the group and to the past hero-kings who symbolize the unity, continuity, and identity of the community. Persons who have prestige, possess status.

As man's control of his environment increases, division of labor begins to develop almost inevitably, and a second determinant of status appears: *social power.* Whereas in technologically simpler societies the members of a group will follow the advice given by experienced and respected individuals, such advisory headmen have no power to compel compliance with their views. But from the time that an increasing division of labor recognizes full-time professional leaders, as well as professional farmers, professional warriors, and professional experts in magic and religion, the situation begins to change dramatically. Society begins to vest authoritative power in individuals, entitling them to coerce recalcitrant members of the group into fulfilling their obligations and abiding by the mores. Most people would rather be the man who gives the orders than the man who carries them out. As the

In simpler societies the village headman may have little or no coercive power, although he speaks with the voice of tradition. M'Baiki elder in formal attire, Republic of Central Africa. (Courtesy of Ministère de la France d'Outre-Mer.)

village headman acquires power, he gains in status. Social power—the ability to persuade others to comply with one's wishes—also contributes to status.

With increasing division of labor we normally find a growth in the conception of private property. The division of labor involves the exchange of services, which means in effect the exchange of *wealth*, the third component of status. Inequalities may arise because some individuals produce more wealth than others and also because some may benefit from the pattern of exchange more than others. Furthermore, once wealth has become personalized, some individuals may consume their wealth almost as soon as they acquire it, while others may be more frugal and accumulate their wealth. All more advanced societies, based upon a division of labor, consequently tend to develop inequalities of income and of accumulated wealth. Since wealth represents control over desired possessions, the possessor of wealth is usually regarded with respect and envy by other members of his community, and to this extent may be said to have higher status.

Equalitarian Societies

Generally speaking, then, in hunting and gathering societies, a man's status depends to a large extent upon his prestige, which in turn reflects his functional role in the community; that is, the contributions he makes towards the welfare and survival of the group and its members. Among hunting peoples production is for immediate consumption, and there are consequently little or no inequalities of wealth. Such societies are sometimes called EQUALITARIAN because their simple subsistence economy restricts differences in status to prestige, and by precluding the accumulation of wealth, prevents inequalities of wealth from developing. Similarly, because they have no division of labor other than between males and females, there can be no inequalities of power except between men, women, and children. When there are no differences in wealth because of the day-to-day basis of subsistence and no differences in power because of the absence of any true division of labor, the only differences in status that can exist will be those based upon personal qualities which contribute toward the maintenance of group values and enhance the survival chances of the group. This is the situation that exists among the Bushmen of the Kalahari, the Arunta of Australia, and the Yahgan of Tierra del Fuego. Adults enjoy a higher status than infants, and men enjoy a higher status than women, but all married adult males have essentially the same rights and privileges. All are hunters. Some have more prestige than others, but there are no differences in wealth or social power.

Rank Societies

In most horticultural, simple pastoral, and fishing societies, some form of authoritative coordinating officialdom has usually developed. Of course it is not always possible to say that in this society we have an authoritative chief, while in that other society we have only an advisory headman. There is no hard and fast dividing line, for authority cannot be easily measured. Nevertheless there is a steady evolutionary transition from equalitarian societies, in which a leader's ability to guide the actions of his fellows depends upon his ability to inspire by words and by example, to those more authoritative systems in which the leader possesses coercive power.

In the more complex horticultural societies the chieftain has an obligation to enforce custom upon his fellows. His judgments may be backed by religious sanctions, or he may have to fall back upon the force of his own hand. When one individual is entitled with the full weight of social approval to coerce another individual, we have authoritative power. Similarly, when some members of society have authoritative power and others lack this power, we have a RANK SOCIETY.[2]

Differences in status in an equalitarian society are based on prestige; in rank societies status depends not merely on prestige but also on the possession of authoritative social power. Authority is more effective when the holder is distinguished by sumptuary marks of status, such as the right to wear an animal skin cloak, a necklace of shells or animal claws, a headdress made from birds' feathers, or a crown of gold set with precious stones. These symbols must not be confused with the jewelry worn in modern societies to display affluence. In a rank society differences in status depend primarily upon prestige and authoritative power, not on wealth, and these symbols of rank are badges of office, not indications of wealth.

Kinship remains the prime basis of social organization in rank societies, and because a tendency toward the hereditary transmission of status will be present, rank societies frequently show a marked preoccupation with genealogies. Nevertheless, rank societies are not rigidly stratified in such a way that all interrank social mobility is prohibited. It is also an essential characteristic of a rank society that higher status does not entitle the individual per se to a larger share in the economic resources available to the group, and the chieftain in a rank society must still labor to secure his own subsistence. Thus an Ariki or Tikopian chief claims descent from a long line of privileged nobles but in reality works in his own fields alongside the commoners. While his person and office may be protected by a complex tradition of religious sanctions and rituals, actual relations between the Ariki and the commoners are surprisingly personal and human, a good deal of badinage and "leg pulling" being customary. Even the banquets which the

[2] Morton H. Fried analyzes "rank" societies in *The Evolution of Political Society* (New York: Random House, Inc., 1967), Chap. 4.

As societies grow in size and complexity, the need for professional coordinators becomes more pronounced. Such persons invariably enjoy high status and their leadership role can be more effectively fulfilled when their office is reinforced by outward symbols of their status. This picture portrays a group of Anjouan notables from the Archipelago of Comores, off the coast of Madagascar. (Courtesy of La Documentation Française, Paris.)

Ariki hosts are supplemented by food contributed by the commoners, since he is not appreciably richer than they. Prestige and power are nevertheless prized, and marriages may often be arranged with the object of securing alliances between the more prestigious families in the community.

SLAVERY may make its appearance at the level of rank societies. While hunters frequently marry captured women and simple horticulturalists such as the Yąnomamö may do the same, in rank societies captive women are less likely to be accepted as wives, and are more commonly treated as concubines. In some cases custom may prohibit sexual relations between owners and female slaves altogether because of the greater emphasis placed upon status differences and because the status of a child may come to reflect, to some extent, the status of the parent.

Caste Systems

As rank consciousness becomes more pronounced and status becomes hereditary in specific kinship units, the rank society emerges as a caste society. A CASTE is essentially an hereditary status group which possesses a distinct occupational role in society, and is endogamous in that it prohibits marriage between any of its members and individuals from a lower status level.

The caste system embodies a principle not present in rank societies. Status in a caste system implies differences not only in prestige, power, and rank but also in wealth—as implied by the restriction on recruitment to the more privileged professions. As shown in Figure 28, in a caste system each social stratum represents a functional area within the society, and a man's occupation and status are determined by ascription at birth. In effect, the caste system seeks to extend the principle of kinship and ascription into societies characterized by a substantial division of labor, thus preventing the rise of social mobility, so that not only does kinship serve as a basis for predetermining the pattern of mutual obligations which hold the group together, but kinship and birthright effectively determine prestige, power, and wealth.

Ideally, in a caste system a man's position in life is rigidly determined at birth and irrevocably ascribed until his death, but there may be some tendency for those who are unable to maintain their position in society to lose their status by their inability to avoid breaking the taboos which attach to the behavior of the members of their caste. A high-ranking caste normally carries with it many prescribed rituals and taboos which can only be complied with by successful and wealthy families, so that those who are incompetent tend to lose their caste status by breaking these rules. Most caste societies have consequently succeeded in maintaining themselves against both internal and external pressures over very long periods of time. Whatever may be lost to a caste society by way of potential talent left undeveloped in the lower castes seems to be compensated for by the absence of friction and the functional efficiency of a society whose various groups cooperate harmoniously in the belief that the different roles and statuses are divinely ordained and morally justified.

The Inca state, though often described as socialist, was essentially castelike in structure, but it is India that is usually cited as the prime example of a caste society. Although it is possible that the Old Indus Valley civilization was organized on a functional-occupational caste basis, the traditional Hindu caste system undoubtedly received its present form following the invasion of India by the pastoral Indo-Aryans some 3500 years ago. Imposing their own castelike three-tier society of nobles, freemen, and slaves upon the indigenous people, the Indo-Aryan conquerors produced in effect a five-tier system. At the head of this system was the *Rajanya* or royal caste, which carried out the leading administrative duties. Below the Rajanya was the *Kshatriya* caste of knightly warrior nobles. Originally subordinate to the Kshatriya caste, but for the last 3000 years superior to the Kshatriya caste, were the *Brahmana*, comprising individuals born into the educated Brahman families, who were destined to be priests, teachers, and judges. Below the Kshatriya and Brahmana were the *Vaisya*, comprising the original Indo-Aryan freemen. The Vaisya served society as farmers or merchants, aided by slaves drawn from the *Sudra* or conquered peoples.[3]

The four upper castes—sometimes grouped as three classes by the merger of the *Rajanya* and *Kshatriya*—claimed descent from the victorious invaders, and were known as *Arya,* which in the Sanskrit language meant "noble." Their privileged roles were validated by their religion, which became the basis of modern Hinduism, on the grounds that they were "twice born"; that is, they were reincarnated beings who had earned their higher status by

[3] See Chaps. 2 and 3, Max Weber, *The Religion of India* (New York: Free Press 1958), for a detailed discussion of the Indian caste system.

FIG. 28   SOCIAL STRATIFICATION

a. Caste System

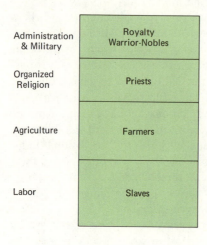

Administration & Military — Royalty / Warrior-Nobles

Organized Religion — Priests

Agriculture — Farmers

Labor — Slaves

b. Estate System

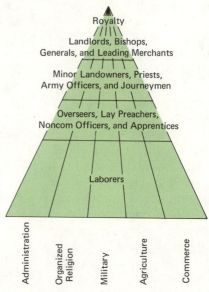

Royalty

Landlords, Bishops, Generals, and Leading Merchants

Minor Landowners, Priests, Army Officers, and Journeymen

Overseers, Lay Preachers, Noncom Officers, and Apprentices

Laborers

Administration   Organized Religion   Military   Agriculture   Commerce

a. Caste System. Rank coincides with functional area in society. Little if any social mobility.

b. Estate System. With increasing complexity, hierarchies now exist within functional areas. Leaders of different functional areas share equal status beneath monarchy. Limited social mobility.

devoted adherence to the social order in their earlier life. In principle, a man who was born into the non-Aryan lower caste might hope to become an Aryan in the next life, *provided* he abided loyally by the religious laws which fortified the existing caste structure, showing due respect to his social superiors and carrying out his menial tasks dutifully during his present life on earth.

The aboriginals, many of whom had formerly been freemen, were downgraded to the rank of Sudras following the Aryan conquest, and as members of the servile caste were required to do manual and unskilled work. The primitive tribal people of India, who had not participated in the Indus Valley civilization and who were darker skinned with low brows and flat noses, were depressed even further. Ranked as *untouchables,* they were employed only for the most menial work, such as washing clothes, cleaning the latrines, hauling the night soil from the villages, and removing corpses from the streets. As untouchables, they had to take care not to pollute their superiors by touch, by the breath from their mouth, or even by allowing their shadow to fall upon an Aryan's food.

It has been observed by some commentators that the caste system operates with greater efficiency in preindustrial, rural economies, and it is true that it is common in agricultural and folk-type societies. Caste systems, such as that of Hindu India, work well in an economy in which most activities are relatively simple and do not require an extensive degree of specialization or coordination. Thus in the type of military activity characteristic of the wars fought by the Indo-Aryans, the unarmed foot

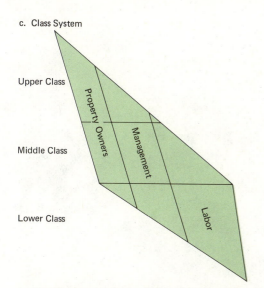

c. Class System

Upper Class

Property Owners

Management

Middle Class

Lower Class

Labor

c. Class System. Maximum degree of social mobility. In general, property owners rank higher than management, and management ranks higher than labor. But the manager of a major enterprise may rank higher than the owner of a small retail business. Skilled craftsmen may rank higher than unskilled labor foremen.

Those who keep written records of transactions and contracts frequently achieve relatively high social status, even though their economic reward may be little greater than that of an artisan working with his hands. Portrayed here is a clerical worker from Northwest India, whose clean, smart, and tidy appearance is in keeping with his respected social status. (Courtesy of the Press Information Bureau, Government of India, New Delhi.)

soldiers were of little effect, and the military nobility, clad in bronze armor and riding in chariots, determined the outcome of battles which were often little more than a series of single combats. Similarly, farming and commerce were essentially small-scale and personal, so that one farmer might enjoy much the same status as another and one merchant could be socially equated with another. But as agriculture advanced technologically, so also commerce developed and the problems of administration became more complex. In the more advanced agricultural societies, such as those of feudal and Renaissance Europe, all the various forms of economic activity began to become increasingly complex and increasingly bureaucratic in organization. In the absence of totalitarian conditions, the caste system tended to become modified into what has been called an *estate system.*

Estate Systems

The estate system of social stratification, which developed out of feudalism and characterized most European societies at the time of the Renaissance, is still a largely closed, caste-like system, characterized by distinctions of

The status of a ruling family, even though validated by kinship ties, can be effectively reinforced by elaborate pomp and ceremonial display. (*Top*) The royal barge of the Kings of Thailand viewed on a Bangkok canal, with the Temple of Dawn in the background. (Courtesy of the Public Relations Department, Thailand.) (*Bottom*) Eighteenth-century European coaches, formerly the property of the royalty and the nobility, now displayed in the Museum of Coaches at Lisbon, Portugal. (Courtesy of the Portuguese Information Service.)

prestige, power, and wealth. Like the caste system, the estate system attributes specific roles to different ranks and rewards high office with greater wealth. But entire functional areas, such as administration, war, religion, and agriculture, are no longer to be equated with a particular status in society. Not all farmers in an estate system enjoy the same status, nor will even all merchants enjoy a similar status. In short, as illustrated in Figure 28, an estate system differs from a caste system in that broad areas of economic specialization no longer correspond to specific status positions.

The reason for this is clear. The estate system is, in fact, a caste system modified to suit the needs of bureaucratic efficiency. Society is conceived of as a single planned organization, with a king, emperor, or republican council at its head, and all functional areas within the social organization are controlled hierarchically and bureaucratically so that there are different levels of status within each functional level. At the same time persons holding equivalent ranks in the various functional areas enjoy equal status with each other, for status depends on one's position in each respective hierarchy, not on the functional area itself.

With kinship still exercising an important role and status remaining largely ascribed, the various strata of society in an estate system preserve a degree of castelike exclusiveness. But instead of political administration being the prerogative of royalty and nobility, a bureaucratic political system has developed, with royalty and nobles occupying the upper positions above a hierarchy of lesser officials whose status reaches down to the lower levels of society.

Parallel to this hierarchical bureaucratic system stands a similar military bureaucracy, with royalty and nobles in the higher ranks commanding an officer core of lesser gentility, and below them "enlisted" men drawn from the lower ranks of society. This bureaucratic system reflects the rising importance of the infantry and the increased size of armies, with all the organizational and supply problems involved. In short, warfare has become subject to a bureaucratic system of organization in the same way that government has ceased to be a personal relationship between the king and his people. Both have become bureaucratic and hierarchical.

In addition to the military and governmental bureaucracy we also find a religious bureaucracy. A single church claims to dominate the religious life of the entire society. The archbishops and bishops who direct this bureaucracy rank on equal terms with the leading nobles of the land, and in eighteenth-century France and Britain they even enjoyed seats in the elite council of nobles. Below the archbishops and bishops various levels of priesthood are hierarchically ordered above a class of lay preachers and an army of junior clerics.

Commerce develops a similar status-conscious hierarchical system as a separate estate. In the cities prosperous merchants control the guilds, whose members are ranked as master craftsmen, most owning their own businesses. Below the elite, the routine work is carried on by journeymen, and beneath the journeymen, apprentices and hired help labor at the more menial tasks. Even in the area of agriculture the land is controlled by estate-owning nobles who employ estate managers and farm managers to work their farms, with the aid of a laboring class of villeins and serfs who may be prohibited from leaving the land in search of better terms of employment in the cities.

But because such bureaucratic systems must work reasonably efficiently, there is usually an element of achievement and some possibility of reward by promotion. Thus loyal service to the king might lead to the grant of a higher hereditary status or to a higher political rank, and in medieval Europe the enforced celibacy of Catholic church officials prevented the inheritance of status in the church hierarchy, meaning that all church offices had to be filled by promotion, based largely on hierarchy achievement. Estate systems are therefore less rigid than caste systems and permit a degree of social mobility. They are also associated with a decline in the significance of kinship, although this may remain an important factor among the elite. Indeed estate systems are commonly associated with the replacement of tribalism by feudalism.

Class Systems

With the development of commerce and especially with the rise of mass production and mass marketing necessitated by industrialization, estate systems and feudalism give way to class systems and industrialization. While the estate system still saw the entire society as a single organization in which all men were essentially role players participating in an integrated system for the mutual good of the total community, industrialization is usually accompanied by the rise of individualism and self-interest.

Class systems arise when the opportunity for personal advancement is so great that individuals are induced to detach themselves from their kinship ties. In times of rapid social change, kinship ties may become a hindrance rather than a benefit to the individual who seeks to better himself. Under such circumstances even immediate marriage and family ties may be represented as restrictions upon individual freedom. In the class system the individual consequently experiences an intense loneliness, in the absence of strong family or kinship bonds, which may lead to new and conscious, but often futile, demands for greater community solidarity. Thus socialism is in a sense a reaction against the decline of kinship and represents the desire to reestablish the bonds of primordial unity and equality in society.

The ideals of the class system are essentially individualistic and competitive. Men are free to move up or down the social hierarchy according to merit. Status in a class system thus appears as an unbroken politicoeconomic continuum extending from the bottom to the top of society without any rigid barriers between classes. Class is still a stratified system, but the emphasis is upon achievement as the moral basis for inequality, even to the point of condemning ascription and inherited prestige, power, and wealth. In reality, however, social mobility still tends to be partially restricted in all class systems because so many of the elements of status must necessarily be identified with heredity—even cultural traits continue to be at least partially ascribed on the basis of kinship, race, and ethnic origin.

Indeed ETHNIC STRATIFICATION is so widespread in complex multiethnic states and in all levels of economic development occurring beyond the hunting and gathering band that it is attracting increasing attention from both anthropologists and sociologists. The fact that ethnic stratification should divide pastoralists from horticulturalists in East Africa, the *Sudra* from the *Arya* in the Indian caste system, and Blacks from Whites in America, exemplifies the tenacity of race as a basis for group endogamy and social, economic, and political status.

Thus mobile class systems survive only where rapid technological, political, or social changes continue to disturb the equilibrium of society. With the decline of innovation in a planned industrial society, a more stable social situation inevitably returns, and with the rise of community loyalty the philosophy of individualism becomes unfashionable. In the event of a decline in the rate of socioeconomic change, social mobility likewise tends to decline and the social system of class stratification tends to revert to a more stable system of estate-type social stratification. Indeed, the future may see the reemergence of estate systems of social stratification in many of the more bureaucratic industrially based societies.

For Further Reading

Eggan, F., 1950, *Social Organization of the Western Pueblos*. Chicago: University of Chicago.

Firth, R., 1963, *Elements of Social Organization*. Boston: The Beacon Press.

Hsu, F. L. K., 1963, *Clan, Caste and Club*. Princeton, N.J.: D. Van Nostrand Company, Inc.

Lowie, R. H., 1948, *Social Organization*. New York: Holt, Rinehart and Winston, Inc.

Majumdar, D. N., 1958, *Caste and Communication in an Indian Village*. Bombay: Asia Publishing House.

Mayer, A., 1971, *Caste and Kinship in Central India*. Berkeley: University of California Press.

Murdock, G. P., 1949, *Social Structure*. New York: The Macmillan Company.

Nadel, S. F., 1957, *The Theory of Social Structure*. Zion, Ill.: International Scholarly Book Service, Inc.

Radcliffe-Brown, A. R., 1965, *Structure and Function in Primitive Society*. New York: The Free Press.

Sahlins, M. D., 1958, *Social Stratification in Polynesia*. Seattle: University of Washington Press.

CHAPTER 19

Magic and Taboo

It was the renowned British anthropologist Sir Edward Tylor who first propounded what has since been called an *evolutionary* theory of magic and religion, claiming that both of these phenomena arose out of primitive man's ignorance of science and consequent fear of what was regarded as the supernatural.[1] Tylor's views were subsequently elaborated and modified by many other writers, including Herbert Spencer, M. Levy-Bruhl, R. R. Marett, and Bronislaw Malinowski, until they became the basis of a branch of anthropology known as COMPARATIVE RELIGION, which is concerned with the study of man's attitudes toward the supernatural as a part of the ideational substructure present in every culture.

Culture—the accumulation of ideas and beliefs—constitutes a vitally significant part of the human environment and plays a powerful role in determining men's choices of action,

which can often be contrary to their own best survival interests. Structurally, all agrarian societies, for example, will undoubtedly tend to show resemblances, resulting from similar responses to similar economic problems, but the cultural content of societies at the same or similar levels of subsistence may differ considerably. Whatever may be the precise degree of significance that attaches to economic forces and to different patterns of subsistence, magic and religion are intimately related to the overall norms and values of a society, and are an essential part of the cultural environment that determines men's choices of action. The case of the Nuer will illustrate this point, for the Nuer steadfastly refuse to eat birds or even birds' eggs, even when near starvation, because they regard them to be totemic and hence sacred creatures. Similarly, the Hindus of India, even during great famines, refuse to eat the meat of the cow because that animal is sacred to them. How does such noneconomic behavior arise?

---

[1] Sir Edward Tylor, *Primitive Culture* (London: John Murray Sons, Publishers Ltd., 1871), pp. 221–259.

242

Animism

According to Tylor, early man thought irrationally, a view which was subsequently endorsed by the psychologist Levy-Bruhl,[2] who devoted much of his energy and attention to anthropological questions. Levy-Bruhl claimed that logical thought is a recent innovation in human history and that in primitive societies men were introspective rather than scientific. Unable to subject their beliefs concerning the nature of the world around them to the test of methodically organized scientific experiments, primitive men could measure the validity of their ideas only by their own emotional reactions to these ideas. Believing that their own actions were deliberately conceived in order to satisfy conscious desires and that their actions were planned and directed toward the achievement of specific goals, early men assumed that all events that took place must similarly be caused deliberately and purposefully by intelligent beings, seen or unseen. In short, primitive men assumed the existence of supernatural beings, and ascribed *teleological* powers to these.

Thus, the early hunter knew that an animal died because a spear was thrown at it, hit it, penetrated it, and "caused" it to die. The spear was thrown because he, the hunter, willed it to be thrown. He observed animal predators, presumably prompted by hunger as were men, carefully and deliberately stalking their prey, and he felt that animals, too, planned their actions and caused events to happen in accordance with preconceived intentions. Things happened because someone or something caused them to happen. If he or one of his family fell sick, it was certainly evident that the sick person had not desired his own ill health, so someone else, or something else, must have willed the sickness. Even today,

[2]L. Levy-Bruhl, *The "Soul" of the Primitive,* trans. by L. Clare (New York: Frederick A. Praeger, Inc., 1966).

when the traditional Azande tribesman, walking along a forest path in equatorial Africa, stubs his foot against an unseen root and breaks a toe, he knows very well that he did not intend to break his toe, and so concludes that an enemy willed the accident.

A similar line of reasoning can be applied to external events which impinge less directly upon the individual. The eruption of a volcano must have been caused teleologically by some unseen and hence supernatural being. Storms and lightning must be caused by supernatural beings with deliberate, teleological wills. Even a severe winter, a *thimbull* winter as the old Norsemen called it, was caused by supernatural

Botanical animism supposes that souls or spirits may reside in plants as well as in animals. Pictured above is a small sacrificial shrine erected in honor of a tree spirit in Bambara, Republic of Mali. (Courtesy of La Documentation Française, Paris.)

beings, possibly out of malice for mankind in general. So primitive men invented the invisible, formless souls or spirits which had both the will and the power to cause unusual natural occurrences. ANIMISM was the name which Tylor gave to this belief in vital forces that lack corporate, visible, or spatial form, but which may will events to happen. He defined animism so broadly that it was virtually coextensive with religion, as "the belief in spiritual beings."

Two types of animism may be identified. In some societies these spirit beings are believed to reside in trees, and the term *botanical animism* has been invented for such phenomena. Botanical animism is widespread in India where the Hindu religion embraces a wide range of animistic beliefs acquired from aboriginal tribal peoples, and the members of the lower castes especially leave small offerings of *ghee* (butter) at the foot of pipul trees which are believed to house spirits.

Among Eskimoes, by contrast, there is a belief in *zoological animism*, for both men and animals are believed to have souls which although nonmaterial, are believed to separate from the body at death. Zoological animism is extremely widespread, and even modern concepts of psychophysico dualism—the belief that the body and mind are separate realities—may be directly traced to the zoological animism of early Greek and Indo-European cosmology and even to beliefs which may date from Cro-Magnon man. Aware of their ability to think and feel emotions, early men regarded consciousness as evidence of the existence of a supernatural soul, which was believed to leave the body temporarily during sleep and permanently at death. Thus Plato has been credited with having invented the concept of psychophysico dualism in the fifth century B.C. when he distinguished between *psyche* or "soul" and *physis* or "body." But Plato did not invent these ideas; he merely developed his philosophy around the only cultural concepts available to him—the cultural traditions of his own already ancient society.

Mana

Animism does not exhaust the range of supernatural possibilities. It was R. R. Marett who, while studying Malayo-Polynesian culture, was impressed by the fact that the Polynesians conceived of a type of supernatural power which did not seem to have any particular will or intentions of its own. Being steeped in Western Judeo-Christian monotheism, many of his contemporaries at once assumed that a "godless" concept of the supernatural must represent a very primitive stage of religious thought, which would have preceded animism. Thus they sought to identify an evolutionary sequence commencing with ANIMATISM, the belief in a diffused, abstract supernatural power. Animatism was supposed to evolve into animism, the belief in souls and spirits, and thence to polytheism, the belief in many gods, and finally to monotheism. This interpretation is now discarded. Many very primitive contemporary peoples, such as the Bushmen, Arunta, and Nuer, have a shadowy conception of a creator god, and if any such scale of evolving sophistication could be validated—which is debatable—the reverse might more likely be the case. Early man thought teleologically, and only at a higher level of abstraction is it possible to conceive of an unseen power field without physical form, possessed of an abstract and amoral causal ability. The concept of animatism is quite close in many ways to modern science.

This more refined concept of an inanimate supernatural force dispensed with the anthropomorphic assumption implicit in teleology. The belief that events in the universe must be willed by some lifelike being is replaced by a concept of causality which, not being comprehensible to man, must still be regarded as supernatural and treated with caution. All matter, nonliving as well as living, is regarded as being permeated by a vague, diffused nonphysical power-force, which may be more heavily concentrated in some objects than in others; that is, which takes a more kinetic form in some objects and a more passive form in others.

Borrowing a name from the Melanesians, Marett[3] called this force *mana*, a diffused supernatural power which has no will of its own, does not exist as a spirit, has no material or spatial form, and may be present in living as well as nonliving things. Mana is related to matter in much the same way as the force of gravity is related to matter, except that man has no way of identifying or measuring mana unless and until it reveals itself in action.

Mana can explain all events without need for recourse to the concept of spiritual wills. Thus, knowing nothing of ballistics, men used the idea of mana to explain why one spear always went straight to its target when thrown, while another, seemingly much the same in appearance, would seldom follow a straight trajectory. To the prelogical mind there was clearly a difference in the mana or power resident in the spears, and even as late as the Iron Age in Europe, some swords which were better made were believed to contain a greater reservoir of natural power than those forged from baser material. Similarly, the sword which had killed a famous warrior must be imbued, by the very evidence of its deed, with more mana than the sword which failed its owner in time of battle. Mana may pervade any or all objects, living or nonliving. It has neither morality nor goal of its own; it is simply a capacity for getting things done, rather like electricity. To those who do not know how to deal with it, however, mana is always potentially dangerous, while those who possess it or understand it have less to fear.

Mana may reside in inanimate objects; thus an odd-shaped stone may be buried in a Melanesian yam plot, and prove its mana when an unusually profuse crop of yams are grown that season. But it may also reside in people, and among the Algonkin Indians of North America mana is recognized by the term *manitou* as a power which may diffuse impersonal objects, which may give skill to medicine men, and which may rest also in the person of the gods. Like the Algonkin Indians, the Indo-Europeans and the Polynesians also believed mana might reside in persons, especially in royalty and nobility, giving leaders of society the ability to influence others and endowing them with a distinctive personality, for which Max Weber[4] invented the term *charisma*. The possession of charisma distinguished kings from lesser folk. Among the Scandinavians the concept of charisma took the form of a vague "luck" force known as *hamingja*, which some men possessed and others lacked. Indeed, it is still common in North Europe for people to use the expression "my luck has run out." Once again, this *hamingja* was generally considered to be genetically transmissible, for there seemed no other way of explaining how a single line of kings could hold power successfully through a number of generations. On the other hand, if bad luck befell a nation, this was a sign that somehow the king had lost his *hamingja*, and a series of poor harvests could lead the people to replace the king by another member of the *hamingja*-carrying royal family.

All the old Teutonic nobility of Europe who claimed descent from Odin were believed to possess mana, and the touch of a king was supposed to cure the sick. Right down to the

[3] R. R. Marett, *The Threshold of Religion*. (London: Methuen & Co., Ltd., 1914).

[4] For an excellent discussion of both charisma and familial charisma (actually called "gentile charisma," as an attribute of the gens, see Rinherd Bendix, *Max Weber* (New York: Doubleday & Company, Inc., 1962).

seventeenth century the king of England was expected to lay hands upon the sick and crippled in the belief that his mana would cure their afflictions. Scrofula, in particular, was known as "the king's evil" because although it was a glandular complaint, it was supposed to be readily curable by the royal touch. Similarly, the laying on of hands by a bishop when consecrating another bishop is rooted in the belief that by this ritual some of the mana or charisma of the first bishop of Rome is passed down through the generations of bishops to the newly consecrated candidate.

Exactly the same belief in transmissible mana was implied by the Viking practice of ring giving. Famed Viking princes customarily rewarded their bravest followers by presenting them with a golden ring, taken directly from their own arm, often on the scene of the battle field. The ring would be proudly worn by the recipient and never sold or traded, for its value was not in the gold, but in the *hamingja* or luck power which the ring had absorbed when worn on the arm of the prince-hero. The ring brought some of the famed donor's luck force with it, which would then diffuse into the body of the wearer, enhancing his own ability to succeed in whatever he undertook.

In Persia it was believed that the Sassanid dynasty was so heavily endowed with familial charisma, that their mana force revealed itself in a circle of bright light that hovered constantly over the king's head. This was reputed to be so bright that Greek travelers recounted that on approaching their king, the Persian courtiers hid their eyes and cried out "misuzam," or literally, "I am burning up," and could never look directly at the king for fear of being blinded.[5] Christianity later borrowed the *xvarənah* or "halo" and introduced it into pictures of the Christian god and his angels and saints as a visible indication of supernatural power.

[5] G. Widengren, "The Sacred Kingship of Iran," in *Numen* (Leiden), Supplement No. 4:242-257 (1959).

Taboo

Since mana is both invisible and potentially dangerous, almost all societies which recognize it believe that it is foolhardy for the ignorant or the unauthorized to meddle with it. People and places known to be imbued with particularly potent mana are potentially dangerous to those unqualified to approach them. Such people and places become TABOO, a word which is like a sign that reads, "Danger! Mana at work." Cemeteries, for example, are generally protected by taboos which warn the layman either to stay away altogether or else to behave in a highly circumspect manner when in their neighborhood.

Taboo also surrounds kings and other semidivine or semisupernatural persons who, being highly imbued with mana, must be treated with care. To lay a hand on a king without authority was a highly dangerous act in many societies, and as we have seen, the Polynesian kings were so taboo that the ordinary citizen might not touch them, eat anything they had touched, nor even eat food from a field through which the king had walked. This extreme emphasis upon royal mana and the subsequent taboo which came to surround the royal personage resulted in the king becoming a virtual prisoner, unable to walk around the village for fear of making things and places untouchable to the common folk. Even the plates from which the king had eaten had to be thrown away, and it is a historical fact that the continued extension of the principle of royal taboo in Hawaiian society led eventually to a complete breakdown of the system.[6] Restrictions became unbearable until the king himself, following a dispute with the priests, decided to destroy the old religion. This he did by deliberately breaking the taboo that surrounded him and by walking around

[6] Malcolm C. Webb, "The Absolution of the Taboo System in Hawaii," in A. Howard (ed.), *Polynesian: Readings on a Culture Area* (Scranton, Pa.: Chandler Publishing Co., 1971).

the public places touching everything he could find, thus proving that no harm would come to anyone as a result.

In a more general sense, taboo may apply to anything unusual. The death of a family member may bring taboo, and this taboo must be observed by those who survive if they wish to ensure that no harm will come to them from the supernatural powers known to be associated with death. The death of a leading member of the community is frequently the sign that powerful supernatural forces are at work, and such deaths in India and certain other Asian countries could lead to a universal *genna taboo*, warning all persons to cease from their normal activities and to become as inconspicuous as possible. Restriction of normal activities on ceremonial days, such as the Christian Sabbath, likewise constitute a form of genna taboo.

Magical Techniques

Yet men are not content merely to treat the supernatural with circumspection. Just as men have succeeded to some extent in controlling the natural world, so sooner or later they will attempt to control the supernatural world as well. MAGIC arises, according to Frazer, when man seeks to bring the supernatural world under his control.[7] Magic is, in a sense, pseudoscience, and although inanimate mana is perhaps more easily manipulated by primitive man than are the animistic spirits, Aladdin was able to control the animistic genie of the lamp, and experts in the occult still claim to be able to control familiar spirits. Through magical spells and ritual, primitive man believes that he can control the unseen forces of the external world. As Malinowski expressed it, magic begins where technology ends.

The magical arts are based on two different principles. The first of these rests on the belief

Magic frequently relies on the mimetic principle, in which the desired events are acted out by those who seek to control the supernatural forces which constantly influence the lives of men and women. (Courtesy of La Documentation Française, Paris.)

we have already mentioned, that supernatural power may be transmitted by touch or contagion. The example of the ring given by the hero-leader to a favorite follower represents an attempt to transfer mana by touch or CONTAGIOUS MAGIC. The laying on of hands by bishops is rooted in the same principle as the curing of ailing subjects by the touch of the royal hand. Anything which has been in contact with a person or object endowed with unusually potent mana will acquire some of that mana. Even today we tend to treasure

[7] Anthropological theories of magic are competently discussed in E. E. Evans-Pritchard, *Theories of Primitive Religion* (New York: Clarendon Press, 1965).

small personal possessions which were physically close to departed friends or relatives. The pen, watch, or ring of a departed parent seems to have some of his personality in it, and will be treasured accordingly. Thus a portion of the "true cross" was believed by medieval Christians to contain special powers, acquired by the principle of contagion, as also were the nails which were believed to have penetrated the hands and feet of god. The relics of saints contain similar mana, acquired by contagion, and Chaucer reports[8] a flourishing trade in medieval England in pigs' bones, sold to the unwitting by itinerant "holy men" as "saintly relics" imbued with miraculous powers.

The principle of contagious magic also reveals itself in the techniques used by Bantu witchdoctors in Africa, who seek to obtain a piece of clothing, a lock of hair, the clippings

[8] Walter W. Skeat (ed.), *The Complete Works of Geoffery Chaucer* (New York: Clarendon Press, 1963), p. 21.

from a man's nails, or even a portion of his excreta to gain supernatural influence over their intended victim. The nails and hair of dead men continue to grow for some time after death, and because of their associations with the mysteries of the afterlife, clippings from dead men's hair and nails are assumed to contain contagious magic, and may be used in magic potions.

If the witchdoctor cannot secure any object which contains, by the principle of contagion, some of his intended victim's mana, he may resort to the second principle of magic: the principle of sympathetic magic.

SYMPATHETIC MAGIC, sometimes called imitative or mimetic magic, arises from the belief that like causes like. A likeness of a man will in some way be associated with his supernatural nature, and will give anyone who knows how to use it the power to exert magical control over him. Many simpler people there-

A Zulu witchdoctor prepares a magical potion. Most Bantu witchdoctors work for hire, receiving gifts of produce from their clients by way of a fee. (Courtesy of South African Information Service.)

fore resent any attempt to make a picture of them for fear that this will give strangers power over them. Witch doctors have to make only a crude effigy of their intended victim, and by crushing this, sticking pins into it, or as among the Baluba of the Congo, setting it afloat on the river in a miniature canoe, the victim will be expected to suffer pain, illness, or even death. Such is the strength in the belief in sympathetic and contagious magic that healthy men have been known to sicken and die, after learning that a spell had been cast upon them, for no reason that could be detected by physical indications.

The concepts of mimetic and contagious magic, first defined by Sir James Frazer in his classic and voluminous anthropological treatise known as *The Golden Bough*,[9] are not perhaps entirely inclusive. Nevertheless, almost all forms of magic seem to relate either directly or indirectly to one of these two principles. For example, the *evil eye* is the name given to the belief that one man may harm another by merely looking at him with evil or malice. In this case no physical object is involved, but as the name evil eye implies, the very act of looking at the victim is a form of contact and allows some of the malice felt by the ill-wisher to enter into the victim's body. In a milder and more general form, in India it is regarded as dangerous to allow a stranger to look enviously at a child, and parents speak disparagingly of their own children, for fear that some evil person, hearing the words of praise, will turn envious eyes upon them. The East Indians of Trinidad in the West Indies believe that a woman should not expose her breasts to the public when nursing her baby, in case a stranger should look with lust upon her breasts and thus poison the purity of the family love that joins mother and child in a separate and private communion.

[9] Sir James Frazer, *The Golden Bough; A Study in Magic and Religion.* (New York: The Macmillan Company, 1951).

Witch from Okoyo in the Congo. Female sorcerers or witches are frequently more feared than male witches. (Courtesy of La Documentation Française, Paris.)

Fetish figures

A belief in the efficacy of sympathetic and contagious magic may also lead to the wearing of *charms* and *talismans*. These are objects which are believed to have the power of attracting beneficial supernatural forces to the aid of the wearer, in the same way that we still speak of lucky charms or lucky horseshoes. Objects which are worn with a view to warding off evil forces are known as *amulets* and may be used as preventatives against disease, witch's spells, and similar dangers associated with the supernatural. *Idols*, or religious images, are representations of supernatural beings, usually of gods, which because of their supposed resemblance to the divinity are believed to house some of the divine being's powers. Charms, talismans, amulets, and fetish figures collectively are known as FETISHES, which may be defined as inanimate objects deemed to contain elements of mana that can be used by man to subvert the supernatural to his will.

Black and White Magic

The expert in magic who knows how to manipulate supernatural powers can use his knowledge for either socially approved or socially harmful purposes. This has led many writers to distinguish between WHITE MAGIC, used in socially approved directions, such as the cure of the sick, the control of the sex of the unborn child, the rendering of barren women fertile, or the prediction of the future (as with Chinese fortune cookies), and BLACK MAGIC, used for socially condemned purposes. Black magic seeks usually to revenge supposed injuries, but may be associated with the enjoyment of vicarious and prohibited pleasures, as with the rituals of the *black mass* in Europe in the eighteenth century. The black mass made use of a common magical technique—the reversal of customary ritual formulae such as verses or prayers. Evil could be worked by repeating the Lord's prayer backward. At other times the reversal of a symbol meant death because the sun was regarded as being reversed during night, and night was associated with death. Either way, the reversal of any customary formula was regarded with considerable superstitious awe.

It is worth mentioning here that *voodoo,* or more correctly *vodun,* practiced among West Indian Negroes, was not originally black magic, although many cult leaders have made use of it in socially undesirable ways in recent times. Vodun arose from a combination of Dahomean ancestral rites brought from Africa with Catholic influences to which the Negroes were exposed when in slavery.[10] Here is a clear case of customs which formerly had a valuable social purpose deteriorating into socially undesirable uses when the structure of society has been dislocated.

DIVINATION may be regarded as a form of white magic, which in the ultimate analysis rests on mimetic principles. Diviners seek to judge the unknown by the examination of the symbolic signs and portents which are deemed to represent the phenomena that interest the inquirer. The fortuneteller in modern times may use a pack of cards or the leaves in a teacup. Astrologers use the position of the planets in the heavens, and Knud Rasmussen, the ethnographer of the Eskimoes, reported that an *angakok* (or local expert in the manipulation of the supernatural) at Nunivak claimed to be able to answer questions by peering into the darkness of a still pool of water, contained in the open entrails of a dead animal. Not only is the similarity to crystal gazing obvious, but we are also reminded of the Etruscans who planned all the more important events in their lives according to the information divined from the entrails of sacrificed animals.

Oracles

ORACLES are a rather special form of divination, in which it is believed that the diviner has communicated with supernatural beings and has been given the answer to his questions by these divinities. In essence, however, it rests upon the interpretation of symbols which are assumed to represent the data under examination. Thus, a Bantu witch doctor may feed poison to a person accused of an offense, and judge his guilt by his fate—death or survival—believing that the answer is dictated by supernatural forces. In medieval Europe the church introduced the idea of *trial by ordeal* as an

[10] See James G. Leyburn, *The Haitian People* (New Haven, Conn.: Yale University Press, 1966).

alternative to the old Teutonic jury trials.[11] In this ordeal the accused was blindfolded and required to walk barefooted across a room, the floor of which had been strewn with red hot pieces of iron. Before the assembled church dignitaries, the god indicated whether the man was innocent or guilty by guiding his footsteps if he were innocent, but allowing him to torture himself on the hot metal if he were guilty. Needless to say, a man with a bad reputation might well prefer to "place his faith in God" and opt for a trial in a church court rather than face a jury in the King's courts. Indeed, the validity of the church courts was one of the major points of contention in the dispute between Archbishop Thomas à Becket and King Henry.

In Africa the Azande have refined the concept of trial by ordeal so as to be able to place the accused persons on trial in absentia. The witch doctor will murmur the name of a suspect over a chicken, while forcing poison down the bird's throat, and if the chicken dies, the suspect is considered guilty. Needless to say, such methods permit considerable manipulation by an experienced operator.

The ancient Greeks of the Homeric Age made regular use of temple oracles to obtain information from their gods. In such cases a priest or priestess acted as the voice of the god, while hidden from the suppliant's view. If the suppliant were in good standing with the god and brought an offering for the oracle, then the oracle would answer his questions, usually being careful to do so with cryptic messages capable of more than one interpretation. Manipulation may have been frequent, and when the Persian armies invaded Europe it is possible that the Delphic oracle may even have been

bribed by Xerxes, for the advice the oracle gave was that Athens should surrender to the invaders. Only after "further consultation" did it advise resistance.

Shamans and Sorcerers

Experts in the manipulation and interpretation of the supernatural—magicians, witches, and witch doctors—have been generally classed together under the generic term SHAMAN. True shamans were first identified among the Paleo-Asian and Altaic-speaking peoples of Eastern Siberia, who like the Eskimoes have no developed religious system and whose concept of the supernatural is basically

Drug taking is widespread among shamans, since any unnatural experience is associated with the concept of the supernatural. Here a South American Indian dances and converses with spirits while under the influence of a hallucinogenic drug. (Courtesy of Napoleon A. Chagnon.)

---

[11] The jury system was systematically revitalized by the English monarchy in the twelfth and thirteenth centuries to replace trial by ordeal. E. Jenks, *The Book of English Law*, rev. by P. B. Fairest, (Athens: Ohio University Press, 1967), p. 78.

animistic. In Siberia and among the Eskimoes shamans may be highly unstable individuals, frequently hysterical and subject to continuous nervous twitching and possibly even epileptic fits. Cultivating the art of feigned trances or imbibing hallucinogenic drugs, they are believed to have the ability to commune with the supernatural, since this seems to be the only possible explanation of their unusual behavior, which is truly "like one possessed by a spirit."

Shamans are usually prepared to hire out their skills for a variety of services from healing the sick to wreaking vengeance upon personal enemies. Franz Boas tells us of one Eskimo shaman who was reputed to practice sorcery for hire too often for the community's peace of mind, and was consequently murdered by common consent of the survivors out of an instinct for self-preservation.[12] But not all experts in the supernatural divide their time impartially betweeen black and white magic. The Shoshone of North America clearly distinguish between those who practice white magic, known as *pohagant,* and those who practice black magic, who are known as *tid-jipohagant.* Anthropologists generally agree in using the North American Indian term MED-ICINE MAN for a shaman who normally seeks to cure the sick and serve the community with white magic and the word SORCERER for one who specializes in black magic.

Magic can obviously be very profitable for self-declared experts, especially when they are masters of the techniques of sleight of hand and ventriloquism. Boas has implied that many Eskimo shamans deliberately exploit their communities without mercy. However, it seems that in many cases the shaman may believe that his tricks work mimetic magic and are genuinely efficacious. Indeed, many sick

patients they attend do get well again, and as is well known, a good "bedside manner" can be a psychological aid to genuine recovery.

Secret Societies

Although by temperament shamans are generally individualists who frequently become bitter rivals of each other, men who work magic may on occasion combine together in SECRET SOCIETIES either for the good of the community or for their own personal advancement. Membership of such societies is not necessarily a secret matter, and anthropologists speak of the men's "secret" societies among the Arunta of central Australia when the entire band knows that all the adult males belong to such groupings. What is secret about them is their closely guarded knowledge of the supernatural and of the techniques for controlling the supernatural. Thus, the medicine men of the Iroquois Indians of North America band together in *medicine lodges,* which are well-respected secret societies whose members practice the magic arts mainly for the good of the community. Among the Masai of East Africa there are age sets, consisting of young men of the same age, which may similarly be described as secret societies, since each has its own secret magical rituals, although everyone knows to which age set a young man belongs.

At other times, secret societies may be made up of sorcerers. The Leopard Men of the Cameroons do in fact keep their membership secret because of the viciously antisocial nature of their activities. They claim that at night they have the power to turn themselves into leopards, and when they ambush their enemies, they claw the corpses with a metal claw to make it look as though the death had been caused by a leopard.

Other secret societies may practice CANNI-BALISM. Cannibalism can be *gastronomic,* where human flesh is eaten out of necessity or for the

[12] For further readings on Shamanism, consult Mircea Elaiade, *Shamanism: Archaic Techniques of Ectasy,* trans. by Willard R. Trask (Princeton, N. J.: Princeton University Press, 1964).

Secret societies possess magicoreligious rites, symbols, and passwords which, as in the case of Western Freemasonry, are divulged only to properly initiated members. But this does not imply that their members do not make public appearances. Secret societies frequently enact important ceremonials in public and may play an important role in the life of the community. Duekoue dancers, West Africa. (Courtesy of La Documentation Française, Paris.)

A member of the Human Leopards of Sierra Leone holding the dreaded magical wand or *Borfina*. This man was subsequently found to be a member of the secret Leopard Society, prohibited by the British colonial authorities, whose members claimed to become leopards at nighttime, attacking and slaying their enemies and consuming a portion of the corpse in a cannibal ritual. (Courtesy of Patrick Mahony.)

253

sake of the preferred flavor, or it can be *vindictive* as among the Ngarigo of Australia who eat the bodies of their enemies after killing them, speaking contemptuously of them, so as to satisfy their anger. In the case of cannibal secret societies, the object is usually *ritual cannibalism*, and the purpose is the ingestion of the mana of the victim. The members of the cannibal societies of the Kwakiutl of Canada formerly ate human flesh as a part of their secret rituals and then rushed back into the throng of the assembled nonmembers, dancing and biting people as though they too were going to be eaten.[13] Ritual cannibalism may be said to rest in the principle of contagious magic, so that when the body of an enemy warrior or chief is eaten, the mana or superior qualities of the victim are believed to be acquired by the cannibal, leaving him a better and wiser man for the experience.

Yet magic is not necessarily the peculiar perquisite of experts. Most societies believe that ordinary men, too, can work magic. The Haida Indians of British Columbia could perform magic, if they knew the secrets, and the Azande of Africa believe that anyone can inherit the powers of a witch. Among the Azande this magical power is believed to rest in what they call a "witch soul," which they believe can be seen in the abdomen if a postmortem operation is carried out on a suspected witch. The power of the witch soul in a child is very small, but that of a grown man may bring about the death of the victim. Witches dispatch their witch soul to harm their enemies, and on a dark evening at an Azande village, a witch soul might be seen as a luminous ball, gliding silently through the air in pursuit of its mission.[14] Men may bewitch

men, but women may bewitch both men and women. In reality, this belief does not work to the advantage of the women, for it means that men can blame women for their misfortunes, accusing them of witchcraft, but no woman can ever retaliate by accusing a man of having bewitched her.

When someone believes that they have been bewitched and may die unless the witch can be persuaded to remove the spell, the Azande will normally consult a poison oracle to determine the identity of the offending witch. Once this is done, the witch will be accused of his or her deed, and must remove the spell. Azande witches are never punished, however, providing they remove the spell if they are identified. Witchcraft is considered very much a part of the daily routine, and every Azande witch is

The filing of the incisor teeth to resemble pointed canine teeth is a frequent custom among cannibals. Here an old man from the Republic of Central Africa smiles to reveal his filed teeth. (Courtesy of La Documentation Française, Paris.)

[13] Franz Boas, *Race, Language and Culture* (New York: The Free Press, 1940), p. 383.

[14] See E. E. Evans-Pritchard, *Witchcraft, Oracles and Magic Among the Azande* (London: Oxford University Press, 1944).

entitled to practise his craft if he can do so undetected.

In the opinion of Sir James Frazer, science and magic were both attempts to control the external world, and as Bronislaw Malinowski pointed out, men resort to magic only when logical methods fail them. As a result, with the advance of science there has been a decline in the role of magic in human society. But the same is not true of religion. Despite advances in scientific knowledge, religious ideas have changed their form, but religion cannot be said to have been forced from the scene by science. Religion and magic are therefore clearly separate phenomena, even though at an elementary level of cultural organization they seem to be closely intertwined. Let us therefore examine the role of religion in human society in our next chapter.

For Further Reading

Eliade, M., 1961, *The Sacred and the Profane*. New York: Harper & Row, Publishers.

Evans-Pritchard, E. E., 1937, *Witchcraft, Oracles and Magic among the Azande*. New York: Oxford University Press.

Fortune, R., 1932, *Sorcerers of Dobu*. London: George Routledge & Sons, Ltd.

Hertz, R., 1960, *Death and the Right Hand*. New York: The Free Press.

Lowie, R. H., 1970, *Primitive Religion*, new ed. New York: Liveright Publishing Corporation.

Mair, L., 1969, *Witchcraft*. New York: McGraw-Hill, Inc.

Malinowski, B., 1954, *Magic, Science and Religion and Other Essays*. New York: Doubleday & Company, Inc.

Radin, P., 1956, *The Trickster: A Study in American Indian Mythology*. Westport, Conn.: Greenwood Press, Inc.

Steiner, F., 1968, *Taboo*. Baltimore: Penguin Books, Inc.

van Gennep, A., 1960, *The Rites of Passage*. Chicago: University of Chicago Press.

CHAPTER 20

Propitiating the Gods

Magic, Sir Edward Tylor said, represents primitive man's attempt to control the forces of the supernatural, but supernatural beings can frequently be very stubborn and may refuse to be controlled. Very often the magical expert can succeed in explaining his failure away by blaming his frustration on countervailing powers greater than his own, or he can claim that the laymen for whom he is working have, by their ignorance of his esoteric techniques, failed to give him adequate cooperation and have therefore neutralized his work. Whatever the excuse, the realization slowly dawns on men that the magical experts have proved themselves unable to control all of the supernatural forces which are at work around them, and men begin to suspect that there are some spirit beings which persistently refuse to be controlled by magical science.

What do primitive men do in such circumstances? Their answer is the essence of pragmatism: If you can't beat them, join them. If there are supernatural beings with a will of

their own and power greater than that of man which man cannot control by magic, then it behooves man to propitiate those powers. Such superior creatures—souls, spirits, or whatever they are—must not be angered, and there is always the hope that if efficiently placated, flattered, and feasted, these divine beings may even be persuaded to use their supernatural powers on behalf of their human suppliants. Thus, according to Tylor,[1] RELIGION is born from the attempt to propitiate those supernatural powers which have failed to respond to magical controls and have refused to subordinate themselves to man. Religion begins when man abandons his attempt to control the forces of the supernatural and instead seeks to propitiate specific supernatural beings. Religion arises from the ruins of magic, but even so, man is slow to reject magic altogether, and

[1] This view developed by E. B. Tylor in *Primitive Culture* (London: John Murray, (Publishers) Ltd., 1871) was also reflected in Vol. I of Herbert Spencer's *Principles of Sociology* (New York: D. Appleton & Company, 1896).

early religion is an intricate and almost indistinguishable network of magical and placatory endeavors.

The concepts of mana and taboo show how closely religion is related to magic. The unusual, the mana-infested, is a subject of awe and respect, protected by taboos. As R. H. Lowie[2] says, man discovers religion when he becomes conscious of the "religious experience"—when with feelings of awe and amazement he comprehends forces which are infinitely greater than his own and which he feels intuitively should be treated with respect. Goldenweiser called it the "religious thrill."[3] Max Weber said that religion results from man's contact with the infinite.[4] The concepts of mana and taboo bring man to the very threshold of the religious experience.

Polytheism

As we have observed, animism does not ascribe souls and spirits only to living men and animals. Spirits may occupy particular trees or even haunt special places of awesome or striking appearance. Nixies may inhabit rivers and waterfalls, ghostly beings may haunt the marshes, and mountains are frequently regarded as the abode of trolls, dragons, and other spirit beings. Hunters and food gatherers are concerned with such spirits, but they camp only temporarily in one place, then move on. Neolithic man, on the other hand, finds himself in a very special relationship to local spirits, geographically rooted in their own particular forest grove or river valley. The inhabitants of a Neolithic village, situated in the meadows close to the river, are more particularly concerned with the spirit that lives in the river,

as the Romans were with the spirit of the river Tiber, because they now share the same territory as a part of the same ecological community. His ill will can bring catastrophe; his goodwill may bring benefits. Permanent villagers must build up a happy relationship—a sort of goodwill and service contract—with the local spirit figures, and in their attempt to do this, they discover religion.

So the supernatural beings that men seek to propitiate become distinguished from other less important and less dangerous spirits and are elevated to the rank of GODS, supernatural beings who are to be placated instead of controlled. Those spirits which are recognized as gods may even be persuaded to assist men in warding off the lesser spirits whom man does not seek to propitiate, and when men entreat the gods for their assistance in this matter, prayer has been invented.

These gods took a variety of forms. Probably the most common were *nature gods,* present in every river, waterfall, mountain, and forest. Forest dwellers may well place a deity in every sacred grove, as did the Teutonic tribes that slaughtered the Roman legions at the battle of the Teutoburger Wald. Mountain dwellers might locate their gods on the mountain tops, as the Greeks placed Zeus on Mount Olympus. Pastoralists, occupying the broad plains, might conceive of *sky gods,* while agriculturalists might also be interested in the sun and the moon because of the regularity of their movements and the importance of the seasons to one who is concerned with raising crops. Sometimes these gods would be hierarchically ordered under a patriarchal *high god.*

To a horticultural people, gods who control the rain will be of particular significance, and the rain god will be a *functional god,* as well as being included perhaps in a pantheon of sky gods. Wind gods were common among American Indians, and the Babylonian Enlil, like the earliest form of the Semitic Jahwe, was also associated with the wind, clouds, and

[2] R. H. Lowie, *Primitive Religion.* New York: Boni-Liveright. (1948)
[3] A. Goldenweiser, "Religion and Society," *Journal of Philosophy, Psychology and Scientific Methods* 12 (1917).
[4] Max Weber, *Essays in Sociology* (London: Oxford University Press, 1946).

storms—counterparts of the Teutonic Thor. But another type of god is particularly characteristic of advanced horticulturalists and elementary agriculturalists: the *fertility god.*

The coming of the Neolithic in Europe revealed an increased interest in the fertility worship which had its roots in the Mesolithic. Venus figures, as they have been called, made from clay and representing pronouncedly pregnant women, appeared in Europe among the descendants of Cro-Magnon man and suggest an early deification of motherhood. But with the emergence of the Neolithic we have increasingly frequent indications of fertility rituals throughout the horticultural settlements of western Eurasia and historical evidence that some of the early Neolithic societies were matriarchal and matrilineal.

Mother goddesses that were widely worshiped in the Mediterranean area in historical times included Isis in Egypt, Astarte in Phoenicia, and Demeter in pre-Indo-European Greece (although the arrival of true Greeks in the Aegean led to a suppression of matriarchal systems because the Greeks were a strongly patriarchal people of originally pastoral origin). These goddesses aided men in ensuring the fertility of the crops, and interestingly, they tended to be associated with immortality as well, as though some symbolic connection existed between the womb through which man entered the world and the afterlife which followed his departure. Protecting his crops from predators, keen to see them multiply and the small fields wave with rich crops of corn, Neolithic man would understandably have expanded his interest in fertility not only as a key to the mystery of life but as a very practical answer to his material needs. In those societies which learned the facts about male paternity, temple prostitutes might appear, symbolizing in the sexual act the mystery of the creation of life, and the sexual organs, symbolized by phallic representations, might achieve religious significance.

Sacrifice

As we have observed, man's earlier essays into the realm of religion retained considerable faith in the efficacy of magic. But when gods have been identified who consistently resist manipulation by magical means, how then shall man go about propitiating them?

The first and most obvious answer is that if the gods have a will then they must also have

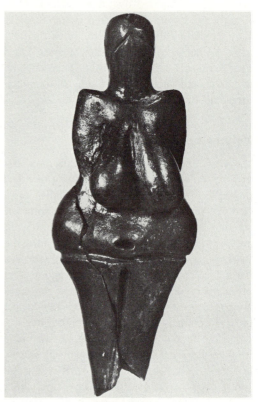

The Neolithic cultures of the Mediterranean and Danubian areas possessed a Mother Goddess fertility cult which was also echoed in many other parts of the world. This appears to have derived from a late Upper Paleolithic and Mesolithic cult evidenced by statues of pregnant mother figures (see also illustration on p. 116) whose heads, for some undetermined reason, invariably lack facial features. Portrayed above is the stone "Venus," typical of such figurines, found at Vestonice in Czechoslovakia. (Courtesy of Moravian Museum, Brno.)

Fossil remains of a sacrificial reindeer thrown into a lake at Meiendorf near Ahrensburg in Germany. Stones inserted in the body cavity to ensure that the animal would sink below the waters can still be seen inside the rib cage. (Courtesy of Dr. Alfred Rust and the Landesmuseum, Schloss Gottorp).

desires, and in man's limited experience these may well be assumed to resemble human desires, for he can conceive of no other needs. Thus, the South African Bushmen of the Kalahari Desert see god in the shape of a praying mantis but still attribute human qualities of thought and reason to the supernatural figure. The ancient Egyptians and the Hindus both recognized animal-headed gods, like the elephant-headed Ganesh of Indian mythology, but still gave them human-type interests. The ancient Greeks went further and saw their gods in human form, so that the phrase "Greek god" has come down to us today, for they represented their gods as the epitome of human beauty, with the clear-cut handsome features that they associated with aristocratic birth. But they also gave their gods very human desires and weaknesses, and these same gods were guilty of jealousy, seduction, vengeance, and adultery.

Men therefore tended to see their gods very much in their own image, a phenomenon known as ANTHROPOMORPHISM. The creation of anthropomorphic gods made it still easier to answer the question: how shall we appease the supernatural powers? Obviously, if the gods are like humans, they will have human tastes and probably human weaknesses. Therefore they may be flattered, and they will enjoy gifts and feasting.

Flattery and submission are apparent in the act of SACRIFICE, the voluntary destruction of one's own goods, even to the point of sacrificing one's own first-born son, as did the Carthaginians and as Abraham was prepared to do before his god Jahwe. To the extent that the gods are anthropomorphic, then it is possible that there may be a way to their heart through their stomachs, and food and drink may be preferred also.

Archeology cannot tell us for sure when the first sacrifice was made, but one of the earliest sacrificial ceremonies seems to have been held at Meiendorf in Germany when Cro-Magnon man tossed valuable deer into the Pleistocene lake (see the photograph above). Evidence of the deed is provided by the heavy stones that had weighted the deer down and were still inside their rib cages when they were found by archeologists some 15,000 years later. What could have been the purpose of such a deed, if it were not an act of sacrifice to some ancient god?

Where food is offered to the gods, such rituals may be accompanied by public feasts

Most traditional alcoholic beverages formerly had magicoreligious significance, and virtually all the folk customs and folklore of Europe are a survival from pre-Christian magical and religious practices. Here the villagers of Winningen, on the Moselle River in Germany, celebrate the ripening of the grape crop by a wine dance, the origins of which may be traced back to pagan antiquity. (Courtesy of the German Information Center, Bonn.)

in which the worshipers imagine that they are partaking of a common meal with their gods. The sharing of meals has always been a symbol of friendship ever since the first protohumans learned to share their food with other members of the intimate, kin-linked group. The modern businessman still seeks to gain a psychological bond with his customer by discussing the most important parts of his business over a common-meal table. Moslems sacrifice a goat at

Ramzan and eat the meat of the sacrificial animal themselves, thus sharing a meal with the supernatural beings.

So it was that the early Indo-Aryans held great horse sacrifices, killing the animals which meant so much to them and consuming the horse meat in sacrificial feasts.[5] However, they ate horse flesh at no other time, since the horse was dearly loved, respected, and useful. At the time of the Norman conquest of England, Scandinavian pagans still practiced horse sacrifices and ate sacred horse meat at sacrificial feasts. Christianity heavily condemned men for taking part in pagan communion, demanding instead that they participate in the Christian communion, and damned the eating of horse flesh so thoroughly that Englishmen still shudder at the thought. Perhaps it is not their Christianity that makes them refuse to eat the old sacrificial dish, but an ancient pagan reverence for horses—the antiquity of which is evidenced by the white horses cut into the English chalk downs—that has still not been totally dispelled.

Where the sacrificial object is not merely animal but also human, elements of ritual cannibalism enter into the banquet. The consumption of the flesh and blood of the slaughtered victim, especially where the victim is of noble birth, implies not only the notion of a meal shared with the god, but also the communicant's desire to acquire some of the mana of the sacrificed being. Thus the Aztec sacrificial victims were chosen from the best warriors, preferably nobles, of the nations they defeated, and there is no doubt that some of the Spanish Conquistadores finished up inside Aztec stomachs. At coronations of the Aztec kings, thousands of victims were slaughtered, and war was a necessary commitment to their god who hungered for fresh hearts torn from the living body. Victims were slaughtered

in vast public religious services, being held spread-eagled over the altar while the priest made an incision in the stomach, thrust in his hands, and tore the heart out while it was still beating. The heart was for the god, but the body was for the worshipers. The skin was deftly flayed from the corpse and handed to the priest, who wrapped himself in the bloody hide before the remainder of the corpse was handed down to the waiting multitude, so that they might consume the sacrificial flesh and benefit from the mana of the victim.

Because of the ancient memory of ritual cannibalism which seems to be implied in the Christian communion service, various Christian sects have in recent centuries dispensed with this part of the Christian ritual, feeling repulsed by what seems to them to be an invitation to eat the flesh and blood of a sacrificed god-king.

Priests and Priesthoods

As we have observed earlier, the introduction of horticulture led to an increasing economic surplus, which made possible the support of full-time nonagricultural specialists in various crafts. Thus in ancient Sumeria, as horticulturalists built temples to their local deities, we may trace the emergence of a regular priesthood whose duty it was to devote themselves full time to the propitiation of the divinities. Similarly, in New Zealand in more recent times, the horticultural Maoris developed a priestly society known as Whare Kura, initiates to which spent a five-year apprenticeship learning the rituals, myths, and prayers of their religion, as well as ventriloquism and sleight of hand—thus implying that they were still only in a transitional stage between shamanism and magic on the one hand and priesthood and religion on the other. PRIESTS are distinguished from shamans in being full-time professionals, trained and organized in the

---

[5] The Indian *rājasūya* or horse sacrifice was an integral part of the ritual conservation of a king or *rāja*.

propitiation rather than the manipulation of the gods.

At first the dividing line between magical and religious practices of the early shaman-priests could hardly have been discernible. Sometimes the members of the priestly society would be derived from a single clan, as with the Levites of the Hebrews or the Magi of Persia (from whom we derive the word *magician*). In other cases they would have been the younger sons of kings and nobles, as the first Indo-Aryan priests may have been. If they practiced endogamy, they inevitably established themselves as a separate caste which might eventually become more powerful than the nobles and kings. Even where the priests accepted recruits from outside their own kinship grouping, the profession was still guarded jealously, and initiates were subjected to rigorous training and tests before being admitted to full membership of the brotherhood.

Once professional and semibureaucratic systems of priesthood had emerged in the civilizations of antiquity, the role of the priests became extremely prominent. In Sumeria, Egypt, Crete, and in the New World among the Mayans and Aztecs, priestly organizations assumed considerable political significance, largely because religion now claimed to control men's moral actions, but also in part at least because in each of these cases the priests were closely associated with the development of a new and increasingly necessary art: writing.

Mass society, characterized by a developing division of labor, needed bureaucrats and clerks who could keep detailed records, and some method of recording data and events. The development of systems of cuneiform and hieroglyphic writing in the city civilizations of the Old World and the trend in that direction in the New World owed much to the priesthood. There was in the first place always something magical about words, especially names. They contain something of the spiritual essence of the object they describe. Many primitive peoples are reluctant to give their name to a stranger—some actually keeping their names entirely secret within their own community—for fear that knowing their name, the stranger may be able to exercise some magical power over them. Words and names, from the earliest days of religion, were therefore inclined to be associated with religious concepts. If spoken words are regarded with such respect, how much greater the mystery that surrounds a semisecret symbol inscribed on an

Wishes spoken aloud could take the form of spells. It is no surprise, therefore, that the written word was regarded as having particular supernatural significance, and the earliest forms of writing were commonly used for magico-religious purposes. This early European Runic stone honored the memory of a dead ancestor. (Courtesy of Landesmuseum, Schloss Gottorp.)

inanimate object, which can convey meaning from one man to another without the two ever meeting.

So the very first written symbols seem to have been associated very largely, if not exclusively, with religious and magical thoughts, and the runes carved on a sword or a tombstone were deemed to have magical power. As specialists in the supernatural the new priesthoods of the city civilizations inevitably found themselves closely involved in early attempts at writing. When literate priests could communicate with each other by means of written symbols, their influence in the community was even further enhanced. Writing gave a degree of political power to the priesthood which cannot be easily appreciated in our modern world in which the skills of reading and writing are taken for granted. Even though the art of writing probably owes more, in its long history, to the merchants than to the priests, in Egypt especially, the close association between priesthood and literacy was reflected in the role of the priests as administrators and statesmen.

Ritual

A horticultural people, concerned with important matters such as the most propitious time for the sowing or reaping of their crops, learn to watch the seasons and judge the passing of time. Here again, religion played a natural and dominant part in the development of a calendar which would serve to determine the correct dates for all annual events in the life of the cultivators. The priests of ancient Sumeria, Egypt, and the Mayan civilization observed the movements of the heavenly bodies and worked out surprisingly accurate calendars in which religious ceremonies and agricultural functions were synchronized and accurately predetermined. Lunar and solar ceremonies aimed at placating the gods could be neatly interwoven with proper husbandry and the

routine of the peasant farmer, and all life assumed a routine but highly religious character. Since the religious ceremonies were so obviously directly linked with the efficient prosecution of horticultural tasks, religious ceremonies began to assume a compulsory nature, all members of society being anxious that none should offend the gods by ignoring the religious duties that they expected from the community. Thus national rituals came to be organized by the priests, scheduled to be held on regular calendrical occasions, and usually representing, at first, a blend of magic and worship.

Regularly scheduled CALENDRICAL RITUALS are usually associated with nature festivals such as spring, harvest thanksgiving, midsummer, or midwinter, and may be intended to assist nature at a dangerous time, as in midwinter when the sun is at its very lowest point in the sky. Midwinter festivals, or winter solstice festivals, are designed to assist the sun in reversing its path, and instead of continuing to sink daily still lower in the sky, to recommence its annual ascent, bringing spring and summer in its wake. Midsummer is generally a period of rejoicing, for the harvest is ahead, even though the sun is about to begin its downward path. In northern latitudes such solstice festivals could take on a very real importance; for example, in Scandinavia where the sun scarcely shows itself above the horizon in midwinter, fiery wheels were rolled down the hillsides at the winter solstice in an attempt to aid the sun in its annual rebirth. Midsummer was also a magicoreligious festival, though more joyous, and Shakespeare tells us of the magical occurrences associated with midsummer night.

Special temples were frequently erected in conjunction with these calendrical rituals, designed by the priests to assist in the observation of the movements of the heavenly bodies. Both Stonehenge in England and the pyramids of the Toltecs in Central America were laid out to help plot the time of the year and to incorporate the movements of the sun into the calendrical rituals held in its honor. Stone circles laid out on the principle of the sundial were also common in Old World horticultural societies, particularly those of the so-called megalithic peoples of North Africa and Western Europe. So also the Hopi Indians in Arizona, probably receiving their ideas from Mexico, traced the rising and setting of the sun behind various mountain peaks, appointing a special sun watcher to do this, and planting and reaping their crops in accordance with his observations.

CRITICAL OR UNSCHEDULED RITUALS may be contrasted with scheduled rituals, since these are not related in any way to the calendrical system. They arise in order to propitiate the gods and cleanse the community of any bad luck whenever disaster threatens or men have reason to believe that the gods are angered with them. Earthquakes and foreign invasions are typical instances of occurrences which call for critical rituals.

The recent translation of the records of the Homeric city of Pylos has given us a new account of unscheduled and critical rites held at a time of crisis.[6] Pylos was a Mycenean city with a literate, cultured populace and a developed economy based upon commerce as well as mixed farming. It would seem, however, that like so many cities of its day, it fell to invading Dorian Greek tribes, self-proclaimed descendants of Hercules who penetrated the more prosperous region of the Aegean from the mountains of Albania. The Pylos tablets record how in the last few days before the destruction of the city, the inhabitants prepared themselves for the coming attack. Along with orders for additional bronze spearheads and instructions for the disposition of the army and the fleet, the tablets record the critical rites undertaken by the priests to cleanse the city of any unintentional impiety on the part of the

inhabitants which may have offended the gods. The rituals apparently failed, for the city was laid in ruins and the tablets are the last we hear from Pylos for some 300 years until literacy came to the descendants of the victorious assailants.

Rites of Passage

Other types of ritual which serve an obvious and direct social function and combine elements of both magic and religion are the RITES OF PASSAGE, ritual ceremonies held by members of a community to mark the passage of individuals from one level or stage to another. Such rituals are customarily regarded as desirable at or shortly after *birth* in order to mark the acceptance of the neonate into society. Similarly rituals are also usually held when *puberty* is reached, and these may or may not be carried out conjointly with *tribal initiation* ceremonies designed to initiate the candidate into full tribal membership and full knowledge of the secrets of tribal lore known only to adults.

The history of western European peoples reveals few traces of puberty customs, although tribal initiation rites were more common. The Romans, for example, recognized the coming of age of their sons by presenting them with a man's toga. Because Western society has no puberty rituals and no truly significant tribal initiation customs, teenagers are never sure when to regard themselves as adults, and no one else is sure either how to treat them—as children or adults. This problem does not exist where puberty and initiation rituals are practiced. Children are treated as children until they have been subjected to the appropriate rituals after which they and everyone else knows that they have attained adult status. The long period of adolescent uncertainty so characteristic of contemporary American society is thus avoided.

In view of the fact that transition from

[6] L. R. Palmer, *Achaeans and Indo-Europeans* (New York: Oxford University Press, 1955), pp. 20-22.

Blood is almost universally regarded as possessing magico-religious significance, and after sacrifices many worshipers smear their bodies with the blood of the dead animals. Ivory Coast celebrant. (Courtesy of La Documentation Française, Paris.)

childhood to adult status represents a very significant change in social status in any society, puberty and initiation rituals are sometimes made deliberately severe in order to emphasize the "rebirth" of the candidate in his new role. The "coming-of-age" ball thrown by parents of debutantes is but a mild echo of the rituals which Arunta children undergo. Arunta boys are subjected to deliberate and protracted torture, during which the older men who are already initiated bite the skin on their heads until it bleeds. Other initiation rituals may even involve staking the candidate down while he is bitten by ants or otherwise maltreated to the limit of his endurance. Such deliberate pain serves to ensure that the new status is traumatically ingrained into the candidate's mem-

(*Left*) Australian aboriginal boy being painted with mystical symbols prior to circumcision rituals. Executed in black, red, yellow, and white, the designs indicate the totemic group to which the boy belongs. (Courtesy of Australian News and Information Bureau.) (*Right*) Guere dancers with heads and bodies painted in preparation for magicoreligious dance; Ivory Coast. (Courtesy of La Documentation Française, Paris.)

ory and that he must now be ready to play his part in defending the community in war. It has been demonstrated that those societies which allow the male children particularly close association with the womenfolk in infancy tend as a rule to make the "coming-out" rituals for males all the more painful in order that the "rebirth" of the child in his new status as a man may be psychologically more effective.

While male rituals more often stress the warrior's role, female puberty rituals are more frequently associated with the need to prepare the initiate for her future role as a wife and mother. Among Nilotic Negroes this may involve cliterodectomy, the removal of the clitoris, with crude flint knives, presumably to inhibit sexual pleasure. Neighboring Hamites, from whom the Nilotic Negroes may have acquired the custom, are usually anxious to ensure virginity before marriage, and conduct similar operations which actually result in a scar formation that prevents sexual intercourse until such time as the scar should be formally broken. Both Hamitic and Semitic peoples also customarily circumcise males at the time of puberty or earlier, and all Moslems are required to be circumcised since the Islamic religion originated among the Semites.

Following puberty rituals young people are sometimes isolated in separate lodges until such time as they are regarded as ready for marriage, when a further public ritual will be arranged. *Marriage rituals* seldom involve any painful or unpleasant experiences. Since marriage marks the formation of a new nuclear family and further involves the alliance of two distinct kinship units, with all the economic, social, and political considerations implied by this, it is generally a family celebration. Nevertheless, community participation and elaborate ceremonial generally serve to impress both bride and groom of the essential solemnity of their undertaking and the religious importance of the new phase of life they are entering.

Old age is not always marked by rites of passage, unless social, economic, or political power is regarded as the privilege of the older generation. When the government and direction of the community is in the hands of the older members of society, we have a situation known as *gerontocracy,* and in such cases ceremonies may be performed when men reach an age which entitles them to participate in such offices. Certainly *death* is invariably marked in all societies by rites of passage, for the "passing over" into the next life is a matter of overwhelming importance and marks a stage in the progress of the soul which is of absorbing interest to survivors. Depending upon how the religion regards the idea of death, so members of one society will meet death contentedly and without fear, while others will live in almost perpetual apprehension of the inevitable day on which they finally depart from the world that is familiar to them.

Mourning and Afterlife

Belief in a soul which was separable from the physical body leads to the assumption that at death the soul merely passes into a different phase of existence. Only a few societies have believed that the soul remains in the body after death, and survivors in these societies might pinch the nose and close the eyes of the corpse to ensure that the soul will remain in the body. The Greeks, however, believed that the soul left the body in its underground tomb and congregated with other disembodied souls in a somewhat dreary, silent, and cold underworld. Happier were the souls of people who believed in a heavenly abode for their gods, for the spirits then might possibly be called to join the gods in their sky palaces. Thus did the Viking heroes hope to be carried up to Valhalla on the horses of the Valkyrie battle maidens, where they could enjoy themselves doing what they seem to have loved the best—jousting and feasting—at least until the dark day of Ragnarok, when gods and heroes would both die fighting the forces of evil, and the world itself would be consumed in flames. By contrast, the Moslems enjoyed a more sensuous Paradise, free from combat and strife, attended in their every need by female attendants known as *houris.*

In apprehension of the supernatural powers which might accrue to the souls of the dead, the surviving relatives understandably believed that every effort should be taken to ensure that such souls should rest in peace. Better by far to take pains to ensure that the departed soul was content in heaven, or perhaps securely trapped in hell, than to risk being haunted by an unhappy ghost. When the departed soul was unable to pass on to the other world because of some omission on the part of the living to comply with the proper rituals, it might be expected to hang miserably around the place where the body died. To avoid this situation, it was necessary to propitiate the ghost of deceased persons in any way that custom demanded. These efforts to propitiate the ghost were called *manism* by Herbert Spencer, after the Latin word *Manes,* the name by which the Romans knew the souls of their departed forebears.[7]

Where the bodies of the dead were laid in recognized burial grounds, these cemeteries would be protected by an elaborate taboo, as with Africans, American Indians, Australian aboriginals, Polynesians, and even more advanced societies. When the Persian army under Darius was laboriously endeavoring to pursue the nomadic Scythians over their native steppes, the Scythians ridiculed the efforts of the Persians to find them, but declared that if indeed the Persians wished to engage them in battle, they had only to seek out the graves of the Scythian ancestors and violate these to "know the Scythian fury."

[7] W. W. Fowler, *The Religious Experience of the Roman People* (London: The Macmillan Company, 1922), pp. 75 ff.

In its earlier stages horticulture exhausted the soil and made it necessary to abandon villages after a few years, but as the Neolithic advanced, settlements became more permanent; thus men were brought into more intimate contact with the dead. Even where deliberate malice was not ascribed to the ghost, there was the constant fear that ghosts might feel themselves neglected and slighted, even if the slight was unintentional. It was obviously very hard for the living to know how to please a ghost, and since neglected ghosts could become angry and malevolent, it was better to be conveniently free from them. In many societies, therefore, the hut in which a man had died would be destroyed; in others, magical devices were developed to protect the living from the dead. Many Bantu and Nilotic Negroes make a hole in the wall of their wattle and daub huts, and remove the corpse through this hole. The hole is then filled in again, and since they believe that the ghost can only re-enter a hut by the same route that the body took when leaving it, the occupants have nothing further to fear.

Fear that the ghost might return from the grave to haunt the living also led to many other magical devices, and the Azande pallbearers weave a zigzag path on the way from the hut to the cemetery in the hope that if the ghost should attempt to return, this will confuse it so that it cannot find its way. For good measure they also toss thorn bushes on the grave to further discourage the ghost from leaving its new abode. Eagerness to keep the ghost contented in the afterlife may also lead men to place food and drink in or near the grave and to bury the dead man's most valuable possessions with him, for who would dare to use the favorite tools or jewelery of a dead person when by so doing he may run the risk of arousing the ghost's jealousy? For similar fear of the departed spirit, widows in New Guinea and some parts of Africa may daub their head and body with white clay to hide their normally dark skin, on the supposition that the spirit of the deceased husband will be unable to recognize them and cause them harm or injury.

Ancestor Worship

The desire to propitiate the spirits of the dead may lead to ANCESTOR WORSHIP in which the souls of the ancestors are worshiped almost as though they were gods. It must not be assumed that all forms of ancestor worship are alike, however, for there are significant differences between those rituals undertaken primarily out of fear of the departed spirit, which may be regarded as malicious, and those rituals designed to comfort and establish communication with a spirit which is believed to be loving and protective. The difference lies in the intentions that are ascribed to the soul as a result of these attitudes. In societies in which the head of the family exercises his power capriciously, fear of the departed soul may be dominant, for the intentions of the deceased are more likely to be suspect. All attitudes toward the spirits of departed relatives will then tend to be self-motivated and may rest primarily upon magical devices intended to avoid the jealousy and anger of the deceased. Such attitudes will not necessarily incorporate strong notions of morality or contribute to the maintenance of social norms and values.

The magical attempts to control the dead or exorcise the spirit of the dead amount to little more than a cult based upon fear and the desire to evade personal suffering at the hands of supernatural forces. However, Shintoism and the ancestor worship of the Hindus, as well as that of ancient Greece and Rome, undoubtedly served to link both the living and the dead in a bond of love and mutual family interest, promoting social unity and imposing social norms on both generations. Such systems of ancestor worship may certainly be regarded as religious systems in their own right, since they serve to promote social consciousness with extreme effectiveness, and indeed have played a very important role in the ideological history of many Old World peoples.

While cults of the dead do not always impose a strong moral obligation to adhere to social norms, true ancestor-worshiping religions tend to subordinate the individual to the customs, traditions, and values of family, tribe, and nation. In such societies the individual may be prepared to sacrifice his life, as was the Japanese *kamikaze* pilot in World War II, for the benefit of family and nation. Where the worship of ancestors is highly developed, the family or phylogenetic continuum is seen as an eternal metaphysical reality, and the individual is regarded as nothing more than the temporary trustee of the name, blood, reputation, property, rights, and privileges of the family—the individual scarcely exists except as a facet of the lineage. Ancestor worship sees the lineage as ideally immortal, surviving in perpetuity and embracing not merely the living but also the dead and those not yet born. Even the nation is seen simply as a very large extended family.

So the Romans of the early Republic believed that the spirits of the departed remained loyal to the continuing family to the extent that each living family member was perpetually attended, protected, guarded, and judged by his own spiritual assistant or *genius*. The term *genius* was derived from the word *gens*, which may be loosely translated as "clan"—the same word that forms the root of our modern words "generation" and "generate," as well as "gentleman," meaning a member of one of the select patrician gens. The genii were always the spirits of departed ancestors who in their devotion to the family undertook the moral guidance and sometimes even physical protection of living family members.

These genii are not feared by their descendants, but the latter are careful to avoid doing anything that would dishonor the family or harm the family heritage which they hold in trust for future generations still unborn. The ancestral genii demand only that the customs and interests of the family be served, including, by implication, the wider community of kinship-linked individuals that makes up the gens, tribe, and nation.[8] Just as in Greece and Rome so also in Japanese Shintoism and to some extent in Chinese Confucianism, ancestor worship validates and reinforces the kinship structure of the community and obligates the individual to dedicate himself to the welfare of his society. With every ritual sacrifice, every remembrance of the ancestors, the obedience to the social values of a familistic society is reinforced. From the devotions of ancestor worship, there consequently arose a particular type of religion which we know as the *ethnic religion*.

Ethnic Religions

Ethnic religions arise out of ancestor worship and the firm conviction that the individual is but a single link in the continuing chain of the generations, and has but a single duty, service to the family and the family-nation. They are religions that belong essentially to the people who have developed them. Their members show little interest in making converts and indeed usually prohibit admission to any who are not born into the community of worship. Since they do not seek converts, they are not jealous of other religions, except and unless such religions attempt to proselytize their members, and like Shintoism, may even be able to permit their members to recognize other religious systems, provided the prime duty to ancestors and to the nation and national gods are not neglected. Hinduism and the ancient religions of Greece and Rome expected the members of other societies to have their own gods and their own beliefs. Their philoso-

[8] Fustel de Coulanges, N. D., 1970, *The Ancient City.* New York: Doubleday & Company, Inc.

phy was essentially this: live and let live.

Because of their exclusiveness, ethnic religions promote a strong sense of group identification, in-group loyalty, and ethnocentrism. Their effect is strongly nationalistic and even racialist, and they are likely to encourage the strict enforcement of endogamous regulations relating to *connubium,* the limits of the interbreeding community. Since ancestor worship places emphasis upon the fame of the forebears and upon the destiny of the progeny, ancestor worshipers will tend to select their wives, as the early Greeks admitted of themselves, "like they choose their horses, by the length of their pedigrees." Emphasis is therefore placed upon purity of descent, and the act of reproduction is regarded as sacred. Newly married patrician Romans actually consummated the marriage on an ancestral wedding couch kept for the occasion and used by the generations before them for this religious rite. Offspring are likely to be put to death if they fall short of the physical and intellectual standards expected by the family. During the feudal period the Japanese were so coldly deliberate about eugenic infanticide that they waited up to two or three years before making a final decision on the fate of the child to be sure of detecting any defects that might be overlooked at a younger age.

When eternal life is obtained through the survival of one's progeny, the tendency for close inbreeding, to ensure that the son will resemble the father and that none of the precious blood of the family will be contaminated by alien admixture, may even lead to strict clan endogamy, as with the Inca kings and certain Egyptian dynasties. Such intense attitudes will be further reinforced by customs such as those of the Roman patrician families who took death masks of all who died and hung these on the walls of the entrance hall, replacing them in later times by ancestral busts, which in turn gave way in Western history to painted portraits.

In addition to promoting national feeling,

ethnic religions are also usually associated with a high degree of social stratification which is invariably castelike in nature. Ancient Greece and Rome, Confucian China, and traditional India and Japan were all highly stratified societies, for the patricians would exclude the plebeians from marriage, and the Brahmans would not mix with lower castes, nor would prerevolutionary Chinese landowners mix their genes with those of the peasants, nor the Japanese warrior-nobles blend their lineages with the farmers or craftsmen. Elements of familial charisma are found in association with all ethnic religions. Wherever emphasis is placed on family and lineage, those who are most closely related to the original heroic or legendary ancestors are likely to rank more highly than those with more remote kinship affiliation. Those whose purity of lineage is in doubt are likely to be socially excluded altogether.

Revitalization

Particularly in those religions which have an ethnic character, political, military, or cultural decay may lead to the emergence of REVITALISM, a religious creed that aims to strengthen the moral fiber of the people and serve as a rallying point for group unity.

Many nations believe that an ancient hero-king or leader will return to save his people should they ever suffer military defeat. If defeat has actually taken place and the nation has been suppressed by alien rulers, a form of NATIVISM (also known as millenarianism or messianism) may persist, promising a return of the god-hero at a later date. Among the Jewish people, this took the form of messianism in which the god was to come down to the world himself to save his chosen nation.

A special case of revitalization occurred among the Indians of the California and Nevada regions in the latter part of the nineteenth century. This took the form of the GHOST DANCE CULT. An Indian named Wodzi-

wob claimed that the ancestors would return and sweep the White men from the land, and special ritual ghost dances were performed to facilitate and advance the date of the ancestral return. The cult spread over a large area, until the Whites began to fear an Indian uprising, and the Indian agents and military stepped in to suppress the cult.

In Melanesia there developed a particularly interesting CARGO CULT which also had nationalist tendencies, heavily reinforced by an appeal to the appetite for material wealth. The Melanesians at Sabai in the Torres Straits, who had become, nominally at least, Christians, saw that ships regularly brought cargoes of desirable manufactured goods, and the idea of revolution developed, again organized around the belief that the ancestors would return by sea in large ships which would bring with them valued goods, and that all the Whites would be killed and driven into the sea.

Various modifications of the theme occurred repeatedly. In some of these it was argued that the White people merely seem to sit in offices and make mystic signs on paper to acquire the goods from the ships. Thus, if the Melanesians took over the office buildings, killed off the Whites, and continued the mystic sign making, the ships would continue to arrive, bringing with them the desired goods.

Missionary Religions

MISSIONARY RELIGIONS stand in sharp contrast to ethnic religions. They tend to be intolerant of rival religious beliefs and seek to convert members of other societies to a recognition of and worship of the one "true god," and to an acceptance of and adherence to the one "true morality" associated with that god. As a result of this monistic outlook, which generally finds expression in MONOTHEISM— the belief in a single all-powerful creator-god—missionary religions have been responsible for a high proportion of the major wars

The great missionary religions have preserved many of the magicoreligious rituals of earlier traditions. Here, Moslem Negroes of West Africa gather for prayer during the annual month-long period of fasting known as Ramadan. The Moslem religion is of Semitic origin, and these African converts dress in costumes of similarly Semitic origin, kneeling on prayer rugs as was the habit of the early Arabic converts. In short, there has been a substantial cultural diffusion involving a well integrated complex of material as well as ideological cultural traits. (Courtesy of the Service Information de la Côte-d'Ivoire.)

Monotheistic religions, which attribute dominant supernatural powers to a single god, are primarily concerned that men should learn the will of this god in order to comply with the deity's wishes. Such religions usually produce "prophets," persons who claim to have communicated with the divine being, and whose "revelations" may be collected in a sacred book. Illustrated above is a copy of the Koran or sacred book of the Moslem Religion. (Courtesy of La Documentation Française, Paris)

of the Old World. Holy wars are frequently preached to convert unbelievers or to protect holy shrines. The Moslems have fought many such *jehad* against the "infidels"; the Christian Crusaders fought against the Moslems; the Christian Franks against the pagan Saxons, and the Christian Teutonic knights against the pagan Slavs. Even religions of "peace" are often carried to unbelievers with the aid of the sword.

But the sword must also be supported by the spoken and written word, and propaganda to win over the unbelievers must be slanted to appeal. In consequence, missionary religions are seldom race-conscious or aristocratic in character; few will convert to a religion that offers them only a subordinate position in society. Missionary religions are therefore usually universalistic and equalitarian in outlook, and have achieved much success in converting the lower orders of stratified societies by promising them social equality—at least in the afterlife. Christianity made wholesale converts by preaching social revolution among the Roman slaves, while in India under the Moghul emperors the Moslem religion won literally millions of converts from the outcastes of Hindu society by offering the converts the opportunity to escape from underneath the hierarchical Hindu caste system.

The fact that until recently Pakistan comprised two quite separate ethnic groups, separated from each other by nearly a thousand miles of Hindu Indian territory, was due to the missionary appeal of the Islamic religion. When the Hindus reached the eastern part of India nearly 3000 years ago, they found the lowlands and marshes of Bengal inhabited by a darker aboriginal population, partly Australoid in character. Because of the ethnic nature of their religion, they established themselves as a thin upper caste over a larger aboriginal population which was relegated to a low ritual status.

Under Moghul rule these aboriginals then converted to Islam. When India was partitioned by popular vote in 1947 into a predominantly Hindu India and a predominantly Moslem Pakistan, East Bengal was carried by this large Moslem convert vote into a political union with West Pakistan a thousand miles away, a region with which the people of East Bengal had few cultural ties other than the Islamic religion and a common legacy of British rule. Renamed "East Pakistan," East Bengal remained subordinate to West Pakistan leadership until 1971 when its people finally won independence under the name of Bangladesh. All contemporary political conflicts are in fact cultural conflicts and can only be understood fully by an anthropological analysis of the problems involved.

But Islam's success does not stem from its appeal to the lower orders alone. It also has something to offer the upper classes as well.

The Moslem religion promises security to the rich in the possession of their wealth. Since all events are the will of Allah, it is not the fault of the wealthy that they are rich. Islam thus supports the status quo in this world, while promising the lower orders equality and happiness in the next life.

The two most characteristic missionary religions of the modern world, Christianity and Islam, are both intimately connected with Judaism and trace their beliefs to the monotheistic ideas which arose among Semitic-speaking pastoralists in the Arabian peninsula. It has been suggested that the seminomadic character of these sheep- and goat-herding pastoralists led them to conceive of a god whose power existed as far as the eye could see, from horizon to horizon, and even beyond the horizon to the ends of the world. Certainly their concept of god was not that of a territorially rooted local spirit like the gods of the Sumerian city states. Indeed, the Hebrews developed the idea of a portable temple to the extent that they transported the things sacred to their god—in particular the Ark of the Covenant—with them when they migrated.

So the basic conditions for an imperialistic, jealous creator-god, seeking recognition and worship from all men, were realized. When the Semitic Assyrians, originally a pastoral people, invaded the settled land of Sumeria and established the world's first large military empire—creating a desert and calling it "Peace"—they closed down all the local temples and set up one supreme god to be worshiped wherever the force of their arms was felt. In this, they sought to weld their empire into a single unified society, just as the Incas 3000 years later taught those whom they conquered to worship the Inca gods in the hope of establishing a homogeneous and permanent empire under Inca rule.

The Assyrian empire was subsequently destroyed by invading Indo-European Persians who endeared themselves to the Sumerians by causing the local temples that the Assyrians had destroyed to be rebuilt, and by permitting freedom of religious worship once again.

Thus was the Assyrian experiment in missionary monotheism brought to an end. But not so the Hebrew version. A similar monotheism also developed among the Semitic Hebrews while these people were still seminomadic pastoralists. The Hebrew idea was distinguished by the novel concept of a contract between the Hebrew creator god and the Hebrew people by which they undertook to serve their god in his drive for world recognition. In return for their aid he promised them the successful annexation of the land of Canaan, a small territory already occupied by horticultural Canaanites, as an initial reward, and furthermore promised that when his vic-

Moslem societies traditionally required their women to be masked from view. Through cultural diffusion the idea may be adopted by other peoples, though often with a different effect. Dancers from Fort Archambault, Chad Republic. (Courtesy of La Documentation Française, Paris.)

tory was complete they would rule the world on his behalf as his Chosen People.

Although the Hebrews won their promised land, their capital city and main temple were destroyed by the Romans, who had begun to fear the disturbing and exciting nature of their religious ideas. But the tenacity with which the worshipers of Jahwe have adhered to their beliefs—and after nearly two millennia have recaptured their city of Jerusalem and in effect rebuilt their temple—is evidence of the significance of ideological factors in determining the pattern of human affairs.

Hebrews abandoned many of the earlier Semitic customs such as blood sacrifice but retained circumcision and other tribal rites. Through the centuries the Hebraic religion seems to have vacillated between the desire to remain a strictly ethnic religion, practicing racial purity and rejecting converts not born of Jewish mothers, and a willingness on the other hand to accept converts to the Judaic religion on the basis of equality. This dispute still divides the more Orthodox from the Re-

form version of Judaism today; but in a sense it was the Christian heresy that was to become the missionary branch of the Judeo-Christian religious tradition.

Christianity arose as an heretical offshoot of the Judaic religion and from an early date declared itself ready to make converts from all nations and races, seeing all mankind as the children of a monotheistic god. Although it almost abandoned its monotheism at one stage, when European converts reared in the pagan tradition insisted on maintaining that "God, the Son, and the Holy Ghost" must logically be three gods, not one, the "Arian" heretics who took this view were overruled, and the monotheistic nature of Christianity was saved by an appeal to mysticism.

Despite its dogmatic character, Christianity, like other missionary religions, tended in practice to become very eclectic in its accumulation of myths and legends. It was easier to assimilate and reinterpret ancient Babylonian, Egyptian, and even Slavic, Celtic, and Teutonic myths than to quash them. All three religions

Many of the customs of pagan Europe still live in the folk life of the people despite Christianity. Here the lighthouse keeper at Tinsdahl, near Hamburg in northern Germany, decorates a small green tree at Christmas in unconscious continuation of the pre-Christian Yuletide ritual, a calendrical ceremony commemorating the Winter Solstice. (Courtesy of the German Information Center, Bonn.)

Buddhist Chedis or shrines in the Wat Po temple compound in Thailand. (Courtesy of the Public Relations Department, Thailand.)

which trace their origin back to the Middle East—Judaism, Islam, and Christianity—actually plagiarized a wide variety of older cultural sources and excellently illustrate the process whereby culture is diffused in the historical evolution of mankind.

Few Christians today realize how extensively pagan traditions were absorbed into the legacy of Christian ritual. No one originally believed that Christ was born on December 25, but the Catholic Church found it more convenient to schedule the festival of his birth to coincide with the pagan winter solstice festivals, known as Yuletide in northern Europe, than to oppose the ancient rituals involving the cutting of holly and ivy, the burning of the Yule log, and much feasting on boar's flesh. The pagan festival of spring, a nature festival named Easter after the pagan goddess Eostra, symbolized the rebirth of the world of nature after the long sleep of winter, and was absorbed into Christianity as the festival which commemorated the resurrection of Christ. The two ideas, resurrection of the slain god-king and the rebirth of life following the winter sleep, were sufficiently similar to permit identification in the minds of the illiterate peasantry. And it is to the pagan past, not the Christian past, that we owe the popular tradition of Easter eggs, indications of the rebirth of nature, as well as the very name Easter. Similarly, All Saint's Day is a memory of early European ancestor worship, when the spirits of the ancestors came back to earth; thus in Brittany today the countryfolk still make a visit to the village churchyard on All Saints' Day and leave little offerings on the graves of the departed.

Another significant missionary religion was to emerge in India, and this was Buddhism.

Like other missionary religions, Buddhism is universalist and essentially equalitarian. But it is deeply rooted in philosophical beliefs that derive from the ancient Indo-European religious scheme, and like the old Indo-Aryan beliefs sees the universe not so much as the creation of a single mind but as a causal nexus. Instead of rejoicing in this causal stream, however, Buddhism sees life as continuous pain, with desire being inevitably frustrated, thus making pain inevitable. Intellectually, Buddhism has become more of a philosophy of self-control, teaching that man's goal should be escape from the pain and from worldly suffering—even from the constant agony of the cycle of birth and rebirth—by attempting to control and if possible to abolish desire. When the mind could succeed in suppressing the desire of the body, then *nirvana* (a state of "nothingness" or "nonbeing") could be attained, and the soul would escape from the prison of life.

Buddhism therefore developed in a direction antithetical to the world-affirming tradition of the Indo-European society that gave it birth. While early Indo-Aryan India had seen the world as a good place and urged men to seek eternity through their posterity or even to yearn for rebirth into the world, Buddhism, like Christianity in its early days, taught that the world was an essentially evil place. But it differed from Christianity in declining, in its purer form, to postulate a better world beyond the grave. Just as the pagan Romans were shocked at the appearance of Christian doctrines teaching "hatred of the world," so too the Brahmans were shocked at a religion which turned away from the world. For a time Buddhism dominated the Indian scene, but eventually the ancestor-worshiping ethnic religion was triumphant, being deeply rooted in the basic kinship structure of Hindu society, and Buddhism virtually disappeared from the land which gave it birth.

Comparison of Ethnic and Missionary Religions

It is no accident, therefore, that missionary religions are generally monotheistic in nature, and equalitarian and universalistic in outlook, and that by contrast ethnic religions tend toward polytheism, since they seem to originate in ancestor worship and are aristocratic and discriminatory in practice. Ethnic religions are usually strongest among the upper classes of a stratified society because they justify social exclusiveness and the emphasis is upon family and lineage pride and racial purity, whereas the lower strata of any society are more likely to respond with alacrity to the appeal of equalitarian missionary religions.

Since ethnic religions have a tendency to deify the ancestors, the upper classes of such societies—known to the Greeks as *aristoi* or *eugenia,* the "well-born"—may even claim to be descended from gods. The later Roman emperors were regarded as living gods, while the Incas claimed to be descended from the Sun. In ethnic religions there is therefore relatively little to fear from the gods, whose deeds the more eminent men endeavor to emulate, nor is the search for knowledge, scientific or magical, condemned. The heroes of ethnic religions have been known to cross-examine the gods and even to force them to reveal their knowledge of the universe and its mysteries, but in monotheistic missionary religions the emphasis is upon blind and unquestioning obedience to the revealed will of an inscrutable and all-powerful creator-god. The ethos of the monotheistic missionary religion clearly states that faith is desirable and doubt is undesirable.

So it was that the ancient schools of Athenian philosophy, founded in the days of pagan civilization, were closed down under the Byzantine emperors on the advice of the Christian clergy because they taught men to question the revealed word of their god as laid down in their holy book. Galileo was arrested and faced the threat of torture for similar reasons. The way out of this religious blanket which suppressed free thought appeared only when men rediscovered the old pagan writings and introduced the Renaissance.

The real conflict between missionary and ethnic religions arose when the former attempted to destroy the tradition of familial charisma vested in the heads of clans and nations. The "divine right" of European kings, based originally on descent from the gods and the possession of familial charisma, was satisfactorily invested with a new concept of church-appointed divinity when a Catholic bishop seized the crown on the occasion of Charlemagne's coronation and placed it on the king's head before the king could do this for himself. By this act he symbolized the supremacy of the church, which in future claimed to extend religious sanctions to kings, including them in God's order of things rather than acknowledging them because they were God-descended in themselves. Henceforth, the kings were merely temporal officials, and the spiritual was divorced from, but theoretically above, the temporal powers.

This is in sharp contrast to the philosophy of societies which maintain an ethnic religion. Even the ancient Sumerian kings had possessed a certain divinity, and the chief priestess in a Sumerian temple was often the king's sister. The Mikado of Japan, into this century, symbolized the combination of both religious and secular offices, and so in tradition does the English queen, if not in fact. Persian kings had sacral responsibilities, as did the earlier pagan kings of Saxon England who were forbidden by their religion to cut their long yellow hair, long hair being associated with familial charisma and nobility of birth—which is the reason why British judges still wear long wigs on ceremonial occasions, since they are dispensing royal powers as the king's deputies.

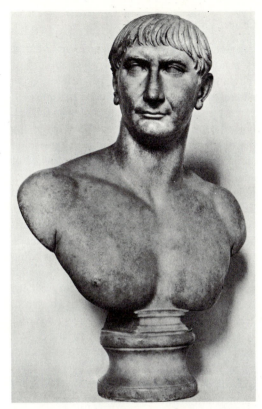

The religions of ancient Rome and Greece centered on the worship of ancestral spirits and nature gods. Death masks of the ancestors were hung on the walls of the sacred altar room (or atrium) of every patrician home in ancient Rome. These were later replaced by sculpted busts of the dead, hence the many busts which have survived to us from the Roman civilization. (Courtesy of the British Museum, London.)

It was thus no accident that when Henry VIII seized church power from the Pope and established the Church of England, his subjects approved his decision to declare himself the head of the Church by virtue of his hereditary office as ritual head of the nation-family. Neither the ancient aristocracy nor the lower classes of Europe were ever fully converted to Christianity; much of the pagan tradition survived in the family pride of the nobles and the folk beliefs of the peasantry.

Other Theories of Religion

Tylor's explanation of magic as an attempt to manipulate the supernatural forces and of religion as an attempt to propitiate supernatural powers that refuse to be manipulated is not regarded as adequate to explain the full power of the religious experience over the mind of man, and subsequent sociologists and anthropologists have put forward a number of additional theories. In general, it is felt that religion serves a far more deeply rooted need in society than Tylor's theory ascribes to it.

One of the most significant theorists in this field has been Émile Durkheim, the French sociologist who was responsible for building a completely new theory of group behavior that has become the foundation of modern sociological thought.[9] To Durkheim, all groups and all societies tend to develop a *social conscience,* an accumulation of norms and values which the group or society will seek to impress upon its members at all times. To Durkheim, religion is the expression of the social conscience. No member of a society can reject the collective conscience or moral culture of his society without feeling alienated or afraid. Religion does not need the idea of a god or of supernatural forces, Durkheim argues, but is likely to invent these to assist in coercing the individual into the acceptance of the group norms. Punishment in an afterlife is prophesied as the fate of those who contravene the social values, while religious services and rituals help to promote a feeling of togetherness, of contact with the infinite, which is actually an awareness of social identity and an awareness of group participation by the individual. Religion does not arise as an answer to fear, according to Durkheim, but invents fear in order to coerce the individual into subordination to the group values.

Durkheim's theories have not been univer-sally accepted, however, and in particular the psychologists have disputed the correctness of his interpretation. Bronislaw Malinowski argued, rather parallel to Tylor, that religion does reduce human apprehension of the supernatural. Religion, according to Malinowski, is a formula which provides answers to man's questions about the universe, and by providing an institutionalized answer, with all the weight of authority that a socially accepted theory carries, it removes that feeling of insecurity which exists whenever we have an unanswered question. Religion tells us who we are, what we are, and even why we are here. Furthermore, he said, religion purports to offer proven ways of placating the supernatural powers, and so also serves the *function* of calming man's fears. Religion would not exist, he agrees, if it did not serve a function, and that function is to assuage doubt and fear. Citing his own observations among the Trobriand Islanders, Malinowski demonstrated that those islanders who lived on the inner lagoon where fishing was less dangerous tended to follow different rituals from those who lived on the outer lagoons or the open sea. In the rituals of the latter, the desire to propitiate the forces of the unknown waters was far more prominent than among those who lived on the safe lagoons, and so, he claimed, the religious function—the calming of fear and doubt—was clearly illustrated.

A. R. Radcliffe-Brown also agrees that religion would not exist if it did not serve a useful function.[10] Society functions like a machine, like a gestalt whole, in which each cog must neatly mesh into the next, and any set of practices which do not contribute to the smooth working of the total social machine will eventually be rejected and discontinued. The purpose of religion is, as Durkheim pointed out, to consolidate the value system and overall cosmogony of society. For this reason religion

[9]Emile Durkheim, *The Elementary Forms of the Religious Life* (New York: The Macmillan Company, 1915).

[10]A. R. Radcliffe-Brown, *Structure and Function in Primitive Society* (London: Cohen & West, Ltd., 1952).

is usually compulsory, while magic is a voluntary pursuit, since magic is not concerned with the social values. Ritual, likewise, serves the social value system. Psychologists explain to us in behavioral terms how habits form as a result of frequently repeated actions. Because rituals are regularly repeated, they tend to be habit-forming, and a particular ideology associated with particular ritual actions, by the process of repetition of thought and deed, becomes deeply ingrained or internalized in the mind. The fact that much ritual is also practiced as a communal activity also serves to identify the individual with the community around him and emphasizes the social nature of the mores.

Although the precise nature and function of religion may still be debated, it is nowadays generally accepted that the definition of religion may be widened to include almost any socially accepted philosophy—even a creed such as communism—that is endorsed and emphatically imposed by society upon its members, even if no specific spirit figures are identified. Such religious systems relieve the individual of the need to worry about the unknowable by providing him with socially accepted propositions concerning morality and metaphysics which are not themselves capable of empirical proof. Religion also serves to integrate the group and reduces tension by imposing a consistent cultural system upon all members of a given society. To the extent that a single religious system succeeds in dominating the whole of society, these goals are achieved. But rival religions can tear a society to pieces and pit one society against another. Religion may therefore have a socially integrating impact in simpler and culturally homogeneous societies, but often exerts a socially disintegrating influence in more complex and diverse societies where rival religions serve as rallying points for opposing systems of normative culture. Whichever way we look at the religious experience, however, there can be no denying the truth of Max Weber's contention that religion, representing as it does distinctive and integrated patterns of ideational programming, has played a very significant role throughout the history of man, as it still does in this present age.

For Further Reading

Burridge, K. O. L., 1960, *Mambu: A Melanesian Millennium.* London: Methuen & Co., Ltd.

Deren, M., 1953, *Divine Horsemen: The Living Gods of Haiti.* London: Thames and Hudson.

———, 1970, *Voodoo: Living Gods of Haiti.* New York: Random House, Inc.

De Vries, J., 1967, *The Study of Religion.* New York: Harcourt Brace Jovanovich, Inc.

Dumézil, G., 1952, *Les dieux des Indo-Européens.* Paris: Presses Universitaires de France.

———, 1934, *Ouranos-Varuna, Étude de Mythologie Comparée Indo-Européenne.* Paris: Adrien Maisonneuve.

Durkheim, É., 1964, *The Elementary Forms of the Religious Life.* New York: Humanities Press, Inc.

Eliade, M., 1962, "Cargo-Cults and Cosmic Regeneration," *Comparative Studies in Society and History,* Suppl. No. 2.

Evans-Pritchard, E. E., 1957, *Nuer Religion.* New York: Oxford University Press.

———, 1965, *Theories of Primitive Religions.* New York: Oxford University Press.

Firth, R., 1967, *The Work of the Gods in Tikopia,* 2 vols. New York: Humanities Press, Inc.

Fustel de Coulanges, N. D., 1970, *The Ancient City*. New York: Doubleday & Company, Inc.

Gelling, P., and H. E. Davidson, 1972, *The Chariot of the Sun*. London: J. M. Dent & Sons, Ltd.

James, E. O., 1964, *The Ancient Gods*. New York: G. P. Putnam's Sons.

Lessa, W. A., and E. Z. Vogt, 1965, *A Reader in Comparative Religion*. New York: Harper & Row, Publishers.

Linton, R., 1943, "Nativistic Movements," *American Anthropologist* 45:230–240.

Littleton, C. S., 1973, *The New Comparative Mythology*. Berkeley: University of California Press.

Maringer, J., 1960, *The Gods of Prehistoric Man*. New York: Alfred A. Knopf.

Middleton, J., n.d., *Gods and Rituals: Readings in Religious Beliefs and Practices*. New York: Doubleday & Company, Inc.

Mühlmann, W, E., 1961, *Chiliasmus und Nativismus: Studien zur Psychologie, Soziologie und historischen Kasuistik der Umsturzbewegungen*. Berlin: Dietrich Reimer Verlag.

Reichard, G., 1964, *Navaho Religion: A Study of Symbolism*, 2d ed. Princeton, N.J.: Princeton University Press.

Spindler, G. D., and L. Spindler, 1971, *Dreamers Without Power: The Menomini Indians*. New York: Holt, Rinehart and Winston, Inc.

Sundkler, B. G. M., 1961, *Bantu Prophets in South Africa*. London: International African Institute.

Willoughby, T., 1928, *The Soul of the Bantu*. New York: Doubleday & Company, Inc.

CHAPTER 21

The Esthetic Adventure

Language grew out of the will to communicate, but as we observed before, there are ways of communicating other than through speech. Art is also essentially a form of communication—and one which is exclusively human; for art represents an attempt to communicate human subjective and emotional experiences.

A Unique Experience

Like animals, men analyze and interpret the events around them in a manner which serves to ensure survival. The snapping of a twig at night means to men, as it does to animals, the possible approach of danger. When men see heavy thunderclouds forming on the horizon, they are able to deduce the possibility of a thunderstorm. In both cases they may share this information with their fellows through the medium of speech, so that they can join together in preparing a proper response. Using their capacity for intelligent rational thought and organizing the information gained by observation and the exchange of information,

men have learned to protect themselves and to harness the forces of nature to their own wills. But they have also developed an emotional sensitivity to the phenomena around them, which seems to have little direct relevance to the problem of survival.

Thus men attempt to understand the universe in all its manifestations—ranging from the sublime panorama of the skies at night down to the smallest detail that may catch their attention—in an emotive sense as well as in a strictly utilitarian manner. They seek to interpret what they see in terms of survival; but what they see and feel also excites them emotionally. From this empathic emotional experience they appear to derive a pleasure which has little or no Darwinian value, but which produces an exquisite thrill. The more men elevate themselves above the immediate pressures of their environment, by gaining control over the forces of nature, the more they pursue this "esthetic thrill." Indeed, civilization itself seems to represent an attempt by man to introduce a pleasing esthetic content into all that

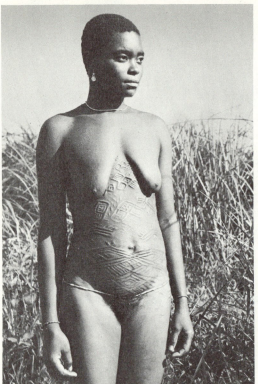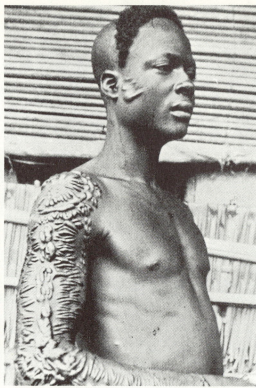

Even before clothes were worn, the body was adorned with cicatrix markings of ritual significance, cut into the skin during puberty or other ritual ceremonies. (*Left*) Woman from Pointe Noire, Congo. (Courtesy of La Documentation Française, Paris.) (*Right*) Sudanese male. (Courtesy of Hans W. Jürgens.)

he makes and does—an esthetic element that adds a certain richness or quality to life. Civilization can consequently only arise when technology and social diversity have developed to the level that permits man to free himself from immediate survival problems and to turn at least some of his attention to esthetic goals. Such esthetic goals can sometimes take quite "unnatural" forms, forms which in their ecological, biological, or other implications have negative survival value; but the only civilization that will ever endure is one with esthetic goals that are attuned to the problems of human survival as an integral part of a total ecological system.

PERSONAL ADORNMENT

Body Mutilation

The emotional pleasure derived from art does not appear to be wholly restricted to man. Chimpanzees have shown obvious signs of enjoyment when allowed to smear colored pigments over large canvases, and in one instance a chimpanzee "fingerpainting" was entered in a children's fingerpainting competition at a modern art gallery, and actually won a prize, much to the chagrin of the judges when the true origin of the prize-winning exhibit was made known. Chimpanzees also dance at rain festivals, as we have already observed, although they do so with little sense of rhythm, harmony, or unison. Yet chimpanzees differ from men in that they do not show any conscious desire to communicate through the medium of art, even though they apparently experience a primitive esthetic emotion. Furthermore, their "paintings" and "dances" lack the benefit of any learned cultural tradition such as characterizes human art.

Experiencing pleasurable emotions from "art," chimpanzees have also been known to derive positive satisfaction from adorning their bodies with pieces of colored rag, but they possess no cultural guidelines regarding body ornamentation and have no preconceived ideas as to how the body might be most advantageously adorned or ornamented. Such is not the case with men, who also derive pleasure from adorning their bodies—surely the most personal form of applied art we know—but do so with deliberation and a degree of consistency, following the dictates of customs learned from the other members of their group. Not content with wearing clothes, men also fix metal and stone objects to their bodies, and even try to change the shape and color of both hair and body by painting and mutilating it, but almost always they do this in imitation of other men and women. When recognized techniques for conveying the desired emotional message exist, we speak of an *artistic tradition*.

Although practices involving bodily mutilation are relatively rare in more complex societies, many peoples in preagricultural societies deliberately mutilate their bodies for magicoreligious and ritual purposes or even as a mark of social status, usually with dramatic artistic effect. The painting of the body and the coloring of teeth, nails, and hair are temporary devices. More permanent mutilations involve the removal of teeth, the removal of hair, the piercing of nose, ears, and even cheeks to

Lip plugs are common in many parts of the world: (*Top*) Mousgoum woman. (*Bottom*) Mongo woman. (Courtesy of La Documentation Française, Paris.)

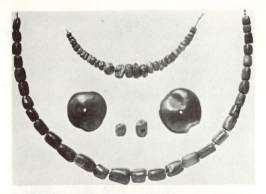

(*Top*) A necklace of beads from European Stone Age, recovered at Satruper Moor, Schleswig. (Courtesy of Landesmuseum, Schloss Gottorp.) (*Bottom*) More elaborate necklaces worn without clothing by a group of Erigpactsa Indians from the Matto Grosso, Brazil. (Courtesy of Musée de l'Homme, Paris.)

receive ornamental bones or valuable stones, and scarification. In the latter case, designs are cut into the skin on either the face or the body, dirt or charcoal being deliberately rubbed into the open wound to ensure prominent permanent scars or *cicatrix*. A more refined mutilation, the *tattoo*, is effected by rubbing dyes into neat punctures of the skin.

Such devices, common to almost all primitive societies, vary in pattern according to the local tradition and the status of the individual. All have esthetic value. Even the deep scars on the head of a Yąnomamö Indian, worn as a symbol of virility and bravery, convey an emotional impression. The dueling scars proudly worn in Germany during the first half of the present century also served to convey the same message by visual means. There is esthetic effect also in the "giraffe-necks" of the Mangegetwe women of Central Africa who have loops of copper wire fixed around their necks while still young girls, the number of rings being increased annually until their necks become elongated. Similarly in Imperial China, girls from aristocratic landowning families, who were not required to work for a living, had their feet bound in infancy to compress the shape of the foot and retard its growth. Though painful, this treatment ensured that as adults the women of upper caste families would walk with dainty and elegant—but crippled—steps.

Despite the fact that many of the more gross body mutilations offend contemporary Westerners, who recoil at the sight of the dramatically sharpened teeth of a cannibal, modern Western culture is not without its own mild forms of body mutilation. Thus men still shave the hair from their faces in the Roman tradition, while women pierce their ears to hold jewelry in a Neolithic tradition, and some even circumcise their sons, following an Asian tradition which presumably dates from the Paleolithic.

Body Ornaments

As with so many art forms, there is a demonstrably close connection between primitive body ornamentation and magicoreligious beliefs. The Australian aboriginal who wears a G-string made from the hair from his father's head does so out of respect for its magical powers. Many primitive ornaments are actually talismans and charms designed to ward away evil forces and attract beneficial spirits to the aid of the wearer. However, with the development of social stratification, body ornaments may also come to reflect status, dramatically indicating the rank or wealth of the wearer. Magicoreligious ornaments constructed from animal trophies may convey a sense of status, since they serve as testimony to the prowess of the wearer, without losing their magicoreligious significance. The crown of a king combined magical powers with status significance, as did the sceptre, which shared a common magicoreligious origin with the fairy's wand. Nevertheless although the first body ornaments were magicoreligious or status symbols, it could not have been long before man's esthetic susceptibilities converted them also into art objects, reflecting the artists' skills. Rare and prized objects in particular are likely to attract the art workers' attention following the emergence of societies sufficiently prosperous to support full-time professional craftsmen and artists.

Clothing

At the earlier levels of social evolution it is sometimes difficult to distinguish between ornaments and clothing. Male and female sex organs may need to be protected from evil powers by magicoreligious shields. It was not the heat nor the cold, nor even a sense of pristine modesty, which gave rise to the first pubic coverings. Instead it was a magicoreligious desire to protect the vital genitals, the seat of supernatural powers, from the many dangers of the supernatural world. Other forms of ornamentation which convey rank, status, or even signify membership in a secret society may become elaborated until a modern observer might choose to describe them as clothes. Yet masks, headgear, and leopard skin cloaks are more properly ritual ornaments or badges of office than clothes in a modern sense. Actual clothing arose only when men covered their bodies for the deliberate purpose of protecting themselves against the elements; but whether the primary intention is ritual ornamentation or comfort, clothes, like ornaments,

eventually become objects of esthetic interest.

Although the Australian aboriginal goes naked except for magicoreligious ornamentation, the Yahgan of Tierra del Fuego may throw a small otter skin or seal skin over his shoulders as a meager protection against the biting winds, and the now extinct Tasmanians draped similar strips of fur over their shoulders and smeared themselves with grease to protect the body against the elemental forces. While animal furskins are luxuries in our modern world, they were originally the most readily available and most effective form of clothing where protection against the cold was required. As long as 30,000 years ago during the Würm glaciation in Europe, Cro-Magnons learned how to stitch hides together, using bone needles and thread made from twine or from strips of leather. Cutting these to shape, they devised tailored clothes probably similar to those which the Eskimoes, the heirs to much of the Upper Paleolithic culture, still wear.

In warmer climates, the first clothes were made from beaten bark and grass, like the grass skirts of Polynesia; as basket making gave rise to techniques of weaving, so cloaks and skirts of woven vegetable fibers were adopted. Probably the greatest innovation in the history of clothing was the discovery of the secret of making sheep's wool into cloth. Accordingly modern Westerners wear suits of cloth which combine the art of weaving, derived from the practice of basket making, with the technique of tailoring and stitching, derived from the Cro-Magnon tradition of leatherworking.

The Upper Paleolithic leatherworking tradition also gave rise to leather shoes and leather boots, as well as to the Indian moccasins. These have greater utility than sandals woven from vegetable fiber in the colder and wetter parts of the world. Nevertheless, the stitched shoe has still not replaced the open sandal in many warmer climates where a sole of leather or wood, attached loosely to the foot by means of thongs passing over and between the toes, still protects the foot quite adequately, while allowing cooling air to reach the skin. To some extent clothes also vary according to the utilitarian requirements of the wearer's occupation as well as to suit the climate. For this reason the horse-riding herdsmen of the Eurasian steppes wore trousers, which were conveniently adapted to a life on horseback, and Westerners still wear trousers as part of the steppeland Indo-European tradition.

At least an element of the esthetic is to be found in virtually all clothing that is superior in sophistication to the single gameskin cloak,

The earliest clothing worn in tropical and semitropical climates appears to have been made from grass and plant materials. Daughters of a Micronesian chief from the Gilbert Isles in the South Pacific wearing grass skirts. (Courtesy of the Smithsonian Institution, National Anthropological Archives.)

worn as a shawl over the shoulders. The emotional and artistic effect can be such that it is a popular aphorism that "the clothes make the man." Men are so impressed by the style of clothes which they wear that they tend to act out the character symbolized by their clothes. Uniforms consequently appear first as simple symbolic badges of office, but later become elaborated as masterpieces of esthetic creativity, designed to convey through art the character of the office which they reflect. Thus the plumed headdress of the Aztec and Inca rulers conveyed the high status of their office, as the toga of the patrician Roman similarly reflected the dignity of classic European civilization. Military uniforms the world over borrow heavily from the artists' inspiration. Indeed stylistic considerations can become overemphasized beyond the requirements of convenience for the deliberate purpose of dramatizing the status role of the actor. In such cases elaborate costumes such as those worn for an Iroquois war dance or for a ceremonial military tattoo in Europe are usually removed before actual combat begins.

Even in modern complex societies clothing thus remains very much a function of ornamentation and social status, and retains many ritual and magicoreligious implications. Apart from the clothes worn for civil and religious rituals, such as the vestments of the Catholic priest and the round collar of the Protestant pastor, the choice of day-to-day clothing reflects through art the religious, moral, and philosophical outlook and even the occupation and class status of the wearer. A man who dresses in a style unacceptable to the members of his class is soon likely to be made aware of his eccentricity by his fellows who will tend to exclude him. In short, the clothes designer knows that clothes are still a badge of status in modern industrial society, just as they are among agricultural, horticultural, and even pastoral peoples, and designs his products accordingly.

Early dancing frequently involved acrobatic feats of magicoreligious significance and the jokers or fools of medieval European Courts may have had an ancient shamanistic origin. Shown here is an acrobatic dancer, Ivory Coast, Africa. (Courtesy of La Documentation Française, Paris.)

A shaman's costume is almost invariably unorthodox. Here a Bateke tribesman wears a costume of leaves and feathers while dancing in an attempt to influence the forces of the supernatural. (Courtesy of La Documentation Française, Paris.)

ART

Although clothing and body mutilations express esthetic concepts in a very personal way, the principles involved in such forms of *applied art* do not differ fundamentally from the principles of the *fine arts*—painting and sculpture—or from the principles of ornamentation on pottery and tools.

In general it may be said that the earlier and more primitive societies have tended to emphasize stylized art forms, in which the stress is upon form, rhythm, and symbolism rather than upon content. This emphasis upon style and form is known as *abstract art*. Abstract art seeks to convey and stimulate the intended emotions by the use of standardized or symbolic forms that emphasize selected esthetic or conceptual elements. African art deliberately, not accidentally, distorts the shape of the human body when creating masks and *fetish figures*—anthropomorphic representations believed to house ancestral spirits or other supernatural forces—ensuring disproportion between the component parts as a means of creating a supernatural impression.

Naturalist art may be described as the attempt to portray an object in a relatively faithful representation of the original, although some emphasis may be placed upon emotional character and an attempt may be made to catch

287

a particular pose or expression. In general, the art of the great civilizations has in many cases tended to favor a degree of naturalism, and in the classical Greek, Roman, and Renaissance traditions of European art naturalism prevailed.

The question is often asked, "What is *primitive* art?" Possibly there is no agreed answer, for some writers use the word *primitive* in one sense, others in another. It is true that in the graphic arts many accomplished primitive artists have not learned the secret of perspective, but perspective and similar technical devices that serve to achieve realism are only of importance in naturalist art. Possibly the best interpretation we can give to the oft used term *primitive art* is that it is the art produced by "primitive societies," those that lack any form of writing, and are characterized by a basic simplicity of social organization and a limited degree of control over their material environment.

So developed is the representative and symbolic form of much of primitive art—which has arisen, let it be remembered, not from spontaneous self expression but as a result of a lengthy evolution of art style through many generations—that modern artists have expressed their deep admiration for the work of many primitive peoples, even though modern artists not reared in the indigenous culture lack the mythological and cultural experience which contributes so much to the message that makes these art works real to the people who construct and use them. Quite naturally, the message contained in such masks and figurines may not be immediately comprehensible to the suburban dweller in the twentieth-century United States. It has been said with some truth that the bodily distortion, elongated faces, contorted mouths, and staring eyes reflect the spirit of a trapped animal trying to escape from a world of fears by means of magic. But although many Western people look at the masks and figures carved by primitive peoples with

uneasy apprehension, the depth of feeling and imaginative creativity of such works cannot be denied. Carved and painted with much skill, African masks in particular have served as an inspiration for modern so-called "primitive" artists. Thus the Museum of African Art in Washington displays reproductions of African masks which seem undoubtedly to have served as models for the works of Picasso and the Cubists.

The Prehistoric Origins of Art

Homo sapiens neanderthalensis is known to have possessed simple color dyes and in at least one case he buried his dead in a bed of flowers, but the evidence of an esthetic sense at this stage of human evolution indicates only a crude esthetic thrill, probably inextricably associated with the supernatural. As we have observed in earlier chapters, the first archeological evidence of conscious art and of clothing and bodily ornaments is associated with the Upper Paleolithic. Although Neanderthals of the Lower Paleolithic had undoubtedly developed magicoreligious beliefs, for they placed utilitarian objects in the graves of their dead, there is no trace in these graves of an ornamental tradition or of clothing, and none of the objects manufactured by Neanderthal man suggests a sense of esthetic appreciation. By contrast, the Upper Paleolithic cultural revolution not only inaugurated the use of clothing and personal ornaments but also left widespread evidence of esthetic sensitivity, revealed in graphic art forms, such as the Aurignacian cave paintings. Cro-Magnon esthetic taste is also indicated by the fact that tools were laboriously worked to produce symmetrical shapes which had esthetic value and involved additional labor that could not be justified on utilitarian grounds.

Many parallels to the cave paintings executed by Cro-Magnon men in Europe have been found in Australia and Africa, being the

Masks help the dancer to "identify." (*Top left*) Masked dancer of Danane, Congo. (*Top right*) Masked dancer of Brazzaville, Congo. (Courtesy of La Documentation Française, Paris.)

(*Bottom left*) This mask from the Ivory Coast clearly illustrates the abstract traditions of African art which inspired Picasso and other European "primitive" painters. (Courtesy of La Documentation Française, Paris.) (*Bottom right*) Head of a poet from Classical Greece. Since the days of Mycenae, traditional European art has characteristically stressed naturalism and realism. (Courtesy of the British Museum, London.)

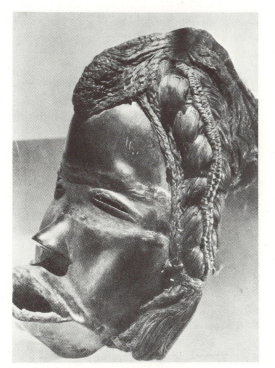

work of Australian aboriginals and Bushmen in recent centuries. Although these are crude in comparison with the sophisticated and colorful work of the Aurignacian and Magdalenian eras, the portrayal of animals tends to follow the same emphasis upon line and form which is found in the earlier Cro-Magnon masterpieces. These are believed to represent a form of sympathetic hunting and fertility magic, in which case they served a definite survival-oriented purpose, even though the emphasis upon form, line, and symmetry testifies to artistic skill (see p. 116).

Other Paleolithic and Mesolithic art forms which may be related to fertility magic are numerous Venus figures found particularly in southern and southeastern Europe (see Venus image, p. 258). Persisting into the early Neolithic in the Balkans, these imaginative and stylized female figures heavily emphasize breasts, stomach, and hips, and undoubtedly reflect a common tradition, probably associated with the cult of a fertility goddess discussed in Chapter 20.

Art and Religion

Since religion pervades all aspects of the life of primitive peoples, it is not surprising that so-called primitive art is generally closely associated with magicoreligious concepts. Religion is essentially an emotional experience and like art, tends to have highly subjective overtones. Religious ritual almost invariably involves the use of sundry material paraphernalia, the emotive value of which can be substantially enhanced by the artist's skill. Such visual aids, artistically designed to convey the appropriate emotional atmosphere, contribute through the "esthetic thrill" to the worshiper's sense of "religious thrill." As all the members of more primitive communities share a similar cultural heritage, the artist who seeks to interpret his own religious experience may be sure to achieve a presentation that will

also be meaningful to his fellow tribesmen. Thus artistic form, rhythm, harmony, and style serve to interpret and reinforce the mythological value of the religious symbols.

Obvious examples of the emotive value of art in religion are provided by the aura of serenity that emanates from the figure of Gautama Buddha in a contemplative pose—so symbolic of the "inner peace" sought by Buddhism—and the stark horror conveyed by the ritual masks of the Kwakiutl cannibal societies of British Columbia.

Not only can religious emotions be enhanced by the visual arts, but the religious experience can also be heightened and dramatized by music, song, and dance. Since the supernatural world is quite as real to primitive man as the natural world, all experiences which involve emotional conditions that differ from the mundane or profane are likely to acquire a magicoreligious significance. As virtually everything which is not mundane and routine is sacred or has sacred connotations, activities such as singing, dancing, and music, which we today regard as purely recreational, generally have magicoreligious significance in primitive societies.

There is a parallel here between the consumption of intoxicating liquor—such as the soma of ancient Aryan India and the drugs of the South American Yąnomamö Indians—and the use of art in religion. The supernaturally distorted experiences of the inebriated alcohol drinker or of the hallucinogenic drug taker become both an artistic and a religious activity when they result in dancing or magicoreligious performances. The Central Asian shaman who dances to a tambourine is performing art with a religious purpose, and the origin of dancing as a form of artistic expression appears to be closely associated with magicoreligious ritual. Through the esthetic impact of the dance the shaman conveys something of the religious thrill. Sometimes, as among the Aztecs and many African peoples, the worshipers may also

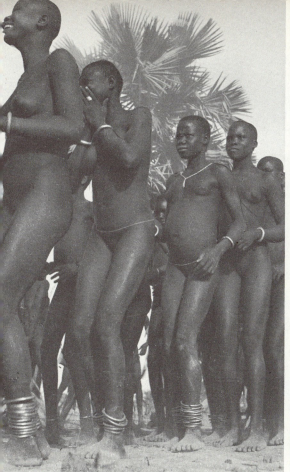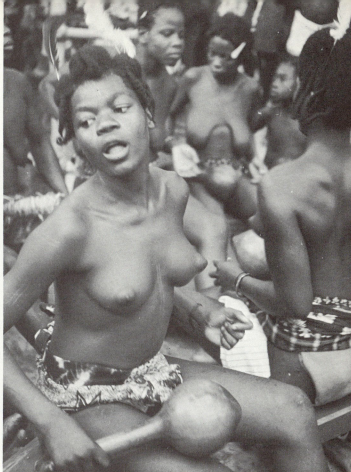

(*Left*) Uninhibited rhythmic body movements are characteristic of African dance forms. Here young women of the Banana tribe (Chad Republic) dance before an audience of males. (Courtesy of La Documentation Française, Paris.) (*Right*) Young Congolese girls use tam-tams to supplement the beat in a traditional tribal rhythm. (Courtesy of La Documentation Française, Paris.)

dance in group patterns as a part of the religious ritual.

Not only did the folk dance derive from religious ritual, but the art of the theater seems also to have evolved out of religious festivities. Even the Yahgan of Tierra del Fuego act out the *Kina* myth to remind the women of their proper place in society. In the same way that the Catholic Church organized religious plays in medieval Europe, the members of secret societies—such as the Iroquois False Face Society, adorned with fantastic masks and ritual clothing—act out the roles of mythological beings and ancestors.

Art and Heraldry

Not only has art served a directly religious purpose, but it has been used in other social applications as in the design of family, lineage, clan, and sodality insignia. From the American Indian totem pole to the feudal coat of arms, art can be harnessed in the service of group unity, helping to stimulate notions of loyalty and group identification. Heraldic art is often heavily stylized, since it seeks to represent an abstract idea, the continuing lineage. Totemic art especially, representing only a crudely conceived impression of animal progenitors, usu-

More complex cultures tend to favor more restrained body movements, usually reducing the impact of rhythm in favor of greater symbolic emphasis. Thai classical dancers. (Courtesy of Public Relations Department, Thailand.)

Classical Japanese culture carried the emphasis upon restrained symbolic verbal and physical presentation to an unrivaled extreme. Here Japanese performers present the Noh play which originated in the thirteenth century. All movement is eloquently symbolic and severely restrained to achieve the Japanese ideals of grace and dignity. (Courtesy of Information Section, Embassy of Japan, Washington, D.C.)

Conscious attempts have been made to revive folk art in this century in a reaction against professional, commercialized art. Folk singer in Portuguese restaurant. (Courtesy of the Director-General of Information, Portugal.)

ally emphasizes symbolic anatomical features in a highly stylized form of imagery of great emotional power, which is appropriate to the mysticism of secret and, to nonkinsmen, unknowable traditions.

Whereas magicoreligious cave paintings, enacted to promote success in the hunt or fertility, frequently create a naturalistic representation of their subjects, the abstraction implied by the concept of a totemic animal or a lineage badge seems to lend itself to stylization. But where individual ancestors are to be honored, in ancestor-worshiping societies like Republican Rome, naturalism will prevail. The object of a Roman bust, for example, was to provide a permanent likeness of the deceased ancestor to join the other ancestral busts arranged around the sacred hearth fire. So also the family portraits that hang in ancestral halls will follow a naturalistic tradition, since their object is to portray the personality of the individual ancestor they commemorate.

Decorative art

Although we cannot hope to enter into the mind or experience of Cro-Magnon man, the fact that he spent considerable time working on his tools indicates what seems to have been a love of art and formal beauty for its own intrinsic value. So also when man began to make pottery, he was not contented to leave it in a crude utilitarian form. Graceful rhythmic forms combining harmonious lines emerged, and all Neolithic societies developed abstract designs, many of which may originally have had religious, mythological, or totemic symbolism, but lost this in the course of time. Certainly such decorations were not spontaneous; indeed the traditional decorations on early pottery and other artifacts usually have a history of the greatest antiquity. Abstract decorative techniques, especially, are customarily very ancient, changing only slowly in

a world which knows little of fashion. Thus archeologists use the decorative styles on pieces of potsherd to assist them in identifying the ethnic origins of the culture they are excavating.

Folk Art, Fashion, and Professional Art

In less complex societies, with more firmly integrated and conservative cultural traditions in which a man's role tends to be ascribed rather than achieved, fashion is a virtually unknown phenomenon. In such societies *folk art*, including music and song as well as drawings, paintings, carvings, and even embroidery, represents not so much a spontaneous creation of the individual artist, as a spontaneous creation of the traditional culture in which the artist and his fellows are thoroughly steeped. In such societies the work of the artist can be understood and appreciated by all the members of the community, for there will be nothing esoteric in his experience or in his method of presentation which they are unable to comprehend. Folk art is consequently a genuine expression of the cultural ideals, experiences, and emotions of the people, to the extent that the people share a common cultural tradition.

In contrast with folk art, which is characterized by cultural continuity, *fashion* is a characteristic of mass societies with but poorly integrated cultural systems which deny the individual the primitive experience of strong group identification and offer him instead a sometimes bewildering kaleidoscope of cultural options. When innovation is regarded as a status-conferring quality, and social status is accorded to those who lead society as agents of change, customary art forms identified with specific social groups and distinctive geographical regions tend to be jettisoned in favor of novelty, the ready acceptance of which indicates an innovative frame of mind and consequently carries status value with it.

Also, as we move away from folk societies in the direction of mass society, increasing division of labor and progressive stratification result in art becoming the professionalized pursuit of a specific occupational subgroup. In societies dominated by a religious hierarchy, art may be used in religious propaganda to convey specific religious experiences to the mass of the people. Similarly, Renaissance and post-Renaissance European art reflected the taste of elegant aristocratic patronage which supported it. But in modern mass society, in which neither the common people nor any religious or aristocratic hierarchy serve as patrons to the artist, the artist has taken over the direction of his own labors. He produces an art which he himself can understand, but which often fails to reflect the emotions, taste, or experience of the majority of the members of his society, who often condemn his work as unintelligible. To the extent that the modern artist still has patrons, these are the art dealers and the critics, themselves professional specialists, representing a narrow subculture within the broader social panorama. Even many of the wealthier members of society who purchase works of art as investments do so under the guidance and tutelage of art specialists. Thus the modern slogan "art for art's sake" represents a state of affairs in which the pronounced division of labor characteristic of mass society has tended to divorce artistic forms from the immediate experience of most of the members of the society in which they are created. To some extent the culture of the masses becomes slowly adjusted to these new art fashions, but the process is slow. In a modern society many fashions—created solely for emotional stimulation and often lacking in social meaning as far as most members of the society are concerned—pass away into history before ever achieving widespread recognition.

MUSIC

The anthropological study of music is called *ethnomusicology*. It is impossible today to say how music began, although it may have become associated with religious ritual at an early date. As one of the most purely esthetic of all human activities, music is almost without a rival as a form of symbolic emotional communication. At the same time, music has been developed in different cultures along quite different lines, so that its message is largely reserved for those who have been enculturated into the tradition that created it. Musical appreciation, even more than the appreciation of the visual arts, seems to depend upon physiological and psychological conditioning.

Musical scales consequently will be found to differ substantially from one society to another, although all musical notes arise from sound waves of varying size, emitted at fixed intervals. Where they differ is in the interval between the fixed points on the scale. Instruments also differ. The first music was probably based on percussion, a primitive rhythm created by knocking hollow objects. Stringed instruments cannot be identified until after the invention of the bow and arrow with its twinging bowstring. Stringed instruments probably appeared in western Eurasia as early as the Mesolithic, and the taut string stretched over a sounding board made possible the elaboration of all kinds of melodic expressions which cannot be produced with percussion instruments. Various wind instruments have added to the melodic possibilities, but these have fixed tonal intervals. Members of societies which lacked such instruments were obliged to direct their ingenuity to elaborating rhythmical beating patterns on hollow instruments.

European music is virtually unique in that it has traditionally stressed pitch, demanding a set of fixed tones, and is consequently noted

Rhythms can also be beaten out on ordinary pieces of wood. The more elaborate xylophone from Mali (*top right*) is probably descended from a more ancient prototype resembling the simpler Central African instrument (*top left*). (Courtesy of La Documentation Française, Paris.) Percussion instruments and rhythmic musical styles are highly developed in sub-Saharan Africa while stringed instruments tend to be more simple. (*Bottom left*) A Bantu tribesman displays a single-stringed musical instrument of a type that might well have been used by Cro-Magnon men in the Upper Paleolithic around the time that the bow and arrow first came into use. (Courtesy of the South African Information Service.) (*Bottom right*) An Ivory Coast musician with his string instrument. (Courtesy of La Documentation Française, Paris.)

295

(*Top*) Large drums used for ceremonial dances, Republic of Central Africa. (*Bottom*) Sacred drum from Madagascar. (Courtesy of La Documentation Française, Paris.)

for its stress upon melody. Rhythm is usually suppressed, following a regular beat with only short phrases, probably to avoid drowning the melody of the wind and string instruments. Marching tunes, following a regular beat, have been cited as typical of European music, whereas syncopation, stressing the off-beat, is traditionally far more characteristic of African music which, relying more on percussion instruments and rattles than on string and wind instruments, has always emphasized rhythm and elaborate arrangements of percussion beats. Jazz reveals its distinctly African origins in the use of drum solos, and in recent years Western popular music has borrowed heavily from the African tribal music, substituting rhythm for melody.

This quality has also had its effect on the character of songs, since the European song tradition was also based on melody rather than rhythm. The attempt to adjust a Western song tradition to the African idiom, in which the drums were seldom accompanied by the human voice, produces many difficulties. The idea of supporting the human voice with a melody played on an instrument is indeed rare in societies lacking an extensive literature. Song would seem to have arisen in Eurasia through attempts to dramatize, as with a harp, the ancient tribal legends and heroic poetry. Such poetry may originally have been chanted to a musical accompaniment, but later came to be sung in melodic patterns, until further elaboration produced not merely the folk song but also European and Oriental opera.

Not all musical instruments have been traditionally used only in a religious and folklore setting, however. Music has been employed in war to inspire courage and to terrorize the enemy. Thus the drum and fife were used in Western society to encourage men to march in straight lines, without wavering, into the mouth of the enemy cannon, while the large metal horns and bagpipes of the Celts were used in battle to drive fear into the hearts of the enemy by the unearthly blare which they produced. Music can be used to soothe and please, to excite, stimulate, irritate, and frighten. But in all cases, music is possibly the most difficult of all the many cultural qualities that the ethnographer attempts to study, for it is concerned so intimately with the communication of emotions, and depends so heavily upon acculturation before the emotive content can become intelligible. Ironically, the more trained the observer is in the techniques employed in music making in his own culture, the greater the difficulties he may experience in understanding the music of other cultures.

For Further Reading

Bascom, W., 1971, *Handbook of West African Art.* New York: Johnson Reprint Corp.
Douglas, F. H., 1970, *Indian Art of the United States.* New York: Arno Press.
Graziosi, P., 1960, *Palaeolithic Art.* London: Faber & Faber, Ltd.
Nettl, B., 1956, *Music in Primitive Culture.* Cambridge, Mass.: Harvard University Press.
Powell, T. G. E., 1960, *Primitive Art.* New York: Frederick A. Praeger, Inc.
Rattray, R. S., 1927, *Religion and Art in Ashanti.* New York: Oxford University Press.
Reichard, G., 1969, *Melanesian Design.* New York: Hacker Art Books.
Sayce, R., 1963, *Primitive Arts and Crafts.* New York: Biblo & Tannen Booksellers & Publishers.
Speck, F. G., 1951, *Cherokee Dance and Drama.* Berkeley: University of California Press.
Westheim, P., n.d., *The Sculpture of Ancient Mexico.* Gloucester, Mass.: Peter Smith.
Wingert, P. S., 1962, *Primitive Art.* New York: Oxford University Press.

PART III

Ecological Adaptation

CHAPTER 22

Studying Cultural Change

Culture, as we have seen, is more than just an accumulation of ideas and attitudes; culture programs people to behave in certain ways. Culture is a vital element in what is in fact an action system, and although action systems may achieve a certain equilibrium when in harmonious adjustment to their environment, they inherently involve some measure of change. Thus cultures and societies seldom if ever remain stationary, but instead continue to react and readjust as a part of the total ecological community to which we as living organisms belong.

Since it is now time to draw together the theoretical data discussed in Part II and illustrate these conceptual generalizations with concrete examples of actual societies at various stages of cultural and social adaptive evolution, we must first explain some of the methods by which anthropologists acquire their data.

So far as living societies are concerned, we can visit these and record all that we see and hear. But living societies cannot be understood except in an historical context, since as we have just observed, culture is a dynamic reality that exists only in time and constitutes action by actors. All social behavior has a causal history that must be pieced together if we are to comprehend its nature. We are therefore obliged to delve into history if we want to understand the present. HISTORICAL RECORDS will give us much useful information when they are available, although we must remember such records are often no more than an account of what happened by the side that won. Similarly, we can learn much about the past culture of a society by an examination of its unwritten tradition of FOLKLORE and verbal legends passed on from generation to generation by word of mouth. But how do we study the culture of ancient societies which have left no written or verbal records—and this includes the overwhelming majority of past cultures from the first hominids on to the present century?

The answer to this question is provided by archeology, the study of extinct societies through the examination of their material remains.

ARCHEOLOGY

The term *archeology* (Greek *archaios,* "ancient," and *logos,* "discourse") means simply "the science of ancient things." Archeologists endeavor to acquire information about the human past by examining fossils and artifacts. FOSSILS are the remains of living organisms, such as skeletons. In some cases they have become mineralized from seeping water in the earth, so that even if the organic material eventually decays, the mineral deposits remain and reveal the original shape. ARTIFACTS are things that have been made or used by man, such as pottery, tools, and weapons—parts of his material culture which tell us how he lived.

Archeology, consequently, provides us with the only means we possess for securing information about human beings and human behavior in the prehistoric past. It can also supply additional information to supplement the written records which survived from the literate periods of human history. Indeed, many historical records have come to light only as a result of archeological excavations, and even where written records exist, these seldom tell us all that we wish to know about past cultures. The reality, as unearthed by the archeologist, may sometimes turn out to be quite different from the impression which we receive from studying the available historical records.

Archeological Sites

Fossils and artifacts may survive in a wide variety of different environments, often coming to light in the most unlikely places. However, archeologists cannot search everywhere, and in the course of time they have developed means for identifying places where fossils and artifacts are most likely to be found, and these are called ARCHEOLOGICAL SITES. Such sites may be classified according to the nature of origin.

HABITATION SITES are among the most obvious places in which to search for evidence of the past. In the Middle East and Asia Minor, settled agricultural villages have survived on the same locations for literally thousands of years, with new houses being repeatedly built on the foundations of the old, so that the accumulated rubble of buildings and artifacts today stands as gigantic mounds, or *tells* as they are locally known, high above the level of the surrounding countryside. Such habitation sites are easy to locate; others can be located by the careful analysis of historical records. Ancient legends, surviving in local folklore, may suggest the existence of camps, houses, and villages which have long since passed away. In other cases the random discovery of tools or other artifacts in the surface soil, possibly turned up by a farmer's plow, may reveal the location of an ancient habitation awaiting excavation by trained archeologists. Still other sites may be identified by discoloration of the surface soil or even by the vegetation growing on the site, which may not be apparent to observers on the ground but is readily noticeable from the air.

Although it is usually difficult to locate the camps of the early hunters and food gatherers, advanced hunters often leave us ample evidence of their culture in KILL SITES. These are usually to be found in places of distinctive topographical character where wild animals were driven over a cliff and butchered where they fell, maimed and dying below, or else in a canyon where they could be slaughtered with ease.

But habitation and kill sites are not the only places in which archeologists may hope to find evidence of former societies. Pastoral peoples who live in tents, for example, may leave no trace of habitation sites, and since they are not hunters, they may leave no kill sites. However, like the Scythians of old, they may bury their dead with elaborate care, creating BURIAL SITES that contain not only human remains but rich hoards of funeral offerings, which provide evi-

Grave sites provide one of the most prolific sources of information concerning earlier cultures, since they usually contain both fossil remains and artifacts. Shown here is a 5000-year-old dolmen, Flensburg, Schleswig. (Courtesy of Landesmuseum, Schloss Gottorp.)

dence of the tools, costume, and jewelry of the age. Even Neanderthal man, who buried his dead in shallow graves beneath the floor of his cave, placed with them some of the personal belongings they had used in their lifetime. Unfortunately, as with the Egyptian pyramids, the more elaborate graves have often been visited by grave robbers hunting for gold and jewelry long before the archeologist was even born.

While Neanderthal man lived in caves, the later Cro-Magnons began to build houses, some of which have been excavated, but continued to use the caves for ceremonial purposes. In addition to habitation sites, kill sites, and burial sites, CEREMONIAL SITES may also be excavated for the evidence they supply of former patterns of life. These may be located in caves or may take the form of giant structures like Stonehenge in England, or the huge sacrificial pyramids of the Mayans in Mexico. Ceremonial sites may include not only remnants of the equipment used in religious rituals but also the bones of sacrificed animals which tell us much about the contemporary fauna, and even magicoreligious pictures which provide one of the richest sources of information we could hope for. Thus we have learned much about Cro-Magnon life from the artistic cave paintings of the Aurignacian and Solutrean eras, while Egyptian temple paintings are renowned for their accurate attention to detail in their representation not only of ancient Egyptian culture but of the many people with whom the Egyptians were in contact.

With the increase in stone and metal working in the Neolithic and Metal Ages, craftsmen of these and later ages began to use large quantities of raw materials which had to be procured by mining, and consequently, QUARRY SITES may also contain evidence of the past. Not only may miner's tools be found in these quarries, but a search of the surrounding area may also reveal habitation sites of a more valuable nature, for one discovery often leads to another.

The Archeologist at Work

Because many sites were used continually or repeatedly over long periods of time, it is necessary for the archeologist to proceed with the utmost care in excavating any site. In the case of the *tell* villages of the Middle East, which survived on the same site over thousands of years, the older and lower levels of the site produced evidence of earlier societies, generally more primitive than those responsible for creating the upper or more recent levels. It is of the utmost importance, therefore, that an excavator keep accurate records of the discoveries made in each successive layer, in order that he may be sure which finds were made at the same level and consequently belong together, thus avoiding confusion with artifacts found at higher or lower levels which will belong to different periods of time. This process of carefully mapping the layers and dating finds according to the relative layer in which they are found is known as STRATIGRAPHY.

Yet, it is also necessary to make accurate records of the spatial location of finds in each separate level or phase. For this purpose it is customary to superimpose grid patterns on the entire area that is being excavated so that the exact location in which all evidence is found, whether in the form of fossils, artifacts, or the remains of buildings, may be accurately charted. Even differences in soil color must be carefully traced because such discoloration is often due to the decay of wooden implements or of artifacts made from other impermanent materials. Samples of such discolored soil can be analyzed to determine the original nature of the decayed material.

Whether the archeologist chooses to expose the site by stripping the area horizontally or by digging into the site against a vertical excavation face, both the grid location and level of all finds have therefore to be carefully noted. If the area is to be stripped horizontally, control pits will usually be dug at intervals so that the different levels of occupation can be identified and kept in mind. Alternatively, if the dig proceeds along a vertical face, certain areas may be stripped horizontally in advance of the main face in order to facilitate a complete three-dimensional perspective and to provide the director of the excavation work with a

The condition of artifacts and fossils recovered by archeologists depends upon both the nature of the materials and the conditions of the soil in which they were deposited. Organic matter decays easily, but occasionally complete human bodies have been found preserved in ice or peat bogs, like this blindfolded corpse deposited 2000 years ago in a peat bog at Tongefassen in Schleswig-Holstein. (Courtesy of Landesmuseum, Schloss Gottorp.)

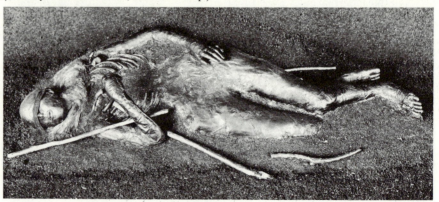

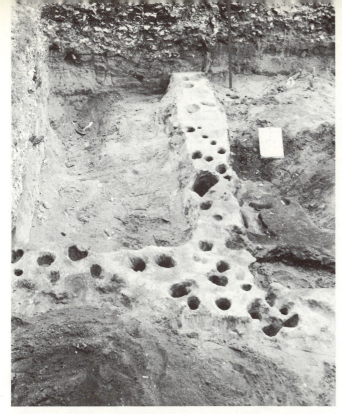

A portion of a Mississippi "Woodland" Indian settlement, date circa 2000 B.P., excavated from beneath a shell midden or refuse heap. Picture reveals holes made by the wooden supports from an upper level wall, penetrating the remains of an older wall uncovered at a lower level. (Courtesy of Dietrich Lüth.)

The decorative designs inscribed or painted on pottery usually follow traditional patterns and therefore provide a useful guide to archeologists in the identification and dating of the site in which they are found. Early Neolithic pottery "sherds" from Denmark. (Courtesy of Landesmuseum, Schloss Gottorp.)

preview of what he may expect to find as the dig progresses.

In addition to the need for accurate descriptions of all finds, accurate dating is necessary if these finds are to be properly interpreted. Few artifacts are stamped with the date when they were made, and few sites contain historical records which may be used to date the material excavated. But through a knowledge of geology it is sometimes possible, particularly where very ancient sites are concerned, to determine at least the geological era in which the artifacts or fossils were deposited. GEOCHRONOLOGY, the dating of fossils and artifacts with the aid of geological data—such as evidence of climatic change and the rate of sedimentation—can therefore be used to date the remains of the more ancient cultures. Where the remains of human food are found, PALEONTOLOGY can also help to date a site, since seeds or bones will be evidence of the type of flora and fauna that lived contemporaneously with the society we are studying. But an even more sophisticated technique, utilizing botanical knowledge, is pollen analysis, sometimes called PALYNOLOGY, which was first developed by a Swedish scientist, Von Post. Specks of pollen that have been preserved in crevices or even in the soil of a peat bog can tell the palynologist what plants were alive at any time in which the archeologist is interested. But of course the most accurate method of objective dating, without references to other objects, is carbon-14 dating, which has already been discussed in Chapter 4.

Since all archeological excavation is essentially destruction, data which is not methodically observed and recorded will be lost to human knowledge forever. Unfortunately, archeology had to have an infancy, and there had to be pioneers whose mistakes provided the basis for more modern scientific techniques. Archeology had therefore to learn by the errors of those same nineteenth-century pioneers to whom we owe so much today.

During the earlier history of archeological exploration many of the richest and most valuable sites of the Old World were enthusiastically excavated in an experimental fashion and were consequently destroyed after yielding only a fraction of the information that more skilled contemporary techniques could have supplied. The ruins of the stone city of Zimbabwe in Rhodesia were similarly stripped of artifacts without adequate and efficient note taking with the result that the evidence which they could have supplied us was destroyed for all times, so that today we still cannot be sure who built this imposing city. This was the inevitable price that had to be paid before archeology could advance to its present level of sophistication. Unfortunately, the course of destruction has continued to be augmented by the untrained depredations of amateur pot hunters and treasure seekers, and as modern cities expand and new roads and airfields are built, much of the heritage of the past is also lost before it can be excavated.

ETHNOGRAPHY

Although archeology provides us with artifacts and fossil remains from earlier cultures, most of our information regarding the use to which these artifacts were put depends upon analogy with contemporary cultures possessing similar material equipment. Our world today is still something of a museum preserving many cultures and societies which are characteristic of earlier stages of human social evolution. Although most of the cultures associated with less sophisticated levels of subsistence are today disappearing, we are fortunate that anthropology developed early enough to ensure that such cultures could be properly studied before they became extinct.

The anthropologist is on somewhat safer ground when it comes to the study of living people. While the archeologist struggles to

The aim of most ethnographers is to become "participant-observers," or in other words to become accepted into the everyday life of the people as far as possible in order that no part of the culture will remain hidden from them. This is not always easy, since the anthropologist is almost always an alien and there must always be some restrictions on the extent to which he is likely to be accepted as "one of the family." A Zulu family is here photographed outside their home, Natal, South Africa. (Courtesy of the Smithsonian Institution, National Anthropological Archives.)

interpret the clues suggested by the scraps of material evidence uncovered by his excavations, the ETHNOGRAPHER, whose function it is to study and describe individual cultures, has much less difficulty when he can visit the society concerned, and if possible become a *participant-observer,* a working member of the community he seeks to analyze.

Analyzing a Society and Its Culture

The ethnographer's work begins long before he ever arrives in the society he intends to study. Ethnographic surveys can only be effective when the surveyor has a broad understanding of ETHNOLOGY, the comparative study of different societies, for he must know what information to look for. In addition, he should be fully acquainted with all existing reports on the society he intends to study, or at least with the culture of its neighbors, so that he will be able to avoid, as far as possible, giving offense to the people whose confidence he needs to

gain. Even a single serious error may be enough to ruin the ethnographer's chances of gaining a sufficient measure of acceptance in order to ensure the cooperation of his subjects.

From the first day of his arrival, the ethnographer will also keep a day-by-day diary of every happening whether or not it seems significant because many of the events that he observes during the earlier part of his research may contain the key to mysteries which will only reveal themselves as his knowledge increases.

The ethnographer should draw up a number of major headings, rather like the chapter headings in a book, under which it is possible to incorporate every facet of life in any society. In order to ensure that his ethnographic survey will be comprehensive, the ethnographer will use these headings as a skeleton outline under which he will endeavor to arrange his observations (see Fig. 29). A systematic analysis and presentation is all the more important, since culture tends to be integrated in constellations of culture traits, each of which will

FIG. 29   COMPILING AN ETHNOGRAPHIC SURVEY

Topics to be included:

   1. Geographical environment. *Also:* changes in geographical environment during the past cultural history of the group.

   2. Linguistic affiliation, including some identification of the generic origin of the language or dialect and also information concerning cultural/linguistic borrowing— evidence of earlier culture contacts and cultural diffusion.

   3. Physical, genetic, or racial background of population. This can be important to researchers endeavoring to recreate the pattern of prehistoric and historic migration.

   4. Method of subsistence. Are the people under study hunters, food gatherers, cultivators, herders, or fishermen?

   5. Technology. Including evidence of cultural traits borrowed from neighboring people and local adaptations.

   6. Marital, kinship, and family systems. These are likely to be central to the description of social structure in preindustrial and nonurban societies.

   7. Nonkinship forms of social association, such as age groups, secret societies, etc.

   8. Economic organization and trading connections (where these exist).

   9. Political organization where this has developed beyond the level of kinship organization already described. Social stratification may be included at this point.

   10. Magical and religious practices, including overall *Weltanschauung* or worldview, calendrical and critical rituals, rites of passage, etc.

   11. Art, recreation, and related topics.

   Remember: at all times endeavor to obtain an overview of the total cultural pattern, indicating the extent to which individual cultural traits are integrated with other cultural elements in a functionally efficient pattern. Seek to obtain the native informant's own interpretation of the significance of the culture you are studying, as well as noting your own impressions. Seek to distinguish between the *ideal* culture, or the way the natives believe they ideally live, from the way in which they actually behave. Furthermore, since social change is apparent to a lesser or greater extent in all societies, do not ignore the utility of historical information.

exert some bearing on every other aspect of the culture.[1]

In analyzing a society, it is important that the ethnographer should first give a general description of the *geographical situation* and *climatic conditions,* as well as of the flora and fauna of the area in which the society is located. The way people live and in particular the way in which they earn their subsistence will be very heavily influenced by their geographical and ecological environment. This is obviously the case in the study of hunting and gathering peoples whose primitive technology renders them subordinate to, and heavily dependent upon, their environment. The pattern of life of the Eskimo quite obviously contrasts

[1] G. P. Murdock, "The Common Denominator of Culture," in R. Linton (ed.), *The Science of Man in the World Crisis* (New York: Columbia University Press, 1945), pp. 123–142.

sharply with that of the Indians of the Florida Everglades because of the geographical differences between their two environments.

It is also desirable that the ethnographer should identify the *dialect, language,* and *language stock* of the society under scrutiny, since this will throw light on the origins, migrations, and cultural history of the people he is describing. In addition a description of the *physical type* of the people can also be important, not only because it may be of direct interest to physical anthropologists, but because, like language, physical characteristics can be a guide to earlier intersocietal contacts. Furthermore a *census* is also valuable, if this can be taken without arousing undue suspicion.

Once these preliminaries have been accomplished, many ethnographers would next describe the *method of subsistence* because as we will see in the following pages, the way in which people adapt their behavior to meet the challenge of survival in different environments necessarily plays a major role in determining their entire pattern of life. Closely related to subsistence and the environment will be the *level of technology.* What type of tools are used in pursuit of subsistence, and what weapons do they possess for hunting or warfare? Because tool technology involves the entire field of *material culture,* this topic may lead into a description of their housing, furniture, and other material possessions.

Having discussed methods of subsistence and material culture, we will come to what many English anthropologists, who like to call themselves social anthropologists, consider the all-important subject: what type of *marital, family,* and *kinship systems* prevail.

Family and kinship ties, derived from the practice of male-female pair-bonding, constitute the basis of social organization in simpler societies. But although kinship is the all-important basis of the simpler society, in more complex societies distinct *political institutions* begin to emerge. Decisions have to be made and

peace must be maintained. Indeed, political systems are intimately linked to the judicial problems involved in *maintaining social order.* In more complex societies, authoritative power to coerce recalcitrant members of society becomes vested in particular individuals.

But no kinship, political, or judicial system is truly meaningful without some explanation of the economic basis of a society. The *economic system* will be intimately related to social and political structure. Every society has to find answers to certain basic questions: What goods shall be produced? Who shall produce these goods? Who shall consume the goods so produced? In the simple society, kinship systems generally provide the answers to these economic questions, but in more complex societies the pattern becomes much more complicated. As inequalities of wealth appear, so inequalities of status become more pronounced, and we begin to talk of *social stratification.* While primitive societies are mainly equalitarian, more sophisticated societies are generally highly stratified.

However, no known society spends all its available time in economic pursuits. All societies engage in *esthetic activities* which are expressed in the things they make and in the way in which they fill their leisure time. Dancing is almost universal, and songs may accompany the dance or may be regarded as an independent pursuit in the more complex societies where division of labor results in professionalization of the artist and the musician. In simpler societies, however, art is closely linked to the ideas of *magic* and *religion,* both concerned with men's attitudes toward the supernatural and in the latter case, especially, with morality and the total ideological system.

Real and Ideal Culture

Yet describing a society is not merely a matter of asking questions and writing down the answers, for people have an "ideal culture" which is not necessarily the same as the "real culture." The members of a society have their own ideas about the way they live and the way they ought to live.[2] Although their IDEAL CULTURE, their folkways and mores, is undoubtedly of importance to the ethnographer—for we cannot understand any society unless we understand its ideologies and value systems and know how the people feel about it themselves—the REAL CULTURE, what people actually do, does not always correspond to what they think they ought to do. The ethnographer therefore must rely upon his own powers of observation and analysis to discover the real culture, to discover how the people in the culture he is studying actually behave.

This same distinction between the real and the ideal culture is particularly apparent in the case of the well-informed informant. There is a great danger in relying too much upon the description of a culture by informants who seem to be particularly well informed, for these are precisely the people most likely to furnish the ethnographer with an overly neat picture which reflects only the ideal culture as the informant himself sees it.

Because of the disparity between the real and the ideal culture, it is impossible for the ethnographer to gain an accurate impression of the society he is studying as a result of a cursory visit. Even if he is aware of the need to search for the real culture, as a stranger it is unlikely that he will be given truthful answers to his questions or, more importantly, that he will be allowed to see the more intimate side of peoples' lives. Unless he stays with a society long enough to become accepted by its members, there will be many aspects of daily and ceremonial life which will remain hidden from him. Not until he is known and trusted will he be able to utilize what Max Weber called the *verstehen* (understanding)[3] approach, and have any hope of discovering what it feels like to be a member of the society he is describing.

[2] David Bidney, "Concept of Culture and Some Cultural Fallacies," *American Anthropologist* 46:30–44 (1944).

[3] Max Weber, *Theory of Social and Economic Organization* (New York: The Free Press, 1964), p. 9.

The ethnographer is also faced with the problem of determining the extent to which he may rely upon the testimony of those members of a society who seem eager to advise him on local practices. This is known as the problem of the "well-informed informer," whose ideas of his own society may actually be quite distorted or even deliberately fictitious. Indeed, many peoples consider it polite to tell a visitor only what they think he would like to hear, whether their statements correspond to reality or not. Shown here is an Arab informant, French Sudan. (Courtesy of La Documentation Française, Paris.)

Emics and Etics

But while ethnocentrism and culture conflict are widespread and seemingly inevitable aspects of daily life, the anthropologist has to endeavor to recognize and control his own prejudices and preferences if he is to succeed in achieving a detached and realistic—an objective and scientific—view of other societies. Whether it is possible for the social scientist to be completely detached from his subject matter is a highly debatable matter, for we are all the product of different societies and have all been molded by the cultural experiences of our lives. Many anthropologists have even taken the position, especially in recent years, that the anthropologist cannot divorce himself from his own value system and must therefore accept the fact that he can only see society through one set of eyes—his own. They argue that what the anthropologist sees is what he is looking for, and that his interpretation of the cultures he studies must therefore inevitably receive the imprint of his own mind and so reflect the pattern of his own cultural biases. At this point the debate can even be carried over into the philosophical analysis of phenomenology and the validity of contemporary scientific methods.

This debate today centers around the idea of *emics* and *etics,* terms first coined by the linguist Kenneth Pike in 1954.[4] Using the analogy of phon*emic* and phon*etic,* Pike differentiated between the *structural* basis of phonemic analysis in language as opposed to the *nonstructural* phonetic approach. This distinction has been carried over into anthropology to stress the fact that the description of the form and meaning of the culture of a society as given by a member of that society will necessarily differ from the description and interpretation of the same culture by an an-

thropologist or, for that matter, by any outside observer whose own culture has taught him a different set of values. The ethnologist may consequently see the culture he is studying in quite a different way from how the people themselves see it, possibly placing great importance on traits which the native ignores, while perhaps overlooking traits which the native would never omit.

The emic/etic dichotomy is not to be confused with the distinction already drawn between the ideal and the real culture. The concept of emics and etics emphasizes the culturally preconditioned nature of all observation, while the contrast between the ideal and the real culture refers to an identifiable discrepancy between the norm and actual behavior.

According to the theory of emics and etics, the view of the society as seen by a native represents the *emic* view, for everything the actor does will be viewed according to his structured cultural background, the total culture of the society. On the other hand, the description and interpretation of the same society by an anthropologist would correspond to *etic* analysis. Is the anthropologist's view any more valid than the native's? This is actually a false question, but it is phrased as a challenge by the exponents of the emic view who in effect deny the validity of any approach that construes meanings different from those implicit in the Weltanschauung of the native.

Emic theory is often extended to cover all cultural analyses that are internally relevant— that is, to dynamic processes within the system—versus crosscultural analyses when relevance is determined by an idea system or model external to the culture. But if anthropology is not to become purely subjective and phenomenological, some yardstick for measuring, comparing, and recording data derived from different societies is needed, and the criteria adopted will determine which data are to be regarded as significant and will also imply

[4] See Kenneth Pike, *Language in Relation to a Unified Theory of the Structure of Human Behavior,* Vol. 1. (New York: Humanities Press, Inc., 1967).

the principles by which such data will be interpreted, we must begin to look for answers to questions such as: What is the mechanism behind cultural change? Why do some cultural traits persist and some disappear? How does the social process work?

THEORIES OF SOCIAL CHANGE

Since culture is *learned,* earlier anthropologists adopted a simple theory of cultural growth known as UNILINEAL EVOLUTION, by which cultural innovations steadily accumulated in a society as a result of *independent invention* in that society. The nineteenth- and early twentieth-century evolutionists like Tylor, Morgan, and Spencer tended to represent all societies as climbing the same evolutionary ladder, some having achieved a higher rung on this ladder than others. European society was conceived as being the highest on this ladder, and other societies were portrayed as representing lower levels of social and cultural progress.

But then came a reaction against the earlier evolutionary theorists, who were accused of overstressing the primitiveness of many contemporary cultures. This reaction was particularly strong in America where many anthropologists, led by Franz Boas, rejected the idea of making comparisons between different societies. They argued that each society should be studied as an independent entity. This has sometimes been described as the PARTICULARIST approach. It stressed the possibility of independent and "parallel" invention, and had the special virtue of emphasizing the need for painstaking ethnographic fieldwork, instead of abstract armchair theorizing.[5]

In time, however, it became apparent that many societies acquired their innovations by contact with other societies and that independent invention was relatively rare. The idea of independent cultural evolution was then rejected, and instead the emphasis was placed upon tracking the *diffusion* of cultural traits from one society to another. The exponents of this school were called DIFFUSIONISTS.

Another school of diffusionists attempted to combine evolutionary and diffusionist theory by accepting the idea of cultural evolution and claiming with much validity that most ideas were invented only once in the history of the world. These then diffused from one society to another, sometimes through trading contacts, but at other times as a result of a migration of peoples who carried their culture with them. Based at the University of Vienna,[6] these theorists claimed that certain societies, located in different parts of the world, had been unusually innovative at certain periods of their history. Consequently it became fashionable in European anthropology to talk about the KULTURKREIS theory, the idea that successive high civilizations had been largely responsible for periods of great innovative achievement which diffused to other parts of the world. This theory, begun by Wilhelm Schmidt, became the basis for the writings of authors such as the historian Arnold J. Toynbee.[7]

On the face of it, the Kulturkreis theory sounded plausible. Western civilization was then believed to have derived from Sumeria, and those societies closest to Sumeria benefited from the inventions taking place there as a result of culture diffusion. After a while, other centers such as Egypt and Crete took over the lead and Sumeria stagnated, and for a time the cultural innovations that occurred in Crete radiated outward to the neighboring Aegean coastal cities. In the course of time the center of innovative progress shifted to the Greek

[5] See also Marvin Harris, *The Rise of Anthropological Theory* (New York: Thomas Y. Crowell Company, 1968), Chapt. 9.

[6] W. Schmidt. *The Cultural Historical Method in Ethnology,* trans. by S. A. Sieber. (New York: Fortseny's, 1939).
[7] Arnold J. Toynbee, *A Study of History* (New York: Oxford University Press, 1955).

mainland, and for a time Greece carried the torch of Western civilization before handing it over to Rome.

"Conflict" and "Functional" Theories of Society

But despite the fact that cultures may enjoy periods of particularly rapid innovation and may substantially influence the cultures of the societies with which they are in contact, just as American engineers and Peace Corps volunteers are changing the cultures of many developing societies today, extreme diffusionist theories undoubtedly represented an oversimplification. In particular, they overlooked the fact that culture cannot be likened to a sack of potatoes which is accumulated in a random fashion and can be distributed in an equally random, mechanical manner by simply emptying part of the bag into one container and part of it into another container. Cultural ideas have necessarily to be a part of a total integrated cultural system, each cultural element effectively meshing in and harmonizing with other cultural traits.

An efficiently operating culture functions rather like a machine, with all the cultural traits acting like cogs, effectively interacting with each other in an overall harmonious pattern. With the rejection of the Kulturkreis theory as an adequate explanation of world cultural history, it became fashionable to talk about a STRUCTURAL-FUNCTIONAL theory of culture, which was less interested in cultural diffusion and social change than in the essential interrelationship of the cultural elements operating as a single efficiently functioning whole. This view was developed first by the French sociologist Émile Durkheim, and then elaborated by the British social anthropologist A. R. Radcliffe-Brown. The structural-functional theory shows how primitive societies which have been left in considerable isolation over a long period of time tend to be well integrated and operate smoothly, whereas more modern societies possess inadequately integrated cultures and consequently suffer conflict and tension as a result of cultural disharmony arising from constant innovations. The structural-functional theory also explains that a society may borrow a new idea only if it can be fitted into the existing traits; as, for example, the refusal of the starving Hindu to accept canned beef because the consumption of beef conflicts with his religious values.

Ignoring the structural-functional approach, certain political theorists—such as the Italian socioeconomist Vilfredo Pareto, reflecting the political right,[8] and Karl Marx, reflecting the radical left[9]—have advanced what has been called a CONFLICT theory of society which has influenced many contemporary anthropologists and sociologists in America. This stresses the fact that with emerging social complexity and the consequent individualization of wealth, social life has become increasingly a conflict for wealth and power between those who "have" these things and those who "have not," and that the social and political structure of a society is wholly shaped by this struggle. Marxist theories, in particular, have resurfaced in the writings of some American anthropologists in the guise of *cultural materialism,* the name given to the claim that culture is but a by-product of the economic process. This interpretation directly refutes the traditional view that culture can frequently cause men to act against their best economic interests, and enjoys little popularity other than among Marxist theoreticians.

The basic difference between leftist conflict theories and those of the right is in their prediction of the future. The cultural materialists follow the nineteenth-century Marxist doctrine

[8] Vilfredo Pareto, *The Mind and Society,* ed. by Arthur Livingston (New York: Harcourt, Brace & Co., 1935).
[9] See Karl Marx, *The Poverty of Philosophy.* New York: International Publishers Co., Inc., 1963, first published in 1847.

of *historical materialism* and believe that economic rivalry is the basic cause of all social conflict. They claim that the needs of mass production and mass planning will eventually make governmental control of the economy unavoidable. With the disappearance of private ownership of economic property, they claim that the prime cause of social conflict will disappear and all human society will inevitably become united in a single worldwide and peaceful communist society. By contrast with the leftist interpretation of the conflict theory, Pareto and the rightist conflict theorists agree that social and political life in complex societies essentially represents a conflict for power, but stress the fact that economic wealth is but one of several types of social power. Even if private property were abolished, inequalities of social power would remain, and social conflict would be transferred from economics to politics, from the struggle for economic power to the struggle for control of the politburo. Such theorists therefore see social conflict not as a conflict between the "haves" and "have nots," but between rival elites, each seeking to control society in the interests of its own group. To them conflict is an inevitable concomitant of complex societies and cannot be dispelled by economic or political measures, for there will always be a governing elite and there will always be a rival elite seeking to overthrow the ruling elite and to seize power for itself. While the scene of the struggle may be further removed from the view of the masses in a planned and centralized industrial society, the principle of conflict will not drop out of history with the introduction of communism or any other totalitarian system.

Structural-functional anthropologists generally deprecate the stress that conflict theorists place on the universality of conflict. Instead they claim that conflict is far from inevitable and that where it exists it represents a normative disequilibrium, a clash of values within a society that lacks effective normative unity. Society exists as a result of patterned cultural order and willing cooperation, not conflict, and cooperation is only possible when people share common ideas and values. It is not and cannot be otherwise, or else society would be destroyed. Excessive tendencies toward conflict lead to civil war, and while all societies permit competition, none can permit conflict and hope to survive. Consequently the functionalists stress the fact that in a complex society, whether it recognizes private economic wealth or not, there must be a number of more influential authoritative persons whose role it is to coordinate the activities of the remainder of the specialized role players. Specialization needs coordination and the elite who direct a complex society are filling essential functional roles. To the functionalist a healthy complex society must function smoothly like a machine with a minimum of conflict; there must be a shared understanding between the members.

Although some anthropologists lean in one direction, emphasizing conflict in all societies, and others lean in the other direction, concentrating on the functional system or the operational structure of the societies they study, all agree that when shared understanding declines, a cultural schism develops between the members of society, and conflict may pass the tolerance level. When this happens, order gives way to violence, and society collapses. Functional integration and conflict may thus be represented as two elements in a dialectical system, with cultural integration and social order representing one extreme, and civil war the other.

Culture Patterns

This viewpoint tends to be reinforced by the fact that most simpler societies consequently exhibit a reasonably integrated system of cultural traits which are organized in *systemic culture patterns* around dominant cultural characteristics.[10] Thus in the culture of the Nuer of the Sudan, the herding of cattle constitutes the dominant Nuer cultural trait around which their entire life is organized. All effectively integrated cultures therefore tend to have a distinctive character known as *ethos*— some being pacific, others militaristic; some praising truth, others, like the Melanesians, admiring the efficient liar; some emphasizing restrained elegance, others loving flamboyance, and yet others reflecting the macabre. Societies whose cultures are effectively integrated—it matters little in which direction—seldom experience serious internal conflicts.

Psychologists such as A. Kardiner[11] have also drawn the anthropologist's attention to another aspect of societal character which is related to ethos: the *basic personality structure.* According to psychoanalysts, a man's personality largely reflects his childhood experiences and the total cultural environment in which he matures. Since cultures and child-training systems differ, it is reasonable to suppose that personality, or human nature, will also differ from society to society. In short, culture shapes the individual's environment, and so helps to mold his personality. To the extent that all individuals growing up in the same society tend to share a similar upbringing and similar life experiences, especially in smaller and simpler societies, such individuals will tend to share a common basic personality structure.

Ecological-Evolutionary Theory

As the pendulum swung from diffusionism to structural-functionalism however, it tended to deemphasize the fact of social and cultural change. Functionalism was more interested in the idea of society as a smoothly operating machine in which every part was effectively integrated with every other part, and became too closely dedicated to an *ahistorical* approach which glorified structure and overlooked the constant presence of change. In time, a dialectical reaction was inevitable. The result was a return to evolutionary concepts, but with a new ecological twist that was at first called "multilineal" evolution but today is better known as the ECOLOGICAL-EVOLUTIONARY approach.[12]

The new ecological-evolutionary school accepts the idea of diffusion of cultural traits and also of independent invention, and recognizes as well the tendency for all living, working cultures to develop a systemic functional interdependence and to reject cultural traits that do not fit into this pattern. Societies that survive and prosper must adjust satisfactorily to the problems of survival in their current environment, and so cultural and social evolution, like biological evolution, are ecologically oriented. Even ideological traditions and religious systems may either contribute toward the problem of ecological adjustment in a positive way, or else may become outdated, divisive, or simply antievolutionary in effect, thus handicapping a society in its struggle to survive. A society whose constituent social and cultural elements do not function smoothly may find itself hampered from a survival point of view. At the same time ecological change often requires cultural changes, which may

[10] See A. Kroeber, *Configurations of Culture Growth* (Berkeley: University of California Press, 1963).

[11] See A. Kardiner (ed.), *The Individual and His Society* (New York: Columbia University Press, 1939).

[12] The rise of modern cultural evolutionism can be traced in A. Goldenweiser "Recent Trends in American Anthropology," *American Anthropologist* 43:153–63 (1945); in J. Steward, "Cultural Evolution," *Scientific American* 194:69–80 (1958); in Leslie White, *The Evolution of Culture* (New York: McGraw Hill, Inc., 1959); more recently, with an emphasis, however, upon cultural materialism, in Gerhard Lenski, *Human Societies* (New York: McGraw-Hill, Inc., 1970); and in Elman R. Service, *Cultural Evolutionism: Theory in Practice* (New York: Holt, Rinehart and Winston, Inc., 1970). Few of these approaches, however, have seen the essential similarity between the principles that control biological evolution and those that control cultural evolution.

temporarily disrupt the structure of society and create tensions but may be conducive to the survival of the society in the long run.

In the following chapters we shall accordingly trace the various processes of social and cultural evolution, using concrete illustrations drawn from archeological, historical, and ethnographic data, organized into an overall ecological-evolutionary framework. We shall see how the many facets of human life change as men abandon the ancient hominid dependence on hunting and gathering to become fisherfolk, cultivators, or pastoralists. We shall further see how the invention of improved agricultural techniques led to the rise of cities and how further technological innovations transformed human society with the coming of industrialism. This approach is a detached, amoral approach; it does not purport to show that cultivating societies are preferable to hunting and gathering societies, or that industrial societies are superior to agricultural societies. All it attempts to do is to record the facts of cultural change—that is to say, the facts of cultural evolution—as they occurred.

In attempting to condense the story of cultural change into a series of ethnographic pen-pictures, some of our material will relate to prehistoric and historic societies now extinct, and some will comprise descriptions of peoples who were still practicing older and simpler patterns of subsistence when first discovered and described by Western travelers. In accordance with the anthropological custom, we shall therefore employ the past tense when describing extinct societies known to us only through archeology and history, but will resort to the convention known as the ETHNOGRAPHIC PRESENT and use the present tense when portraying cultures and societies that were still vital when first described by ethnographers. In this way we see such societies through the eyes of those who studied them at first hand before further contact with Western culture drastically modified their traditional customs. Many

FIG. 30   THE EVOLUTION OF METHODS OF HUMAN SUBSISTENCE

Although more advanced methods of subsistence are generally accompanied by more complex social and economic systems, the exact course of evolution followed by any one society will depend upon the local environment and upon opportunities to borrow technology from other more advanced cultures.

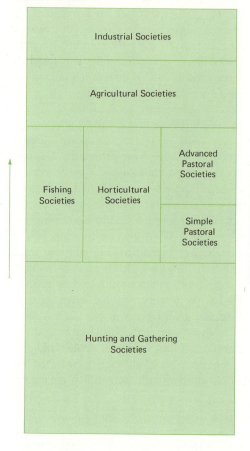

of the peoples so described in the present tense, such as the Haida of Canada, the Nuer of the Sudan, and the Baganda of East Africa, still survive today, but their present way of life is in many cases drastically changed as a result of the acculturating influence of contact with European civilization. For our present purpose we will therefore study such cultures as they were when they still retained the vital richness of character which is to be found in any culture that has been able to develop a distinctive and holistic pattern of its own and, while not reject-ing all innovative ideas, has been able to integrate such inventions into its own cultural system.

For Further Reading

Barnett, H. G., 1953, *Innovation: The Basis of Cultural Change.* New York: McGraw-Hill, Inc.

Casagrande, J. B., 1960, *In the Company of Man.* New York: Harper & Row, Publishers.

Evans-Pritchard, E. E., 1951, *Social Anthropology.* London: Routledge & Kegan Paul Ltd.

Hole, F., and R. F. Heizer, 1973, *An Introduction to Prehistoric Archeology,* 3d ed. New York: Holt, Rinehart and Winston, Inc.

Hume, I. N., 1969, *Historical Archeology.* New York: Alfred A. Knopf.

Kaplan, D., and R. A. Manners, 1972, *Culture Theory.* Englewood Cliffs, N.J.: Prentice-Hall, Inc.

Libby, W., 1955, *Radio Carbon Dating.* Chicago: University of Chicago Press.

Pelts, P. J., 1970, *Anthropological Research.* New York: Harper & Row, Publishers.

Piggott, S., 1965, *Approach to Archeology.* New York: McGraw-Hill, Inc.

Royal Anthropological Institute of Great Britain and Ireland, 1957, *Notes and Queries on Anthropology.* London: Routledge & Kegan Paul Ltd.

Sahlins, M. D., and E. R. Service, 1960, *Evolution and Culture.* Ann Arbor: University of Michigan Press.

Service, E. R., 1971, *Cultural Evolutionism: Theory in Practice.* New York: Holt, Rinehart and Winston, Inc.

Sorokin, P. A., 1970, *Social and Cultural Dynamics.* Boston: Sargent Porter.

Spindler, G. D., 1970, *Being an Anthropologist: Fieldwork in Eleven Cultures.* New York: Holt, Rinehart and Winston, Inc.

Steward, J., 1955, *Theory of Culture Change.* Urbana: University of Illinois Press.

Williams, T. R., 1967, *Field Methods in the Study of Culture.* New York: Holt, Rinehart and Winston, Inc.

CHAPTER 23

Marginal Survivors from the Paleolithic

The simplest level of human social and cultural evolution is that of the small band of adults and children, occupying a distinct territory and supporting themselves by predatory techniques of hunting and food collecting, just as our primordial hominid ancestors must have done. Such hunting and gathering societies can be classified as *foragers* (simple hunters and gatherers) or as *advanced hunters* (or advanced hunters and gatherers) on the basis of their technology and their sources of food.

Simple Foraging Societies

Simple foraging societies depend primarily on gathering fruit, nuts, berries, roots, cereals, fungus, shellfish, rodents, lizards, and eggs, rather than on big game hunting. Armed only with spears, throwing clubs, and sticks, they are still essentially subordinate to their ecological environment. Although their primitive tools serve to supplement their biological equipment, making them more effective predators, they are still restricted to a low density

of population by the overall ecological system, the actual volume of which will depend on the fertility of their environment. If they begin to overprey upon their food supply, they have no means of artificially stimulating their food resources. Although they often endeavor to promote the fertility of the herds on which they prey by magical rituals, thereby attempting to escape from ecological controls by pseudoscientific methods, they have no effective means of manipulating the constituent elements of their environment, and there is little that they can do to upset the overall ecological balance.

Man, the elementary hunter and gatherer, is therefore still just another animal in the ecological community, even though his primitive tools may make him the dominant animal. In more harsh environments, a small group of 20 to 30 individuals may, in a day or two, strip their immediate neighborhood of all fruit, berries, nuts, and roots, and drive off the animals they hunt. All hunters and gatherers are therefore to a greater or lesser extent nomadic. Although a band may return to the same camp site periodically, it is obliged to move on to fresh land, and hunters and gatherers consequently wander continually over a limited and usually well-defined territory. This does not mean that they will be prepared to fight to defend their territorial boundaries. Most simple hunters and scavengers lack adequate group coordination for effective combat, and their attitude to an invasion of their territory is likely to depend largely upon the availability of alternative territories.

Since Paleolithic peoples possess no beasts of burden, nor any wheeled vehicles, they are obliged to carry everything they possess on their backs, on their heads, or in their hands, so there is little incentive to accumulate cumbersome possessions. The weapons which they use for hunting, a digging stick used for unearthing roots and insects, and possibly a grinding stone to break the hard covers of nuts and seeds, are the usual essentials. Other material possessions tend to be an inconvenience. Furthermore, when moves are frequent, there is also little incentive to build sophisticated shelters. While our earlier hominid ancestors must have slept under the open skies, as our primate relatives still do, many contemporary foragers erect only primitive lean-tos to act as wind breaks, to hold off the night dew, and to give some protection from the rain.

Simple hunting and scavenging societies seldom have any means of storing food. Consequently those days on which food is not secured are days of hunger. The procurement of food provides their lives with meaning and purpose and the comfort of routine. For hunters and food gatherers, the meal constitutes the prime goal of the daily activity. The fact that this meal is shared by the members of the band also serves to bind the community together in a close social communion unknown to other primates.

Also significant to early man, from both a cultural and psychological point of view, was the possession of fire. Most hunters and food gatherers know and desire little privacy. They have no yearning for walls behind which to escape from the other members of their small primary face-to-face group. Instead, the camp fire serves to bring the group together, reinforcing the sense of group unity in a deeply emotional, virtually religious, experience of togetherness. Those who know what it is like to sit around a camp fire under the starlit sky know the intense sense of in-group solidarity that is created by the flickering firelight, reflected in known, trusted, and predictable faces. Furthermore, fire gives a sense of security from other predators. Animals live and sleep close to the other animals that prey upon them, with no protection but the brief warning which their senses may give them of approaching danger. The camp fire brings security to man, for the animals of the wild still fear fire, while man has learned to use it, has overcome his fear of it, and knows it to be his ally. Fire gives protection to hunters and gatherers almost as surely as do the walls of a house. Thus it is treated as a supernatural benefactor which protects its possessors from the dangers that lurk in the dark behind their backs. Many simpler people who do not know how to kindle a fire are forced to carry their fire with them when they move. If their own flame dies, they have to find a brush fire, or obtain new fire from another band. The importance of preserving the living glow of "fire life" looms large in their cosmology.

Notwithstanding this idyllic picture, infanticide is common. Since all hunters and gatherers have to face the hard realities of survival, too many children, especially deformed children, would be an unbearable burden upon the community. Similarly, should the food supply become inadequate in times of severe hardship, some members of society will have to die. In some cases it will be the children who are killed, but in others it may be the old and infirm, for they have already fulfilled their biological function of reproduction, and can no longer aid the other members of the band in the struggle to obtain subsistence. Such persons may either voluntarily wander off into the snow to die, as among the Eskimoes, a technologically advanced hunting people, or else may be murdered and eaten by their own descendants with full ritual ceremony in accordance with the dictates of customary norms and magicoreligious sanctions. In the absence of any division of labor between males, however, simple hunting communities usually have only part-time shamans so that few rituals are elaborately developed.

Lacking any concept of economic property, simple hunting and gathering societies have frequently been described as equalitarian. Apart from the social distinction between men and women, and between adults and children, it may be said that relatively speaking all members of a hunting and gathering society share a common heritage, a common culture, and similar life experiences—all men being hunters and fathers, and all women food gatherers and mothers. Since there is no division of labor other than on the basis of sex and age, and their communities are so small, there is neither need nor opportunity for any hierarchical or authoritative structure, and none are elevated politically over the others. Because of their sparse populations, each band frequently lives in relative geographical isolation, and due to the infrequency of outside contacts, the ancient pattern of endogamy may prevail. Among present-day hunters and gatherers, endogamy is the exception rather than the rule, but it is quite possible that the reverse was the case at earlier stages of hominid social evolution.

Advanced Hunters and Gatherers

While most foragers usually have only a few elementary cutting tools powered by crude human force, advanced hunters depend more heavily upon killing larger animals and are equipped with more sophisticated tools and weapons. Thus advanced hunters and gatherers have developed more elaborate spearheads which may be barbed so that once having penetrated the victim's body, they cannot be withdrawn or dislodged, except after creating a terrible wound. Similarly, spearheads may be "waisted" in such a way that after penetrating the body of the victim they cannot fall out or be brushed off, and any pressure on the external part of the projectile will cause the head to snap off inside the victim's body.

Another more sophisticated invention of the advanced hunters of the Upper Paleolithic was the spearthrower, a piece of wood with a crook at one end which by effectively lengthening the human arm increased the force as well as the accuracy of flight. The bow and arrow is another attempt to find an answer to the same problem: how to project a spear further and faster. The bow enables the human muscles to be concentrated behind the projectile, increasing its velocity. While the more primitive bows do not shoot with the accuracy that a man can throw a spear, their range is greater, and as bow-making skills improve and arrows become more sophisticated, the efficiency and accuracy of the bow and arrow also improves.

Another weapon, the blowpipe has also impressed modern observers with its sophistication. The principle is analogous to that of the Western gun, but although human lung power is concentrated into the small-gauge tube through which the dart is blown, the necessary lightness of the dart means that blowpipes without poison are useless. A simpler but often more effective projectile, suitable for use in treeless country, is the *bola*, which comprises two or three lengths of rope-like twine. Each has a weight tied to one end while the free ends are tied together. When thrown at the legs of a running animal, the weight causes the twine to wrap around the victim's legs, making the animals stumble and fall.

Because the use of such weapons as the bola requires skill in the tying of knots, the bola is usually only found in societies which have learned how to weave vines and to make rope from vegetable twine. But rope can also be woven into nets which can be used to catch birds and fish and even to snare larger animals. Plaiting and weaving similarly lead to basket making, and baskets are an important asset to the women who need something in which to put the nuts, seeds, fruit, fungus, caterpillars, and lizards which they collect for food.

Once weaving and stitching have been invented, advanced hunters begin to construct more sophisticated, usually tentlike, shelters from plaited plant produce or from stitched animal hides. Advanced hunters often wear clothes for greater protection against thorns, insects, and elements. Sometimes these clothes are made from the bark of trees, which

Advanced hunters are usually equipped with a reasonably sophisticated collection of weapons. (*Left*) Yupa Indian from Venezuela, South America, armed with barbed spears. (Courtesy of A. G. de Díaz Ungría.) (*Right*) Mentawei tribesman from the forests of Sumatra, armed with bow and poisoned arrows. (Courtesy of Smithsonian Institution, National Anthropological Archives.)

is pounded until it becomes flexible, but in colder climates furs may be stitched together to produce tailored clothes, the hides being chewed in the mouth and rubbed with animal fat to keep them flexible. As we have seen, such tailored and stitched fur garments were already common in Europe by the Mesolithic.

Because of their more sophisticated technology, advanced hunters and gatherers are capable of supporting a denser population within any given ecological environment than foraging societies. Gerhard Lenski[1] has suggested that simple hunters and gatherers may be restricted to an average density of population as low as one person per square mile, but that advanced hunters and gatherers, who are technologically able to exploit the available food supplies more efficiently, can often support as many as 15 or 20 persons per square mile. In consequence of this greater density, more frequent contacts facilitate exogamy, and exogamy lays the foundations of linguistic unity and interband cooperation over a number of adjacent territories as a result of the repeated exchange of womenfolk in exogamous marriages through the generations. Thus, socially as well as technologically the advanced hunter and gatherer has the advantage over the simpler endogamous hunting and gathering bands.

Hunting and gathering represents the primordial hominid method of subsistence. However, while the advantages of ascribed order, deriving from the network of kinship ties that arise out of pair-bonding, give the human band an evolutionary advantage over the troop, more complex tribal systems, associated with larger Neolithic communities, have a higher competitive value than the band system. Consequently in the history of man, horticultural

[1] Gerhard Lenski is to be congratulated on his attempt to reorientate sociology in a broader ecological-evolutionary framework, more in line with the original macroscopic approach of Auguste Comte. A useful discussion on hunting and gathering and other types of human societies is to be found in Part II of his *Human Societies*, (New York: McGraw-Hill, Inc., 1970).

and pastoral societies expanded over virtually all those parts of the world suitable for these more advanced methods of subsistence, expropriating the hunters and gatherers as they went—just as the Bantu cultivators spread out over the grasslands of Africa in the past few centuries, eliminating or partially absorbing the Bushmanoid hunting and gathering proprietors. Hunters and gatherers, who can place only a few fighting men in the field, have seldom proved a match for encroaching cultivating or pastoral tribesmen. Consequently the hunters and gatherers of the modern world have only survived in those more remote or marginal lands which for one reason or another did not attract populations with more advanced methods of subsistence. Typical of these more impoverished simple hunting and gathering band-type societies, surviving down to the twentieth century only in a harsh and marginal area, are the Yahgan of the extreme tip of South America.

FIG. 31   THE YAHGAN

The southern tip of America is broken into many rugged islands, well populated by birds, but bleak and unattractive to cultivators. This is the home of the Yahgan.

THE YAHGAN OF TIERRA DEL FUEGO

A glance at the atlas reveals that the South American continent becomes more narrow as it protrudes southward, until it finally culminates in the large and rugged island of Tierra del Fuego, beyond which there is nothing but a chain of small islands and the cold and troubled waters of the stormy Cape Horn. Here, at the very end of the earth, is the homeland of one of the most primitive of human societies to survive into modern times.[2]

Although the Yahgan who inhabit this rocky, barren, and inclement land are now almost extinct, Europeans visiting the area in the nineteenth century left us a number of accounts of their way of life which have been reinforced by the research of more recent ethnographers. From these we learn that the Yahgan were traditionally hunters and food gatherers who possessed a band-type social structure and a Stone Age technology which was far below that of the people of Upper Paleolithic Europe of 30,000 years ago. The poverty of their economy and the simplicity of their social life matched the cold unattractiveness of their environment and placed them, like the Athabascans who inhabit the tundra wastes of Canada, far beneath the evolutionary level of most other American Indians. Despite the fact that their culture is now extinct, we will follow the anthropological convention and describe them in the ethnographic present.

[2] The Yahgan are today practically extinct, and the best ethnographic sources are therefore from the nineteenth and early twentieth centuries. Charles Darwin commented on them in his *Journal of Researches into the Natural History and Geology of the Countries Visited during the Voyage of H.M.S. Beagle Round the World, under Command of Captain FitzRoy, R.N.* (London, 1845), but a more recent summary of information can be obtained in M. J. Cooper "The Yahgan," in J. H. Steward (ed.), *Handbook of South American Indians,* Vol. 1. (Washington, D.C.: Smithsonian Institution, 1946) and in the book by the missionary E. L. Bridges, *Uttermost Part of the Earth* (New York: E. P. Dutton and Co., Inc., 1949).

Prehistoric Origins

The Yahgans are probably descended from one of the early groups of settlers who arrived in the Americas at some time between 15,000 and 20,000 years ago. Presumably they were pushed continuously southward, as later immigrants with more advanced cultures followed behind them, until they finally found refuge in their present remote homeland. Archeological evidence suggests that their ancestors completed the long trek down the west coast of the Americas to arrive in Tierra del Fuego some 7000 or 8000 years ago. While it is possible that they may have suffered some cultural regression as a result of the harshness of their environment, with its rain, sleet, fog, high winds, and rough water, there is no archeological evidence to substantiate this. The example of the Eskimoes, who settled the even more unattractive arctic lands on the northern extremity of the American continent and who have maintained a more advanced cultural level despite the hardships they faced there, militates against this suggestion.

At the time of the first European contacts, there was probably a total population of some 3000 Yahgan, but the arrival of Europeans exposed them to new diseases against which they had little biological resistance, and as a result sickness has since reduced the Yahgan population to the point of extermination. The name *Yahgan* is actually only a place name, and the term by which they know themselves is *Yamana* which means simply "men."

The Yahgan people are divided into a number of territorially separate bands whose members are generally endogamous, marrying among themselves, but who do not seem to be prohibited from marrying outside their own territory, should the opportunity arise. The earlier unity of the Yahgan is indicated by their common language, but as a result of geographical dispersal this language has become divided into five or six separate dialects.

An early photograph of a Yahgan man and woman. The Yahgan normally went entirely naked, despite the extremely cold winds and driving rain of Tierra del Fuego, until they acquired clothing from occidental explorers and missionaries. The man in this picture proudly wears a necklace of beads he has been given. (Courtesy of Musée de l'Homme, Paris.)

Social Organization

The only clearly identifiable social units are the band and the individual nuclear family. Yahgan social organization consequently hinges upon the pair-bonds established between male and female. Such relationships are basically monogamous, each man taking a single wife, although it is the duty of a man to support the widow of a dead brother, accepting her into his family with the status of a second wife.

The pair-bond between male and female is treated with great respect by all members of the Yahgan community, and there is no adultery, no wife lending, no prostitution, and seldom even any divorce. The society may be said to be patrilineal, since children are regarded as belonging to the father, and the children of a dead man will be brought up as part of his brother's family, the widow having no rights over them.

For food, the Yahgan rely upon collecting berries and edible tree fungus, mussels, limpet, and shellfish, and whatever catch they can obtain by spear fishing. They have no knowledge of cultivation nor any domesticated animals except for the ubiquitous dog. Fire is carefully preserved at all times, and since they spend much of their time on the water, a small hearth place is constructed in the center of their frail canoes so that they can carry their fire with them. Indeed, they spend so much of their time in their canoes that they were once described as "canoe Indians" to distinguish them from their relatives, the Ona, who live inland.

However, the Yahgan supplement their diet with birds' eggs and even birds' meat. Since they do not have any nets in which to snare birds, and their bows and arrows are too inaccurate to kill birds on the wing, they rely upon stalking them with their bare hands. Just like an animal predator, they wait until nightfall when the birds have nested on the cliff faces, and then climb quietly to the birds' nests. Silently grabbing one bird at a time by the neck to prevent it from making a noise and alarming the rest of the colony, the hunter quickly bites off its head, and then steals silently onward to seize the next bird, killing as many as possible before the alarm is given.

Despite the cold weather the Yahgan live in the open and erect only a simple lean-to of branches and skins for protection against the biting winds. Rubbing their bodies with fat for protection against the cold salt water and driving rain, the Yahgan go naked except for a seal skin draped around the body for warmth in winter. No clothing or ornaments are worn, apart from the small covering of furskin sometimes worn by women over the pubic region. Similarly, they take little interest in their appearance—except for plucking out the odd facial hair with mussel shells used as tweezers—and allow their long head hair to hang in tousled, uncombed masses. However they do tattoo the flesh in a primitive fashion at the time of puberty rituals, and cut and slash themselves at funerals.

The Yahgan canoes are so frail that they cannot be beached. In consequence, they have to be lifted out of the water and carried ashore, or else anchored well away from the bank. Paddling the canoes is the woman's job, and when coming into the land, the woman normally paddles close enough to the shore to allow the man to jump out, then takes the canoe out into deeper water. After securing the canoe, the woman jumps overboard and swims ashore. Since all diving for shellfish is done by the women, they are usually excellent swimmers; many men cannot swim at all. The only division of labor is that which separates the roles of husband and wife. The men make all the tools and spear fish with sharpened wooden sticks hardened in the fire. The women take care of the children, gather fungus and berries, dive into the icy waters for shellfish, and when they have nothing else to do, weave baskets. Nevertheless, because of the absence of any suprafamily organization, husband and wife are very close to each other, and the women enjoy a high status. Since there is no big game hunting, and consequently no male hunting groups, there are no hunting expeditions, and the principle of male superiority is not strongly enforced. Each Yahgan family is considered the equal of the next, and the wife and husband make a team in which the husband is only slightly dominant.

Interpersonal Relations

The absence of any clan system also results in bilateral kinship ties, with the kinship responsibilities to the mother's relatives being regarded as equivalent to those due to kinsmen on the father's side. However, the mother's brothers and sisters are distinguished by different names from those given to the father's siblings. All cousins on both sides of the family are collectively known as brothers and sisters, but a man's nephews and nieces are distinguished from his children. Marriage with sons, daughters, nephews, nieces, and even first cousins is prohibited, but otherwise there are no restrictions on the choice of a mate. Since there is no suprafamily organization, there are no endogamous or exogamous requirements, but geographical contiguity normally assures that marriages take place within the band.

A man is expected to show respect for his father-in-law, and in particular may expect assistance from his mother's brother. Children are highly valued, and legitimate children are not subjected to infanticide. On the other hand, should an unmarried girl become pregnant, abortion may be attempted; if this fails, infanticide is common. Following the birth of a child, the afterbirth is burned, but the umbilical cord is preserved for its magical value. Almost immediately after birth the mother cleanses herself and her newborn baby by bathing in the almost ice-cold sea, while the husband is expected to rest from the ordeal for several days. The Yahgan understand the connection between sexual intercourse and pregnancy, and unlike Australian aboriginals, seem to place importance on genetic relationship.

Following birth every child receives a personal name, normally that suggested by its

An early photograph taken in 1882 of a Yahgan woman paddling a canoe constructed from a wooden framework covered by hides. (Courtesy of the Musée de l'Homme, Paris.)

A Yahgan family huddles in front of their brushwood shelter. Customarily free from clothing, except for an animal hide thrown over the shoulders, the members of this family have been given woven blankets which they are using as a protection against the cold wind. (Courtesy of Musée de l'Homme, Paris.)

place of birth, but this is regarded as having an almost magical significance and is not used in terms of address. Consequently the practice of teknonymy prevails, meaning that people normally address each other according to kinship title instead of by their personal name.

The only suggestion of professional specialization to be found among the Yahgan is that of the part-time shaman or medicine man. These are believed to be able to control the weather, to divine the future, and to heal the sick by pretending to extract foreign objects from that portion of the body which is giving pain. Sickness is believed to be the work of evil shamans, who are supposed to be able to cause a man's death by stealing his soul from him. There is a general fear of the spirits of the dead, and whenever a man dies, the camp at the place of death is immediately abandoned. The name of a dead person is never mentioned, and their fear of departed spirits is unmitigated by any belief that the dead will intervene on behalf of the living in either the supernatural or the natural world. Some belief in a personal protective spirit which guards each individual man, woman, and child has been evidenced, but the character of this spirit is not clearly determined.

There are but a few ceremonial rituals among the Yahgan, and there is no special ceremony when a child is named. At puberty girls are expected to refrain from eating for three days and to bathe in the sea, the event being celebrated by a small feast. Probably the most important Yahgan ceremonial is the *ciexaux* in which boys who have reached puberty are tatooed and submitted to various tests, including sea bathing. On this occasion the entire band gathers to sing magical formulas designed to keep an evil giant, Yetaita, at bay until the youths have been fully inducted into adult status. Another important Yahgan ceremony is the *kina*, at which the adult males paint themselves with clay and appear before the women and children as spirit figures. This event commemorates a mythical age when the women were believed to have gained ascendency over the males by disguising themselves as spirit figures. Eventually the men discovered how they were being tricked and regained their dominant position in society. The *kina* ritual is designed to remind the women to keep their properly subordinate positions.

The Yahgan dead are disposed of by cremation, and since the tools, weapons, and other sparse property of the deceased are believed to be closely associated in a magicoreligious sense with their owner, they cannot be used by the living and are consequently destroyed with the body. Cremation is followed by mourning rituals, involving abstinence from food and bodily mutilation, the latter apparently intended to protect the survivors from the ghost of the deceased.

Despite the poverty of their existence, the Yahgan make no attempt to store food from one day to the next, since all that they need is readily available at all times of the year. They spend only a fraction of the day in hunting or gathering food, and the rest of their time is free for conversation and recreation. Yet it is important to note that with so much leisure time the Yahgan have invented few games and even their ritual activities remain primitive and relatively brief. The suggestion made by some anthropologists that dance, song, and ritual developed to fill the time made available by advanced technological systems cannot be maintained after examination of the life of the Yahgan and other very primitive societies. Apart from occasional spontaneous wrestling, the Yahgan do little except relax and talk when they are not hunting or gathering. They have no musical instruments, no proverbs, no legends, and no poetry. Even the myths which are recounted at their occasional ceremonies seem to be borrowed from other peoples and to have become simplified rather than enriched after absorption into the Yahgan culture.

FIG. 32　THE ARUNTA

The Arunta are situated in the geographical center of Australia in arid semidesert, the extent of which is shown by the shaded area.

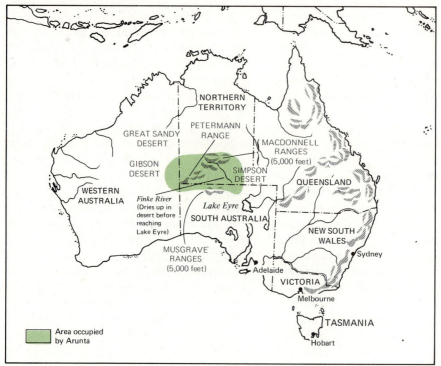

Area occupied by Arunta

THE ARUNTA OF CENTRAL AUSTRALIA

While the Yahgan of Tierra del Fuego live in predominantly endogamous bands, the Arunta of Central Australia provide a well-studied example of an exogamous hunting and food gathering band-type society. Dark-skinned, with receding foreheads, prominent brow ridges, broad noses, and straight black hair, and speaking a language belonging to the South Australian stock, the Arunta number some 2000 men, women, and children, and occupy around 40,000 square miles of semi-desert in the geographical center of the Australian continent.[3]

Ecological Adaptation

Since their environment presents a severe challenge to survival, the Arunta and other Australian aboriginals have been much praised for the skill—and even more, the tenacity—with which they have managed to perpetuate

[3] The Arunta are one of the most studied and most quoted of Australian aboriginal peoples. For a general survey of the Arunta and other Australian aboriginals read H. Basedow, *The Australian Aboriginal* (Adelaide, Australia, 1925) and Sir Baldwin Spencer and F. J. Gillen, *The Arunta*, 2 vols. (London: Macmillan, Ltd., 1927).

themselves. As in other semidesert areas the heat of the day is intense. But in the winter months of June and July the night air can fall to 12 or 13 degrees below the freezing point. Although the soil is potentially fertile, rain is sparse and irregular, and the desert vegetation is therefore limited to a few wiry shrubs, some coarse tufts of grass, and a few acacia trees. However, when rain does fall, floods of water pour down the shallow river beds, causing these to overflow their banks, and the desert is suddenly converted into a carpet of luxuriant vegetation and birds, frogs, lizards, and insects appearing as if by supernatural command.

During the irregular rainy season, small bands of Arunta wander in search of food, each keeping to his own territory. These wandering bands usually contain only two or three families at the most, but during the dry season neighboring bands gather at a convenient waterhole and build lean-to shelters made from forked sticks set upright to give protection from both wind and sun. In these periods of social celebration they carry out their initiation and other rituals.

The technology of the Arunta is that of a Stone Age people, equipped with tools and weapons that originated in the Paleolithic. Unlike some Australian aboriginal peoples who are ignorant of the art of fire making, the Arunta know how to create fire with the aid of wooden rubbing sticks, but still prize their camp fire as a symbol of group unity and prefer to carry the embers from camp to camp rather than to allow the precious flame to die. Time is designated in terms of "sleeps" and "moons," but since they can only count as far as the five digits on a man's hand, their time keeping is only vague. They possess little sense of history.

The Arunta do not wear clothing, and their only body attire comprises ornaments of magicoreligious significance. In the case of the women, this usually takes the form of a string of red beans, while the men attire themselves in a G-string made from the hair of a dead relative. The women crop their hair short, but the men wear theirs long, dying it with red ochre and greasing it with blood on ritual occasions, before dressing it with feathers. Ritual mutilation of the body is universal, ranging from circumcision and the insertion of bone ornaments in the nasal septum, to the knocking out of the incisor teeth, the raising of scars on the body and arms with a stone knife, and the amputation of fingers.

Males, especially the older males, dominate the Arunta society, and a rigid division of labor separates the activities of males and females. Hunting is the prerogative of males, who spend long hours stalking kangaroos, and lacking bows and arrows, they lay in ambush to kill the unsuspecting marsupials with sharpened sticks which serve as spears. Many Australian aboriginals also keep half-wild hunting dogs which can pull down wounded or stupefied animals. But since the supply of marsupials is sparse, snipe, pheasant, and pigeon provide most of the meat in the Arunta diet, although even these are difficult to kill without nets. Emus are sometimes drugged by poisoning their waterholes with *pituri*, a narcotic plant juice, and some birds can be knocked down with the boomerang or throwing stick. Needless to say, the Arunta do not understand the aerodynamic theory of the boomerang, which ideally returns to the thrower if it misses its target, and they have only a rough idea of the desired shape. The boomerang is therefore regarded as an effective throwing stick, and if it reveals a tendency to return to the thrower, it is all the more highly valued. Those which do not come back, however, are not discarded, provided they can still be used as effective missiles.

While the men are engaged in their attempts to kill larger game, the women and children busily employ themselves in collecting the

An Australian aboriginal woman from the Krickhauf ranges. Note the ritual scars acquired during rites of passage. (Courtesy of the Australian News and Information Bureau.)

An aboriginal "wurley" or brushwood shelter. This photograph was taken in the Northern Territory, 150 miles west of Alice Springs. (Courtesy of the Australian News and Information Bureau.)

Australian aboriginal from the Pintubu group, Northern Territory, with "dingo" or half-wild hunting dog. Australia possesses the world's longest fence comprising some 5200 miles of dog-proof wire netting. This makes a continous barrier extending from the great Australian Bight around the sheep lands of Queensland and South Australia to New South Wales, and was built by the Australian Government to protect Australia's millions of sheep from the dingos kept on the aboriginal reservations. (Courtesy of the Australian News and Information Bureau.)

basic elements of the Arunta diet. Using a simple digging stick, they delve for edible roots and overturn stones in search of lizards, snakes, frogs, snails, caterpillars, and larvae. Ants are well-liked, anthills being ground down with a stone until a fine powder is produced and is then baked in the fire and eaten like cakes—without troubling to separate the clay from the ants. When animals were killed, early reports state that the meat was eaten in a semicooked condition, being placed in the fire to burn off the hair, without any effort being made to extract the intestines and other internal organs.

One or two days spent in the same camp will soon exhaust the food resources of the immediate neighborhood, and the band is therefore obliged to move camp every few days. Since the Arunta make neither pottery nor baskets, the only containers available for transportation of their possessions are crude wooden trays and woven fiber handbags. As a constantly wandering people who have to carry everything they possess with them, they have little incentive to accumulate much in the way of material possessions. Men carry their throwing sticks and spears in their hands, while the women carry the embers of the camp fire in a crude wooden trough, any babies who are unable to walk by themselves, and all the other odds and ends, most important of which is the precious grinding stone used to crush berries and seeds.

Social Organization

Although Arunta communities are small and lack tribal organization, the kinship system is remarkably complex. There is no distinction between consanguineal kin and in-laws related only by marriage. Like the Papuans of Papua New Guinea, until their first contact with Europeans, they were seemingly unaware of the genetic fact of biological paternity, believing that a woman became pregnant when the spirit of a deceased relative entered her body to seek rebirth. "Wife lending" is consequently common, but is usually restricted to persons whom they would normally be entitled to marry. The privilege may be extended to strangers on the rare occasion that they arrive on the Arunta scene. When the Arunta offered their wives to early European pioneers, they explained the lighter color of the resultant half-caste children by supposing that the mother must have eaten something that was white.[4] However, the Arunta have their own social and sexual proprieties, and brothers and sisters may not have sexual relations with each other or with their parents. Furthermore a wife who has sexual relations with another man without her husband's permission can be severely beaten, while no man may as much as look directly upon the face or body of his mother-in-law.

Because all females become married immediately when they reach maturity, and the Arunta are largely ignorant of the basic facts of biological paternity, they have no conception of illegitimacy. Every child has its legitimate parents, and kinship provides the fundamental key to both the economic and social structure. Such being the case, the choice of marriage partners is not left to personal option, marriages being arranged by the kin groups between cross cousins before the bride has

---

[4] The Arunta are nevertheless aware of the fact that the physical act of intercourse is necessary before the spirit can pass into the female womb, thereby initiating pregnancy. These hybrid offspring were killed by the aboriginals, who rejected them as abnormal, until this practice was prohibited by the Australian government.

even been born. Although in the absence of any authoritarian enforcement system, Arunta society is governed only by informal social controls, and marriage contracts are occasionally violated, no marriage is ever contracted against the wishes of the kinship group or between individuals who are not eligible to marry. Marriages are generally monogamous, but a widow is expected to marry her deceased husband's brother, not so much for his sexual enjoyment as for the socioeconomic protection of herself and her offspring.

Since all members of the same totemic group and age level are regarded as brothers, and all marriageable females of the appropriate degree of kinship are "wives," there is no separate word for *wife* to distinguish a man's wife from all the other women who would be eligible as marriage partners. In fact the men do enjoy sexual relations with these women at periodic corroborrees when there is a considerable degree of promiscuity. A man uses the term *father-in-law* or *mother-in-law* to apply to the father or mother of any of the many girls who are eligible to become his wife. This practice is known to anthropologists as a *classificatory* system of kinship terminology. Although elaborate genealogies are not kept, the Arunta possess an extremely elaborate kinship system, involving not less than 54 distinct kinship terms, which completely determines the social relationship of the individual to all other members of his group.

Essentially the territory of the Arunta band is regarded as the ancestral or spiritual home of a specific lineage, traced through the male line. Ignorant of genetic paternity, however, the unity of the lineage is believed to reside in the reincarnation of the original spirits in the bodies of the children. Since the soul of a man cannot be reincarnated in his own son during his lifetime, alternate generations are believed to be closer to each other than adjacent generations. As a result, the patriline-

The aged and wrinkled Pintubi woman in the background and the well nourished infant in the foreground vividly illustrate the ability of the Pintubi to obtain sustenance for all age groups despite their harsh environment. The Pintubi were first contacted by a Northern Territory patrol as recently as 1957. (Courtesy of the Australian News and Information Bureau.)

Australian aboriginal "corroborees" or ritual dances sometimes tell the story of recent hunting incidents and at other times recapitulate the exploits of mythic folk heroes. These Arunta dancers are miming the events of a recent kangaroo hunt. The printed loin clothes have been given to them in deference to the esthetic susceptibilities of white Australian tourists. (Courtesy of the Australian News and Information Bureau.)

FIG. 33   THE ARUNTA KINSHIP SYSTEM

The "Four Section" System[1]

	Moiety A		Moiety B
Generation 1	Panunga	=	Purula
	↕		↕
Generation 2	Bultara	=	Kumara

[1]Children belong to the same moiety as their father, but to a different generation.

The "Eight Section" System[2]

		Moiety A		Moiety B	
Generation 1		Section a	=	Section a	
	→	Panunga		Purula	←
		Section b	=	Section b	
	→	Knuria		Ngala	←
Generation 2		Section a	=	Section a	
	→	Bultara		Kumara	←
		Section b	=	Section b	
	→	Pungata		Mbitjana	←

[2]Children belong to the same moiety as their father but to a different generation and a different section.

age or patriclan is divided into distinct generations—*generations* 1 and 3 being regarded as separate from 2 and 4.

At the same time all patriclans are divided into two groups or *moieties:* moiety A and moiety B. Thus a man from generation 1 of moiety A must marry a woman from generation 1 of moiety B, for all women of generation 1 of moiety A, regardless of their specific patriclan, are his "sisters." His son, however, will belong to generation 2 of moiety A, and may only marry a women from generation 2 of moiety B. This system has the great advantage of preventing the older men from hoarding all the females—as their high status might otherwise allow them to do—since they can only marry women from the prescribed generation.[5]

Totemism

From a biological point of view it will be easy to see how the Arunta population, closely inbreeding over thousands of years, has become a distinctive population isolate in which all the genetic parts are evenly distributed throughout the whole. All the members of an Arunta band share a virtually identical genetic heritage, for the intricacies of the kinship sys-

[5]The Australian kinship systems are analyzed in detail by A. R. Radcliffe-Brown in "The Social Organization of Australian Tribes," *Oceania*, Vol. 1 (1930–1933).

tems require a constant circulation of genes. In such a situation kinsmen will not necessarily share a closer genetic identity than those who are not recognized as immediate kinsmen. Kinship in Arunta society is a social convention, not a genetic relationship, while the whole society comprises a single well-integrated gene pool.

Nevertheless, the Arunta place great social importance upon their totemic lineages. Believing that particular kinship groups are descended from specific animals, they also believe that their totemic animal is closely associated with territory in which the lineage resides, so that their totemism serves to reinforce the principles of territoriality. The Arunta band is consequently intimately and irrevocably tied to the territory in which its members are born, not merely by habit but by religious conviction. The idea of deliberately invading an alien territory with a view to conquest is unknown to the Arunta, and organized war is an impossibility, for no man desires to stray from his ancestral homeland where the totemic mysteries are kept.

The ancestral or totemic spirits of the Arunta include kangaroos, lizards, rats, and birds, each lineage having its own totemic animal. No Arunta will ever kill the totemic animal of his lineage when hunting, but periodic totemic rituals are held to ensure the fertility of the totemic species. On these occasions, but at no other time, the flesh of the totemic creature is freely eaten in a kind of primitive communion ceremony. However, there is no attempt to prevent the members of other lineages from killing and consuming such animals at any time, and the prohibition applies only to the members of a lineage in respect of their own totemic animal.

The relations between neighboring Arunta bands are normally friendly. Such disputes as do arise between the members of different bands are usually settled amicably, each group

chiding the individuals concerned, but should a friendly settlement fail, mock fights may be enacted between the rival bands in an attempt to release tension. Only when these measures also fail, does a serious blood feud ever develop, and even then territorial isolation serves to reduce the significance of such feuds, for contacts are necessarily infrequent and time is a great healer.

Blood has a deep magico-kinship significance. On the rare occasions that the Arunta are driven to seek blood revenge, the men first rub themselves with the hair of the slain kinsman and then cut their own veins and smear each other with their blood in order to commit themselves more deeply to the common task of revenge. An earlier tradition of cannibalism, based on the belief that men may acquire the magical properties of those whose blood they consume, is indicated not only by the incidence of blood drinking at the puberty rituals, but by the fact that an ailing elder may be fed blood drawn from one of the children in the belief that the magical properties inherent in the child's healthy body will give new vitality to the consumer.[6] Needless to say, if the condition of the patient is aggravated by undernourishment, the improved diet may actually be a stimulus to recovery.

Metaphysical Beliefs and Ritual

When a marriage is negotiated, the mother of the still unborn bride presents her future son-in-law with a pair of fire-making rubbing sticks with which to light a new hearth fire. However, the birth of children involves little ceremonial, and a woman will usually return to her normal food gathering duties within a few hours after childbirth. Twins are invari-

[6] The practice of drinking the blood of a child or of a younger man, and of medicinal cannibalism in general, is by no means peculiar to the Arunta. The underlying principle is one of contagious magic.

ably killed, since multiple births are regarded as unnatural and evil, and eugenic infanticide is also practiced in obvious cases of genetic malformation. In addition, since a woman has to carry the entire family's possessions whenever the group moves camp, any child born before the previous baby is old enough to walk by itself or keep up with the adults is usually killed by the simple process of immolating it alive in the sand. However, babies which are fit and healthy and do not arrive too soon after a previous birth, are welcomed, although without elaborate ritual. It is customary to burn the afterbirth, but the umbilical cord will be carefully preserved to make a necklace which the baby wears as a talisman. The infant's paternal grandfather fashions a special *churinga* for the child from a piece of wood or stone.

According to the Arunta every person has two parts to his soul. One of these resides in his physical body, but the other takes up residence in the magicoreligious *churinga* object fashioned by his grandfather. The *churinga* is stored with those of all other members of the totemic group, living and dead, at the totemic storehouse, actually just a geographical location close to a sacred tree or other natural object. Each child also receives two names, a personal name which will be used by the other members of his group and a secret *churinga* name which will only be known to the elder men who have been fully initiated into the secrets of the band. This name is the one that will be used in all subsequent rituals such as the puberty ceremony.

When boys reach the age of puberty, they are required to undergo a number of elaborate secret rituals before they can be admitted into full adult male status. Since the only authoritative figures in the Arunta band are the initiated adult males who have learned the age-old magicoreligious secrets of the group, the initiation and puberty rituals are of enormous significance and involve many painful trials of

physical endurance. In the course of these rituals the candidate is tortured with fire, cut with stone knives, and ritually circumcized. The exuvia, or portion of flesh removed in this operation, is eaten by his younger brother, who expects thereby to acquire some of the merits of his elder relative. In addition, the candidate's penis is also cut to the urethra with a crude stone knife in a practice known to anthropologists as *subincision. Bull-roarers,* or flat stones which are whirled through the air at high speed on the end of a length of twine, are used at such ceremonies, the roaring sound which they make being interpreted as the voices of ancestral ghosts. Most male ceremonies, particularly those involving the use of the bull-roarer, are strictly banned to women and children, and a woman who inadvertently hears a bull-roarer will be put to death.

Girls also undergo puberty rituals, although these are not of the same intensity as those experienced by boys because girls do not acquire political authority with adulthood and are not admitted to the secrets of the tribal lore. However, in view of their approaching eligibility for parenthood, a girl who is reaching puberty has her breasts rubbed with animal fat and red ochre to encourage their growth, after which a group of the older men take her off into the bush, fracture the hymen with a flint knife, and after having sexual intercourse with her, give her a new adult name and declare her ready for marriage.

Sorcery and Death

The Arunta believe that death is the result of sorcery, and any man may harm an enemy by reciting a ritual curse, while pointing a sharpened bone in the direction of his victim. Consequently, when death occurs, it is customary to ask one of the group who specializes in the arts of magic to name the magician who caused the death. Since those consulted usually name a member of some distant and unfriendly

An aboriginal from the Northern Territory pointing a bone at his victim while intoning a magical curse. Although such ceremonies are usually performed in secret, news of the curse inevitably reaches the victim, who in many cases has been known to die. (Courtesy of the Australian News and Information Bureau.)

band, deaths do not normally create new disputes but merely serve to perpetuate the traditional suspicion reserved for alien bands, with whom social contacts are irregular.

The entire life of the Arunta is actually spent in an aura of magic and sorcery, for they cannot conceive of natural forces, but only of forces motivated teleologically by ghosts and sorcerers. Although any man or woman may practice sorcery, there are some who are believed to be specialists in the black arts, and these may be identified by a hole pierced through the tongue in secret initiation rituals carried out by other ordained sorcerers. As might be expected, there is a great fear of death. Bodies are consequently quickly buried in shallow graves beneath a pile of loose earth and brush wood before they can begin to putrefy, although a small hole is left through

which the soul may leave or reenter the body at will. Ghosts are feared, never revered, and not only is the lean-to of the deceased man invariably burned down, but his personal possessions are destroyed for fear that his ghost would be jealous if they were used by someone else. This is no great loss, since primitive tools do not take long to make, but the camp must be immediately abandoned, and the survivors hasten to move away from the vicinity of the deceased spirit. The name of a dead man is never spoken again, and during the long period of mourning, the length of which depends on the kinship status of the deceased, the survivors must lacerate their bodies and follow other rituals. When this mourning period is over, the band revisits the site of the grave, and a second funeral ceremony is held at which the adult males dance and shout to drive away the ghost, trampling on the remains of the now-disintegrated body in order to ensure that the spirit leaves the gravesite and joins its *churinga* double in the ancestral storehouse.

Dreams are regarded as supernatural experiences, and the distant past is regarded as a "dream-time." It was during this *alchuria,* or distant dream-time, that the totemic ancestors are believed to have lived. Since the past is characterized by its dreamlike timelessness, the Arunta have no concept of history and dismiss the past as mystical and unknowable. When asked their opinion as to how the world came about, they simply refer to the legend of a certain Numbakulla, or "one who came out of nothing"—who created the land, trees, plants, animals, and all other living and nonliving things, but himself enjoys eternal life.

THE PYGMIES OF THE AFRICAN FORESTS

Both of the hunting and gathering societies which we have just described, the Yahgan and the Arunta, survived in harsh environments. Indeed, it could even be said that they owe the fact of their survival to the unsuitability of their lands for cultivation or herding, for as a general rule it was only in those areas which were unattractive to Neolithic and Metal Age cultivators and herdsmen that the earlier Paleolithic hunters were able to retain control of the land.

It is therefore not to be assumed that ancient gatherers always lived as poorly as the peoples whom we have just described. Just as the primates still flourish in the fertile tropical and semitropical lands, so the hominid hunters and gatherers who lived in these fertile regions had little difficulty in finding ample food. While some *Homo sapiens* subspecies fought a struggle for existence in the harsher climates of Europe and Asia, those *H. sapiens* subspecies which were fortunate in inheriting territories

in the richer tropical and semitropical climatic zones found that their ancient hunting and gathering techniques supplied them with all that they needed. Thus today, in those depths of the Congo rain forests which have not yet been penetrated by Negro cultivators, the Pygmies still maintain an age-old hunting and gathering culture which enables them to live in comfort in their lush environment, enjoying a plenitude of resources such as the Yahgan and Arunta have never experienced.

The Friendly Forest

To the Pygmies, the forest is not the fearful, dark, and silent place that men who are unaccustomed to the arboreal world believe it to be. Anyone who has experienced life in an African rain forest knows that once the fears and tensions of the unfamiliar have disappeared, the forest becomes a cool and restful place, illuminated by a soft light which filters down through the canopy of leaves above. Rain is heavy most of the year round, falling regularly during late afternoon thunderstorms, and the humidity is always high, except during the relatively dry season in January and February, when the sky may be overcast and rain is less frequent.

The forest is never silent and no one in it is ever lonely, for it is full of life, and living things make sounds. Brightly colored birds flit between the trees, singing as they go; monkeys leap from branch to branch; and elephants trample through the thick undergrowth of bushes and liana leaves. Surrounded by a wide variety of plant and animal life, the Pygmies have no difficulty in finding food, and while the men hunt game with bows and arrows, the Pygmy women and young girls gather mushrooms, fruits, nuts, and edible roots. In fact, the forest is so generous a provider of food that the Pygmies do not have to trouble to hunt every day, and they happily laze around their camp whenever the previous day's work has

FIG. 34   THE PYGMIES

Most surviving Pygmies are found in the eastern Congo between Stanleyville and Lake Albert on the borders of Congo and Uganda.

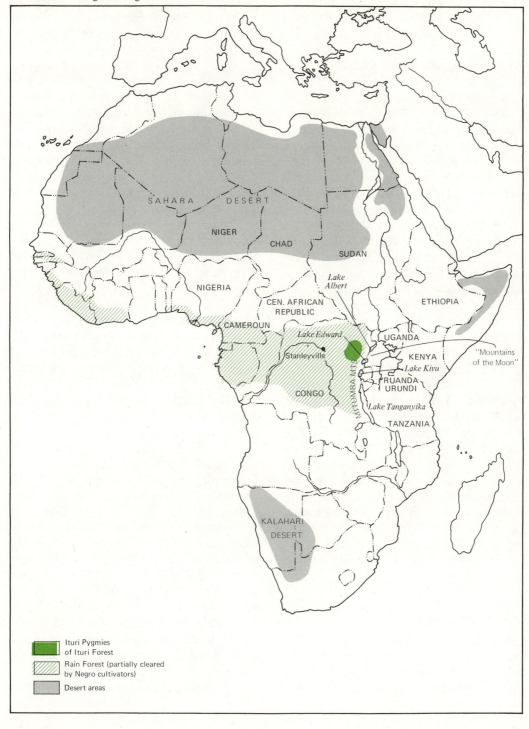

Ituri Pygmies
of Ituri Forest

Rain Forest (partially cleared
by Negro cultivators)

Desert areas

brought them all that they need. In such a paradise there is no need to think of the morrow, and Pygmies have no fear of the future. They know that the forest will always provide for them, for as the Ba Mbuti song says, "The Forest is good, the Forest is kind."

Thus the lives of the Pygmies illustrate the contentment and simplicity of a hunting and gathering people who live in a world of plenty. Although it has been customary to portray the lives of early man as short, brutish, and cruel, mainly on the basis of the evidence of those less fortunate hunters and gatherers who only survived into our present age in the more remote and unwanted corners of the earth, the life of the earliest hunters and gatherers of tropical lands was probably relatively carefree. With little knowledge of black magic and largely free from fears of the supernatural, and with simple needs that were abundantly supplied by a friendly environment, and a poorly developed technology that required no toil, no drudgery, and relatively little time, our earlier forebears may well have had all the leisure they needed for storytelling, laughter, and dancing.

Unlike so many hunting societies which have tended to migrate over considerable distances during the past few millennia, we know from ancient Egyptian records that the Pygmies were already living in their present location as long as 4000 years ago. Possibly they represent a very ancient central African population, but we have no evidence of their history before that date, for there is a complete absence of fossil evidence. Improvements in technology were slow in entering the African rain forests, and prehistoric artifacts are also nonexistent.

Relationship to Negroes

Some physical anthropologists have assumed that Pygmies are simply the dwarfed descendants of a larger Negro subspecies. They argue that as a general rule of mammalian adaptation,

those members of a species which live on the open plains tend to develop long limbs and grow to a considerable height, like the tall Watusi of the Urundi grasslands. On the other hand, mammals of the same species that live in heavily forested areas generally tend to become reduced in size with the passing of generations to create a new dwarf subspecies, since in thick forests height can be a handicap to mammals, and short stature will have a positive survival value. Thousands of years of continued residence in the Congo rain forests, which they share with the pygmy hippopotamus and pygmy chimpanzees, would therefore explain the Pygmy stature.

The original language of the Pygmies is unknown, for like other hunters and gatherers they never developed a written script. Today they speak the dialects of their Negro neighbors. However, they still use a number of words which do not appear to belong to the Congo-Kordofanian languages of the Negroes, and these may well be survivals from an original Pygmy language. Linguists also note that Pygmies speak with a sing-song intonation quite distinct from the speech of the Negroes, who find it difficult to understand them.

Pygmy Technology

Although contact with Western peoples has led to the virtual elimination of the Yahgan, and is also currently exerting a similar, drastically modifying influence on the Australian aboriginal culture, the first modern European intrusion into Central Africa took place only a century ago, and in the protection of their forests the Pygmies have managed to retain much of their traditional way of life. At the present time there are still probably 40,000 Pygmies in the Congo, although rapid increases in the surrounding population of Negroes, following the control of malaria and other tropical diseases since World War II, has led to increasing forest clearance. In consequence, the survival of the Pygmies, with their ancient hunting and gathering tradition, is today threatened by the further expansion of cultivation in Africa and the disappearance of the last forest reserves.

Fortunately the Ba Mbuti Pygmies, who live in the Ituri forest just west of the Ruwenzori mountains in northeastern Congo, have been comprehensively studied by an English anthropologist, Colin M. Turnbull, who lived with the Pygmies and knew them intimately for a number of years.[7] As wandering hunters and gatherers, the Pygmies have few possessions and need no more than they have. Their simple equipment is easy to make, and much of what they use is abandoned when they move camp, and made anew when required. Crude beehive huts are constructed from saplings twisted together in a beehive frame, which is then covered with large leaves that somewhat imperfectly waterproof it against the rain, while allowing the smoke to seep out around their edges. As far as personal equipment is concerned, leaf cups serve as containers for drinking water, and simple clothing is made from bark which has been stripped from the trees, soaked overnight in a stream, beaten, and then allowed to dry. The flattened bark fibres actually make a soft though not very durable cloth, which is usually decorated with dyes, obtained from the juices of the gardenia and other plants, drawn in free designs with the fingers. Hunting nets are made from shredded pieces of *nkusa* vine, rolled by hand on the inside of the thigh. Pottery was originally unknown, but has since been acquired from the Negroes who trade pots, axes, spear heads, and knives for fresh meat. Before contact was established with

A Pygmy hunter from Gabon carrying his hunting net on his head. The net seen in this picture is modern, having been acquired by trade. Traditional nets were woven from creepers. (Courtesy of La Documentation Française, Paris.)

the Negroes, the Pygmies had only sharpened wooden spears, with points hardened over a fire like those of the Yahgan.

As bowmen the Pygmies are not good marksmen, for their bows are only primitive, and their technique is to steal up on their quarry and pump it full of arrows before it can escape. But in addition to bows and arrows, the Pygmy hunters often use nets made of liana fibers. While the men wait behind the nets, concealed from view by the dense foliage, the women tramp through the forest, striking the undergrowth with sticks as they go, and shouting and crying to drive any wild animals into the nets. Antelope are their prime quarry, and

[7]This description is largely based on the ethnographic studies by Colin Turnbull and P. Putnam. See Colin Turnbull, *The Forest People* (New York: Simon and Schuster, Inc., 1961) and P. Putnam, "The Pygmies of the Ituri Forest," in C. S. Coon (ed.), *A Reader in General Anthropology* (New York: Holt, Rinehart and Winston, Inc., 1948).

once an animal is caught in the nets, the men spear it before it can escape.

Despite their small stature the Pygmies enjoy an elephant hunt, which is a major adventure since their bows are too weak to drive an arrow deep enough into the heavy hide of an elephant to kill or even incapacitate this forest giant. Success, therefore, depends upon the dexterous use of a spear combined with the element of surprise. When stalking an elephant, one Pygmy creeps forward in advance of the others. If he succeeds in reaching the elephant's side, he quickly jags his spear into the animal's soft underbelly, jerks it out again, and freezes, knowing that the elephant will not detect him unless he moves. Waiting until his quarry begins eating again, he repeats the act and continues to sink his spear into the elephant's hide until it finally moves away. If the hide was penetrated deeply enough to injure the internal organs, the elephant eventually dies of peritonitis. The Pygmy hunters have only to trail it until it finally collapses, its body bloated with pus and the decaying contents of its stomach.

Social Organization

The Pygmy community is a band organization. Each band is politically autonomous and all decisions are made by community discussion. There are no headmen and no one seeks authority. All adult males assume the responsibilities of a father to all children whenever aid or assistance is needed, and all women will fill the duties of a mother if need be. All the men in a Pygmy band are "brothers," and the Pygmies possibly reveal the world's greatest talent for mutual cooperation. Families are usually monogamous, mainly because there is generally a shortage of women due to the fact that Pygmy women are often persuaded by the prospects of village "luxury" to leave the forest and become second wives to Negroes. Pygmy marriages are consequently usually arranged at puberty, two Pygmy families agreeing to provide wives for each other's sons, with little ceremony. Divorce is as casual as marriage, and remarriage is regularly permitted.

All Pygmies are regarded as equal, except for the respect due to men and to the aged, and the women enjoy a considerable amount of freedom. Even the division of labor between males and females is not highly developed, for the men are not embarrassed to pick mushrooms and fruit or to clean a baby, while the women on occasion participate in the hunt.

Although they are a remarkably peaceable people, occasional disputes between husbands and wives or between families do arise, and

Two Pygmy females. Note the pronounced curvature of the spine, a feature characteristic of the Pygmy physique, which contributes to the marked distention of the abdomen. (Courtesy of Hans W. Jürgens.)

A Babingas Pygmy family from the rain forest of Ouesso in the Congo seated in front of their leaf-covered dwelling. (Courtesy of La Documentation Française, Paris.)

since a Pygmy will seldom admit to being wrong about anything, a domestic quarrel can lead to divorce. In the majority of cases husband and wife prove to be too fond of each other to allow a quarrel to break the marriage, and an excuse is usually found for reconciliation without loss of dignity to either party. When a family quarrel does become far advanced, the wife may begin to pull the leaves off the outside of the hut as a symbol of the approaching breakup of the marriage, and unless her husband stops her from demolishing their home, everyone knows that after uprooting the framework she must leave him and return to her parents.

Disputes between families do not usually last long, and Pygmies have no tradition of the blood feud. However, when a disagreement arises between two families in the same band, whose stick and leaf huts are adjacent to each other, one family may construct a loose wattle fence to separate the two houses from each other so that they do not have to look at each other all the time. Since these "spite fences" are only loosely put together, they fall down after a few days, by which time the disagreement has usually been forgotten.

In moments of unhappiness Pygmies do not attempt to control their emotions, and freely burst into tears. On the other hand, laughter comes readily, and having no inhibitions about extroverted behavior, they may laugh until

343

they can no longer stand, and fall to the ground still laughing. Not only do the Pygmies cooperate in brotherly fashion with each other, but there is a relative absence of suspicion between band members. The idea of witchcraft is unknown. Consequently, while the more sophisticated Negroes believe that every death is caused by witches or evil spirits, Pygmies accept death as natural, having no explanation for it and merely regarding it as "a big thing," and "a matter of the Forest." Nevertheless when a member of the band is sick, the womenfolk wail aloud in sympathy, and when a Pygmy dies, there is a genuine grief among the survivors.[8]

The killing of an elephant is an occasion for great merrymaking, and all other pursuits are put aside in favor of singing, dancing, and feasting. The Pygmies believe in a God of the Forest who shows them affection and love, and on an important occasion like an elephant feast they celebrate the *moliemo,* a religious ceremony comprising ritual dancing and singing. The ceremony is held in the evening, the men gathering in three groups: the elders or "Great Ones" sitting in one place, the adult male hunters in another, and the youths in a third. Women are permitted to watch the dances from an outer circle, and also to paint their bodies with black *kangay* juice, stick pieces of vine in their hair, and perform their own dance. Music is made by blowing crudely worked wooden trumpets, and the young men shout hunting cries, lashing around themselves with sticks, and sometimes even knocking down huts as they become more excited.

The Pygmy Camp

A Pygmy camp is usually situated in a small clearing in the undergrowth, deep in the forest. Here the little circle of huts, one for each nuclear family of husband, wife, and children,

[8] Turnbull, p. 42.

faces inward toward a common plaza, where the earth is worn bare by dancing feet. Although fire is a prized possession, the Pygmies have not learned how to make it; consequently whenever they move camp, they have to carry the glowing embers from their last fire with them, borrowing new fire from a neighboring group if ever the flame is lost.

While the adults congregate in the central plaza, the children gather to play in a small clearing at one end of the camp, known as a *bopi,* where a couple of vines will be rigged up as a swing. Many of the children's games involve tree climbing, vine swinging, or acrobatics. They also like to play "house," the girls building a miniature hut with sticks and leaves like the huts of their parents, while the boys go off on "hunting trips" with their toy bows and arrows. As "hunters" the children love to catch a frog and pretend that it is an antelope which they are hunting, although they do this without deliberate cruelty. If they are lucky, they may persuade one of the elders to play the part of the hunted animal, jumping upon him and beating him with their fists. But, except in fun, the children are respectful toward their adults, for whenever they get out of hand at any time, they are likely to receive a quick smack or even a thorough spanking.

The contact between Negroes and Pygmies seems to be a long-established relationship. Since the Pygmies know the forests far better than do the Negroes, who cultivate the clearings and are essentially horticulturalists, the Pygmies not only trade meat for tools and horticultural produce, but also act as scouts to give warning of raiding parties from other Negro tribes. They do not admire the Negro cultivators, regarding them as clumsy giants who cannot live without destroying the good forest, but they value Negro tools and pottery, and have also developed a respect for the Negroes' command of the supernatural, taking their children to the Negro villages to be circumcised and to join the Negro secret societies.

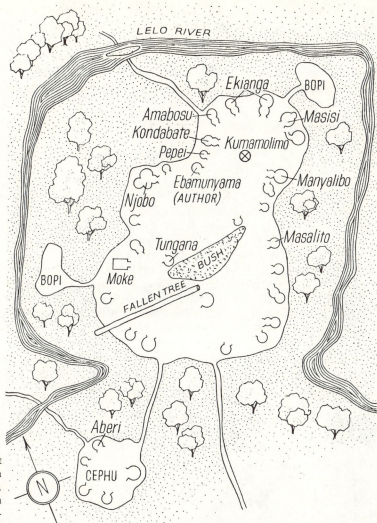

Plan of a Pygmy encampment in the Ituri Forest. (From Colin M. Turnbull, *The Forest People,* p. 10. Copyright 1961 by Colin M. Turnbull. Reprinted by permission of Simon and Schuster.)

Their precise attitude to Negro magic is ambiguous, however, for they believe that the forest will protect them from all evils. Some observers claim that they participate in the Negro rituals mainly for the novelty, for the gifts they receive, and for the pleasure of feasting—in much the same way as many tribal Negroes patronize missionary stations without necessarily becoming true converts to the missionary faith.

The Negroes regard the Pygmies as lesser beings, lacking in civilized refinements, and classify the zoological species into four categories: Negroes, Pygmies, chimpanzees, and "other animals." However, the Pygmies seem to be happier than the Negroes, innocently describing themselves as "children of the Forest." The forest, they say, is their father, mother, and friend. They feel secure in it and show love and affection for it. Knowing its ways intimately, they sing and dance in its honor. While the neighboring Negroes toil in their fields, fight sanguinary wars, and live out their lives under the dark pall of sorcery, the Pygmies dance and put their faith in the goodness of Nature. It is perhaps symbolic of the good life which hunters and gatherers enjoy in a lush environment that the peak of their contentment comes during the honey season, when they dance to assist the bees in gathering honey, and all hunting is abandoned in favor of the more peaceful art of honey collecting.

For Further Reading

Bicchieri, M., 1965, "A Study of the Ecology of Food Gathering Peoples." Unpublished doctoral dissertation, University of Minnesota.

Clark, G., 1967, *The Stone Age Hunters.* New York: McGraw-Hill, Inc.

Dentan, R. K., 1968, *The Semai, A Non-violent People of Malaya.* New York: Holt, Rinehart and Winston, Inc.

Elkin, A. P., 1964, *The Australian Aborigines.* Garden City, N.Y.: Natural History Press.

Hart, C. W., and A. R. Pilling, 1960, *The Tiwi of North Australia.* New York: Holt, Rinehart and Winston, Inc.

Lee, R. B., and I. DeVore, 1968, *Man the Hunter.* Chicago: Aldine Publishing Co.

Lévi-Strauss, C., 1963, *Totemism.* Boston: The Beacon Press.

Porteus, S. D., 1931, *The Psychology of a Primitive People.* London: E. Arnold & Co.

Putnam, P., 1947, "The Pygmies of the Ituri Forest," in C. S. Coon, ed., *A Reader in General Anthropology.* New York: Holt, Rinehart and Winston, Inc.

Service, E. R., 1960, *The Hunters.* Englewood Cliffs, N.J.: Prentice-Hall, Inc.

Spencer, B., and F. J. Gillin, 1927, *The Arunta,* 2 vols. London: Macmillan, Ltd.

———, 1947, "The Ancestors Walk," in C. S. Coon, ed., *A Reader in General Anthropology.* New York: Holt, Rinehart and Winston, Inc.

Strehlow, T. G. H., 1947, *Aranda Traditions.* Melbourne: University of Melbourne Press.

Turnbull, C. M., 1968, *The Forest People.* New York: Simon and Schuster, Inc.

van Gennep, A., 1960, *The Rites of Passage.* Chicago: University of Chicago Press.

Wheeler, Sir M., 1954, *Archaeology from the Earth.* New York: Oxford University Press.

CHAPTER 24

Horticulturalists: Warlike and Peaceful

The late Upper Paleolithic is commonly known as the *Mesolithic* or Middle Stone Age since it essentially represents a transitional stage in which the hunting and gathering cultures of the Upper Paleolithic evolved into the plant cultivating and animal domesticating societies of the Neolithic or New Stone Age. The term *Neolithic* was formerly used to refer to a level of technological evolution at which polished stone tools were first used, but is today applied to any Stone Age food cultivating society. Because such societies are generally settled in more or less permanent village communities, they are able to accumulate considerable material wealth, and this usually includes an array of pottery domestic utensils, which since they do not decay in the soil provide archeologists with a paradise of useful information.

The transition from hunting and gathering to horticulture reflected a process of gradually improving skills, and was by no means an instantaneous or sudden "revolution", as we might erroneously imagine from the expression "the Neolithic revolution" so often used in this connection. While it is true that cultivation did introduce revolutionary changes in the pattern of human life, these were by no means abrupt, for the Neolithic emerged as a result of a steady process of evolutionary change which took the entire length of the Mesolithic to convert the Upper Paleolithic advanced hunters and gatherers into settled Neolithic cultivators.

While there were settled villages of advanced food gatherers who herded pigs in the forests of southeastern Europe as early as 7500 B.C., the first regularly sown and harvested crops appear to have been cultivated in the highlands of Anatolia, Persia, and the European Balkans by 7000 B.C. or earlier. From these areas the art of cultivation spread rapidly up the Danube and into the Rhineland, as well as into the so-called *Fertile Crescent*, comprising the valleys of the Tigris, the Euphrates, and the Jordan.

The Transition from Hunting and Gathering

The history of the cultivation of the soil has two main phases. The first of these is known as HORTICULTURE and implies the use of crude tools such as the hand hoe and the digging stick in the process of simple soil exploitation, in which no conservation of natural resources is involved. A more advanced phase is known as AGRICULTURE and implies not merely the use of sophisticated tools such as the plow but also the application of measures designed to prevent erosion and even to enrich and fertilize the soil. So far as the pattern of human life

Because women were normally food gatherers while the men concentrated on hunting, women are generally given the credit for having invented horticulture. Woman cultivator of the Ivory Coast. (Courtesy of La Documentation Française, Paris.)

is concerned, the essential difference between the two is that horticulture customarily exhausts the soil, requiring periodic changes of residence, while agriculture not only produces substantially larger crops for the same amount of work but also makes continued occupation of the same settlement possible from one generation to another.

It has been suggested that horticulture arose as a deliberate invention forced upon the population of one area by a change of climate, but this cannot be substantiated. In fact the drift to horticulture seems to have been undertaken without the pressure of environmental necessity, since there is no evidence of any radical change of climate at this time. In all probability there must have been a steady drift toward horticulture as a purely deliberate local specialization—an attempt to make the most of local conditions, with wild grain being regularly harvested by hunting and gathering bands who probably began to protect the richer beds of grain from the enchroachments of wild animals.

The first steps toward cultivation may have consisted of nothing more than the removal of weeds and the protection of wild grain from the depredations of wild animals, and actual transplanting or sowing of seeds probably came later. We must surmise that the first experiments in planting grain took place in the upland areas, for it was in these areas that the grain grew wild in profusion and the oldest permanent settlements were located. But it could have been only a matter of time before men found that it was better to plant their crops in the lower meadows where the soil was richer and the water supply was more reliable, and deliberate clearings of lowland vegetation by fire and axe were undertaken to prepare for transplanted upland grain.

Along with the planting of wild grain, there are ample signs of the domestication of wild goats and sheep as well as of asses and dogs. Thus the first farming may well have been mixed farming—as distinct from pastoralism, a way of life centered on nomadic herding of animals. Speculation as to the motives for the domestication of animals by settled farmers generally rules out the suggestion that they were first captured for food. If *domesticated* animals are defined as those whose territorial behavior has been modified to enable them to live in a symbiotic relationship with men, it may well be that the first domesticated animals were young animals adopted by hunters and kept as pets after the mother had been slain, while for food men continued to prey upon the ample herds around them.

Few hunters would accept the toil of keeping unruly animals in captivity when they could easily hunt down a whole herd of wild animals in a stimulating and enjoyable exercise, without any of the work or responsibility attached to the care of domestic animals. In the course of time, pets may have been employed as decoys for the wild animals, a hunting trick still used by many hunters to this day, but wholesale domestication may not have taken place until by unintentional selection, men had already succeeded in breeding into existence several generations of tame and docile animals. Assuming that men would kill and perhaps eat the more unruly pets out of sheer convenience, in the course of time a new breed of less ferocious, more docile domesticated animals would develop, and might be permitted to increase in number once their food potential was realized.

Thus the less advanced horticulturalists seldom depend wholly upon the produce of their fields. Unless deprived of the possibilities of hunting, as are the Hopi Indians of Arizona, the men will customarily continue to hunt wild animals partly for sport and partly for the variety which the meat will provide in their diet. Many horticulturalists of Oceania augment the produce of their fields substantially by fish caught at sea or in the coral lagoons. On the other hand, the horticulturalists of Africa rely mainly upon the produce of the land, while those of Southeast Asia are so densely settled on the available land that there is little wildlife for them to hunt, and too few fish to make river fishing profitable.

Historical Centers of Horticulture

The earliest indications of horticulture are thus found by 7000 B.C. in Kurdistan, southern Turkey, and the Balkans where small bands of advanced collectors settled in semipermanent communities, using flintstone sickle blades to harvest the wild cereals which grew in abundance on the rolling uplands.[1] Fossilized human excrement contains abundant evidence that the diet of members of these communities included a wide variety of different plant foods. In fact, the erosion and exhaustion of these areas over the past 10,000 years has been such that these ancient settlers may well have enjoyed a better diet and a higher standard of living than do the present-day inhabitants of the same now sadly deforested, despoiled, and eroded hills.

Archeological evidence suggests that even at this early time there was a population density of some 27 people to the square mile, or about the same level as exists today, notwithstanding the more advanced technology available to the present population, which barely compensates for the devastated condition of the landscape. The tragedy of the Middle East is that as the first area of experimental horticulture, it suffered from early man's ignorance of soil conservation.

As horticulture developed, the older more

[1] See E. C. Curwen and G. Hatt, *Plough and Pasture: The Early History of Farming* (New York: Abelard-Schuman, Ltd., 1953). Although this work does not distinguish clearly between horticulture and agriculture in the anthropological sense and does not include the latest material from European archeology, which shows European cultivation to be as old as that of the Middle East, it may be used as a valuable introduction to the study of the origins of cultivation in the Old World.

FIG. 35   THE ORIGINS OF HORTICULTURE AND SETTLED FARMING

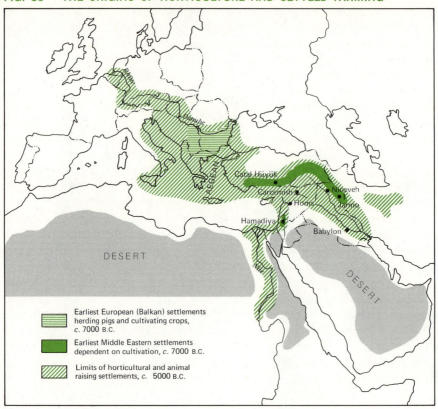

Earliest European (Balkan) settlements herding pigs and cultivating crops, *c.* 7000 B.C.

Earliest Middle Eastern settlements dependent on cultivation, *c.* 7000 B.C.

Limits of horticultural and animal raising settlements, *c.* 5000 B.C.

highly specialized hunting and food gathering tools began to give way, in archeological sites, to new artifacts devised to suit horticultural needs. The evidence of these tools and other archeological remains shows that by 6000 B.C. horticulture had begun to move down into the broad alluvial lands of the valleys of the Tigris, Euphrates, Upper Danube, Rhine, and Aegean.

Horticulture appears to be one of the few innovations which may have been invented independently in several places. The fact that certain crops are naturally indigenous to particular areas means that the earliest attempts at cultivation in different environments had to depend upon the local plants available. This creates the impression of quite distinctive re-

gional horticultural culture traditions, even though in some cases the *idea* of cultivation may have been carried by migrating populations who found that they could not grow their traditional crops in their new environment but that they could domesticate indigenous wild plants. Nevertheless, few of the different crops raised by man throughout the world are indigenous to the areas in which they are today cultivated. Most have been introduced by man from other areas.

The main centers of early cultivation were located in Southwest Asia and the European Balkans. The Anatolian uplands were probably the home of wheat, millet, rye, peas, apples, pears, plums, and many other crops well known to us today. On the other hand, the Mediterranean was certainly the home of the fig and the olive as well as the broad bean. Northern China enjoyed a separate agricultural tradition, although the idea of cultivation and some of the earlier crops seem to have been brought into China from western Asia. Nevertheless the soya bean is undoubtedly indigenous to China. Southeast Asia, by contrast, appears to have a very ancient and possibly independent tradition of cultivation, and this part of the world is the home of rice and sugar cane. Although western Africa, south of the Sahara and north of the forest of the Congo, has a very ancient horticultural tradition, many of the crops grown in Africa, such as millet, yams, coconuts, and bananas, are not indigenous African plants, but appear to have been brought to Africa from Southeast Asia by sea-going Malayo-Polynesians who crossed the Indian Ocean to settle Madagascar and parts of the east coast of Africa.

But the New World is another source of many of the crops well known to modern cultivators. Horticulture appears to have originated independently among American Indians in Central America some 3000 years ago. When the first Europeans arrived in the Americas in the fifteenth and sixteenth centuries they found manioc, potatoes, pumpkins, tomatoes, tobacco, maize, cotton, pineapples, peanuts, papaya, guava, and many other species of cultivated plants which were until then unknown in the Old World.

The cultivation of crops in northern Europe lagged behind central Europe some 1500 years because wheat and other Middle Eastern grains will not grow in northern latitudes. However, rye and oats will grow in northern latitudes, and although these were apparently regarded

Manioc is widely cultivated in both Africa and the Americas, but is poisonous until it has been soaked in water to remove the acidity. (Courtesy of La Documentation Française, Paris.)

as weeds by the more southerly cultivators, it is easy to see how attempts to introduce wheat into northern Europe would lead to good crops of weeds and poor crops of the desired grain. Nevertheless rye and oats are nourishing, and in the course of time persistent cultivators would begin to appreciate their value and cultivate the "weeds" for their own virtues.

Horticulture reached northwestern India, presumably from the Middle East, by 4000 B.C., thus laying the foundations for the later Indus Valley civilization. The cultivation of crops had spread to the Upper Nile Valley by 5000 B.C., and to West Africa at a much later still disputed date. No crops appear to have been cultivated in northern China until approximately 3000 B.C., but the first crops found in northern China suggest a West Asian origin.

Social and Cultural Implications

The most important change introduced into the lives of the food gatherers by the invention of horticulture was the abandonment of nomadism in favor of semipermanent settlements, although the transition from nomadism to regular settled life probably took a thousand years or more to accomplish. This earliest method of cultivation probably required a *slash-and-burn* pattern of shifting cultivation which exhausted the fertility of the soil and caused the cultivators to clear fresh soil every one or two years for their crops.[2] However, even the possibility of settling in one place for as long as a year at a time meant a substantial reorganization of early man's life style.

Where land suitable for cultivation was plentiful, it was even possible for horticulturalists to occupy the same village site for several years at a time, so that horticulturalists no longer had to think of carrying everything

they owned with them on a daily trek in search of food. This made possible the accumulation of increasing quantities of material artifacts, allowed the development of heavy equipment for grinding cereals, baking food, and storing grain, and even led to the appearance of elementary furnishings for personal comfort. Men no longer abandoned much of what they made every few days when they broke camp. When an artifact was made for long-term use, it was worth putting more time into designing, finishing, and even ornamenting it. Similarly, with horticulture, permanent or semipermanent huts became a possibility.

Equally significant is the fact that larger populations become possible. Like the old hunting and gathering bands, the horticulturalists still lay claim to a given territory, but instead of roaming around this territory, they are able to settle in a central village, and because of the larger and more dependable food supply, they are able to increase in number. Horticulturalists also soon learn ways and means of preserving the surplus of food accrued at harvest time, and because they are no longer a wandering people, food storage presents fewer problems. Pottery making techniques improve and a wide variety of large and small pots appear, replacing the older baskets which were simply smeared with mud to prevent seeds and liquids from falling through the holes. While nomadic hunters and gatherers undoubtedly had the intelligence to invent pottery, they did not have the need for heavy utensils which would have to be left behind when they moved camp. Pottery for the storage of liquids and food is just another of the bonuses that come with settled residence.

On the debit side, the Neolithic revolution also marks the beginning of human population problems. Hunting and gathering societies are essentially subordinate to natural ecological systems, but when the Neolithic brought with it the secret of cultivating crops and rearing animals, men gained an element of control over

---

[2] See S. P. Ottenberg, *Cultures and Societies of Africa* (New York: Random House, Inc., 1960) for numerous illustrations of shifting cultivation and slash-and-burn techniques.

Horticulture makes possible the construction of more or less permanent dwelling places. Women carry straw while men thatch the roof of a new hut in the Central African Republic. (Courtesy of La Documentation Française, Paris.)

their environment which enabled them to expand their population beyond the optimum limits of a balanced ecological system. From the earliest Neolithic times onward, there has consequently been a continuous and substantial rise in the hominid population of the world, which has reached disaster-dimensions in the present century.

Also significant is the fact that larger societies require some system of authoritative social control. The old equalitarian freedom of the individual in a small band-type society of 10 to 20 people is no longer practicable in a village of 100 or 150 men, women, and children. The problem of enforcing order in horticultural societies is very real, and one or more individuals may be authorized to coerce and punish those who offend against the customs of the group. Since all men and women are still essentially food producers, however, the

quantity of food produced is still inadequate to support any full-time nonfood-producing specialists, and such officers are likely to be part-time.

The Hamitic-speaking Berber villagers of North Africa still reflect to a large extent a pattern of social organization which appears to date from the early horticultural villages of the Middle East. Life is still dominated largely by the concept of kinship; in fact kinship often achieves more clearly defined and more precisely rationalized experiences in horticultural societies than in the simpler and more territorially oriented bands. A primitive democracy prevails, in which each family is represented on the village council by the family head. Each village has its headman, an office primarily hereditary, and beyond the village there are the bonds of clan, all clan affairs being managed by clan councils. Although these councils have little or no power of coercion, the bonds of kinship and custom command compliance and enforce social pressures, so that consensus and harmony are easily maintained.

In such societies the traditional culture of the community dominates the individual mind, and the traditional standards of the past are regarded as the only possible way of living—all new situations being judged by the application of custom and precedent. Thus as yet there is no separation of judiciary, legislative, or executive functions of government. Where political, religious, and other specialists become full-time practitioners, they will be supported by some system of economic redistribution, but many horticultural societies have need only for part-time specialists. Although tasks such as the supervision of the fields, the allocation of work loads, the judging of disputes between rival families and lineages, the appeasement of the supernatural beings, and the direction of war parties will continue to be assigned to different individuals largely on a kinship basis, some consideration may also be given to the candidate's ability to fulfill these roles effectively. This is particularly the case with appointments to positions of magicoreligious significance, and shamans, witchdoctors and other experts in supernatural manipulation are frequently recruited from among the epileptic, the mentally abnormal, or in the case of witches, the aged widows.

Horticulturalists rely on human muscle power and a simple digging stick or at best a hoe. Plows only appear with agriculture. Senegal hoe cultivators. (Courtesy of Service Info Sénégal and La Documentation Française, Paris.)

House-Communities and Village-Communities

At the horticultural level of evolution, each band, settled in a village in its own territory, is usually still autochthonous and self-governing. In a few cases the members of these communities will still marry among themselves, but in most cases they may be expected to find their wives in the neighboring villages, thus cementing a number of adjacent villages together in a pattern of friendship and mutual cooperation. Nevertheless, there is seldom any governing authority above the level of the village settlement. In the equalitarian tradition of their hunting and gathering predecessors there are also few differences in wealth because the land is still regarded as communal property even though different plots may be allocated out to individual families or lineages for cultivation.

Where marriage is exogamous, the settlement resembles a single large extended family. This kind of settlement is also sometimes called a HOUSE-COMMUNITY because not only the land but even the produce is shared. In Europe, an example of these house-communities survived into the present century in the form of the southern Slavic *zadruga* of the Balkans. Each *zadruga* was virtually self-governing and represented in effect a single large family, owning the land and livestock communally, allocating all work communally, and sharing the produce communally. The government of the *zadruga* was essentially a kinship matter, the heads of all nuclear families being entitled to participate in a democratic manner in the village assembly. However this assembly could meet and deliberate only in the presence of the *domatchin*, or village chief.[3] This office was hereditary in the seniormost family, but the

[3] Philip E. Mosely, "The Zadruga," C. F. Ware (ed.), in *The Cultural Approach to History* (New York: American Historical Association, 1940), pp. 95–108.

actual appointment was usually elective, the election being made from among the various men of this family on the basis of competence. In Melanesia and Southeast Asia villages may be found which are in effect autochthonous kin groups, living together as a house-community.

In other cases, however, especially where marriage is permitted within the village, the existence of separate kinship groups in the same community may lead to a greater individualization of wealth. We then have what many archeologists call a VILLAGE-COMMUNITY, comprising a number of family and clan units which possess a degree of economic independence from each other. In such cases, the land is allocated to families who are entitled to retain the product of their own labors. Since each family constitutes a separate household, differences in wealth may develop in terms of the accumulation of simple commodities such as tools, weapons, clothing, blankets, mats, and ornamental jewelry. Even a surplus of food may give more status to those families which can host banquets. The headman may be given some measure of coercive power over the several kinship groups in the settlement, and may be entitled to receive gifts from the other members of the community to remunerate him for the additional efforts which he has to make on the behalf of the community. Some competition may also arise for appointment to such official roles, not so much for the sake of any incidentally economic benefit, but rather for the status and prestige attached to the position.

The Elaboration of Culture

One factor common to all horticultural societies is the elaboration of culture. Horticulturalists live a more varied life than hunters and gatherers, not only out of necessity but also in fulfillment of their social conventions. Their life is full of festivals, elaborate banquets, religious dances, and tribal rituals. In

Horticulturalists can store food for the winter, since they are not obliged to move camp every few days. A woman of the Banana tribe on top of a storage hut. (Courtesy of La Documentation Française, Paris.)

many cases the customary modes of address and courtesy associated with kinship are also elaborated beyond all potentially useful purposes, almost as though they are trying to invent ways and means of making life more interesting. While the hunter and gatherer tramps around his territory, spending most of his leisure time simply talking or sleeping, the horticulturalist has something to keep him busy all his waking hours. There is always something of social importance, if not of practical importance, that the horticulturalist has to be doing.

But settled residence and the accumulation of material wealth bring with them something new in the history of mankind: war. Hunters and gatherers do not possess adequate economic resources to permit them to indulge in the luxury of war. Since they must gather their food daily, a protracted state of war is virtually an economic impossibility. By contrast, many horticulturalists have to labor for only a few weeks in the year in order to lay in sufficient food to supply themselves for the remainder of the season. Under such circumstances war may become an exciting recreation, something

of a gamble. There are always reserves of food and material wealth to be looted from neighboring villages, and more important in the eyes of most horticulturalists, there are women who may be seized after their menfolk have been slain. Women are important in the social and economic life of horticultural societies because they care for a man's physical comforts, provide him with children, and also undertake most of the manual labor.

Many horticultural societies, in particular those of South America, Africa, and Melanesia, have developed strong militaristic traditions. In such cases villages are protected against surprise attack by wooden palisades, mud walls, and lethal booby traps. In many cases warfare has acquired a religious significance, with ritual headhunting and even cannibalism becoming obligatory upon all young men who wish to prove themselves healthy-minded and successful members of the adult community. To horticulturalists war is frequently a recreation rather than a curse—a luxury which would have been impossible at the more impoverished hunting and gathering level of development.

But not all horticultural societies become

militaristic. In Old Europe between 6000 and 4000 B.C., archeological evidence indicates relatively peaceful horticultural societies, in which the status of women was high and which particularly stressed the concepts of fertility and reproduction. Similarly, in a number of surviving horticultural societies of the present day in which hunting is unimportant, much social power rests in the women as the inheritors of the food gathering tradition. In these societies, in which horticulture provides only a precarious existence in a harsh environment, militarism may be weak, and life more peaceful. While the Yąnomamö Indians of South America reflect a warlike horticultural society, the Hopi Indians of North America, who have benefited technologically from their closer proximity to several centers of high civilization but whose economic life is more precarious, reflect a more peaceful outlook, even though they seem to retain a complex of military traditions from an earlier age.

THE YĄNOMAMÖ OF SOUTH AMERICA

Far up in the headlands of the upper Orinoco River, where the borders of Venezuela meet the borders of Brazil, live a horticultural people who have had very little contact with Western civilization. These are the Yąnomamö Indians. Gathered in scattered villages averaging 70 to 80 people, they probably total some 10,000 men, women, and infants, though no one has ever counted them.[4] But it would be wrong to assume that they live an idyllic carefree existence far from the tensions of the modern world. Although the work in their plantations is not hard, their life is actually full

[4]This description of the Yąnomamö is partly based on Napoleon A. Chagnon's *The Yąnomamö: The Fierce People* (New York: Holt, Rinehart and Winston, Inc., 1968). Chagnon's *Studying the Yąnomamö* (New York: Holt, Rinehart and Winston, Inc., 1974) points out the rather large variability that exists within the Yąnomamö subpopulations.

FIG. 36   THE YĄNOMAMÖ

The Yąnomamö are a warlike horticultural people who live in the forested headwaters of the Orinoco River.

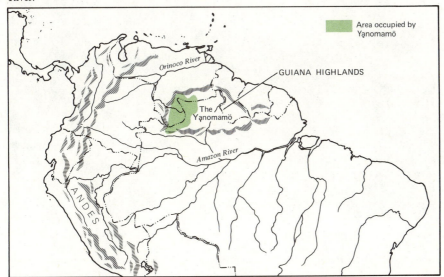

of tension, for their prime interests lie in raiding and warfare.

The territory the Yạnomamö occupy is very fertile, and most of their villages are situated in heavily forested plains broken only by gently rolling hills. The whole area is covered by dense forests, comprising a mixture of palm and hardwood trees which grow so thickly that the sun is rarely able to penetrate the overhead canopy of leaves. Nevertheless, the ground beneath the trees is covered by a rich matted tangle of undergrowth. Because of the sharp spines that protrude from the palms and the ever present danger of snakes, men are obliged to restrict their passage to established jungle trails. For this reason Yạnomamö villages are connected by a network of leafy paths, so narrow as to be scarcely perceptible to the untrained eye.

Where these trails are broken by streams, the ground vegetation grows even more densely, encouraged by the constant moisture of the running water and by the sunshine which is able to pour through the breach in the forest. Such streams are crossed by narrow foot bridges made from poles slung across the water and tied together by vines, but in the months of May, June, July, and August, the constant downfalls of rain convert the streams into raging torrents and all bridges are then washed away. Since most low-lying land is also turned into marshy lakes at this time of the year, travel becomes virtually impossible, and each village becomes a separate island of human life.

The deeper and more slowly flowing rivers can be used for transportation, but the Yạnomamö make such clumsy canoes, comprising

Although the Yạnomamö seldom travel great distances from the comparative safety of their own territory, the rivers provide excellent waterways through the dense rain forests of the Upper Orinoco region. Seen above, three Yạnomamö Indians paddle a dugout canoe, made without any joins from a single tree trunk, along a muddy jungle stream. (Courtesy of Napoleon A. Chagnon.)

A Yąnomamö village situated in a forest clearing, with the "garden" seen in the lower part of the picture. Life is intensely public in this single structure, and the Yąnomamö know little privacy. (Courtesy of Napoleon A. Chagnon.)

only a crude framework of sticks covered with bark, that they are too unwieldy to be paddled against the current. Thus river traffic generally follows one direction, downstream.

Village and Garden

Yąnomamö villages are distinctive, usually comprising a single building made of poles, vines, and leaves collected from the surrounding forest, protected from alien raiders by a palisade of logs raised to a height of about 10 feet. This large building is called a *shabono*. It is round in shape and is covered by a conical

roof which opens to the sky in the center to allow the smoke from the fires to escape. Underneath this central opening there is a communal plaza around which each family has its own living area. Every family builds its own section of the *shabono*, the men raising the heavier poles into position while the women gather leaves and vines for them to weave into the thatched roof. Although fresh and attractive when first constructed, the *shabono* naturally attracts cockroaches, scorpions, and vermin, and after one or two years, when the leaves begin to rot, the entire structure will be burned to the ground and built anew. Because of the constant fear of surprise attack, precautions are taken including occasional booby traps which are set in the jungle paths approaching the village, and even the village vegetable and fruit plantation may be protected against raiders by sharpened bones concealed in the ground.

The greater part of the Yanomamö food supply comes from horticulture, based on slash-and-burn techniques. Land selected for a garden must be near a source of drinking water and should be well drained so that it will not turn into marshlands during the rainy months. It should have only a light covering of jungle and undergrowth because of the primitive stone tools that the Yanomamö have to depend upon for clearing wild vegetation.[5] Larger trees are seldom felled, the main object being not to remove the trees but to defoliate them so that the sunshine can reach the soil. This is accomplished by setting fire to as much of the trunk and branches as possible. After the undergrowth has been cleared this is also burned, although no attempt is made to use the ashes to enhance the fertility of the soil. Not only are the Yanomamö ignorant of all techniques for fertilizing the soil, but the rapidity with which weeds gain a hold on the cleared garden land makes it easier for them to abandon older cultivation sites and clear fresh land than to attempt to weed the old land and keep it in production. The gardens consequently tend to "creep" as fresh land is taken into cultivation at one end and land at the other end is allowed to return to the jungle.

The main crops are plantains, bananas, maize, and a variety of root crops including "South American" taro and sweet potatoes. Also, sweet and bitter manioc are grown, the latter being a poisonous plant which must be soaked in water to remove the poison before it can be eaten. Cane is grown for making arrows while palm trees supply wood for bows.

[5] In recent years the Yanomamö have acquired metal knives and axes through trade.

Cotton is also regularly cultivated, being used to make twine, and tobacco is grown as a luxury item—men, women, and children all being accustomed to chewing dried tobacco leaves.

Yanomamö technology is relatively unsophisticated. Stone axes are the basic implements used for woodworking, and sharp knives are made from the teeth taken from the jaws of the *aguti* rodent. These incisors are long, slender, and extremely hard as well as being sharp, but are limited in utility because of their small size. For weapons men depend primarily upon the bow and arrow. Arrows are tipped with curare poison which is slow acting, causing a relaxation of the muscles, so that a wounded monkey will loose its grip and fall to the ground, where it can be easily killed. Arrowheads are designed so that the tip will break off inside the target animal's body, thus ensuring that the poison has time to do its work.

The Yanomamö diet is further supplemented by wild fruit, honey, and insect grubs, and by the meat of monkeys, turkeys, wild pigs, and even armadillos, tapir, and alligators killed in the jungle. Napoleon A. Chagnon, who spent three years with the Yanomamö, observed that they come very close to practicing animal domestication in their deliberate rearing of insect grubs. In order to encourage the large white grubs that grow in the decaying pith of dead palm trees, the Yanomamö deliberately cut down a number of palm trees and allow them to rot. After a few months, when the decaying pith has produced a fat crop of crawling grubs, they dig the pith out of the tree, pick out the grubs, and then bite each grub behind its squirming head, pulling off the head complete with intestines. Some of these grubs are as large as a mouse, and the bodies are carried triumphantly to the village where they are roasted on hot coals, to produce one of the delicacies of the Yanomamö table, with a flavor reported to resemble bacon.

Characteristic Aggressiveness

Kinship ties have not developed to the level that they entirely supplant a basic pattern of dominance and submission. The men regard the women largely as property to be traded back and forth for the sake of political alliances, and women are frequently ill-treated by their husbands who beat or even mutilate them when they cause displeasure. Marital infidelity is common. Secret meetings are frequently arranged for the early dawn, while the ground is still damp from the dew and the air is chilly, and the individuals concerned can leave the village by foot on the pretext of going into the forest to defecate. Secretly meeting each other at the trysting place, they later return to the village by separate routes.

Women are important property not only for sexual exploitation but because they represent a labor force. It is the women's job to procure firewood and drinking water, to prepare food, to care for the children, and to do the routine work in the fields. When not thus engaged, the women employ themselves in twisting cotton fibers into yarn from which they manufacture hammocks, waistbands, and other Yąnomamö necessities.

Female children are largely ignored by their father, and have but a short childhood. At 6 or 7 years of age they may play happily at house, but by the age of 10 they spend most of their time helping their mothers in their work. With the onset of menstruation they are segregated for one week, during which time they are expected to eat their food with a stick for fear of contaminating it with their hands. After this short period of confinement they are bartered as wives by the male members of their family. A lazy wife will be beaten regularly by her husband, who may belabor her with a stick simply because of a delay in the preparation of the evening meal. Indeed, Chagnon reported that men occasionally chopped their wives with the sharp edges of their machetes and shot barbed arrows into their buttocks or legs; one man even shot a barbed arrow into his wife's stomach. Infidelity may likewise be punished by mutilation—by angrily chopping off the ears or even, in a few cases, actually killing the unfaithful wife. Any annoyance can prompt a husband to grab his wife by the wooden ornaments worn in the pierced lobes of her ears with such violence that the ear lobes may be torn open. When women enter their 30s and begin to lose their sexual attraction, their status deteriorates still further, and they generally adopt a vindictive and caustic attitude to life. Only when their sons reach adulthood and afford them some protection and even a degree of affection does their situation begin to improve.

Male children, on the other hand, receive considerable attention from their fathers who endeavor to make them fierce. Young boys are encouraged to strike their parents and to develop aggressiveness by beating the girls of the village. Those slow to show a combatant spirit will be mercilessly teased in order to arouse their fury. The entire community approves a spirited attitude in a male child and the Yąnomamö mother especially shows considerable pleasure in seeing her son attack his father in a bout of anger. The Yąnomamö boy therefore learns to be fierce, aggressive, and callous. Young boys torment small animals; for example, catching a lizard, they will tie it to a piece of twine and shoot it full of miniature arrows from their toy bows until it finally dies.

Husbands often allow a brother to share one or more of their wives. In fact the internal politics of the Yąnomamö village largely revolve around the possession and access to women; indeed the same is largely true of relations between villages. If an individual is not aggressive in the assertion of his rights, in particular of his rights over his womenfolk, he will quickly find himself without women.

Among adults interclan conflicts frequently divide a village into two combatant groups. A fight may begin between individuals, usually as a result of a conflict over women, but in a short time friends join in and a brawl may develop which involves the entire village while the headman makes an attempt to calm his fellow villagers. The long stakes used for clubs are usually sharp at one end, so that as tempers rise, someone may be driven to use his pole as a spear, and at this point the melee may become deadly. Customary forms of intra-village conflict have consequently developed which appear to be designed to restrict hostilities to nonhomicidal forms of combat. Chest pounding is possibly the most innocuous of these. Two quarreling tribesmen will pound each other on the chest with closed fists in an attempt to stun their opponent; in some villages a rock is clenched in the fist to reinforce the blow. Although they are not supposed to inflict external wounds, the participants in such a contest often cough blood for several days after the ordeal. Yet even more dramatic are club fights, using poles torn from the walls of houses. Custom requires the offended individual—often a cuckolded husband—to challenge his rival by offering the top of his skull as a target. Once he has sustained a blow on the head, sufficient to open the flesh, he is entitled to take a return blow at his opponent's head.

In consequence of the status attached to aggression, the Yanomamö are very proud of the complex of scars which they carry deeply engrained on the crown of the head—proof that they have survived many club fights. In consequence, a veteran of numerous conflicts may shave the crown of his head to show these scars more clearly, allowing the remainder of his stiff, coarse black hair to grow to a length

The Yanomamö actively encourage their male children to play cruel games. Here three small boys amuse themselves by shooting at a lizard, whose legs have been tied to prevent it from escaping. (Courtesy of Napoleon A. Chagnon.)

The feast is over, and a chest-pounding duel has broken out, which at the time the photograph was taken was about to break into an open fight. The shaven heads, displaying dueling scars, can be plainly seen in this picture. (Courtesy of Napoleon A. Chagnon.)

of two to three inches before cutting it off in a straight line just above the level of the eyes and ears.

In order to maintain some semblance of village unity, the weaker group will usually be expelled from the village after a fatality; thus Yąnomamö villages are seldom much larger than 100 to 150 individuals. With increasing size, the possibility of deadly conflict is enhanced, and the expulsion of the weaker group will result in a reduction in size of the village to a more harmonious level. Despite the fact that larger villages have a greater competitive advantage in intervillage wars, the inability of the Yąnomamö social system to maintain order in larger communities prevents the rise of larger social groupings.

The Village Headman

The village headman exercises very little real authority and is obliged to lead by example rather than to require compliance because of his office. A headman owes his position partly to kinship ties but mainly to the wisdom of his advice, to his aggressiveness, to his reputation for personal bravery in war, and to his ability to retain the respect of his fellows. A headman will be obliged to exert himself to maintain internal order in the village, but can only advise a dissident villager against the follies of any proposed course of action. However, if internecine fighting breaks out, the headman is expected to intervene and may slay any troublemaker who is threatening the cohesion of the group. If he fails to exert the necessary leadership at the risk of his own life, there are always other putative leaders in the village who seek through bluffs, threats, and chicanery to undermine his authority in order to supplant him. In such cases there may even be a constant rivalry between the headman and an influential rival for status, which will be expressed in feast giving and martial gallantry.

The headman who does not lead his fellow villagers effectively and cannot protect them against the raids of an enemy may soon lose his position, if his rival can demonstrate superior bravery and greater tactical skill. But not all the Yąnomamö warriors are as brave as they boast. Many are nervous and ill at ease while preparing for a raiding expedition, and may invent all kinds of excuses in order to drop out of a raiding party and return to their village before the arrows start flying. Yąnomamö warfare, in fact, is almost entirely restricted to ambushes, night raids, and deliberate treachery, pitched battles being avoided as altogether too dangerous.

Intervillage Relations

Relations between villages consequently also depend largely on the principle of dominance and submission. This condition is to some extent mitigated by marital alliances, but even the obligations due to those who have provided a village with wives sometimes fail to prevent intervillage warfare. The more powerful and aggressive villages constantly make surprise raids on the weaker in order to steal women and to exact revenge for earlier killings. The members of a village which has suffered from repeated enemy raids may decide to evacuate their settlement, abandon their crops, and establish a new village in a safer location. Alternatively, a village that has been reduced in size by internal dissension and the expulsion of some of its members may attempt to form military alliances with neighboring villages to ensure its survival. Such alliances can usually be secured only by the transfer of women from the weaker to the stronger group, and again represent a form of exploitation of the weak by the strong, who offer friendship and protection at a price. Smaller villages may become so debilitated by the loss of men in combat and by the loss of women, either to enemy raiding parties or as gifts to other villages as the price of friendship, that the entire village may be eliminated, leaving the survivors to attach themselves as dependents to the weaker faction in a more powerful village. In this way the men from the abandoned village find security, while their benefactors find their own intravillage political position strengthened by the acquisition of additional fighting men. In return for these needed reinforcements, they may go so far as to provide the refugees with wives or else allow them access to certain of their own womenfolk. Such alliances are not made fortuitously of course, and a claim for friendship and protection is usually based on some previous kinship relationship.

Alliances between villages, negotiated through the exchange of women and by reciprocal feasting, also provide the only framework which exists for trade. These alliances tend to be stabilized by the fact that a village which accepts women as a gift is under the obligation to return the compliment at a later date. Theoretically this pattern of reciprocity reinforces the affinal ties periodically, but such obligations are not always kept. Village alliances are usually best maintained when external pressures make it necessary for one group to secure the active military collaboration of the other; even then the mutual responsibilities are not always honored. While the men of a weaker village are absent on a raid against the common enemy, their more powerful allies may seize the opportunity to attack their sparsely defended homes and carry off the women and any valuable goods which may be on hand. Even the friendship feast to which a village is invited by its allies may turn out to be an ambush,

Yąnomamö Indians approaching a friendly village. The structure on the left is a portion of the village roof. (Courtesy of Napoleon A. Chagnon.)

A Yąnomamö warrior in a contemplative mood, while observing a mourning ceremony at which a portion of the ashes of the deceased are eaten by the mourners. (Courtesy of Napoleon A. Chagnon.)

a club fight being deliberately started by the hosts as the pretext for slaughtering their male guests in order to steal the women.

Religious Beliefs

The religious beliefs of the Yąnomamö center on the idea that men have souls. There are, however, three distinct aspects of the soul. In the first place, each man has a *buhii*, or will, which separates from the body after death. The body of a dead Yąnomamö is burned; the ashes ground into a fine powder and eaten by the relatives of the deceased. By contrast, the *buhii* becomes an incarnate spirit known as a *no borebö*. As among the ancient Egyptians, there is a belief in a judgment after death when each *no borebö* is judged by a good spirit known as Wadawadariwa who asks it whether it was generous or mean during life, directing it to a place of punishment or reward according to the response. Nevertheless, the Yąnomamö believe they can avoid punishment by simply lying to Wadawadariwa, and are little troubled by the belief.

Since children are believed to be lacking in strength of will, the *buhii* is something that develops to the fullest only in adults. As a result those who die in childhood do not leave a *no borebö* behind them. However, even children have the second portion of the soul known as the *no uhudi*. Following death the *no uhudi* wanders perpetually in the jungle and may become malevolent. In consequence, when camping in the jungle at night on their way to raid an enemy village, the Yąnomamö always light fires—if they are not too close to the village they intend to surprise—so as to ward away not only wild animals, such as jaguars, but also the *no uhudi* spirits of the dead.

In addition to the *no borebö* and the *no uhudi*, all Yąnomamö have a *noreshi* spirit. These are animals which live as a kind of twin to the man or woman with whom they are linked, doing everything that the individual does in the course of his life. If a man is sick or goes insane, then the *noreshi* animal does the same. A man may never meet his *noreshi*, for a man and his *noreshi* live quite separate existences, even though they mirror each other's lives. This mirror relationship is reciprocal, and if a *noreshi* animal is killed by a hunter, then the man with whose soul he is linked will also die.

The well-being of every individual is so intimately linked to the *noreshi* that should the *noreshi* part of the soul leave the human body, the owner will fall sick in its absence. The Yąnomamö consequently have shamans, known as *shabori,* whose efforts are directed toward preventing evil spirits who live in the jungle from capturing the vital part of the human soul and thereby causing the death of its owner. To combat such evil spirits, shamans employ other spirits. In a war between two villages the shamans will recruit spirit forces from the jungle to attack the souls of their human enemies, the pattern of human warfare being replicated by spirit warfare.

The role of *shabori* is not hereditary, and any man can become a *shabori* provided he abstains from sexual relations and can lure *hekura,* or spirit beings, into his body by a process of fasting and drug taking. Hallucinogenic drugs obtained from the ebene tree are consequently widely used. These are derived from the bark, the inner part of which is mixed with ashes and ground together to make a fine powder. Drug takers assist each other by blowing a small quantity of this powder down a hollow tube into their partner's nostrils. After considerable coughing and choking, the drug taker vomits a little and develops an excessively runny nose, the green-stained mucus running freely from his nostrils. In a few minutes he will be behaving in an intoxicated fashion, unable to focus his eyes. Seeing colored visions, he believes himself to be in communication with *hekura* and begins chanting and dancing in order to subordinate these spirits to his will (see picture on p. 251). In this way he finds escape from the narrow and oppressive existence of the Yąnomamö settlement.

THE HOPI INDIANS OF NORTH AMERICA

Arizona, the desert state high in the southwestern mountains of North America, is renowned for its deep blue skies, its crystal clear landscape, and the pastel shades of its mountains. Rain is very sparse, being mainly confined to the summer months when desert flowers appear as though from nowhere to blossom and scatter their seeds before their short life comes to a sudden end. Although the shortage of rain makes life hard, the dry desert conditions are a boon to archeologists, for they have resulted in the preservation of many fossils and artifacts from the American Indian past. The information supplied by the archeologist's spade has also been amply supplemented by the valuable accounts of the Arizonian Indian culture left to us by early Spanish explorers in the immediate post-Columbian period. Thus, this area provides us with one of the most complete and coherent accounts of American Indian cultural history in the annals of anthropology.

Historical Background

The Hopi Indians still preserve much of their old culture on the reservation lands. Although the soil is mostly arid today, it seems that Arizona formerly enjoyed a better climate, and the cultivation of maize was first introduced into this area from the south as long as 4000 years ago. At that time, although horticulture was widespread in Central America, the greater part of the North American continent was still inhabited by hunters and food gatherers. Arizona was therefore a border territory separating the higher Central American cultures from the nomadic hunters and gatherers of the northern plains and mountains.[6]

With the introduction of cultivation the life of the Arizona Indians began to reflect a relative degree of prosperity. Semipermanent set-

[6]The Hopi Indian culture has been described and analyzed in a multitude of publications. Among these the student may be advised to consult R. H. Lowie, "Hopi Kinship," *Anthropological Papers of the American Museum of Natural History* (1929); and L. Thompson and A. Joseph, *The Hopi Way* (Chicago: University of Chicago Press, 1965).

FIG. 37   THE HOPI

The Hopi Indians live in Arizona close to the Colorado River and adjacent to their old enemies the Navaho. Note area formerly occupied by old "Basket Maker" culture and location of other surviving "Pueblo" Indian peoples.

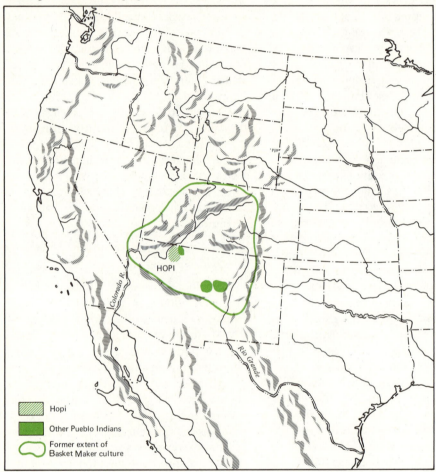

HOPI

☐ Hopi

■ Other Pueblo Indians

◯ Former extent of Basket Maker culture

tlements were established, and though the first cultivators did not know how to make pottery, they were skilled in basket making. This early Arizonian culture has consequently been labeled the *Basket Maker culture.* But around 2000 years ago a warlike hunting and gathering people, carrying bows and arrows, invaded Arizona from the north, seized the land, and settled down to learn the arts of cultivation. These were the forebears of the Hopi, Zuni, and other "Pueblo" Indians—as the Spanish called them because of their stark hill-top villages of mud brick, clustered tightly together like fortresses (Spanish *pueblo*, "village"). When the Spaniards first encountered the Hopi in the seventeenth century, they recorded a

The Hopi village of Walpi stands typically atop the Mesa cliffs, affording protection to the inmates against surprise attacks by Navajo or other enemies. By contrast, the fields are situated beneath the cliffs, where water seeping from the Mesa keeps the soil moist. (Courtesy of the Smithsonian Institution, National Anthropological Archives.)

total population of around 20,000 men, women, and children, dispersed in 66 villages, but today the Hopi number only 4000.

Nevertheless, the earliest Hopi settlers did not build masonry villages like those described by the Spaniards. Indeed they originally seem to have lived in pit houses comprising a rectangular hole in the ground, roofed over with timber and mud, and entered by way of a ladder or notched pole through a small opening in the roof. Such pit houses are somewhat reminiscent of Cro-Magnon man's semisub-

The Hopi have inherited the traditions of the ancient Basket Maker culture, and Hopi women are still renowned for their skill at weaving baskets, ornamented with elaborate designs. (Courtesy of the Smithsonian Institution, National Anthropological Archives.)

terranean dwellings in Upper Paleolithic Europe some 20,000 years earlier. These pits would undoubtedly have been cool in summer and warm in winter, but must have been difficult to defend. Accordingly, when a more aggressive people began to harrass the settled Hopi food producers some 1500 years ago, the Hopi abandoned their pit houses and began to construct their characteristic masonry houses on hill-top eminences, closely huddled together so that they could be easily defended. From these they had a commanding view over the surrounding countryside and were relatively safe from attack.

Desert Horticulture

At about this time, however, Arizona began to suffer a deterioration in climate, and the rainfall decreased to its present very low and irregular level. This severely restricted the Hopi farmers in their choice of village locations. Indeed, today's rainfall would be quite inadequate for the cultivation of crops but for the fact that the part of Arizona in which the Hopi have survived is characterized by flat table-top mountains or *mesas* which drop suddenly into broad low-lying desert. Any rain falling on these mesas drains downward through the rock strata and emerges at the foot of the mesas to keep the soil there perpetually moist, thus permitting the cultivation of sparse crops in these small but favored areas.

Despite the shortage of water the Hopi have not developed any system of irrigation, probably because there is no permanent water supply available for this. Because of the dryness of the soil the productivity of their fields is very low. Although the Hopi must be classified as horticulturalists because they lack any sophisticated farming technology and merely scratch the surface of the soil, they are not shifting cultivators, and Hopi fields are cultivated perennially. This is possible partly because the lack of water necessitates the wide spacing of

plants, thereby reducing the chemical strain on the soil, and partly because the desert winds continually redistribute the surface soil, regenerating the fields with fresh dust from the virgin desert. Consequently, although the Hopi are ignorant of fertilizing techniques and of the theory of crop rotation, and never allow their fields to lie fallow, they are able to raise food on the same land year after year.

The Modern Hopi

Physically the Hopi Indians are still like their hunting and food gathering ancestors who first entered Arizona 2000 years ago. Their high cheek bones, broad faces, straight black hair, and rather short, stocky appearance is highly suggestive of the Mongoloid origin of American Indians, although their custom of lashing babies into a flat wooden cradle has the effect of flattening the back of the head while it is forming, creating a distortion of the skull which stays with them throughout life. Some observers have also suggested that the Hopi custom of strapping their babies into these cradles so tightly that they cannot move their limbs also tends to inculcate that spirit of individual subservience to society which is so characteristic of the Hopi personality.

Linguistically, the Hopi language is distantly related to that of the Aztecs, Aztecs and Hopi having once shared a similar hunting and gathering way of life. But while the Aztecs became a victorious warlike people, the Hopi have not been famed as warriors, and even hunting became less important in their lives as steady climatic deterioration slowly reduced the availability of game in the Arizona area.

The Matriarchal Tradition

The decline of hunting also appears to have had another interesting effect on Hopi society. The customary dominance of the male in hunting societies seems to be derived from the basic division of labor which groups the men together in hunting bands and leaves the women to gather berries and roots, tend to the children, and possibly hoe any root or corn crops which may be cultivated close to the camp. In societies in which males customarily engage in hunting or in warlike activities, they are invariably dominant, but the relatively peaceful horticultural Hopi society is customarily described as matriarchal.

The decline of hunting may also have reduced the military effectiveness of the Hopi male, and from 500 A.D. the Hopi tended to become subject to raids from more aggressive neighbors. As the climate changed and game became more scarce, the males brought home less meat from the hunt, and the community became correspondingly more dependent on cultivation for survival. As this happened, we suppose that an original patriarchalism may have given way to the present matrilineal and partially matriarchal system, a state of affairs not uncommon among settled and more peaceful horticulturalists. Today, therefore, it is the females who inherit and own the land, and in the absence of other more prestigious occupations, the men customarily toil in their wives' fields. Interestingly, however, the male Hopi derives much of his status from ceremonial weaving roles, an occupation which in patriarchal societies would normally be reserved for women.

The men still hunt but more out of a traditional and religious sense of ritual than for the quantity of meat they can hope to procure. Thus, the Hopi diet is almost entirely limited to agricultural produce—maize, beans, squash, and pumpkin being the staple crops. The only livestock kept in pre-Columbian days were the dog and turkey, neither of which were eaten, the turkey being reared only for its feathers. Since the coming of the Spaniards, the Hopi have learned to keep a few sheep and an occasional donkey, both being animals brought by the Spaniards from Europe.

Hopi technology is Neolithic, but their skill at basket and pottery making is renowned. While basket and pottery making, as well as house building, are regarded as women's work, the manufacture of cotton blankets is undertaken by the men on simple upright looms. Renowned for their artistic geometrical designs, their clothing takes the form of a sleeveless robe, worn by the women to the knees, while the men wear kilts and a poncho, a piece of material with a hole cut in it for the head to pass through. Fur wraps made from rabbit skins are also worn in cold weather, and the feet are protected by sandals made from yucca leaves or by moccasins of deerskin for hunting. There is a considerable amount of commerce in new clothing, but as the owners of all property and real estate, women carry on all such trading negotiations.

Unlike the Yąnomamö whom Chagnon portrays as a somewhat dirty people, the Hopi keep their villages quite clean and are deeply concerned with their personal appearance, ornamenting themselves with necklaces and earrings made from turquoise shells and beads. Although they sometimes paint their faces with red ochre, they do not mutilate their bodies in any way. They take a particular interest in their hair, washing and dressing each others' hair with the greatest care.

Social and Political Organization

The Hopi social system revolves around exogamous clans, which are known by totemistic names, such as the Snake Clan, the Rabbit Clan, the Coyote Clan, or the Bear Clan. Most clans possess a small figure of their totemic animal which is closely revered. In accordance with the matrilineal tradition, membership of the clans is inherited through the female line, and although the clan chieftains are males, succession to office is likewise through the female line, the chieftainship customarily belonging to the eldest brother of the senior clan

Hairdressing plays an important part in the lives of Hopi men and women. On formal occasions the Hopi women wear their hair in large rolls on each side of the head, using wooden frames to give form and rigidity. (Courtesy of the Smithsonian Institution, National Anthropological Archives.)

mother. Each village or pueblo contains families belonging to several different clans, so that marriage is usually within the village.

The size of a Hopi village is strictly regulated by the limited availability of land suitable for cultivation. As with the buildings, all fields are inherited through matrilineal descent groups or *sibs*. Since married daughters remain with the household of their mother, and the members of any one clan in a particular village tend to live as a single extended family group, there is little need for a division of property according to nuclear families. Although some individual concept of field ownership does exist, in so far as a woman's husband is responsible for working particular fields, any kinswoman may demand a share in the crop produce if the supply from her own fields is inadequate. Any disputes that may arise between the members of the clan will be settled by the "clan mother," who is the guardian of the clan fetish and other ceremonial equipment.

Although the Hopi clans are grouped into a total of 12 exogamous phratries, there is no

Hopi girl with completed coiffure. (Courtesy of the Smithsonian Institution, National Anthropological Archives.)

tribal organization, and each village, with its own fields and hunting lands, is consequently an autonomous political unit. The village government is in the hands of hereditary clan officials, such as the village chief, usually recruited from the Bear Clan, who makes daily prayers for the village and supervises all routine activities. In addition there is an hereditary sun watcher whose duty it is to observe the daily rising and setting of the sun, marking its daily progress along the horizon against the panorama of peaks and valleys, in order to determine the date, in much the same way as the Aztec priests of Central America kept a check of the time by the calendrical movements of the sun and other heavenly bodies. All agricultural operations are scheduled according to the sun calendar, and so the sun watcher in effect determines the entire routine of the village.

Each village also has its hereditary town crier who summons the villagers to public

Despite the matrilineal organization of the Hopi kinship system, most ritual functions are fulfilled by the males. In this picture Hopi men participate in a ritual snake dance. (Courtesy of the Smithsonian Institution, National Anthropological Archives.)

ceremonies and publicizes all matters of communal importance, as well as a house chief who assists the village chief in his various duties. There are also a leader of the rabbit hunt—a rather pitiful memory of the days when hunting was more important than it is today—and a war chief who in times of peace serves as a policeman but in war takes charge of all defensive and aggressive operations. It is the particular duty of the war chief to ensure that a permanent guard is mounted day and night on the village rooftops, and when marauding Navaho or Apache are known to be in the locality, it is he who decides whether to lead an expedition in an attempt to ambush the raiders. Although the Hopi are known for their generally pacific attitude—their name actually means "the peace-loving people"—the Hopi warrior is nevertheless expected to take the scalp of any enemy he kills, fixing this to a scalp pole on his return to the village in order that victory dances may be performed in front of it.

Courtship and Family

At peace in their villages the Hopi lead a busy life. The complexity of their ritual and etiquette gives them plenty to gossip about when discussing the day's events, and they occupy themselves with weaving, religious rituals, and songs and music of both a religious and a profane nature. Music is made by percussion and wind instruments, and there are a variety of traditional songs, many of which have a bawdy character. Sexual relations are in fact very free before marriage.

The family exercises very little influence in the choice of marriage partners, the selection being left to the young people. Courtship is informal and any girl is considered ready to entertain suitors by the time she is 14 or 15 years of age. Boys, on the other hand, normally commence courting immediately at puberty.

Most courting is done at night, by assignation, in a custom known as *dumaiya*. Often attempting disguise, an eligible youth stealthily visits any girl who has invited him to spend the night with her. Both girls and boys, consequently, have ample opportunity to try out a range of prospective marriage partners, and although the actual proposal is made by the girl, no boy is supposed to return for a second visit unless he is prepared to marry the girl. In consequence of this widespread premarital promiscuity, the first child born to a married couple may not necessarily be biologically related to the husband. Such cases are not regarded as important, since the child will belong to the mother's clan and will inherit its name and status from the mother's lineage.

During the daytime boys and girls have considerable opportunity to mingle, and on the day following important ceremonies, girls invite the boys of their choice to informal picnics. Assignations for the night are frequently made at such picnics, and the girl who has determined on her future husband may use the occasion of the picnic to present her lover with a *gömi* or cornmeal cake, which amounts to a proposal of marriage and normally should not be rejected by the boy. Nevertheless, it is obligatory upon the bride-to-be to present a large quantity of ground cornmeal to the boy's mother. Should her prospective mother-in-law refuse to accept this gift, the wedding will not proceed. If the gift is accepted, the bride-to-be must also work for three days at her prospective mother-in-law's house, grinding cornmeal for her future in-laws, before the marriage can be consummated on the fourth day, following a ritual washing of the bride's and bridegroom's hair by their new affinal relatives.

Because the Hopi are matrilocal, it is the husband who goes to live with his mother-in-law after marriage. Each matrilineal clan owns a group of houses in the village, and each extended family is dominated by the maternal grandmother. In his mother-in-law's home a man is a person of relatively little importance. Even the upbringing of his own children is left largely to the control of his wife's eldest brother, and should he displease his wife she may divorce him by simply placing his few personal possessions outside the door of the house. On the other hand, a husband is also entitled to divorce his wife and go home to his mother should he so choose. Marriages are consequently very brittle and divorce is frequent. However, divorced children always remain with their mother, since they belong to her matriclan.

Women give birth to their children attended only by their mother, who leaves the room briefly at the actual moment of birth in deference to her daughter's modesty. Although most Hopi mothers desire "a quiver full of children," abortion is not unknown, this being effected by binding the abdomen tightly. The fact that the Hopi men were formerly hunters is still reflected in the postnatal ritual which requires the umbilical cord of a male child to be wrapped around a bow before being stored in the rafters of the house. By contrast, the umbilical cord of a female child is wrapped around a stirring spoon, reflecting the traditional division of labor between men and women in a hunting society. Children are often breast-fed until they are four or five years old.

Hopi children are reared under a reasonably permissive system, with most punishments being of an informal nature and taking the form of ridicule, scolding, or the withholding of favors. Although physical punishment is sometimes administered to a child by his mother's brother—never by his father—the major weapon of coercion is fear of *kachina* spirits who will "eat them up." By warning the child that his misdeeds will bring supernatural cannibal spirits to the house in search of him, the parents succeed in threatening difficult children without alienating their affections

from themselves. They can pretend to hold the door against the cannibal spirits and even to offer the spirits alternative food, thereby giving the impression that they are protecting the children whom they are actually punishing.

Spirit Worship and Secret Societies

Religious ritual revolves heavily around the idea of the *kachina* spirits and permeates almost every aspect of Hopi life. Ritual governs not only social ceremonies but also the production of food and even recreational activities.

All Hopi ritual is rooted in a strong *cult of the dead,* based on the belief that the physical body contains a soul or "breath body" as they call it. The souls of the dead are feared rather than revered, and it is incorrect to use the term *ancestor worship* in relation to Hopi attitudes toward the dead. Corpses are buried with care in a graveyard at the bottom of the mesa, and lines are traced in the dust across the path which connects the village to the grave, to serve as a spirit barrier to guard against the return of the disembodied spirit. However, the ghosts of children who die before they have been initiated into adult status are not feared, and it is believed that such souls are reborn into the clan in the body of the next baby. Adult ghosts are not believed to hover for long over their graves. Shortly after they depart from the world of the living, it is believed they take up residence in a supernatural "skeleton house" where they exist much as they did in the living world, planting and harvesting crops, except for the fact that the seasons are reversed in the ghost world.

Elaborate religious ceremonials are held during the winter when there is no work to be done in the Hopi fields. It is believed that the *kachinas*—who are ancestral clan spirits, not representative of any particular individual, but symbolizing the clan as a whole—visit the village at this time of the year to occupy underground *kivas,* or religious clubhouses. These *kivas* resemble the ancient underground homes of the earlier Hopi, comprising rectangular subterranean rooms which can only be entered by a ladder through a hole in the roof. Just as Cro-Magnon man continued to use caves for religious rituals long after they had been abandoned as residences, so the Hopi continue to preserve the ancient tradition of underground houses, using them as chapels for their various religious fraternities. Only men

are permitted to belong to these religious fraternities, and *kivas* are off limits to unauthorized persons.

Although the worship of the *kachina* ancestors probably represents one of the more ancient elements in the Hopi culture, Hopi religion has also absorbed many magicoreligious practices from diverse sources, particularly from Central America. Consequently, there is a Fire God as well as a Sun God, while the mountains and the stars are all believed to house different spirit figures. When the fields are sown with seed, prayers are offered to a

A photograph taken around 1900 A.D. of the La-la-kon-ti altar in an underground Hopi kiva. (Courtesy of the Smithsonian Institution, National Anthropological Archives.)

Corn Mother; when rain is needed, prayers are given to the Sky God; and there is an Earth Goddess who is believed to care for the crops while they are growing.

Many of the Hopi rituals are very colorful. In a tradition that appears to have been derived from Central America, turkey feathers are used to adorn the emblems of religious ritual. The priests of the Snake Society use live snakes in their rainmaking rituals, and phallic symbols are employed in fertility rituals. But by far the most important ceremony in the entire Hopi calendar is the *Powamu* ceremony, which is associated with the planting of beans and is believed to be attended by the *kachina* ancestors. It is on this occasion that male youths and girls alike are initiated into the status of adulthood, after being flogged by the male members of the *kachina* secret society wearing *kachina* masks.

In addition to these various religious rituals and ceremonies, the Hopi also practice sorcery, bringing sickness upon their enemies. Others belong to a brotherhood of medicine men and are believed to be able to cure sicknesses caused by the sorcerers by massaging, by the application of herbal poultices, and by the sleight-of-hand removal of alien objects from the body.

However, life in a horticultural Hopi community is generally well regulated and relatively free from brutality and cruel practices. Despite the ancestral nature of the *kachinas*, the Hopi religion leads to a close and intimate association with the elements, as befits a people who depend upon the raising of crops. Every aspect of daily life and recreation is vested with a symbolic nature-appreciating significance. Clearly, while the Yąnomamö and the Hopi share certain cultural similarities, both being dependent on horticulture, there can be no denying the fact that wide divergencies of cultural traditions and life styles can and do separate different societies despite similarities in the pattern of subsistence.

For Further Reading

Chagnon, N., 1968, *The Yąnomamö: The Fierce People.* New York: Holt, Rinehart and Winston, Inc.

Curwen, E. C., and G. Hatt, 1953, *Plough and Pasture: The Early History of Farming.* New York: Abelard-Schuman Ltd.

Dozier, E. J., *The Pueblo Indian of North America.* New York: Holt, Rinehart and Winston, Inc.

Forde, C. D., 1931, "Hopi Agriculture and Land Ownership," *Journal of the Royal Anthropological Institute* 41:357–405.

Harner, M. J., 1970, "Population Pressure and the Social Evolution of Agriculturalists," *Southwestern Journal of Anthropology,* 26:67–86.

Hogbin, H. I., 1964, *A Guadalcanal Society: The Kaoka Speakers.* New York: Holt, Rinehart and Winston, Inc.

Jacobsen, T., 1943, "Primitive Democracy in Ancient Mesopotamia," *Journal of Near Eastern Studies* II(3):159–172.

Josephy, A. M., Jr., 1968, *The Indian Heritage of America.* New York: Alfred A. Knopf.

Malinowski, B., 1922, *Argonauts of the Western Pacific.* New York; E. P. Dutton & Co., Inc.

———, 1966, *Coral Gardens and Their Magic,* Vols. 1 and 2. London: George Allen & Unwin Ltd.

Meggers, B. J., 1971, *Amazonia.* Chicago: Aldine Publishing Company.

Mellaart, J., 1965, *Earliest Civilizations of the Near East.* London: Thames and Hudson.

———, 1967, *Catal Hüyük: A Neolithic Town in Anatolia.* London: Thames and Hudson.

Murray, J., 1970, *The First European Agriculture.* Edinburgh, Scotland: Edinburgh University Press.

Pospisil, L. J., 1963, *The Kapauku Papuans of West New Guinea.* New York: Holt, Rinehart and Winston, Inc.

Service, E. R., 1958, *Profiles in Ethnology.* New York: Harper & Row, Publishers.

Sanders, W. T., and B. J. Price, 1968, *Mesoamerica: The Evolution of a Civilization.* New York: Random House, Inc.

Uchendu, V. L., 1965, *The Igbo of Southeast Nigeria.* New York: Holt, Rinehart and Winston, Inc.

Ucko, P. J., and G. W. Dimbleby, 1969, *The Domestication and Exploitation of Plants and Animals.* Chicago: Aldine Publishing Company.

von Fürer-Haimendorf, C., 1969, *The Konyak Nagas: An Indian Frontier Tribe.* New York: Holt, Rinehart and Winston, Inc.

CHAPTER 25

Fishing Societies

Fishing societies may be defined on the basis of primary dependence rather than exclusive reliance upon fishing as a means of subsistence. Virtually all societies which have advanced beyond the level of general hunting and food gathering tend to combine diverse methods of food seeking. Just as horticulturalists may supplement their vegetarian diet with meat dishes procured by herding or hunting, so fishing societies will generally supplement river and sea food with meat obtained by hunting and trapping, and may also cultivate some cereals or vegetables where conditions permit such pursuits.

General Characteristics

Because of the predatory nature of both hunting and fishing as a means of subsistence, some writers have given way to the temptation to regard fishing societies as a rather specialized type of hunting society, but this is not the case. Fishing communities differ sharply from hunting communities in a number of ways. In the first place, they are not nomadic. The fisherman's food resources are localized quite specifically in certain rivers, lakes, and coastal waters. With the limited mobility that their boats provide, fishing people are able to build permanent settlements, usually located close to the water's edge. Thus in the permanency of their settlements fishing communities resemble horticultural rather than hunting societies. Indeed, even horticulturalists may have to move to a new location from time to time if they exhaust the soil by primitive techniques, whereas fishing communities seldom if ever have to face the necessity of migration.

Again, fishing societies will differ from hunting societies in another crucial manner. Fish have a high reproductive rate and are not as easily depleted by human predators as are animal populations occupying restricted territories. Animal populations are limited in potential density and may be overhunted by a slight increase in the size of the human hunting bands above the ecological optimum; however, it requires very heavy fishing, with modern equipment, for men to deplete a fish population in an open network of rivers or in the open sea. As a result, fishing communities tend to be both richer and larger in size than hunting communities. While hunting and food gathering bands average 30 or 40 members, settled fishing communities frequently exceed a hundred or more members. In such cases hereditary clan and village chieftains come to be respected and are sometimes even given a measure of authoritative power. Private law normally prevails, however, all controversies being regarded as disputes between kinship groups.

Because of the permanency of their settlements, fishing people are able to construct durable houses. They can accumulate substantial reserves of food, usually dried and smoked fish, and heavy containers of wood or pottery can be made in which to keep such food. Famine is therefore a rare and virtually unknown experience.

The possession of permanent and often large houses and the accumulation of natural wealth, including large quantities of luxury items such as furskin rugs, add considerable comfort and interest to the life of fishing people. Freed from fear of famine, with ample leisure and with permanent houses in which to keep their wealth, fishing societies commonly develop elaborate art styles, giving considerable attention to the ornamentation of everything that they make, from weapons, pots, and household utensils to their boats and even their houses. A sedentary existence and a growth in the size of the population also lead to elaborate rules regarding the disposition of property such as fishing rights and house sites. Particular house sites come to be regarded as the habitual right of lineages which occupy them generation after generation. Similarly, there is a tendency for particular lineages and clans to claim the right to fish specific areas of water and even to launch their boats from particular beaches, so that slowly the concept of inherited land

rights begins to emerge. The idea of trading or bartering the family claim to a house site or a fishing site may be still unknown, but the territory is no longer entirely communal property. Similarly, the accumulation of manufactured material possessions is most certainly regarded as private property, although trade within the tribe is rare. Such trading as may take place is usually between separate communities, not between members of the same community. However, an interest in the concept of accumulated wealth may lead to piracy and Viking-type raids, facilitated by the mobility that the possession of boats provides.

Wherever there is a large economic surplus, the possibility of inequalities of wealth and of stratified society must appear. Lenski[1] has calculated that while slavery is very infrequent in hunting and gathering societies, it is present in around one third of fishing communities. Hunting and food gathering societies are almost invariably equalitarian in character, with no traces of any hereditary upper class, but a fairly large percentage of fishing communities not only practice slavery but also reveal fine grades of social stratification, while some even have hereditary nobilities. Along with stratification the existence of an economic surplus has led many fishing societies to attach economic transactions to the marriage ceremony—financial arrangements which are generally absent in societies that live on a hand-to-mouth basis.

Nevertheless, dependence upon fishing does set certain restrictions upon the demographic and cultural possibilities open to such societies. They are obviously tied to rivers, lakes, and coastlines, wherever their food resources are located. Although their population may increase and they may achieve a fairly sophisticated style of life and a complex degree of social stratification, they cannot migrate from their fishing waters or send out colonies to seize inland areas from more primitive neigh-

[1] Gerhard Lenski, *Human Societies* (New York: McGraw-Hill, Inc., 1970), p. 292.

Fishing communities can conveniently settle in permanent villages, and thus benefit from the opportunity to construct solid dwellings and accumulate more bulky material possessions. Individual families also often acquire traditional "property" rights to particular house sites. This fishing village is located on the Ivory Coast. (Courtesy of La Documentation Française, Paris.)

One of the simplest ways of catching fish is to enter the water and use one's hands. Here, on the island of Vanau Balavu in the Lau Group of the Fiji Isles, virtually the entire village community take time off from a fish hunt to wave to the photographer. After rubbing coconut oil over their bodies, they enter the water to stir up the muddy lake bed with their feet, pursuing the escaping fish with their hands. This method of fishing serves to supplement their diet, but would seldom provide adequate sustenance for a community primarily dependent upon fish. (Courtesy of Fiji Public Relations Office.)

bors. They are certainly unlikely to build empires or to achieve a complex culture or even to achieve any marked division of labor and literacy, except in those instances, such as ancient Crete and Venice, where fishing—and possibly piracy—led to large-scale mercantile trading operations. So long as they remain primarily dependent upon fishing, there is a definite ceiling to their potential capacity for development and expansion. This ceiling can be broken only by modern technology and economic innovations leading to a market economy, such as have transformed the historical fishing communities of the Norwegian and Japanese coastal areas into subsocieties within a larger and more highly diversified industrial economy.

Fishing Technology

The evolution of fishing societies was intimately related to a corresponding advance in primitive technology. Many Paleolithic peoples who are primarily dependent upon gathering shellfish and molluscs endeavor to supplement beachcombing with the spearing or harpooning of fish. In such societies the woman not only frequently undertakes the gathering of food but may also be responsible for paddling a primitive log canoe while her husband stands in the bows and concentrates on the more interesting work of spearing the fish. As technology progresses, however, primitive bone fishhooks appear at the Mesolithic level, and fishing with a baited hook enables the fishermen to catch fish in deeper waters than those in which a harpoon can be employed.

The Neolithic produced many distinctive fishing techniques; the Chinese, for example, developed a sophisticated style known as kite fishing, which later spread to the South Pacific. A baited hook and line are tied to a kite which is then flown out over the deeper waters by a fisherman, thus enabling him to fish in waters where he cannot conveniently take a boat. This method is particularly useful when rough seas or other hazards make it undesirable to take a boat out on the water.

Net fishing also seems to have appeared by the Neolithic, being of particular value in trapping fish in shallow waters. Some of these nets were designed simply to be dipped into the water, like the picturesque butterfly nets used by the Aztecs on the high lakes of Mexico, while others were weighted and cast into the water. Still more sophisticated nets were provided with elaborate sets of floats and weights so that they could be used to entrap whole shoals of fish. But best of all the Trobriand Islanders trained their dogs to swim in formation, driving a shoal of fish toward the nets which, supported on one side by the floats and held down to the bottom of the water by weights on the other side, engulfed the fish as they attempted to flee from the disturbance created by the splashing canines.

Techniques for drying the surplus fish landed during a good season make possible the storage of food reserves for the less prosperous months, thus providing greater security and enhancing the survival chances of fishing societies. In addition, although most simpler fishing societies produce only for their own consumption, those which are adjacent to prosperous horticultural or agricultural settlements may develop a system of commerce. This system may be based on barter or on some kind of primitive coinage, like the dog's teeth used in Melanesia, and the rudiments of a market economy may appear. Where this leads to large-scale fishing operations, requiring several men, large catches of fish will then be sought. One way of obtaining a large yield is the use of poison, already widely known in many hunting societies, to kill or stun the entire fish population of whole streams and lakes.

Prehistoric Fishing Societies

Because of the greater prosperity of fishing communities, we are not surprised when we find the very sophisticated Maglemosian fishing folk of the shores of the Baltic during the European Mesolithic paving the streets of their villages with planks—the first boardwalks in Western history. The Maglemosians of the North European plains and Baltic coast were the lineal descendants of the Upper Paleolithic Cro-Magnon population of western Europe. The passing of the fourth ice age toward the end of the Pleistocene slowly transformed the landscape of Europe from tundra into thick forest, and the herbivorous animals customarily hunted by the Paleolithic population declined in numbers as they became restricted to shrinking forest glades, riverside meadows, and coastal plains. In their reduced territories they would easily have been overhunted by men armed with bows and arrows, and Mesolithic man had to find alternative sources of food if he was to maintain his population at the higher level that now prevailed. Fish provided the solution.

The name *Maglemosian* is taken from the large bog (in Danish *magle mose*) at Mullerup on the Baltic, one of the first archeological sites at which the new culture was identified. At first the Maglemosians must merely have camped along the river banks, lakes, and seashores, while they continued to hunt water fowl and the surviving herbivorous animals—elk, aurochs, and red deer. Birds were shot with arrows tipped with small microliths, and fish were harpooned with barbed, bone-tipped spears, developed thousands of years earlier. But fishing which had formerly been a subsidiary activity now became increasingly the mainstay of subsistence as the mammalian food resources declined in these more northerly Mesolithic communities.

In Europe the basic technological equipment common to most fishing societies had probably developed in the Maglemosian culture by around 6000 B.C. While horticulture reached the Rhineland and the lowlands of what is now Holland as early as 5000 B.C., the Middle Eastern types of grain which were cultivated there would not flourish in the Baltic. North of the Rhine the Mesolithic hunting and fishing communities therefore survived without benefit of horticultural produce down to around 2500 B.C. Even so, their general technology reflected a high level of workmanship not inferior to that of the horticulturalists who occupied Central Europe and the Balkans.[2]

Not all the Maglemosian communities that emerged in the warmer weather of this *neothermal period* were dependent upon fishing. Those farther inland combined hunting with

[2] J. G. D. Clark, "A Survey of the Mesolithic Phase of the Pre-history of Europe and Western Asia," *Atti del VI Congresso Internazionale delle Scienze Preistoriche e Protoistoriche. I Relazioni Generali* 97.

The earliest known fishing societies appear in the European Mesolithic, around the shores of the Baltic and along the edges of the major North European rivers. Illustrated here are some of the first fishhooks and harpoons known to archeologists. They are made from carved bone and come from Neustadt, Kreis Oldenburg, in Germany. (Courtesy of Landesmuseum, Schloss Gottorp.)

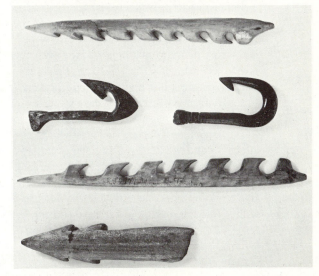

river fishing, but along the Baltic shore, sea-food became the main source of subsistence. The settlements of the coastal Maglemosians are marked by huge accumulations of waste bones and seashells known as *kitchen middens,* or kitchen "muck heaps" to translate the Danish term literally, which collected precisely because the settlements were occupied continuously over many generations.

The predicament of these Mesolithic people who found themselves obliged to concentrate upon fishing was paralleled in a number of other societies around the world. Many people who lived by lakes, along rivers, or close to coastal waters in which fish could be easily harvested, found fish catching a solution to their problems when game became sparse. Accordingly, they developed fishing techniques from a general Upper Paleolithic, Mesolithic, or Neolithic level. In the South Pacific, especially, the Malayo-Polynesians who settled the multitude of small coral atolls known as Micronesia found that horticulture was restricted by the poor quality of the soil, but the coral lagoons were rich in fish, and fishing consequently became an important occupation. These Micronesians were also great raiders, as so many fishing people became, and their style of life has certain parallels to that of the Haida whom we shall examine shortly.

In northeastern Asia, too, the severity of the climate made horticulture impossible, and the hunting of land animals provided only a precarious existence in many parts. However, the rivers teemed with fish, and the Paleolithic Paleo-Asians became highly skilled in extracting a living from the rivers, lakes, and even more turbulent coastal waters. Some of these Paleo-Asians slowly made their way across the Aleutians and the Bering Strait and eventually began to move southward down the mainland of North America in the extension of a primitive economy which nevertheless showed great ability to adapt itself to new environments.

In the more favorable climate further south, the Paleo-Indians, as these first settlers in America are called, were able to adapt once again to big game hunting. But those that settled in the densely wooded northwestern coastal areas, around what is now British Columbia, concentrated on fishing and developed rich and prosperous settled communities, hunting only to vary their diet and perhaps for recreation and prestige.

These fishing communities have survived right down to the present century, achieving a higher standard of living than many of the big game hunting societies further inland—a standard of living that even exceeded that of the less successful horticulturalists in other parts of the Americas. Notable among the modern representatives of these fishing communities are the Haida, whose wealth is greater than they know how to consume by normal methods and who consequently have developed a remarkable custom of conspicuous waste that is shared by the Kwakiutl and various other fishing societies in the same general area.

THE HAIDA OF BRITISH COLUMBIA

The Haida occupy a beautiful and well-wooded archipelago of islands off the coast of British Columbia. While the land is mountainous and full of game, the coastline is richly indented by channels and rivers which teem with fish. There is a suggestion that the Haida may have come by sea from the South Pacific by way of the East Asian coast and the Bering Strait. Any such migration, however, must have been on a small scale, since today the Haida look like typical coppery-complexioned brown-eyed, black-haired American Indians, and they speak a language which shows affinities with the Athabascan linguistic stock. As is so often the case, the name *Haida* by which

FIG. 38   THE HAIDA

The Haida live on a group of well-wooded islands off the coast of British Columbia, where the many inlets and rivers are rich with fish.

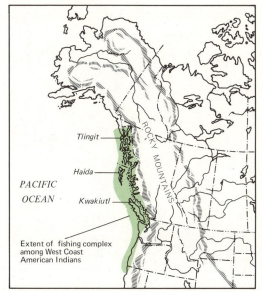

PACIFIC
OCEAN

Tlingit

Haida

Kwakiutl

ROCKY MOUNTAINS

Extent of fishing complex
among West Coast
American Indians

they know themselves means simply "people."[3]

The Haida practice no horticulture other than the cultivation of a little tobacco and possess no domestic animal other than the ubiquitous dog. The women and children collect clams, cockles, and mussels as well as fruits and berries in wicker baskets. The men are fairly active hunters, using dogs to hunt bear, which are killed with solemn ceremonial reminiscent of the bear cults of the Ainu of Japan and of Upper Paleolithic Cro-Magnon man in Europe. Deer, seals, and sea lions are slain with bows and arrows and clubs; wild birds are caught in snares. But the main source of subsistence and livelihood is fishing. Despite their Stone Age technology, the Haida lovingly

[3] This account of the Haidas is based primarily upon the publications of G. P. Murdock listed at the end of this chapter.

carve their canoes from forest timbers, decorating them with the most elaborate patterns of ornamentation.

The rivers, creeks, and ocean waters around the Haida islands are full of fish. Salmon are plentiful in the rivers, and are caught with nets and wicker baskets planted across holes in artificially constructed weirs. Herring are captured with dip nets, while hook and line are used for halibut, cod, and dogfish in the deeper waters. Food is abundant during the summer and also fairly plentiful in winter, but reserves of steamed and dried fish are laid in to guard against any possible emergency.

The Haida Village

Depending primarily upon water for both food and transport, the Haida build permanent villages of rectangular wooden buildings arranged in rows facing the waterfront but well above the high water mark. These are constructed from solid planks of cedar wood, worked with stone tools and reinforced by massive posts which are deeply carved and ornamented, representing months of labor. Each house has a giant totem pole in the center of the front wall, which may rise to a height of 60 to 80 feet, and is heavily and imaginatively carved with animals representing clan and lineage crests. The entrance is a relatively small opening at the base of the pole. Although the Haida did not in recent times practice human sacrifice, it was formerly customary when building a new house to throw a living slave into the hole dug to receive the base of the totem pole, so that he would be crushed to death when the pole was erected into position.

Inside the house, mats and furskins cover the floor, carved ceremonial masks hang on the walls, and a fire burns in the center of the long room, the smoke from which escapes through a small hole in the roof. There is no pottery,

The Haida community suffered from considerable cultural dislocation following contact with Europeans who were technologically much further advanced. This photograph shows a finely carved totem pole, in the traditional position at the front entrance to the house, on which metal sheeting has replaced the traditional handhewed wooden planks. (Courtesy of British Columbia Provincial Museum.)

for the Haida have not learned the art of pottery making. However, they know how to beat copper into plaques adorned with the clan crests, the copper being acquired by trade, and a wide range of finely finished wooden plates and spoons adequately fills all household needs.

Clans and Moieties

The household is the basic unit of Haida society. Each household constitutes an extended family, numbering perhaps a couple of dozen members and all sharing the single

building. Up to as many as 20 lineages or households make up a clan, and some forty-odd clans together constitute the Haida nation. These are grouped in two exogamous, matrilineal moieties, known respectively as the Ravens and the Eagles, titles which may be a memory from earlier hunting and gathering days.

The Haida have no tribal organization above the moieties, and indeed the moieties themselves are only significant in regulating marriage and similar kinship matters. Thus the clan is the major social and political unit, each possessing its own crests, belonging to the member lineages, and each possessing traditional rights over hunting and fishing territories as well as over house and village sites. For historical reasons villages may sometimes have come to include families drawn from two or more clans, but probably villages were originally populated exclusively by the members of a single clan.

Clans and lineages, like moieties, are matrilineal; thus descent and inheritance of property and authority descends through the female line, even though the clan chieftainships are normally held by males. When there are no male heirs, women may inherit both property and titles in their own right. The equality of the sexes is indicated by the fact that both males and females customarily eat together. Because of the matrilineal tradition, the mother's brothers significantly influence the life of a younger man, who must obey them in all customary matters. In ceremonials, on the other hand, the *sqan,* or paternal aunts, play important roles, and since *collective* nomenclature is employed, the term *sqan* includes all the father's sisters and the father's female cousins, just as all the father's brothers are known as "father" and all the mother's sisters and female cousins are known as "mother." The Haida people also have particular responsibilities to cousins, so that, as is common in kinship-based societies, the relations between all members in the community are knitted tightly together by a precise and all-inclusive network of kinship obligations.

Though names, titles, and house rights pass through the female line, the men nevertheless play an important role in all family and clan affairs, and work ardently to create and acquire wealth. It is the men who hunt, fish, and make war, the object of which is the acquisition of slaves and loot. It is also the men who work long hours to produce the ornately carved artifacts and ceremonial masks, richly decorated goods being highly valued not only for esthetic reasons but as symbols of status; and Haida society is status conscious.

Wealth and Slavery

Haida society is characterized by a great emphasis upon the acquisition of wealth. Material possessions are not used for trade so much as valued for the status they confer, and prosperity reveals itself not only in the elaborately carved artifacts, rich accumulations of fur cloaks and rugs, and the year-round adequacy of food but also in substantial slaveholdings. Slaves, acquired by war or by purchase, do all the menial tasks. Their status is hereditary, although they may not legally marry, nor can they own property. Treated with contempt and abuse while they are alive, after death they are not even afforded a burial ceremony, their bodies being casually thrown into the water in order to dispose of them in the easiest possible fashion.

The slave-owning free men and women consequently live a life of considerable comfort. The women dress in skirts woven from vegetable fiber and cloaks of tanned leather, while the men wrap a vegetable fiber cloth around their buttocks and loins and throw a cloak of furskins over their shoulders. The feet are kept bare. For ceremonial occasions the men paint their faces or don finely carved and painted masks, which are inlaid with shells and adorned with eagles' feathers and pieces of fur. Tattooing is common, and bone or shell nose ornaments are worn by both sexes. Women will not appear in public unless they are wearing the conventional long wooden lip plug through their pierced lower lip.

As is common among fishing peoples who have at their disposal the means of easy transportation, the Haida turn their maritime prowess partially toward commerce, and trade once a year with the Indians of the mainland, who are their enemies at other times. But waterborne mobility also leads to piracy and slave raiding. Plundering expeditions are cooperatively organized, with each household fitting out its own canoe. The men put on war helmets and armor made from wood and leather, and arm themselves with wooden war clubs, bone-pointed spears, and stone knives. Their usual tactic is ambush. Such war parties are usually accompanied by a shaman who determines the lucky days on which the expedition is most likely to be successful.

When a village is ambushed, the captives are enslaved, and the heads of those that are slain are mounted on poles and taken by the raiders as trophies for victory celebrations. The main purpose of these expeditions is to obtain slaves and booty, and those who resist, even women and children, are slain without mercy. Since it is generally regarded as a matter of shame to be related to a man or woman who is a slave, prisoners may be ransomed where their relatives are wealthy enough to pay a handsome fee.

The Potlatch

Prior to the coming of Europeans, the opportunities for trade were severely restricted, and the surplus wealth acquired by fishing and war expeditions, as well as by their craftsmanship, tended to be consumed in *potlatches*.[4] These are ceremonial feasts at which the host and hostess give lavish gifts to their guests in an attempt to earn status. They are also social festivals which entertain those who participate in them and add variety to the social life of the Haida. Following the death of a clan chief, the heir to the chief's title and possessions must give a funeral potlatch before he can inherit. On these occasions he and his wife invite the members of the moiety opposite to his own, and entertain them for several days while they carve and erect a memorial column to honor the deceased. After work there will be feasting and dancing every evening, but the actual potlatch will be reserved until the com-

[4] See also Stuart Piddocke, "The Potlatch System of the Southern Kwakiutl: A New Perspective," *Southwestern Journal of Anthropology* 21:244–264 (1965).

pletion of the project. Then a vast quantity of the inherited wealth, including even slaves, is given away. The object is to win honor and shame the guests by the enormity of the host and hostess's generosity. Since the guests belong to the same moiety as the husband, the wife concludes the distribution by turning to her husband and mockingly presenting him with some small, last-remaining, and trivial present, thus humbling the moiety to which he and the guests belong.

Similarly, a prosperous couple who wish to erect a new house will not attempt to build this by themselves, but instead will work to accumulate sufficient wealth to hold a house-building potlatch. A year before they are ready to hold the potlatch, they may further multiply the hoard of gifts they are collecting by lending out some of the accumulated wealth to members of the wife's clan, who must then return the borrowed furs or blankets with additional furs and blankets by way of interest on the loan. When the guests from the opposite moiety arrive for the house-building potlatch, they are welcomed with a ceremonial dance, and may remain as guests for as long as several months, working without pay to collect the timber, cut it into shape, raise the walls and the roof, and finally carve and erect the totem pole in position by the front entrance. During this time every day's work will be alleviated by nightly entertainments and a good deal of teasing and merrymaking. The potlatch ceremony is held after the house has been completed at the conclusion of the long period of labor. In some ways such potlatches can be regarded as a reward for the labor of the helpers, while in other ways they can be seen as "housewarming" parties. But in all cases the potlatch is regarded as a prime indicator of the giver's status.

Potlatches will also be held when a family has been insulted, but on these occasions wealth is deliberately destroyed instead of being given away, and beautifully carved tools

An early photograph of four Haida Masset Indians, attired in ceremonial costume for a Potlatch. From left: dancer, clan chieftain, shaman, and tattooed dancer. (Courtesy of the British Columbia Provincial Museum, Victoria.)

and wares are smashed to pieces. This is done to challenge the offender who will be permanently disgraced unless he likewise destroys an equivalent amount of wealth.

Such vast distributions of wealth, including also the destruction of wealth in the last instance, earn prestige for the clan and social status for the family. Only those families which by reputation have given and continue to give potlatches are regarded as "noble," and these families regularly snub the remaining majority, known as the "commoners."

Should a "commoner" family accumulate sufficient wealth to give a potlatch, it will gain status but will have to repeat the potlatch generation after generation before the stigma of having originated in a lower non-potlatch-giving class is eliminated. There are, indeed, practical values attached to the status that results from this conspicuous waste and generosity, for the status of a family, as determined by its record of potlatches, will determine the amount of compensation to be paid if one of its members is injured, robbed, insulted, or killed. Needless to say, a family which may demand a large compensation for injury to any of its members is in a more secure position than one which has low status and whose members may be insulted, beaten, robbed, or even slain with impunity by anyone who can afford the low compensation money which attaches to the victim's inferior status.

Personal Relations

When disputes arise between clans, kinsmen are regarded as being corporately responsible for the acts of their relatives and also for extracting vengeance. The kinsmen of the offending party will gather before the house of the accused, who will have to raise the compensation payable for the particular crime from among his relatives. Once the appropriate compensation has been paid, however, the two opposing parties sit down to a feast of friendship, at which a "dance of reconciliation" is performed, and the matter is closed.

As is common in many matrilineal societies, there is considerable sexual freedom before marriage, since the paternity of the child is relatively unimportant provided the father be-

An elderly Haida woman, seen in profile. (Courtesy of Vancouver Public Library.)

longs to the opposite moiety. Even after marriage men are permitted to have semisecret adulterous relations with their sisters-in-law. Adultery in general is not regarded as a very serious offense, although a husband may expect compensation from his wife's lover should he be able to prove the offense. The right of divorce is permitted to both husband and wife, and where this takes place, the children remain with their mother.

Children not only belong to the mother's clan, but are named by the mother, usually after one of her deceased forebears whose soul is believed to have returned to the world in the body of the child. A shaman will be invited to assist in determining the correct name for the child, and if a child falls sick, this is taken as an indication that the wrong name has been selected. The shaman may then be consulted again in order to rectify the error and determine the correct name.

As the children mature, cross cousin marriages are preferred, the status of the two families being important. Marital arrangements are usually made between the respective mothers, but consideration is also given to the wishes of other kinsmen and to the boy and girl involved. Prior to marriage, the intending bridegroom must take up residence for as long as a year in his intended bride's household, during which time he is not allowed sexual liberties and must work for the bride's mother. If all passes well, at the end of this period of time a simple wedding ceremony is held in the bride's house. After speeches by the menfolk and the exchange of gifts—the bride receiving useful household articles—the father of the bride makes the gift of a slave or some other object of value to his new son-in-law.

Shamans and Spirit Figures

The Haida believe that spirits inhabit a wide variety of natural objects, and among the more important of these spirits are a Sky God and a Thunderbird which produces thunderstorms when it flaps its wings. The ocean is peopled by many different spirits, and whales are regarded as the reincarnation of the souls of drowned men. There is a Creek Woman who must be propitiated if fishing is to be successful. The bears, too, have spirits or souls which must be placated by appropriate rituals when the animal is killed, in much the same way that the Eskimoes propitiate the souls of the animals they kill. The shaman, who may be a woman, can be called in to assist with special magical powers, should an antagonistic spirit cause sickness. Shamans may be bitter rivals to each other, and their powers, which are hereditary through the female line, reveal themselves through unusual physical or behavioral manifestations.

Magic, however, is not the prerogative of the shamans. Anyone who is sick or who is about to undertake an important venture may purify himself by ritual feasting, avoiding sex, ritual bathing, or purging his bowels with salt water, if confident of his own adequacy in the magical arts. Ordinary people may work magic by reciting ritual verbal formulas over pieces of hair or clothing belonging to the person they wish to harm. When a man falls sick and sorcery is suspected to be the cause, the victim or his relatives must catch a mouse and repeat the name of all who are suspected of causing the illness. If the mouse nods its head at one of these names, the person so identified must produce the fetish and destroy it, or may protect himself by declaring that it was one of his slaves who was responsible for the spell. When this happens, the suspected slaves are bound hand and foot and thrown into the creek in an attempt to identify the sorcerer, on the principle that the guilty slave will float higher in the water than the others.

Following contact with Europeans during the nineteenth century, the introduction of diseases against which the Haida had little resistance substantially reduced their population by a process of natural selection, until only the offspring of the more resistant survived. But the Haida culture was less fortunate. Missionaries superimposed Christian traditions upon the pattern of Haida animism, and the older social system rapidly collapsed. Today even the handicrafts have been replaced by mass-produced factory goods and the old skills have been forgotten.

For Further Reading

Clark, J. G. D., 1948, "The Development of Fishing in Prehistoric Europe," *Antiquaries Journal* 28:45–85.

———, 1952, *Prehistoric Europe: The Economic Basis.* London: Methuen & Co., Ltd.

Drucker, P., 1955, "Indians of the Northwest Coast," American Museum of Natural History Handbook 10. New York: Natural History Press.

———, and R. F. Heizer, 1967, *To Make my Name Good: A Reexamination of the Southern Kwakiutl Potlatch.* Berkeley: University of California Press.

Duff, W., ed., 1959, "Histories, Territories, and Laws of the Kitwankool," *Anthropology in British Columbia Memoir 4,* pp. 1–45.

Duff, W., and M. Kew, 1957, *Anthony Island, a Home of the Haidas.* Victoria, B.C.: Provincial Museum.

Fraser, T., 1966, *Fishermen of South Thailand: The Malay Villagers.* New York: Holt, Rinehart and Winston, Inc.

McIlwraith, T. F., 1948, *The Bella Coola Indians,* 2 vols. Toronto: University of Toronto Press.

Murdock, G. P., 1934, "The Haidas of British Columbia," in *Our Primitive Contemporaries*. New York: The Macmillan Company.

———, 1934, "Kinship and Social Behavior among the Haida," *American Anthropologist* 36:355–385.

———, 1936, "Rank and Potlatch among the Haida," *Yale University Publications in Anthropology* 13:1–20.

Piddocke, S., 1966, "The Potlatch System of the Southern Kwakiutl: A New Perspective," *Southwestern Journal of Anthropology* 21:244–264.

Rohner, R. P., and E. Rohner, 1970, *The Kwakiutl: Indians of British Columbia*. New York: Holt, Rinehart and Winston, Inc.

Suttles, W., 1960, "Affinal Ties, Subsistence and Prestige among the Coast Salish," *American Anthropologist* 62:296–305.

Vayda, A. P., 1961, "A Reexamination of Northwest Coast Economic Systems," *New York Academy of Science, Transactions*, Series 2, 23, 7:618–624.

CHAPTER 26

Simple Pastoralists

Pastoral or herding societies tend to be more dependent upon a single source of subsistence than either horticultural or fishing societies. This is often out of choice rather than necessity, for few pastoralists hold the cultivation of the soil in high regard. Some obtain a quantity of grain and vegetables by trading animal produce with nearby cultivators, but others contrive to subsist without horticultural produce, even though the opportunities for cultivation and trade may be present. So low is their esteem for agriculture and horticulture as occupations that where pastoralists do cultivate the soil, they usually delegate this work to slaves, or where they do not possess slaves, to their womenfolk.

General Characteristics

Because of the seasonal fluctuations in climate, particularly in rainfall, most pastoralists are nomadic, and it is no accident that the word *nomad* comes to us from Arabia where it meant simply "herdsman." The most common form of pastoral nomadism is known as TRANSHUMANCE, a regular seasonal migration between summer and winter grazing lands. Upland pastures which may be rich in the summer are frequently quite unsuitable for occupation during the winter, and flocks and herds that are grazed at high altitudes during the summer must usually be moved to lower-lying pastures during the winter. As a consequence of this necessary mobility, not all animals are suitable for domestication among nomadic pastoralists. Sheep, goats, cattle, horses, camels, and even reindeer are ideal in the right locations, but animals such as pigs are usually kept only by settled farmers.

SIMPLE HERDING SOCIETIES are those which do not possess domesticated riding or draft animals, whereas ADVANCED HERDING SOCIETIES possess either or both of these animals. The difference is much more than academic. Members of simple pastoral societies have to follow their herds on foot; therefore there is a limit to the size of the herds which they can control. Similarly, pedestrian herdsmen cannot travel the greater distances that are open to mounted pastoralists. Because of these restrictions they are obliged to sustain themselves in smaller communities or at a lower level of living. In particular, simple pastoral societies are severely limited in their ability to accumulate material artifacts because without pack animals they are obliged to carry virtually everything that they possess on their backs when they migrate, and in this sense are but little advanced beyond the primitive hunter and food gatherer. By contrast the advanced pastoralist can manage large herds, riding with these over the greater distances that are necessary to find sustenance for them. Having pack or draft animals, he can accumulate material possessions in far greater quantities. The Mongolian pastoralists of central and eastern Asia, for example, even build portable houses on large wheeled wagons[1] in which their women and children are able to travel in comfort, maintaining their domestic routine while the entire community is on the move.

Simple Herding Societies

Simple herding societies normally migrate only relatively short distances and maintain less extensive community contacts. As a result, their societies are much smaller in number and are concentrated over a relatively smaller area than is the case with animal-riding pastoralists. But even the simple pastoralist tends to be somewhat warlike because of the constant need to defend his flocks from sudden raids by hostile tribes. Animals are an easily movable form of wealth, and the herders who fail to achieve skill in the art of war have little chance of long-term survival. Not only will they lose their herds if they are unable to defend them from attack, but if they are not militantly aggressive, they will miss the opportunity to rebuild their herds when these are depleted by

[1] E. D. Phillips, *The Mongols* (New York: Frederick A. Praeger, Inc., 1969), p. 29.

sickness, drought, or enemy raids, by the simple process of raiding someone else's herds. Unlike land which can only be appropriated as a result of outright conquest and settlement, the entire wealth of a pastoral community can be lost in one night as a result of a single cattle raid.

The pastoral way of life consequently differs from that of the hunter, the fisher, and the horticulturalist. Unlike the fishing people and the horticulturalists, the simple pastoralist is still essentially seminomadic and cannot accumulate much natural wealth, for he has to carry everything with him when he drives his flocks from one pasture to another. Unlike the hunter, however, he does have a relatively assured food supply. When his herds are not decimated by disease or stolen in war, they can be relied upon to provide him and his dependents with food all the year round; even in winter he can bleed his animals and drink their blood, or kill them and consume their flesh.

In another way, also, the simple pastoralist differs from the hunter. Hunters seldom have any economic property; but as herding peoples must part company at those times of the year when upland grazing is ample, there is a tendency for separate families to acquire some degree of proprietorial rights in the animals which they customarily herd. The land, however, generally remains public property, and as among the Nuer, social organization is often little developed beyond the level of autonomous bands.

It is probably due to the constant emphasis upon cattle rustling and warfare that herding societies are almost invariably patriarchal and patrilocal. The herds have to be protected and cannot be effectively guarded by a lone man and his children. Nuclear families cannot muster a proper defense force, so that there is a tendency for the sons to remain with the parent family after marriage instead of setting up house on their own. In some cases where militarism has become highly developed, as among the Masai of East Africa, hereditary chieftains possessing considerable authority may emerge, and warrior sodalities become an important feature contributing to the survival of the tribe.

With the emphasis upon the breeding of herds, human reproduction will understandably come to be thought of in terms analogous to the breeding of livestock. Women are the means by which human children are produced, just as cattle are the means by which calves are produced, and men who are herders will therefore be ready to accept the idea that if they want a wife they will have to pay for her. In consequence, the payment of a bride price is common among pastoralists, and women may have a low status. If a wife petitions for divorce from her husband for bad treatment, her relatives must repay the cattle or sheep which they acquired at the time of the wedding. Should these have already been spent to procure a wife for her brother, her family is likely to pressure her to stay with her husband rather than face the economic disadvantages of refunding the purchase consideration and taking the divorced wife back into their own huts. But despite the use of animals as units of wealth for the stabilization of marital arrangements, commercial activity per se generally remains muted.

The Origins of Pastoralism

Most simple pastoral societies were located in the Old World, perhaps because hunting, fishing, and horticulture provided an adequate living in most parts of the New World, and the New World seems to have had fewer animals which were suitable for domestication. In South America a number of settled farming communities did domesticate the llama, but distinct pastoral or herding societies were not found until after the Spaniards brought sheep and horses to the Americas. Taming wild horses which had escaped from the Spanish

settlements, the Navaho and certain other plains Indian tribes then adapted themselves to pastoralism with remarkable alacrity and changed their entire pattern of life to accord with the new method of subsistence, even to the point of becoming notoriously warlike and aggressive.

There are essentially two ways in which nomadic pastoralism may develop. In the first place, a hunting people may make a practice of following a particular herd of animals upon which they prey regularly. Should this herd become severely depleted by the ravages of rival predators, such as wolves, the security of the human hunters will be endangered. Such a hunting society will consequently tend to protect its regular prey from rival predators. Through such a relationship a direct transition from hunting and gathering to pastoralism may be effected.

An example of such a transition is provided by the case of the Lapps of Lappland in northern Europe. There is no historical evidence to suggest that the Lapps were ever a horticultural people. Although formerly hunters, they appear to have attached themselves to the herds which they hunted, following these through their seasonal migrations. In order to protect the reindeer from other predators, they began to keep them in corrals, and in the process the more unruly and vicious reindeer were the first to be killed. Thus by a process of selection a relatively domesticated breed of reindeer was evolved.

The second way in which nomadic pastoralism may emerge is from a regional specialization among mixed farming societies resulting in a concentration on animal tending and a decline in cultivation. In both the Middle East and Europe the evidence of archeology suggests that cultivation preceded pastoralism. In such areas the more prosperous settlements of horticulturalists, supplementing their crops with milk and meat from a number of domesticated livestock in a pattern of mixed farming, saw their population steadily increase generation by generation. As the population increased, new farming colonies were established in virgin land until all the rich river valleys most suitable for cultivation had become fully settled. When this point was reached, it became necessary for new settlements to be established on poorer essentially marginal land scarcely suitable for cultivation. With a continuing rise in population, new colonies were established on grass downlands where there was ample grass for grazing animals, but where the top soil was thin and the return from cultivation disappointing. Such farming colonies consequently tended to depend more and more upon animal produce and often abandoned their at-

tempt to cultivate anything except the richer pockets of soil. Without ever losing their knowledge of horticulture, such mixed farmers found themselves effectively converted into pastoralists over a number of generations.

Prehistoric Pastoralism

Archeologists are frequently prone to overemphasize the role of the settled horticulturalists in prehistory at the expense of the pastoralists, mainly because nomadic herders do not build permanent houses and do not accumulate so many material artifacts—and therefore leave less material debris for the archeologists to discover. Nevertheless, there

FIG. 39   TYPES OF PASTORALISM

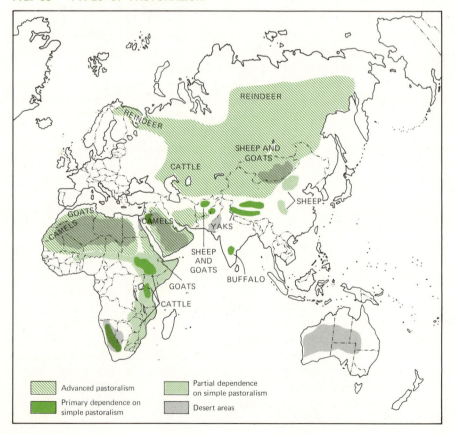

is reason to believe that while horticulture was spreading throughout the "fertile crescent," the Aegean and the Danube valleys between 7000 and 5000 B.C., the marginal lands adjacent to this area were developing a simple pastoral way of life.

The earliest nomadic pastoralists seem to have been shepherds who followed their flocks on foot. Those who roamed to the north and east of the fertile crescent probably spoke Indo-European languages; those further afield in eastern Asia spoke Ural-Altaic languages; and those that occupied the marginal land between the fertile crescent and the Arabian desert spoke Semitic or Hamitic languages. The first domesticated animals were probably sheep and goats; the domestication of the cow is believed to have taken place at a somewhat later date. The cow was originally a wild woodland grazing animal, probably inhabiting the European forests, but once it was domesticated, the practice of herding cattle seems to have spread very quickly across the Asian steppes, southward into India and southwest through the Middle East to Africa, wherever the terrain and climate made this the most suitable form of subsistence.

The poorer lands which bordered the agricultural regions may in some instances have been marginal even for the pastoralists, and during droughts the Arabian grazing lands in particular seem to have reverted to desert. It is therefore likely that pastoralists, being already warlike by inclination, were tempted to raid the more outlying horticultural settlements in times of hardship. They were usually able to loot a settlement and retire into the vast plains before the villagers could organize their resistance or come to each other's aid. In the course of time, these raids might have become more frequent, until a larger body of pastoralists, perhaps an entire tribe or even a group of tribes, would decide to expropriate the villagers altogether from their richer land and would attack with permanent settlement as

their intention. Being more martial and more mobile, the pastoralists frequently prevailed over the cultivators. Much Old World history, not only in Europe and western Asia but in eastern Asia and Africa as well, can only be understood in terms of the conflicts between pastoralists and settled horticultural and agricultural populations.

The first evidence of the existence of pastoralists on the fringes of the fertile crescent to come to the attention of archeologists is associated with signs of dislocation among the settled cultivators. As a patriarchal herding people, probably similar to those described in the Old Testament, they would strike their tents and move their flocks into the richer land already settled by cultivators. Thus the Hebrew pastoralists invaded Palestine, driving out the earlier horticulturalists, and it may well have been a famine that drove Jacob and his people into Egypt where they met with an unexpected reception from that more highly organized civilization.

There is ample evidence also that the pastoralism of Africa originated in the poorer lands of Arabia. Pastoralists undoubtedly entered Africa through the Sinai peninsula and Egypt, moving westward along the northern coast, and there were also incursions of mainly Semitic-speaking peoples over the Straits of Bab-el-Mandeb to Abyssinia and the Horn of Africa. According to G. P. Murdock,[2] during the first millennium A.D. these pastoral migrations brought a new wave of cattle, sheep, and goats, as well as Hamitic and Cushitic languages and Caucasoid genes, to the great African savannahs. Many of the African horticulturalists were dislodged from their lands, but in most cases the cultures of the indigenous peoples amalgamated with those of the immigrants, resulting in mixed pastoral-horticultural economies. While horse- or camel-riding pastoralists were eventually to dominate North Africa and

[2]G. P. Murdock, *Africa: Its Peoples and Their Cultures* (New York: McGraw-Hill, Inc., 1959), p. 44.

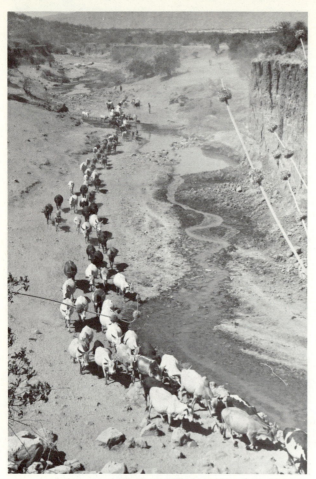

Cattle have become the center of a cultural complex among East African foot-herding pastoralists from the Sudan to South Africa. African cattle watering at a river during the rainy season. (Courtesy of Alan H. Jacobs.)

the Asian grazing lands, simple foot-bound pastoralism survives to the present day over large parts of sub-Saharan Africa.

Pastoralism had many advantages over horticulture on the savannahs of Africa. Vast grasslands extend westward through the Sudan from the mountains of Abyssinia as far as the Atlantic ocean; animal husbandry spread westward along this belt, at first without milking animals. A second wave brought true pastoralism, accompanied by milking practices, along this same belt during the first millennium A.D. The

high cultures which stretch across Africa from Uganda to the Niger arose from a combination of horticulture and animal husbandry. The entire range of Chad-Sudanese and Nilo-Saharan languages represents an amalgam of Hamitic-Cushitic and the languages of the Niger-Congo area, the former having been associated with the immigrant cattle tenders, and the latter with the indigenous Negroid population.

Pastoralism could not flourish north of this fertile Sudanese belt, for northwards the soil becomes steadily more arid until the moving sands of the Sahara defy settlement. To the south of this belt, the trees become increasingly more dense until the thick rain forests of the equatorial Congo and the Cameroons similarly check the pastoralists. In these forests the Pygmies were allowed to continue their pattern of hunting and gathering without interference, sharing their reserve with gorillas and that wide range of African fauna which still delights those who seek to see something of the world as it was before more advanced methods of human subsistence upset the ecological balance. Some observers have commented that we owe much to the tsetse fly, as one of the greatest of African conservationists, for the tsetse did much to discourage Neolithic man from encroaching on these last major nature reserves. One of the greatest tragedies of the last 20 years has been the conquest of the tsetse by modern insecticides, thanks to the well-intentioned efforts of international agencies, so that men will now probably complete the ecological destruction of those remaining central African lands which escaped the attentions of the Neolithic developers.

But not all the pastoral immigrants went westward across Africa. Some turned southward where a similar vista of great open grasslands rolled away into the distant blue. Avoiding the flat and unhealthy coastlands to the east and also the humid, low-lying rain forests of the Congo to the west, cattle, sheep, and goat herders drove their animals slowly southward. As they went, they amalgamated with the Negroid, Bantu-speading horticulturalists and became absorbed into these. Their martial descendants, speaking Bantu languages (a subdivision of the Niger-Congo linguistic stock), continued the triumphant southward drive down the East African highlands during the second millennium A.D., dispossessing and annihilating the older Bushmanoid hunters. Eventually as Zulus, Bechuanas, and Basutos, they took a mixed pastoral and horticultural economy over the Zambezi and Limpopo rivers. Contemptuously driving before them the remnants of the indigenous tribes, they entered the high veldt of the Transvaal. There they came into conflict with small groups of Caucasoid immigrant farmers who had trekked northward from the Cape in ox-drawn wagons, but were equipped with a more advanced technology. So the seeds of South Africa's race problems were laid as two migrant populations, with widely different cultural systems, attempted to cohabit the same land.

From an economic point of view, East African Bantu pastoralism is a hybrid affair, representing a newer acquisition which dominated but did not supercede the older horticultural basis of subsistence. But the usual ideologies of pastoral societies dominate the culture, and all work with the hoe is delegated to the women as beneath the dignity of cattle herders and warriors. One is sometimes inclined to wonder whether the attention lavished on the cow in these mixed East African economies is economically justified, for the Bantu do not make butter or cheese, and they breed their cattle for quantity only without regard to quality, so that their herds are a poor lot in comparison to those further north. Yet such is their adoration of the cow that no one would consider using them as beasts of burden, and all loads have consequently to be carried by the women.

The most southerly of African pastoral economies is that of the Hottentots. Expropriated from richer lands by the invading Bantu, the Hottentots are the survivors of the non-Negroid peoples who formerly occupied large areas of Africa. Before losing their best lands, they managed to acquire the art of cattle herding from their Bantu enemies. Today they struggle to make a living herding cattle and cultivating the soil on the fringes of the Kalahari Desert, fighting off attacks from the wiry Bushmen, armed with poisoned weapons, who have never abandoned their ancient hunting and gathering tradition.

Looking at the map of sub-Saharan Africa, one is struck by the distribution of pastoral cultures, neatly determined by the climatic and topographical conditions but varying in character and becoming steadily less Hamitic or Cushitic in speech and culture the further one penetrates in a southerly direction.

THE NUER OF SOUTHERN SUDAN

Probably one of the best studied examples of a simple pastoral society, at the lower level of organization, is that of the Nuer of the southern Sudan.[3]

The Nuer are a Nilotic people, numbering perhaps one third of a million in all, who are of predominantly Negroid origin with possibly an ancient admixture of Caucasoid genes. The name *Nuer* is actually given to them by the Dinkas, neighboring pastoralists who share a similar culture and with whom they maintain a more or less constant state of war. The Nuer, however, call themselves the *Nath,* which like the names Haida and Yạnomamö means simply the "folk" or "people."

Under British rule the Nuer remained little

[3] This description is based upon E. E. Evans-Pritchard, *The Nuer* (New York: Oxford University Press, 1940) and *Nuer Religion,* by the same author (New York: Oxford University Press, 1956).

FIG. 40   THE NUER

Map showing the location of the Nuer in the tropical swamps of the Upper Nile. During the dry season, these swamplands are transformed into arid semidesert.

"Nations" were created which have no historical, cultural, racial, or linguistic justification or unity whatsoever. Many ethnic peoples found themselves divided between two or more political states, in each of which their members continued to live as a powerless political minority, separated from their kinsmen by artificial political boundaries. Many who had never before been subordinated to rule by their neighbors, now struggle with spears and clubs against modern armies, recruited from and controlled by alien tribes which have inherited the mantle of colonial power by weight of numbers.

disturbed in their sparse tropical grasslands. Unfortunately following the withdrawal of the British, the Sudan acquired a government dominated by the Arabs of the northern provinces, the descendants of former slave owners and traders. The Nuer have since suffered very considerably from the attacks of the Sudanese army, equipped with modern weapons, and have alleged deliberate genocide by the Arabs.

The plight of the Nuer today is one which is reflected in many parts of Africa. Unfortunately, during colonial rule the direction of Africa fell under the control of European statesmen who had little interest in cultural, linguistic, or tribal affairs, so that political boundaries ignored ethnological considerations and were determined by the accident of exploration and political opportunism. This situation actually mattered little under colonial rule which was generally based on a policy of noninterference in tribal affairs except to suppress warfare, cannibalism, and any other activities that offended against Western mores. But when the old colonies were given independence, no effort was made to correct the meaningless political boundaries of the colonial period, and these assumed a new and vital importance.

Environment and Ecology

The Nuer territories seem unattractive to anyone but the Nuer. During the dry season when the land is scorched and arid, the people congregate together in small villages made up of a number of related households. When the summer rains come, the White Nile floods, and the entire territory turns into a swampy morass, with small islands of higher ground and myriads of mosquitoes. But the grass grows tall, and with the coming of the rains, the villages break up, and each household drives its own animals away to take advantage of the ample grazing, establishing temporary family camps on the islands of higher land.

In consequence of this annual dispersal, the extended family household is the basic unit of the Nuer economy, comprising the father and his wives, his sons, and his sons' wives and children. All camp together in a cluster of small wattle and daub beehive huts, with an adjacent cow shed and corral for the cattle. Beyond the household there is only the winter village community—and a shadowy pattern of clans and tribes. There are no authoritative officials whatsoever, and the Nuer have been portrayed by some writers as idyllically democratic.

The Nuer tribesmen are tall and lithe. They wear no clothes, but are seldom seen without a spear. This is often a valued heirloom inherited from the ancestors. (Courtesy of Hans W. Jürgens.)

Social Structure

Nuer social organization is therefore hardly more complex than that of an endogamous band of food gatherers. Nuer folklore says that they have clans only because an early culture hero known as *Gaa*—who also gave them cattle and taught them to wear clothes—originally separated them into two exogamous groups, which subsequently subdivided into the present variety of clans. Each clan has its own totemic bird symbol—thus the Nuer refuse to eat birds or even birds' eggs—but there are no clan chiefs, and clans are little more than a means of systematizing marriage arrangements. Thus winter villages comprise permanent groups of biologically related families,

A Nuer home constructed from mud walls surmounted by a conical grass roof. There are no windows, the door opening being barred at night by a bamboo screen to keep out animals. (Courtesy of the Musée de l'Homme, Paris.)

and closely resemble endogamous bands, except for the fact that genealogies are carefully remembered, and heirlooms, such as ancestral spears, passed down from generation to generation, are highly treasured.

Beyond the clans there are loose tribal groupings, numbering up to 5000 members in each, but again there is no system of tribal government. The tribes are held together solely by the link of identifiable clan membership and contiguous territorial holdings. The only office of any significance is that of the Leopard Skin Chief, so named because he is entitled to wear a leopard skin which serves as his badge of office. However, even this official has only advisory powers, and although he may be called in to settle an interfamily dispute he cannot enforce his decisions if the parties refuse to accept his judgment. Some influence is exercised by part-time shamans who use magic and sleight-of-hand tricks to extract solid objects from the bodies of the sick. Rainmaking and divination also come within their province, and the more successful diviners may even earn a reputation as prophets beyond the limits of their own tribe.

Domestic Economy

The Nuer take a great pride in possession of cattle, but during the dry winter months the supply of milk can run low, and they are therefore obliged to supplement their diet of milk and cheese with the produce from horticulture. Work in the fields, in which they grow maize and millet, is despised, however, and is assigned entirely to women. The men do a little fishing, and some hunt, but although game is plentiful, hunting is also a despised occupation, regarded as a fit pursuit only for those who do not own cattle. When the cattle are unable to give milk therefore, the bullocks are used as an additional source of food, blood being extracted from their necks using a special hollow arrow which is skillfully shot from a short

distance into one of the veins. The blood thus obtained is roasted until it can be eaten in solid form, making a highly nutritious dish. So great is the Nuer dependence upon cattle that cattle are butchered only when they become too old for milking or breeding purposes. Even then no cattle are ever killed except as a sacrifice to one of the gods, following which the meat is consumed as a sacrificial ritual. As the Nuer themselves say, "Cattle beget children." Without cattle to give in payment of the bride price, there can be no wedding, and without a wedding there can be no children, and life would not continue. The cow is therefore conceptualized as the central figure in Nuer religious ritual.

Little cattle produce is ever wasted. The animal hides provide leather, and the dung is used as fuel for the homestead fire. The smoke from the dung fires keeps mosquitoes away, and the ashes make an effective tooth-cleaning powder. The urine from the cattle is used for washing, since it serves to repel body pests, and also as hair oil. Depending so much on their cattle, the men spend long hours caring for them in the corral, grooming them, picking off ticks and leeches, crooning songs to them, and decorating their horns with tassels. As one anthropologist remarked, the young Nuer men talk incessantly of cattle and women, and of the two topics, the former is the more favored.

Age Sets

The life cycle of the Nuer is not very complex. As boys grow older, they are expected to leave their mother's hut and sleep in the cattle sheds which serve as a young man's clubhouse. When approaching the age of 15, they undergo puberty and initiation rites. These rituals are supervised by one of the elders, who is known as the *Wut Ghok*, or "Man of the Cattle," and include circumcision and the cutting of cicatrix markings on the forehead. At the conclusion of these painful ceremonies, the initiate is ceremonially pelted with cow dung and presented by his father with his own herd of cattle.

All the young men who have passed through the initiation ceremonies at the same time become members of a male sodality known as an *age set*. This institution appears to be of Hamitic origin and is common to many East African pastoralists among whom it usually constitutes a warrior society, representing a form of compulsory military service. Those of the Nuer, however, are not true warrior societies, although their members are expected to take part in cattle raids against other tribes.

While the men tend the cattle, the women are responsible for care of the children, the cultivation of the crops, the milking of cattle, and the preparation of food. This seems to leave little for the men to do, but in actual fact the protection of the cattle from both animal and human predators is not an easy task. Herds may be lost in a night, and military readiness is an essential condition for survival.

The Position of Women

Following the puberty rituals young men and women are allowed a great deal of sexual freedom and are normally permitted to find their own mates. The approval of the bride's father is needed before marriage but can generally be secured by payment of an appropriate bride price in the form of cattle. Such financial arrangements will be taken care of at a betrothal feast at the bride's home, and the ensuing wedding involves two feasts, one at the bride's home and the other at the bridegrooms' household. The marriage is consummated only after the third of these three feasts, during the course of which the bride's head is shaved and anointed with butter in token of her new status. Even then the bride must stay with her own family until a child is born. After this event, the husband may move into the bride's father's household to live with her until the child is

weaned, and only after this has been successfully accomplished will the bride be admitted to her new father-in-law's household.

At her father-in-law's household the bride receives her own hut in which she will bring up her children. Polygyny is practiced, and there is some jealousy between wives, although all are supposed to be treated equally. Widows are protected by the levirate, the custom by which the younger brother or some other close relative of the deceased husband takes the widow into his own household as his wife and cares for her and her children. Such marriages are not necessarily consummated, however, since they are devices designed to ensure the protection of the widow and orphans rather than to provide sexual pleasure for the brother. If, on the other hand, a man should die without heirs, his brother will be responsible for marrying his widow and raising up heirs in his name, for the Nuer believe that the spirits of the dead will be angered if a lineage is permitted to die out.

Ghosts and Sky Gods

The Nuer believe in ghosts and also in a number of sky spirits. Since death is in accordance with the will of these beneficent spirits, it is considered incorrect to fear death. However, the Nuer do fear the ghosts of the dead, and corpses are carefully wrapped in a cowhide before being buried, with the legs drawn up in a fetal position. To ensure the contentment of the ghost, the deceased is mourned not only by his relatives but also by the members of his age group. Mourners may neither cut their hair nor wear any ornaments for six months after a man's death or for three months after a woman's, months being counted by the moon. It is significant that the mourning rituals are observed out of fear of the departed spirit, the purpose being to propitiate the spirit and prevent its return to seize the widow, children, or possessions—for even though they fear ghosts, the Nuer do not bury a dead man's possessions with him. Should a man die suddenly without warning, it is believed that one of the sky gods has seized his soul. In such cases there is no fear that the spirit can linger around the settlement, so mourning ceremonies are dispensed with.

The Nuer believe that their gods lived in the sky, which is not unreasonable for a people who live in flat open plains. The gods are nature spirits who control all major natural functions such as thunder, rain, sickness, and even war. It is to these gods, especially the rainmaking god, that cattle are sacrificed when old. A great deal of the social life revolves around religious ceremonies, and it is interesting to find that the Nuer religion prompts them on occasion to build earthen pyramids of no small size, an idea which they must have acquired from Egypt many centuries ago. Unlike the Egyptian tradition however, these pyramids do not serve as graves, since no Nuer is sufficiently elevated above his kinsmen to justify such a distinction. In their equalitarian society the pyramids represent nothing more than an attempt to honor and propitiate the gods that control their everyday lives.

THE MASAI OF EAST AFRICA

Distantly related by culture and language to the Nuers are the Masai of East Africa.[4] Their homeland is the great Rift Valley which runs from Uganda through Kenya into Tanzania. Advancing southward from the area west of Lake Rudolf, they originally seized the rich grasslands of this gigantic valley and the up-

[4] This description is largely based on C. D. Forde's account of the Masai in his *Habitat, Economy and Society* (New York: E. P. Dutton & Co., 1963) and J. Thomson, *Through Masai Land* (London: Sampson, Low & Co, 1885), one of the earliest published accounts of the Masai, written truly in the "ethnographic present."

land plains on each side of the valley from an earlier aboriginal cultivating people, but have themselves disdained to cultivate the soil in any way. Fortunately, because the soil is fertile and reasonably well watered, they enjoy a considerably higher standard of living than that of the Nuer.

Like the Nuer, however, the Masai have also had political troubles since independence, finding themselves dominated by the more numerous Kikuyu with whom they formerly had little contact. Until the coming of the British they had always been independent. Today their position is made worse by the fact that they are divided between Kenya, Uganda, and Tanzania, so that in all three countries they are merely a small minority group with little or no political power to influence decisions which will intimately affect their future history.

Also like the Nuer, the Masai are a tall people, somewhat dark-skinned, but with finer and more aquiline features. In general it may be said that their culture reveals an even stronger Cushitic or Hamitic tradition, still surviving from the days when pastoralists first crossed the narrow Straits of Bab-el-Mandeb into the Horn of Africa and surged down the Nile Valley from the Sinai peninsula. Earlier scholars described them as Nilo-Hamites or half-Hamites, because of the Hamitic elements in their language. However, the term *Nilotic* is used today to refer to both the Masai and the Nuer languages as well as other languages in adjacent areas which similarly reveal both Niger-Congo and Hamito-Cushitic influences.

Social Structure

Thanks to the rich grasslands which they control, the Masai have been able to retain their proud dependence upon pastoralism without the need to accept any agricultural techniques. Not only do they despise cultivation, but they also dominate the various horticulturalists around them, such as the Lumbwa, whom they regard contemptuously as mere hoe wielders, not proper warriors. Like most pastoralists, they are seminomadic, grazing their herds in the lower grasslands of the Rift Valley during the wet season and moving onto the higher plateaus on each side of the valley during the dry season, since the uplands receive more rain all the year around. However, they do not attempt to penetrate the thick rain forests which cover the slopes of the higher mountain ranges, such as the Aberdares, be-

A group of Masai. Note the long metal blade of the Masai warrior's spear, the pigtails worn by the young men, and the heavy metal armbands of the woman. This and the ensuing pictures are contemporary, and they show the Masai wearing cloth wraps draped round their bodies, instead of the more traditional animal hides customary in the "ethnographic present" when the Masai were first encountered by European explorers. (Courtesy of Musée de l'Homme, Paris.)

Cattle entering a kraal camp for the night. The low structures on the right are the mud-dung covered huts of the Masai. (Courtesy of Alan H. Jacobs.)

FIG. 41   THE MASAI

Map of Africa showing the Masai grazing lands situated in the Rift Vally.

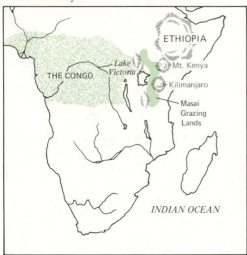

cause these have nothing to offer their herds. As might be expected, the life of the Masai revolves round the acquisition, possession, and care of cattle. In consequence, grass is virtually sacred to the Masai, even to the point of becoming a symbol of goodwill and peaceful intention. Strangers approaching a Masai camp will therefore pluck a handful of grass and hold this high, using it like a white flag as a request for safe conduct. Milk is similarly revered, and despite the hot climate, is never boiled, for this would be regarded as a sacrilege.

The basic social and economic unit of Masai society is the polygynous family. Cattle are owned by individual families, but since the land supports far larger herds than do the poorer lands of the Nuer, the size of settlements tends to be larger. The typical kraal or *enkang'* of the Masai therefore consists of several independent polygynous families, drawn from different clans. Each kraal is surrounded by a circular thorn bush fence to keep out wild animals, and the cattle share the camp with their owners at nighttime, when the area

within the fence becomes a crowded cattle byre. Entrance to the kraal is made through a number of separate gates, each owned by an independent family. Wives of heads of families build themselves houses on either side of their husband's gate along the interior perimeter of the fence, and the total number of gates to a kraal generally indicates the number of economically independent resident families.

While ultimate control and ownership over livestock rests with the individual family heads, the Masai believe that "the grass belongs to every man," and the animals belonging to the different families in a kraal are generally pastured and watered as a single herd, besides being coralled communally at night in the open center of the kraal for protection against predators. The kraal community is, however, a voluntary association, and although most kraals maintain a core of congenial members over several years, a personal dispute or a difference on opinion over management of the combined herd can cause dissidents to break away and join another kraal camp, taking their own cattle with them.

The clans are exogamous and are grouped in two phratries, known as the Black Ox and the Red Bullock, respectively. These two phratries are not exogamous, and some clans regard themselves as being more "pure" in descent than others. All kinship ties are patrilineal, and Masai society is very decidedly patriarchal in the pastoral tradition.

Marriages are negotiated while the intended bride is still young, sometimes even before she has been born, but do not take place until the bridegroom has retired from warrior service. A bride price of cattle and honey beer is payable, but this is not generally handed over to the bride's family until she has produced her first child, for divorce may be expected in the case of barrenness. Women are well treated, and each wife brings up her own children in her own hut. She must build this hut herself, however, for all menial tasks are customarily the privilege of the female. Such huts are made of branches covered with a mixture of wet mud and cow dung, and must have cowhides thrown over them when it rains hard, to prevent the mud-dung plaster from washing away. About 9 feet long by 5 feet wide and only 4½ feet high, they have no windows—only a low, doorless opening which must be entered on all fours, and a small hole in the roof to let out the smoke. The interiors are therefore always dark, but this does not matter much, since the Masai are an outdoor people and use their huts only for sleeping and as a place of refuge in bad weather.

The climate is warm and Masai clothing is simple. The women wear a goatskin around the waist; the young warriors wear calves' skins, and the elders wrap themselves in more prestigious oxhides. Adult women shave their heads completely, but the men have short pigtails: one to the front and one to the back of their heads. Boys have their ear lobes pierced while young, and the resulting loop of skin is stretched methodically until it hangs down almost to their shoulders. It is then decorated with large ivory or brass objects, sometimes up to 6 or 8 inches in size, or else more simply with long twists of monkey hair.

The "Age Set"

Historically the Masai have seldom been seriously harassed by their neighbors, despite their large cattle holdings, because of their well-established reputation for martial prowess and their efficient system of compulsory military service based on age sets. The Masai age sets are more complex in function and organization than those of the Nuer. Commencing around the age of 15, youths are initiated into age sets in ceremonies which take up to four years to complete. Circumcision, a practice of seemingly Hamitic-Semitic origin, plays a major role in these rituals, as also does ceremonial head shaving.

Masai mother shaving her son's head at the *eunota* junior warrior's ceremony. The warrior, with legs painted, sits on a cowhide while his mother scrapes off the braided hair at the roots. (Courtesy of Alan H. Jacobs.)

All who undergo the Masai rites of passage at the same time are regarded as being of the same age group. Those initiated during the first four years are circumcized "to the left," those initiated during the next four years are circumcized "to the right." The two successive age groups are known as the Age of the Left and the Age of the Right, and together make up an age set. Each age set possesses its own secret rituals and crest, as well as its own title, which always has a military connotation, such as "the Raiders" or "the White Knives." After their initiation is complete, all members of each age group take up residence in one of the warrior kraals that are scattered throughout the country at strategic points, where they constitute a permanent and ready fighting force for the defense of the Masai nation.

A Masai warrior kraal. (Courtesy of Alan H. Jacobs.)

Masai elders lead the young warriors in a dance around the special "ritual house" or *osinkira* during the head-shaving ceremony. (Courtesy of Alan H. Jacobs.)

While on active service in the warrior kraals the young men are not expected to engage in any menial work, and they are therefore attended by a body of young women who work for them. These also serve as their mistresses, for no man is permitted to marry or own cattle while serving in a warrior kraal, since this might reduce his willingness to dedicate himself to the nation on the battlefield. In view of the historical dominance of the Masai, the prime activity of the warrior kraals has historically centered on cattle-rustling raids directed against non-Masai tribes, sometimes as far away as the Coast, the object of which was loot rather than slaughter. But should the Masai be threatened by a powerful alliance of enemies, it is always possible for them to marshal several thousand youthful warriors all anxious for combat and fame, at no more than a moment's notice.

In preparation for a preplanned raid the warriors, who are at all times restricted to a diet of milk, beef, and cow's blood, gorge themselves on beef for several days, believing that the meat will build up their reserves of energy. They then smear their bodies with fat and colored dye, donning a headdress of ostrich feathers and attaching to their legs tufts of long black hair taken from the colobus monkey. Since no warrior is allowed to own cattle, each gives the cattle that he is able to capture to his father.

Masai warriors are renowned for their proud bearing and haughty demeanor. They carry elliptical shields, which are covered with oxhide and display clan or age set symbols, heavy spears with flat leaf-shaped blades of iron, and wooden clubs or knobkerries. Surprisingly the Masai refused to use firearms when these first appeared due to the ritual significance of their traditional weapons, which had served their ancestors so well in the past. These iron weapons were prized, in fact revered, as being possessed of magical powers, because of their superiority over the stone spears of old. They

are still made by an inferior caste of smiths (*Ilkunona*) who maintain few cattle of their own and are dependent upon the products of the forge for their livelihood. Metalsmiths are regarded with awe for their alleged supernatural abilities, but at the same time they are despised for not being warriors and cattle owners. As a result, the smiths form a quite separate endogamous group with whom the ordinary Masai warrior has little social contact, seldom even attempting to seduce their womenfolk.

At the end of their military service the young men are retired by generations, but even after they have returned to civilian life and settled down in their own kraal with their own wives and cattle, the age set continues to operate as a powerful social bond, crosscutting the lineages and uniting the entire society. Thus the age sets continue to unite old soldier friends, who give each other hospitality and assistance when needed, attend the funerals of those of their number who die, and mourn their dead members for the appropriate ritual periods.

Religious Systems

Warrior kraals are given supernatural guidance in their military operations by the *oloiboni*, a ritual expert who uses magic and divination to forecast the success of intended raids. But military plans are not left entirely to magical preparations: the Masai maintain an efficient network of spies among their neighbors, who keep them informed of all that goes on around them.

For ritual dances and other special occasions such as cattle-rustling raids, the Masai men adorn themselves with feather headdresses reminiscent of those worn by early Indo-Europeans in the Aegean 3000 years ago, from which the Greek and Roman crest and medieval European plumed helmets were derived. At other times Masai clothing is very simple, comprising only a calfskin wrapped around the buttocks, a larger ox hide for the elders, and goatskin aprons for the women, one of which is hung round the hips, the other thrown over the shoulder.

Ritual and religion come under the direction of another ritual expert, the *Laibon,* an hereditary official whose clan, the *Laiser,* also provides the shamans. The Laibon has only advisory authority, but being backed by the weight of religion and respected for his supernatural skills, his influence is actually very extensive. In view of the Hamito-Cushitic background of the Masai, some writers have commented on the resemblances between the office of Laibon and that of the Chief Priest of the Israelites, as well as between the Laiser clan and that of the Israelite Levite clan.[5]

Both the Nuer and Masai share certain cultural traits derived from a common Cushitic or Hamitic heritage. Comparisons have also been made between the *impi,* or warrior regiments, of the Zulu of South Africa and the age groups which the Masai share with Nuer, Galla, and so many other Nilotic and Hamitic peoples. Although it is easy to make unwarranted assumptions, and research must proceed with caution, the example of Africa shows that there is a pressing need for much more work to be done in historical anthropology before we can ever hope to understand the nature of contemporary societies.

Neighboring Pastoral-Horticultural Economies

While the Masai have maintained a purely pastoral economy, backed by religious sanctions, other East African peoples with a similarly pastoral economy, like the Bakitara,

[5] The similarities between certain culture traits of the Masai and those of various Hamitic and Semitic peoples are mentioned, among other writers, by C. Daryll Forde, *Habitat, Economy and Society* (New York: E. P. Dutton & Co., Inc., 1963), p. 300, but many anthropologists question the extent to which such parallels may be regarded as evidence of Hamitic incursions into Sub-Saharan Africa.

superimposed themselves upon an original Bantu-speaking millet-growing population, retaining their own cattle-herding traditions and establishing themselves as an upper caste over the horticulturalists. Semidivine kings live in fortified kraals while freemen tend the cattle and horticulture is relegated to the descendants of the aboriginal hoe cultivators who live next to their fields in small beehive huts made from grass. The semifeudal caste system is strongly reminiscent of the relationship between the Scythians and the indigenous cultivators in the European steppes during the first millennium B.C., and of the relationship between the Celts and the pre-Celtic people in western Europe around the same time. However, this represents a different stage in the story of the evolution of our modern world, which will be dealt with in a later chapter.

THE TODAS OF SOUTH INDIA

One weakness which must always handicap a relatively young science like anthropology is the temptation to oversimplify. Man is a very complex physicochemical organism, and the human brain is capable of initiating an almost infinite variety of responses to differing stimuli. In consequence, human culture may be equally complex and diverse. While it is entirely scientific to postulate general principles of social behavior, real life situations involve such a variety of causal forces that no anthropological generalization can be expected to apply universally in an unmodified and constant form. The true challenge for the ethnologist is the problem of explaining how exceptions to the expected patterns of behavior arise. Our ecological-evolutionary analysis is not invalidated by the discovery of societies which do not really fit into the evolutionary scheme, providing we are able to explain how such exceptions arise and why they differ from the expected pattern.

FIG. 42   THE TODAS

The Todas are a polyandrous buffalo herding people who live in the Nilgiri uplands of Southern India.

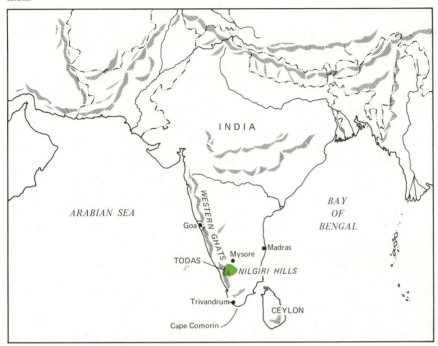

General Characteristics

One of the most unusual pastoral societies, which seems to differ in many ways from the simple pastoral societies we have just described, is that of the Todas of the Nilgiri Hills in southern India.[6] The Todas are an autochthonous people who inhabit an area of undulating hills in the interior of the southern part of the Indian subcontinent some 6000 feet above sea level. The Toda language, like that of most southern Indian people, is of Dravidian origin, but physically the Todas differ from the majority of South Indian Dravidian-speakers in their lighter complexion, coarse heavy beards, extensive body hair, and relatively tall stature. The shape of the head and of the fleshy parts of the body suggests the possibility of a partially Australoid origin. Largely isolated in the past, they still refuse to practice horticulture and depend almost entirely on dairy produce obtained from their herds of water buffalo, supplemented only by a quantity of wild fruit, berries, bamboo shoots, thistles, and nettles, and some grain and vegetables obtained from their neighbors, the agricultural Badagar. Around their all-important herds of water buffalo they preserve an elaborate religious cult which dominates almost every aspect of their material and social life.

[6] This description is based primarily upon W. H. R. Rivers' classic description entitled *The Todas* (London: Macmillan Company, 1906), describing the Todas before the impact of missionaries had seriously disrupted their lives. An updated account of the Todas is contained in D. G. Mandelbaum, "Cultural Change among the Nilgiri Tribes," *American Anthropologist* 43:19–26 (1941).

Like other pastoralists the Todas are strongly patriarchal, but instead of being polygynous and permitting a man to possess several wives, they practice polyandry, following a marital tradition under which several brothers customarily share a single wife. In addition, far from being warlike, they are a peaceful people, possessing only a few crude clubs and employing models of bows and arrows only as ceremonial equipment.

The Toda lack of militarism can be readily explained. Anyone who is acquainted with the water buffalo knows that it is a ponderous animal which is so slow-moving that the thought of buffalo rustling is quite farcical. As the objective for livestock rustling raids, the buffalo can hardly rank highly, for the surprise

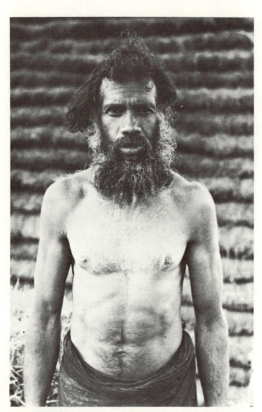

A Toda priest, showing the slightly Australoid cast of the Toda features. (Courtesy of Susanta Chatterjee.)

hit-and-run attacks so characteristic of cattle and sheep raiding would be impracticable. While it is impossible to make any historically verifiable statements about the earlier relations between the Todas and their agricultural neighbors, time seems to have consolidated these into a pattern of peaceful coexistence. Not only do the Todas have nothing to fear from their Badagar neighbors, but the Badagar even pay them an annual tribute in the form of plant produce. Again the circumstances under which this tribute originated are unknown, but the Badagar declare that the Todas were the original occupants of the land and that the tribute is paid to keep their goodwill, for they fear Toda sorcery. In short, it seems that they prefer to seek the friendship of the Todas rather than risk magically-induced droughts, crop disease, and famine.

The explanation of Toda polyandry is possibly even simpler. Toda society emphasizes patriarchalism to the extent that women are regarded as ritually unclean, like corpses. Not only are women forbidden to attend religious ceremonies, but they are kept well away from the prized buffalo herds at all times. Indeed, they are not even permitted to cross the paths that the buffalo use, and are obliged to enter and leave the village by special routes so that they will not contaminate the world of buffalo and men. Since the Toda men consequently milk the buffalo themselves, women are economically unproductive, being restricted to housework and to the production and rearing of children. In short, the Toda regard women as an expensive luxury, and in their preoccupation with male interests they must have discovered early that one woman can adequately serve the needs of an entire family of men. From the masculine viewpoint, the idea of sharing a single wife among a group of brothers represents an intelligent rationalization of resources. The uneconomic surplus of unwanted women is eliminated by female infanticide.

Social Structure

The Todas preserve a creation myth which reveals how the god *On* brought a large herd of buffalo from out of the earth, following which his wife also created an even larger herd of buffalo. Following the buffalo brought by On, a man came holding onto the tail of the last animal in the herd. This man was the first Toda. The first female Toda was created from one of this man's ribs, and as man and wife they became ancestors of all the Toda tribe. It fell to the privilege of the Todas to become stewards over both herds of buffalo, as a result of which the Todas have ever since regarded themselves as superior to all other men.

But within the Toda tribe there are two major divisions, known to anthropologists as *moieties,* for the herd of buffalo created by On is regarded as sacred, whereas that created by On's wife is not sacred. Consequently, those who serve as stewards to the sacred buffalo descended from On's herd are known as Tarthars and are regarded as superior to those who care for the buffalo descended from the herd created by On's wife, who are named Teivali. Members of the Tarthar moiety do not intermarry with the Teivali.

The Toda social system revolves primarily around household and clan. All Todas belong to one single tribe, but there is no chief, and tribal affairs are managed by a council of five men, appointment to which is hereditary in particular clans. The authority of this tribal council is restricted to mediation in disputes between clans, families, and individuals and to decisions regarding the proper conduct of religious ritual. In general, however, the Toda are a pacific people among whom murder and theft are unknown, and most disputes amount to offenses against ritual traditions concerning the care of the buffalo, which regulate virtually every aspect of daily life.

The material culture of the Todas is relatively undeveloped. For shelter they build small thatched huts, comprising a barrel-shaped thatched roof standing directly on the ground, with vertical end walls made from planks of wood. These huts have no windows. Inside, the earth is smeared with wet buffalo dung which provides a smooth, hard floor surface when dry.

Toda custom prescribes that the milk from sacred buffalo must be processed in sacred dairies which are small conical thatched huts constructed some distance from the ordinary village houses. A special order of dairymen-priests is responsible for manufacturing dairy products from the milk of the sacred buffalo, and no one may consume the milk taken from the sacred herd before it has been ritually processed into ghee or butter by one of these priests. On the other hand, the milk of an ordinary buffalo may be processed by any male member of the Toda tribe.

The polyandrous family

Newborn female babies which are surplus to the social requirement are placed in the buffalo pens to be trampled to death by the sacred animals. Thus the convenient elimination of the unwanted female children takes the form of a sacrifice. Because of the resultant scarcity of females, marriage is normally arranged while girls are still only one or two years old. Since all the members of a Toda village belong to the same clan, wives must be found from neighboring villages. The simple marriage negotiations are made by the two fathers. No bride price is payable, but a small gift may be made. Once the marriage has been arranged, the affianced usually remains with her parents until she reaches the age of puberty, but receives periodic gifts of clothing from her future husband.

Before a girl reaches puberty, it is customary for members of her own clan to have intercourse with her. This familiarity will continue until some months after puberty when she leaves the village to join her husband. Al-

A typical though rather large Toda house, with the housewife standing in front of the main door opening. (Courtesy of Susanta Chatterjee.)

though there is no formal wedding ceremony on this occasion, the bridegroom and his brothers will be feasted by the bride's family. Because neither the bride nor the bridegroom are consulted at the time of the betrothal, each is entitled to cancel the arrangement, but this seldom happens, since both have learned to look forward to the event from their earliest childhood days.

In her husband's hut, a wife shares her life not just with her husband but with all of his brothers. Although Toda huts contain only a single room, when one of the brothers wishes to associate with the communal wife, he merely leaves his cloak and wooden staff leaning against the outside of the hut as an indication that he is engaged inside. Marital rights are enjoyed equally by all the brothers of the household, and it would be literally irreligious for one brother to dispute with another over such privileges.

When a child is born, no attempt is made to determine biological paternity, since the absence of any concept of individualism among groups of brothers renders this meaningless. However, as a social convention a father must be appointed, and this will normally be the eldest brother. In order to give public confirmation of the legitimacy of the expected child, the brother who has been chosen to serve as the child's father makes a crude facsimile of a bow and arrow and publicly presents it to the wife before the conclusion of her pregnancy.

Under normal circumstances childbirth takes place in the family hut, and after a short period of postnatal seclusion in a special woman's hut, mothers rear their children in the tightly packed little household. Male children are prepared for their adult role by being given toy buffalo to play with. Girls at an early age learn to assist their mother with sweeping, mending clothes, and carrying water.

Toda childhood seems to be a happy experience. Parents are indulgent, and since all the adult members of the village belong to the same clan, they are regarded as uncles and aunts, and treat the child much as though it were their own.

Wife hiring

The Todas place no value upon sexual exclusiveness, and as we have seen, a woman loses her virginity prior to puberty. By the time she is married, she will have experienced sexual relations with a number of males, and usually knows how to handle men effectively. Due to the vagaries of life in an unsophisticated society, however, a high proportion of Toda women die in childbirth, and because girls are usually betrothed soon after birth, widowers may find it impossible to find a fresh wife immediately. As a result, a system of *consort-mistresses* has been developed, whereby a group of brothers may agree to lend their wife to a wealthy widower and his brothers in return for an appropriate payment. All children produced as a result of such arrangements belong to the lineage of the official husband and not to the borrower. Such cohusbands merely visit the household periodically whenever they wish to claim their privileges, or if the payment is sufficiently substantial, it may be agreed that the wife will leave her husband's house and take up residence in that of the cohusband for long periods at a time.

An even more formalized solution for a widower—and in polyandrous societies it is a statistical probability that widowers will greatly outnumber widows—is to purchase a wife from among those already married. In such cases, if the girl's father and the council of elders agree to the arrangement, a wealthy widower may purchase a wife from an impoverished group of brothers for an agreed number of buffalo. In this way the widower solves the problem of finding a wife, while the ex-husbands now find themselves in an improved economic condition and have only to negotiate a fresh child marriage and wait patiently until the affianced girl is old enough to assume her marital responsibilities.

In reality, the life of the Toda women is not too severe. Their contentment shows itself in their demeanour, which is generally passive but reveals an air of goodwill and satisfaction. Since the menfolk carry out most of the important economic functions, the Toda housewife merely has to sweep the tiny hut, clean and repair the few clothes that the men use, and prepare the food. Since she will nurse her children for several years, she is unlikely to produce more than three or four offspring during the course of her life; consequently she has a considerable amount of leisure time which she spends curling and greasing her hair and adorning herself with ornaments. The Toda woman is never left without a husband, and lonely spinsterhood is unknown. Although socially subordinate, Toda women are fairly

A Toda being greeted by his wife, who shows her respect by lowering her head to touch his feet. (Courtesy of Susanta Chatterjee.)

self-assured in their ability to handle masculine whims. While they never challenge the traditional authority of the menfolk, they are able to express their views with frankness on all matters which are not taboo to them. In short, the Toda household may be regarded as one large happy family.

Property, ritual, and religion

Property ownership among the Todas is quite simple. Land and dairies belong communally to the clan. Each clan owns several villages, for as the seasons change it becomes necessary for them to move their buffalo from lowlands to highlands and vice versa. The house sites and the buffalo belong to individual families, while men and women own their own clothing, ornaments, and other small personal possessions. Inheritance is through the male line, all sons taking an equal share in the household possessions. Grandsons inherit any portion due to their father, should he die first. Since brothers normally live together, there is no need to subdivide the herd of buffalo inherited from their father, but if the circumstances necessitate a subdivision of the household, the herd is divided equally, except that the eldest and youngest son receive an extra animal each. Since the Todas recognize the lending and borrowing of property, debts are inherited by the sons along with the rest of their inheritance.

The Todas believe in a large number of nature gods and spirits which are said to have inhabited the Nilgiri Hills prior to the arrival of the Toda ancestors. These gods herd spirit buffalo to spirit dairies situated in the more remote mountain peaks, and it is believed that they punish breaches of ritual and custom. The Toda religion therefore revolves around the dairyman-priesthood, with the dairies of the Tarthar clans serving as temples. When a Toda visits another village, his first action is to visit the sacred dairy for worship and prayer.

From the moment a Toda crawls out of his hut and raises his hand to his forehead to salute the sun, the daily routine is punctuated by recitations and ritual. Each day of the week has its own special religious function, and one day of every week is set aside for rest in the manner of the Christian Sabbath. Thus, there are days on which the household equipment should be cleaned, on which clothes should be washed, on which people should bathe, and on which name-giving and marriage festivals should take place.

Breaches of ritual and violations of the sanctity of the sacred dairy by unauthorized persons require lengthy ceremonies to cleanse both the individual and the site from impurity. Although the Toda are dependent for subsistence upon dairy produce, they never eat buffalo meat except in token quantities on sacrificial occasions. Nevertheless, after sacrifices the meat may be traded for plant produce with the neighboring cultivators, thus reflecting an attitude similar to that of the Arunta who refuse to eat the meat of totemistic animals but do not object to members of other clans killing and eating the totem animal.

In addition to the dairyman-priests, the Todas also recognize diviners, sorcerers, and medicine men whose ability to manipulate the supernatural is regarded as hereditary. In cases of sickness a medicine man may be called in to work a magical cure or to invoke the aid of the gods by the repetition of age-old formulas. When other misfortunes strike, a diviner may be called in to determine the cause of the trouble, which could be either sorcery or a breach of ritual. Should a man enter a sacred dairy immediately after having had sexual intercourse, he could incur the wrath of the gods, and a diviner will advise him to propitiate the gods by making the appropriate sacrifice of one or more of his buffalo. However, atonement may sometimes be achieved by merely dedicating the animal to the gods instead of actually slaughtering it. Animals thus dedicated may be kept with the herd and may be milked by the owner until they die a natural death.

Ill luck is a more serious problem when the diviner declares it to be a product of sorcery. Sorcerers usually only work harm upon those who have harmed them. When this happens, they obtain a piece of hair or some other symbol of their intended victim, and after binding it into a small parcel with a number of small stones, to the accompaniment of the appropriate magical incantations, they hide the fetish in the thatch of the victim's house. Toda sorcerers are greatly feared, but should the victim be able to determine the identity of the sorcerer through the services of the diviner, he can have the spell removed if he is able to assuage the sorcerer by appropriate gifts.

Cultural Conservation

A study of Toda culture leaves the impression that it is an attenuated survival of an older, more rational system, the meaning of which has been largely lost, although the form survives. There can be no doubt that the form of ritual is rigidly preserved, but the prayers and recitations seem to be an involved, almost unintelligible repetition of ritual words by a people who slavishly imitate the traditional formulas used by their parents without understanding their meaning.

W. H. R. Rivers, who studied the Todas before their culture had undergone substantial modification through contact with the British, believed that the Toda culture represented a degenerate survival from a more elaborate cultural tradition,[7] possibly acquired by cultural

---

[7] This observation reflects the "diffusionist" viewpoint of W. H. R. Rivers as incorporated in his original ethnography. The implication of "cultural deterioration," in particular, was subsequently criticized by "particularist" writers of the Boasian school. The current revival of interest in diffusionism, as a result of the continued accumulation of archeological evidence for cultural decay in many societies, has also revived interest in a more cautious form of Rivers' diffusionism.

diffusion. However, Toda life is so fully integrated in all its aspects that the Todas have shown a marked resistance to modernization. While the more sophisticated Hindu agriculturalists of the surrounding countryside have in many cases succumbed to the chaos of modernization, the Todas have shown a strong tendency to adhere to their own way of life and to reject alien ideas which are incompatible with it. The pleasant climate of the Nilgiri Hills attracted many English and Eurasian settlers during the long period of British rule in India, and the Todas consequently received more than an average exposure to Western cultural traditions. However, the Toda culture remained fundamentally intact during the period of British rule in India.

Throughout the British Empire the imperial authorities generally pursued a policy of noninterference with the cultural and religious customs of the diverse people over whom they ruled, although the ethics of Christian religion led them to prohibit many practices such as headhunting and infanticide. The one vital element in Toda culture to be prohibited was female infanticide, and under British imperial rule the percentage of females in Toda society eventually rose to match the male population. Despite this trend the Todas still refused to abandon their polyandrous tradition in favor of monogamy, and a form of polyandrouspolygyny developed, under which several brothers shared several wives.

The only other major incursion into Toda tradition under British rule was the arrival of Christian missionaries, whose activities were not always encouraged by the British administration. When the missionaries early found that they were unable to achieve any success in India in their attempt to convert caste Hindus, they directed their attention to the conversion of the more primitive, non-Hindu tribal people. A number of Todas were accordingly converted to Christianity, tending to disrupt the framework of Toda society and leading to the establishment of a number of separate Christian villages detached from the rest of the Todas. However, the main attack on Toda culture came only after the Independence of India in 1947 when Western-educated politicians, inspired by Utopian ideals and a new nation-building spirit, attempted to integrate all non-Hindus into the main stream of Indian society. Accusing the British of having treated the Todas and other tribal people as museum pieces, the Indian government has made strenuous efforts since Independence to destroy the cultural separateness of the non-Hindu tribal people, while at the same time attacking aspects of the Hindu tradition which would retard the introduction of what they hope would be a more egalitarian, socialist society. Schools, traveling cinema shows, and the constant intervention of agents of the central and state governments have managed to produce a new generation of more outward-looking Toda youth. In consequence, it is no longer possible to regard the Toda as an independent society, still preserving their ancient traditions. The Todas are becoming inevitably caught up in the turmoil of social and cultural change which pervades the Indian scene today.

For Further Reading

Coon, C. S., 1961, *Caravan: The Story of the Middle East.* New York: Holt, Rinehart and Winston, Inc.

Evans-Pritchard, E. E., 1940, *The Nuer.* New York: Oxford University Press.

————, 1951, *Kinship and Marriage among the Nuer.* New York: Oxford University Press.

Fage, J. D., and R. A. Oliver, 1970, *Papers in African Prehistory.* New York: Cambridge University Press.

Forde, C. D., 1963, *Habitat, Economy and Society.* New York: E. P. Dutton & Co., Inc.

Hafez, E. E., 1962, *The Behaviour of Domestic Animals.* Baltimore: The Williams & Wilkins Company.

Herskovits, M. J., 1926, "The Cattle Complex of East Africa", *American Anthropologist* 28:230-62.

Imanishi, Kinji, 1954, *Nomadism: An Ecological Interpretation.* Kyoto: University Research Institute of Humanistic Science, 466–479.

Klima, George, 1970, *The Barabaig: East African Cattle Herders.* New York: Holt, Rinehart and Winston, Inc.

Leakey, L. S. B., 1930, "Some Notes on the Masai of Kenya Colony," *Journal of the Royal Anthropological Society* 60:186–209.

Murdock, G. P., 1959, *Africa: Its Peoples and Their Culture History.* New York: McGraw-Hill, Inc.

Myres, John L., 1941, "Nomadism," *Journal of the Royal Anthropological Institute of Great Britain and Ireland* 71:19–42.

Rivers, W. H. R., 1967, *The Todas.* New York: Humanities Press, Inc.

Stamp, L. D., 1961, *A History of Land Use in Arid Regions.* Paris: UNESCO.

Thomson, J., 1885, *Through Masai Land.* London: Sampson, Low & Co.

Ucko, P. J., and G. W. Dimbleby, 1969, *The Domestication and Exploitations of Plants and Animals.* Chicago: Aldine Publishing Company.

Zeuner, Friedrich E., 1963, *A History of Domesticated Animals.* New York: Harper & Row, Publishers.

CHAPTER 27

Advanced Pastoralists

Advanced pastoral societies may be distinguished from the simple pastoral societies described in the last chapter by the possession of domesticated animals which have been trained for use as transportation. Although sheep and goats can be effectively herded on foot and even small herds of cattle can be managed without the aid of riding animals, large herds of faster animals can only be successfully tended if the herdsmen have learned to ride animals themselves. Also, larger herds need to graze over much broader tracts of country, and with a seasonal change of climate they may also need to migrate over much greater distances. Societies which wish to enjoy greater economic security by maintaining larger herds of animals will therefore need to incorporate the art of riding in their cultural tradition.

Associated with the riding of animals is the idea of using animals for baggage-carrying purposes. Clearly, a pastoral society whose members have to carry everything that they own on their backs will be confined to a rela-

tively impoverished material culture by the strict baggage limitations that this entails. On the other hand an animal which can be ridden can also be trained to carry baggage, and most advanced pastoralists possess both riding animals and pack animals which can be used to carry tents, furniture, and as much baggage as may be needed. Not content with training animals to carry pack saddles, however, the early pastoralists of Asia soon learned to train their animals to pull sledges. With the invention of the wheel, two-wheeled chariots and four-wheeled wagons appeared on the steppes, and covered wagons were used as portable homes by the Scythians, Mongols, and several other steppeland dwellers.

General Characteristics

Advanced pastoralists therefore differ from simple pastoralists in a variety of ways. Generally speaking, their larger herds provide them with a higher standard of living and greater economic security. In addition, the fact that

Baggage animals make it possible for advanced pastoralists to carry with them the materials with which to erect effective shelters, even when living in temporary camps. Seen above are tents made from woven vegetable fibers in the French Sudan. (Courtesy of La Documentation Française, Paris.)

they are able to accumulate very substantial quantities of material possessions means that they can enjoy greater comfort. Although many advanced pastoralists possess permanent houses which they use during the winter months, they may use elaborate tents or even portable huts when trekking with their animals during the grazing season.

Because the possession of riding animals extends the effective range of social contact, advanced pastoral societies usually embrace a larger number of communities than is the case with simple pastoralists, horticulturalists, fishing peoples, or hunting and gathering bands. Although the size of the individual community remains fairly small because of the need to disperse widely during the grazing season, advanced pastoral communities are able to maintain fairly frequent contact with each other. The total size of the society, enjoying a fairly uniform cultural tradition, may number several thousand families grouped in a hundred or more communities.

Most advanced pastoralists develop a keen interest in the selective breeding and genetic improvement of their animals. This concern may arise from the fact that after the breeding season vast herds can be grazed on the summer pasture, but with the coming of autumn and the need to retire to winter pastures in which the food supply is inadequate to support such large numbers of livestock, it is customary to slaughter the weaker animals in order to reduce the herd to match the seasonal reduction in food supply. By selectively weeding out those which look less able to withstand the rigors of winter, the herders are in effect introducing a form of artificial selection, which may be unintentional at first but later becomes deliberate.

Because of the need for incisive and authoritative control of their large herds, the kinship units of advanced pastoralists are generally organized in extended families under the direction of a patriarch whose orders must be obeyed explicitly. Despite the vast distances which may separate clans and tribes, making direct rule by tribal chiefs impracticable, ad-

The lives of advanced pastoralists are built around the care of their animals, for whom they frequently develop a very real affection. Portrayed above is an Arab and his riding camel, from the Republic of Mali, on the borders of the Sahara Desert. (Courtesy of La Documentation Française, Paris.)

vanced pastoral clans belonging to the same tribe, and even tribes belonging to the same society, have frequently been known to unite under a charismatic clan chieftain to embark on ambitious and far-reaching campaigns of loot, plunder, and conquest. Not only did Indo-European pastoralists extend themselves into Iran, Anatolia, and Central Europe, but the exploits of the Ural-Altaic speaking Turks, Huns, and Mongols are also well known in history. Indeed, the attractiveness of raiding operations often leads to the appearance of semipermanent, mobile war bands. Just as the Nuer and Masai of Africa both maintained warrior associations, so the chieftains of the advanced pastoralists of Asia normally main-

tained bodies of mounted and well-armed young men of heroic and noble descent who lived permanently at the chieftain's house ready to take up arms at a moment's notice.

As would be expected under such conditions, the blood feud is common, and fierce legal disputes may develop between families, lineages, and even entire clans, for systems of public law have not yet appeared. Clan and tribal chieftains are normally part-time officials who are self-supporting. However they sometimes receive a larger allotment of summer grazing lands. This enables them to maintain bigger herds, which can be cared for by slaves. Although there is seldom any system of economic redistribution to support clan officials, a redistribution of animals is sometimes made to aid the members of a clan who have lost their herds through disease or theft by rival tribesmen.

The Emergence of Ritual Stratification and Caste Systems

Since the mobility provided by riding animals facilitates sudden cattle and sheep raids, a family may lose its entire herd as a result of a single night raid by the members of another tribe. Disease may also decimate the family herd. Inequalities in the wealth of individual clans and families are far more common among advanced pastoralists than among simple foot-herders. The willingness of the more fortunate to assist the less fortunate by a redistribution of animals, characteristic of the Tungus, is less marked among the Kazaks because the possession of larger herds creates opportunities for the employment of prop-

ertyless wage earners and slaves. Hereditary slavery is also very common among advanced pastoralists. Despite the example of the more impoverished reindeer-herding Tungus, advanced pastoral societies are usually more heavily stratified than simple pastoral or other societies so far described.

Not only do the economic circumstances contribute to the introduction of slavery and to inequalities of wealth among the freemen, but it would seem that the idea of stock-breeding places an ideological emphasis on the concept of inherited qualities. Many advanced pastoralists consequently become "blood" conscious and carry over the idea of selective animal breeding into human life, choosing their wives only from pedigreed "proven stock." Keeping careful record of their genealogies, aristocracies arise which pride themselves not only on the size of the herds driven by their slaves but also on the heroic deeds of their ancestors. When these aristocracies separate themselves genetically from the rest of the

The grassy steppelands of Asia have provided man with an age-old highway between the East and West. Today the Trans-Siberian Railway replaces the caravans known to Marco Polo. This photograph shows a Kazak woman waiting at the railway station at Arys in Kazakstan for the train to Tashkent. (Courtesy of Musée de l'Homme, Paris.)

population by selective mating practices, the society acquires a castelike structure. In such cases the members of the same kinship group are no longer necessarily regarded as equals in status, and the more senior lineages, able to claim closer descent from the ancestral heroes, become socially preeminent.

Although advanced pastoralists are seldom literate, their interest in genealogies and in the deeds of their ancestors usually leads to the development of a sophisticated oral literature. This will comprise songs and epic legends which are learned by heart, even though they may extend to thousands of verses.

In consequence of their elitist philosophy, ancestor worship is also common in pastoral societies. However, because of the wide social contacts which horse-riding people are able to maintain over extensive areas, ancestor worship may succumb to universalist missionary religions, such as that of Islam. Whether their religion is based upon ancestor worship or on a universalist missionary religion, the nomadic habits of advanced pastoralists discourage the construction of elaborate religious shrines. This in turn militates against the emergence of an organized bureaucratic priesthood, and most religious ritual usually remains under the direction of the patriarchal family head. Such professional religious specialists as do exist are mostly itinerant magicians, preachers, and prophets, who attempt magical cures or who claim to reveal the divine will by dreams, vision, and hallucinatory experiences, for which they usually receive some kind of economic reward.

Historical Background

For thousands of years the grass-covered steppelands of Central Asia have served as a corridor linking Europe to the distant centers of human settlement in eastern Asia. Starting from the rich "black earth" of the Ukraine in Europe and extending through Turkistan and Kazakhskaya in Central Asia, crossing the Tien Shan and Altai mountain ranges by way of the Dzungarian Gates and skirting past the Gobi Desert, these grasslands finally reach the fertile valley of the Yellow River of China (see Fig. 43).

At the western extremity of this grassland corridor, the rich Ukrainian soil, amply watered by rainfall, is ideal for cultivation. As the steppes extend eastward, the rainfall becomes less reliable and the soil becomes poorer, so that the steppelands adjacent to the Gobi Desert are but sparsely covered with grass. Nevertheless, stretching the entire width of Asia and bordered by the high mountains of Persia, Afghanistan, and Tibet to the south and by the coniferous forests of Siberia to the north, this corridor is ideally suited to the development of pastoral economies. Probably the earliest advanced pastoralists were to be found in the European and West Asian steppes where Caucasoid, Indo-European-speaking, horse-riding pastoralists once herded vast numbers of cattle, while draft oxen pulled four-wheeled carts containing their household effects. Then in Central Asia a similar pattern of steppeland pastoralism emerged among the Uralic-speaking peoples, concentrating on sheep instead of cattle because of the poorer soil. In the East Asian steppes a purely Mongoloid people known as the Mongols herded sheep on foot until they acquired horses and cattle and the wheeled wagon from the west and also became typical steppeland pastoralists.

It is now known that there were horse-riding, cattle-herding pastoralists living in the European steppes at least 7000 years ago. Cattle seem originally to have been a woodland animal and were probably first domesticated somewhere in Europe. But while the settled agriculturalists of the Danube valley kept cattle and other livestock as a part of a pattern of mixed farming, it was in the area north and northeast of the Black Sea, where the European woodlands gave way to the grass-covered steppes, that cattle herding became a way of life. Here as men learned to ride horses which were

FIG. 43 ADVANCED PASTORALISM IN ASIA

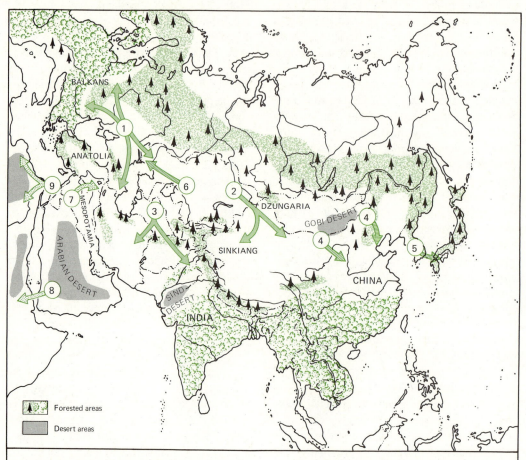

Forested areas

Desert areas

 EXPANSION OF ADVANCED PASTORAL/INDO-EUROPEAN SPEAKERS (CAUCASOIDS)/WITH HORSES CHARIOTS AND CATTLE, c. 3500-1500 B.C.

1) Enter Europe and Asia Minor, overrunning old European cultivators, to become ancestors of Greeks, Slavs, Celts, Teutons, Latins, Hittites, etc., establishing a semi-feudal hegemony over earlier cultivating populations.

2) Carry cattle, horse, and chariot complex into Central Asia (Indo-European speaking Tokharians in Sinkiang until c. 800 A.D.) Chariots and horses move on eastward into China.

3) As Iranians invade and settle Iran, c. 2000 B.C., and as Indo-Aryans invade and settle northern India, c. 1500 B.C.

 EXPANSION OF ADVANCED PASTORAL URAL-ALTAIC SPEAKERS (MONGOLOIDS), c. 1500 B.C.-1250 A.D.

4) Equipped with chariots and horses early dynasties invade and settle China, to be followed by repeated Hun, Mongol, and Manchu invasions.

5) Horse riding Japanese warriors cross from Korea to settle Japan. Although no longer pastoral, Japanese culture had early roots in Asian advanced pastoralism, c. 600 B.C.

6) Huns invade Europe c. 550 A.D. Turks invade Asia Minor c. 1050-1250 A.D. Mongols invade Middle East and India (Moghul Dynasty).

 EXPANSION OF ADVANCED PASTORAL SEMITIC SPEAKERS (CAUCASOIDS), c. 3200 B.C.-800 A.D.

7) Semites enter Fertile Crescent and establish Akkadian and Assyrian Empires, c. 3200-1800 B.C.

8) Semites enter East Africa as Tigrē and Amharic herdsmen (date unknown)

9) Arabs conquer North Africa c. 700 A.D., introducing sheep and goat herding.

native to the East European and Asian plains, advanced pastoralism had its earliest beginnings. It produced an aggressive, horse-riding warrior people who tended vast herds of horses, cattle, and sheep and used draft oxen to pull four-wheeled covered wagons containing their women and children and household effects.

It is probable that these pastoralists spoke Proto-Indo-European, a language which was to evolve into the Celtic, Italic, Germanic, Baltic, Slavic, and Greek languages, being carried by warrior clans in migrations across the length and breadth of Europe, as well as southeastward by the Iranians into Persia and by the Indo-Aryans into India. Some of these pastoralists, the Tokharians, even spread eastward over the Asian steppelands as far as Chinese Turkestan (today a part of the Peoples Republic of China) whence, mixed with the Mongoloid footherders of the eastern steppes, their descendants may have reached China.

THE SCYTHIANS

The first historical accounts which we possess of this pastoral culture are provided by the Greeks who described the fierce Scythians, a Caucasoid people who lived on the east European steppes and spoke an Indo-European language. The Scythians were a warlike people who herded their cattle and sheep on horseback, leaving all the menial tasks, such as the cultivation of the soil—for they practiced some horticulture—to slaves descended from prisoners taken in war. They appear to have been ancestor worshipers, to whom the home fire was sacred, and who swore solemn oaths at the king's hearth. Social order was maintained by the principle of the blood feud, the entire lineage or clan being responsible for the good behavior of their kinsmen.[1]

[1] For further details see T. T. Rice, *The Scythians* (New York: Frederick A. Praeger, Inc., 1957).

Scythian society was highly stratified, comprising three classes: nobles, freemen, and slaves. In addition, certain of the noble families claimed divine descent, and it was from these royal families that kings were always elected. All freemen were organized in patrilineal clans with a clan chieftain or nobleman at the head of each. Clans were normally exogamous, and a group of clans joined together under a common king constituted a tribe. The king presided over all religious rituals but also exercised considerable political power, maintaining a court and being at all times accompanied by a group of armed riders or "companions" recruited from the ranks of the warrior nobility. This mounted war band, which appears to have been parallel in function to the *hauscarls* who attended the Danish kings in tenth-century England, served the king not only out of tribal loyalty but also in a spirit of chivalry, like the knights of King Arthur's Round Table. Although every freeman served in the tribal militia in time of war, it was the king's companions who spearheaded all offensive operations and stood in permanent readiness to defend the community against surprise attacks. Whenever the Scyths were on the move, the armed tribesmen rode around the edges of their herds while the women and children of the freeman class traveled in covered wagons and the families of the slaves walked behind.

The royal household thus served as the center for the national life. As in the private household, all meals there were eaten communally, with the band of knights dining at long trestle tables while the king and his immediate family sat at a head table on a raised dais. During the day, when not engaged in war or in cattle rustling, these knights whiled away their time horse racing, hunting wild animals with trained packs of hounds, and coursing birds with falcons. Their nights were spent in gambling and romantic amours. Intoxicating drinks were popular, and bards sung heroic songs and legends, recalling mythical deeds in the tribal past.

Monogamy was the general rule, but royalty and noblemen usually kept several wives, and all noblemen seem to have kept concubines. However, these rich pastoralists were not only rank-conscious but also genealogy-conscious, believing that both luck and skill were inherited qualities. Legitimate wives were therefore carefully selected from families of the purest and most renowned lineage. Only the children of legal wives could inherit their parent's rank, and children born to concubines acquired their mother's status. If the mother were a slave, the child would be a slave; if the mother were free, the child would be free. Only if both the father and mother were of noble descent would the child be awarded noble status.

In time, many Scythians established themselves as feudal lords over settled villages of cultivators. These lived in fortified hill-top castles, protected by earthworks and a wooden palisade, while the commoners resided in villages of timber, daub, and thatch at the bottom of the hill. Although the more settled Scythians controlled large agricultural estates worked by slaves, they retained their herds, and cultivation remained a despised pursuit, inferior in status to the herding of cattle.

Royal Burials

The Scythian funeral rituals were particularly impressive. When a king died, he was buried under a great *barrow,* or burial mound, with his favorite horses and servants and other possessions. His favorite wives also committed suicide and were buried with him. Furthermore, 50 or 60 of his warrior-companions, selected from among the knights of his court, were strangled, their bodies being mounted on horses killed and stuffed for the occasion, and set up in a ring around the burial mound.[2] Then, as darkness fell, the remainder of the warrior-knights rode around the barrow by torchlight, chanting heroic songs in a final dramatic farewell to their divinely descended hero-king. These lavish burials illustrate a tradition widespread among Indo-Europeans. They also reflect a curious parallel with the

[2] See M. I. Rostovtzeff, *Out of the Past of Greece and Rome* (New York: Biblo and Tannen, Inc., 1963), Chap. 1.

Detail of silver-gilt Scythian vase showing Scythian horsemen hunting a lion with hounds. (From M. I. Rostovtzeff, *Out of the Past and Present.* By permission of Yale University Press.)

lavish royal burials of ancient Sumeria, suggesting a cultural connection between the early Sumerians and the steppeland peoples to the north which is still not adequately explored.

THE TUNGUS OF SIBERIA

As we move eastward across the steppes, the soil becomes poorer, and the climatic differences between winter and summer become greater. Mixed farming becomes less profitable, and settlements inevitably give way to seasonal nomadism. Horticulture declines in importance until pastoralism becomes the only way of life. It is thus in the central Asian area, around Lake Baikal, that we still found fully developed advanced pastoral societies at the beginning of this century which provide a crude but basically similar reflection of earlier Eurasian pastoralism as represented by Scythian society. But the pastoral tradition spreads even further into Asia than the limits of the favorable steppeland. Let us first examine the lives of the Tungus of Siberia, a rather impoverished but still advanced pastoral society which depends for its existence upon herds of domesticated reindeer. From an evolutionary point of view, Tungus society reflects a much simpler pattern of social organization than is found among the more sophisticated cattle and horse herders of the richer steppelands to the west.

The Tungus, a northeastern Siberian people, whose language is related to that of the Manchus of Manchuria and belongs to the Altaic branch of the great Ural-Altaic family of languages, today combine reindeer herding with a hunting and fishing economy. Clearly Mongoloid in racial type, some 20,000 Tungus still live in eastern Siberia between Lake Baikal and the Kamchatka peninsula.[3] They drive their herds northward to the subarctic tundra during

[3] See Shirokogorov, S. M., *Social Organization of the Northern Tungus* (Shanghai: Commercial Press, 1929).

FIG. 44   THE TUNGUS

The Tungus herd reindeer in northeastern Siberia, where land temperatures vary more widely between summer and winter than almost any other part of the inhabited earth.

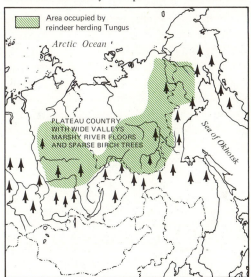

Area occupied by reindeer herding Tungus

Arctic Ocean

PLATEAU COUNTRY WITH WIDE VALLEYS MARSHY RIVER FLOORS AND SPARSE BIRCH TREES

Sea of Okhotsk

the summer to graze on lichens, willow shoots, and reed grass while they themselves hunt wild reindeer and catch fish with nets in the rivers. During these months both men and animals are tormented by mosquitoes and midges, so at night the Tungus and their reindeer gather closely around the camp fires, the smoke from which tends to keep the myriads of flying insects at bay. In winter the Tungus drive their herds south again toward the fringes of the Siberian forest belt, and then they have to build fenced compounds to protect the animals from the attacks of hungry wolf packs.

Ecological Adaptations

In the absence of rich pasturelands, the Tungus population is spread extremely thinly, and warfare and livestock raiding are made impracticable by the vast distances that separate groups from each other. In consequence, the only threat to the survival of the herd comes from wolves and from disease, both of which are sufficiently real threats, however, as entire herds are frequently decimated by predators and sickness.

The Tungus may be classified as advanced pastoralists, since although the climate is too severe for horses, they train reindeer to serve as riding and baggage animals, capable of carrying loads up to 150 pounds or more over a distance of 50 miles a day. Buck reindeer, with antlers sawed short for safety, are usually used for riding or baggage because the females are not strong enough to carry heavy loads.

A Tungus woman riding a reindeer, with a herd of reindeer in the background. This is a recent photograph, and while the costume remains essentially traditional, it will be seen that the cloth is machine-made. The tent in the background is also of a modern design, presumably having been obtained by trade. (Courtesy of the Novosti Press Agency, Moscow.)

Not content with domesticating their reindeer as riding and pack animals, the Tungus also train many of them to pull large sledges. During their migrations it is common to see a rider leading a trail of reindeer on a rope, each harnessed to a sledge similar in design to the dog sledges used by Eskimos.

During the summer the Tungus live in sturdy tents made of birchbark, fixed to a frame of sticks to make a permanent conical-shaped structure. During the winter permanent settlements are impractical because of the poor grazing available, and temporary camps are constructed of conical tents made simply of reindeer hides. Nevertheless, since they possess baggage and draft animals, the Tungus are able to accumulate a considerable quantity of material effects. In historical times they have learned how to forge iron tools from metal obtained by trade with the distant peoples of China and Russia.

The Household

The effective unit of Tungus social organization is the family household which is almost invariably monogamous. Each household normally embraces a family of three generations, dominated by the grandfather. Descent is through the male line, and in common with other pastoral peoples the Tungus are patriarchal.

Although the men assist the women in driving the herds at the time of migration, the care of the reindeer is generally regarded as a woman's work because hunting expeditions frequently take the men away from the camp for several weeks at a time. Elk, deer, wild reindeer, and bear are the main animals hunted. The Tungus rely on their bows and arrows to bring their quarry to the ground and finish the animal off with spears.

Nevertheless, the efficient care of a herd of reindeer requires more people than a single family can provide, so Tungus households usually migrate in company with two or three other families who are generally related to them by marriage. A man normally marries his mother's brother's daughter, in the pattern known to anthropologists as cross cousin marriage.

Marriage and Kinship

Weddings are arranged by parents while the bride and bridegroom are still infants, and a bride price is paid to the parents of the bride which is raised by the members of the bridegroom's clan. No definite bride price, or *turi* as it is known, is fixed by custom, the amount varying with the social status of the families concerned. However, at the time of marriage the bride also brings with her a dowry provided by the members of her clan, which will include most of the necessities of household equipment from the tent to the kitchen utensils so that she will not represent an economic burden upon her new in-laws. Polygynous marriages occur only when the first wife proves to be barren.

Beyond the household Tungus society is organized into patrilineal exogamous clans. Each clan lays claim to a definite territory and has its own legendary ancestors and its own gods. However, the looseness of the Tungus kinship-political structure is indicated by the fact that there is no hereditary clan chieftain, and clan affairs are managed by a council which includes all the heads of households. This council can only meet during the summer months when the summer vegetation on the tundra makes it possible for separate households to come together in a clan gathering. Although there are no permanent clan officials, those who have offended against the rights of other clan members may be physically punished upon the decision of the clan council. Corporal punishment such as beating is customary and the death penalty is not uncommon. Since clans sometimes trespass on each

other's territories, clan disputes do occur. Open combat may occasionally break out, and when this happens, there is no mechanism for enforcing peace between the combatants. Only in time of war is a war chief elected from among the more respected household leaders, but prolonged conflicts are rare.

Although the individual household owns its own reindeer, the sense of clan unity is sufficiently strong to ensure a periodic redistribution of animals in order to compensate any families which may have suffered severe losses as a result of epidemics or the attacks of wolves. Within the clan the right to particular hunting and pasture land is also redistributed from time to time to suit the needs of the different households where one household has diminished in size and another has increased as a result of disparities in the birth and death rate. In short, the Tungus conception of property rights in both land and animals is based on need rather than upon the concept of individual rights. So far as the means to the production of food and wealth are concerned, families—not individuals—share in the common clan property according to their needs and to their ability to use this property. Consequently, no family is ever allowed to become totally impoverished, and the Tungus therefore have neither slaves, serfs, nor any propertyless class of wage earners.

Beyond the clan there are no true tribes in the political sense but only in the sense of an aggregate of clans linked by regular intermarriage, by territorial propinquity, and consequently by the symbolically unifying factor of a shared dialect. The importance of speech similarities in holding human groups together in the absence of more formal bonds is clearly indicated among the Tungus, and of course it is only due to periodic social contacts that these speech groups retain their unity. However, there is nothing to stop a Tungus clan from transferring its allegiance to another "tribal" group, except for the traditional marriage ties which tend to keep groups of clans together.

The social organization of the Tungus is therefore of a very simple kind, corresponding to that of a highly developed, exogamous band system. The rules of exogamy have resulted in a relationship between groups of bands or clans in which kinship rather than territory is the determining factor. However, no supraclan authority has developed, and although many writers talk about Tungus "tribes" in a general sense, there is no tribal authority to give political reality to these "tribes" which are nothing more than groups of intermarrying clans occupying loosely contiguous areas. More sophisticated and truly tribal societies tend to develop only when the ecological environment is sufficiently rich and the technology suffi-

ciently advanced to sustain a denser population, whose members will be thrown into closer interaction with each other. Such is more nearly the case with the Kazaks of the more fertile Asian steppelands.

THE KAZAKS OF THE CENTRAL ASIAN STEPPES

Although agriculture has replaced advanced pastoralism in the western steppes, the Kazaks who live adjacent to the Tien Shan mountains of central Asia still provide us with an example of steppeland pastoralism.[4]

[4] This account is largely based on C. D. Forde, *Habitat, Economy and Society* (New York: E. P. Dutton & Co., Inc., 1963).

FIG. 45   THE KAZAKS

The advanced pastoral life of the Kazaks preserves into the ethnographic present much of the ancient culture of the Scythians.

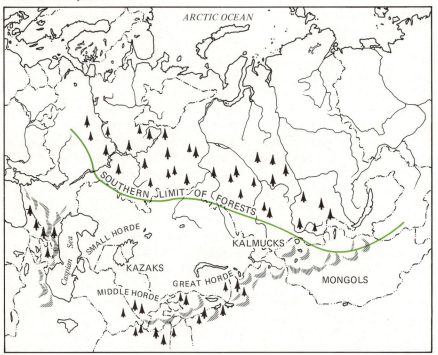

Physically, the Kazaks of today are more or less intermediate between Caucasoids and Mongoloids. They are relatively light-skinned, short in stature, and broad-headed, with prominent cheek bones. Mongolian characteristics—such as the epicanthic fold of the eye, the Mongolian spot (the patch of dark blue which appears at infancy near the base of the spine), and the Mongoloid straight, coarse hair—are common. Nevertheless, the cast of their features and the lower frequency of blood group type B suggest they are closer to the people of Europe than to those of eastern Asia. The Kazak language, a Turkic tongue, belongs to the Ural-Altaic stock and is closely related to Kalmuck in the west and less closely to the Mongol language to their east.

Culturally, the Kazaks are typical advanced pastoralists. Since the pastures of central Asia are not as rich as those of the western steppes, sheep rather than cattle are the mainstay of their economy, although they also keep substantial herds of cattle, goats, horses, and camels. While horses are an essential and prized possession—for it would be impossible to handle large flocks on foot—two-humped Bactrian camels are invaluable for the transportation of tents and other heavy baggage. With the aid of these camels the Kazaks are able to transport substantial quantities of household equipment with them when they move.

The Kazaks treat camels with great respect and carefully seek to protect them from the extremes of winter cold. But it is the horse which is their physical ideal. Since they consider the horse to be the most beautiful creature in the universe, they will compliment a woman by comparing her to a mare. Mares are used only for milking and breeding, and riding horses are almost invariably gelded since it is considered shameful to ride a mare. However, a few stallions are kept for breeding purposes and stallions dominate the Kazak herds of horses, protecting the mares and the foals against wolves and other predators.

Ecological Adaptations

Rain is sparse in the Tien Shan steppes and falls mainly in the winter, but the grass is richer than it is farther to the east in Mongolia, and in the river valleys small clumps of trees add variety to the scenery. Nevertheless, the Kazaks are obliged to migrate seasonally, for when the uplands are swept by blizzards in the winter, they provide neither food nor shelter. On the other hand, the low-lying river valleys are intolerable in the intense heat of the summer when the air is filled with flies during the day and mosquitoes at night.

Kazak winter quarters are permanent structures made from sods of turf, with a floor of trampled earth and a roof of thick branches covered first with leaves and then with a layer of turf. A hearth fire burns in the center of the room, the smoke escaping through a small hole in the roof. In many ways these vermin-infested huts are barely advanced beyond the houses built by Cro-Magnon man in the European Mesolithic. However, woven carpets of wool cover the floor, and there are windows made from the stretched membranes of animal bladders. Every nuclear family has a separate house, and with the turf and stick barns erected for the animals, a camp usually totals some 20 to 30 buildings, protected by a surrounding wall of earth mixed with animal dung. By contrast, since the summer camps are occupied for only a few days at a time the Kazaks construct only semiportable tents known as *yurts*. These are made from a light frame of wood covered with felt, and look rather like beehives, the felt being strapped down against the wind by an outer web of ropes.

The Kazak diet is very heavily oriented around meat and dairy produce, with few vegetables being eaten. During the summer especially they survive almost entirely on a menu of milk, butter, and cheese. Mare's milk is also fermented to make an intoxicating drink known as *kumiss,* which is highly nutritious.

But in autumn when the flocks are moved into the more confined *auls,* or winter settlements, large numbers of surplus animals are slain, and great quantities of meat are consumed in the ensuing months. Meals are a communal ritual for the entire family; the food is heaped on a large central plate from which everyone eats with his fingers. However, the patriarchal nature of the Kazaks again reveals itself in their eating customs, for the men dine first and the women and children eat only after the men have finished.

Although Kazaks vary their diet of animal produce with a small quantity of cultivated foods, the art of horticulture is a despised occupation which is undertaken only by paid servants and was formerly allocated to slaves before the abolition of slavery. To a small extent the Kazak diet is also supplemented by the produce of the chase, but the Kazaks hunt primarily for sport, pursuing foxes on horseback with packs of hounds in much the same way as the Indo-Europeans who entered Europe have hunted foxes, deer, and boar with hounds down to the present day. Falconry is another favorite sport which also supplies food, and the streams and rivers are fished with spears and nets, substantial catches being recorded.

Social Structure

As is to be expected in pastoral societies, the men dominate the social scene. Descent is traced through the male line, and wives leave their families to join their husband's kinsmen after marriage. The basic social and economic unit is an extended family, comprising the family head, his wife, and unmarried children, and his married sons with their wives and children. Attached to each extended family as an integral part of the household are a number of free dependents or retainers and, in former times, the slaves.

This large household is known as an *aul,* and

several *auls* together make up a clan or *taypas.* The *taypas* is the main property-owning unit and theoretically owns all herd animals and all rights to summer grazing lands and winter pastures. Each *taypas* possesses its own crest, which may have had a totemic origin, and is headed by a clan chief known as a *beg,* who arbitrates any disputes between the member families. Beyond the limits of the clan are the *sok* or phratry, which has no chief, and a rather shadowy tribe or *uruk* which has no hereditary chief. Tribal affairs are conducted by a council of clan chiefs who elect one of their members as a *bi* to preside over meetings or to lead the tribe in times of crisis. Nevertheless the pattern of social organization does not stop here. Because the extreme mobility of advanced pastoralists makes possible extensive contacts over very large areas, the ultimate Kazak social unit is a grouping of tribes known as a *horde.* The horde, however, is not so much a kinship organization, like the clan or tribe, as it is a convenient territorial-cum-political amalgam. A tribe may transfer from one horde to another, and tribal membership in any one horde is not necessarily permanent. There are three hordes in all—a Great Horde, a Middle Horde, and a Small Horde—which together make up the Kazak "nation," but which unite only to act as a concerted group under the leadership of exceptional individuals in times of great political turbulence.

Property and Social Stratification

The lands and livestock are held communally by the clan, and livestock are branded with the clan crest in the same manner that American ranchers still brand their livestock with their ranch insignia. However, there is a tendency for families to acquire an entitlement to specific animals for ecological convenience. During the winter when the Kazaks congregate along the river valleys, each household occupies its own traditional site, living in a small settlement separate from, but adjacent to, those of the other families in the clan. In these winter camps the animals are fed from hay grown in the preceding summer. But when spring comes, the winter camps are abandoned and each family treks with its own herds to summer pastures in the rolling uplands. Ample grass is then available, and in contrast to the winter quarters the summer grazing lands are not regarded as being private to any one family, although each clan lays claim to a distinct territory and no family grazes its herd outside of the clan pastures. Because of the summertime dispersal, however, individual families procure a semiproprietorial right to the animals which they herd during the summer months and to the animals born at this time. Nevertheless, the obligation to share livestock with any clan family which suffers misfortune remains an accepted part of the Kazak system.

As among other advanced pastoralists, Kazak society is stratified into castelike groupings which cut across the tribal divisions. The upper caste comprises those families which claim to be descended from Genghis Khan and other heroes of the past. It is from these elite clans that the Khans or horde leaders are elected, and genealogies are therefore kept assiduously—the legendary Genghis Khan being credited with a genealogy of aristocratic forebears extending to some 28 generations. This upper caste of nobles is known as the White Bone, a *bone* being a large kinship grouping, and the remainder of the clans are grouped together in the Black Bone, comprising a lower caste of commoners. Below these two free castes was a slave caste, comprised of persons taken captive in war. Not only are the key tribal and horde positions filled by elected members of the White Bone, but members of the noble caste enjoy privileges in the allocation of pasture lands, possessing larger and richer holdings than the commoners of the Black Bone. In consequence, they are able to maintain larger herds of sheep, cattle, and horses and are wealthier as well as politically and socially superior to members of the Black Bone.

Inequalities of wealth between different clans easily arise because of the ease with which a clan can lose its animals through war, theft, and disease. Should one family lose its livestock, other members of the clan will come to their aid and redistribute their share of the clan livestock with their kinsmen. Should an entire clan suffer severe losses, the only alternatives open to them are to attempt to recuperate their losses by successful raids against their neighbors or else to abandon the attempt to be independent and hire themselves out, family by family, as paid freemen tending the large herds of the nobles.

Militarism

Traditionally the Kazaks have long been famed for their warlike and predatory habits. No Kazak will steal from a member of his own clan; indeed, as we have seen, all major property is nominally owned by the clan. Nevertheless, sheep, horse, and cattle rustling betweens clans and tribes is a regular pastime; thus the Kazaks had to be warlike to protect their herds.

Before the introduction of firearms they were armed with bows and arrows, a long cavalry lance for horseback fighting, and a battle-axe for foot combat. Perhaps the most unusual weapon in the Kazak armory is the leather whip. These massive whips, tipped with a heavy lash, can be wielded with such efficiency by a Kazak rider as to kill a man. But unlike the Indo-Europeans who made use of the axe and the short sword and reveled in pitched battles, the Kazaks prefer to avoid formal conflicts and specialize instead in ambushes and night raids. All prisoners were formerly enslaved, but torture was unknown.

Although fierce and predatory, the Kazaks place great emphasis on hospitality, and any traveler who presents himself at a Kazak *aul* will be welcomed and will be safe until his departure. Once he has left the clan territory, however, there is nothing to stop him from being waylaid and robbed by his erstwhile hosts.

It is interesting to observe the existence of traveling metalworkers and silversmiths who do not own herds or grazing land. These small family groups of professional smiths travel continuously from one settlement to another without fear of assault, manufacturing new items of houseware and repairing older damaged tools and jewelry.

Marriage and the Family

Kazak clans are exogamous, and marriages are negotiated at an early age, usually before puberty but sometimes even before birth. All Black Bone marriages take place within the tribe, and marital arrangements are negotiated by the bride and bridegroom's male relatives. A bride price or *kalym* of up to 40 or 50 horses is usually payable, and the bride herself receives a dowry of clothing, bedding, or household equipment from her father.

The actual marriage does not take place until both the bride and bridegroom are of mature age. The *kalym* is often large, and is normally paid in two parts. Accordingly the wedding involves two ceremonies. The first of these is held at the bride's home where both the bride and bridegroom are required to hide themselves away while the guests enjoy themselves in games and feasting. Eventually, after considerable teasing, the bridegroom will be permitted to emerge and must then make an attempt to catch his bride-to-be. After a show of resistance she will allow him to carry her off to her father's tent where the marriage is consummated. These mock wedding chases and fights suggest that at some earlier times the Kazaks practiced wife capture. Even in historical times, many Kazaks were known to

A Kazak man, wearing quilted clothes and traditional fur cap. A portable *yurt* or tent can be seen in the background; the grassy plains sweep gently into the distance. (Courtesy of Musée de l'Homme.)

steal wives from the neighboring Kalmuck pastoralists.

The bride and groom are not permitted to live together until after a second ceremony, held at the bridegroom's *aul,* which will be postponed until the bridegroom has effected payment of the second part of the bride price, although he will be allowed to continue to pay nightly visits to his wife at her father's encampment. It is customary for the bride to show signs of pregnancy before the second ceremony is concluded, thus demonstrating her fertility before she goes to live with her husband. But should she develop a distaste for his company during the intervening period, she will be entitled to refuse further advances, and if her family agrees to repay the first installment of the bride price, the marriage will be cancelled.

Kazak women are responsible for the general management of household affairs, including the making of felt for the tents, the weaving of rugs, and the sewing of clothes for the entire family. They also milk the animals and prepare all food. The women occupy a position of considerable respect and are entitled at any time to divorce their husbands if they suffer cruelty or negligence; divorce is permitted at the wishes of either husband or wife. In reality, divorce is not common, but when it does occur the bride price is returned and since the children belong to their father's clan, the divorced wife must return to her own clan without them.

Inheritance is through the male line, but when the eldest son reaches manhood, he is expected to marry and set up his own household. His father will procure winter quarters for him and will also give his son a share of the family herd. As other sons grow to their majority, they may also be provided for in the same way, so that the father's wealth is steadily diminished as he is freed from his responsibilities. However, the youngest son will normally remain with his father even after his marriage in order to continue the parental household. After his father's death the remaining property will pass to him, unless there are other sons at home when it will be divided equally among them. Those older sons who have already received their share of the family wealth have no claim on the estate of their father at his death. However, a small provision is made for the widow in order to give her a degree of independence following her husband's death. Her property will also be equally distributed among her sons upon her own demise.

Upon the death of her husband, a wife who has not produced a male heir to inherit his name and property is required to marry his next younger brother in order that she may produce an heir who will carry the deceased's name. In this position she will be relegated to the position of second wife if the brother is already married, and will cease to head her own household. Rather than face this possibility, women are anxious to fulfill their duties to their husband's lineage by producing male children, for if a wife has already produced an heir before her husband's death, she is not obligated to remarry. Instead she may raise her children in her own tent, acting as a trustee of her son's affairs until he comes of age.

Great value is placed upon the birth of children and Kazaks do not practice infanticide. Abortion is also unknown except among unmarried girls. Children receive a great deal of affection and are breast-fed up until four or five years of age, even though milk is supplemented by other foods. The physical punishment of children is virtually unknown, but in the tight family circle, informal methods of social control are adequate to enforce discipline, and children consequently grow up in complete subordination to their parents. Boys and girls are groomed for their different roles in life by separate play activities, the girls playing with dolls and the boys receiving gifts of toy domestic animals and bows and arrows.

Folklore, Custom, and Religion

Like many other pastoralists, Kazaks have little use for literary skills, and although contact with Islam introduced them to the Arabic alphabet, few Kazaks can read or write. The Kazaks also have a calendar which originated in China and came to them by way of their eastern Mongol neighbors. This divides the year into 12 months, but instead of numbering the years in successive order, it recognizes a series of 12 successive years by names—years of the mouse, ox, leopard, hare, fish, serpent, horse, sheep, ape, fowl, dog, and hog—repeating the series in 12-year cycles.

Having no writing of their own, the Kazaks possess only an oral tradition of law which is best called custom. Offenses are regarded as disputes between families and clans to be settled by arbitration before a *beg*. Once a decision has been made on the basis of the testimony of witnesses as to which party is guilty, custom prescribes a range of payment for compensation of the offense. A *kun* or wergild of 100 horses or 50 camels is payable for the slaying of a freeman, one half of this amount being payable for the murder of a woman or a slave. Such payments are distributed among the relatives of the injured individual. Cattle rustling, when proven, requires the return of the stolen cattle, together with a penalty of twice the number that were stolen. Seduction is punished by the obligation to marry the seduced girl, after payment of the full bride price plus an additional penalty. Judgment in these disputes is passed only after the hearing of all testimony, but should the relatives of the party found guilty refuse to pay the composition fine to the relatives of the deceased, the

A group of Mongol women. The Mongols depend more upon sheep herding than the Tungus, since cattle do not thrive in the more severe Mongolian climate so well as in the milder climate of the West Asian steppes. (Courtesy of Musée de l'Homme.)

onus is upon the complainants to seize the equivalent value of property from the defendants. Such action is likely to be resisted and a blood feud will then result, there being no supraclan authority to enforce a settlement.

Although the Kazaks have been Moslems for centuries many memories of shamanism have survived, and itinerant *baksa* or shamans travel from one camp to another. Singing and dancing to the beat of a small tambourine held in the hands, these *baksa* work themselves into a state of frenzy, frequently injuring themselves while in conversation with spirits and demons. They also claim to be able to cure the sick by beating the prostrate patient with clubs and whips to drive out the evil spirits, and practice divination by placing the shoulder blade of a sheep in the red-hot embers of a fire, reading the future from the cracks that appeared on the bone in a widespread practice common to the Etruscans in Europe, the Chinese diviners of the Shang dynasty, and many New World hunters. This may derive from a common Upper Paleolithic tradition, evidence of the custom being found in European Upper Paleolithic sites.

Ceremonial horse races are still held, which again seem to reflect the pagan past, for the winning stallion is treated as a sacred animal, and ribbons are fixed to its mane and tail. Until recently it was also still customary to bury a man's favorite horse with him, and periodic feasts are still held in honor of the dead forebears.

Kazak customs also still retain elements of a fire worshiping tradition, often associated with ancestor worship. None may spit into the fire on the family hearth, and no fire may be blown out with human breath. An earlier belief in reincarnation is suggested by the fact that a woman who is experiencing difficulty in childbirth may be given a magic potion made with earth taken from one of the clan graves. After the birth of the first child, mothers make an offering of fat at the hearth fire as though to the ancestors of the household, and when the new bride enters her husband's *yurt* for the first time, she is expected to kneel down by the hearth fire and pour fat into the flames in honor of her husband's ancestors. This family fire must never be quenched and is treated with respect at all times. There are also traces of tree worship, certain trees being regarded as possessing spirits which should be propitiated. Barren women sometimes sacrifice sheep before a sacred tree, and an earlier paganism also expresses itself in a belief in prophetic dreams—a dream of fat body lice is believed to foretell prosperity.

For Further Reading

Barth, F., 1961, *Nomads of South Persia: The Basseri Tribe of the Khamseh Confederacy.* New York: Humanities Press, Inc. (originally published by Oslo University Press).

Czaplicka, M. A., 1914, *Aboriginal Siberia.* Oxford: Clarendon Press.

Downs, J. F., 1961, "Origin and Spread of Riding in the Near East and Central Asia," *American Anthropologist* 63 (11):1193-1203.

———, and G. S. Downs, 1971, *Nez Chi'ii: A Pastoral Community of Navajo Indians.* New York: Holt, Rinehart and Winston, Inc.

Ekvall, R. B., 1968, *Fields on the Hoof: Nexus of Tibetan Nomadic Pastoralism.* New York: Holt, Rinehart and Winston, Inc.

Forde, C. D., 1963, *Habitat, Economy and Society: A Geographical Introduction to Ethnology.* New York: E. P. Dutton & Co., Inc.

Krader, L., 1955, "Ecology of Central Asian Pastoralism," *Southwestern Journal of Anthropology* 11:301-326.

—— , 1963, *Social Organization of the Mongol-Turkic Pastoral Nomads.* Bloomington: Indiana University Press.

Maksimova, A. G., 1959, "Epokha bronzy vostochnogo Kazakhstana" ("The Bronze Age of Eastern Kazakhstan"), Akademiia Nauk Kazakhskoi S.S.R., Institut Istorii, Arkheologii, i Etnografii, *Trudy* 7:86–161.

Meakin, A. M. B., 1903, *In Russian Turkestan.* London: George Allen.

Nicolaisen, J., 1963, *Ecology and Culture of the Pastoral Tuareg: With Particular Reference to the Tuareg of Ahaggar and Ayr.* Copenhagen: National Museum.

Phillips, E. D., 1969, *The Mongols.* New York: Frederick A. Praeger, Inc.

Rice, T. T., 1957, *The Scythians.* New York: Frederick A. Praeger, Inc.

Sahlins, M. D., 1968, *Tribesmen.* Englewood Cliffs, N.J.: Prentice-Hall, Inc.

Shirokogaroff, S. M. 1929, *Social Organization of the Northern Tungus.* Shanghai: Commercial Press.

Sykes, E. C. and P. M. Sykes, 1920, *Through Deserts and Oases of Central Asia.* London: Macmillan and Co.

Zhdanko, T. A., 1963, "Semi-nomadism in the History of Central Asia and Kazakhstan," Moscow: *International Congress of Orientalists, Proceedings* 3:176–184.

CHAPTER 28

Centralized Chieftainships

In earlier chapters we have followed the course of human evolution in relation to the dominant means of subsistence. We have shown how the culture of hunters and gatherers reflects the economic necessities of their way of life. We have shown how settled horticulturalists develop a more complex culture, although there is no one particular style of life common to all horticulturalists. Indeed, as man's control of his environment grows, the number of alternative life styles tends to increase, and cultures begin to acquire their own ethos, free from a narrow dependence on ecological necessities. We have also dealt with the cultural traits characteristic of fishing societies and pastoral societies, but beyond this level of social and cultural evolution it becomes necessary to introduce a new concept that is more directly political than ecological. This is the CENTRALIZED CHIEFTAINSHIP, a situation in which a chieftain has succeeded in imposing his authority upon a number of different peoples of the primitive state.[1]

[1] The concept of centralized chieftains and the "primitive state" is discussed in Elman R. Service, *Primitive Social Organization* (New York: Random House, Inc., 1971).

Centralized chieftainships do not occur at random without appropriate ecological conditions. Purely horticultural societies seldom lead to the centralization of power in the hands of a single individual. Pastoral societies likewise generally retain a kinship structure which ensures that clan chiefs exercise their authority within limits laid down by a reciprocal system of kinship ties rather than arbitrarily on the basis of personal power. Centralized chieftainships normally arise only after a considerable degree of stratification has developed, as may be the case when advanced pastoral clans impose themselves upon settled horticultural peoples. Certainly most centralized chieftainships reveal a fairly diversified basis of subsistence and the system is not common among societies that are wholly dependent upon a single means of subsistence.

Historical Background

The record of history shows that centralized chieftainships commonly resulted from the conquest of one community by another. In the Western world the settled cultivators of Old

Europe and the Middle East were overwhelmed and subjugated by militaristic pastoral peoples, such as the Indo-European-speaking Hittites and the Semitic-speaking Assyrians. In Europe especially, a similar trend led to the establishment of a protofeudal system in which the victorious war leaders set themselves up as kings, allocating political and territorial offices to the more loyal members of their war bands. Whole villages were granted as estates to the loyal members of the conqueror's *comitatus* or band of warrior-knights; thus the village headmen who derived their authority from customary kinship bonds were replaced by "lords of the manor" ap-

pointed by the king. As a result of a constant succession of invasions and conquests from the fifth millennium to the first millennium B.C., the indigenous European cultivators were subordinated to a new horse-riding aristocracy of Indo-European warrior-nobles originally of pastoral origin, of the type portrayed in the saga of Beowulf. Serving charismatic war leaders, these warrior-knights looked forward on retirement to the grant of substantial estates as a reward for loyal service to the chieftain of their choice, in whom all effective social power was vested.

The transition to a centralized chieftainship does not mean to say that all vestiges of traditional elective systems and kinship structures disappeared overnight. No chieftain wishes to rule by fear alone because this involves a constant military effort and prevents the enjoyment of office. All successful officeholders, whether they are elected to office, inherit it, or seize it by conquest, attempt to *constitutionalize* their position by winning the willing support of those over whom they rule. The chieftain who rules rather than reigns may still validate his position by acquiring acceptance through the trappings of constitutional rule. Most centralized chieftains consequently claim a long and honorific genealogy, purporting to show descent from past heroes or even tribal gods, and ancestor worship—centering on the royal ancestors—may bestow a mantle of "divinity" on the ruler's shoulders.

Bronze Age Europe constituted a highly stratified "heroic" society, dominated by a martial aristocracy that claimed descent from semidivine heroes and gods similar to those of Homeric Greece. Pictured here are the hilts of Bronze Age swords dating from the second millenium B.C. from Schleswig-Holstein in Germany. (Courtesy of the Landesmuseum, Schloss Gottorp.)

HOMERIC GREECE

The arrival of the Indo-European-speaking Greeks in the Aegean provides an excellent example of a conquest-based centralized chieftainship. The Homeric courts of the thirteenth century B.C. are typical of the patchwork of small kingdoms which covered most of Europe prior to the rise of the Roman Empire, and spread over large areas after the collapse of

Rome, surviving in Germany until the nineteenth century.[2] Thus, in Homeric Greece all agricultural and other manual labor was undertaken by the original Pelasgian agricultural population, who continued to live in equalitarian and property-sharing villages according to the tradition of the old European agricultural system. But close by every major village was a manorial estate, granted to a member of the conquering Greek warrior-nobility by the local king.

In return for the grant of such estates, the warrior-nobility were required to serve the king loyally in time of war. They were also expected to supply at least one man to join the band of knights who lived at the royal court and constituted a permanent standing army. All justice was administered by the king who was believed to be divinely descended from one of the great heroes or from the gods themselves, and all executive decisions were made by the king-in-council, which in effect meant the king in consultation with the leading nobles. The king's rule was "constitutionalized" by referring all important decisions involving war or peace to the mass of freemen for approval. The freemen were periodically called together in the *agora*, the assembly place located in front of the king's *polis* or fortified palace, by the king-in-council to hear and approve new decisions. At such meetings, however, the freemen never debated an issue, but merely indicated their assent by a traditional shout of acclamation.

Yet, no king could hope to retain his position if he were a fool or a coward. Although each noble family held its estate only in return for the obligation to support the king in time of war, much of the king's authority was derived from his band of companions, the young warriors of noble families who wined and dined

[2] See T. D. Seymour, *Life in the Homeric Age* (New York: Biblo and Tannen, Inc., 1965), for a detailed account of life in Bronze Age Greece, which exemplifies European life at that time.

The chieftainships characteristic of Homeric society still reflected a pattern of life which developed in the earlier advanced pastoral Indo-European culture from which both Homeric and a Classical Greek civilization developed. Indeed, the Greeks continued to reverence the horse as a near sacred symbol of aristocratic virtue until the very close of Greek Classical tradition. Horse of Selene from the pediment of the Parthenon. (Courtesy of the British Museum, London.)

at the royal palace and served as a permanent standing army, ready to die for their hero-king whenever required. Should a king lose the respect of his warrior band, its members might stray away in search for more inspiring and successful leaders from whom they might receive better awards and greater scope for future loot.

A somewhat analogous system appears to have been taken into sub-Saharan Africa by Hamitic-speaking, cattle-herding warrior bands, who shared a culture parallel to that of the Semites of Arabia. Although these early Hamites were absorbed into the larger Bantu-speaking Negro population, many of their cultural traditions survived in a remarkable blend of Hamitic and Negroid cultural traits. One of the best known examples of a centralized chieftainship of conquest origin in Africa is that of the Baganda of Uganda. The Baganda kingdom was essentially feudal in character, and provides an example of a centralized chieftain who wielded power with a degree of

FIG. 46   THE BAGANDA

The Baganda are today incorporated in Uganda, between Lake Victoria and Lake Albert.

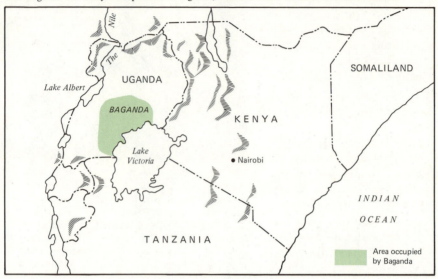

arbitrariness hardly matched in any other continent, but whose arbitrary rule was nevertheless constitutionalized by an impressive network of political and religious sanctions.

THE BAGANDA OF EAST AFRICA

The Baganda of Uganda in East Africa are typical of African tribal chieftainships. When European explorers penetrated the interior of Africa in the nineteenth century, they found a series of feudal kingdoms stretching from east to west along the grass and woodland belt which separates the rain forests of the Congo from the shifting sands of the Sahara Desert. From the conquest states of the Ashanti and the Dahomeans in West Africa to the kingdoms of Baganda and Bunyoro on the shores of Lakes Victoria and Albert in Uganda, contact between the Congo-Niger language speakers of true Negro type and Afro-Asiatic Hamitic speakers of predominantly Caucasoid type has produced a series of societies speaking languages which arise from an admixture of these two distinct speech families. These societies exploit a combination of horticultural and herding techniques.[3]

Although the people are generally of characteristically Congoid or Negro type, the evidence of an infusion of Caucasoid genes is to be found among people like the Watutsi, who for several centuries held a Bantu-speaking population in subordination, maintaining their feudal rule by means of a centralized chieftainship. Today many of the older traditions are changing, and Watutsi domination did not long survive the end of colonialism. Under European rule, members of the subordinate Bantu clans were recruited into colonial regi-

---

[3] The traditional centralized kingship of the Baganda was replaced under colonial rule by a semidemocratic and semibureaucratic system under which Baganda chiefs acted as servants of the colonial government. However, the traditional system is described in John Roscoe's *The Baganda* (London: Macmillan & Co., 1911). Lucy Mair, *An African People of the Twentieth Century* (London: George Routledge & Sons, 1934), may also be consulted.

West Africa also possessed several important central chieftainships. Pictured here is an Ivory Coast king attended by the state officials. (Courtesy of the Service Information de la Côte d'Ivoire.)

ments and were trained in the use of modern weapons. When they found that independence from the Europeans did not mean independence from their traditional Watutsi overlords, revolting Bantu troops, backed by the mass of villagers who greatly outnumbered the Watutsi, hunted down every Watutsi man, woman, and child they could find throughout the rolling grass-covered hills of their homeland, all but annihilating their former rulers.

Essentially typical of these African conquest states, the high culture of the Baganda in the uplands of Uganda also owes much to interaction between the Bantu of central Africa and the Hamites from the north. In fact the royal family of Baganda claims descent from the royal family of the ancient Hamitic conquerors, but the extensive polygamous practices of the Baganda kings, who customarily maintained literally hundreds of wives, must have rapidly led to the genetic homogenization of the two elements, creating the genetically uniform Bantu-speaking Baganda nation of today.

Since colonialization undermined the traditional Baganda society, converting the formerly despotic Baganda chiefs into salaried government officials, let us describe the unacculturated Baganda as they appeared to the first European visitors of the nineteenth century, so as to capture the feudal complexity of a society which had become authoritatively integrated under the rule of a single chieftain. We shall use the convention of the "ethnographic present."

Ecological Adaptations

The Baganda live on the northwestern shores of Lake Victoria. Although Uganda is situated in equatorial Africa, its climate is attractive because its high elevation modifies the worst extremes of heat and humidity usually associated with inland tropical areas. A considerable variety of crops are grown, but the main cultivated foods are bananas and plantains. All cultivation is undertaken by women. Because of the richness of the soil and the favorable nature of the climate, the yield is high, and one woman is said to be able to tend enough land to feed four men. Since most men have several wives, neither men nor women have a very arduous existence. In addition to the produce obtained from cultivation, there is also a profusion of milk and meat available from the flocks of goats and cattle tended by boys.

The essentially feudal character of the Baganda kingdom centralizes all effective power in the hands of the king, and all land is regarded as his personal property. The king always retains sufficient of the best land under his own control to support the royal herds which number several thousand cattle. The land that he does not need for his own livestock, he allocates to local chiefs. They in turn subdivide it among subchiefs who break it into still smaller plots which are made available to the ordinary tribesmen.

Baganda tribesmen are not tied to the soil like serfs, and may transfer their allegiance from one territorial chief to another should they so desire. However in return for the lease of land on which their wives can raise crops, they must render a share of all produce to their chiefs who in turn must contribute to the sup-

The Baganda are polygynous, and the women are responsible for all manual work. Baganda women hoeing their husband's vegetable garden. (Courtesy of the Uganda Government, Ministry of Information.)

port of the royal household. Taxes are also levied directly by the king upon all chiefs and freemen in the Baganda state. Although these are not collected regularly, whenever the royal treasury is empty a commissioner is appointed to tour the land, calculating the contributions that all householders must make.

The Baganda nation is organized in a state of constant military preparedness, for apart from the dangers of an unexpected enemy attack, periodic expeditions are organized against the hereditary Baganda enemies. All freemen are therefore liable for military service, and a subchief must be ready to provide fighting men for the service of the chief whenever these are needed.

The Centralization of Authoritative Power

The royal authority is maintained with the aid of spies who serve as a kind of secret police. Even a chief might be arrested on the basis of the thinnest shreds of evidence, including anonymous information or even simply an ill omen in a royal dream. Few processes of law are observed when the accused is placed on trial, but he may be saved from execution if his relatives are able to persuade the king of his innocence with the aid of valuable gifts intended to convince him of their loyalty.

However, the Baganda king is more than a feudal overlord—he is a divine figure, the descendant of an ancient line of kings who were deified upon their deaths, and are thus worshiped by the entire nation. Since the living king also becomes a god on his death, the future of the nation will one day depend upon his willingness, when his spirit sits among the great nature gods, to exercise divine influence on the behalf of the living. It is only to be expected therefore that he should be treated as semidivine during his life, and no Baganda ever denies the king any wish. His power is complete, and all who approach his presence

are required by custom to throw themselves face down on the ground, kick their legs behind them, beat their hands on the earth, and strike their forehead repeatedly in the dirt.

The position of the king is skillfully reinforced by the system of bureaucratic feudal appointment subject to his control. Immediately below the throne is the *katikiro,* or prime minister, and the *kimbugwe* who is in effect the Keeper of the Royal Umbilical Cord and supervisor of the national shrines. Through the *katikiro,* the king controls the appointment of the district chiefs, or *basaza,* through whom the subchiefs are also appointed. Through the *kimbugwe,* the king controls the priesthood and all religious activities. In addition there are a multitude of lesser feudal appointments at the royal court, each of which is prized for the opportunities which the officeholder has to reach the king's ear.

Clan loyalties are exploited by making these many offices hereditary in specific clans. The Royal Guard is always drawn from the Rat Clan, whereas the Keeper of the Royal Tombs is drawn from the Monkey Clan. The men who carry the royal chair on their shoulders are selected from among members of the Buffalo Clan and the Royal Drummers are recruited from the Hippopotamus Clan. The chief of the Lungfish Clan has the privilege of supplying one of his own sons to be beaten to death at the royal court, in order that his skin may be made into a whip for the king, and his back muscles may be made into anklets for the royal legs. Historically it would seem that the feudal system was superimposed upon an original Bantu clan system in such a way as to bind the clan loyalties to the new regime while still retaining central power in the hands of the king.

The Baganda actually enjoy one of the highest standards of living in Africa. Young men are customarily raised with their father's brother at whose kraal they help with the herding of the sheep and cattle. As adults, however, they become liable for military service. As warriors they are entitled to wear a girdle of skins and carry a spear with a long iron blade, a knobkerrie, and an oval shield made of wickerwork. On military expeditions the army is always accompanied by war drums and fetish objects, the war drums acquiring magical powers through sacrificial rituals carried out whenever they are re-covered. Prisoners of war are slaughtered at special places of sacrifice, according to a variety of rituals, varying from starvation to the more dramatic procedure of breaking the prisoners' arms and legs and leaving them by the river to be devoured by crocodiles. Female prisoners become concubines for their captors, but are usually freed and recognized as wives when they bear children.

Social Structure and Life Style

A few boys find positions in the household of the chief or even in that of the king. There they learn to be properly servile, and hope for promotion to a higher office. Those not selected become eligible at the age of 15 or 16 to seek a grant of land for cultivation from a local chief, in return for which they will be obliged to pay taxes and render military service. Once he has land, a man needs a wife to cultivate it, but he is not permitted to marry any of his immediate cousins. Consequently marriages take place between families who live some distance apart.

Polygyny is made possible by the high death rate among Baganda males, so that grown women normally exceed adult men in the ratio of 3 to 1. If the first child of a newly married woman is a male, it is strangled, for a first-born male is belived to augur the early death of the father. Because of constant insurrections and warfare many young men never live to be married. Chieftains and their male retainers may be slaughtered merely on suspicion of an intended insurrection. The number of males is

further depleted by human sacrifices offered at the coronation or death of a king, and in commemoration of deceased kings, so that if it were not for polygyny, the majority of Baganda females would never be married.

Once a girl's father has indicated his willingness to consider a suitor by accepting a token gift of salt, marital negotiations are conducted through the girl's brother and paternal uncle who act as intermediaries. It is customary to pay a bride price in cattle, goats, or cowrie shells to the relatives of the bride, and the extent of this payment is carefully negotiated. Once an agreement has been reached there is a beer drinking ceremony at which the uncle asks the girl whether he should drink of the beer offered by her suitor; if she consents, he then ratifies the negotiation by drinking from the proffered gourd.

No marriage ceremony will take place until the bride price has been paid. Once the negotiations are complete, the bride will be encouraged to eat well so as to be suitably plump for the wedding, and her skin will be regularly washed with butter. Eventually, veiled with bark cloth and adorned with all her jewelry, she is ready for the wedding.

The wedding ceremony takes place at the husband's kraal, where she will be expected to show her reluctance with tears and wailing until the bridegroom has bribed her with cowrie shells to enter his kraal. Further gifts are required before she agrees to participate in the marriage feast and again before she agrees to retire to a bed in her husband's kraal. However the marriage is not consummated until the third night. If the bride is then found not to be a virgin, she may be returned to her parents, and the repayment of the bride price will be demanded. Should the husband be satisfied with her, the bride will remain in seclusion for several weeks before assuming duties as a wife under the direction of her mother-in-law, who will then present her with a hoe and show her to her plantain patch.

The bride price paid by her husband actually serves as a guarantee of the wife's good behavior. In theory she is entitled to return to her family for good reason, but if she does decide to abandon her husband, her relatives will have to return the bride price, and she is unlikely to receive a warm welcome.

The Baganda household comprises a nuclear polygynous family of husband, wives, their offspring, and slaves. Each wife has her own circular grass hut within the fenced kraal in which she rears her own children. Babies are usually born in the plantain garden as their mother clutches on to the branch of a banana tree. Unlike many primitive people the Baganda look upon the birth of twins as a blessing. Since the afterbirth is believed to be a dead twin, it is carefully buried in the banana orchard. The living children are reared without any outward signs of affection; in fact, the Baganda language has no word for "love" or "affection."

The naming ceremony is the first important ritual in the child's life, and is carried out under the direction of the child's grandfather. Since Baganda clans are patrilineal, tracing descent and membership through the male line, it is first necessary to determine whether the child was legitimately conceived. This is done by dropping the umbilical cord into a pot of beer; unless the cord floats, the child will be regarded as illegitimate and consequently cannot be admitted to the clan. If the child is legitimate, the naming ceremony is held the following day, when the child's grandfather repeats the names of the dead ancestors in an attempt to determine which ancestral soul entered the mother's body to be reborn into the clan. The identification is made by the soul itself which will cause the child to laugh when its own name is mentioned. The child's head is then shaved, and in order to prevent any evil person from securing these clippings to use them to harm the child through black magic, they are buried alongside the afterbirth.

When a man is wealthy enough to have several wives, it is his duty to be fair to each of them, each being entitled to share his bed in rotation, but this does not stop jealousy, and disputes between wives are common. In polygynous households the eldest wife assumes direction of younger wives and is also responsible for the household fetish objects in which protective ghosts are believed to reside.

Religious System

The religious system of the Baganda is quite complex, since they worship both ancestors and nature spirits. The most notable spirit is Kadtonda, the "Father of the Gods" who is believed to have created the universe, but Mukasa, the god of the Great Lake (Lake Victoria) nevertheless supersedes Kadtonda in practical importance, since he is the god of fertility, the god of fishing—an activity of some importance in the Baganda economy—and more importantly, the protector of the crops. In what seems to be an echo of ancient Egypt, the Baganda also believe in a certain Walumbe, the god of death, who judges the departed souls according to their record of behavior in life. Other gods each have their own sphere of influence, such as Nabuzana, the goddess responsible for the care of pregnant women, who is the patron deity of a cult of midwife-priestesses.

Second in importance only to the nature gods are the deified spirits of former kings. The Baganda, like all Bantu, are ancestor worshipers. Although an ancestor may be worshiped only by his own descendants, the ancestors of the king may be worshiped by all members of the Baganda nation.

The Problem of Succession

One of the great problems which face centralized chieftainships is the question of an orderly transfer of power following the death of the chieftain. While the Baganda king lives, despite frequent insurrections and constant warfare, life in the Baganda kingdom can be enjoyable. Men bind themselves to their chiefs by personal as well as economic ties, and as long as the chief is not suspected of political subversion, the lives of the ordinary people may be relatively routine. But the peace of the nation is shattered by the death of the reigning king. The primary weakness of the Baganda political system lies in its failure to designate a royal successor during the lifetime of the king, mainly because the kings live in constant fear of uprisings, and an heir-apparent would become a rallying center for dissident elements.

Following the demise of the king, the Keeper of the Royal Flame outside the royal hut is strangled, the Royal Drummers beat out the news to all corners of the kingdom, and in the interregnum that follows, chiefs and subchiefs take advantage of the kingless state of the nation to take revenge on their enemies and to plunder weaker neighbors. The key members of the court confer to decide which of the multitude of princes will inherit the kingdom, the eldest son being barred from the kingship, for fear that if primogeniture were the rule the heir would plot to murder his own father. Civil war may break out when one or more of the disappointed candidates seeks to seize the kingdom by force of arms, and when all disputes have been finally settled, it is customary for the successful candidate to have his several hundred brothers and half-brothers put to death in order to prevent them from leading insurrections in future years.

This arrangement may be supervised by the Queen Mother who will ensure that the unsuccessful princes are rounded up and imprisoned in a fenced stockade where they are starved to death. Since descent is through the male line only, princesses cannot inherit the throne. Although they are provided with small estates and are permitted to take as many lovers as they wish, they are forbidden to marry or produce children, and all babies born to a princess are quietly murdered.

After the succession has been decided and the dead king's body has been mummified, hundreds of slaves are clubbed to death in order that their bodies may be arranged around the royal tomb. But the funeral rituals do not conclude with the burial of the royal body. Six months after death the tomb is opened up, the mummified head is removed, and any remaining shreds of decaying flesh are cleaned off the skull. The skull is filled with beer mixed with magic potions from which a priest-wizard then drinks in order that he may acquire the power of communicating with the royal spirit and interpret the wishes of the dead king to his people.

The royal remains are permanently attended by selected priests under the direction of an official known as the Keeper of the Royal Tombs. During the reign of the king's successor a further commemorative ceremony is held at which the reigning king sacrifices hundreds of living subjects in his ancestor's honor.

Not only are kings deified following death. The spirits of the original clan founders are also ranked among the gods. Like the nature gods and the kings, each clan founder has a shrine which is attended by its own priests. These clan gods are responsible for ensuring the good behavior of their descendants, in particular, the adherence of the living to the rules of exogamy and endogamy.

A man's spirit remains a member of his clan and his tribe even after death. Such ghosts feel pain, suffering, and pleasure. It is in their power to assist the living in time of need, but they can show anger should the living fail to honor them, dispute with other members of the family, or in any way break the Baganda traditions. Thus ancestor worship is a strongly unified force, binding members of the same clan closely together, and unifying—in the worship of the royal ghosts—the entire Baganda nation beneath the living king.

FIG. 47   THE POLYNESIANS AND OTHER SEA-GOING MALAYO-POLYNESIAN PEOPLES

Map showing the location of Hawaiians, Tahitians, and Maoris.

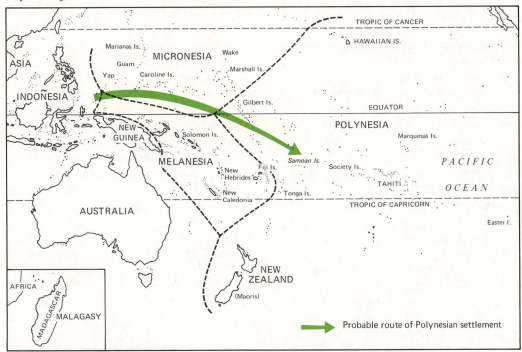

Probable route of Polynesian settlement

THE POLYNESIANS OF OCEANIA

While Baganda despotism makes rather fearful reading for those who have been acculturated into a different morality, contemporary Westerners usually react more favorably toward the Polynesian social system which also took the form of a centralized chieftainship, especially in Hawaii and Tahiti, but was inspired by a sense of noblesse oblige. Nevertheless, Polynesian society was also militaristic, the nobles being particularly proud of their martial skills, and it was even more rigidly stratified on a strictly hereditary basis than that of the Baganda. Like the Baganda the Polynesians vested all authoritative power in the person of their kings, who were also believed to be divinely descended and imbued with such inherited magical mana that no commoner might touch anything which had been in physical contact with them.

The Settling of the South Pacific

The South Pacific is one of the largest relatively homogenous culture areas in the world. Stretching from the equator to the waters of the Antarctic and from Samoa and New Zealand to the Easter Isles—almost due south of Denver, Colorado—this multitude of South Pacific islands is inhabited by a well-proportioned, moderately tall, light brown people with black hair, straight noses, and relatively broad heads. Although the residents of different groups of islands are customarily inbreeding in their habits, the entire area was settled so recently that not enough generations have passed to allow a substantial physical or cultural divergence. In the same way, all the languages spoken in these many islands can be readily identified as belonging to a single Polynesian branch of the Malayo-Polynesian linguistic stock.

Despite the possibility of earlier contact between the more easterly of the South Pacific islands and South America, it would seem that the ancestors of the Polynesians originated somewhere in the general Southeast Asian or Malayan region. Genetically, the Polynesians are believed to reflect Australoid, Mongoloid, and Caucasoid elements,[4] and some legends suggest ties with India in the distant past.

[4] Pearl Buck, *The Vikings of the Pacific* (Chicago: University of Chicago Press, 1959), is a stimulating account of Polynesian society.

Certainly there is an interesting parallel between the concept of inherited magicoreligious powers among the Polynesian aristocracy and the *familial charisma* of the upper castes of the Indo-Aryans.

As far as it is possible to reconstruct the migration of peoples and cultures in Oceania, it would seem that the western part of the area was at an early time inhabited by hunting and gathering Australoids and Negritoes who were later overrun by an Asian horticultural people. Possessing advanced marine skills, these people began a series of oceanic migrations eastward from the Asian mainlands. Skirting Australia and New Guinea, some settled the islands of Melanesia where they admixed with the Negrito population. Others moved in a more northeasterly direction, leaving the Philippines to settle the islands of Micronesia, most of

The islands of Oceania were first settled by man less than 1500 years ago. Although subject to violent storms during certain seasons, the climate is generally attractive and many offer a most attractive habitat for man, providing plentiful food at a cost of minimal effort. Portrayed above is the island of Moorea, in the Polynesian Society Isles. (Courtesy of La Documentation Française, Paris.)

which were at that time unoccupied. This element of the population may also have acquired some Negrito admixture before leaving the Philippine area, so that the Micronesian population may also reflect some Negrito elements. Generally speaking the islands of Micronesia were not so large as those of Melanesia, and consequently the Micronesian settlers had to depend to a greater extent upon fishing to supplement their horticultural techniques.

While all this was happening, other groups of Malayo-Polynesians sailed westward across the Indian Ocean and established settlements on the eastern coast of Africa, completely colonizing the large island of Madagascar which, because of its isolation, had no indigenous human population nor even any anthropoids, the most advanced form of life being prosimians of the lemur type.

Then, at a fairly recent date, around 1000 to 1500 years ago, a further eastward migration of these same Asian people seems to have skirted past the Melanesian and Micronesian islands, since these were already settled, to colonize the rich but empty island archipelagoes of Polynesia farther out into the Pacific, while a small group of them swung backward to the southwest to become the progenitors of the New Zealand Maoris. These people absorbed very few Negrito genes. The lands which they settled had never before been colonized by any mammalian species, but were rich in plant life, and in many cases the surrounding waters teemed with fish. Traveling literally thousands of miles in large canoes equipped with stabilizing outrigger devices, and guiding themselves by the stars, the Polynesians brought pigs and chickens with them, and settled down to enjoy what was to be in most cases a relatively peaceful existence in an ideal climate surrounded by ample food resources. Planting coconut palms, banana, and breadfruit trees, yams, taro, and sweet potatoes, catching wild pigeons in nets, and fattening their pigs to make a centerpiece for their sacrificial feasts, the Polynesians built themselves what has been frequently portrayed as an idyllic culture.

Importance of Genealogies

Organized into clans, each of which claims descent from a distinguished common ancestor, and inbred closely in their island homes to the point that all the residents of each island look to outsiders like brothers and sisters, the Polynesians believe that their chiefs symbolize the unity and history of the social group. They pay deep respect to those who are the most directly descended from the ancestral heroes by either the male or female line, and award the highest status to the first-born regardless of sex. Polynesian kings possess inborn magical abilities, inherited from their predecessors, and each successive generation of kings is believed to be more powerful and more elevated than the previous. It is therefore not surprising that great attention is given to the keeping of genealogies. Many authentic genealogies record as many as 30 generations with apparent historical accuracy, while mythical genealogies, which may also be rooted in a degree of historical fact, extend for up to 70 or 80 generations. In some cases the legends which surround these mythical ancestors also indicate the direction of the migration which brought the clans and tribes to their present homes.

Mana and Taboo

Although the inheritance of the royal office is usually restricted to the male line, the first-born child, regardless of its sex, inherits more *mana* than its younger siblings. Thus a king may be socially inferior to his elder sister, to whom he must therefore show due deference. Many kings find this tiresome and go to great lengths to avoid meeting their elder sisters in

Polynesian kings were believed to inherit mana, each generation possessing more mana than the last. They were consequently surrounded by many taboos and could be approached only by close relatives or persons of noble status. The above drawing by a nineteenth-century French traveler portrays the Polynesian king of the Sandwich Isles, reclining in the privacy of his royal hut. (Courtesy of the Smithsonian Institution, National Anthropological Archives.)

public. But even greater problems arise from this principle of sexual equality in the inheritance of rank, for on the death of a king, his title usually passes to his eldest sister's son instead of to his own son, and this can be a constant source of conflict in Polynesian society. One solution to the problem, as adopted in Hawaii, was for the king to marry his elder sister, thus keeping all the inherited mana in the family.

Because of this inherited mana, everything that a king touches becomes *taboo*, or prohibited, to commoners. Only a few close relatives or special servants are permitted to have physical contact with the king's person, food, eating utensils, or clothes, or indeed to enter the royal household. In some islands the principle is so highly developed that a field has to be abandoned should a king so much as walk across it, and Polynesian royalty has to be carefully

secluded from contact with the property and possessions of lesser mortals in order to prevent the complete disruption of the social and economic system.

The Tahitian Culture

Tahiti, in the Society Islands, may be regarded as largely typical of a complex Polynesian society. Tahiti itself is about 35 miles long by 15 miles wide, and contains two volcanic mountains rising to 7000 feet in height. It is almost entirely surrounded by an outer coral reef, which creates an attractive lagoon, the waters of which are normally calm. The climate is mild, the temperature remaining within the 70s all the year round. The volcanic soil is rich, so that with the aid of rain brought in by the regular sea breezes, the islands produce a rich growth of tropical vegetation.

As in other Polynesian societies, there are three classes in Tahiti: the chiefly lineage known as the *Ari'i*, the nobility known as *Ra'atira*, and the commoners known as *Nanahone*. All have tribal status, presenting a picture of a large kinship group in which some families are elevated far above others because of the directness of their descent from the original heroic ancestors. As in other centralized chieftainships, peace and order in Tahiti are maintained by royal authority, not by blood feud; violations of customs and law are seen as offenses against the religion and the royal power, not as private matters involving only the disputants.

Although the Tahitians do not practice excessive bodily mutilation, tattooing is widespread. Traditionally the men wear only a loin cloth, while the women wear a skirt covering the lower portion of their body—both loin cloth and skirt are made from bark cloth in the absence of woven animal hair. Like all Polynesians the Tahitians are clean in their body habits, devoting particular attention to the care of their hair, and all buildings and paths are brushed regularly so that they stay clean and tidy. The Tahitian love of beauty, which finds ample inspiration in their South Seas landscape, expresses itself in wood carvings which reveal a strong artistic sense. Great care is taken in the style and form of these carvings, but there is surprisingly little interest in color, and most Tahitian artists prefer natural tones rather than bright or contrasting colors.

Tahitians follow an easy daily routine, taking a light meal in the morning, resting in the afternoon, and feasting in the evening. Because of the heavy emphasis on status—which invades even the household where important differences of rank exist even between brothers according to the priority of birth—most social relations are heavily regulated by tradition. Notwithstanding this, the Tahitian attitude toward sex is well known: commoners tend to look upon sex as a pleasurable pastime,

rather like feasting. Although children of the genealogically-conscious nobility are the subject of arranged marriages, those of common parentage are permitted to choose their own mate, and premarital promiscuity is widespread. The concept of romantic love is regarded as childish, and although divorce is rare among royalty and nobility, marriages between commoners are very brittle. The children of broken marriages normally remain with their mother or with their mother's family.

A heavily tatooed Maori chieftain. In Polynesia, the right to wear tattoo marks is restricted to persons of noble descent. These marks, which follow traditional scroll designs, are cut deep into the skin, and involve a lengthy and extremely painful process. (Courtesy of Musée de l'Homme, Paris.)

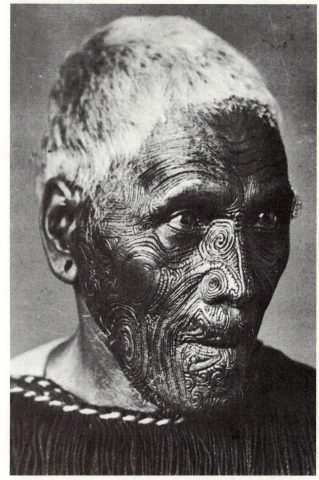

Religion

The Tahitians have a number of gods, and each island has its own favorites. Professional priests maintain elaborate temples where involved rituals are performed to the honor of the state gods and the ancestors of the kings and chieftains. In addition to the priests whose role it is to supervise the ritual ceremonies, there are also a number of diviners and oracles who serve as a medium for the gods by interpreting omens or allowing a god to express himself through their voices.

As in many other Polynesian islands, the temples are taboo to commoners, who are obliged to congregate outside the temple precincts while royalty and nobility worship inside. Frequent sacrifices are made to the gods: pigs and dogs being the most customary offer-

An old Hawaiian in native garment made of leaves, carrying a long pole with bundles balanced on both sides. (Courtesy of Smithsonian Institution, National Anthropological Archives.)

The cloaks worn by Maori women are greatly prized, being handed down from generation to generation. That on the left is made from kiwi feathers; the other is of flax trimmed with feather tufts. (Courtesy of the New Zealand Embassy, Washington, D.C.)

ing, but following a war, human prisoners are also sacrificed in a thanksgiving ritual. Attention to ritual detail in all ceremonies is greatly emphasized in Polynesian religion, and if any error is made, the entire ceremony has to be done over again.

The Polynesians believe in the existence of a human soul and envisage an afterlife for the souls of royalty and noblemen on a heavenly island of peace and plenty, situated somewhere over the western horizon in the direction of the ancestral homelands. Thus the ghosts of royalty and nobility are not feared. On the other hand, the souls of commoners are believed to proceed to an underworld situated beneath the ocean. Since this world is not so happy a place as the paradise island to which the spirits of the nobility retire, it is believed that the ghosts of commoners often return during the night to visit the world of the living.

All funeral rituals are carefully attended to, in an attempt to ensure that in the case of dead royalty the spirit will reach its joyous destination safely, and to ensure that in the case of commoners the spirit will be securely consigned to its predestined underworld, thus freeing the living from its unwelcome atten-tions as a ghost. While attention to ritual detail ensures the success of the project, the ghosts of men who remain unburied, such as those of men who are drowned at sea, pose a constant problem, haunting their old homelands and threatening harm to the living.

For Further Reading

Beattie, J., 1960, *Bunyoro: An African Kingdom.* New York: Holt, Rinehart and Winston, Inc.

Bascom, W., 1969, *The Yoruba of Southwestern Nigeria.* New York: Holt, Rinehart and Winston, Inc.

Buck, P. H., 1959, *Vikings of the Pacific.* Chicago: University of Chicago Press.

Childe, V. G., 1970, *The Aryans.* Port Washington, N.Y.: Kennikat Press.

Codrington, R. H., 1969, *The Melanesians.* New York: Oxford University Press.

Cohen, R., 1961, *The Kanuri of Bornu.* New York: Holt, Rinehart and Winston, Inc.

Goodenough, W. H., 1970, "The Evolution of Pastoralism and Indo-European Origins," in G. Cardona, H. M. Hoenigswald, and A. Senn, eds., *Indo-European and Indo-Europeans.* Philadelphia: University of Pennsylvania Press.

Harding, T. G., and B. J. Wallace, 1970, *Cultures of the Pacific.* New York: The Free Press.

Malinowski, B., 1922, *Argonauts of the Western Pacific.* New York: E. P. Dutton & Co., Inc.

Middleton, J., and D. Tait, eds., 1958, *Tribes without Rulers: Studies in African Segmentary Systems.* London: Routledge & Kegan Paul Ltd.

Palmer, L. R., 1955, *Achaeans and Indo-Europeans.* New York: Oxford University Press.

Richards, A. I., ed., 1960, *East African Chiefs.* London: Faber & Faber, Ltd.

Roscoe, J., 1911, *The Baganda.* London: Macmillan & Co.

Sjokerg, G., 1952, "Folk and 'Feudal' Societies," *American Journal of Sociology* 58 (3):231–239.

Stanley, H. M., 1899, *Through the Dark Continent or the Sources of the Nile around the Great Lakes of Equatorial Africa and Down the Livingstone River to the Atlantic Ocean,* 2 vols. London: George Newnes Limited.

Williamson, R. W., 1924, *The Social and Political Systems of Central Polynesia.* New York: Cambridge University Press.

CHAPTER 29

The Rise of Urban Civilizations

The term *civilization* is perhaps one of the most ill-defined terms ever to be employed by anthropologists. Some writers try to avoid the use of the term altogether, but since the idea of civilization is so deeply ingrained in the Western mind, it is better to attempt a definition and to recognize the fact that as students of man we cannot sidestep such widely used concepts simply because no agreed definition has yet been found.

Most writers who have discussed the concept of civilization generally agree that it contains substantial normative or value elements, and that these generally imply a degree of urbanity or esthetic consciousness as well as a degree of security or comfort, the existence of a high degree of division of labor, an extensive degree of social stratification, sophisticated systems for the maintenance of social order, and some form of writing or permanent, non-verbal communication. Bearing these qualities in mind, we can immediately see that the development of a civilization may be roughly equated in ecological-evolutionary terms to the

appearance of certain levels of subsistence which may be regarded as essential prerequisites to the evolution of civilization, although it cannot be said that a civilization will inevitably develop once these conditions are present. Artistic appreciation, physical comfort, a division of labor, complex social stratification, and even the emergence of writing all require a level of technological and ecological evolution that frees men from the immediate problems of short-term survival, and results in the production of an adequate surplus of material wealth that will support a class of specialist hand workers and metal workers who can provide the specialist goods and specialist services essential to the maintenance of civilized standards of comfort and order. All these conditions are provided for by agricultural societies.

Like the transition from hunting and gathering to horticulture, the transition from horticulture to agriculture was a slow and steady evolution, without any revolutionary changes which would have transformed society overnight. Nevertheless, several essential innovations distinguish an AGRICULTURAL SOCIETY from a horticultural society. In the first place, the agriculturalist has learned how to regenerate the soil by the rotation of crops, or even by the application of manure and natural fertilizers. Such improvements lead to the disappearance of the old "slash and burn" techniques of the shifting horticulturalist, which are usually highly wasteful, and the agriculturalist is not exploiting the soil and then abandoning it. This means that he and his descendants can settle permanently on the same plot of land, and that all suitable land can be brought under permanent cultivation, thus making the maintenance of a much larger population possible.

In the second place, the more advanced agriculturalists also learn how to utilize the heavier and richer loam soils, by harnessing animal power to pull a heavy plow, capable of turning over the richer soils to a greater depth than the hoe and other hand tools permit. This will further increase the output of the land. Most agriculturalists are actually *mixed farmers,*[1] who combine crop raising with some animal breeding, and utilize animal power to supplement human muscle power. The agricultural societies of the Old World have also learned how to utilize the wheel to provide transport, and consequently they can haul heavy loads of agricultural produce over larger distances—an innovation without which the surplus crops would have been of purely local and limited value.

The Appearance of Urban Centers

Although successful horticultural societies frequently support a number of overgrown villages, true urban connurbations are found only in agricultural and industrial societies. By

[1] Mixed farming implies the domestication of large animals by settled agriculturalists, without migratory pastoralism.

definition, CITIES are aggregations of occupational specialists who do not produce their own food. A large village may contain a number of full-time craftsmen, but the villagers produce sufficient food to maintain the entire village population. In the case of cities, this is no longer true. Cities do not produce their own food and must therefore rely upon bartering or trading their specialist services with the inhabitants of the surrounding villages in return for food. With the coming of agriculture, society becomes divided into urban and rural communities which are by nature vastly different from each other.

In a sense, cities are a human luxury which become possible only when advances in food-producing technology free large numbers of people to enter specialist occupations, thereafter obtaining their food by trading their specialist produce with the food producers. Cities can arise only when improved methods of food production create an economic surplus of sufficient proportions to permit a large segment of society to devote its labors to activities which are not directly related to the problem of basic subsistence. And they are only possible when technology has advanced to the level that permits the wholesale transportation of large quantities of food from the surrounding farmlands to the urban centers.

Although pack animals were undoubtedly in use from an early date, boats offered the first solution to the problem of transporting heavy quantities of merchandise, and in consequence the earlier cities were usually located close to rivers or to the sea. Early urban civilization developed on the Tigris and the Euphrates, on the Nile, the Yellow River, the Indus, or even as in the case of Tenochtitlan in Mexico, on lakes. It was the invention of the wheel that made inland transportation possible. Without wheeled transport to carry large quantities of grain and meat from the rural areas to the emerging cities, urban civilization would have been restricted to the waterways of the world.

The wheel was one of the most significant inventions of the Old World Neolithic. Pictured above is a contemporary Lebanese potter using a potter's wheel to mass produce his wares by techniques first developed by the potters of ancient Sumeria and related areas. (Courtesy of the Lebanese Tourist Office.)

The invention of the wheel also stimulated agricultural and urban progress in other ways, since it could be used to convert animal power into mechanical power, to draw water from wells, to convert wind power to mechanical power (as through windmills which harnessed the wind to grind flour), and also for sundry other industrial purposes such as pottery making.

One other invention was essential to the rise of urban civilization. No complex society, requiring the movement of substantial bodies of food and other resources and the management of hundreds of thousands of people, can survive for long without some method of keeping records. All civilizations need some form of writing. The Incas of South America managed astonishingly well with simple devices for recording mathematical statistics, but without writing there is a limit to what can be accomplished.

The Market Economy

Since the farmer must necessarily specialize in the management of his farm, he is unable to transport this produce or distribute it to those who need it. Consequently, the gap which divided the farmer from the ultimate consumer is inevitably filled by one or more merchants or middlemen. Even during the Neolithic, European and Middle Eastern societies knew professional trading families and clans. Just as an entire village might concen-

Urban civilization led to great improvements in artistic skills, as all manufacturing work became the task of specialized professionals. Red-figured cup from Attica in Greece, circa fifth century B.C. (Courtesy of the British Museum, London.)

trate on the collection of amber, the manufacture of stone spears, or the mining of flint, other trading clans traveled over large areas, bartering these specialized local products and dealing in any produce which was not readily available in every area, but which was easily transportable. Transport, in fact, was one of the main problems restricting the rise of cities in the Neolithic world. Agricultural surplus is usually bulky, and unless it can be transported to the areas in which it is needed, it is valueless. Thus the primeval subsistence economy in which men produced primarily for their own needs could only give way to an urbanized MARKET ECONOMY in which men deliberately produce food or other merchandise for exchange, specializing in those products that they can most efficiently produce rather than those they need for their own consumption.

The Management of Commerce

In many of the earlier city-state civilizations, such as that of Persia, the old administrative nobility frequently entered into commerce, operating it as a state monopoly. Thus the Persian nobility often ran large agricultural estates and even mining operations as though they were state corporations. In Crete and the Mycenean cities of ancient Greece the local kings frequently entered into international trade because of its profitableness. But in most advanced agricultural civilizations there developed a new class of urban-dwelling merchants who became both prosperous and influential. In some cities, such as Venice, the merchants eventually came to dominate the entire community, socially, economically, and politically. In most agricultural civilizations less intensely oriented to international trade than Venice, Crete, and the Mycenean cities, the administrative nobility were able to retain political control even though their economic position was frequently undermined by the new merchant class.

With the coming of a market economy, the foundations for capitalism were laid. CAPITALISM is an economic system in which the ownership of the means of production is vested in private individuals or corporations rather than in the community as a whole. This involves a complete reorientation of attitudes. The administrative class, including the nobility and clergy, and the peasants who work on the land may continue to think in terms of an ordered total socioeconomic system, seeing the society as a functioning whole in which each individual role player has his own contribution to make to the survival and well-being of society. However, the merchants base their claim to all that they own on the principle of individualism and on the idea of private enterprise for personal gain. Thus the landowning nobility justify their status, role, and income on the basis of their services rendered to the community, and they are rewarded by traditional rents and taxes. But the merchant's motive is more obviously private gain, and this will clearly be greater when he can profit from famine or scarcity. It is obvious to all that the merchant owes his success to his own acumen and initiative. It is only natural therefore that successful merchants may feel ill at ease in a rural environment, where roles and rewards are more traditional. In the city, by contrast, where he is also close to his market center, the merchant lives among other persons who are more achievement-oriented, more individualistic in outlook.

To the extent that merchants lack political power, a concealed rivalry may arise between the merchant classes and the administrative nobility, with the latter seeking to impose taxes upon the former, and the former striving to acquire a measure of self-government in their cities in order to develop their own subculture and free themselves from the constraints of the traditional mores which do not suit their more individualistic pattern of life. To the extent that the corporate tradition survives, merchants may organize themselves in trade guilds, fixing prices and benefiting to some extent by cartels or monopolies, but the spirit of revolt against the corporate concept of society is present. In almost every case of social and political change, it was the merchant class that first undermined the authoritative position of the older administrative nobility.

Religious Bureaucracies

If the merchants were one of the main beneficiaries of the new urban societies that developed as a result of the agricultural revolution, the priests were the other beneficiaries. Experts in the supernatural draw together in regular priesthoods, restricting membership in their profession and introducing regular training programs for new initiates as they build up a coherent system of dogma and ritual. The economic surplus produced by the farmers and peasantry offers a challenge which the new organized priesthoods seldom fail to exploit. The larger and more prosperous population can readily support a number of full-time religious advisors. A bureaucratic priesthood, efficiently organized under a hierarchical system of archpriests, is easily able to produce a convincing set of arguments as to why the now prosperous community should support the one true union of religious specialists with generous financial contributions.

Yet there was seldom any clash in the early city civilizations between the administrative nobility and the organized church. To some extent the pyramid of power was still too small to permit serious rivalry, and the ancient idea of corporate national unity was still too strong. In most cases the kings were themselves divinely descended or else became gods upon their own deaths. Thus church and state worked closely together in ideological harmony, the one reinforcing the position of the other by mutual agreement.

Decline of Descent Groups

Few urbanized societies have preserved their descent groups intact. Although the rural population in an advanced society may still preserve a pattern of descent groups, city life is too turbulent, in most cases, to tolerate the rigid patterning of obligations which is the purpose of the kinship system. As the extended families weaken, the full weight of social responsibility falls on the unsupported nuclear family.

In reality, however, complex societies frequently differ considerably from one stratum to another in their style of life. Many urbanized societies have preserved extended families and even a rudimentary clan system among the aristocracy, for the kinship system gives a man allies. An aristocracy is more likely to retain its privileged position if it retains its kinship and familial loyalties, and works as a team, than if it allows individualism to divide its ranks. Similarly, even in the modern Western world, many ethnic groups, such as the Lebanese in America, who have retained strong kinship ties have found that kinship loyalties help them to maintain a favored position. In India groups such as the Mahwaris and Parsees, some of whom are among the world's richest men, preserve the extended family system and are to this day painstakingly loyal to kinship obligations. In China the upper classes maintained extended families and kept extensive genealogical records while the peasantry suffered a collapse of the cooperating descent groups as their extended families broke down into nuclear families. A team of effectively cooperating and loyal kinsmen possesses a certain competitive efficiency in any society, and is more usually found among those who are successful than among those who are failures.

In the transition to urbanized societies, therefore, the first casualties were among the lower strata who drifted away from the villages, in which they had been protected by their descent groups, to become a proletariat without kinsmen in the cities. While the aristocracies and wealthy merchants still preserved kinship ties and loyalties, the masses lost their kinship basis of support and were left with only the nuclear family. It is therefore not surprising that the new landless, kinless proletariat frequently became a political problem. Many city civilizations of the past, just like those of the present day, found it necessary to introduce some kind of welfare in the urban areas, as the rulers took upon themselves the protection of the plebeian masses who were now without any kinship organization to support them in ill health, old age, and misfortune.

ANCIENT SUMERIA

We have already indicated how as their knowledge of horticulture improved, the early cultivators of the Middle East moved down from the highlands, in which they had first learned to harvest the wild grain, into the richer alluvial valleys. In the broad plains of the Tigris and Euphrates rivers, then better watered and more fertile than today, further improvements in the art of cultivation took place until the stage that we know as agriculture was reached. It is probable that the alluvial plains were first cultivated around the sixth millennium B.C., and during the next 2000 years men slowly learned how to rotate their crops and how to build elaborate systems of irrigation, using the wheel for lifting water in a series of small cups. The wheel also provided the basis for wheeled transport, in carts drawn by onagers, small donkeylike animals.[2]

From the Middle East, through Anatolia and into the Balkan area of Europe, we find evi-

[2] See S. N. Kramer, *The Sumerians: Their History, Culture and Character* (Chicago: University of Chicago Press, 1963).

FIG. 48   ANCIENT MESOPOTAMIA

Map of Mesopotamia showing some of the main Sumerian and Assyrian sites. The Persian Gulf formerly extended inland to the limits indicated by the dotted lines.

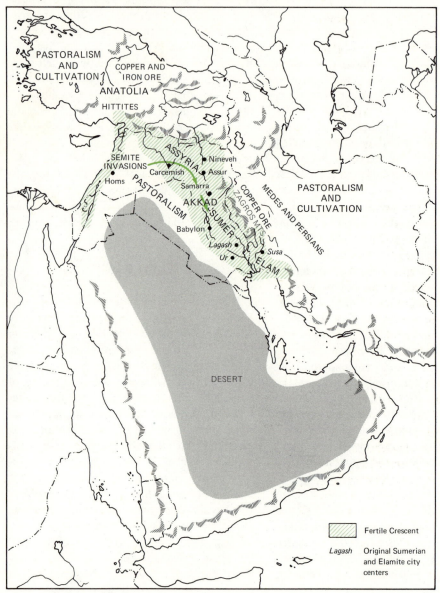

462

dence of settlements known as *tell* villages, resulting from occupation over continuous periods of thousands of years. As old houses fell down, new houses were erected on their foundations, until with the accumulation of compressed rubble, the villages steadily rose higher above the surrounding ground. Today, especially in Asia Minor and the Fertile Crescent, both inhabited and uninhabited tell sites stand up as large mounds, dominating the surrounding flat lands.

Examination of the archeological evidence indicates that the earliest Sumerians were typical Mediterranean Caucasoids, although at a later date a broader-headed strain, possibly similar in type to living Armenians, may have entered into the population from the Anatolian region. Their society was tribal, with semisacred warrior kings. Their religion was polytheistic, comprising hero-gods whose battles with dragons and other evil powers were recorded in epic legends, such as that of Gilgamesh, which contain within them the original versions of many of the legends and precepts of the Bible, the Talmud, and the Koran—the holy books of later Middle Eastern religions.

The Invention of Metallurgy

In the course of time technological improvements and the increase of population led to greater occupational specialization. Around 5000 B.C. the smelting of copper ore was invented in the mountain regions of Anatolia and western Persia, and metallurgy began. Needless to say, the large Neolithic villages of the Sumerian region offered a ready market for the things that could be made from metal. Although the mountain dwellers of Luristan became famous for their skill as jewelers, it was only a matter of time before professional metalworkers began to establish themselves in the Sumerian towns.

From the beginning, copper ore was never plentiful, and copper artifacts were conse-

Statuettes representing worshippers, found in the remains of the Abu Temple at Tell Asmar. (Courtesy of Iraq Museum, Baghdad, and Oriental Institute, University of Chicago.)

quently expensive. Nevertheless, petty chieftains and kings controlled sufficient resources to pay the cost of manufacture and transport. If disputes arose about the cost of the metal, we know from historical sources that the kings of the alluvial settlements were not slow to make war upon the smaller but prosperous mountain kingdoms, on a suitable pretext, and having subjugated the mine-owning towns, they would levy a tribute to be paid in free metal in the future.

Copper was also too soft to be used for anything except ornamental and decorative ware, but once the art of adding an amalgam to the copper to produce bronze, a much harder metal, was learned, the nobles began to equip themselves with bronze armor and bronze weapons. This equipment served to increase their efficiency in war over that of the peasantry still further, and the Homeric poems of the parallel Bronze Age civilization in Ancient Greece tell us of the eagerness with which the greatest heroes would have their men strip the body of a slain enemy leader of its valuable armor, even before the battle had been finally won.

During the next few centuries the Sumerians developed most of the known ways of working metal. They learned how to heat it and beat it into required shapes. They learned how to make fine wire from it, with which to do filigree work. They also learned how to cast both copper and bronze in molds, made by carving wax into the desired shape and then covering the outside of the wax with heat-resisting clay. The hot metal was then poured onto the wax, which melted and ran out, while the metal cooled in the shape of the wax, as preserved by the outer clay covering. Many of the designs developed by Luristan and Sumerian jewelers 3000 to 4000 years ago are still followed by jewelers in Persia, Afghanistan, and India to this day.

Fortified City States

Neolithic Sumeria also developed pottery making during the fifth millennium B.C. and subsequently invented the potter's wheel. The replacement of horticulture by agriculture steadily increased the yield of the peasant farmers, and wheeled transport made it possible for this surplus food to be transported reasonable distances. With these advancements the Neolithic villages began to grow into towns, and some of the towns began to develop as regional cities. Merchants and bankers appeared to handle the growing trade, arising from the increasing division of labor and the constant flow of goods from one area of regional specialization to another. The local chieftains emerged as hereditary nobility, ruling over towns and cities. Sumeria became transformed into a patchwork of petty kingdoms, each with its own capital city and its accompanying cluster of villages, most of which still lived in the Neolithic. Each Sumerian city-state was independent of its neighbors; each had its own protective deity, its own temple and priesthood, its own *lugal* or king, nobles, and army; each made its own preparations for war, signed its own treaties, and protected its central city with tremendous defensive walls.

These Sumerian city-states usually embraced several acres within their huge earthen walls, the front of which was commonly faced with several layers of baked bricks. Inside the city there was no proper provision for sanitation, and the Sumerian city dwellers retained their ancient tradition of burying their dead under the floors of their houses, just as some Melanesians still do to this day. Because they did not always bury the corpses too deeply, and had no toilet or other sanitary devices, a house that had been lived in for some time tended to become somewhat noisome. Most wealthy families consequently owned two or more houses in the city, moving from one to the other periodically while the last house "sweetened" for a while.

If the rich lived well, the kings lived in literally palatial style. They were believed to become divine on their death, and as among the early Scythians, the death of a king was the occasion for the most lavish funeral rites. Not only were the earthly remains of their kings buried with great pomp, but they were usually accompanied to the grave with vast treasures and by wives, courtiers, slaves, and other assorted attendants who were expected to follow their king in death as they had done in war. Needless to say, since the kings were deified at death, no city would wish to offend the spirit of its dead king by not providing him with all that he might need to enable him to live in the next life in the style to which he had become accustomed.

In war the survival of the Sumerian city states depended upon the bravery and courage of their kings who were expected to lead their troops into battle personally, either striding ahead of them on foot, or else riding in a four-wheeled battle chariot drawn by diminutive donkeylike onagers. So far as we can ascertain, the Sumerians may have been the first people to train their infantry to drill and fight in close formation. Lacking horses, they had no cavalry or mounted troops, and instead the warriors formed close phalanxes behind a wall of shields, the identical formation used by the soldiers of Alexander and Rome in later millennia.

In this stratified society, which had already emerged to the level that we are describing by the early part of the third millennium B.C., slavery was an established institution. Prisoners of war were regularly enslaved, but slavery was also used as a form of punishment. The idea of the blood feud was dead, and in Sumeria all justice was properly handled in courts of law responsible to the king. A man who was found guilty of an offense against a fellow citizen and was unable to pay the appropriate fine might be ordered to serve his victim as a slave for the rest of his life, or else for so long as was regarded necessary in the light of the severity of the offense. Similarly, a man who borrowed money—for the Sumerians were minting their own coins—might also be made a slave until the debt had been paid off. The system seems to have worked well, and avoided the need for costly prisons, since each man was held responsible for the correct behavior of his slaves. Female slaves normally became concubines to their masters, and on his death they and any children they had borne by him were customarily given their freedom.

Emergence of a Market Economy

Marriage was normally monogamous, although wealthier men might keep a number of concubines. The old clan system disappeared among the city dwellers, and the individual nuclear family household was the basic unit of economic and social structure. The status of women was high, and property was usually jointly owned by man and wife, so that the women were even entitled to run the family business in the absence of their husbands. Interestingly enough, if the husband were away on business for too long, a wife was entitled to take a lover, but any children that she might produce by this temporary arrangement never-

Golden head of a bull, decorating a musical stringed instrument or lyre, found at the Sumerian city of Ur. (Courtesy of University Museum, Philadelphia.)

theless belonged to her husband, not to their genetic father.

This complex society could not operate on the age-old basis of barter, and of necessity the Sumerian cities developed a metal currency to replace barter. Gold and silver coins were cut, and in order to avoid any disputes about their value, individual bankers stamped each metal piece with their own family seal as proof of its correct value. These bankers received money on deposit and loaned money at interest rates running from 25 percent to as much as 200 percent per annum.

To facilitate expanding commerce, mechanical devices such as the *abacus* were invented. Useful for calculations and also for recording data, the abacus was a counting device comprising counters mounted on parallel strings or wires; it is still used in India and the Middle East. They also invented the device known to anthropologists by the term *quipu*. This constituted a collection of knotted strings which could be used to record simple statistics. However, these mechanical aids to arithmetic were in due course supplemented by a form of writing based upon a phonetic system. Sumerian CUNEIFORM writing was effected by pressing a wedge-shaped wooden stylus repeatedly into a soft clay tablet, which was then usually baked to render it hard, in a series of regular patterns that represented identifiable speech sounds. The technique was so efficient that thousands of baked clay tablets have survived, the majority of which still await translation, even though the script has been deciphered. These provide us with accurate historical information about almost every aspect of Sumerian life, leaving us with the impression that they were essentially modern people.

Those of the tablets whose contents have been translated and published include private letters, legal documents, bills of sale, merchants' accounts, royal decrees, and even schoolboys' exercise "books." Almost the complete code of Sumerian laws has come

down to us in written form. As might be expected, however, although writing was used for numerous purposes as in the modern world, it was also inevitably associated with the mysteries of religion. Thus, the Sumerian schools were attached to the temples, so that all educated men had the training of a priest behind them.

The Power of the Temple

Organized bureaucratic religion played an essential role in Sumeria, and each city state had its own god-protector in whose honor an imposing temple was raised in the center of the city on an artificial mound or tower known as a *ziggurat*. It was the building of these high ziggurat mounds, raising the temple in the direction of heaven, that seems to have inspired the biblical story of the Tower of Babel. The Sumerians also gave the Bible another of its legends, the story of the Flood, which may relate to some earlier flooding of the Tigris and the Euphrates. The Hebrews were, in fact, heavily influenced by the high civilization of Sumeria when they were slaves in the Mesopotamian city of Babylon—just as they had earlier learned much from Egypt when in slavery there.

But religion was not just one other aspect of life in a Sumerian city. It engulfed almost every facet of life. Not only did the temples serve as educational centers, but the political structure of the state, involving the deification of dead kings, was fully integrated with the religious system. Priests managed the official state sacrifices of animals on behalf of the king and made prophecies that might affect the future policy of the administration or at least served to sway the people to loyal support of the king and state. Since the god was the nominal owner of all land, the priesthood was supported by tithes levied upon the farmers as a form of rent payable to the god. In addition, however, the temples seem to have entered into a good deal of trade on their own initiative, and some of the priests spent their entire lives as clerks and salesmen. The state god was also served by a harem of *Sal-me* or temple prostitutes, who were permitted to marry mortals but were not permitted to have children by their husbands. They therefore indulged in primitive forms of birth control, and when this failed, probably resorted to secret infanticide. Any temple concubine who produced a living child was liable to summary execution. Laymen also had access to temple concubines, as a way of heightening their "religious experience."

One might anticipate some conflict between the church and state because religion was so highly organized, but this does not seem to have happened very often. To avoid such a conflict, which would have torn the tiny states asunder, a close family relationship was usually maintained between the royal family and the chief priests. Indeed, the chief priestess who controlled the god's harem of concubines was usually the king's own sister. Where any struggle for dominance arose as a result of personality clashes, therefore, it was a family struggle as often as not, and both parties would find it in their interest to keep the dispute from the ears of the public. Sumerian city life integrated the entire political, social, economic, and religious structure into a single body of unified institutions, every aspect of daily life having religious implications. Any possibility of conflict between theological and administrative interests was out of the question.

Semitic Incursions

Throughout the Old World the fate of the early civilizations based upon settled agriculture seems to have been to become the prey of more militaristic pastoralists. The Sumer-

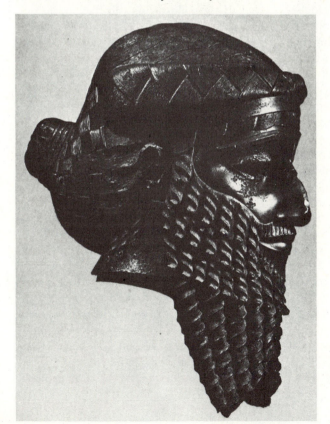

Bronze head of the Assyrian king Sargon, from Nineveh. (Courtesy of Iraq Museum, Baghdad. Photo, Max Hirmer.)

ians warred against each other but never attempted to overthrow the local city god after a victory, believing his power to be territorially delimited, and consequently each city-state tended to retain a measure of cultural autonomy even in defeat. But the arrival of Semitic pastoralists bent upon permanent conquest changed the pattern of life drastically. These came out of the Arabian peninsula and swept into the upper reaches of the Fertile Crescent before moving southward to establish the Akkadian dynasty of Sargon (*c.* 2360 B.C.), and thus coming into conflict with the Sumerian cities of the lower Tigris and Euphrates valleys.

Later generations of Semites, known as Assyrians, succeeded in brutally suppressing all Sumerian opposition by eliminating the inhabitants of cities which resisted their armies. They thus established what might be regarded as the world's first military empire. The Assyrian language now supplanted Sumerian for official state purposes, and Semitic ritual replaced Sumerian ritual. However, being themselves warriors rather than clerks, the Assyrians were obliged to retain an army of Sumerian bureaucrats to administer their new empire, and much of the old Sumerian culture therefore survived, even though the language eventually disappeared.

Contemporary illustrations portray the bearded Semitic kings and nobility in sharp contrast to the shaven heads and skirts of the Sumerian clerks and petty bureaucrats in their older tradition of Sumerian clothing. It was around this time that the upper class women began to wear a heavy veil when appearing in public places, for the Semites secluded their women in a more directly patriarchal tradition. This custom, being later adopted by the Moslems, still survives in many Moslem countries to the present day as the practice of *purda*.

Around 1700 B.C. a Semitic king known as Hammurabi made his capital city at Babylon, elevating the local city god Marduk above all other gods. Demolishing the temples of rival gods in all the cities which were conquered, he began the fashion for monotheism which since then has remained a characteristic of the Semitic peoples. Gathering together the old Sumerian laws, he caused an edited and revised version to be published, which has come down to us as the Code of Hammurabi and which also played a vital role in shaping the Ten Commandments of the biblical Old Testament. It was in Babylon, as is well known, that the Israelites, a politically insignificant people, were held in captivity until the Babylonian empire was eventually overthrown by Indo-European speaking Persians who called themselves Aryans, or "nobles," like their close relatives the Aryans who later invaded India—a title still reflected in the modern name for Persia which is Iran. Destroying Semitic control in Sumeria, the Persians reinstigated local religious freedom, allowing the cities to rebuild their old temples to their own gods, and released the Israelites, who returned to Palestine with many new ideas garnered from their contact with Babylonian and Sumerian civilization.

The Appearance of Iron

As we have already intimated, the Copper and Bronze Ages were dominated by a class of warrior-elite, for communities were mostly still small enough to encourage personal rule, and copper and bronze were so expensive that only the administrative class, directing the resources of their society, could afford its use. But around 1900 B.C. iron ore began to be smelted in Anatolia. Since iron was much more plentiful throughout western Eurasia and was also a much harder metal, a new age was around the corner. However, the area in which iron was initially developed fell within the control of the Hittites, another expastoral ruling caste, who had built a military empire—

which they administered very efficiently—in Anatolia.

Speaking an Indo-European language, which suggests a steppeland point of origin, the Hittites tried to keep the smelting of iron a military secret because they realized that this new hard metal, which was much more readily available than copper, could be used to equip entire armies with superior weapons and armor. Riding in fast two-wheeled "steppe-wagons" or chariots and equipped with iron weapons and armor, the Hittites built an empire which covered the whole of Syria and much of Palestine. At one time it appeared as though they might even dominate Egypt as a similar band of warlike pastoralists, the Hyksos, had done before them. For a thousand years they managed to preserve their empire intact, until they finally exhausted themselves in their efforts to overthrow the Egyptians. The use of iron, however, was to spread over most of Europe and Asia and much of Africa. In Europe especially, the cheaper, harder metal was put to use in agriculture, and the metal-shod plow, pulled by bullocks, made it possible for European farmers to cultivate the heavy but rich loam soils effectively and thereby contributed in no small way to the subsequent rapid advances in European culture and economy.

ANCIENT EGYPT

The long valley of the river Nile and the broad delta at its mouth flood annually, irrigating the rich alluvial soil, and thus providing an excellent environment for the introduction of cultivation. So dark with humus was this soil that the Egyptians called their country *Keme,* the Black Land, and our name *Egypt* is actually derived from the Homeric Greek word *Aiguptos,* referring to the Nile Valley. Egypt was therefore one of the first countries to develop a high civilization, and since its dry

climate had bequeathed us a vast wealth of archeological information, many former archeologists erroneously believed that the Nile Valley was the original center of Western civilization.[3]

However, subsequent excavations in the Middle East and even more recently in Europe have now revealed that this was not the case. Instead of being a center of cultural innovation, the Nile Valley and the rich delta lands have played only a secondary, though still important, role in Western cultural history. In fact, the Nile was situated just beyond the main center of cultural activity, so that it acted rather like a large cul-de-sac or reservoir, absorbing successive waves of cultural innovations and integrating these into its own distinctive traditions to produce one of the most exotic and long-lived civilizations the world has ever seen.

The early hunting and gathering cultures of prehistoric Egypt first gave way to horticulture with the arrival of immigrants from the Middle East around 6000 B.C. who spoke a Hamitic language, closely related to the Semitic tongues of Arabia. These immigrants found great expanses of rich land, covered with fish, wild birds, antelope, lion, and elephant, not to mention crocodiles. Caucasoid and Mediterranean in type, like the hunters they supplanted, these immigrants brought with them a pattern of horticulture based upon the Natufian culture of the Palestinian area, and they and their descendants drained the land and established a pattern of mixed farming throughout the rich delta area which was to become Lower Egypt. Then, as their population expanded, some of the horticulturalists began to migrate further southward up the river Nile, settling on the fertile land on each side of the river where the annual flooding of the Nile made cultivation possible.

The delta area of Lower Egypt eventually

[3] See J. A. Wilson, *The Culture of Ancient Egypt* (Chicago: University of Chicago Press, 1968).

FIG. 49   ANCIENT EGYPT

The Nile Valley, showing major sites in Upper and Lower Egypt.

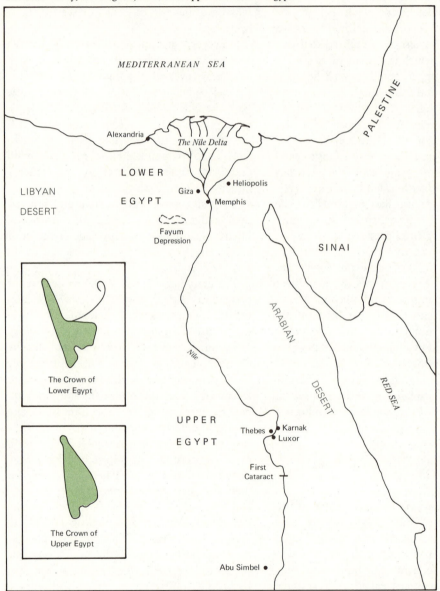

became united under a divine king around 4500 B.C., and Upper Egypt similarly achieved an independent unity under a separate dynasty. For the next 1300 years, known as the Pre-dynastic period, Lower and Upper Egypt existed as autonomous nations, Lower Egypt being symbolically represented by a Red Crown and a Cobra Goddess and Upper Egypt

Pyramids and Sphinx at Giza, on the outskirts of the modern city of Cairo. These date from the great era of pyramid building in the Old Kingdom.

by a White Crown and a Falcon God. Eventually, in 3200 B.C. the Pharaoh Menes, the ruler of Upper Egypt, succeeded in conquering Lower Egypt and united both kingdoms under his own rule, recognizing the local traditions of each.

Following the unification of the two nations Egypt entered the Dynastic period, which lasted until 30 B.C., when the suicide of Cleopatra left Egypt a fief of Rome. During these three millennia as many as 31 dynasties ruled Egypt, the last dynasty being that of the Greek Ptolemies, following the conquest of Egypt by Alexander the Great.

Pharaoh Worship

Immediately after the unification of Upper and Lower Egypt, there was a period of rapid cultural progress. Horticulture gave way to agriculture, and clans and tribes disappeared in favor of a loose nuclear family system.

However, the Egyptian state continued to be divided into some 40 *nomes* or provinces which probably corresponded to the original tribal territories, each *nome* being placed under the control of a *nomarch,* or hereditary regional viceroy, responsible to the Pharaoh. Thus during the Dynastic era Egyptian society came to resemble the great pyramids which were built for the dead Pharaohs—becoming converted into a vast centralized bureaucracy, with the commoners at the base of the pyramid, supporting an elaborate administrative structure which tapered toward the top where all ultimate authority rested in the Pharaoh.

The Egyptians worshiped their Pharaohs as reincarnated gods, and because of their divinity it was customary for the Pharaoh to marry his own sister in order to preserve the purity of the lineage. Many of the Pharaohs who ruled Egypt were distinguished men of letters and science, and their courts were filled with an organized body of architects, writers, priests, and generals selected from among the intellectual elite of the nation, while the local officials who ruled the provinces were usually drawn from the ranks of the old tribal nobility. Nevertheless, considerable opportunity for promotion existed for officials who demonstrated individual talent, notwithstanding class origin. In order to maintain the efficiency of this massive bureaucracy, an army of scribes and accountants was employed to keep accurate records of all transactions, from the number of sacks of grain supplied to the tax collectors by individual peasants, to the vast expenditures involved in the maintenance of the army.

Much of the conservatism of Ancient Egypt may be attributed to the power of its priesthood and to the importance of religion in the Egyptian culture. Indeed, even education was controlled by the priests, and most Egyptian schools were managed by the temples, so that many members of the professional classes were actually trained religious specialists.

Egyptian temples employed two classes of priests, one being concerned with the supervision of ritual ceremonies and the other serving as oracles who claimed to be the medium through which the gods expressed their views. As oracles such priests were also believed to be able to forecast the future, making such predictions in a state of ecstasy, or else basing their forecasts on numerology or upon the movements of the heavenly bodies. In addition, Egyptian temples usually maintained prostitutes, which latter introduced an element of orgiastic physical experience into the religious mysteries. All through their long history Egyptians were always deeply interested in the fate of the soul after death, and it was in Egypt that we first find the idea of a Day of Judgment when the souls of the dead are expected to give an account of their behavior during life.

During the dynasties of the Old Kingdom only royalty and nobility were deemed to possess souls which would outlive the death of the body, but in later centuries it was believed that all men, including commoners, possessed an eternal soul. Since the soul ideally required the preservation of the physical body in order that it might serve as a vehicle in the afterlife, funeral experts developed sophisticated techniques of mummification, not only preserving the flesh by chemical means but also placing life-giving amulets in the wrappings which enclosed the corpse, in the same way that Upper Paleolithic Cro-Magnons appear to have placed charms in their graves to help restore the body to vitality in the world beyond the grave. In order to satisfy the needs of the soul of the Pharaoh after death, hundreds of thousands of Egyptians labored to build the vast pyramids which served as tombs for dead Pharaohs, and skilled craftsmen, numbering tens of thousands, labored to fill these pyramids with rich furniture and equipment. Unfortunately for our archeologists, the vast majority of these treasure hoards were subsequently stolen by professional thieves who developed the art of pyramid entering to the point that even the most refined system of false passages and double doors seldom seemed to have frustrated them.

Government by Bureaucracy

By 2000 B.C. Egypt had therefore acquired a governmental bureaucracy and all the elements of a mass society, while the older caste-like stratification had given way to a class system permitting a degree of social mobility through promotion within the bureaucracy. In this new agrarian society all peasants were entitled to the use of a parcel of land, on which they paid taxes but which was not theirs to sell. In the cities, by contrast, freemen were able to enroll in various crafts or professions, but each occupational group was restricted to a separate residential area. Women were entitled to hold property in their own right and even to occupy high bureaucratic positions. In the absence of a strong clan system, individuals

The Egyptians were deeply preoccupied with the problem of life after death, especially the continued well-being of the soul of the sacred pharaohs. Much of the resources of Egypt were therefore diverted into the construction of mammoth buildings to house the bodies of the divine pharaohs or god-kings and to serve as temples for the priests who served the pharaohs. Valley of the Kings at Luxor. (Courtesy of Egyptian Government, Ministry of Tourism.)

Hieroglyphic inscriptions painted on the plaster walls of a royal tomb at Luxor. Figure on right is the Goddess Isis. (Courtesy of the Egyptian State Tourist Administration.)

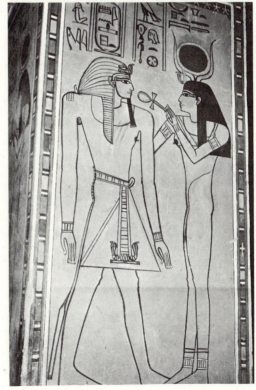

were permitted to choose their own marriage partners. However, although monogamy was common, the richer men frequently had several wives, in which case the senior wife exercised authority over subsequent wives. Matrilineal descent was common, as was adultery, which is frequently the case, as we have seen, when paternity has little legal significance.

Egyptian civilization differed from that of Mesopotamia in a number of ways. At its peak, the population of Upper and Lower Egypt probably reached five or six million, but Egyptian society always remained essentially agrarian, the cities being little more than administrative and religious centers. While the system of writing developed in Mesopotamia was cuneiform, based upon phonetic sounds, that which emerged in Egypt was hieroglyphic. Egyptian HIEROGLYPHIC WRITING comprised pictorial symbols which stood for complete ideas by themselves. Instead of being impressed on clay tablets, the Egyptian signs were inscribed with an ink on *papyrus*, a form of paper derived from the papyrus plant, or else painted or incised on some other surface such as pottery, wood, or even stone walls. In the course of time certain stylized hieroglyphic symbols came to represent phonetic sounds and Egyptian writing also developed a phonetic basis, although the transition was more difficult than in the case of the more geometrical cuneiform script of Mesopotamia.

The Egyptians were a very practical and realistic people despite their absorption with horoscopes and their concept of the afterlife. Not only did they develop an advanced science of astronomy, but it was the Egyptians who first invented glass, and as jewelers and enamel workers the quality of their work is virtually unmatched. They were excellent woodworkers and their architectural and sculptural skill is well known. Their art was highly stylized, but retained sufficient naturalism to distinguish between the various racial types of the people with whom they came into contact. Not content with ornamenting their clothes, furnishings, and buildings, the Egyptians developed a sophisticated science of cosmetics, using eye shadow, rouging their cheeks, painting the palms of their hands and the soles of their feet with henna—as many rural people still do in the Middle East and India—and making wigs of human hair for their womenfolk. Men shaved not only their faces but also the tops of their heads, thus presenting a startling contrast to the hirsute inhabitants of Europe. Men

wore a short skirt drawn tightly round the waist with a belt, while women wore a longer skirt; both went bare above the waist, ladies of fashion frequently painting their breasts with gold paint.

Being preoccupied with the ideas of death and the afterlife, the Egyptians never became a truly militaristic people, and the vast armies maintained by the Pharaohs were often recruited from neighboring tribes and subject peoples. In the New Kingdom especially, mercenary soldiers became the rule, and as the centuries rolled by, a large proportion of the vacancies in the Egyptian army were actually filled by slaves. In consequence, Egypt owed its longevity as a civilization to its isolated position on the perimeter of the civilized world, largely protected from the more turbulent centers of Europe and the Middle East not by its own military ability but by the Mediterranean Sea and the Sinai Desert. Relatively secure in this position, the Egyptian civilization maintained a substantial degree of cultural continuity for a total of six millennia until its conquest by Islamic Arabs in 639 A.D. wiped out the memory of the old Egyptian culture, with all the later Greek, Roman, and Christian influences. Invading Arabs replaced the old Hamitic language by Arabic throughout the land, except among a small sect of Coptic Christians who kept the language alive until the present century.

THE MINOAN CIVILIZATION

Recent excavation in the Communist Balkan and Central European countries and revised carbon-14 chronologies for European artifacts have now refuted the popular myth of a barbaric prehistoric Europe which was "enlightened" by the diffusion of culture from more advanced Middle Eastern countries. Although some crops, such as wheat, may have been first

FIG. 50   OLD EUROPEAN AND THE MINOAN CIVILIZATIONS

Map showing the Chalcolithic (stone-copper) age civilization of Old Europe, 5300–3500 B.C. This had developed a written script, probably ancestral to Cretan Linear A. (Courtesy of Prof. Marija Gimbutas and *Journal of Indo-European Studies.*)

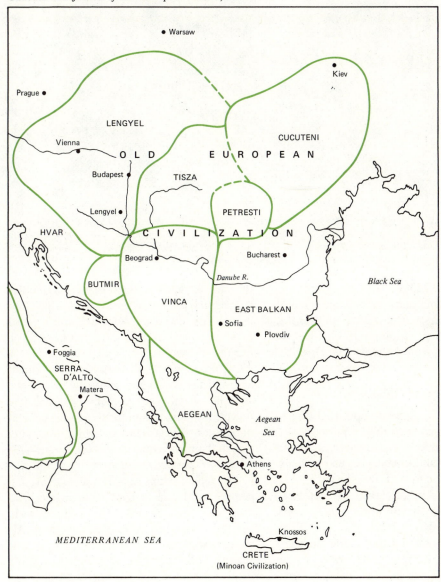

As European horticulture was steadily replaced by agriculture and the ox-drawn plow replaced the hoe, large farmhouses were built, with simple partitions that separated the living quarters of the farmer's family from the animals. Reconstruction of an early North European farmhouse, circa 3000 B.P. (Courtesy of Landesmuseum, Schloss Gottorp.)

cultivated in the Middle East, many animals, such as the dog, pig, and cow, are now believed to have been first domesticated in Europe, and the antiquity of farming in Europe is now known to match that of the Middle East.

The Civilization of Old Europe

Archeology also shows a population of settled villages, each probably representing a zadruga-type single clan settlement, from the Euphrates to the Danube. Regular trading contacts may have existed over the entire area from a much earlier date than was formerly suspected. The inhabitants of these settlements are believed to have owned the land communally, cooperating together as the members of a single extended family. The crops raised in any one area would have depended to some extent upon climate and local conditions, as would the animals first domesticated in different regions. Certainly pottery-making styles differ from one region of this horticultural belt

to another, and the early Balkano-Danubian culture, named by archeologist Marija Gimbutas as the *Old European Civilization*, seems to have placed considerable emphasis upon fertility rituals, as would be likely among a horticultural people. Elaborate religious rituals involved the wearing of masks by actors, and an echo of this old religion seems to have survived among the original Aegean population, known as Pelasgian, which was later overrun by invading Indo-Europeans—the Greeks of classical antiquity.[4]

The people of this area were already making pottery by the seventh millennium B.C., and ships with sails traversed the Mediterranean, doubtless engaging in trading operations. Although Scandinavia was still relatively unattractive because of the slow recession of the Würm glaciation, and northern Europe was

[4] See M. Gimbutas "Old Europe *c.* 7000–3500 B.C.: The Earliest European Civilization before the Infiltration of the Indo-European Peoples" *Journal of Indo-European Studies* 1:1-20 (1973).

still too cold for crops at this time, the Adriatic, the Balkano-Danubian area, and the Aegean Sea all participated in an advanced civilization independently inventing copper smelting as well as producing the oldest written script yet known to archeologists, both prior to 5000 B.C.

This early Old European script has not yet been deciphered, but its hieroglyphic symbols suggestively resemble those of the undeciphered Linear A of the Minoan civilization of Crete. Even the Etruscan script may ultimately prove to be related in some way to this ancient Old European script, while the runes of northern Europe and the Ogham alphabet of the Celts may be a primitive form of writing derived from an older script already in use before the ancestors of the Scandinavians and the Celts arrived in their present homelands.

The island of Crete, situated between the Aegean and the Mediterranean, appears to have escaped conquest by the Indo-Europeans until around 1500 B.C. when Dorian Greeks stormed its cities. The arriving Greeks, Slavs, Latins, and other Indo-European warrior peoples destroyed the memory of the older society but absorbed much of its material culture. A new form of writing known to archeologists as Linear B then replaced the still undeciphered Linear A script of the older Cretan civilization. This fortuitous survival of an Old European civilization into the second millennium B.C. gives us much valuable information which fits well with the older archeological evidence on the mainland, dating from the second and third millennia back to the eighth and ninth millennia, in a more or less unbroken chain of cultural continuity. Only one obvious reservation must be made: Crete represents the coastal trading form of this ancient civilization, and with the passing of centuries, undoubted influences from Egypt and other eastern Mediterranean sources enter into the Cretan or Minoan civilization. These influences must be disassociated from the Old European elements.

Examples of what is now believed to have been the world's earliest written script: a) Linear symbols that appear on figurines, pottery, and cult objects from Vinča archeological sites. b) and c) Inscribed spindlewhorl from Fafos in southern Yugoslavia. d) An early Vinča bowl with an inscription on the inside wall. (Courtesy of Marija Gimbutas and *Journal of Indo-European Studies*.)

Maritime Commerce

The original Cretans or Minoans were typically Mediterranean Caucasoids in type. Dark-haired, dark-eyed with aquiline profiles, light-skinned, fine-boned, and of moderate height, they appear to have possessed an ancient horticultural tradition, but the soil of Crete is poor. Thus, since its island situation in a strategic position athwart the sea lanes of the eastern Mediterranean placed it in an admirable position for seagoing commerce, Crete became heir to the ancient Mediterranean naval tradition. Excavations in the Messara plain of eastern Crete show that by the fourth millennium B.C. Cretan merchants were importing copper ore from Cyprus, manufacturing bronze, silver, and gold ornaments, and in particular producing olive oil for export in attractive pottery jars. A flourishing ship building industry, which was later to denude the island of its forests, was already established, producing *galleys,* ships which could be rowed with oars against the wind and could also harness favorable winds with the aid of a large square sail. The bows and sterns of these ships swept upward in a picturesque curve, and the bows were shod with pointed metal rams for use in sea combat against other ships. These galleys were also equipped with anchors, which were traditionally credited as an invention of the Cretans but more probably belonged to a much more ancient Mediterranean sea culture.

The evidence of archeology suggests that the

A 2000-year-old mosaic from Coimbra in Portugal. The design illustrates the strong maritime tradition of the Mediterranean area, already over 6000 years old when this mosaic was made. (Courtesy of the Director-General of Information, Portugal.)

Cretans probably lived in large extended families like the old zadruga settlements of the mainland horticulturalists, and their later literature implies that they may have possessed matrilineal traditions. Their most important deity was an earth goddess—who seems to reflect the ancient tradition of Venus figurines and fertility cults of Old Europe—to whom they offered agricultural produce in their religious festivals. By 2000 B.C. the Minoan cities indicate, by the size and frequency of their dwellings, a large and prosperous merchant class, presumably representing the merchants who engaged in overseas trade with the coastal towns on the mainland of Europe, Asia, and Africa. However, Crete also produced warriors, armed with spears and swords, and clad in bronze armor and plumed bronze helmets.

Houses were built, as on the mainland, of timber and stucco but differed from those of the Balkans in being flat-roofed, this being doubtless a local adaptation to suit the Mediterranean climate. But by far the most impressive building was that of the Minos or priest-king, from whose title the name Minoan has been derived and applied to the entire Cretan civilization. Situated at Knossos, the palace of the Minos had over a thousand rooms. Some of these rooms obviously represented warehouse space; it is believed from this and other evidence that the priest-king himself engaged in the export trade, having dealings with the Pharaohs of Egypt among others.

Minoan cities were elaborately equipped from the point of view of sanitation. They were the first cities in the world to possess bathrooms and toilets and the first to use the rain water collected from the roofs to flush out the system of underground drains or sewers, in much the same way that modern Western cities still harness rainwater to flush out their sewer systems. Undoubtedly the Minoans lived a comfortable and indeed, luxurious life. Their art shows a distinctively *European* naturalism which has been identified by many historians as setting it apart from the art traditions and ethos of the Middle East and Egypt. We have to thank these naturalistic pictures for the story that they tell of Cretan life. Vivid frescoes revealing colorful plants, land- and seascapes, decorate the walls of some rooms, giving us a detailed knowledge of what the Cretans looked like and the gay life that they lived. One thing is quite sure: they liked to use elegant furniture and to surround themselves with beautiful objects, but in the balmy Mediterranean climate they never lost their love of the outdoors.

While younger men and persons of lower status wore only a brief loin cloth, drawn up around the waist by means of a belt, more prosperous people attired themselves in a long loose gown similar to the later Roman toga which undoubtedly belonged to an ancient Mediterranean tradition. Women wore high heeled shoes, blouses, and either skirts or else loose pajamas. When out of doors, the women wore large and stylish hats, doubtless to protect their fair complexions from the strong sunshine, for women of status are portrayed as being ivory-skinned. Both men and women wore lavish quantities of exquisitely worked jewelry.

The Legend of the Minotaur

Later Greek legends tell how the Cretan ships seized young men and sacrificed them to the Minotaur, a fearsome creature, half man and half bull, which the Cretans were said to keep in a labyrinth. Some light on these legends can be obtained from frescoes excavated at Knossos which show young men and women, clad only in loin clothes and sandals, leaping over bulls in what appears to be a display of acrobatics. So far as we can put the story together, the Cretans kept sacred bulls which were first subjected to some kind of ritual ceremonial, possibly involving the display of acrobatics that is portrayed on frescoes

more than once, and then sacrificed to the gods. Many pottery symbols of horned bulls' heads and of dancers wearing horned masks have been unearthed from the mainland Old European civilization. These seem to be related to the Minoan bull-teasing ritual, and there seems to be good reason to speculate that the popular Spanish bullfighting tradition may be directly descended from an ancient Mediterranean religious ritual, involving the teasing or taunting of a bull prior to its sacrificial death.

Much of what we still do not know about the earliest European civilization would doubtless be revealed if we could only succeed in deciphering the ancient Linear A of Crete, the old hieroglyphic script of the Balkano-Danubian area, and possibly also the Etruscan writing. The later Linear B, used after the Greek or Dorian conquest of Crete in the middle of the second millennium B.C., has been

Seascape from a Minoan fresco. (Courtesy of Alison Frantz.)

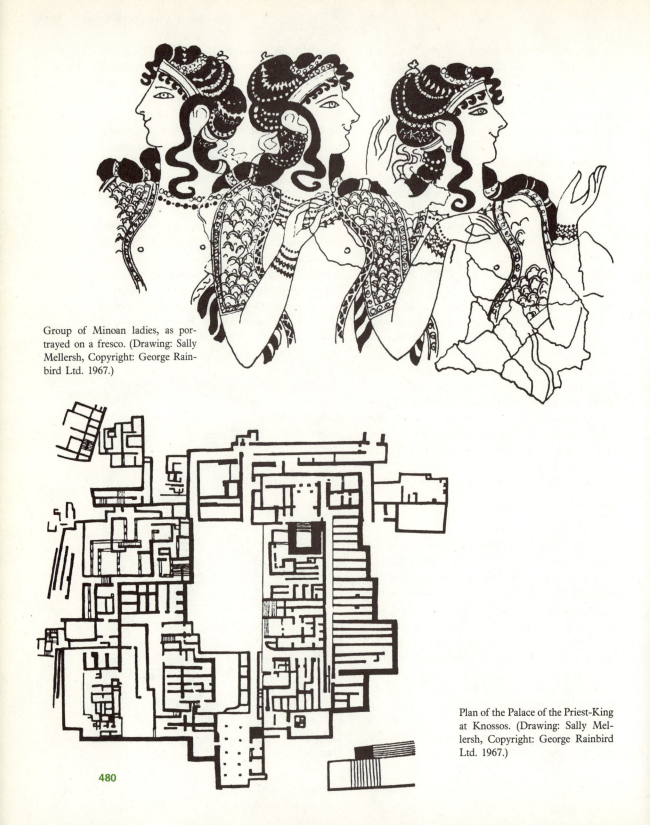

Group of Minoan ladies, as portrayed on a fresco. (Drawing: Sally Mellersh, Copyright: George Rainbird Ltd. 1967.)

Plan of the Palace of the Priest-King at Knossos. (Drawing: Sally Mellersh, Copyright: George Rainbird Ltd. 1967.)

480

deciphered, but the knowledge gained was disappointing, for most of the tablets related only to trading records. In any case, the entire pattern of life changed with the Dorian conquest. Typically Indo-European *polis* or castles were built, and Crete became more famous for its mercenary war galleys, which could be hired by anyone willing to pay the price, than for commerce. With the fall of Knossos to the Indo-Europeans, one of the last outposts of Old Europe disappeared, and the new Europe bore little resemblance to the older tradition. As the Indo-Europeans spread themselves as a warrior aristocracy over Europe, the old pattern of horticultural civilization gave way to a patchwork of principalities, dotted with castles in which kings and nobles, attended by their band of warrior companions—just as we have described in the case of Homeric Greece—laying the foundations of feudalism. Under special circumstances, the Indo-European conquest gave birth to three new civilizations: Celtic, Greek, and Roman. But each of these is worth a library in its own right, and we will not attempt in this volume to describe how the classic European civilizations evolved out of their Homeric-style prototypes.

THE INDUS VALLEY CIVILIZATION

The Neolithic culture entered India from the direction of Persia and Sumeria, and indeed it would seem that as early as 3500 B.C., horticulture was spreading eastward across Persia, through Seistan and entering the Indus Valley through Baluchistan. Early Kulli pottery in the Indus Valley is decorated with pictures of bulls tethered to trees, which are virtually identical to similar pottery decorations in early Dynastic Sumeria.[5]

[5] See M. Wheeler, *The Indus Civilization* (New York: Cambridge University Press, 1968).

The builders of the early Indus Valley civilization were also of a general Mediterranean Caucasoid variety, differing sharply from the older, partially Australoid hunters and gatherers and from the Dravidians of modern southern India, although there is evidence that some elements from each of these populations may have been absorbed into this new society. One image of a prostitute or dancing girl reveals especially Australoid features, indicating that at least among the lower classes some elements of the older population may have survived.

However, although horticulture itself penetrated the Indus Valley from the west and trading connections were maintained with the Tigris and Euphrates area, the newly developing urban civilizations, Harappa in the north-central portion of the Indus Valley and Mohenjo Daro in the southern area, soon acquired their own distinctive character. Trade objects excavated indicate the existence of regular commercial contact between Sumeria and the Indus region, but each culture had its own distinctive character. Considering the fact that both the Sumerian and the Indus Valley civilizations had the same Iranian-Anatolian origin, their subsequent differences impress us more than their similarities.

Unfortunately, although we have vast ruins to excavate, the Indus Valley language remains a mystery to us, and we have no historical information. However, the physical evidence implies an elaborate sociopolitical and economic system, for the culture maintained itself from around 2300 B.C. down until 1500 B.C. over an area at least 1000 miles in length, embracing several cities which nevertheless reveal a remarkable degree of cultural homogeneity. These were carefully planned. The city of Mohenjo-Daro covered around one square mile—much smaller than the Sumerian cities—but the streets were carefully laid out on a grid system, and although they were not paved, the roads were equipped with brick drains.

FIG. 51   THE INDUS VALLEY CIVILIZATION

The Indus Valley, showing major Indus Valley civilization sites and the course taken by invading Indo-Aryan advanced pastoralists.

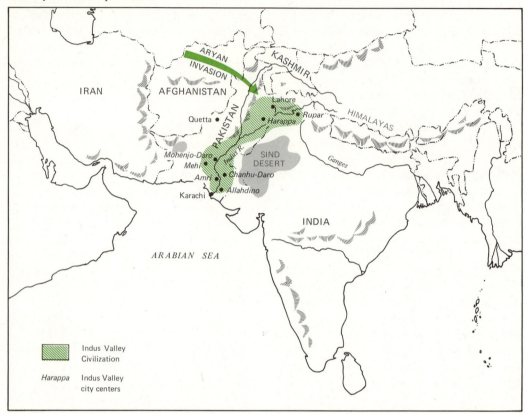

The houses of the wealthier citizens were segregated from those of the lower classes; indeed it is possible that India already possessed, in the Indus Valley civilization, a caste system similar to that which it has preserved to the present. However, there can be no doubt that the Indian caste system of today owes much to the arrival of the pastoral Aryan, Indo-European speakers who arrived just as the Indus Valley civilization was collapsing in the middle of the second millennium B.C. The dominant classes lived in houses of baked brick built around courtyards and equipped with bathrooms, while the lower classes occupied smaller cottages erected in rows adjacent to what appear to be workshops and factories.

The cities of the Indus Valley also reveal another peculiarity. Dominated by a fortified citadel, they always reveal a central group of buildings built around a large artificial pool or water tank, rectangular in shape. Remembering the ritual bathing practiced in India since the earliest times, and also the ancient pools which still house sacred crocodiles in present-day India, it has been suggested that these buildings might have accommodated a priestly bureaucracy. Again, circumstantial evidence to support this interpretation is supplied by the knowledge that the invading Aryans, who succeeded the Indus Valley civilization, borrowed many religious ideas, in particular that of a powerful priesthood, from the older culture.

The Coming of the Aryans

What led to the decay of the Indus Valley civilization, with its striking pictographic seals and its red and black painted pottery, is still not known. The invading pastoral Indo-Europeans who gave India its Aryan character have been blamed, but archeologists believe that the great cities of the Indus were already declining before the arrival of these warrior kings and their retainers, whose courts so closely resembled those of the Scythians and the Homeric Greeks. Instead, soil exhaustion has been suggested as a possible explanation.

The Indus Valley civilization has left us a wealth of material evidence but no literature. Strangely, the succeeding Aryans have left us a wealth of literature and a group of languages spoken by literally hundreds of millions of Indians today, but virtually no material remains. The reason for the dearth of archeological material is simply explained. We know from their literature that the invading cattle-herding warriors, who reached India around the fifteenth century B.C. from the direction of Iran and the Asian steppes, lived in wood and stucco houses and burned their dead on funeral pyres, thus leaving archeologists neither habitation sites nor tombs to excavate. Only a few settlements have been identified, and these reveal little more than the foundation marks of their house timbers, for they seem also to have been a reasonably tidy people who left little litter lying around.

Nevertheless, the rich oral literature which they brought with them was elaborated after their arrival in India and came to be written down soon after the eleventh century B.C. as the art of writing spread among them— roughly simultaneously with the spread of iron. Rejecting social and cultural admixture with the Indus Valley, Dravidian, and Austro-Asiatic Munda peoples whom they conquered, the Indo-Aryans brought their own highly stratified caste system with them and possibly elaborated this with traditions borrowed from the older Indus Valley civilization which may also have practiced a rigid system of occupational classification. Although 3500 years have elapsed since the arrival of the Aryans in India, much of their culture has survived into modern India. Even the village of Gopalpur, which we shall describe in Chapter 31, retains to this day much of the Indo-Aryan inspiration, despite the fact that the people of Gopalpur are South Indians who do not claim descent from the Aryan invaders of the north, but accepted Aryan domination and the Aryan-based Hindu religion.

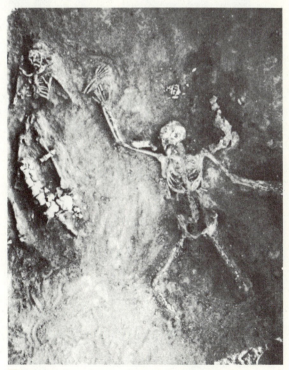

Skeletons of massacred residents of Mohenjo-daro, lying in the streets where they were slaughtered. (Courtesy of Sir Mortimer Wheeler.)

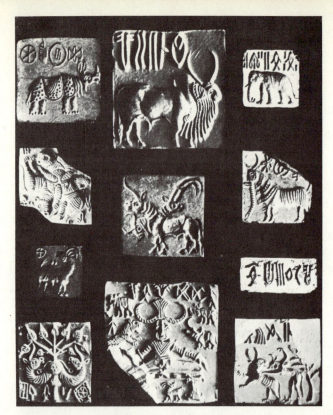

Seals from Mohenjo-daro and the Indus Valley cities frequently portray animals. These include the "brahmin" bull, elephant, rhinoceros, and various mythical creatures. (Courtesy of Sir Mortimer Wheeler.)

The "Great Bath" at Mohenjo-daro, believed to have been used for religious ceremonies. (Courtesy of Dr. George F. Dales.)

THE FAR EAST

The increase in archeological activity within the USSR during the past two decades has greatly clarified Asian prehistory and brought about a realization of the immense cultural significance of the steppeland corridor which links Europe and western Asia to the Far East. Marco Polo was by no means the first traveler to reach the Orient by this route. Indeed, it would now seem probable that even before the Upper Paleolithic, Neanderthal men may have extended the area of human settlement across Central Asia to make contact with the populations of Northern China. The discovery of the remains of a Neanderthal boy at Teshik-Tash, near Samarkand, and of Lower Paleolithic artifacts in areas still further east are highly suggestive that this was the case.[6]

Whatever may be the facts regarding Neanderthal settlement in Asia, evidence of the spread of Upper Paleolithic traditions eastward from Europe and western Asia is quite conclusive (see Fig. 16). Neolithic culture reached southern Turkmenia, in southwestern Asia, by the fourth millennium B.C., and had reached a comparable level in northeastern Central Asia by the third millennium. While considerable local differences do exist in the Neolithic traditions of eastern and western Asia, it is permissible to refer to a circumpolar Neolithic tradition, marked by pit houses, extending across Eurasia from west to east.

Although some scholars still attempt to maintain the independent invention of cultivation in northern China, chronologically it is agreed that the first evidence for cultivation in northern China dates around 2500 B.C. with what is known as the Yang Shao culture in the Valley of the Yellow River, close to Peking, the ancient capital of China. This was some 5000 years later than the beginnings of culti-

---

[6] A. L. Mongait, *Archaeology in the USSR* (Baltimore: Penguin Books, Inc., 1961), Chap. 2.

vation in southwestern Asia. In view of the increasing evidence for cultural contacts throughout the Asian steppelands, the probability that the idea of cultivation traveled from the West to the East is therefore high.

The early Yang Shao villages of northern China were constructed on small elevations above the flat plains which flooded when the rivers overflowed. These first Chinese horticulturalists used painted pottery closely similar to that of the West Asian tradition, and in addition to millet, a seemingly indigenous crop, they cultivated wheat and barley both of which are believed to have originated in western Asia. In addition to dogs, they kept pigs, sheep, and cattle—all animals which were most probably derived from western Eurasia. Nevertheless, as we would expect there were many inventions that were local. In addition to the cultivation of millet, the Yang Shao villages kept silk worms, making fine clothes from silk as well as coarse cloth from hemp. At a later date they also developed the cultivation of rice, which was to spread to so many parts of the globe from eastern Asia.

The Grey-eyed Hsia

The Chinese have always been historically-minded people, and the early historians of dynastic China commendably strove to collect and record the many legends from the early twilight of their country. According to such quasi-historical works as the Book of Changes, Neolithic China was ruled by an upper caste of red-haired and green or grey-eyed *Hsia* nobles, known as the "Hundred Clans," who ruled over a "myriad black-haired people." These may have been descendants, in part at least, of the aboriginal possibly Australoid *Miao,* against whom the Hsia warred, and who are described as having dark skins. Even today "grey" eyes are not uncommon among the peoples of Central Asia and Siberia, and it may be significant that the *Hsia* royalty were

FIG. 52   ANCIENT CHINA

Map of China showing center of earliest Shang civilization situated in the valley of the Yellow River. The route from the steppeland corridor lies westward along the Yellow River, south of the Gobi Desert.

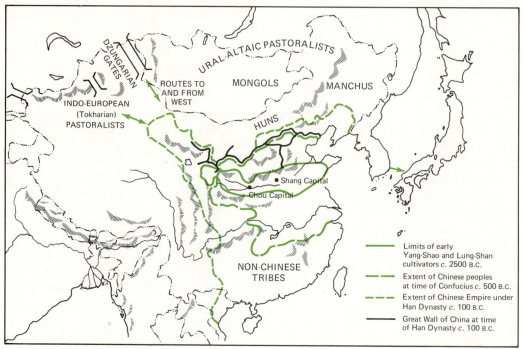

priest-kings, who worshipped sky gods, similar to those of the pastoralists of the West Asian and European steppes.

The coming of these invaders, who presumably descended upon the Yang Shao from the steppelands of the west, may have occurred at the time that archeologists trace the replacement of many of the lightly fortified or unfortified villages of the Yang Shao by larger fortified towns. Rectangular shaped houses appear in place of the older round houses at this time and improvements in the quality of pottery indicate the introduction of the potters' wheel. Similarly, agriculture replaces horticulture.

Shang Charioteers

According to the early Chinese histories, a new people seized the government around 1750 B.C., and established the Shang dynasty. Archeology supports the historical record by tracing the sudden appearance of a new and highly developed bronze culture. The Bronze Age in China appears suddenly fully developed, with little evidence of local evolution, and is most easily explained by immigration of the new Shang rulers whose ancestors may have come from the steppes, bringing with them a knowledge of metallurgy which presumably originated in Europe and western

Asia. Piecing together the data derived from the earliest records and the more dependable evidence of archeology, we find that Shang society resembled early European feudal society, and showed all the marks of a stratified society arising from the superimposition of a warlike horse-owning aristocracy on a settled farming peasantry. Clad in bronze armor as they drove their chariots into battle, at the head of their more lightly armed foot soldiers, the heroic Shang warrior-nobles were ancestor worshippers who offered numerous animal and human sacrifices to the departed spirits. Superbly cast animal and bird-shaped bronze urns and tripods were used in the rituals honoring these ancestors. The Shang kings were buried lavishly, along with their horses, chariots, servants, womenfolk, warrior companions, and in one case at least a favorite dog. Indeed these burials closely resembled those of the Scythian kings, and axes found in Shang graves are similar to those of the Scythians. Another old European Paleolithic tradition, which has survived among Siberian shamans until present times, was also commonly practiced by the Shang kings. This was divination by heating the shoulder blades of a sheep and reading the answers to specific questions from the pattern and frequency of cracks in the bones. The Shang costume—trousers and coats with sleeves—was also suggestive of a western steppeland origin.

A unique cultural trait was a form of pictographic writing, using some 5000 rectangular seal characters. Some of these have been deciphered and a typical inscription, painted in black on an oracle bone, reads "Day *huei mao,* oracle examined by augur *Huan;* sacrifice of a dog to the ancestor *chia.*" The style of these characters cannot be traced to any other source outside of China, but Shang mathematical records were kept by means of knotted cords, virtually identical to those used by the ancient Sumerians.

According to Chinese historical records, the sophisticated Shang society was itself overrun by a horse-riding tribal people from the west, and the last Shang emperor was politely deposed in 1122 B.C. The Chinese empire was still restricted, it must be remembered, to northern China and the basin of the Yellow River, although its boundaries were steadily being pushed southwards.

The "Son of Heaven"

These new invaders were the Chou, who were probably of Ural-Altaic stock, closely related to the Huns who later invaded Europe. In China they established themselves as benevolent feudal lords, like the Shang nobility they replaced, differing from the barons of

A Manchu man of the landowning class, photographed against a background of Western style furnishings. (Courtesy of the Smithsonian Institution, National Anthropological Archives.)

feudal Europe primarily in the fact that each Chou noble held his appointment directly from the emperor, instead of from the next most senior nobleman above him. Like the Shang, the Chou were ancestor worshippers, their lives being strictly bounded by religious ritual. Although they introduced a penal code to control the behavior of the peasants and commoners, this code did not apply to the nobles, whose behavior was effectively dictated by the requirements of an elaborate code of ritual.

The Chou nobility were elegant, highly literate, and well-educated, receiving as children systematic training in the arts of architecture, music, charioteering, ceremonial ritual, mathematics, and writing. Each local baron maintained his own court, in which he was attended by a body of companions comprising the members of his own family and such warriors of noble birth as might take service with him. Holding the joint family as its ideal, Chou society was strongly patrilineal and familistic. Beyond the joint family there was a larger "name group" or clan which was strictly exogamous. On marriage, women were admitted to the worship of their husbands' ancestors, but unlike the women of ancient Greece and Rome they were not permitted to worship their fathers' ancestors, even when young.

From the centuries of Chou rule we may trace the origins of the traditional pattern of the Chinese social system. Only the peasants, who could not afford the luxury of a large household implied by the joint family system, appear to have retained a nuclear-family pattern of social organization.

Claiming divine descent as "the Sons of Heaven," the royal Chou dynasty lasted for nearly a thousand years. During this time the use of iron and also of swords was introduced to China from the West, and the crossbow was invented, an indigenous innovation. In the latter part of the Chou period, however, the central government seems to have lost control over the nobles, and internal warfare became common.

As the nobles became increasingly concerned with the problem of personal survival, they tended to delegate administrative matters to professional bureaucrats recruited from among the commoners, thus laying the foundations for the literate bureaucracy which was to become one of the outstanding features of later Chinese civilization.

Confucius and Lao Tzu

This literate bureaucracy constituted a major force for stability during the next 2000 years of Chinese civilization. It also provided a number of great philosopher scholars, whose writings greatly influenced the subsequent pattern of Chinese history until Communist armies overran the country in the present century. In the northern portion of the empire, where the ancestor worshipping tradition of the steppes was most firmly ensconced, Confucius preached a paternalistic and unchanging moral system reflecting the ancestral pastoral traditions of the Shang and Chou nobility. The state itself was seen to be but a single large family, with the emperor at the head of this family. Every individual inherited an ascribed status and role. The obligations attached to this role, similar to those of son to father, brother to sister, wife to husband, or cousin to cousin, were to be adhered to faithfully. If all men adhered to their duty effectively, there would be a general freedom from tension, and society would be prosperous and happy. Only if men failed to act out their proper roles could unhappiness and misery result.

In southern China, which was less affected by the steppeland tradition, and where the old Neolithic peasant traditions were stronger, another teacher named Lao Tzu, laid the foundations of the more mystical doctrine of Taoism. Taoism was rooted in Neolithic nature worship. It expounded two principles, the Yin (female) and the Yang (male). The female and the male polar elements dominated the universe in an amoral sense. Life was not seen as a struggle of good against bad, but simply as a mechanistic operation of the male and female principle fertilizing the world of nature and causing constant rebirth and rejuvenation. Confucius stressed the social need for familistic loyalties and moral behavior, and even implied that an emperor who failed his people might be overthrown. Taoism, by contrast, required the ruler to rule wisely but benevolently, in the sense that nature is benevolent but firm. However, it portrayed the governmental structure as a part of the natural order of the universe and denied the right of the people to question the actions of a ruler who failed to govern wisely.

The Confucian and Taoist doctrines were subsequently elaborated by numerous scholars into complex philosophies, with the power of religions. Taoism, especially, became highly mystical, but being philosophies rather than missionary religions both Confucianism and Taoism tolerated the appearance of missionary Buddhist priests when these arrived from India and Tibet.

Centralization under the Ch'in State

The Chou dynasty finally collapsed in disorder in 221 B.C., as the nobility slaughtered each other unmercifully, and was replaced for a short 15 years by a Ch'in dynasty from the Hunnish state of Ch'in on the edge of the steppelands. Like the Chou, the Ch'in were originally militaristic pastoralists with a strong disciplinarian tradition. Equipped with a powerful cavalry they soon overran the disorderly Chou realms, establishing a new empire under the personal rule of their leader Shih Huang Ti. The new emperor attempted to impose a uniform pattern of culture on the conquered feudal states, destroying the last relics of tribalism and making China into a centralized state. He thought to reeducate the population

A Mongol peasant farmer of the stock that raided China constantly, despite the protection afforded by the Great Wall. (Courtesy of Musée de l'Homme, Paris.)

into accepting the Ch'in system by seeking to eliminate all memory of the previous culture, in much the same way as the rulers of the modern Chinese state have attempted to exercise complete mind control by eradicating the traditions of the earlier culture. Virtually all existing books and records were ordered to be destroyed, except for copies which were placed in the imperial library for the restricted use of approved scholars. Developing the breach between the nobility and the new bureaucracy still further, the Ch'ins separated military and administrative roles, placing the former in the hands of professional generals and the latter in the hands of a bureaucratic order of imperial

A Chinese barber shaving the front half of a man's head. Although the ruling landowning classes wore rich clothes, the peasant classes of China always dressed in a somewhat sober fashion. (Courtesy of the Smithsonian Institution, National Anthropological Archives.)

clerks. The officers of these military and administrative bureaucracies were appointed by the emperor, and regularly transferred from one position to another to prevent them from acquiring too much personal influence or becoming corrupt. By these measures it was possible to impose a centralized code of law. One other achievement of the Ch'in, during their brief rule, was the construction of the greater portion of the Great Wall of China, in an attempt to prevent further invaders from the steppes from repeating history.

The Ch'in dynasty was replaced by the Han dynasty in 206 B.C. and at this stage we enter historical times. The Han emperors endorsed Confucianism as an official philosophy and also introduced a system of competitive written examinations for all appointments to the clerical bureaucracy, the members of which now ranked higher than the richest merchants. These examinations were heavily classical in flavor, being based on the candidates' ability to write scholarly essays and poetry. By 100 A.D. a Han government census revealed a population of some 60 millions in China, all living under the rule of a central imperial regime. Despite subsequent insurrections and invasions (such as that of the Ural-Altaic Manchus), the basic configuration of Chinese culture was finally settled. Life in China thereafter retained a consistant and stable pattern until the late nineteenth century, when the rule of the Son of Heaven was rudely disturbed by increasing contact with seaborne Europeans, who arrived on the Chinese shores equipped with a more advanced technology and many alien and politically corrosive ideas. What kind of cultural synthesis will eventually result still remains to be seen.

490

Japan

Continued pressure upon China by warlike pastoralists was to have little effect after the Han dynasty. The Ural-Altaic speaking Manchus succeeded in settling Manchuria and also in establishing themselves as the Manchu dynasty in China, but they failed to change the basic pattern of Chinese civilization to any marked extent. Other Ural-Altaic speaking peoples moved further eastward, however, and as Koreans established themselves in the peninsula that we today know as Korea.

At that time, the island of Japan was occupied by two different peoples. The northern two-thirds were held by a hunting and gathering people, who reflected the old Circumpolar Upper Paleolithic culture, and possessed Bear cults similar to those of the ancient Cro-Magnon men in Europe. However, a horticultural Jomon people were established in southern Japan, and these warred constantly with the Ainu. This situation was drastically changed when, around the third or fourth centuries B.C., the islands were invaded by a horse-riding military aristocracy, who were equipped with bronze armor and bronze weapons and who brought with them pottery and the knowledge of agriculture. These invaders came from Korea, speaking a tongue which was related to Korean and to the other Ural-Altaic languages of Central Asia. As Japanese, they soon dominated the Neolithic population in the southern part of Japan, and proceeded to wage an intermittent war against the Paleolithic Ainu hunters, steadily pushing them backwards, until today the Ainu survive only in the northern islands of Hokkaido and Sakhalin.

These Bronze Age invaders, who were to give Japan its name, its language, and its traditional civilization, were organized into clans

Ainu man and woman standing in front of a traditional thatched house on Hokkaido Island, Japan. The house has a small aperture just beneath the ridge for the escape of smoke, and also a hole in the roof, which can be closed with a shutter. A mat may be dropped over the front door at night. (Courtesy of the Smithsonian Institution, National Anthropological Archives.)

and tribes, with a nobility comprising clan and tribal chiefs. For several centuries both clans and tribes retained their local independence. The clansmen toiled as farmers while the nobles constituted a warrior *samurai* class, with their own *bushido* code of ethics and ritual, which forbade them ever to surrender to an enemy and required suicide in the event of defeat or dishonor. Below the free tribal members were the *eta*, to whom was delegated all the ritually unclean work. Although the freemen never intermarried with the eta, there nevertheless appears to have been a considerable amount of genetic mixture, and there is today no sharp physical distinction between families of eta origin and those of the ancient freeman class. The nobles, similarly, often took concubines from among the freeman class, and their children by these concubines were en-

Ivamatjou Taro, a Japanese Samurai nobleman, who became Japanese ambassador to Paris in 1862, following Japan's enforced entry into diplomatic and trading relations with the Western powers. (Courtesy of the Musée de l'Homme, Paris.)

titled to enjoy the status of their father. This was in accordance with the general Ural-Altaic custom which allots the father's status to the children, regardless of the status of the mother, and contrasts with the Indo-European tradition which relegated the offspring of concubines to the social status of the inferior parent.

Eventually, following a series of internecine wars, one noble clan emerged to a position of preeminence above the others, to establish itself as the imperial, ruling house. Claiming divine descent from the sun, the new emperors segregated themselves above the other nobility, although the male members of the imperial family customarily took concubines from among the noble families, and granted imperial status to their children by these concubines. Under imperial, centralized government, the last vestiges of tribal organization broke down, but the powerful loyalties of the extended family unit remained among the noble and the farming classes. In addition a class of merchants emerged, but these were regarded as having low status, inferior to the farmers, even though they often amassed more wealth.

In the course of time the imperial family began to lose effective control, becoming increasingly subjected to the burden of heavy ritual sanctity, and in 1192 the direction of the central government fell into the hands of another noble family, which established itself as Shoguns or hereditary prime ministers, restricting the activities of the divinely descended emperors to strictly religious functions. Thereafter until the eighteenth century the Shoguns maintained military rule, which was supported by an efficient system of tax collectors. Indeed, in fiduciary matters Japan had a unique tradition. Instead of allowing the feudal nobles to collect taxes themselves, as in medieval Europe, all taxes were collected by the central government, disbursements being made to the samurai classes from the central exchequer. Although the Shoguns effectively controlled the feudal nobility by requiring them to send members of their families to the court, where as courtiers they served as hostages for the good behavior of their kinsmen, Japan did not develop the efficient, centralized bureaucracy of China, and the power of the nobles was never effectively destroyed.

Japanese religion developed from a combination of ancestor worship and animism. Stressing a myriad of nature spirits, seeing the state (like Confucianism) as a large family with the emperor at its head, teaching unbending rules of ritual and moral behavior, compliance with which was a duty to the ancestors, the Japanese developed their own ethnic religion, Shintoism. Under Shintoism, each family worshipped its own ancestors, although there were specialist Shinto priests to serve the nature spirits. Shinto shrines honoring the latter were usually placed in locations of great natural beauty, and the Japanese love of natural landscapes, combined with their highly developed artistic tradition, made Shintoism a religion of marked beauty and refinement.

Shintoism's patriotic and national potentials, as an ethnic religion that revered the ancestors, led to the development of a state-supported official Shinto religious system after Japan's placid and relatively peaceful feudal existence had been rudely shattered in 1853 when the American Admiral Perry compelled the Japanese at gun point to permit the import of American manufactures. Since that fateful

Interest in natural art forms is highly developed in the more advanced civilizations, as evidenced by the traditional Japanese art of flower arrangement known as *Ikebana*. This combines esthetic and ethical principles, each flower arrangement being intended to symbolize the relationship between "heaven," "earth," and "man."

year, the Japanese have completely modernized their technology along Western lines. So successful have they been that only 120 years after the Americans forced them to enter into the arena of international commerce, Japanese manufacturers are now competing so effectively in the American market that many American voices have been raised in favor of reversing Admiral Perry's demands, and of raising American barriers to restrict the import of Japanese goods into America.

For Further Reading

Belenitsky, A., 1968, *Central Asia*. New York: World Publishing Company

Clark, Grahame, 1969, *World Prehistory*. New York: Cambridge University Press.

Eichhorn, W., 1969, *Chinese Civilization*. New York: Frederick A. Praeger, Inc.

Fairservis W. A., Jr., 1963, *The Origins of Oriental Civilization*. New York: Mentor Books.

Forbes, R. J., 1964, *Metallurgy in Antiquity*. New York: Williams Heinemann, Ltd.

Frankfort, H., 1948, *Ancient Egyptian Religions*. New York: Columbia University Press.

———, 1956, *The Birth of Civilization in the Near East*. New York: Doubleday & Company, Inc.

Gimbutas, M., 1965, *Bronze Age Cultures of Central and Eastern Europe*. The Hague: Mouton and Co.

———, 1973, "Old Europe c. 7000–3500 B.C.: The Earliest European Civilization before the Infiltration of the Indo-European Peoples," *Journal of Indo-European Studies* 1 (1):1–20.

Gurney, O. R., 1961, *The Hittites*. Baltimore: Penguin Books, Inc.

Kramer, S. N., 1963, *The Sumerians: Their History, Culture and Character*. Chicago: University of Chicago Press.

Mallowan, M. E. L., 1965, *Early Mesopotamia and Iran*. London: Thames & Hudson, Ltd.

Myres, J. L., 1967, *Who Were the Greeks?* New York: Biblo & Tannen Booksellers & Publishers.

Renfrew, C., 1969, "The Anatomy of the South-East European Copper Age," *Proceedings of the Prehistoric Society* 35:12–47.

———, 1971, "Carbon 14 and the Prehistory of Europe," *Scientific American* 225:63–72.

Watson, W., 1966, *Early Civilization in China*. London: Thames & Hudson, Ltd.

Wheeler, Sir Mortimer, 1968, *The Indus Civilization*. New York: Cambridge University Press.

Wilson, J. A., 1968, *The Culture of Ancient Egypt*. Chicago: University of Chicago Press.

CHAPTER 30

Civilization in the New World

Although a few scholars have been tempted to suggest that Neanderthals entered North America some 50,000 years ago, it is generally accepted that the ancestors of the American Indians were primarily of Mongoloid and Paleo-Asian stock. These colonized the New World from the vast expanses of Siberia, entering what we today call Alaska around 20,000 years ago, by way of the Bering Strait.[1] Traveling southward along the valleys that lie between the coastal mountains and the Rockies, some fanned eastward to occupy the Great Plains and eventually to settle the Eastern Woodlands, while others slowly moved farther southward to settle Central and South America.

These early immigrants were hunters and gatherers, and the first waves were equipped only with an Early Paleolithic technology of the kind that survived until late in eastern Asia. Later immigrants, or possibly simply cultural

diffusion, introduced Middle and Upper Paleolithic traditions after these had reached eastern Asia. By 10,000 B.C. distinctive styles of American stoneworking technology, characterized by the remains found at Folsom in North America, were already in existence. These possessed grooves or channels incised in the stone blade, a trait not found in Old World tools of a comparable type.

Most North and South American Indians retained their ancient hunting and gathering pattern of life until very late, as exemplified by the Yahgan and the earlier predecessors of the Hopi, but Central America appears to have undergone a Neolithic revolution which quickly spread to Peru and also eventually influenced many of the North American Indian cultures. Although situated in tropical latitudes, the Mexican highlands enfold fertile valleys at elevations of up to 8000 feet, and seem to have attracted human settlement from a very early date. The Indians in other parts of the New World did not materially disturb the ecological balance of their environment and

---

[1] See G. R. Willey, *An Introduction to American Archeology* (Englewood Cliffs, N.J.: Prentice-Hall, Inc. 1966), Chap. 2.

remained primarily dependent upon hunting and gathering. However, it is believed that a combination of circumstances, which would have included the relative freedom from disease in the highland valleys of Mexico, allowed the population of these somewhat arid areas to expand to a level at which the wildlife became depleted. This would have forced the Mexican Indians to depend more heavily upon advanced food gathering, and they consequently appear to have paid more attention to the cropping of wild grain as the centuries passed by.

As early as 5200 B.C. the American Indians who resided in the Tehuacan Valley were already systematically gathering maize.[2] This development seems to have been independent of the Old World Neolithic tradition, although the domesticated dog, which appeared in Tehuacan around 3400 B.C., is believed to have entered the New World via the Bering route. Meso-America, as this area is generally known to anthropologists, moved from the Paleolithic into the Neolithic under its own inventive ability, so far as we presently know, without influence from other cultures. Thus the cultivation of maize and beans developed in Mexico during the period known as *Incipient Cultivation* between 4000 and 2500 B.C., and had spread southward by 2500 B.C. to Peru where many new crops of distinctively Peruvian origin came to be cultivated. By the middle of the second millennium B.C., crude pottery, basketry, and wickerwork were being made in settled village communities, comprising one-room subterranean dwellings.

While cultural evolution proceeded very slowly in other parts of the Americas, cultural invention was now beginning to accelerate in the Peruvian and Mexican areas. As both areas developed their own distinctive characteristics, anthropologists sometimes speak of *Nuclear America* to refer to the two separate civilizations which were in the process of

making. During the second millennium B.C., the *Early Formative* phase in the Mexican area reveals the growth of a number of large villages, dependent upon full-time horticultural specialization which utilized maize and beans and an increasingly wide variety of supporting crops, the quality of which was steadily improved by means of selection until the domesticated varieties of grain came to contrast sharply with the poorer wild varieties.

Then around 800 B.C. a *Middle Formative* tradition begins. At La Venta on the gulf coast of Mexico, archeologists have found the beginnings of that great tradition of gigantic ceremonial buildings for which the Meso-American civilizations are so well known. Excavations at La Venta reveal what was already a highly developed architectural tradition, the antecedents of which have not yet been traced. The settlement centers on a large rectangular plaza at one end of which a huge pyramid of earth had been raised, with smaller mounds at each of the corners of what was clearly a ceremonial square. Diggers unearthed stone stelae or monuments, weighing many tons and worked with representations of human figures with ferocious expressions, as well as a rich variety of figurines, ornaments, and carved jade, some of which were executed in materials that must have been transported for distances of up to several hundred miles.

By the *Late Formative* period, between 300 B.C. and 300 A.D., this remarkable architectural style seems to have moved up into the higher valleys of central Mexico where another large ceremonial plaza with pyramids was built at Teotihuacan, with numerous buildings that were later to multiply until they covered a total area of some seven square miles. The largest pyramid here is stone-faced and rises to a height of some 200 feet. Its pinnacle is flat, however, not pointed like those of ancient Egypt, and it is believed that these pyramids were used as platforms for sacrificial altars, not as tombs like the Egyptian pyramids. Close by

[2] See Willey, Chap. 3.

FIG. 53   MAYANS AND AZTECS

Meso-America, showing the locations of the Mayan and Aztec civilizations.

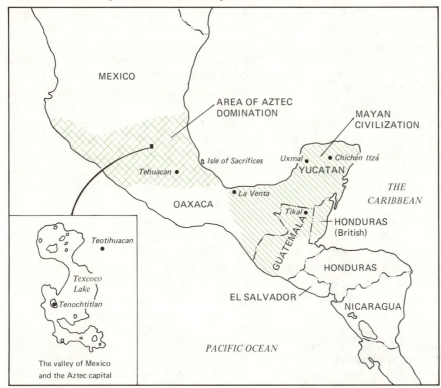

MEXICO

AREA OF AZTEC
DOMINATION

MAYAN
CIVILIZATION

Isle of Sacrifices

Uxmal • • Chichén Itzá
YUCATAN

Tehuacan •

THE
CARIBBEAN

• La Venta

OAXACA

Tikal •

GUATEMALA

HONDURAS
(British)

HONDURAS

EL SALVADOR

NICARAGUA

PACIFIC OCEAN

Teotihuacan

Texcoco
Lake

Tenochtitlan

The valley of Mexico
and the Aztec capital

this ceremonial site stood a large city containing sufficient homes to house as many as 100,000 people.

MAYAN CIVILIZATION

Too little is known about this obviously highly advanced Neolithic people, but the Late Formative culture seems to have served as the antecedent, by way of a culture known as the *Olmec,* for the later *Classic Mayan* civilization about which we are much better informed.[3] Interestingly enough, the Mayan civilization developed in the tropical lowlands of Yucatan

[3]G. H. S. Bushnell, *The First Americans,* (New York: McGraw-Hill, Inc., 1968), pp. 36 ff.

in eastern Mexico and Guatemala—the only high civilization known to develop in a lowland and truly tropical environment. Here, clearing away patches of jungle, the Mayan horticulturalists lived in small clan-villages and—another unique aspect of the Mayan civilization—built few true cities, although in Late Classic times one such city did emerge at Tikal. However, they regularly built elaborate ceremonial plazas with huge stone-faced pyramids for their sacrificial religious rituals.

The Mayans never gave up hunting. Richly colored birds were eagerly sought for their plumage, as were animals for their skins, and colored feathers and jaguar skins seem to have been used for ceremonial attire. Spread out in their small villages, the Mayans were divided into lineal clans, each tribe having its own hereditary ruler. In many ways their social and political organization closely resembled that of ancient Sumeria, with kings who were regarded as being the head of separate civil, religious, and military organizations.

Bureaucratic Priesthood

But what was most significant in Mayan culture was the highly organized, bureaucratic priesthood. Every aspect of Mayan life was regulated by religious dogma, and the priesthood therefore exercised great power. The Mayans believed that the world was the arena for a struggle between benevolent gods, who gave rain and brought fertility to living things, and various evil spirits who caused sickness, crop failure, and death. Especially in later Post-Classic times, wholesale sacrifices were organized by the priests for ceremonial occasions, human sacrifice being central to the

Mayan religion. Captives of war, naked and daubed with blue paint, were stretched out one after the other over the sacrificial altars in front of the assembled peasantry, while they were slaughtered by the priests, the populace being given the sanctified flesh to consume in an act of mass communion with the gods. At Chichén Itzá, living men, women, and children were hurled into a deep well, while in other places victims were tied to stakes and executed with arrows.

In order that these important rituals could be performed on the correct dates, careful calendars were developed to chart the movements of the heavenly bodies. The Mayans actually possessed two calendars, one with 365 days broken down into 18 months and the other, used for religious ceremonies and possibly the older of the two, based on a year of 260 days. The art of mathematics was highly developed; the Mayan priests used the zero sign and understood the principle of positional enumera-

Mayan civilization was based upon a rural village culture rather than on an urbanized city society. Contemporary Indian temples at Las Latas in Mexico, taken during the Peyote Festival. The large circular building on the right is the "Temple of the Grandfather Fire." (Courtesy of the Smithsonian Institution, National Anthropological Archives.)

tion. Only in one other part of the world was the concept of the zero sign invented independently—that was among the Indo-Aryan speakers of India, whence the sign and concept were introduced to Europe by Arab scholars.

The Mayan priesthood also developed an elementary technique of hieroglyphic writing using picture symbols. Numbers of religious records kept in this script were unfortunately destroyed by the Christian missionaries, who arrived in the wake of the Spanish conquest, because of their "superstitious" and "heretical" content. Happily, a few priests realized the value of these early manuscripts, and it is to the foresight of these priests, and some Spanish laymen, that we owe much of our knowledge of Mayan civilization.

Mayan stone carving, in particular, achieved astonishing though often grotesque beauty of a virtually unique character. Yet with all their intellectual arts, which were harnessed to the service of religion above all else, the Mayans remained essentially Neolithic and indeed never learned to use the wheel[4] and never learned to build an arch. Although the possibility of contacts between the Central American civilization and Oceanic and North African-European civilizations does exist, in general the much publicized theories of Thor Heyerdahl, based upon seagoing migrations, have not been accepted by anthropologists or archeologists. While no New World precedent has yet been found for the already highly evolved culture of La Venta, which suddenly appears in a fully developed state on the gulf coast of Mexico, the separate evolution of horticulture in the New World implies an ancient and indigenous civilization which developed independently in the Americas over a period of several thousand years.

[4] A number of children's wheeled toys have been found, which indicate a pre-Columbian origin, but no satisfactory explanation has been afforded as to why the wheel should be used on toys but not applied to any useful purpose. See also E. L. Stendahl, "Wheeled Toys," *South West Museum Masterkey* 24 (5):161 (1950).

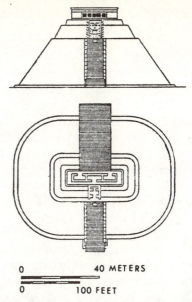

0   40 METERS

0   100 FEET

Frontal elevation and plan of the northeastern pyramid at the Mayan site of Uxmal. This edifice dates from between the seventh and ninth centuries A.D. (Courtesy of George Kubler.)

Aztec relief illustrating dedication ceremonies at the temple of Huitzilopochtli where 70,000 victims are believed to have been sacrificed. (Courtesy of W. H. Prescott.)

THE AZTECS

The Mayan civilization appears to have experienced a weakening of lineage ties during the Late Classic period and collapsed from internal decay around 900 A.D. Meanwhile a number of Nahuan-speaking tribes, closely related to the Shoshones of the western United States, had been moving southward, attracted by the opportunities for pillage and loot. The Teotihuacans of the high valleys of Mexico succumbed to one of these tribes, the Toltecs, in the seventh century A.D. Absorbing the fundamentals of Teotihuacan civilization, the Toltecs began to construct urban centers. But by 1200 A.D. the Toltecs were themselves under attack from the Nahuan Aztecs, who finally established themselves in the valley of Mexico and constructed their own city of Tenochtitlan on Lake Texcoco, which today lies under the foundations of the modern Mexico City.

The Aztecs were rather short in stature, with a light brown complexion, straight noses, coarse black hair, and like other North American Indians, little facial hair. According to their legends they came south in search of sacrificial victims to feed to their blood-thirsty Sun God, Tonatiuh, a warrior god who demanded a constant supply of living hearts as tribute from the Aztec nation. Protected by the mountains that encircle the valley of Mexico, they literally built an island for their settlement on marshy land in the center of the Lake Texcoco, by sinking baskets of mud in the shallow waters. This city actually comprised a number of islands, and as in Venice transportation was mainly effected by boat along the canals that served as streets. The palace of the king stood in the center of the city, adjacent to a great plaza, alongside which the temples of the tribal gods stood on giant pyramids. The hierarchical nobility of officeholders also lived close to the royal palace, in a series of large single-storey buildings arranged around garden courtyards planted with flowering plants and shrubs. The peasantry lived in the outer suburbs, in mud and thatch huts, each with its own "floating" vegetable garden surrounded by the shallow waters of the lake. Contact with the mainland was by causeways with drawbridges which could be raised at a moment's notice in the event of an enemy attack.

At first the Aztecs were subordinate to the neighboring Tapanec tribe, but as their strength grew they were able to throw off the Tapanec yoke. Enlisting other Nahuan tribes as allies, they succeeded in building a rambling empire that extended from the Pacific to the Atlantic, and embraced not only the uplands in which their own city was located but many tropical valleys to the southeast and southwest of their highland fortress. No attempt was made to incorporate the conquered nations into the Aztec tribe, nor indeed to interfere with their separate cultural traditions. Thus the Aztec empire was not truly an administrative empire but merely a loose assortment of tribute-paying nations.

Technology

This extensive tribute-levying empire was created with essentially Neolithic weapons. The Aztec military equipment comprised a wooden bow strung with human hair, arrows pointed with bone or obsidian, short hand-spears, and *atlatl* or spearthrowers. For close fighting the Aztecs carried wooden swords with razor-sharp microliths of obsidian set in a row along the leading edge, which according to Spanish reports were capable of decapitating a horse in a single blow. To protect themselves from enemy missiles, the common soldiers carried small lightweight shields made of cane and decorated with feathers, while the Aztec noblemen wore quilted cotton armor and wooden helmets, designed in the likeness of

Huichol Indian, Mexico. (Courtesy of the Smithsonian Institution, National Anthropological Archives.)

animal heads. Some of the wealthiest of the nobles even had suits of armor manufactured from gold plate.

Although the Aztecs, like the Mayans, remained essentially Neolithic, they worked copper, silver, and gold into ornaments by a simple process of heating and smelting. Gold, which they called the "excrement of the gods," was hammered into thin foil and wire with which filigree work could be accomplished. But because of the softness of these metals and the Aztecs' ignorance of bronze and other amalgams, metalwork was restricted primarily to ornamental purposes.

If the Aztecs knew the wheel, they never learned to apply it to any mechanical purpose. They therefore had to make their pottery by hand, and lacking beasts of burden, they had to carry everything they manufactured on their backs. Nevertheless, they were accomplished weavers and produced a rich variety of finely woven materials. In addition, they became extremely competent stone masons, applying their Neolithic tool-making skills to the construction of architectural monuments of the greatest magnificence. Although they never learned how to build an arch, they erected extravagantly ornamented stone public buildings which reflect remarkable, if somewhat macabre, esthetic imagination.

Social and Political Structure

One of the most interesting aspects of Aztec society is that, like republican Rome, although urbanized it never lost its essentially tribal structure; thus it was both democratic and yet aristocratic. Traditionally the Aztecs were organized in endogamous clans, called *calpulli,* each occupying a number of contiguous villages, one to each village. *Calpul* leadership and seats on the tribal council were elective on the basis of individual merit, but key positions went customarily to individuals from *cacique* families of aristocratic background.

The office of *tlacatecutli* or "chieftain of men," the title of the king, was hereditary in a single family but passed always to a younger brother or to one of the royal nephews, never to the son of a reigning king. Originally it was a strictly constitutional office, but as the Aztec military power became stronger so did the position of the king, for the king assumed total power over the tribe in time of war. War became an almost permanent state of affairs, and indeed the very first obligation of any newly elected Aztec king was to subjugate an alien tribe in order to obtain the thousands of sacrificial victims which were necessary to celebrate his coronation. These defeated peoples were obliged to pay a regular tribute of young men and women, gold, precious stones, food, feathers, or any other commodity the Aztecs could use.

Since colorful animal pelts and birds' feathers played an essential part in the regalia of the royal court, the Aztec kings kept zoo-farms at the capital to ensure an ample supply of the more rare hides and plumage just in case of a temporary failure in the normal tributary sources of supply.

Immediately below the king, one other officer stands out in importance, that of the *ciuacoatl,* which meant literally "the snake woman." Despite the title, the "snake woman" was always a man whose duty it was to assist the king in the command of the army in times of war and to preside over the tribal council, thereby in effect directing the administration of both the military and the judiciary.

Penal System

Among the Aztecs the concept of the blood feud gave way to a system of centralized criminal law. All offenses were regarded essentially as offenses against the state or more precisely against a particular god. Under this system the idea of the payment of compensation to the injured party disappeared in favor of a range of penalties which would be regarded as extremely severe by contemporary Western standards. If a man were proved guilty of slander, he was liable to have his lips cut off. A debtor who failed to pay his debts would be enslaved; an adulterer might be impaled on a stake or have his head ground between two heavy stones; and public intoxication, except in the course of religious rituals, was regarded as a profanity and was punishable by death.

The death penalty was imposed by a variety of methods, depending upon the status of the criminal and the nature of the offense. Aztec nobles and clansmen were always beheaded, while the laboring classes, who were not members of the Aztec tribe, were normally hung. In this respect the Aztec customs resembled medieval England where nobles were also generally beheaded, while commoners were invariably hung. Where the offense was deemed to warrant greater severity, death could be brought about by flogging, stoning, drowning, burning, or tearing the limbs from the body.

Slavery

In a culture which lacked both animal power and wheeled transport, and in which even the king had to be carried "piggyback" when traveling on long journeys, the Aztec nobility nevertheless enjoyed a standard of living which surprised the Spaniards who after their experiences in the Carribean had expected to find only impoverished savages. This standard was achieved by the effective exploitation of human labor, and as in all the civilizations of the ancient world, progress was possible only by the utilization of slave labor, reinforced by the contributions made by a landless and politically powerless class of free laborers.

These landless laborers lacked tribal status but were entitled to earn food and wages and to transfer their services from one employer to another. Their position was actually not far superior to that of the slaves, for the conditions attached to slavery were peculiarly mild for a nation which punished lawbreakers with such severity. An owner could not kill a slave nor even sell him without his consent. Slaves were entitled to marry each other and to possess property of their own. More importantly, the children of slaves were born free. However, since they were not members of an Aztec clan, they had no political privileges and joined the class of landless laborers. Because nobody was born into slavery, recruitment into this important class of workers had to be from other sources. Laborers who could not pay their debts were enslaved into the service of their creditors, or else sold their children into slavery rather than suffer enslavement themselves. Certain classes of criminals were also enslaved as a punishment for their crimes, but when these sources did not provide sufficient labor, the conquered tribes were ordered to supply the necessary number of men and women to make up the shortage in the slave market.

Religious Festivals

Like the Mayans, the Aztecs were intensely religious people. Every aspect of their daily life had a religious meaning. Immediately after rising, they had to make offerings to the god of the household fire. Similarly all agricultural operations, such as sowing and reaping, were scheduled in accordance with the religious calendar and initiated with appropriate religious ceremonies. The Aztec calendar was, in fact, a compilation of ritual ceremonies—public religious festivals—in which communal dancing played an important symbolic role as myths and legends were acted out in dramatic form. Religious music, played on flutes and kettle drums, was used to guide the dancers and to provide a background sound to the sacrifices, drowning the cries of the human victims. Temples maintained choirs to chant religious poetry which usually emphasized death and human suffering. Even warfare involved religious ceremonial. No expedition would be undertaken unless the occasion were regarded as propitious by the priests, and further religious rituals were necessary before the army could be committed to battle.

Probably the most imposing of the Aztec cultural achievements that have survived to impress visitors to Mexico are the gigantic pyramids which served as a base for the sacrificial altars. Every one of the Aztec gods required propitiation. While the populace offered all kinds of foodstuffs to the gods at their respective temples, human sacrifice was the central religious activity around which the Aztec nation, oriented as it was toward warfare, revolved. The Aztec religion required a constant supply of human blood for the gratification of the deities. In all fairness, the priests who carried out these cruel sacrifices also constantly mutilated themselves in order to be able to make daily offerings of their own blood to the gods. Most priests pierced holes through the lobes of their ears and kept these plugged so that they only had to remove the plug and drain off further blood for the offerings which they made every few hours, day after day, year after year.

Aztec religious ceremonies were mostly bloody. In sacrifices to the War God human victims were held naked and splayed across the sacrificial altar while an incision was made in the stomach, and the heart was torn out before it could stop beating. Some of the minor festivals, such as the Spring Flower Festival held on March 14, required only the sacrifice of a virgin, several children, and a number of snakes. The June festival of Ueitecuiluitl involved only the beheading of a woman, held on the back of a priest, while the nobles danced by torchlight; but that of Ochpaniztli in August involved the slaughter of captives by a priest wearing the skin of a woman whom he had just flayed alive. The festival of Xocouetzi in the same month required the sacrificial victims to be roasted alive in a huge fire, being dragged out just before their death so that the hearts could be torn out while still beating. In November the feast of Panquetzaliztli involved the slaughter of war captives and slaves whose blood was then mixed with dough and baked into bread for consumption by the masses in communion with the gods. But it was the annual festival of Tlacaxipeualiztli that required the mass slaughter of both male and female prisoners of war whose skins were flayed from their living bodies to be donned by the priest-dancers while still oozing blood, as the populace consumed the bodies.

But one must not get the impression that these rituals were carried out with calm, cold deliberation. Every important ceremony was preceded by several days of fasting, followed by the excitement of processions and communal dancing. As the time of sacrifice approached, the hungry masses surged around the base of the pyramids or around the open temple doors, and entered into an orgy of drinking so that by the time they came to consume the raw human meat they were deeply intoxicated.

Life among the Aztecs was anything but dull. Every simple daily action had a symbolic meaning, and the religious calendar was so full of ceremonies that the nation spent a very large part of its time either making war, which in itself was a religious requirement, preparing

for the next sacrifice, or actually participating in the religious rituals. The ordinary Aztec tribesman had little time or need for labor. His life was filled with war and with the excitement and intoxication of sacrificial ceremonies. But he lived in an atmosphere steeped in death and bloody mutilation.

It needs only the most superficial comparison between life in American suburbia and life in pre-Columbian Tenochtitlan to realize how different cultures can fashion human life in very different molds. If there is one thing which we can learn from anthropology it is that human life need not necessarily be dull or mundane. The record of culture reveals an almost endless variety of diverse life styles, each with its own ethos or emotive content.

THE INCAS OF THE ANDEAN MOUNTAINS

Meso-America was not the only area in the New World in which the Neolithic gave rise to exotic civilizations. Further to the south the high Andean range of mountains thrust snow-clad peaks more than 20,000 feet above the warm waters of the South Pacific. There advances in agriculture, weaving, and general technology, stimulated by diffusion from the high cultures of Central America, led to the appearance of an equally spectacular civilization of a somewhat contrasting character.[5]

This Andean region embraces a wide range of environments. The Andean mountains, which are broken by deep ravines and fast-flowing rivers, comprise two major ranges, separated by a high plateau some 100 to 200 miles in breadth. Beyond the crest of the eastern or major Andean range lie the dense rain forests of the Amazonian jungle. The moun-

---

[5] As in the case of the Aztec, the archeological evidence relating to the Inca civilization is confined to early Spanish eyewitness acounts, from which we obtain most of our information concerning customs and ritual.

FIG. 54   THE INCA EMPIRE

The Incas established a successful empire by educating the peoples whom they conquered to worship the Inca emperor and his gods.

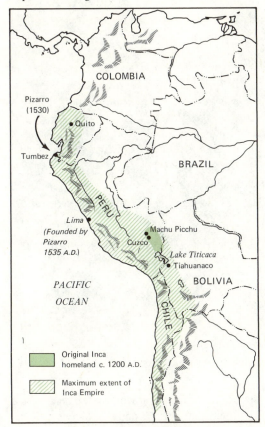

Early Peruvian Civilizations

Everywhere the scenery is dramatically impressive, and since the range of flora is considerable, the potential for agricultural progress is high. As early as 1000 B.C., therefore, horticulture had already evolved to a sophisticated level in the Peruvian area, a wide variety of vegetable and root crops being grown. Only animal life was relatively impoverished, and the only animals which the Peruvians were able to domesticate, other than the dog, were the llama and the alpaca. Nevertheless, the llama provided wool and meat and could be used as a baggage animal even though it was only able to carry weights up to 100 pounds and could not be used for riding; thus the Peruvians possessed baggage animals, something that the Mayans and Aztecs never had. By 500 A.D. a high Neolithic culture existed on the shores of Lake Titicaca in the area today known as Bolivia. Using only stone tools, the people of this culture built a city at Tiahuanaco of huge precisely-cut boulders of stone which were fitted together with such precision that no mortar or cement was necessary. In northern Peru the Yanca Indians developed another civilization which is noted for its advanced agricultural techniques, its elaborate systems of irrigation, and its skill in producing ornaments of gold, silver, and copper. Known as the Chimu civilization, its potters are famous for their lifelike figurines which portrayed scenes from Chimu daily life with extreme realism, while its weavers produced some of the most sophisticated materials ever to be made by a Neolithic or Chalcolithic people.

The social pattern of these early Peruvian cultures was closely parallel to that of ancient Sumeria and the early agrarian civilization of Europe. The village unit was an *ayllu* or exogamous clan whose members traced their descent from a common ancestor. In many tribes descent was traced through the female line, but whether matrilineal or patrilineal rules per-

tains of the western range fall sharply toward the narrow tropical coastal plain—sometimes densely-forested, sometimes arid—which separates them from the waters of the Pacific. Within a relatively short distance, therefore, a traveler journeying eastward from the humid coastal plains climbs through fertile upland valleys and crosses the arid deserts of the high plateau to reach the frozen mountain peaks of the eastern Andes, before descending into the profuse tropical forests of inland South America.

Indians from La Paz, Bolivia, wearing traditional costume. (Courtesy of Musée de l'Homme, Paris.)

tained, clans were held together by the common worship of ancestral and tutelary spirits. In a tradition probably surviving from hunting and gathering days, these spirits were often totemic animals such as jaguars, pumas, condors, serpents, or fishes.

Each *ayllu* inhabited a single village in the center of its own territory, often with a fortified encampment on a nearby hill or mountain crest which served as a place of refuge in time of war. Such villages usually comprised a hundred or more nuclear families, each occupying its own thatched hut built strongly of stone or clay but lacking windows. Even where descent was matrilineal, the husband was the head of the individual household and was re-

sponsible for directing work in the fields. Each clan held the pastures and woodlands as common grazing lands, but the arable land was divided into *tupus* or strips of equal size, each large enough to support a childless husband and wife. These plots were allocated by the clan chief to the clan members every year, each household receiving one *tupu* for each man and his wife, an additional *tupu* for every male child, and half a *tupu* for every female child. A number of plots were also reserved to be cultivated communally by the members of the clan for the maintenance of the lame and elderly. As in the Russian *mir* and the Anglo-Saxon village, every family enjoyed the produce derived from its own lot.

The Inca Empire

These early Andean cultures appear to have suffered from several vicissitudes before the Incas appeared on the scene around 1100 A.D. The origin of the Incas is still something of a mystery, although Inca legends claimed that the first Inca was a child of the Sun God who arose fully grown out of the waters of Lake Titicaca with a divine mission to teach mankind how to cultivate the soil and how to live in a well-ordered society, worshiping the Sun God and treating his earthly representative, the Inca, with proper respect and obedience.

In order to ensure that their god-descended Inca line might be kept pure, according to legend the Sun God gave Macnopac a sister, named Mama Ocllo, and brother and sister cohabited to produce numerous offspring who became the royal Inca clan. These legends appear to have been taken very literally; thus, no Inca was ever allowed to marry outside the royal clan, and the reigning Inca invariably married his own sister. The lineage must have been genetically healthy for there were no genetic complications, and the inbred Inca emperors were all men of exceptional ability. Indeed, under their personal guidance they built one of the greatest empires the world has known, and it was during the reign of the tenth Inca emperor, Huayna Capac (1485 to 1525) that their empire attained its maximum power, reaching a preeminence which was shattered only by the arrival of the Spanish conquistadores.

At its peak in the reign of Huayna Capac, the Inca empire extended along the ridge of the Andean Mountains from central Chile to southern Colombia, a distance of some 3500 miles, engulfing the populous coastal plains to the west and even penetrating into the jungles east of the Andes. Keeping a total of 10 million people in submission, it was held together by an efficient network of roads, 10,000 miles in length, which stretched out in all directions from the imperial capital city of Cuzco.

These roads extended over mountains, deserts, marshes, and deep gorges, and where they had to cross a ravine or canyon, thick rope cables, a foot in diameter and made from woven cloth fibers, carried a swaying path of wooden planks across the deepest crevices. Indeed, the conquistadores reported that these rope bridges were sufficiently strong to be able to take the weight of horses and armor. How the Spaniards managed to persuade horses to cross such bridges, as they gyrated back and forth, swinging dizzily hundreds of feet above the rocky river beds beneath, is not explained.

Commoners were not permitted to use these royal roads which were reserved for the imperial army and state employees, even com-

Peruvian figure of a llama, made from thin silver foil. (Photograph by Andreas Feininger. © Time-LIFE Books.)

merce being a government monopoly. Nevertheless, the roads were lined with post stations at which uniformed *chaquis* or relay runners constantly waited to carry official messages to all parts of the empire at a speed of more than 200 miles a day. Inns known as *tambos* were also maintained at these post stations to accommodate traveling officials, and there are still a number of towns in Peru which incorporate the term *tambo* in their names. All traffic was on foot or by pack animals, for like the Aztecs the Peruvians did not understand the use of the wheel, and there were no riding animals, since the llama cannot carry a load of more than 100 pounds. Consequently, when the Inca traveled across his domains, he rode in a hand-carried ornamental litter, similar to the ancient European palanquin.

From Cuzco the Incas made war against their neighbors constantly, but unlike the Aztecs they were not content to impose tributes upon defeated enemies. Instead, conquered tribes were forcibly incorporated into their system, being taught to worship the Sun God and the divinely-descended, culture-bearing Inca race. The Inca sense of cultural superiority was such that when primitive forest tribes were incorporated into the empire, they were required to pay a mock tribute of live lice until they had become sufficiently civilized to make useful contributions to the imperial economy.

Although more primitive peoples had to be substantially reeducated, the Incas never attempted to destroy the old clan system of the more advanced Peruvian peoples but used it as the basic substratum for a bureaucratic system which has been described as national socialist in its character. With the members of the ruling Inca family elevated like a superrace above the conquered peoples and with a hierarchical system of bureaucratic administration in which appointments were ascribed by family and kinship rather than by personal achievement, the Incas nevertheless created a socialist-type welfare state in which no man was permitted to starve but in which all were obliged to contribute to the maintenance of the aristocracy and to the welfare of the whole.

State Socialism

Steadily modifying the ancient clan system, the Incas reshaped it into a standardized feudal structure, which only reached its final form by the reign of the eighth emperor, Pachacutec. In this state-socialist system, the nuclear household remained the basic unit of economy, 100 householders being regarded as the optimum size for a standardized clan. In a remarkable parallel to that of the Roman system, these clans became known as *pachaca* or centuries, with the clan chief becoming in effect a centurion. Each *pachaca* retained the ownership of the old clan lands, but by a novel innovation the *pachaca* were divided into 10 subclans or *chancunku*, each made up of 10 householders, one of whom acted as an officer above the other nine. On a larger scale, 10 clans or *pachaca* were organized into a *huranca* or phratry, 10 of which constituted a *hunu* or tribe. As the Inca domains expanded, distinct *guaman* or provinces were also established, each comprising four *hunu* and each under an Inca-appointed governor of the royal Inca clan. These provinces were further grouped into four Quarters, each of which was administered by a *capaco* or viceroy appointed from the royal clan.

It is calculated that at the peak of the empire there were probably some 1300 state employees for every 10,000 members of the population. But what is really remarkable about the Inca bureaucracy was that it was maintained without the aid of any developed system of written language or any advanced system of mathematics. The only effective aid to the human brain known to the Incas was the *quipu*, a knotted collection of strings which facilitated simple decimal calculations and was also used to record elementary statistics.

The strict decimalization of Inca *pachaca* or clan-villages was of course more of a norm than a reality, since the pattern of births and deaths constantly prevented the actual community from corresponding completely to the ideal. Nevertheless, an annual census was taken, and any community which substantially exceeded the ideal of 100 households was required to send its surplus young men and women to help populate new colonies in outlying areas of the empire, with a view to consolidating the imperial borders against alien attack. Alternatively, *yanacuna* or male conscripts were drawn from the overpopulated villages and assigned to work on the private estates of priests and bureaucrats, or else were located in cities where they were trained as laborers, runners, or craftsmen. The young women who were drafted from the overpopulated villages were first taken into convents where the more capable learned to become priestesses, while the less capable were assigned as concubines to the nobility or as wives to the *yanacuna*. Although such men and women lost their clan rights, their life appears to have been more interesting and better rewarded than that of the villagers.

Appointments to the leadership of clans and phratries remained hereditary in the old chiefly families, but when a new tribe was annexed to the empire, the sons of the tribal chieftains were taken to Cuzco as hostages, where they were reeducated into the Inca system of emperor and Sun God worship before being sent back to rule their own people as officers of the Inca emperor.

One dramatic change that the Inca did effect in the social system was the replacement of clan exogamy by a pattern of local endogamy, in which men were required to marry women from their own village rather than from a neighboring village. Marriage was also made obligatory under the Inca laws, but commoners were permitted to possess only one wife. Only officials of the state were granted secondary wives or concubines, and polygyny and concubinage were regarded as among the privileges of higher office.

While local government remained in the hands of minor bureaucrats recruited from the older Peruvian tribal nobility, the key positions were filled by members of the Inca clan. The Inca clan was actually quite large because although the Inca had only one legitimate wife—usually his eldest sister—both the emperor and his Inca relatives maintained a large number of concubines who produced numerous offspring. Thus political power was concentrated in the hands of one man, whose public appearances were always surrounded by much pomp and ceremony. On official occasions the Inca wore a plumed headdress and carried a mace of office. He wore only the finest garments of silky vicuna wool which were destroyed after they left his person. His table was set with gold and silver plates which were likewise destroyed after they had been used but once. The task of manufacturing the clothing and equipment used by the Inca was reserved for a special priestly class, his clothes being spun by virgin priestesses who were kept constantly employed at this task.

The imperial capital at Cuzco became a center for the accumulation of an enormous wealth of richly-worked and ornamented gold, silver, and copper objects. The walls of the imperial palace were covered with decorative gold and silver panels, and the Temple of the Sun God had a golden garden in which even the trees, plants, flowers, birds, and butterflies were made of gold. Even the homes of the ordinary nobles were filled with riches beyond the imagination of the Spanish adventurers. The goldsmiths were reputed to be able to beat gold into sheets one tenth of a millimeter in thickness, making gold butterflies which were so light they would glide through the air when thrown.

In order to support the imperial bureaucracy, every century or village was required to supply labor for state projects, and every able-bodied man was required to contribute a portion of his time and labor to the construction of the state roads and public buildings, as well as the cultivation of the agricultural estates which supported the officials and priests. This service was made a religious virtue, and communal work days were treated as "holy days" or holidays. Each village or century worked as a unit, having a definite acreage of state or temple land to maintain. On the days they labored for the state, the householders wore their best clothes, singing in chorus as they worked and being fed and entertained at the end of the day at state expense.

But it was undoubtedly the army that played the most important role in the maintenance and expansion of the Inca empire. The Incas continuously worked for the expansion of their empire and even maintained a system of spies in neighboring countries, who attempted to persuade independent peoples voluntarily to join the empire and kept the Inca army informed of the defenses and strength of all such unincorporated neighbors. Service in the army was compulsory for all, and each *chankunku* of 10 householders was required to maintain one man on active service at all times. Military service was subject to rotation so that all adult freemen received training as soldiers, and the military potential of the Inca empire was actually many times greater than the 150,000 to 200,000 soldiers who were maintained under arms at all times.

To maintain the desired social distance between the various castes, *sumptuary laws* restricted the types of clothing and ornaments that could be worn by each social level according to status. Thus commoners were forbidden to wear clothes made from the finest alpaca or altuna wool and were also not allowed to enjoy the richer foods or to drink cocoa or any intoxicating beverages.

Only the children of the nobility received any formal education. They attended schools in Cuzco where they were taught mathematics, poetry, engineering, history, and of course, religion. After four years at the college in Cuzco, students had to pass a number of tests, largely military in character, before being eligible to graduate. This they did at an impressive passing-out ceremony which was presided over by the Inca emperor who personally pierced the lobes of their ears in order that they might insert the large ornamental plugs which served as the Inca badge of office and caused the Spaniards to know the bureaucrats as *orejones* or "big ears."

Since all law derived from the divine emperor and was supported by religious sanctions, there was no system of composition or fines. All felonies were crimes against God and were punished by physical penalties such as flogging, by forced labor, or by death—which was always administered in a dramatic fashion, some condemned criminals being thrown over a cliff and others cremated alive, depending on the offense. Nevertheless an element of communal responsibility survived, in the sense that a father was held responsible for the misdeeds of his children, father and son both being punished alike. Clan and phratry officials were also held liable for offenses committed by the persons in their jurisdiction.

The Inca state was probably the most advanced attempt ever made by man to reshape society into a single organizational unit. Even Roman society recognized individual citizens as persons endowed with certain basic rights as freemen, and conceived of society as being an aggregate of free individuals bound together by kinship and common interests. However, the Inca philosophy saw society ideally in terms of a social organization, serving communal purposes and subordinating all members to the same societal goals. In short, it regarded society not as an aggregate of free individuals voluntarily collaborating together for their own mutual benefit, so much as a deliberate, goal-oriented amalgam in which individuals were mere role players with all the obligations and duties attendant upon their particular role.

Despite their impersonal and ruthless efficiency, the Incas were nevertheless deeply religious. Indeed social uniformity and efficiency were probably made possible only by the fact that compliance with the orders of the divinely-descended Emperor was a religious obligation as well as civil necessity. Lawbreaking was therefore a sin, and breaches of his law were acts of profanity which might bring sickness and even death upon the wrongdoer.

Under Inca rule the old clans continued to worship their own tutelary spirits or *pacarina,* and each household retained its own guardian spirit, believed to reside in a fetish object, such as a stone of a peculiar shape, which would be kept in a shrine or niche in the wall. Instead of attempting to eliminate traditional Peruvian peasant beliefs, the Incas superimposed on these the worship of their trinity of sky gods: the great Sun God known as Inti, the Moon God, and the Thunder God. Below them were a number of lesser gods such as the Sea God, the Earth Mother, a fertility goddess, and a god who was responsible for maintaining order in the universe but who was actually subordinate to the Sun God. Each of these divinities had its own cult and priesthood. Some serious research into the mysteries of the universe was attempted by the priests, although most of this took the form of magical experimentation, as in the case of the order of eunuch monks who practiced self-mutilation and black magic. At the lower level of religious activity the minor priests served as oracles and soothsayers for the peasants while intoxicated with narcotics. But the most important cult was always that of the royal ancestor, the Sun God, at whose temple virgin priestesses constantly tended a sacred fire like that of ancient Rome.

The Arrival of the Conquistadores

The first European to discover the Inca empire was a Portuguese adventurer who accompanied a number of savage Guarani tribesmen in a raid upon an outlying Inca province.

But it was Pizarro who, in 1527, visited the Inca port of Tumbez, and being impressed by the obvious accumulation of gold, silver, and jewelry, developed a plan to conquer the Inca empire, notwithstanding the vast army of trained warriors at the Inca's disposal. Returning in 1531 with just 183 Spanish adventurers, mostly of noble descent, and 27 horses, he arrived at a time when the Inca empire was divided by civil war. The last Inca emperor, Huayna Capac, had broken the traditional law of primogeniture and had attempted to divide the empire upon his death between his legitimate heir, to whom he left Cuzco and the southern part of the empire, and a second son to whom he had willed Quito and the northern portion. This breach of tradition had resulted in war, with the younger son overcoming the legitimate heir to the united throne.

The defeated forces of the legitimate Inca welcomed the arrival of Pizarro, believing that this might give them a chance to overthrow the imposter, and with typical conquistador courage Pizarro and his small troop rode into the presence of the usurper. At a preplanned signal he seized the usurping Inca in full view of the Inca army, and since control of the empire centered on the person of the emperor, organized resistance was impossible. After executing the usurper, Pizarro made no attempt to restore the legitimate heir but instead placed himself in the Inca's position, and for some years the bureaucratic structure continued to function under Spanish orders.

But Spanish rule lacked the religious sanction of the indigenous Sun-worshiping religion. Since the Spanish were themselves subordinate to the control of the Roman Catholic Church, large numbers of Christian priests and inquisitors arrived and began the systematic suppression of the Inca religion and priesthood. As its moral basis was destroyed, the bureaucratic administration broke down, and internal chaos spread. For a time, a group of Incas managed to survive in a city today known as Machu Picchu, high up on an

18,000-foot mountain top, in a position which was virtually impregnable. Although the Spaniards knew of the existence of this undefeated Inca township which they called Vilcabamba, they never succeeded in locating it, for the few Catholic priests and friars who may have found their way to Machu Picchu never returned alive.

For Further Reading

Adams, R. M., 1966, *The Evolution of Urban Society*. Chicago: Aldine Publishing Company.

Baudin, L., 1962, *El Imperio Socialista de los Incas*. Santiago de Chile: Empresa Editora Zig-Zag S.A.

Brainerd, G., 1954, *The Maya Civilization*. Los Angeles: Southwest Museum Press.

Coe, M., 1966, *The Maya*. New York: Frederick A. Praeger, Inc.

Jennings, J. D., 1968, *Prehistory of North America*. New York: McGraw-Hill, Inc.

Josephy, A. M., Jr., 1968, *The Indian Heritage of America*. New York: Alfred A. Knopf.

Leakey, L. S. B., and others, 1972, "Pleistocene Man at Calico: A Report on the International Conference on the Calico Mountains Excavations, San Bernardino County, Calif." Bloomington, Calif.: San Bernardino County Museum Association.

Sanders, W. T., and M. Josephy, 1970, *New World Prehistory*. Englewood Cliffs, N.J.: Prentice-Hall, Inc.

———, and B. J. Price, 1968, *Mesoamerica: The Evolution of a Civilization*. New York: Random House, Inc.

———, and B. J. Price, 1968, *An Introduction to American Archeology*. Englewood Cliffs, N.J.: Prentice-Hall, Inc.

Spencer, R. F., and others, 1965, *The Native Americans*. New York: Harper & Row, Publishers.

Thompson, J. E. S., 1927, *Civilization of the Mayas*. Chicago: University of Chicago Press.

Vaillant, G. C., 1941, *The Aztecs of Mexico*. New York: Doubleday & Company, Inc.

Willey, G. R., 1966, *An Introduction to American Archaeology, Vol. 1: North and Middle America*. Englewood Cliffs, N.J.: Prentice-Hall, Inc.

———, 1971, *An Introduction to American Archaeology, Vol. 2: South America*. Englewood Cliffs, N.J.: Prentice-Hall, Inc.

CHAPTER 31

Peasant Societies

Midway between primitive societies and industrial societies stands that class of people known as peasants. Historically peasants are important because they appear with the beginnings of agriculture and survive until the advent of industrialization. From the point of view of our contemporary world, peasants are important because there are probably more peasants in the world than any other class of people.

Like primitive cultivators and modern farmers, peasants live close to the soil, and as rural dwellers they belong to that great category of nonurban peoples that Robert Redfield referred to as "folk societies." People who live in towns are exposed to contact with a variety of different occupational, social, and even ethnic groups, but those who live in rural societies are more uniform in their experiences and have much more tenuous connections with the outside world. A FOLK SOCIETY is a rural society whose members live in intimate face-to-face contact with each other, largely isolated from outside contacts. As may be expected, such

societies are traditional but at this point the similarities between peasant and tribal societies cease.

Unlike tribal cultivators, peasants do not live in self-governing communities.[1] They lack the economic and political independence of primeval man. Peasants also differ from the farmers of contemporary Western industrial society in that a peasantry is economically, socially, and politically subordinate to an administrative ruling class.

Peasant societies, by definition, never exist as economically or politically independent and autonomous units; they are essentially a segment of a more complex society. Indeed we might have dealt with them in our last chapter, because peasants provided the backdrop for the glittering civilizations of both the Old World and the Americas. But peasants justify a separate chapter since they enjoy a cultural existence of their own, identifiably separate from

[1] Eric R. Wolf, *Peasants.* (Englewood Cliffs, N.J.: Prentice-Hall, Inc., 1966), Chap. 1.

513

the dynamic urban centers of agrarian civilization. The culture of the peasants often outlives the fall of a city civilization, preserving a dim reflection of its glories long after the city has died.

Thus instead of controlling their own destiny and laboring to produce commodities only for their own consumption, peasants are but a part of a larger and more complex *market* economy. Although they grow their own food, they also toil to produce surplus crops. A portion of this surplus is paid over, either in kind or in cash, as taxes or tithes to support specialist administrators and priests, while the balance is traded for luxuries produced in the cities and distributed by a professional merchant class.

Peasant societies similarly seldom control the land and resources which they utilize. Their culture is frequently an admixture of innovative forces that are derived from the more virile urban centers of culture, as reflected in banks and schools, and of older cultural traditions combining ancient tribal memories with elements drawn from past urban civilizations, often long dead. The culture of a peasant people is consequently a synthesis of traditional elements combined with more innovative traits borrowed from contemporary urban centers. On the basis of their agricultural labors, high civilizations frequently arise. However, although they are a part of a larger market economy, subordinate to outside forces, and purport to accept the teachings of an externally controlled bureaucratic church, in other respects they tend to remain conservative cultural cul-de-sacs, reluctant to absorb too many new ideas and tenaciously holding on to older traditions.

It should not be assumed, because of the foregoing statements, that life in a peasant society cannot be psychologically highly satisfying. The traditionalism and the slower tempo of life, the intimate contact with nature, and the freedom from tension all seem to be conducive to a healthy mental life. Although our contemporary urbanized Western culture trains us to eagerly welcome cultural innovations, anthropological fieldworkers who have participated in the life of a peasant community know that such societies are often far more contented than our own and that the life of a peasantry is by no means emotionally unsatisfying.

Social and Economic Status

Peasant societies arise when the economic surplus produced by the introduction of agriculture makes larger and more complex societies possible. Horticultural societies do not produce sufficient goods to support an elaborate superstructure of merchants, craftsmen, and administrators. Agriculture does produce such a surplus. With the development of full-time occupations which are not directly related to cultivation of the soil, most specialist workers tend to congregate in urban centers; thus, society becomes divided between two polar types: the urban and the rural. As division of labor increases, political and economic power falls into the hands of those who coordinate the society, and history witnesses the rise of an estate-owning agrarian ruling class. This ruling class, exemplified by the landed aristocracy of eighteenth-century Europe and by the *caciques* of Central America, may eventually be supplanted by the merchants and bureaucratic administrators of the cities, but in both cases those who work the land seldom exercise great political or economic influence. In effect, the peasantry constitute a politically powerless subculture which is but a part of a larger and more complex society.

Land Distribution

Peasant communities can take several forms. The simplest of these is the village comprising a single lineal clan, like the zadruga described earlier, or even a multilineal organization like the Russian mir. In both cases cultivation is

Peasant societies have frequently been associated with very sophisticated urban civilizations. Portrayed above is a contemporary view of the center of the beautiful city of Lisbon, constructed in the seventeenth century following an earthquake which destroyed the old town. The planned layout of its elegant buildings reflects the civilized tastes of the ruling classes in the highly stratified estate-type society. (Courtesy of the Portuguese Information Service.)

undertaken according to a common plan, although in the mir the produce belongs to individual families.

In other cases some or all of the village land may be privately owned, and this may lead to relative inequalities of wealth. However, even where land is privately owned by peasant families, the entire community continues to be welded together in a tight primary group, as is characteristic among folk societies.

Since the peasant is politically weak, the center of social power resides either in the cities or in a ruling aristocracy that "camps" among the peasantry, as the feudal barons of Europe camped in their manorial halls next to the villages they controlled, or as the feudal Watutsi of Africa camped among the Bahutu peasantry of Ruanda Urundi. Thus the peasants find themselves in the position of paying *rent* for the land they cultivate to those who have *domain* or effective political power over them. This rent is in effect a payment for the administrative, military, and other services rendered to them by these occupational specialists, although the amount of such rents tends to be determined according to the principles of monopoly rather than by those of a free market economy.

The existence of a dominant administrative class is a characteristic of peasant societies, for no peasant is truly the sole owner of the land he tills. All peasants pay rent in one form or another—if not to an aristocratic lord of the manor, then as profit to a dominant class of traders or as taxes directly to a government so remote that the peasant has little control over it regardless of whether it is democratically elected. Indeed, there would appear to be a built-in tendency for agrarian societies to develop an extreme and relatively static division of labor separating those who till the land from those who wield political power, either through the sword or the pen. In consequence, agrarian societies reveal substantial inequalities of wealth, influence, and power. Because of the slow rate of innovation in agrarian societies and the consequent tendency toward conservatism which is characteristic of most people working on the land, castelike structures emerge naturally and are usually not difficult to preserve.

With the passing of time it therefore seems only inevitable that a great deal of the power in such stratified agrarian societies would eventually come to reside in the hands of the ruling class. In many agrarian societies the ownership of the majority of the land will be found to fall under the control of a privileged minority of under 5 percent of the total population. As long as this ruling minority retains its alertness and its intellectual preeminence, there is little reason why such a situation should change. In short, most agricultural societies are highly stable, and the opportunities for social mobility are heavily restricted.

Although it is customary to associate the idea of peasantry with the reciprocal concept of an aristocracy, many countries have experienced social revolutions that have overthrown the old landed aristocracy without actually liberating the peasantry, who merely pass under the domination of a new ruling elite. Such revolutions are seldom if ever generated by the peasant classes themselves but are usually stimulated by a *speculator elite,* members of the educated classes of the cities who wish to overthrow the existing power structure and may seek to use the peasants' eternal hunger for landownership as a tool toward achievement of their goal. Thus in Russia the Bolshevik revolution overthrew the old landed aristocracy, but the coming of Communism did not eliminate the peasantry despite the collectivization of all cultivating operations. The peasants of Russia did not become owners of their own land nor did they assume the right to make their own production choices or to dispose of their own crops, but found themselves working under the direction of an impersonal state bureaucracy which manages their activities and takes control of their surplus produce.

The Peasantry and the Church

One peculiarity of peasant societies is the readiness with which they accept international *missionary* religions where these are managed by powerful priestly bureaucracies. In early levels of society a man's family or local loyalties determined the god or gods whom he would worship, but in peasant societies highly organized churches tend to dominate the scene. Thus Christianity spread across Europe with relative ease after the appearance of peasant communities. Similarly in India the old ancestor-worshiping religion became for a time subordinate to Buddhism, which like Christianity possessed a great universalistic priesthood and offered monasteries into which men who wished to escape from the world might retire. A third universalistic religion has also prospered among agricultural and pastoral societies alike; this is the Islamic religion.

The reason for the success of such religions among the peasantry lies in the fact that an agrarian peasantry produces an attractive economic surplus and is capable of supporting an hierarchical religious bureaucracy which can organize missionary projects, coordinate the activities of local village priests, and is also powerful enough to deal with those who hold administrative power. Since the peasantry represent a subordinate class tied to the land which they do not truly control, they welcome any religious system which will introduce into their lives something of the sophistication of the higher urban culture. Local tribal religions usually lack the resources to compete with a broad-based and organized missionary priesthood and consequently give way to the more universal religion. However, many ancient practices, denounced by the new church, often survive in folk practice as witchcraft and demonry.

Modernization

In view of the large peasant population in the less developed countries, many anthropologists with an interest in social change have examined the problems affecting the *modernization* of peasant societies. One of the most obvious forces resisting change is that most members of an agrarian society are actually strongly attached to past customs and derive a positive pleasure from following the familiar patterns of social behavior which they have known from childhood. As a result there is frequently a psychological reaction against innovations, even where these may bring economic benefits. This psychological reaction tends to be reinforced whenever an experiment fails, as for example, when attempts to introduce fertilizers fail due to an overdose or to the use of the wrong type of fertilizer in the absence of a proper chemical analysis of the soil.

In many agrarian societies religion has helped the population to accept its difficulties with a fatalistic philosophy, teaching acceptance of the hardships of life. Peasants who have learned to achieve psychological contentment by deliberately limiting their aspirations to objectives which are within their foreseeable grasp are seldom anxious to experiment with radical new ideas. The substantial rewards that technological change can bring in terms of productivity are not always immediate, and it takes a relatively sophisticated mind to be capable of deferring gratification in anticipation of greater rewards.

Even the peasant dependence on familism acts as a conservative force resisting social experimentation. Any innovations which may affect the traditional patterns of family and kinship responsibility will be strenuously resisted, for the family is not just a companionship group—it is the individual's insurance against unemployment, economic depression, and even ill-health. In consequence, peasants cling tenaciously to their traditional pattern of family and kinship responsibilities, and to this extent are likely to oppose any social changes which may act to the detriment of the prevailing family and kinship structure.

It is consequently among the upper strata of any agrarian society that innovation and change is usually first accepted, not among the peasants. Once the intellectual leadership of a traditional society has been subverted from the traditional ideologies, the lower strata will be left in a strictly defensive position. Breaches in the defenses of the older system may be created by exposure to new ideas through literacy and the mass media as well as through interpersonal contacts with persons dedicated toward bringing about social and cultural change—persons who are commonly known as *change agents*. If respected members of the local elite accept the new ideas and openly identify with the goals of innovation, social change comes more easily than when the society as a whole resists change. On the other hand, if the existing social leaders reject the proposed goals of innovation, the innovators find themselves in opposition to the dominant social elite and can then bring about social and cultural change only in the form of a cultural or political revolution.

The entire subject of social change in agrarian societies is examined in some detail by Everett M. Rogers in *Modernization among Peasants: The Impact of Communication,* which attempts a crosscultural comparison of social change in agrarian societies in both the Old and the New Worlds. In particular Rogers detects three main variables which contribute toward modernization. The first of these is the capacity for communication between members of the agrarian society and the external world. Such communication is probably strongest where peasants make visits to industrialized cities, failing which the mass media and mass education can be used to introduce the norms and aspirations of the urban innovators into the minds of the peasant population. The second major variable is the existence of a younger generation which, through exposure to contacts with the seemingly more glamorous external world, may become disenchanted with the traditional culture and will be prepared to work actively for a social and cultural revolution. The third essential variable is the existence of a cadre of professional change agents dedicated to the task of bringing about social, cultural, and possibly even political revolution.

But times of rapid social and cultural change are not always happy times for peasants, any more than they are for other societies. Those who become change agents may obtain a degree of vicarious excitement from their role, but for those whose society is being changed, in particular for the older generation, a feeling of insecurity overshadows other considerations. Where previously village or even township consensus gave a feeling of security, in times of change interpersonal cohesion declines and individual gain tends to become the dominant goal. Thus changes that seem desirable to the outsider may be seen by those adjusted to the older culture as evils, threatening the breakup of the community spirit, the decline of traditional morality, and the replacement of group consensus by self-seeking and self-indulgent passions.

To gain a clearer impression of life in a rural peasant society, let us now look at two such communities. One of these, the village of Gopalpur in India, is still essentially traditional. The other reveals the impact of change more sharply, for Tepoztlán, Mexico, having lost its aristocracy in a violent revolution, is now witnessing the disruption of the traditionally rural fabric of life as it is slowly drawn into the modern industrial world.

GOPALPUR, A VILLAGE IN INDIA

The Indian subcontinent is unusually rich in the diversity of its cultures. Although Europe and the Middle East possess civilizations much older than that of India, an advanced urban civilization existed in India long before it emerged in the Far East or Meso-America, and small pockets of aboriginals of proto-Australoid origin have also managed to maintain their own distinctive way of life in the more remote forests and upland plateaus. India consequently offers a kaleidoscopic panorama of political, religious, and esthetic traditions, ranging from the band-type organizations of the aboriginal peoples to sprawling industrial urban communities of very recent origin.

Agrarian India

Nevertheless, for some 5000 years the culture of India has been characteristically agrarian. The Indus and Ganges valleys were cultivated long before the coming of the

FIG. 55 GOPALPUR IN INDIA

Gopalpur is a common village name in India, but the Gopalpur we are describing was situated in the former princely state of Hyderabad, until annexed by India shortly after the dissolution of the British Empire in India.

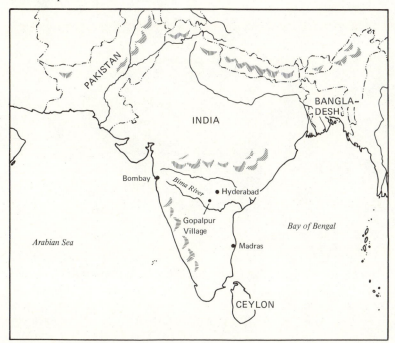

warrior-farmer Indo-Aryans who brought the Sanskrit language and so much of the Hindu tradition to India. Even though modern industry was introduced during the British *raj*, more than three quarters of the Indian population remains rural to this day. The life of the Indian farmer is extremely rich because he is the heir to one of the most exotic and varied traditions of religion, folklore, and mythology that the world has known. It is rich also because of the complexity of Indian village social structure, with its wide variety of occupational distinctions. It is rich because the Indian villager has the feeling that he is a cultured and refined individual, the heir to an ancient civilization, and the master of his own destiny, within the narrow limits permitted him by nature and by the gods.

There is therefore something particularly timeless and consequently restful about life in the Indian countryside. Every event seems important, however trivial it may be, and even though famine and pestilence return periodically, there is no sense of impending doom nor any reason for unseemly haste. All men are important as individuals, no matter what their status is in the rigidly stratified Hindu social system. However lowly a man's social rank may be, others realize that he has his own life, his own joys, and his own problems, and that these are just as real to him as other peoples' joys and problems are to them. Social rank in India carries with it a sense of responsibility, of noblesse oblige, so that even the members of the lowest social orders are able to derive satisfaction from life. To the Hindu it is this

Indian villagers in everyday costume. (Courtesy of G. D. Kumar.)

world, not the next, that is real, and the belief in reincarnation releases men from the need to fear the passing of time. Nor is there the slightest element of the suburban monotony that haunts the residents of modern America. Life is far too real in India and far too earnest, yet at the same time, far too poetic for monotony. The rising of the sun, the gathering of the storm clouds, the coming and going of a heat wave, all demonstrate the vitality of nature and provide, along with the village's latest news, adequate material for conversation and gossip.

Perhaps it is because of the ancient and relatively slow-changing pattern of a settled agricultural economy that the villagers of India have time to detach their minds from unsatisfying and unrealizable goals and to concentrate them instead on the very human and personal problems of daily life. The Indian villager is indeed a socially-oriented person, valuing his dignity, but unable to feel remorse for personal failures because his position in society has been allocated to him by forces greater than himself. When the social structure

is rigidly ascribed and validated by religious doctrine, the pressure to prove oneself in constant competition with other members of the community no longer exists as a pressing psychological necessity, even though it may occasionally assert itself as an economic convenience.

Historically, Hindu Indian society comprised a clan of royalty known as *Rajanya,* a landowning warrior-noble caste known as *Kshatriya,* a caste of priests or *Brahmans,* a caste of merchants and farmers known as *Vaisya,* and a landless caste of manual workers and slaves known as *Sudra.* A man's birth irrevocably determined his subsequent profession and status in life. Today we still use the word *caste* in its original Indian sense to represent a group of people who occupy a particular status in society, who are expected to fulfill specific occupational functions, and who may not engage in any work regarded as inappropriate to their status. The members of a particular caste may marry only within their caste, and society is therefore rigidly structured into a hierarchy of endogamous status groups, each with its own privileged economic functions validated by religious sanctions.

The village of Gopalpur in Southern India has been dramatically described by the Californian anthropologist Alan R. Beals,[2] who provides us with a microcosmic picture of the seemingly timeless pattern of agricultural life in rural India. It is a pattern which has only recently become subject to substantial stresses as a result of the introduction of modern farming technology and the impact of reformist legislation and modern Western medical techniques. Its people are the descendants of a thousand generations of villagers who have tilled the same soil before them. They speak Kannarese, a tongue belonging to the Dra-

vidian group of languages common in southern India. Serious-faced, with dark skin, black straight hair, dark eyes, slightly prognathous jaws, and noses which are rather broad at the base, they probably descend from some early admixture of a basically Caucasoid people with an early proto-Australoid population.

Most of the people of Gopalpur are Hindus, but during the Mogul empire the area was ruled by Moslems who managed to remain politically dominant during the subsequent era of statehood under British rule. There are consequently still many Moslems in the district, who have been more or less integrated into the Hindu social system, being accorded a separate caste status of their own, which they readily accept. The great strength of the Indian rural tradition is revealed in its ability to absorb alien immigrant groups. More primitive

[2] A. R. Beals, *Gopalpur: A South Indian Village* (New York: Holt, Rinehart and Winston, Inc., 1962).

An Indian rajah and his retainers—a survival from the early Indo-Aryan invasions of 3500 years ago. (Courtesy of Musée de l'Homme, Paris.)

cultural systems would have collapsed in competition with such powerful cultural systems as those of the Moslem and British conquerors of India. However, the Hindu culture, rooted in the agrarian tradition, has been able to modify and absorb alien traditions in much the same way as the agrarian Chinese culture also successfully absorbed immigrant cultural traits and managed to retain its cultural integrity for a period of more than 3000 years.

The Village

The village of Gopalpur has only 500 inhabitants, but its people believe that they belong to the soil and that the soil belongs to them. External dynasties and empires have come and gone—they cannot even remember all the different governments who have ruled over their land—but they and their way of life have survived triumphantly. With only 500 inhabitants Gopalpur may be regarded as a small community, yet its size is adequate, for in an agrarian society villages do not have to be entirely self-sufficient. Consequently, the people of Gopalpur do not produce important commodities such as bananas, coconuts, cigarettes, beetle leaves, cooking oil, or even blankets or leather goods, since they can purchase these economically from neighboring villages with the funds left over from the sale of their own surplus produce. Few villages in India are large enough to be able to maintain the large variety of specialist craftsmen required to supply the different commodities and services that a sophisticated agricultural society is accustomed to consuming. Villages such as Gopalpur are but a part of a larger regional economy.

The days have passed when rajahs were ensconced in hill-top fortresses and constantly warred with each other, and the villagers no longer live in danger of attack by *dacoits* or bands of robbers. However, the houses in Gopalpur are still built like individual fortresses, providing each family with security for itself and its possessions. Built around a small courtyard, every house is encircled by a win-

A South Indian village in the Deccan. (From Alan R. Beals, *Gopalpur: A South Indian Village.* Copyright © 1962 by Holt, Rinehart and Winston, Inc. By permission of the publisher.)

dowless outer wall in which the cattle are kept at night, safe from cattle raiders. Constructed of mud and stone, the rectangular buildings cluster closely together so that the village is like a stronghold which would be difficult to attack without artillery. Since there are no windows in any of the walls, the only light and air that enter a house are admitted through the open doors and through small holes cut in the flat roofs, which are covered over when it rains. On the front of each house, facing the street is a small raised veranda, some 6 to 8 feet in width, from which a large wooden double door provides the only means of access to the interior.

No one really lives inside these houses, which are used primarily for the protection of property. During the daytime the able-bodied men work the fields, unless they are craftsmen like the blacksmith who works in his smithy. If the men are too old to toil physically, they sit in the cool shade of a tree, occupying themselves with simple tasks such as rope making. At noon the men return from the fields to rest in the shade of the veranda; then as the afternoon begins to cool, they go back to the fields to work until dusk. The womenfolk, on the other hand, work on their verandas and the children play in the streets or in the cattle yard. Meals are taken on the front veranda, and except when the night is wet, the villagers sleep on string cots on the cool flat roofs. Since there is no street lighting, the entire village goes to sleep early on moonless nights, but during the full moon the moonlit streets resound with laughter, songs, and dancing.

There is only one latrine in Gopalpur, an innovation located in the house of the relatively wealthy *Gauda* or Brahman landowner. While adults leave the village to relieve themselves, young children who are not allowed out of the village by themselves are permitted to defecate and urinate in the streets. Young children run naked, but men wear a shirt and a loin cloth or *dhoti*, and women drape their bodies with a length of colored material known as a *sari*.

Family and Marital Traditions

Ideally, the basic economic and social unit is a joint family, a household comprising two or more generations which share all property under the direction of a patriarchal head. Although the senior male is listened to and obeyed, every child born into the joint Hindu family becomes an equal shareholder in the common property from the moment of birth. The ambition of the Gopalpur youth is to win the respect of his peers by making a successful marriage, by producing a large family of children (preferably sons), by marrying these children successfully, and by living to see numerous grandchildren. But the harsh reality does not permit many to fulfill this goal without experiencing many mortalities and economic hardships. The constant drama of suffering and death teaches the people of Gopalpur to appreciate the value of good health and regular meals in times of good fortune. Although their ideal is a large, happy, and contented joint family, and there is no generation gap to prevent the younger members of the family from respecting, admiring, and even loving and enjoying the company of their elders, many a family is broken by premature deaths or prevented from expanding to its desired size by infertility induced by sickness and disease.

Since marriages are contracted when the brides are still children, wives begin to live with their husbands immediately after puberty, producing a continuous series of babies during their entire fertile life. Although from time immemorial the infant mortality rate has been extremely high, and many wives are also lost in childbirth, as modern techniques slowly begin to control disease, India is experiencing a population explosion which is creating serious economic problems. Nevertheless, children are traditionally regarded as a joy and a bless-

An Indian farmer with two fine Punjabi bulls yoked to a primitive plow. (Courtesy of G. D. Kumar.)

ing and as a guarantee of support for the parents in their old age. Whether or not the inhabitants of Gopalpur can be brought to understand the macroeconomics of overpopulation from a national point of view is questionable so long as individual families clearly benefit from a large number of offspring and the biological pleasure of raising children remains the main joy in an essentially simple pattern of life.

Gopalpur is so small that it has only one landowning family of the elite Brahman upper caste. This is the family of the *Gauda,* or village headman. In the Brahman tradition, it is essential that a father must see his children successfully married, and Brahmans must traditionally give a large dowry with a daughter at the time of her wedding. For Brahmans it is therefore particularly desirable that children should be males, for a series of daughters can mean economic bankruptcy. Among the other families of Gopalpur, who belong to the lower

jati or castes, daughters are almost as welcome as sons, for the lower castes pay no dowry, and the cost of the wedding is borne by the bridegroom's family. Furthermore, a family benefits by the alliance that marriages provide with other families, for a marriage is not an individual matter, since it serves to link two complete lineages. In a society which hinges on kinship, marriage constitutes a social and political bond between two kinship groupings, and neither the bride nor the bridegroom have any influence in the choice of their mate.

Marriage between the members of castes with different social statuses is impossible. It follows that the members of each *jat* or caste have been interbreeding among themselves for countless successive generations. In consequence, each caste contains, in effect, two phratrylike kinship groupings because no daughter is permitted to marry into the same lineage as that to which her father belongs. All the boys and girls of the same generation in the father's lineage are regarded as brothers or sisters, and a marriage partner must therefore be found from the mother's lineage. Similarly, as far as a male child is concerned, all the women in his mother's lineage are classified either as "mothers" or, if they belong to his own generation, as "wives." Ideally, a man therefore marries his sister's daughter, and since girls are married early in life and begin producing children at a young age, there are usually several sister's daughters available.

A number of prospective wives may be found in the village or in the neighboring villages, but the selection will depend on the outcome of negotiations arranged through intermediaries with considerable social ceremony and much excitement. The economic status of the husband is important, not simply to ensure that the girl will be well provided for but also because the alliance made will reflect the status of both families. Once a bargain has been reached, a betrothal ceremony is held at the bride's house, followed by a banquet, but the wedding does not take place until both parties are old enough. When bride and bridegroom have both reached the age of puberty, a wedding ceremony is held at the groom's village, attended by as many friends and relatives as the groom's family can afford to entertain. Weddings are important social events, and the status of the host family is reflected by the number of guests they are able to feed.

In many cases the bride and bridegroom see each other for the first time at the conclusion of the wedding ceremony. This is a fact which often astonishes Westerners, but arranged weddings usually work out very well because a better match could seldom be made if the bride and groom were to be chosen by computer. In the first place, such marriages are invariably arranged between families of similar social status and cultural background. In the second place, the wedding has the full support of kinsmen and friends, so that the marriage is sustained at all times by the community approval. And in the third place, no man or woman can ever think his partner is ugly, for they will invariably be close relatives, looking similar to their own brothers and sisters. In short, as Indians say: "In the West you love, then marry. In India we marry, then love."

Despite the relative poverty of the inhabitants of Gopalpur, wedding ceremonies are an occasion for everyone to wear their best clothes. In particular, the bride wears the most expensive new *sari* she is ever likely to own, embroidered with real gold thread, and there is no married woman in Gopalpur who does not possess some genuine jewelry to call her own. Although almost every villager is in debt, none would allow his wife to forego the dignity of possessing at least a few poor pieces of jewelry made from genuine gold and genuine precious or semiprecious stones.

Migrant Specialists

Gopalpur still possesses an institution which has been characteristic of rural village life since the beginning of the Neolithic: the regular visits by traveling craftsmen and merchants who provide specialized services to smaller communities. Such people do not belong to the Gopalpur community but visit the village at regular intervals, sometimes only annually, performing their services, receiving payment, and passing on. There can be no marriages between the families of the visitors and the people of Gopalpur, to whom they are simply itinerant strangers, coming from no one knows where. Nevertheless, they are a regular feature of Gopalpur life.

Probably the most wealthy of these migratory specialists are the goldsmiths or jewelers whose caste has a low status, but who eat well and always seem to have all they need in life. Of lower economic status are the traveling performers, deer hunters, tinkers, and religious mendicants, but all add richness to the life of the people of Gopalpur, not only through their wares and services but by bringing with them some of the mystery of strange lands which gives the villagers a sense of adventure and worldly knowledge—even though few have ever traveled more than a score or so miles from their homes.

Caste in Gopalpur

In addition to these itinerant specialists, there are other professional specialists in neighboring villages, upon whom the farmers of Gopalpur also rely for particular services. Thus Gopalpur has no resident astrologer but uses a neighboring astrologer who serves three villages. Astrologers have a high caste status, being classified as Brahmans, and their services are necessary for reading horoscopes, determining auspicious dates for weddings and other ceremonials, and even predicting success or failure in farming experiments. Similarly,

singers are necessary professionals whose duty it is to chant religious songs on ceremonial occasions. Again Gopalpur has no singer, but is able to employ the services of a singer living in a neighboring village. Despite their religious function singers have a low caste status, as does another essential specialist, the washerman. Before ritual ceremonies all clothing must be ritually cleansed by a member of the washermen *jati*. Again, since Gopalpur is not large enough to support a washerman of its own, it uses the services of the washerman from the neighboring village when the occasion requires. Every specialist has a right to monopolize his profession in his own district, and it is impossible for a villager from Gopalpur to take his business to a rival washerman—the concept of competition simply does not exist. Indeed, even fees are traditional and take the form of gifts.

Since the concept of economic competition

Itinerant male dancers, dressed as females, pose for the camera at an Indian village fair. (Courtesy of Government of India Information Service.)

is totally foreign to the traditional ties of inter-dependency that bind the villagers together, the pattern of economic life in Gopalpur may be said to be based upon the concept of reciprocity of service between the members of the various specialized castes, not upon the ideal of a free market economy. Barter and trade for profit come into the picture only when the farmers seek to sell their surplus crops to the merchants who reside in the larger district towns, are not a part of the community, and are alien to the principle of communal reciprocity. These merchants invariably make a profit whether the crop is good or bad, and much of the wealth of India's peasantry is siphoned off by those who are not a part of the system, the townsmen having replaced the old royal caste of rajahs as the main beneficiaries.

Although in the distant past caste status in India appears to have been roughly equated to economic status, this has not been the case for a number of centuries. Today, Brahmans who beg for a living as religious mendicants are common, and there are extremely wealthy Vaisya caste merchants who are among the wealthiest multimillionaires of the world. The most immediate indicator of caste status is today not wealth but the dietary taboos to which the members of a caste are subject. Brahman priests are vegetarians. Salt makers, who fill a very unprofitable economic role, also have a relatively high caste status and neither eat mutton nor drink beer. The farmers and shepherds of Gopalpur rank below the salt makers in status and are consequently permitted to drink beer as well as eat mutton. Stoneworkers, on the other hand, are of even lower status, and they may eat pork, while the lowly leatherworkers are so inferior that their customs permit them to drink beer and eat mutton, beef, and pork.

The continuing vitality of the caste system is demonstrated by the fact that even Moslems have been fitted into this system of hereditary status. As we have already observed, the Moslems were once a dominant political group. But their position in the caste hierarchy places them below the farmers and shepherds, and only just above the stoneworkers. The Moslem religion permits them to eat beef, which is banned to the "twice-born" *arya* or higher Hindu castes, but "commendably" prohibits them from eating pork.

However, it would be wrong to say that caste no longer plays any part in the determination of economic status. Even the Brahman mendicant who begs for a living will receive larger gifts than a begger of lower status, and a number of the more profitable occupations, such as that of the village accountant, are reserved for Brahmans. Furthermore, although some stoneworkers have purchased their own fields in Gopalpur, this is regarded as a breach of tradition and has caused considerable tension, even physical violence in some cases. In modern India the socialist policies of Indira Gandhi seek to destroy the principles of caste exclusiveness and other characteristic aspects of the agrarian Hindu tradition, such as the giving of dowries at the time of marriage, but the laws passed in Delhi are weakly enforced and have little effect in Gopalpur. In the Indian countryside, the traditional cultural structure still functions, adapting itself to changing conditions, despite the attempts of the central government to introduce radical change. In the eyes of the inhabitants of Gopalpur, it is therefore still regarded as unfair for the members of one *jat* to compete in occupations traditionally reserved for the members of other *jati.*

TEPOZTLÁN IN RURAL MEXICO

As we have already seen, at the agricultural level of social evolution society becomes divided into rural and urban communities. In this situation innovations occur in the urban communities, which place them ahead of the

FIG. 56   TEPOZTLÁN

Tepoztlán is a Mexican peasant township which has been the subject of several ethnographic studies.

dependent rural areas. Thus, in ancient Sumeria the cities developed a substantial division of labor and an advanced Bronze Age technology while the surrounding rural areas preserved an essentially Stone Age technology and social structure. But between the villages and the cities there arise a number of market towns which not only act as local administrative and commercial centers but serve to articulate the relationship between the conservative villages and the more progressive cities.

It is through these market towns that technological, social, and political innovation reaches the rural areas. The culture and social structure of such towns consequently represents a blend of the rural tradition tempered by sociopolitical innovations filtering in from the cities. Such towns underline the fact that more complex cultures are generally in a state of constant change. Torn between conservative adherence to the values of the past and the socioeconomic temptations of urban innova-

tion, they may give an outward appearance of tranquillity, but beneath the surface their inhabitants live in an uneasy state of cultural disequilibrium.

The vital role of such rural centers, as intermediaries between the dynamism of the cities and the conservatism of the villages, can be clearly appreciated from Oscar Lewis' study of Tepoztlán, a village situated in the State of Morelos not far from Mexico City.[3] Throughout its entire history Tepoztlán has been a rural center through which innovation has been transmitted to the Indian villagers. Geographically it serves as the nucleus to a group of villages occupying a broad alluvial valley in an area that has been continuously inhabited for at least 2000 years. Beyond the Tepoztlán valley, imposing cliffs rise 1200 feet or more above the fields, and because of its elevation the climate is temperate and healthy—the en-

[3] Oscar Lewis, *Tepoztlán: Village in Mexico* (New York: Holt, Rinehart and Winston, Inc., 1960).

tire area being too high for the malaria-carrying mosquitoes which plague the lowlands. From the point of view of the peasant population, the main problems are the irregularity of the rainfall and the shortness of the growing season, for the long, dry winter lasts up to seven months. Nevertheless, the flora is semitropical, and in addition to the main crops of corn, papaya, avocado, mango, and banana, a variety of other fruits and herbs are easily grown.

The Pre-Columbian Background

The population of Tepoztlán is predominantly Indian in origin, with some admixture of Spanish genes. The Indian Nahuatl language was still universal prior to the political revolutions of 1910 to 1920. Since then, however, the establishment of a government school in Tepoztlán has introduced Spanish, and the ancient Nahuatl language has come to be despised by some of the younger generation of Tepoztlán Indians as a sign of rural unsophistication.

In pre-Columbian days Tepoztlán society was highly stratified, and a few noble families, representing the tribal elite, dominated the mass of commoners. The community was organized entirely on kinship lines. All property was owned communally by the clans under the direction of the clan chief, political office being hereditary in specific families. But Tepoztlán was not independent, and the Tepoztlán nobility paid tribute first to the Toltecs and then to the Aztecs. Life was highly structured, every detail being validated by religious sanctions. Tepoztlán had its own special cult of Ometochtli (literally "Two Rabbits"), the deity of an intoxicating drink known as *pulque,* whose worship involved collective orgies.

Since the old Indian culture had neither wheeled vehicles nor beasts of burden, Tepoztlán served as a local center for hand industries, its craftsmen weaving the cotton that was grown in the fields and making building materials, clothing, and all the basic essentials of the material culture. During this early period Tepoztlán was a center of innovation, identifying itself with the conquering Toltecs by adopting a new local god, Topiltzin (later known as El Tepozteco) who was believed to be the son of the Toltec emperor Mixcoatl by

Mexican peasant from Jalisco, Sierra Madre. (Courtesy of Musée de l'Homme, Paris.)

a local woman. Under the Aztecs the Tepoztecans also sacrificed prisoners of war to the Aztec War God, tearing the beating heart out of the chests of their living victims, and on necessary occasions they even sacrificed their own children to the Aztec Rain God.

Under Spanish Rule

With the conquest of Mexico by Cortez in 1521, Tepoztlán did not lose its importance but became a local center for the bureaucratic governmental structure of the Spanish empire in Mexico. The old Indian nobility retained its power, merely transferring its allegiance to the new government. But Spanish rule destroyed the clans as property-owning kinship groups, thus clearing the way for the replacement of the extended family by the nuclear family. The old clan lands were divided between the *caciques* or clan nobility and the Catholic Church. With the disappearance of the clan system, Tepoztlán social structure consequently came to revolve around the ideal of the nuclear family, and the individual's status became tied to that of his family, beyond the limits of which he was left without protection.

Under Spanish influence Tepoztlán acquired much of the appearance of a Spanish town, with a town square, a park, and later even a bandstand. A church was built in the town center, and a monastery was established nearby, staffed by members of the Dominican order. Because of the Indian tradition of polytheism, Christianity was readily accepted by admitting the Christian Trinity to the existing pantheon of gods. However, once the new church was built, the priests rejected the concept of religious coexistence and energetically set about the expurgation of the old beliefs, persecuting members of the indigenous priesthood as witches. Bloodletting sacrificial rituals were consequently replaced by colorful church services and outdoor fiestas, as the church rapidly accumulated great wealth and became a substantial landowner, dominating and directing all religious activities in the district.

Following the French Revolution, the Spanish colonies in the New World took the opportunity afforded by the Napoleonic conquest of Spain to seize their independence. In 1810 Mexico became independent of Spain under the rule of conservative Spanish and *mestizo* colonists—mestizos being Spanish-speaking persons of mixed Spanish and Indian descent (Latin *mixticius*, "of mixed descent"). Nevertheless, this revolution at first made little change in the life of the inhabitants of Tepoztlán, and the pattern of continuity was not disrupted until the Juarez reforms of 1857 which broke the power of the church and led to the confiscation of all church property and its distribution among the local caciques. Enriched by the additional lands, the old Indian nobility built impressive Spanish-style houses. Not only did they maintain their dominant position in Tepoztlán society but they also began to hire labor in imitation of the estate systems of the nearby Spanish haciendas, further increasing their wealth by becoming market crop producers. When the church retrieved its political power a generation later, the caciques managed to preserve their position by reasserting their support for the church and effectively succeeded in maintaining their ancient preeminence until the revolutions of the present century. Renowned for its cultured and sophisticated mestizo and Europeanized cacique population, Tepoztlán was in 1900 known as the "Athens of the State of Morelos," boasting even its own lending library and its own museum, and local cacique families provided the State of Morelos with many doctors, lawyers, priests, and other educated professional men.

Revolution

Socialist revolution finally broke out in Morelos in 1912, led by an Indian known as Zapata. Aided by active revolutionary elements from other parts of Mexico, the peasants of Tepoztlán turned on the local caciques, killing many and looting their houses. During the ensuing fighting between rebel and government troops, the town was severely damaged, and for a time there was only disorder. Arson and robbery were accompanied by murder, assassination, and rape, until finally the revolution succeeded. The power of the caciques and the church was broken, the local monastery being used as stables for the horses of the rebel troops. During this time Tepoztlán suffered terribly, the population falling to one half of its former level, but the changes wrought were to be permanent.

With the end of the disorders the surviving members of the cacique class returned to their wrecked homes and even managed to reclaim a portion of their lands, but their political power was lost and the larger part of their land was redistributed. In particular, the nearby Spanish hacienda was completely broken up; its estates were divided among landless families in the district. Nevertheless, the new social and economic order that began to emerge embodied much of the old tradition despite the violent economic and social changes introduced by the revolution. The Catholic Church once again reestablished itself in the lives of the people, and many of the cacique families which had survived the upheaval built up a new, though modest, level of prosperity by frugality and hard labor. In addition, a new commercial and professional class began to emerge, many of whom came from outside Tepoztlán.

Economic Stagnation

Unfortunately for Tepoztlán, with the modernization of transportation, small towns of its size now began to lose their importance as local centers of industry. Unable to compete with factory goods the old craft industries of Tepoztlán consequently withered away. Although the town gained a new government high school, financed by the federal government, it lost much of its local autonomy. By 1930 the central plaza and park were neglected, and a state of decay engulfed the town center. The general state of chronic neglect was only temporarily alleviated once a year when the square was swept and the main fountain cleaned for the annual carnival. Improved communications, linking the town with the nearby city of Cuernavaca, further undermined its importance as a local commercial center. Thus, market stalls were small and ill-attended, and Tepoztlán remained mainly dependent upon subsistence cultivation for its survival, augmented only by the wages of women workers in two small mills established by national entrepreneurs to take advantage of the cheap local labor.

In this state of depression the pattern of cultivation in the Tepoztlán valley reflected the survival of horticultural traditions in what was becoming an increasingly industralized economy. Only the land in the valleys could be cultivated with plows because of irrigation problems and the steepness of the hillsides, and this superior land was and still is privately owned. Meanwhile improvements effected by international agents in the control of disease have led to a rapid expansion in the local population; thus, one quarter of the present families are again landless, despite the redistribution following the bloody 1910–1920 upheaval. Land on the sloping hillsides above the valley is regarded as communal property but is allocated in small grants, known as *tlacolol*, to individual families. Because of the steep gradients, primitive hoe culture is necessary on these plots, and not only is this work laborious and back-breaking but it is less profitable. There is therefore a very sharp separation of wealth between those who own the rich plow land of the valley and those who have to make a living working the *tlacolol*. Those families which are not even in the happy position of holding *tlacolol* land hire themselves out to work for those who own plow lands.

Market scene in a Mexican village (Courtesy of Museo Nacional de Antropologia, Mexico City.)

The Indian tradition of horticulture has consequently survived in the *tlacolol* plots alongside the Spanish tradition of plow culture in the valley fields. Other Spanish innovations, such as the herding of cattle originally brought in from Europe, do not play a large part in the Tepoztlán economy. The few cattle that are to be found are thin and poor. However, oxen play a vital role as draft animals, pulling plows and carts—another Spanish innovation—and there was still no mechanical tractor in Tepoztlán as late as 1956.

Despite the revolution which overthrew the old cacique aristocracy, Tepoztlán society is still stratified and a wide income gap separates the wealthy from the poor. Twenty-five percent of the total land is once again owned by

4 percent of the population. These new landowners represent the more industrious families who, by their own efforts and economy, have accumulated wealth since the revolution; ironically many are descendants from the old cacique families, who have applied themselves energetically to the recuperation of their lost fortunes, and now work manually alongside their employees. Since an Old World tradition of courtesy and mutual respect still pervades the entire township, polite forms of address are used at all times. The descendant of a cacique family will use the friendly *tu* to address hired landless laborers of his own age and the respectful *Usted* when speaking to employees who are older than himself. However, there are few domestic servants in Tepoztlán because

domestic service is regarded as humiliating, and the memory of the revolution is still strong enough to ensure that those rich families which have succeeded in recuperating their wealth prefer to avoid too open a demonstration of their prosperity. Consequently houses are allowed to remain decayed and impoverished looking on the exterior, even though the interiors are often well furnished and comfortably equipped.

Family and Barrio

Tepoztlán life essentially revolves around the nuclear family, following the disappearance of the old clan system and the extended families of the pre-Hispanic period. Family bonds are cohesive, held together by economic ties, inheritance, and a close psychological interdependence. Outside the family, except for the church, there is no organization that the individual can turn to for protection.

As in most Latin American societies, the Tepoztlán family is strongly patriarchal. Men consciously seek to acquire the spirit of *machismo* or manliness, and a man who is submissive to his wife tends to be despised by males and females alike. Although many wives today work for wages outside the family, men still claim to rule the household, and this tradition is accepted by the womenfolk. Furthermore, men claim the right to extramarital sexual relations, though not publicly, but wives and daughters are kept under strict surveillance.

A few men drink heavily, and wife beating is sometimes reported. But there is a general belief that wives who are beaten may take revenge upon their husbands by witchcraft, or at least by dropping a herb known as *toloache* into their coffee, which can make a man *tonto* or stupid. Children are generally loved and valued, although they are brought up under strict discipline and taught to be passive toward their parents and unobtrusive. Fathers are expected to treat their children with sternness, while mothers are more sympathetic, seldom using physical punishment—although they may threaten to abandon their children if they do not behave themselves properly.

In the absence of clan ties the system of *compadrazgo* or godparenthood plays an important role in Tepoztlán family life and provides a degree of social security for children who may be orphaned. Each child has *compadres* or godparents, often relatives, whose duty it is to care for them should their parents die prematurely, and who also ensure that the child is brought up correctly by the parents in accordance with the Christian religion.

There is one other social grouping of great importance which still serves to fill the gap left by the decline of the old clans. This is the *barrio* or local community, which appears to descend directly from the pre-Columbian *ayllu* or local kinship community. Tepoztlán is divided into seven barrios, which are socioreligious units. Each has its own chapel, religious festivals and fiestas, and its own patron saint. Most people marry within their barrio or in a neighboring barrio, and membership is determined by ownership of a housesite within the territorial limits of the barrio. Because housesites are passed on from generation to generation within the same family, there is a great deal of continuity through the generations in barrio membership, and the members of a barrio are also closely interrelated by marriage and kinship.

But each barrio is also a socioeconomic group with its own mayor or *mayordomo* and its own taxes. The funds raised through taxation are used to keep the chapel and surroundings in repair and to hire dancers and musicians and pay for the cost of fireworks for the annual fiesta in honor of the patron saint. The selection of the *mayordomo* is by common consent rather than by election and is usually awarded to the head of one of the wealthier families in the barrio, since its duties may be onerous and it carries with it no economic advantages. Under such circumstances the honor is not always accepted with enthusiasm.

Future Directions

So far as spending patterns and life styles are concerned, the wealthier farmers consequently reflect a conservative "yeoman" pattern of life, and it is the merchant and professional classes which have become the main innovators. These classes often affect modern fashions in costume and may even send their children to school in Cuernavaca. Since they also usually read newspapers from Cuernavaca, they can be influential in swaying local opinion on any national or international issues that may stimulate their interest.

There has been no leisure class in Tepoztlán since the revolution, and sex, age, kinship, and occupation are the basic determinants of social status. With the overthrow of the old Indian nobility, Tepoztlán reverted at least temporarily to the *Gemeinschaft* relationships of a rural community, but inequalities of wealth have inevitably reemerged. Such inequalities are becoming more marked as a result of a recent influx of tourists and the establishment of a foreign "colony" attracted to the town by the quaintness of the colonial architecture and the healthiness of the climate. For the present time most of the professional people—the carpenters, bakers, barbers, and merchants—come from peasant families and still work part-time on the land; but with the development of communications, tourism, the rise of new industry, and the appearance of a foreign residential section, all the signs point to an intensification of the division of labor and to a corresponding diversification and stratification of society.

For Further Reading

Anderson, R. T., and B. G. Anderson, 1964, *Vanishing Village: A Danish Maritime Community*. Seattle: University of Washington Press.

Banton, M., 1966, *The Social Anthropology of Complex Society*. New York: Frederick A. Praeger, Inc.

Beals, A. R., 1962, *Gopalpur: A South Indian Village*. New York: Holt, Rinehart and Winston, Inc.

Fei, H. T., 1939, *Peasant Life in China: A Field Study of Country Life in the Yangtze Valley*. London: George Routledge & Sons, Ltd.

Halpern, J., 1970, *A Serbian Village*. Santa Fe, N.M.: William Gannon.

Hsu, F. L. K., 1971, *Under the Ancestors' Shadow: Kinship, Personality and Social Mobility in China*. Stanford, Calif.: Stanford University Press.

Jones, E., 1966, *Towns and Cities*. New York: Oxford University Press.

Lewis, O., 1960, *Tepoztlán: Village in Mexico*. New York: Holt, Rinehart and Winston, Inc.

Moore, D. R., 1939, *A History of Latin America*. Englewood Cliffs, N.J.: Prentice-Hall, Inc.

Potter, J. M., M. N. Diaz, and G. M. Foster, 1967, *Peasant Society: A Reader*. Boston: Little, Brown & Company.

Redfield, R., 1947, "The Folk Society," *American Journal of Sociology* 52(4):293–308.
———, 1956, *Peasant Society and Culture*. Chicago: University of Chicago Press.

Rogers, Everett M., 1969, *Modernization among Peasants: The Impact of Communication*. New York: Holt, Rinehart and Winston, Inc.

Spindler, G. D., 1973, *Burgbach: Urbanization and Identity in a German Village.* New York: Holt, Rinehart and Winston, Inc.

Wolf, E. R., 1966, *Peasants.* Englewood Cliffs, N.J.: Prentice-Hall, Inc.

Wylie, L., 1964, *Village in the Vaucluse: An Account of Life in a French Village.* Cambridge, Mass.: Harvard University Press.

Young, M., and P. Willmot, 1957, *Family and Kinship in East London.* London: Routledge & Kegan Paul Ltd.

CHAPTER 32

Industrial Societies

Industrial societies are inherently different from any other kind of society that we have so far discussed. These differences may be traced directly to technological advances which require specialization in the production of tools and tool parts so that standardization replaces older methods of individual craftsmanship. By definition, INDUSTRIAL SOCIETIES may therefore be said to arise from the combination of technology with an extensive diversification and specialization of labor. This results in a FACTORY SYSTEM which utilizes new sources of power to replace human and animal muscles in the mass production and mass distribution of standardized products.

Historical Background

The invention of the wheel in the Neolithic may be seen as the first precursor of the series of innovations which were to lead to the *Industrial Revolution,* a period of rapid technological, industrial, and social change which began in England, a small country off the western coast of Europe, during the latter part of the eighteenth century. The first signs of this industrial revolution appeared in the textile industry and took the form of technological innovations which led to the replacement of handlooms, operated by the women in their homes, by mechanical looms powered by machinery, concentrated in central factory work areas.

Events moved rapidly after an invention known as the Spinning Jenny enabled workers to spin a number of threads simultaneously, and the further innovations by Richard Arkwright and Edmund Cartwright led to the introduction of sophisticated power looms. Mechanical sources of power were harnessed for these early machines by placing waterwheels in millstreams and connecting them to the machines in such a way that the running water turned the working parts of the loom. Where an adequate supply of water was not available, human muscles were utilized as a machine-driving force using devices such as the treadmill, a unique device which required no water, being powered by men, women, and children who constantly tramped on a revolving wheel, thereby converting human muscle power and gravity into machine power. The treadmill was not particularly economic of human effort, but it represented an attempt to adapt mechanical systems to traditional sources of cheap energy such as prison labor and solved the problem of exercising the prisoners while converting their energy into a useful purpose. Thus while France was undergoing social and political revolutions and the dictator Napoleon was attempting to introduce a new totalitarian social order into Europe backed only by the resources of an agrarian society, England was already an industrialized power, selling machine-made textiles to clothe the armies of its French enemies—and subsidizing the European nations in their resistance against France from the large profits which its new factory system produced.

The revolution in textile manufacturing brought a complete industrial revolution to England, for not only did the demand for iron for machinery lead to the establishment of an iron and steel industry, but the demand for new sources of power led to an unprecedented expansion of coal mining. Industrialization also led to centralization, and manufacturing ceased to be a cottage activity carried on by small groups of craftsmen in every market town. Instead, industrial settlements began to emerge, which were at first organized rather like agricultural estates, with the houses of the owners and supervisors grouped in one area, the factory workshops in another, and the houses of the workers in yet another, until the entire community sometimes comprised the supervisors and workers employed in a single factory. As new factories were established, these settlements grew in size to become industrial cities, often dependent for survival upon a single industry.

In consequence of the centralization of industrial production in convenient locations, the transportation of vast quantities of raw materials and finished goods over substantial distances became necessary. Horses and carts were inadequate to meet the transportation needs, and the industrialists therefore turned to the solution devised by Neolithic man: water transport. Since many of the new cities were inland, the industrial inventive genius produced the idea of a network of inland canals which would permit the transportation of heavy loads of merchandise in boats even where no natural water link existed between the cities concerned. Yet the canals had not been established for long when the invention of the steam engine, converting heat from coal into mechanical power, introduced a revolutionary new concept in transportation: the mechanically propelled vehicle.

The first steam engines were relatively inefficient, and the vehicles which they powered could not be driven over the rough surfaces of the existing roads, which were in any case impassable to most wheeled vehicles after heavy rains. The new vehicles were therefore placed on metal tracks laid on wooden supports, and the world's first railway was constructed in 1825. By 1850 England was covered by a network of railways, and other Western nations soon copied England's example and built similar rail networks. The steam engine was in due course followed by the development of the petroleum internal combustion engine; it was then only a matter of time before road, sea, and air transport developed to their present level of efficiency.

Mass Society

This improvement in communications has meant that human populations become more mobile from a geographical point of view as the time taken up by travel is substantially reduced and distances correspondingly decrease in importance as social and political boundaries. Inventions such as the airplane and radio have reduced the size of the world in a sense that it is proportionately smaller today than the average German principality of two centuries ago. Even as late as 1815, the year of the battle of Waterloo, the fastest a man could travel was the speed of a galloping horse, and messages flashed by the heliograph were regarded as a novel and rapid means of communication. Today air travel, radio, and television greatly facilitate effective political control of extensive areas.

The mass production of goods in centralized industrial cities has also led to the decline of local industry; and with improved means of communication and transportation, the need for large markets to support the new system of mass production has led to an increased trade over wider areas. With industrialization, political units have consequently tended to increase in size so that political participation in government has tended to become less personal than it was in band, tribal, or even agrarian societies. Local communities lose much of their economic and cultural autonomy and eventually become integrated as separate subcultures into a much wider MASS SOCIETY in which the direction of the overall activities of the total population tends to be controlled and given direction by a central core of uniform political, economic, social, and other institutions. Such mass societies not only involve the mass production and mass marketing of goods but may also involve welfare measures made necessary by the decline of the older kinship system which provided economic security to all its members. Mass societies are also essentially urbanized, for industry and commerce concentrate in the cities, while in the course of time the percentage of population employed in agricultural activities decreases as a result of the mechanization of agriculture and increased productivity per agricultural worker.

With the movement of population from rural centers to the mushrooming cities and with the growing interdependence of local communities in an increasingly integrated and specialized economic system, the larger political units have tended to suppress the political and cultural autonomy of local areas and there has been a corresponding decline in the authority of local traditions. Since culture grows out of communication, it is only natural to assume that in most traditional rural societies, where communication is restricted to word-of-mouth contact between father and son and between neighbors, a relatively conservative, unchanging cultural tradition will persist. But in modern industrialized societies, mass communication has broadened the field of personal contact, and mass media such as books, newspapers, radio, and television have brought new and hitherto alien cultural traditions into almost every household. Compulsory schooling and the standardization of education throughout larger areas have further repressed local cultural autonomy, imposing a uniform set of approved cultural values and attitudes throughout the political state. When the entire society is intellectually integrated and directed by these means, deliberate social and cultural change may be implemented on the basis of planned programs. Where effective political control has been acquired by an effectively integrated political group—as in totalitarian societies such as National Socialist Germany, Fascist Italy, Communist Russia, or Communist China—complete sociocultural revolutions can be produced within the period of a single generation, especially when dissenters are physically suppressed.

Decline of Family and Kinship Ties

From the earliest known hunting and gathering societies, men have traditionally been territorial animals, acquiring a deep psychological attachment to a particular locality and responding to the ties, real or imaginary, of "blood and soil." But in industrial societies sudden changes in the pattern of production

Machinery has drastically reduced the percentage of the world's population that need engage in food production, resulting in the continuing urbanization of the more advanced countries and the revolutionary changes in human social organization that this implies.

following upon technological innovations can affect the whole structure of society, throwing many people out of work and requiring others to migrate substantial distances to find employment, thus breaking kinship and local ties.

Industrialization also offers opportunities not only for geographical mobility but also for vertical social mobility, making it more common for individuals to rise out of the social class of their kinsmen, thus disrupting the community of interest and placing a social distance between kinsmen. Indeed, industrialization weakens the traditional forms of social stratification in preurban societies, which tend to place the members of the same family in the same social class, restricting social mobility and emphasizing birth as a determinant of social status. The older castelike societies are replaced by more mobile class systems (see Fig. 28) in which status comes to be more competitive than inherited.

Industrialization has consequently undermined the kinship system wherever it has taken hold, and even the family system has been weakened as a result of the decline of the family as a unit of production. In agricultural and nonindustrial societies the basic unit of production is the household, usually comprising either a nuclear or an extended family. Thus, family members are tied together by common economic interests as well as by emotional and personal links. In industrialized societies, however, the household ceases to be the basic unit of production, and to the extent that the head of the family becomes a wage earner, employed in an external economic organization, instead of a director of the family economic corporation, his status is weakened.

In many industrial societies, husband, wife, and children all find employment as wage earners, often in different enterprises, and since their experiences and life interests are no longer linked to a single common family venture, the sense of shared interest and shared concern is lost. Furthermore, children who have completed a modern education, preparing them for specialized roles in industry, usually become independent of their parents and may even move upward into a higher income and social group, making social communication difficult. In such cases the resultant social and cultural differences can make relationships between even the closest kinsmen tension-ridden and embarrassing to all.

Bureaucracy

With the decline of kinship and the replacement of the household by the factory or workshop as the unit of production, new methods of social organization become necessary, and these lead to the emergence of *bureaucratic systems,* hierarchical forms of social organization rationally planned to facilitate co-

A Haida Indian sitting on the back porch of his house in the Old Masset Indian Reserve, Queen Charlotte Islands, British Columbia. This photograph poignantly illustrates the plight of many ethnic peoples whose traditional culture has been shattered by contact with contemporary Western industrial society. Even the Western style tombstone (in the foreground) commemorating a dead family member has since been removed to a local cemetery in accordance with the prevailing customs of Euro-American society but in violation of traditional Haida mores. (Courtesy of the Canadian Government Photo Center.)

operation and goal achievement in a society characterized by a substantial division of labor. Eliminating local self-sufficiency and forcing local political and cultural groups to participate in larger and more highly integrated societies, bureaucracy expands with mass production and mass marketing as the seemingly inevitable answer to the organizational problems which industrialization has created.

Bureaucracy is by no means restricted to departments of government. All larger organizations in an industrial society are run on a bureaucratic basis, whether publicly owned or not. When the scope of any industrial, commercial, or military operation becomes too large to be effectively controlled by a single man, a division of labor must develop and there must be some delegation of duties to subordinates. As these subordinates proliferate in number, a regular chain of responsibility and control develops and the bureaucratic system is born.

The bureaucratic system has been frequently criticized, but as Max Weber, one of the pioneer authorities on the subject, points out, bureaucracy arises simply because it is the most efficient solution that man has yet found to the problem of organizing any work force characterized by an advanced division of labor. The division of labor requires, and bureaucracy supplies, an hierarchical chain of authoritative control. Arising out of the system of mass production, bureaucratic systems necessarily play down the value of individual personality. In an efficiently integrated workforce, comprising diverse highly specialized but integrated roles, every worker becomes essentially a role player, a cog in a larger machine, and the efficiency of the entire operation will depend on the efficiency with which each individual acts out his specific role.

Thus bureaucratic officeholders soon learn that they have a better chance of succeeding if they become like the man in the gray flannel suit: faceless but versatile. In a prebureaucratic society a man is to a large extent valued because of his individual personality, but in an industrialized society a man is valued for his ability to fill the required role, and individual idiosyncrasies are regarded more as a handicap to efficient role playing than the reverse. To succeed in a bureaucratic system the worker must become an "organization man" who will owe his first obligation to the organization which he serves, and his family duties will be relegated to a secondary position. This situation frequently leads to feelings of alienation and boredom, a loss of personal self-respect, and a sense of antagonism against "the system" and "the establishment" among those who find themselves depersonalized and left without any decision-making powers.

This sense of alienation and resentment is largely peculiar to industrialized societies. Decision-making seems to play an important role in contributing to human satisfaction. Agrarian and preagrarian societies seem to offer their members a wide range of socially approved choices which may not be politically significant in their implications but seem to be significant according to the values of the society in question. Thus, in a familistically-oriented society the decisions involved in negotiating marriage alliances can prove highly satisfying to those concerned. But because of the interdependence of roles in a bureaucratic system, all socially "significant" decisions tend to be taken at the upper levels of the hierarchical pyramid, and all sense of individual responsibility and creativeness is lost at the lower levels.

In place of the face-to-face contact characteristic of most preindustrial societies, in which a man's reputation and character becomes widely known throughout his community, industrialization has also promoted anonymity and has consequently led to what has been described as a *marketing orientation,* a situation in which individuals learn to disguise their true character, feelings, and beliefs, and strive instead to promote an artificial image of themselves—a false front—for the express purpose of easing their relations with the members of the diverse subcultures with which they come into contact daily. Instead of being an ethnocentric, loyal, and outspoken supporter of his own social group, a successful man tends to become something of a supersalesman, learning how to sell himself and how to "win friends and influence people" by pretending to espouse the ideals and attitudes of other groups even though these may be alien to the segment of society with which he identifies himself.

In time a state of *anomie* or normlessness may develop. Men will cease to hold any cultural values seriously, becoming cynical and placing their individual interests above the values of any social group whatever. Those at the peak of the bureaucratic pyramid come to regard themselves as "emancipated" from the cultural values of the society they dominate, seeing society as an organization which, properly manipulated, may be made to accept the imprint of their values and their goals. Those who are successful in bureaucratic systems develop a "higher amorality," conceiving of themselves as being above the moral and cultural traditions of the society they dominate. Their activities may often be opportunist and contrary to the cultural traditions of their society and to the wishes of the more conservative mass of the more heavily acculturated population.

From an aesthetic and psychological point of view, the anomie created by the bureaucratic system is reinforced by the decline in the psychological satisfaction which men receive from the act of producing goods. From the Upper Paleolithic until the coming of mass production, the individual craftsman took a personal satisfaction in the perfection of his product and found joy in his work. Such satisfaction, however, is denied to the modern machine operator, who feels little personal pride in the mass-produced products created under his supervision, since he is prevented from regarding his work as a form of personal self-expression.

In addition there is an emotional divorce between industrial man and the things he uses. The disappearance of the individual character of artifacts has destroyed the close psychological bond that exists in preindustrial societies between men and the objects they use. This loss comes about not only from the anonymity of standardized articles but from the fact that cheap replacements have led to a "throwaway" economy which not only is wasteful from an ecological point of view but also inhibits any emotional bond between the owner and the objects which he uses so fleetingly.

Ethnic Tensions

Because the increase in the size of industrial societies leads to the incorporation of different ethnic minorities under the rule of a single government and because increasing geographical mobility may destroy the original pattern of geographical segregation which formerly distributed ethnic and racial groups in separate provinces, most industrial societies suffer from racial, ethnic, and religious tensions. Even though urbanization and the factory system tend to break down the geographical segregation of different cultural groups, this does not prevent men from seeking to associate with those who share their own cultural experiences and attitudes. In consequence, there is a constant tendency toward ethnic residential segregation in the large multiethnic cities of the industrialized societies. Relations between different ethnic groups may also become more tense because the ethnic cleavages tend to be reflected in different levels of social stratification. Quite obviously, the individuals from one cultural group may find that their cultural background aids them in the competition to climb the social ladder, while the cultural tradition of other groups may actually serve as an impediment to social mobility.

Such a tendency toward segregation on cultural lines also reinforces existing tendencies toward genetic segregation, so that industrial societies do not necessarily become the melting pot that they outwardly appear to be. Indeed, there is evidence that in the faceless anonymity of large industrial societies men search for identity, trying to find a personal niche in the world, as an alternative to being but one individual among millions. The destruction of the elaborate kinship systems has deprived men of the multitude of links which made each individual an integral part of the larger society to which he belonged. Faced with a feeling of loneliness, helplessness, and insecurity, an individual finds some comfort in belonging to an identifiable ethnic group within the larger mass society, providing some of the psychological security which the old descent groups ensured.

The significance of this quest for human identity must not be underestimated. As smaller nations disappear politically, through absorption into larger units, the search for

identity fosters nationalism anew, leading to demands for autonomy by even the most diminutive ethnic groups in a striving to reverse the trend toward centralization. Members of minority groups, especially, find solace in emphasizing ethnic identity, and minor languages are often zealously preserved by their speakers as a symbol of group identity and cultural autonomy.

Ecological Disequilibrium

The psychological sense of alienation arising from a loss of identity is perhaps not so immediately serious as the threat to ecological equilibrium created by the vast expansion of the hominid population of the world and man's wholesale and largely shortsighted exploitation of his environment with the aid of modern technology. Demographic statistics predict a continued increase in world population, particularly in the less industrialized tropical and semitropical countries. The population of India has increased by 200 million in the last 52 years—and is increasing every 3 months by as much as the total population of Norway, a country which gives financial aid to India, but whose aid will soon become a meaningless drop in an ocean of misery. Indeed, the population of Asia alone is expected to reach 3.5 billion by the year 2000, and there are similar increases in Central and South America, and Africa. While the birthrate of the nations of northern Europe is falling close to replacement level, or even below replacement, the countries experiencing this population explosion are caught in a vicious circle—the population increasing as fast as the food supply increases or faster. This problem has already brought disaster to most higher forms of wildlife, many species being now in imminent threat of extinction as men take over their last remaining territories. And most population experts are too concerned with the horrific dimensions of this explosion to even contemplate what could be an equally serious problem—the build-up

FIG. 57   THE HUMAN POPULATION EXPLOSION

The ecological balance has been substantially disrupted by the human population explosion. Ancient horticulture and fishing both resulted in an increase in the density of human populations, but agriculture and medical innovations have converted a world population estimated at around a quarter of a billion in the year 1 A.D. and a half billion in 1500 A.D. into a rapidly expanding multitude estimated to reach 7 billion early in the twenty-first century.

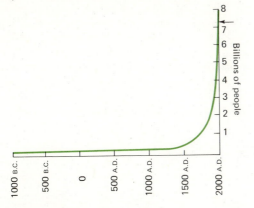

of defective genes due to the relaxation of natural selection in the more advanced industrial countries.

It is true that despite these population increases industrialization has led to a rise in the "standard of living," by which we mean the level of consumption in the industrialized countries; however, the degree of satisfaction resulting from this increased rate of consumption of the world's natural resources is not easy to assess. As Socrates said on visiting the Athenian market, long before the advent of industrialization: "How many things are there here which I can well do without!" Much of this material wealth, used only to satisfy ephemeral desires, is produced at the cost of considerable depredation of the earth's natural resources and frequently involves by-products of a poisonous nature which are modifying the ecological environment in directions inimical to the survival of the more complex life forms. Unless this process can be halted at an early date, mankind may face an ecological disaster, for a new ecological balance will be reimposed with or without human cooperation. The whole of mammalian life, as well as that of many other life forms, may be at stake. Certainly man is—or ought to be—fighting for his own survival. It is a struggle for human racial survival. Indeed the rivers, lakes, and seas—such as the Mediterranean and Baltic seas, and Lake Michigan in the U.S.A. and Lake Baikal in the U.S.S.R.—are slowly decaying and dying from pollution. Three thousand acres of oxygen-producing land in the United States alone are going under cement or tar macadam daily, and if world population continues to race upward, there is a real possibility that men may one day have to produce oxygen as well as food. But those who wish to may take heart by pointing out that if men do succeed in destroying the conditions which make life possible for more complex plants and animals, it need not be the end of the evolutionary story. Numerous bacteria and other simple living organisms are sure to survive, and in the course of time natural selection may be expected to raise a new hierarchy of life forms from whatever organic wreckage survives the failure of the human experiment.

For Further Reading

Banton, M., 1966, *The Social Anthropology of Complex Societies.* New York: Frederick A. Praeger, Inc.

Dubos, R., 1965, *Man Adapting.* New Haven, Conn.: Yale University Press.

Durkheim, E., *The Division of Labour in Society.* New York: The Free Press.

Goldschmidt, W., 1960, *Exploring the Ways of Mankind.* New York: Holt, Rinehart and Winston, Inc.

Schneider, D., 1968, *American Kinship.* Englewood Cliffs, N.J.: Prentice-Hall, Inc.

Sombart, W., 1927, *Der Moderne Kapitalismus.* Leipzig and Munich: Duncker and Humblot.

Sorokin, P. A., 1959, *Social and Cultural Dynamics.* New York: The Free Press.

Stein, M., 1960, *The Eclipse of Community.* Princeton, N.J.: Princeton University Press.

Weber, M., 1947, *The Theory of Social and Economic Organization.* New York: The Free Press.

Whyte, W. H., 1956, *The Organization Man.* New York: Simon and Schuster, Inc.

Postscript

The Evidence of Language

We have already seen that human culture arises out of the ability of men to communicate with each other. Such communication is primarily verbal, but at a more advanced level men find ways of translating verbal communications into written form. It is obvious, therefore, that language must bear a very close relation to culture, for ideas, beliefs, values, and sentiments which have not been expressed in a language that we understand will remain alien to us. Language, more than political boundaries, tends to restrict the diffusion of ideas, making possible the coexistence of different cultural systems.

The patchwork of diverse languages which divide the people of the world today did not arise accidentally, and is not without very far-reaching anthropological significance, for there is an ecology of languages which is intimately related to the cultural history of the speakers of these languages. But we shall return to this after we have first taken a closer look at the more technical aspects of language as a form of communication.

By definition, LANGUAGE may be regarded as a system of arbitrary verbal symbols by which members of a society are able to communicate complex ideas and experiences. In other words, every language has a particular structure, grammar, vocabulary, and function of its own, employing sounds as meaningful symbols in a coherent and consistent manner. If a language is to convey meaning efficiently, it is important that the persons using that language employ such sounds in a conventional and widely understood fashion. In themselves, the vocal symbols that are used in any language have little or no objective meaning but are arbitrarily endowed with meaning by the users. Language not only transmits culture but is an integral part of culture. As ideas, values, sentiments, and beliefs increase in complexity in order to convey the ideas contained within a culture, so language tends to increase in complexity to transmit these ideas. Language, more than any other manifestation of culture, demonstrates the vast debt that we owe to the untold generations of men and women who preceded us on this earth.

Linguistic Science

The study of language and languages is known as linguistics. It is customarily subdivided into two disciplines, synchronic or structural linguistics and diachronic or historical linguistics.

STRUCTURAL LINGUISTICS is concerned with the study of languages as coherent, homogeneous entities. It includes PHONOLOGY, the study of the sounds in a language. These may be broken down into *phonemes,* the smallest recognizable units of sound, and *morphemes,* those clusters of sounds normally used together in a particular language which represent the smallest units of meaning. SYNTAX is another important area of structural linguistics, being concerned with the arrangement of words in meaningful order. No languages merely string the verbal symbols together in an unarranged mass. The syntax or arrangement of these symbols in sentence order usually contributes substantially to the meaning conveyed by the individual words.

Since the principle of communication rests on the use of symbols, whether these are verbal or visual, an important aspect in the study of language is concerned with SEMANTICS. Semantics deals with the relationship between a symbol and its meaning or referent. Although the English language, for example, may seem to possess many words that express a similar idea, in actual usage every word carries a slight difference of implication. Similarly, while we may believe that we recognize an English word in French or German or Latin, we will usually find on closer examination that although the two words which sound so similar may have had a common historical origin, in the course of time they have come to acquire slightly different shades of meaning in the two different cultures. Even in everyday speech much misunderstanding arises when two members of the same society use the same word in a slightly different sense, usually because of different social backgrounds, without realizing that they are not discussing the same thing. Many lengthy debates could be avoided if only the speakers could realize that they were applying different meanings to the same symbols.

A fourth aspect of the study of structural linguistics involves PRAGMATICS, the relationship between symbols and their users. A language develops to serve the culture to which it belongs; for example, the Eskimo language may have several different words for "ice" but no words for any aspect of nuclear physics. Even when an object is precisely identified, the connotations that it may suggest to people of different cultural backgrounds may vary substantially, and communication cannot be truly effective between individuals whose pragmatic conception of the object identified is widely different one from the other.

DIACHRONIC OR HISTORICAL LINGUISTICS is concerned with the study of languages from the point of view of their evolution through time. One particular subarea, known as *linguistic paleontology,* is of particular interest to anthropologists, since it is devoted to the analysis of the vocabulary of the earlier forms of a language with a view to deducing evidence concerning the culture and life style of the former speakers of that language. Thus, it may be demonstrated that the proto-Indo-European language had a word for "horse," a word for "wheel," and a word for "axle" before the emergence of the separate Indo-European languages of historical times. This information tells us that the original speakers of the proto-Indo-European language possessed horses and wheeled vehicles before they spread outward, lost contact with each other, and developed the different daughter languages so well known to us today.

The Sapir-Whorf Hypothesis

Any society which is relatively isolated over a period of time from contact with other societies will undergo changes in pronunciation, grammatical usage, and even in vocabulary.

When the speakers of a language divide into two groups and lose contact with each other, the process of linguistic change will continue independently in each group. In time two separate *dialects* will emerge, still intelligible to each other but recognizably different, and in the course of linguistic evolution these will continue to undergo differentiation until they become separate *languages,* so different from each other that their speakers will be unable to understand each other.

Such separate languages will each be adjusted to the speaker's own distinctive needs, and each language will reflect in its symbols the distinctive experiences and personal culture of its speakers. Not only does a language serve and reflect the culture of the society that uses it, but the language will itself be a part of that culture and will help to shape the thought of succeeding generations of neonates who speak and think in the terms used in that language. Thus two distinguished linguists, Edward Sapir and B. L. Whorf, have stated that the language a people speak conditions their thought and determines the way in which they will look upon and judge their environment.

According to the *Sapir-Whorf hypothesis,* language is not simply an inventory of the experiences of a particular society. The entire way in which a member of a society looks at life will tend to be shaped by the language that he speaks. Language actually defines experience for us by interpreting all experiences in terms of traditional symbols because of our unconscious projection of its implied expectations into the field of experience. Language therefore tends to shape our way of thinking because it comprises symbols which we have learned to use, and these tend to unconsciously shape the thoughts that take root in our mind.

According to Sapir, the languages of Europe, for example, stand in sharp contrast to the indigenous languages of Africa, America, and other non-Indo-European-speaking territories in the type of ideas and attitudes which they will inspire. Putting this to the test, Whorf made a comparison between the Hopi language of North America and a number of Indo-European languages from Europe. He found that the differences between European languages were insignificant when compared with the differences between the European languages as a whole and the Hopi language—so insignificant that he lumped the European languages together under the general title of SAE (Standard Average European) for the purpose of further comparative studies.

Language and Ecology

But the study of historical linguistics is important to anthropologists for another reason. The science of GLOTTOCHRONOLOGY analyzes the historical process of linguistic change to determine the historical links between related languages. By the comparison of vocabulary and grammatical structure, it can even indicate the date at which two related languages first became separated from each other and even provide some picture of the level of culture and the pattern of subsistence employed by its speakers at this time. During the Paleolithic, when all men were hunters and gatherers and lived in small bands scattered thinly over the inhabitable parts of the world, we may safely assume that as a result of relative isolation the linguistic pattern of the world revealed literally thousands of local languages, many of which probably merged into others through a series of local dialect changes where some degree of interband contact existed. This picture of a multitude of Paleolithic languages is substantiated by our knowledge of contemporary primitive societies. In New Guinea, for example, there are today still hundreds of different languages, each population having developed its own characteristic forms of speech because of its relative isolation from the others.

This primordial pattern of small local languages was disrupted when those peoples who had developed a more evolved technology expanded at the expense of their less developed neighbors. Thus Upper Paleolithic culture expanded at the expense of Lower Paleolithic peoples. With the Neolithic and the invention of cultivation we see the rapid, and still continuing, expansion of tribal cultivators at the territorial expense of band-type hunting and gathering communities. Again, pastoralists have demonstrated a potential for military expansion and an ability to establish themselves as a ruling caste over more settled horticulturalists, while urban civilizations have built extensive empires and industrialists have colonized whole continents formerly occupied by small bands of hunters and gatherers. The result is that small and relatively isolated populations of hunters and gatherers, speaking a multitude of separate languages, today survive only in marginal lands. Elsewhere, by contrast, the quiltwork of minor local languages has been replaced by a comparatively limited number of major languages, the languages of the expanding and triumphant pastoralists, cultivators, and industrial peoples. These major languages can easily be grouped together into *families* of languages and traced back by historical linguistics to the original speakers who, through more advanced subsistence techniques, were able to expand at the territorial expense of their less fortunate neighbors.

A study of the relationship between historical linguistics and ecological adjustment is therefore, in effect, a summary of world cultural history. To attempt such a summary, it is convenient to divide the world into a number of major natural areas within which peoples, cultures, and languages tended to interact, while contacts with other peoples and languages outside each area remained restricted by geographical barriers. The case of the Americas is a very obvious example of a distinct natural area, shut off by the oceans from connection with the cultures and peoples of the Old World, except by way of the Bering Strait, and therefore apparently subject to largely independent cultural and linguistic evolution until the arrival of Columbus.

Other natural areas also tend to have their own distinctive cultural history because of their geographical position. Sub-Saharan Africa, for example, is an identifiable natural area, which has been constantly influenced by migrations from North Africa and from Asia but has still been sufficiently isolated to escape many of the cultural experiences of the lands to the north of the Sahara. So far as prehistory is concerned, Europe, on the other hand, must not and cannot be regarded as a separate natural area in its own right, as so many historians have represented it to be. The history of Europe is intimately associated with the history of southwestern Asia and with the history of Africa north of the Sahara. It was only after the rise of the Moslem religion, which established itself throughout North Africa and the Middle East, that Europe became culturally disassociated from these neighboring lands.

India is a very clear-cut natural area in its own right, due entirely to geographical considerations. Some migration and diffusion has taken place between India and the lands which lie to the north and east, but the Himalayas and the jungle ridges of the Arakan have restricted this severely. By contrast, continuing culture contacts bind India to western Asia through the mountains of Afghanistan and Persia.

Turning to Asia, we may identify another, less sharply defined, natural area that might be loosely termed Central Asia. This area includes the broad grasslands known as the steppes which sweep from Europe to the southern edge of the Gobi Desert. The steppes have historically served as a link between eastern and western Asia, forming a broad and attractive corridor, skirting north of the mountains and south of the coniferous forest belt, with only one narrow neck—the Dzungarian Gates, a relatively broad pass separating what is sometimes called Russian Turkestan from Sinkiang or Chinese Turkestan. North and northeast of the steppes lie the vast expanses of Siberia, never a center of high culture, unsuitable for cultivation, and therefore settled only by Stone Age hunting and food gathering bands.

To the east of the steppes, once the Gobi Desert has been skirted, an entirely separate natural area opens up as the migrant enters China. China is closely linked also to Manchuria, Korea, and of course Japan, although the history of Japan has always been somewhat different from that of the mainland because of its relative isolation as an island and because of its maritime contacts with the Pacific cultures.

To the south of the East Asian area, Southeast Asia may be identified as a separate natural region with its own distinctive history—an area receptive to immigration from the north and west, and significant also as a path leading south toward Oceania in which we may include the entire Indonesian area. Australia and New Guinea, separated from Indonesia by rigid cultural-historical barriers along the path of what has been called the Wallace Line (and possessing a much older flora and fauna, protected from competition with the more evolved life forms of Asia) are clearly recognizable as a separate unit. Thus, while Sumatra and Java may be examined in conjunction with New Zealand, Hawaii, and the distant Easter Isles, all contrast sharply in culture with the nearby Australian and New Guinea cultures.

These geographical barriers, comprising oceans, deserts, forests, and mountain ranges, remained linguistically distinct until the Portuguese, Spanish, Dutch, and English mariners first crossed the Atlantic and sailed around the southernmost cape of Africa to trade, colonize, and bring Western culture and languages to every corner of the world.

The Ancient Mediterranean-Asianic Languages

We also know little about the languages of the early horticultural and agricultural peoples of Europe and the Middle East. However, it seems possible that there may once have been a single Mediterranean family embracing all languages of Old Europe. This would have included the languages of the early Neolithic civilization of the Aegean and Danube; the Etruscan language; the language of Crete, used in the Linear A script which has not yet been deciphered; and the Basque language, still spoken in northeastern Spain and southwestern France. Similarly, there may be some connection between the early languages of the ancient civilizations of Sumeria and those which are still used in the Caucasian Mountains that separate Europe from Iran and Anatolia. Indeed, another ancient language, known as Burushaski, which still survives on the borders of Pakistan and Afghanistan, seems to be related to these Caucasian languages. Thus arises the possibility that the ancient language of the Indus Valley civilization may have been a part of an Asianic group of languages stretching from the Caucasus Mountains to the Indus.

The Indo-European Languages

The reason why we know so little about languages formerly spoken in the agricultural civilizations that once stretched from the Indus to the Rhine is that the early farmers were overrun by pastoralists, some emanating from the European and Asian steppes and others from Arabia. Successive waves of militaristic Indo-European-speaking advanced pastoralists, who also practiced some cultivation, succeeded in establishing themselves as an aristocracy over the indigenous farmers from the Atlantic to the Bay of Bengal. Indo-European languages consequently suppressed most of the older languages of the early Mediterranean-Asianic group, and on the Atlantic coast of Europe a militaristic, chariot-riding, Celtic-speaking group of nations settled France, Spain, and the British Isles. Of these the Goidelic-speaking Celts gave their name to ancient Gaul, the name by which the Romans knew the area today called France, and left us the Gaelic language of the highlands of Scot-

FIG. 58   LINGUISTIC SUMMARY

For the purpose of this summary, the following major culture areas may be identified, bearing in mind that this analysis is by no means intended to be exclusive or rigid and that the regions identified refer primarily to natural geographic areas in which there has been a close interchange of ideas and frequent internal contact among residents and/or migrant populations.

(1) Europe, Middle East, and North Africa
(2) Central Asia
(3) Eastern Asia
(4) Southeast Asia
(5) Indian Subcontinent
(6) Oceania
(7) Australasia and New Guinea
(8) Sub-Saharan Africa
(9) America
(10) Circumpolar

Dead languages are shown in square brackets.

---

1   Language families originating in EUROPE, MIDDLE EAST, AND NORTH AFRICA

1a.

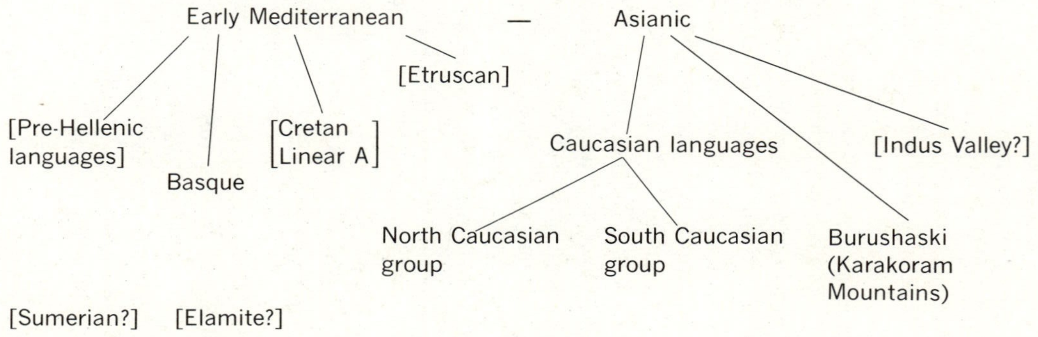

```
                Early Mediterranean  ———  Asianic
                     /        \
      [Pre-Hellenic       [Cretan
       languages]     |    Linear A]
                    Basque

                                        [Etruscan]

                                   Caucasian languages     [Indus Valley?]
                                        /        \
                              North Caucasian   South Caucasian   Burushaski
                                 group             group         (Karakoram
                                                                  Mountains)

      [Sumerian?]    [Elamite?]
```

1b.   Indo-European or Aryan

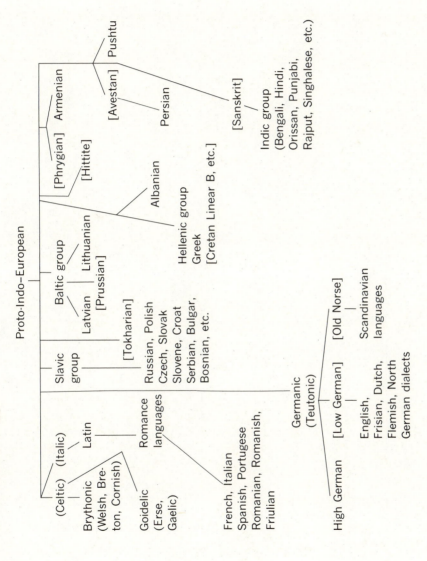

FIG. 58   LINGUISTIC SUMMARY (continued)

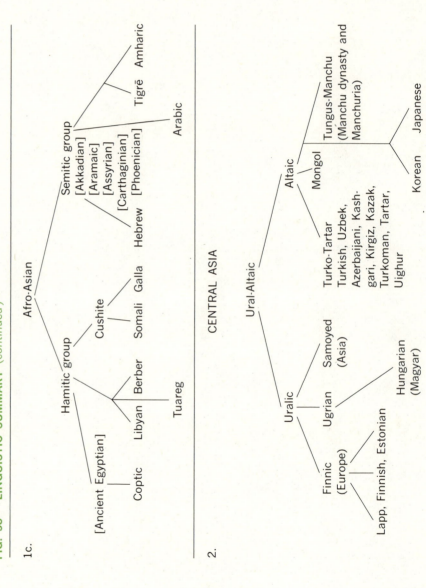

3.

EASTERN ASIA

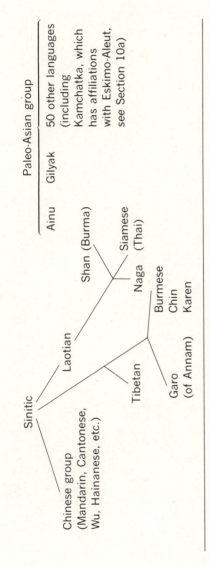

Sinitic

Chinese group
(Mandarin, Cantonese,
Wu, Hainanese, etc.)

Laotian

Shan (Burma)

Siamese
(Thai)

Naga

Tibetan

Burmese
Chin
Karen

Garo
(of Annam)

Paleo-Asian group

| Ainu | Gilyak | 50 other languages (including Kamchatka, which has affiliations with Eskimo-Aleut, see Section 10a) |

4.

SOUTHEAST ASIA

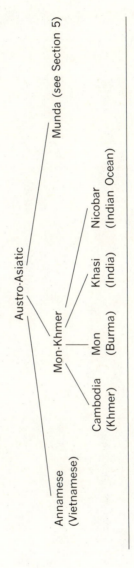

Austro-Asiatic

Annamese
(Vietnamese)

Mon-Khmer

Cambodia
(Khmer)

Mon
(Burma)

Khasi
(India)

Nicobar
(Indian Ocean)

Munda (see Section 5)

5.

NON-INDIC INDIA

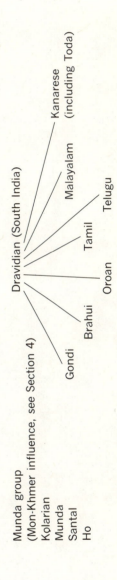

Munda group
(Mon-Khmer influence, see Section 4)
Kolarian
Munda
Santal
Ho

Dravidian (South India)

Gondi

Brahui

Oroan

Tamil

Telugu

Malayalam

Kanarese
(including Toda)

FIG. 58   LINGUISTIC SUMMARY (*continued*)

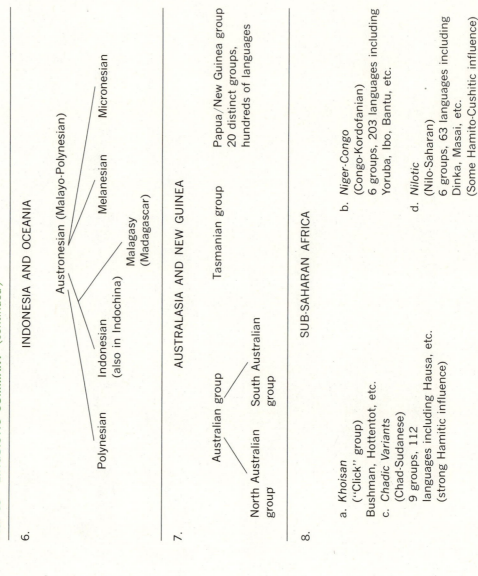

6.   INDONESIA AND OCEANIA

Austronesian (Malayo-Polynesian)

Polynesian   Indonesian   Melanesian   Micronesian
                 (also in Indochina)

                 Malagasy
                 (Madagascar)

7.   AUSTRALASIA AND NEW GUINEA

Australian group   Tasmanian group   Papua/New Guinea group
                                             20 distinct groups,
North Australian   South Australian   hundreds of languages
group   group

8.   SUB-SAHARAN AFRICA

a. *Khoisan*   b. *Niger-Congo*
   ("Click" group)   (Congo-Kordofanian)
   Bushman, Hottentot, etc.   6 groups, 203 languages including
c. *Chadic Variants*   Yoruba, Ibo, Bantu, etc.
   (Chad-Sudanese)
   9 groups, 112   d. *Nilotic*
   languages including Hausa, etc.   (Nilo-Saharan)
   (strong Hamitic influence)   6 groups, 63 languages including
                                             Dinka, Masai, etc.
                                             (Some Hamito-Cushitic influence)

America had over 900 languages averaging 10,000 persons per language in 1600 A.D.

9a.

NORTH AND CENTRAL AMERICA

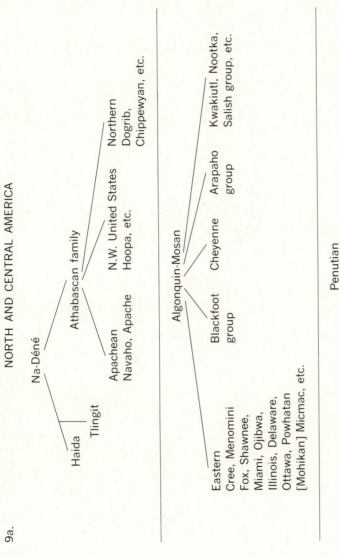

FIG. 58 LINGUISTIC SUMMARY *(continued)*

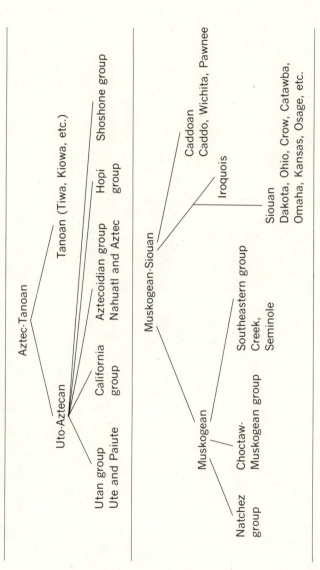

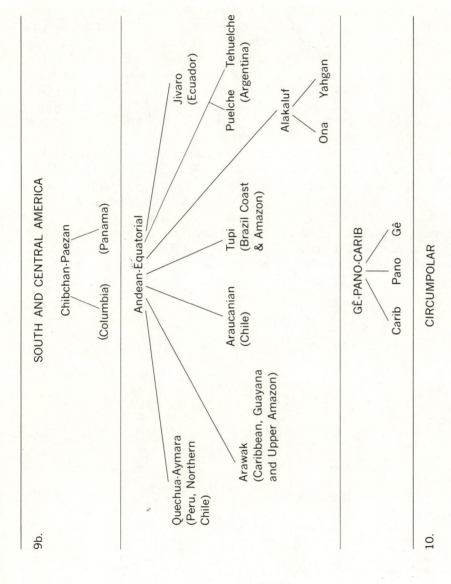

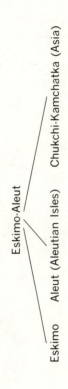

land, the Erse language of modern Ireland, and the Manx language of the Isle of Man. A second group of Celtic speakers, just behind them, represented the Brythonic family of Celtic languages and gave us the Breton language extending from Brittany to Belgium and Britain, while the Welsh language, still spoken in Wales to this day, also belongs to the Brythonic group.

Closely related to Celtic speech is the Italic group of languages which gave Italy its name. Breaking away from the Celts, the Osco-Umbrian Italic speakers migrated southward down the Italian peninsula, and one group of these, speaking Latin, founded Rome. The Latin language was carried by the Romans over most parts of western, southern, and eastern Europe where it survived the collapse of the Roman empire in various local forms to become the French, Spanish, Portuguese, Italian, and Roumanian languages of today, collectively known as the *Romance languages.*

Another group of Indo-Europeans, speaking a Germanic family of languages, established themselves in the plains of northern Europe, and some crossed the Baltic Sea to settle Scandinavia. The language of those who settled Scandinavia developed into Old East Norse, which became parent to the Swedish and Danish languages, and Old West Norse, which became parent to Icelandic and Faroese. Rural Norwegian is derived from Old West Norse, but an East Norse form was later adopted as the official language of Norway as a result of many centuries of Swedish and Danish domination.

An Old East German language was the basis for the Gothic tongues spoken by the Ostrogoths and the Visigoths who sacked Rome and later settled Spain to become the ancestors of the Spanish Castilian nobility. Old South German developed into modern High German, the official language of modern Germany, and a hybrid form known as Yiddish was subsequently

FIG. 59   THE LANGUAGES OF EUROPE (see map on p. 559)

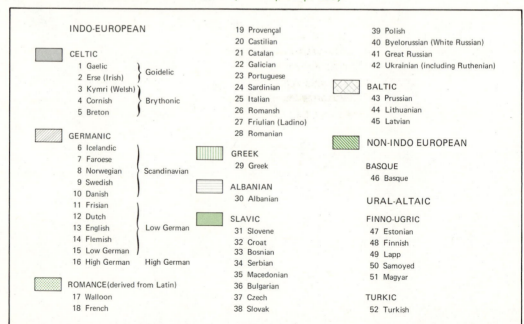

INDO-EUROPEAN

CELTIC
1 Gaelic
2 Erse (Irish)   } Goidelic
3 Kymri (Welsh) }
4 Cornish   } Brythonic
5 Breton   }

GERMANIC
6 Icelandic
7 Faroese
8 Norwegian   } Scandinavian
9 Swedish
10 Danish
11 Frisian
12 Dutch
13 English   } Low German
14 Flemish
15 Low German
16 High German   High German

ROMANCE (derived from Latin)
17 Walloon
18 French

19 Provençal
20 Castilian
21 Catalan
22 Galician
23 Portuguese
24 Sardinian
25 Italian
26 Romansh
27 Friulian (Ladino)
28 Romanian

GREEK
29 Greek

ALBANIAN
30 Albanian

SLAVIC
31 Slovene
32 Croat
33 Bosnian
34 Serbian
35 Macedonian
36 Bulgarian
37 Czech
38 Slovak

39 Polish
40 Byelorussian (White Russian)
41 Great Russian
42 Ukrainian (including Ruthenian)

BALTIC
43 Prussian
44 Lithuanian
45 Latvian

NON-INDO EUROPEAN

BASQUE
46 Basque

URAL-ALTAIC

FINNO-UGRIC
47 Estonian
48 Finnish
49 Lapp
50 Samoyed
51 Magyar

TURKIC
52 Turkish

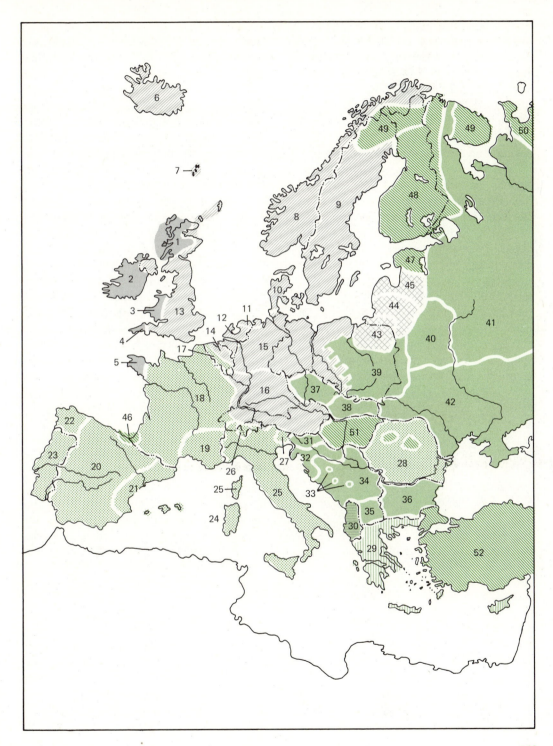

developed by immigrant Jews. West German, sometimes called Low German, developed into Flemish, the language of the Flemings of northern Belgium; Frisian, the language of Frisia in the northern Netherlands; Dutch, the language of Holland, and Old English.

Other Indo-European speakers established themselves in the Baltic countries, where they retained archaic forms of Indo-European speech known as Old Prussian, Lithuanian, and Lettish, the language of Latvia. Yet more Indo-European speakers, belonging to the Slavic group, settled eastern Europe, giving rise to the Russian, Ukrainian, Polish, Czech, Slovak, Croatian, Slovenian, Serbian, and Bulgarian languages. A further group was responsible for the modern Albanian language.

Another branch of these Indo-European-speaking migrants established themselves as a military aristocracy over the early cultivators of the Aegean area. Thus the Hellenic or Greek group of languages, spoken by the Homeric heroes, belongs to the Indo-European family, as does modern Greek. In Anatolia, or Asia Minor, Indo-European settlers were responsible for the Phrygian and Hittite languages as well as for modern Armenian.

But not all the Indo-European pastoralists settled in Europe or in Asia Minor; some went southeastward toward Persia and India. In Persia they established themselves as Iranians while others invaded India and as Indo-Aryans established the classic Sanskrit language of India from which most of the languages of northern, central, and eastern India are today derived. These include Hindi, Punjabi, Bengali, Rajput, and even Singhalese, the language of Ceylon.

Africa

Just as the Indo-European speakers spread out over wide areas of Europe and Asia, so the Afro-Asiatic group of languages expanded across North Africa and the Middle East from the Atlantic to the Arabian Sea. In the Arabian peninsula Semitic languages dominated; these included Assyrian, the language of the first advanced pastoral conquerors of Sumeria; Hebrew, the language of a group of simple pastoralists who seized Palestine; and the Arabic language of today, which was carried widely through the Middle East and Africa by advanced Arab pastoralists—dedicated missionaries working to spread Moslem monotheism with the aid of the sword.

In North Africa the Afro-Asiatic Hamitic speech spread widely with the first horticulturalists. The ancient Egyptian language, which survives today in the ritual language of the Coptic Christians of Egypt, was a branch of Hamitic, as is the Berber tongue still spoken by fierce horticultural tribesmen and herders of the North African mountains. The languages of Abyssinia and Somaliland in the Horn of Africa are of both Hamitic and Semitic origin, the Semites having penetrated into Africa as advanced pastoralists from southern Arabia. Cushitic, the most important of these, is associated with Hamitic.

South of the Sahara Desert we find literally hundreds of languages. These are customarily classified in four main groups. In the Kalahari Desert of southwestern Africa the hunting and gathering Bushmen and the simple pastoral Hottentots (formerly hunters) speak Khoisan languages, notable for the distinctive "click" with which certain sounds are pronounced. These are the last remnants of the old hunters and gatherers who formerly inhabited all the grasslands of sub-Saharan Africa and who are even postulated as having inhabited North Africa in pre-Hamitic times. As might be expected, by far the largest group of sub-Saharan languages are those spoken by the horticultural Negroes of the Congo in the West African forests and the simple pastoralist Bantu who displaced the Khoisan hunters from the East and South African grasslands. Because of its wide dispersal there are today some 203 lan-

FIG. 60   THE LANGUAGES OF AFRICA

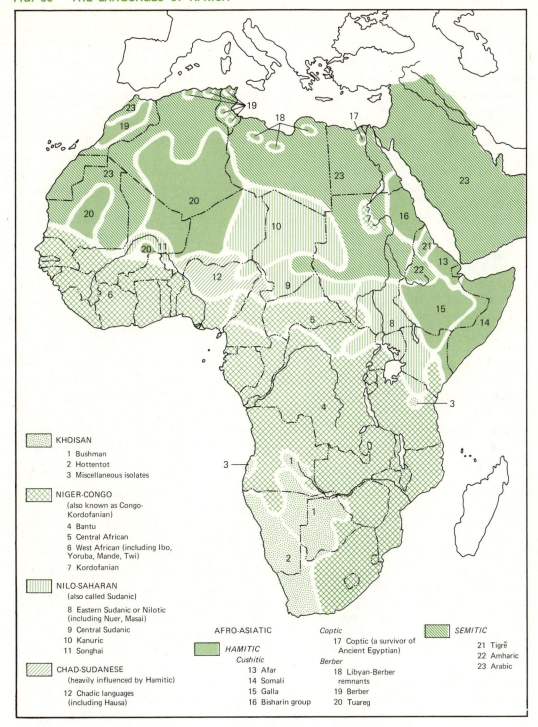

KHOISAN
1 Bushman
2 Hottentot
3 Miscellaneous isolates

NIGER-CONGO
(also known as Congo-Kordofanian)
4 Bantu
5 Central African
6 West African (including Ibo, Yoruba, Mande, Twi)
7 Kordofanian

NILO-SAHARAN
(also called Sudanic)
8 Eastern Sudanic or Nilotic (including Nuer, Masai)
9 Central Sudanic
10 Kanuric
11 Songhai

CHAD-SUDANESE
(heavily influenced by Hamitic)
12 Chadic languages (including Hausa)

AFRO-ASIATIC

HAMITIC
Cushitic
13 Afar
14 Somali
15 Galla
16 Bisharin group

Coptic
17 Coptic (a survivor of Ancient Egyptian)
Berber
18 Libyan-Berber remnants
19 Berber
20 Tuareg

SEMITIC
21 Tigrē
22 Amharic
23 Arabic

guages in this Niger-Congo or Congo-Kordofanian group, which includes the Yoruba and Ibo of West Africa and the large Bantu family extending from the Congo down to South Africa—all ultimately descended from a common origin.

Between the Niger-Congo languages and the Hamitic languages of North Africa are two more large families both of which derive linguistically from different blends of Niger-Congo and Hamitic languages. At the head of the Nile there are some 63 languages belonging to a Nilotic or Nilo-Saharan group, and these include Nuer and Masai. Further to the west, but also in the Sudanese grasslands, 112 additional languages belong to the Chad-Sudanese group. These are spoken between the Sahara and the forests of the Congo, and are similarly of Hamitic and Niger-Congo origin, reflecting the historical cultural interaction between Hamitic-speaking Caucasoids from the north and the Negroids from the tropical rain forests of the Niger and Congo rivers.

As we have already commented, the Pygmies may once have had their own languages, but acquired the languages of the culturally more advanced Negroes after contact with them.

The Ural-Altaic Languages

Prior to the Russian conquest of Siberia, Central Asia was seemingly dominated by languages belonging to the Uralic and the Altaic families. The Uralic languages appear to have had their roots in both eastern Europe and Asia and to have been spoken by Paleolithic hunters and gatherers. Thus the Samoyeds speak a Uralic tongue which is related to the Finnish language of Finland and the Estonian language of the Baltic coast. By contrast, those Uralic speakers who lived on the steppes became warlike advanced pastoralists and migrated extensively. Thus Hungary is named after the Huns who invaded Europe under Attila, and the language spoken there, Magyar, is a Uralic tongue.

Similarly the Altaic branch of the Ural-Altaic group also spread out over an even vaster area, being carried both eastward and westward by warlike advanced pastoralists who had acquired horses, cattle, and chariots from the Indo-European pastoralists. The Turko-Tartar branch of the Altaic family of languages fought its way westward until the Turks invaded Anatolia and established themselves in what is today known as Turkey. Other Turkish-speaking pastoralists who still live in the central Asian steppes include the Kazaks of Kazakstan and the Uzbeks of Uzbekistan.

Another Altaic people closely related to the Turko-Tartars are the Mongolian speakers whose homeland lies slightly to the east of Turkestan and who have given their name to Mongolia. Through the course of history these fierce pastoralists invaded China, the Middle East, and even India where the Moghul dynasty was derived from Mongol conquerors. But it was the Tungus-Manchu group of pastoralists who seem to have expanded furthest to the east. Of these, we have already mentioned the Tungus pastoralists. Although the Tungus never built an empire, the Manchus invaded China, established a Manchu dynasty at Pekin, and also gave their name to Manchuria.

Some philologists find an identity between the Korean language and the Tungus-Manchu group. Historical and archeological evidence would also support the possibility of such a relationship, and since Japanese is also related to Korean, and horse-riding Japanese warriors originally invaded Japan from Korea, it seems reasonable to suppose an original connection between Japanese and all the Altaic languages of Asia, including the Turkish language spoken in Europe and Asia Minor.

Paleo-Asian Languages

The marginal hunters and gatherers who still survive to the northeast of the Ural-Altaic speakers in the wastes of northeastern Siberia

FIG. 61 THE LANGUAGES OF ASIA

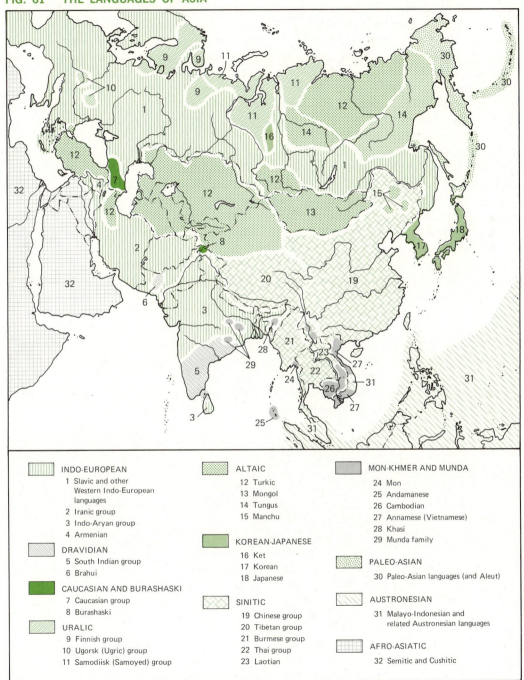

INDO-EUROPEAN
1 Slavic and other
  Western Indo-European
  languages
2 Iranic group
3 Indo-Aryan group
4 Armenian

DRAVIDIAN
5 South Indian group
6 Brahui

CAUCASIAN AND BURASHASKI
7 Caucasian group
8 Burashaski

URALIC
9 Finnish group
10 Ugorsk (Ugric) group
11 Samodiisk (Samoyed) group

ALTAIC
12 Turkic
13 Mongol
14 Tungus
15 Manchu

KOREAN-JAPANESE
16 Ket
17 Korean
18 Japanese

SINITIC
19 Chinese group
20 Tibetan group
21 Burmese group
22 Thai group
23 Laotian

MON-KHMER AND MUNDA
24 Mon
25 Andamanese
26 Cambodian
27 Annamese (Vietnamese)
28 Khasi
29 Munda family

PALEO-ASIAN
30 Paleo-Asian languages (and Aleut)

AUSTRONESIAN
31 Malayo-Indonesian and
  related Austronesian languages

AFRO-ASIATIC
32 Semitic and Cushitic

preserve some 50 different languages which are generally labeled Paleo-Asian because of their ancient Paleolithic origins.

The speakers of these remote languages have been isolated for so long that it is only with difficulty that their languages can be grouped into families, for any generic unity they once possessed has been largely lost due to linguistic drift. Gilyak is perhaps one of the most widespread Paleo-Asian languages on the mainland of Asia, while Ainu, the language of the aboriginal hunters of the islands of Sakhalin and Hokkaido north of Japan, is probably the best known of the group. But just as the Ainu are in the process of being absorbed into the Japanese population in Hokkaido, so also the other Paleo-Asian speakers are but the remnants of a formerly much more widespread Mesolithic population which long ago lost the richer areas of Asia. Today they hang on, a politically and economically subordinate population, only in lands which have remained unsuitable for even the most modern methods of economic exploitation. According to the evidence of ecological evolution in other parts of the world, their languages may well disappear in the course of time unless they are able to adapt their culture to the point that it becomes once again a viable competitor with that of other technologically and ecologically more advanced societies.

Australia and New Guinea

A similar patchwork of languages survives in Australia and New Guinea. Each group of exogamous hunting and gathering bands in Australia has its own language, but we can classify the numerous languages of Australia into two main groups, North Australian and South Australian, because the entire population of aborigines appears to be descended from only a very few original bands who entered Australia not more than around 15,000 years ago at the most. The extinct peoples of Tasmania also had their own group of Tasmanian

languages. In nearby New Guinea, where the Papuans live in isolated, warring horticultural communities, the lack of social contact is reflected in the diversity of the linguistic pattern, for each small society has its own separate language. In New Guinea, sparsely populated as it is, there are no less than 20 distinct groups numbering hundreds of languages.

The Austronesian Languages

North of Australia and New Guinea, however, and eastward across the South Pacific, we find large areas occupied by a single stock of languages known as the Austronesian or Malayo-Polynesian group. These appear to have originated somewhere in Southeast Asia and include the Melanesian family of languages, spoken by the darker and more woolly-haired, partially Negrito Melanesians; the Micronesian family spoken on the smaller atolls to the north; and the Polynesian family which extends across the Pacific, reaching as far north as Hawaii, as far east as the Easter Isles, and as far to the southwest as New Zealand, where it includes the Maoris. In Malaya, Sumatra, Java, and Borneo, Indonesian and Malayan are spoken.

It would appear that these languages all descend from an original language spoken by a people who knew the arts of cultivation and seamanship and were therefore able to expropriate the original population of Indonesia. They then sailed further eastward to colonize the islands of the entire South Pacific which had remained uninhabited by man until the time of their expansion, between 2000 and 800 years ago.

Not content to sail eastward to settle the whole of Oceania, Malayo-Polynesian speakers also sailed westward across the Indian Ocean to establish small settlements along the east coast of Africa and to populate Madagascar, which isolated by water, had no hominids of any kind prior to the arrival of these seaborne argonauts. Although the Malayo-Polynesian settlements along the east coast of Africa subsequently disappeared before an invasion of Bantu-speaking Negroes from the Congo, the island of Madagascar was still wholly Malayo-Polynesian at the time of the arrival of the French in the nineteenth century. Today, however, it is heavily settled by Bantu-speaking Negroes imported as labor by the French colonists for work on their agricultural plantations.

Mon-Khmer

North of the Malayo-Polynesians, in what we call Southeast Asia, which includes Burma and Indochina, there survive a number of ancient languages that belong to the Austro-Asiatic or Mon-Khmer group spoken by people who have been agriculturalists for centuries, but were originally horticulturalists at the time of their expansion. The language of the Vietnamese, properly called Annamese, belongs to this group, as also does the Khmer language of Cambodia. It would appear, however, that the Mon-Khmer languages may at one time have covered the whole of Southeast Asia, except for small pockets of formerly hunting and gathering Negrito speakers. As evidence, we find a remnant of this group in Burma among the Mon-speakers and also as far west as India where a small group of horticulturalist hill-dwellers on the eastern frontier still speak the Khasi language. Mon-Khmer also survives in the language of the inhabitants of the Nicobar Islands in the Indian Ocean.

The Sinitic or Chinese Group

The original unity of the Mon-Khmer languages in Southeast Asia appears to have been broken by a southward expansion of agriculturalists who spoke Sinitic or Chinese languages. China itself contains many different languages, ranging from the Mandarin of the north to Cantonese and Hainanese in the south. In fact, the differences are so great that earlier in this century it was customary for a merchant from southern China to converse with a merchant from northern China in English!

Sinitic speech, which originated in northern China, originally spread over the whole of present-day China as a result of an early expansion by horticulturalists who later became agriculturalists. It was even carried by some of these same immigrants into Tibet where it became the basis of the Tibetan language. Other Sinitic-speaking cultivators invaded Burma, bringing with them the Burmese language as well as the Chin and Karen languages spoken by horticultural colonists in the hills bordering India. Still another group pressed through the mountains between Burma and India where they established themselves as the horticultural Naga headhunters, Mongoloids now living within the basically Caucasoid state of India. Further east, a group of Sinitic-speaking agriculturalists invaded the old Cambodian empire and established themselves in what we today call Thailand less than 1000 years ago. These were the Thai or Siamese speakers. Another group, speaking Laotian, settled in present day Laos.

The Indian Subcontinent

Northern, central, and eastern Indians today speak Indo-European languages as a result of the invasion of warlike advanced pastoralists who spoke Vedic, a language related to Russian, Greek, Latin, German, and English, which later evolved into Sanskrit.

There are still a number of tribal languages in the more remote mountains and uplands of India which appear to have survived among remnants of the earlier aboriginal populations. These include Kolarian, Munda, Santal, and Ho, all of which contain elements of the Old Mon-Khmer languages of Southeast Asia, thus suggesting that the Mon-Khmer speakers were

FIG. 62   EXPANSION OF INDO-EUROPEAN AND SINITIC LANGUAGES IN SOUTH ASIA

The immigration of Indo-European and Sinitic speakers has fragmented the original pattern of indigenous languages, leaving scattered remnants of these older tongues in isolated pockets from India through Southeast Asia.

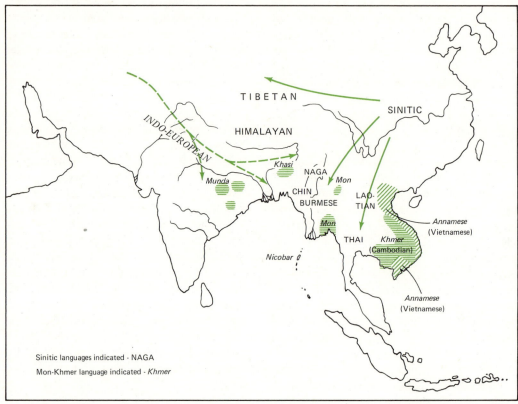

Sinitic languages indicated - NAGA

Mon-Khmer language indicated - *Khmer*

once aboriginal to a much larger area than they presently occupy. A few of these people are still hunters, but others practice elementary forms of horticulture which they probably acquired from neighboring Dravidian speakers.

We cannot trace any surviving language of the Indus Valley civilization because we have not yet deciphered the original tongue. But in the Dravidian group of languages from southern India, including Malayalam, Tamil, Telugu, and Kannada, we have a survival of a formerly more widespread family of languages spoken by the agriculturalists who dominated much of

lowland India prior to the arrival of the Indo-European Aryans over the passes from western Asia.

Language in the Americas

Since most of the Americas were still living at either a hunting and gathering or a horticultural level at the time of Columbus, it is not surprising that the linguistic map of the Americas was extremely complex. The dispersal of even a single people over such a wide area, at a hunting, food gathering, or horticultural level of evolution, would inevitably lead to a multiple fragmentation of nonwritten languages and dialects so that after some 20,000 years the linguistic diversity would be so great that it would be difficult to identify the original tongue. Add to this the fact that America was not populated by a single wave of migrants but was settled by the descendants of successive migrations which crossed the Bering Strait at various intervals over a period of more than 15,000 years, and the linguistic complexity of the American continent will be readily understood.

It has been estimated that when Columbus reached the Americas in the fifteenth century there were around 20 million people in the New World, speaking probably some 900 distinct languages, most of which would have been divided into numerous dialects. Careful research has managed to group most of these into language stocks, and in some cases the evidence of language has helped to throw some light on prehistoric migrations. In North America the most recent immigrants are known to be the Eskimoes who, in the short span of the 2000 to 5000 years which have elapsed since their arrival from Asia, have retained what is essentially a single Eskimo language. Yet even this has become diversified to the extent that the speech of an Eskimo from Labrador is unintelligible to one from Alaska, despite the fact that there is no sharp break in the continuity of dialects which stretches across the continent from west to east. The Aleutian language of the Aleuts of the Aleutian Isles is akin to that of the Eskimoes, but in northwestern Canada the Na-Déné or Athabaskan group of languages marks out a slightly older group of immigrants, who were obliged to content themselves with hunting and gathering in the cold and undesirable wastelands left unoccupied by earlier immigrants who pressed southward. To the east of the Na-Déné linguistic territory lies the Algonkian-Mosan language group, which also occupies much subarctic and undesirable land, but which succeeded in penetrating southward in the Illinois area and along the eastern seaboard.

Located amid the Algonkians in the woodlands to the east of the Great Lakes are the Iroquoian speakers who achieved a horticultural "Woodland" tradition, and developed a complex social system which led them to be known as the "seven civilized tribes." As members of the Iroquois League they maintained a working unity on a national rather than a tribal basis. This language group is now believed to be closely associated with that of the Siouan-speaking tribes of the Great Plains, as well as with the Muskogean speakers of Mississippi, Alabama, and Florida.

Further south in Central America, the Mayan languages are located in the Yucatan peninsula, while in the upland valley of Mexico we find Aztec speakers who are now known to be related linguistically with the Azteco-Tanoan speakers of northern Mexico. The history of this group reveals the migrations that brought the warlike Aztecs deep into Central America from an earlier home in the southwestern Rockies, for the group also embraces the Hopi, the wild Comanche, and the simple hunting and food collecting Utes and Paiutes who still live in the areas whence the fierce Aztecs set out on their southward invasion of the older Toltec empire.

Because of Aztec migrations, Meso-America is closely tied linguistically to the lands on the north of the Rio Grande, and there is no essential language barrier between the indigenous languages of Mexico and those of the United States of America. However, south of Mexico and Guatemala there is a more dramatic change. As we move southward to Panama we come into an area of Chibchan speech which extends down through Columbia. The West Indies are dominated not by North American languages but by the Arawak and Carib tongues which are also firmly established over large areas of Venezuela and Brazil on the

South American mainland. As is well known, there are no Indians left in the Caribbean (named after the Carib-speaking Indians) this area being today occupied by Negroes who acquired English, French, and Dutch speech during the colonial era and by persons of mixed Spanish descent still speaking Spanish.

In South America the same patchwork of languages is found among the predominantly horticultural populations, even though in Peru, Bolivia, and northern Chile the Quechua language of the Incas gained a certain prominence under Inca rule. However, Aymara also survived in this area, despite Inca domination.

In the subsequent struggle to throw out the Spanish and Portuguese colonists from southern America, it is interesting that the newly formed independent states corresponded to some extent to the major cultural and linguistic divisions in that subcontinent. Not only does Chibchan coincide roughly with Colombia, but

Jivaro corresponds to some extent with the borders of Ecuador, and Guarani with the boundaries of Paraguay. The old Portugese colony of Brazil was too large to reflect any one major language group, but combines Tupi, Arawak, and Ge as dominant linguistic groups, with some Carib. The Guianas combine Arawak on the coast and Carib further inland. Argentina is divided mainly between the Puelche on the rich pampas grassland to the north and the primitive Tehuelche of the poorer desert to the south. Central Chile is the home of Araucanian-speaking horticulturalists, and Alakaluf dominates southern Chile. Only in the extreme southern tip of the Americas do we find the remnants of Ona and the related Yahgan tongue, spoken by the descendants of the earliest hunting and gathering bands to penetrate to the extremity of the South American continent, to whom the inclement conditions provided protection against horticulturalists.

FIG. 63   NORTH AMERICAN INDIAN LANGUAGES (see map on p. 569)

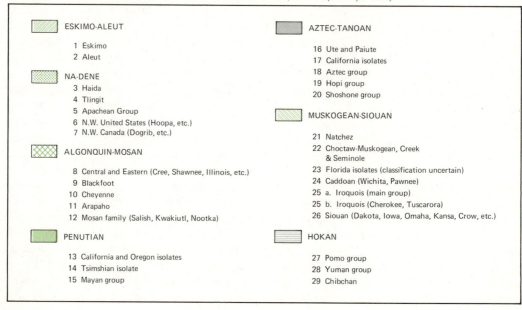

ESKIMO-ALEUT

1 Eskimo
2 Aleut

NA-DENE

3 Haida
4 Tlingit
5 Apachean Group
6 N.W. United States (Hoopa, etc.)
7 N.W. Canada (Dogrib, etc.)

ALGONQUIN-MOSAN

8 Central and Eastern (Cree, Shawnee, Illinois, etc.)
9 Blackfoot
10 Cheyenne
11 Arapaho
12 Mosan family (Salish, Kwakiutl, Nootka)

PENUTIAN

13 California and Oregon isolates
14 Tsimshian isolate
15 Mayan group

AZTEC-TANOAN

16 Ute and Paiute
17 California isolates
18 Aztec group
19 Hopi group
20 Shoshone group

MUSKOGEAN-SIOUAN

21 Natchez
22 Choctaw-Muskogean, Creek & Seminole
23 Florida isolates (classification uncertain)
24 Caddoan (Wichita, Pawnee)
25 a. Iroquois (main group)
25 b. Iroquois (Cherokee, Tuscarora)
26 Siouan (Dakota, Iowa, Omaha, Kansa, Crow, etc.)

HOKAN

27 Pomo group
28 Yuman group
29 Chibchan

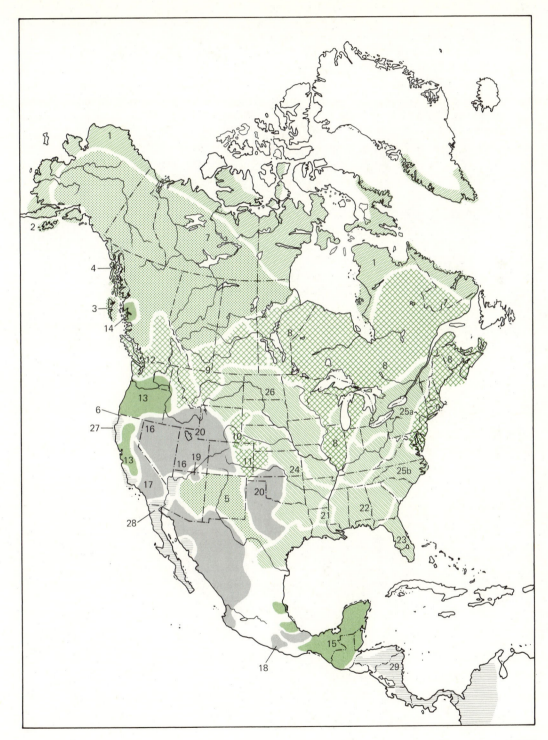

FIG. 64   THE LANGUAGES OF SOUTH AMERICA

CARIB

CHIBCHAN

ARAWAK

CARIB

PAEZAN

PAEZAN

ARAWAK

PANO

TUPI

QUECHUA–AYMARA

GÊ

TUPI

TUPI

GUAYCURI

TUPI

ARAWAK

CHARRUA

AURACANIAN

HUELCHE

TEHUELCHE

ALAKALUF
(including Ona and Yahgan)

	CHIBCHAN-PAEZAN
	ANDEAN-EQUATORIAL
	GÊ-PANO-CARIB

For Further Reading

Anttila, R., 1972, *An Introduction to General and Historical Linguistics.* New York: The Macmillan Company.

Bloomfield, L., 1961, *Languages.* New York: Holt, Rinehart and Winston, Inc.

Cleator, P. E., 1962, *Lost Languages.* New York: Mentor Books.

Greenberg, J. H., 1968, *Anthropological Linguistics: An Introduction.* New York: Random House, Inc.

Jensen, H., 1969, *Sign, Symbol and Script: An Account of Man's Efforts to Write.* New York: G. P. Putnam's Sons.

Lockwood, W. B., 1969 *Indo-European Philology: Historical and Comparative.* London: Hutchinson University Library.

————, 1972, *A Panorama of Indo-European Languages.* London: Hutchinson University Library.

Miller, R. A., 1972, *Japanese and Other Altaic Languages.* Chicago: University of Chicago Press.

Murdock, G. P., 1964, "Genetic Classification of the Austronesian Languages: A Key to Oceanic Cultural History," *Ethnology* 3:117–126.

Pei, M., 1960, *The Story of Languages.* New York: Mentor Books.

Samarin, W. J., 1967, *Field Linguistics: A Guide to Linguistic Fieldwork.* New York: Holt, Rinehart and Winston, Inc.

Sapir, E., 1921, *Language.* New York: Harcourt Brace Jovanovich, Inc.

Sommerfelt, A., 1954, "Speech and Languages," in C. Singer, ed., *A History of Technology,* Vol. 1. New York: Oxford University Press.

Swadesh, M., 1971, *The Origin and Diversification of Language.* Chicago: Aldine Publishing Company.

Glossary

Abacus A counting device comprising a number of beads mounted on parallel rods.

Abbevillian A Lower Paleolithic technique of biface core tool making formerly widespread in Europe but also found in Africa where it is usually known as *Chellean*.

Acculturation A process of cultural adjustment occurring when two distinct cultures come into contact.

Acephalous Society A society lacking in formal political offices or statuses, sometimes described as *equalitarian*.

Acheulian An improved biface core tool technique associated with Swanscombe man in the later, more highly evolved phase of the Lower Paleolithic in western Europe, Africa, and Southwest Asia. Characterized by elegant hand axes and a wide range of flake tools.

Acropolis The fortified center of a Greek city, usually situated on its highest point, wherein the palace of the king and the chief temples were located.

Adaptation The response of an organism to its environment involving some kind of adjustment which will enhance its chances of leaving more numerous descendants.

Adaptive Radiation Diversification resulting from evolution, leading to the creation of divergent forms of life with different life patterns.

Affinal Relationship Marital relationship, as distinct from relationship by consanguinity or birth.

Age Set A group of persons of similar age who cooperate for specific purposes.

Agriculture An advanced method of cultivation implying the possession of domesticated animals, and some knowledge of fertilizing techniques or crop rotation.

Alleles A pair of genes appearing at the same locus on a chromosome but producing contrasting characteristics.

Allotrophs *See* Autotrophs.

Amino Acids Organic compounds which may be regarded as the fundamental constituents of living matter. Each protein molecule in a human cell comprises hundreds of thousands of amino acid molecules.

Amulet A fetish object intended to protect the wearer against potentially harmful supernatural forces.

Analogies Anatomical, physiological, and cultural similarities which arise from parallel environmental needs instead of from descent.

Anasazi The Pueblo Indian culture located in the southwestern United States which first emerged with the Basket Makers and is still represented by the Hopi culture.

Animatism A belief in a supernatural force which may inhabit either organic or inorganic matter, but which does not possess self-will.

Animism The belief in the existence of supernatural beings possessing self-will. As souls or spirits these may inhabit either living or nonliving organisms.

Anthropocentrism A tendency to regard man as of central importance in the universe, usually to the detriment of other living species.

Anthropoid A member of the suborder Anthropoidea (of the primate order) comprising Hominidae, Pongidae, and monkeys.

Anthropology The science of man. In its widest sense anthropology is today a synthesizing discipline drawing its data from the findings of specialists in such fields as anatomy, ethnology, genetics, paleontology, psychology, linguistics, sociology, and any other disciplines relating to the origin and evolution of man, culture, and society.

Anthropology, Cultural The study of those aspects of behavior which are learned, including such patterns of instinctive behavior as may become modified by cultural factors.

Anthropology, Physical The study of human biology, dealing with the evolution of the human organism, the relation between environment and the human organism, and genetic variations between human individuals and groups.

Anthropometry That branch of physical anthropology which is devoted to the physical measurement and description of individuals and races.

Anthropomorphism The ascription of human qualities to nonhuman objects or phenomena.

Apes A variety of large anthropoids, today represented by the gorilla, chimpanzee, orangutan, and gibbon.

Arboreal Adapted to life in or among trees.

Archeology A branch of anthropology which attempts to identify and interpret artifacts and fossils surviving from past cultures.

Archeozoic The era of "archaic life," from 3.7 to 1.2 billion years ago, characterized by unicellular life forms.

Arthropoda One of the largest phyla in the animal kingdom. Includes centipedes, insects, spiders, and crabs.

Artifact Any object manufactured by man.

Associations Social groups formed for a specific purpose and possessing their own administrative officials.

Atlatl The Aztec name for a spearthrower, a mechanical device first devised by Cro-Magnon man in the Upper Paleolithic.

Aurignacian A stage of West European Upper Paleolithic culture associated with Cro-Magnon man and characterized by refined aesthetic concepts displayed in the design and decoration of tools as well as in the renowned cave paintings found in France and Spain.

Australopithecinae Literally, "Southern Apes." A term now used generically to refer to a general level of hominid evolution during which manlike creatures are believed to have attempted toolmaking. A subfamily of the family Hominidae, including both *Australopithecus africanus* and *Paranthropus robustus,* now usually called *Australopithecus robustus.*

Autochthonous Aboriginal; literally, "springing from the soil."

Autotrophs Living organisms that are independent of outside organic sources for the provision of their organic constituents. Most plants are autotrophic, manufacturing organic materials from inorganic sources. By contrast, most animals are *allotrophs*, requiring external sources of organic substances and being ultimately dependent on autotrophs for their existence.

Avoidance A pattern of socially required behavior restricting relations between certain relatives as, for example, between son-in-law and mother-in-law.

Azoic An era "without life" associated with the earliest part of the geological Precambrian period, dating from the formation of the first rocks, over 4.5 billion years ago, until approximately 3.7 billion years ago.

B.P. "Before Present."

Baboon A large, predominantly terrestrial monkey of the genus *Papio*.

Band A small face-to-face social group occupying a single district or territory, economically dependent on hunting, scavenging, or food gathering, and politically autonomous.

Barrio A Spanish word used to refer to a distinctive neighborhood group found in many Central and South American cities, particularly in Mexico and Peru. The barrio is actually a survival of the older localized descent groups of the Aztecs (*calpulli*) and Peruvians (*ayllu*), whose members customarily constituted a separate community.

Barter The exchange of goods for profit in the absence of money or some other widely accepted symbol of value.

Bifurcate-Merging A system of kinship terminology whereby a clear distinction is made between the mother's and father's families (which are thus "bifurcate") while groups of relatives on the respective sides are "merged" for naming purposes.

Bilophodont A dental characteristic found in Old World monkeys, tapirs, and certain ungulates, in which the summits of the opposite cusps of the molar teeth are linked by cross crests.

Biometrics The application of mathematical and statistical theory to biology.

Bipedalism The ability to walk erect on the hind limbs, thus freeing the hands for use.

Blood Feud A conflict between distinct descent groups in which the members of one group are obliged to revenge themselves on the second group for an assault, injury, or insult suffered by a kinsman.

Bola A throwing device consisting of a number of weights attached to each other by thongs, which will wrap itself around the legs of a running animal, bringing the victim to the ground.

Boomerang A throwing stick, usually shaped in such a way that it will return in the direction of the thrower if it fails to hit its target.

Brachiation A technique by which certain primates are able to move rapidly through an arboreal environment by swinging from their forearms—resulting in substantial physiological adaptation, especially of the forelimbs.

Brachycephalic Broad-headed to the extent of possessing a skull with a width at least 81 percent as great as its length.

Broken Hill A site in Northern Rhodesia (now Zambia) where the remains of Rhodesian man were found.

Breeding Population A group of males and females who customarily reproduce only among themselves.

Bride Price A payment of cattle or other wealth made by the groom or his relatives to the family of the intended bride.

Bride Service Labor supplied by the groom to the relatives of the bride in lieu of payment of a *bride price*.

Bronze Age A level of technological evolution associated with the use of bronze tools, a pronounced degree of social stratification, and a substantial division of labor.

Bull-Roarer A flat device which makes a roaring noise when whirled at the end of a string.

Bureaucracy A method of human cooperation involving an extensive division of labor organized and directed by a hierarchy of coordinators.

Burin A stone blade with a chisel-shaped edge.

Cacique A Central American Indian clan chief.

Calendrical Rites Magicoreligious rituals scheduled for routine performance at specified times of the year.

Calotte The bones of the skull which together comprise the skull cap.

Canine Teeth The pointed teeth which are located between the incisors and the premolars.

Capitalism An economic system in which control over the means of production, distribution, and the exchange of wealth is in the hands of private individuals.

Capoid A racial group, once widely extended over the grasslands of southern and eastern Africa, today represented mainly by Hottentots and Bushmen speaking Khoisan languages.

Capsian A late Upper Paleolithic/Mesolithic culture of North Africa and Spain, noted for the abundance of microliths.

Carbon-14 A radioactive substance found in living organisms which disintegrates at a regular rate. By measuring the rate of disintegration of carbon-14 (C. 14) it is possible to estimate the approximate age of organic remains. Reasonably accurate up to 50,000 years only.

Cargo Cult A religious cult in which the believers seek to secure the material wealth of advanced cultures by magicoreligious means.

Caste An endogamous group characterized by a distinctive set of norms and a defined position in the social stratification of the society of which it is a part.

Catarrhine A term used to designate the "long-nosed" Old World apes and monkeys.

Caucasoid A member of the broadly defined geographical "White" race.

Ceboidea A simian superfamily corresponding to the platyrrhine or New World monkeys.

Cell A microscopic living structure comprising a nucleus surrounded by cytoplasm enclosed in a semipermeable membrane.

Celt A prehistoric stone or metal tool used as an axehead. (Not to be confused with the Celtic [or Keltic] linguistic division of the Indo-European family of languages; that is, *Celt:* one who speaks a Celtic language.)

Cenozoic The most recent geological era lasting from 65 million years ago to the present.

Central Chieftain The head of a *centralized chieftainship* who possesses effective means of coercion over his "subjects" and no longer relies wholly upon the spontaneous and voluntary support implied by superior kinship status, illustrious descent, or inherited ritual functions.

Cephalic Index A skull measurement designed to show the relative length and width of the human skull, calculated by expressing the width as a percentage of the length.

Cercopithecoidea That superfamily of primates that corresponds to the Old World monkeys.

Cerebral Cortex The layer of gray matter covering the cerebral hemispheres which is believed to be associated with the process of abstract thought. First found in the record of evolution among reptiles, but well developed only in mammals.

Chalcolithic A term used to refer to cultures using pure copper without bronze alloys.

Charm A fetish object believed to have the supernatural ability to attract good fortune.

Chellean A Lower Paleolithic hand axe culture. *See also* Abbevillian.

Chellean Man *Homo erectus* fossil remains found at Olduvai in East Africa, dated about 500,000 B.P.

Chopper An early or Lower Paleolithic technology using *pebble tools* held in the palm of the hand, which survived in parts of East and Southeast Asia until recent times.

Chordates Animals possessing a spinal cord or central nervous system.

Choukoutien A cave site close to Peking where Peking man (*Homo erectus*) was found as well as a number of human remains from the Upper Paleolithic.

Chromosome A threadlike chain of DNA molecules which contain the genetic code.

Churinga Sacred objects found in most Australian cultures.

Cicatrix A scar raised on the skin for ornamental or ritual purposes.

Civilization A complex system of integrated cultural traditions, normally but not necessarily associated with the existence of urban centers, which generally involves a considerable division of labor and a degree of technological advancement, as well as the possession of some form of writing.

Clavicle A slender collar bone which facilitates free arm movement among man and the primates.

Clan A unilineal cluster of relatives, part of a larger society, membership of which is determined by descent from a common ancestor, real or imaginary.

Class, Social A social unit in a hierarchical system of stratification, membership in which is determined by the extent to which different individuals and groups of individuals possess wealth, power, and status. Class systems generally imply some degree of vertical mobility.

Cleaver A cutting tool with a flat edge and no point.

Clitoridectomy A somewhat crude operation frequently performed on the clitoris in Hamitic and some other cultures, the effect of which is to reduce sexual sensation.

Clovis A distinctive type of stone blade found in the New World and named after the archeological site at which such blades were first discovered.

Coccyx The vestigial internal tail in man.

Codon The smallest combination of bases in DNA or RNA; hence the ultimate unit of the genetic mechanism.

Comitatus A small but permanent band of armed warriors, usually of noble descent, who served an Indo-European king in the relationship of loyal friends and kinsmen.

Community A social group or area in which cooperation and competition and other interpersonal relations exist; the smallest unit of a society capable of independent existence.

Compadrazgo A system of ritual kinship or *godparenthood* in Latin America.

Competition Impersonal rivalry for identical goals without the necessary existence of social communication.

Connubium A Latin word used by the Romans to define the limits of the social group within which marriage is permitted.

Consanguineal Relations Persons claiming relationship by common descent from the same ancestor, biological or fictitious, as distinct from persons related by marriage.

Core Tools Tools manufactured by chipping flakes from a stone core until the core eventually assumes the desired shape.

Couvade The practice whereby husbands simulate the birth pains of their wives and/or "lie in" following the birth of the child. Found among the Amazonian tribes and formerly present among some Mediterranean peoples.

Cranial Capacity The interior measurement of that part of the cranium which houses the brain. Normally expressed in cubic centimeters, differences in the cranial capacity of extinct hominids have been used as an indication of evolutionary progress.

Critical Rites Rituals held *only* at a time of crisis, designed to attract supernatural aid by magical or religious means.

Cro-Magnon A variety of *Homo sapiens sapiens* associated with the Upper Paleolithic period originating in Europe and West Asia about 35,000 B.C.

Cross Cousin The father's sister's or mother's brother's child.

Crowd A temporary gathering of people brought into a collective behavior pattern by identical excitatory stimuli, as distinct from a *social group*.

Cult A system of rituals or a group of persons centering upon specific sacred symbols, wherein participation tends to be individualistic or involves only a part of the community. Cults differ from religions in that they do not serve to bind the entire community tighter by the unifying bonds of common veneration and worship.

Cultural Diffusion The dissemination of the traits of one culture among those who possess a different culture, involving the geographical transmission of culture as distinct from *cultural heredity.*

Cultural Heredity The dissemination of cultural traits from one generation to another within the same society.

Cultural Materialism The theory that cultural behavior is determined solely by economic forces—favored by Marxists.

Cultural Pluralism The existence of a variety of diverse cultural and/or ethnic groups within the framework of a larger society.

Cultural Relativism The anthropological doctrine that people's values are primarily the product of their social and cultural environment, and that their ideas of right and wrong will therefore reflect the normative systems characteristic of their own culture. According to cultural relativism, culture therefore determines the rightness and wrongness of actions, and there is no external set of values which applies to all societies.

Culture That complex whole which includes knowledge, belief, art, morals, law, custom, and any other capabilities acquired by man as a member of society.

Culture Area A geographical area throughout which a distinct pattern of culture traits may be found.

Culture Conflict The rivalry of two conflicting cultures or subcultures within the same society and the tension created by this mental conflict.

Culture, Ideal The normative patterns of behavior as described by the members of a society.

Culture Pattern A set of cultural traits that tend to be found together.

Culture, Real Patterns of actual behavior as distinct from the *ideal culture* of the society as defined above.

Culture Shock The reaction experienced by an individual who finds himself suddenly confronted by an unfamiliar cultural system which differs sharply from that into which he has been enculturated.

Cuneiform Script An early form of writing characterized by wedge-shaped impressions.

Dating, Absolute Dating of an artifact or fossil by radiocarbon or any other method which establishes an approximate age without reference to stratigraphy or to other objects found with the item.

Dating, Relative Dating by reference to other artifacts or fossils associated with the object by location or similarity of designs, the age of which has been determined.

Deme A predominantly inbreeding local population.

Demography The statistical analysis and description of population aggregates with reference to distribution and vital statistics such as age, sex, race, and social status.

Dendrochronology A dating technique based on the measurement of patterns of tree rings, usable whenever a profusion of timber remains has made it possible to chart the years of rich or poor tree growth.

Deoxyribonucleic Acid (DNA) An organic substance which has the power to reproduce itself and is therefore fundamental to the survival of life.

Descent, Bilateral A descent system which reckons kinship equally through both parents, resulting in the formation of kindreds instead of clans.

Descent, Bilineal (*also* duolineal descent) The custom of recognizing a dual system of descent groups in which the individual inherits certain functions and responsibilities through his father's line, and other functions and responsibilities through his mother's line. Each individual is, in fact, a member of two separate clans or lineages: one traced through the male ancestors; the other through the female ancestors.

Descent, Unilineal A method of tracing kinship or inheritance through either the father's male ancestry or the mother's female ancestry.

Descriptive Kinship System Ideally, a system of kinship terminology in which there is a distinctive form of address for each individual kinsman.

Determinism The belief that chance (and hence free will) does not exist in the universe and that all events result from natural "laws" or "sufficent cause."

Dialect A regular pattern of variations within a language, usually restricted to a particular locality or social group.

Dimorphism, Sexual Morphological differences between the sexes.

Divination The attempt to foretell the future, to discover hidden knowledge, or to discern the wishes of supernatural beings.

DNA *See* Deoxyribonucleic Acid.

Dolichocephalic A condition in which the breadth of the skull is less than 76 percent of its length.

Double Descent *See* Descent, Bilineal.

Dowry Property transferred to the bride or to the groom by the bride's relatives at the time of marriage.

Dryopithecinae A subfamily which embraced most varieties of nonhominid Hominoidea living in the Miocene and Pliocene.

Dysfunctional A cultural condition arising when certain cultural traits conflict with others, thus preventing the smooth functioning of the culture as an integrated system.

Dysphoria The state of tension which exists when rapid changes in the culture of a society result in a poorly integrated and hence contradictory and dysfunctional assortment of values.

Ecology The study of the relationship between an organism and its environment, especially the spatial-functional patterns which arise as a result of the process of symbiosis.

Ecological Community A community of diverse species occupying the same territory and hence interdependent upon each other.

Economic Surplus Food and material goods produced in excess of subsistence needs.

Education An institutionalized process by which certain aspects of the culture of the group are deliberately transmitted from generation to generation.

Enculturation The transmission of the culture of a group to newcomers (including children).

Endogamy A social convention confining mating to members of a defined group; the custom of mating only within a specific group.

Environment, Physical All external physical forces that affect the life of an organism.

Eocene A division of the Tertiary period in which Prosimii have been identified.

Eolithic Age A lengthy period in hominid evolution when manlike creatures, notably Australopithecines, were believed to be using eoliths.

Eoliths Chipped flints found in association with early hominid remains which do not reveal conclusive evidence of deliberate manufacture but whose shape would suggest that they may have been used as crude chopping or scraping tools.

Epoch A division of geologic time smaller than a *period*.

Estate System A system of social stratification in which persons holding equivalent ranks in functionally distinct areas of society enjoy equal status in an integrated hierarchical structure.

Estrus The period of greatest sexual responsiveness among mammalian females.

Ethnocentrism The tendency to judge other societies by the standards or norms dominant in the observer's own society.

Ethnographic Present An ethnographic convention on the basis of which ethnologists describe cultures as they were immediately prior to contact with Western civilization, thus ignoring modifications arising from subsequent acculturation.

Ethnography The systematic description of different races, societies, and cultures.

Ethnology The comparison and analysis of diverse cultures and societies.

Ethology The study of animal behavior.

Ethos A distinctive style or quality of life implicit in the total culture pattern of a well-integrated society.

Eugenics The scientific application of genetic knowledge to the problem of raising the survival potential of human populations by a process of guided evolution.

Eutherian Mammals A subclass of higher mammals whose offspring are nourished in the prenatal stage by means of a placenta, thus freeing the fetus from dependency upon the limited food content of an egg yolk.

Evil Eye A magical power, the possessors of which are believed to be able to cause harm by simply gazing upon their victim. The evil eye utilizes the principle of contagious magic, transmitting the ill-intentions by visual contact.

Evolution A process of selective adaptation to environment resulting in a proliferation of diversified species, each specialized to meet the challenge of survival in its particular environment, and frequently resulting in the replacement of simpler life forms by more complex forms capable of producing varying responses to diverse stimuli.

Exogamy The custom of mating only with persons chosen from outside the defined social group.

Facet Flake Tradition A Lower Paleolithic technique of manufacturing finely shaped stone tools, which are struck as flakes from a carefully prepared core stone.

Family A group of people bound together by ties of marriage, ancestry, or adoption, sharing special economic, residental, psychological, and legal obligations in respect to each other.

Family, Extended A group of related families united by economic and other ties.

Family, Joint Two or more related families sharing a common residence and common property.

Family, Nuclear A small family group comprising husband, wife, and first-generation offspring only.

Family (taxonomic) A taxonomic subdivision of an *order*.

Fayum Depression An area in Egypt south of Cairo in which many hominoid remains have been found.

Femur The thigh bone.

Fetish An inanimate object believed to contain supernatural forces.

Fetus A term used to refer to the developing young of an animal while still in the prenatal stage.

Fictive Kinship "Honorary" kinship. In kinship-based societies virtually all rights and obligations are rooted in kinship ties, without which there can be little basis for trust or cooperation. In such instances "blood brotherhood," or similar fictitious kinship ties, may be invented in order to justify social, political, or economic cooperation between nonrelated individuals.

First Fruits Rituals Harvest rituals celebrating the first fruits of the harvest.

Flake Tool A stone tool comprising a flake which has been struck off a larger core.

Fluorine Dating A process by which the age of bones may be estimated by measuring the amount of fluorine that they have absorbed.

Folk Society A relatively isolated society operating largely through primary contacts. As originally conceived by Redfield the *folk society* was the opposite of an *urban society*.

Folkway A characteristic behavior pattern positively sanctioned by the members of the group.

Folsom An archeological site in New Mexico in which a large number of fluted stone spearheads revealed a distinctive New World technique of manufacture, without parallel among Old World artifacts.

Fontéchevade A site in France revealing incomplete fossil remains of an early *Homo sapiens* subspecies, dating from the Third Interglacial period.

Foramen Magnum The opening in the base of the skull through which the spinal cord joins the brain.

Fossils The remains of prehistoric life forms, sometimes mineralized by the absorption of mineral deposits.

Fraternity A voluntary association or club usually possessing its own ritual and ceremonies.

Fratricide The killing of a "brother" or kinsman, widely regarded by kinship-based societies as the most heinous of all crimes.

Gemeinschaft Society One in which the human relations are predominantly personal and traditional.

Gene Flow The exchange of genes between different populations.

Gene Pool The total genetic heritage possessed by a distinct breeding population. The term "pool" is used since with each successive generation the genes from the common pool are redistributed among the individual members.

Genes A term used by geneticists to refer to the mechanism by which particular sets of inherited characteristics are transmitted from generation to generation.

Genetic Drift A change in the frequency of specific genes within small and relatively isolated populations occurring "accidentally" rather than as a result of natural selection.

Genetic Load An accumulation of harmful or undesirable genes in the gene pool of a given population.

Genetics The science of heredity, concerned with the inheritance of similarities and the rise of dissimilarities in related organisms.

Genna Taboo A universal taboo applying to an entire community.

Genotype The entire content of the genetic heritage transmitted from parents to offspring, including not merely the dominant genes responsible for the structure of the organism but also the corresponding "latent" genes which may nevertheless contribute to the genetic heritage of subsequent generations.

Gens An aristocratic Roman kinship group (*gentes*) which might otherwise be described as a patrilineage. The root *gens* has survived in many English words, such as *gent*leman (the member of an aristocratic lineage), eu*gen*ic (well-born), *Gent*ile, and so on.

Geochronology The chronology of the geological history of the earth.

Gerontocracy Government by the elder members of a society.

Gesellschaft Society A society in which impersonal factors are dominant and social contacts are mostly deliberately conceived for definite ends.

Ghetto Formerly, in ancient Europe an area wherein privileged alien communities, usually comprising merchants or craftsmen, were permitted to live in accordance with their own customs. Today used to refer to slum areas occupied by socially or economically subordinate ethnic groups.

Ghost Dance Cult A nationalistic revival movement which arose among American Indians at the end of the nineteenth century.

Glottochronology The comparative and historical study of related languages in order to deduce the probable date at which they separated from the common parent language.

Gods Supernatural beings of such power that they cannot be controlled by man and must therefore be propitiated.

Gorilla A large ape (Pongidae) found in parts of central Africa.

Group, Descent A social group linked by the ties of kinship and common descent.

Group, Ethnic A group of men and women united by recognition of a common cultural, linguistic, national, and/or racial heritage.

Group, Formal A small group which evolves for a definite purpose.

Group Identification Positive recognition of one's membership in a group and of the responsibilities of such membership.

Group, Informal A social group which evolves without specific design.

Group, Primary A group with intimate and frequent communications among its members, in which the members have intimate knowledge of each other's social personality.

Group, Secondary A social group with impersonal, segmentalized relations among its members, who share a common set of purposes but seldom are aware of each other's behavior outside of this setting.

Group, Social A number of people who possess distinctive elements of culture in common as a result of shared communication.

Günz The first of the four major Alpine glaciations of the Pleistocene.

Hallstatt A Central European culture belonging to the early Iron Age, about 1500–500 B.C., named after a noted archeological site at Hallstatt, near Salzburg in Austria.

Hammurabi, Code of One of the oldest codes of laws known to anthropology, being a compilation of earlier Sumerian laws effected around 1700 B.C. by the Babylonian ruler Hammurabi.

Headman A community leader with advisory rather than executive authority. The office may be elective but in tribal societies will more frequently be hereditary, especially in the case of unilocal lineages.

Herding Societies Otherwise known as *pastoral societies,* these depend primarily upon the care of the larger domesticated animals such as sheep, goats, and cattle.

Heroic Age A period of protofeudal social organization frequently associated with Bronze Age and early Iron Age societies when centralized chieftains, attended by bands of knights, warriors, or "companions," were the dominant power in society.

Heterodont Possessing teeth which are variously specialized for different functions.

Heterozygous Possessing different alleles at the same locus on corresponding chromosomes.

Hieroglyphics Pictorial symbols arranged in rows, constituting one of the earliest forms of written communication.

Holism The theory that to a greater or lesser extent all parts of an operative culture must be interrelated. (Adjective, *holistic.*)

Holocene The latest division of the Quaternary period, which commenced around 12,000 B.P.

Hominidae Any creature whose anatomical structure approximates to our current concept of *Homo sapiens* rather than to that of the Pongidae. Technically distinguished by an adaptation of the lower limbs to permit habitual bipedal locomotion and by the absence of the heavy canines of the apes. A subdivision of the superfamily Hominoidea.

Hominoidea A primate superfamily comprising Pongidae (apes) and Hominidae (man).

Homo A genus of the family Hominidae, including Pithecanthropines, Neanderthals, Cro-Magnons, and all living hominids.

Homodont Possessing teeth lacking specialization according to function.

Homo erectus A term now used collectively to refer to a general level of hominid evolution after a permanent erect stance had been adopted for walking. *Homo erectus* fossils date from 900,000 years to 250,000 B.P.

Homo modernus A term formerly used to refer to a group of fossil remains found in Europe including Swanscombe man. These reveal certain "modern" features and are believed by some to have been directly ancestral to Cro-Magnon man. Also known as *Homo steinheimensis.*

Homo neanderthalensis *See* Neanderthal Man.

Homo sapiens A term originally used by the Swedish naturalist Carl von Linné (Linnaeus) in the eighteenth century to identify living men and subsequently used by the nineteenth century archeologists to distinguish living Caucasoids from Neanderthal and other earlier occupants of Europe. Today used generally to refer to Neanderthals and all extant survivors of the hominid assemblage.

Homo sapiens sapiens A term first used to distinguish Cro-Magnons from Neanderthals, but now loosely applied to include all Upper Paleolithic subspecies and their extant survivors.

Homozygous Possessing identical *alleles.*

Horde A loose aggregate of local communities lacking any consistent basis for authoritative leadership.

Horticultural Societies Neolithic societies which depend primarily upon the cultivation of plants, using hand tools rather than plows, with little knowledge of soil fertilization or other advanced agricultural techniques.

Household A social, economic, and sometimes political group comprising one or more nuclear families sharing a common area of residence and a common set of resources.

Hunting and Gathering Societies Societies which have not yet developed pastoral, advanced fishing, or horticultural arts.

Hybrid The offspring of cross-breeding between members of two distinctive races or subspecies.

Hylobates Members of the anthropoid family Hylobatidae, of which the main surviving representatives are the gibbons and the siamangs.

Ideology An integrated system of values or preferences.

Idol A manufactured three-dimensional object believed to be associated with a supernatural being.

Incest An act contravening mores which restrict sexual relations between persons regarded by society as being related (whether or not they are in fact biologically related).

Independent Invention An indigenous innovation, not acquired by diffusion from another society or group.

Industrial Society A society which is characterized by mass production and which depends primarily for its energy supply upon inanimate sources rather than upon human or animal muscle.

Infanticide The deliberate killing of infants for eugenic, economic, or ritual purposes.

Instincts Potential courses of action which are genetically programmed and will be readily followed upon receipt of the appropriate stimulus.

Institution A fairly permanent cluster of social usages relating to functions and values which are regarded as necessary for the survival of the group.

Interglacial A warmer period intervening between periods of major glaciation.

Intersocietal Selection A process of selection which eliminates some societies and cultures while permitting the survival of others more suited to meet the environmental challenges.

Interstadial The warm periods between glacial phases within a major glacial age.

Invention An innovation arising from a new combination of information or concepts.

I.Q. Intelligence quotient; an arbitrary scale designed to indicate innate reasoning ability.

Jati An Indian subcaste.

Java Man A *Homo erectus* fossil from Java.

Joking Relationship Insulation techniques designed to reduce the possibility of friction and to reinforce social bonds between specific individuals.

Kachinas Spirits of the ancestors in the Hopi culture, represented by male dancers wearing masks.

Kindred A kinship group comprising bilateral relatives.

Kinship A socially defined relationship regulating the various aspects of social order on the basis of actual or assumed genetic relationship.

Kinship, Classificatory A system of kinship which awards the same statuses and titles to a variety of relatives of diverse genetic relationship.

Kraal A type of enclosed settlement, comprising several families and their animals, common to many cultures in eastern and southern Africa.

La Chapelle-aux-Saints Archeological site in France associated with Neanderthal remains.

Language A system of verbal symbols by which a relatively sophisticated degree of communication can be attained. Some writers use the term *language* only when a written form is present and employ the term *speech* for strictly verbal forms of communication.

Laws Norms of behavior which have been codified by a society, the contravention of which attracts specific penalties.

Legends Narrative accounts of real or fictitious events of unusual significance in the past history of the group, often involving supernatural beings or forces.

Leisure Any time available to man after laboring to produce the material wealth considered necessary for the maintenance of the desired standard of living.

Lemuroidea A primate superfamily within the suborder Prosimii represented mainly by the lemurs of Madagascar.

Levalloisian A relatively highly-evolved Lower Paleolithic technique of stoneworking by which flake tools were struck off a prepared core.

Levirate The custom whereby a woman marries the brother of her deceased husband.

Lineage A unilateral kinship group (smaller than a clan) tracing descent from a known ancestor.

Linguistic Paleontology The analysis of the vocabulary of an earlier form of a language in order to obtain information concerning the culture and style of life of its speakers.

Linguistics, Diachronic The study of languages from the point of view of their evolution through time. Also known as *historical linguistics.*

Linguistics, Structural The study of languages as coherent homogeneous entities. Also known as *synchronic linguistics.*

Magdalenian The last major Upper Paleolithic culture in Europe, associated with Cro-Magnon man and marked by a highly refined esthetic sense.

Magic A technique or formula aimed at achieving control over the forces of the supernatural. Significant since it appears to represent a prescientific attempt to employ the concept of causality in the control of the environment.

Magic, Imitative The belief that the construction of images or symbols will give the possessor power over the subject so represented.

Magic, Contagious An attempt to manipulate the supernatural on the principle that supernatural power can be transferred by touch or physical proximity.

Maglemosian A hunting and fishing culture of northern Europe which was equipped with many advanced technological skills of a Neolithic level, but which lacked horticultural techniques appropriate to the severe climatic conditions of the Baltic area, and is therefore classified as Mesolithic.

Mana A term borrowed by anthropologists from the Melanesian language and applied generally to the idea of a vague and diffused supernatural power that may pervade inorganic as well as organic matter. The concept of *mana* should be distinguished from that of a spirit or soul which possesses a will of its own. *See also* Animatism.

Mandible The lower portion of the jaw.

Market Economy An economic system in which the problem of production, distribution, and consumption are decided by the free operation of the price mechanism.

Marriage A socially recognized pair-bond between one or more males and one or more females.

Marriage, Preferential Marriage within a traditionally preferred category.

Mass Society A society in which the activities of the component groups have become differentiated and specialized to such an extent that integration is based upon a functional interdependence and behavior tends to be directed by a central core of institutionalized structures.

Mastoid Process A bony projection appearing on the base of the skull just behind the ear.

Matrilineal Descent Descent traced through the female line.

Matrilocal Residence with or near wife's parents.

Medicine Man A specialist in the manipulation of the supernatural who is generally believed to use his powers for the good of the members of his community rather than for nefarious or purely personal goals.

Meiosis A stage in the process of sexual reproduction during which the number of chromosomes are reduced by one half, prior to the combination of the male and female gametes.

Melanin A dark pigment which is primarily responsible for protective coloring in hair, eyes, and skin.

Mendelian Population A population which customarily inbreeds among its own members and only occasionally outbreeds with neighboring populations.

Mesocephalic Possessing a skull of medium width, that is, in which the width is 76 to 80.9 percent of the length.

Mesolithic The Middle Stone Age; a transitional stage between the Upper Paleolithic and Neolithic cultures often regarded today as an extension of the Upper Paleolithic but distinguished from the latter by the existence of primitive pottery-making techniques. Usually characterized by settled fishing or swine-herding village communities.

Mesozoic The era of "middle life," characterized by large reptiles and the appearance of flowering plants and mammals, between 225 and 65 million years ago.

Mestizo A word of Spanish origin indicating a person of mixed Caucasian and American Indian descent.

Metabolism The chemical life processes that occur within a living organism, by which autotrophs build up organic compounds from external nonorganic sources such as sunlight, and allotrophs break down complex organic substances to secure energy.

Metatheria A mammalian subclass represented by the kangaroo, wombat, wallaby, and koala bear of Australia and the more widely distributed opossum. The females produce eggs with small yolks, but retain these in their own bodies for a brief period of "pregnancy." The offspring are still immature at birth, following which they are carried in an abdominal pouch and fed from teats.

Metazoa Multicellular life forms in which some specialization or division of labor has developed between the member cells. (*Porifera*, or sponges, are not usually regarded as Metazoa, being instead described as colonial *Protozoa*.)

Microliths Small, usually geometrically shaped stone tools.

Mimetic Magic *See* Magic, Contagious.

Mindel The second of the four major Alpine glaciations of the Pleistocene.

Miocene A period in the Cenozoic, extending from 26 to 12 million years ago, during which substantial hominid evolution took place.

Mir A traditional pattern of village government in Russia, under which all property and all wealth produced was deemed to belong to the villagers as a whole. This late survival of the collective kin-group, sharing the means of subsistence, was destroyed following the introduction of the Communist "collective farm," which though superficially parallel in concept ignored kinship ties—moving families from one collective to another to suit production needs—and deprived the villagers of effective ownership rights by placing their operations under the control of distant urban bureaucrats.

Mitosis A stage in the reproductive process by which the nucleus divides into two, enabling the parent cell to divide into two daughter cells, each complete with its own nucleus.

Mixed Farming A pattern of subsistence combining the cultivation of crops and production of food from domesticated animals.

Mobility, Social The ability of the individual to change his *situs* in the social matrix, usually implying vertical social mobility, that is, the ability to move up or down the class structure. *See also* Class, Social.

Moiety A major kinship grouping, usually exogamous, which arises when a tribe is divided into two parts.

Molars The large posterior mammalian teeth used for grinding.

Monotheism The belief that a single god created and guides the world.

Morpheme The smallest unit of speech that may possess a distinct meaning.

Morphology The study of the form and structure of an organism.

Mongoloid One of the major geographical races of living hominids, centered on eastern Asia.

Monogamy Marriage of one man to one woman.

Mother-in-law Taboo A social custom requiring a man to avoid or severely restrict social contact with his wife's mother.

Motor Habits Routine patterns of body movement which have socially determined origins.

Mousterian A culture associated with the Neanderthals of the Middle Paleolithic, which subsequently extended eastward and southward into Asia and Africa.

Mulatto A word of Spanish origin indicating a person of combined Caucasian and Negro descent; literally, "little mule."

Multilocal Household An extended family which may formerly have shared a single roof but has since become diversified into separate households.

Mutation A sudden and permanent change in the number or structure of the genes or chromosomes which is genetically transferable to subsequent offspring. Mutations are random and usually caused by radiation. Thus evolution occurs as a result of natural selection, not directed change.

Myths Legends which explain the origin of customs, rituals, and magicoreligious beliefs.

Natal Kinship Kinship traced by birth, that is, consanguineal kindred.

Nation A political grouping of people with an independent government and a common territory, united by the common recognition of a shared cultural, linguistic, and genetic heritage.

National Character A distinctive system of norms, values, attitudes, and behavior associated with the members of a particular national group.

Nativism A messianic movement among peoples subject to culture contact often heralding the return to a precontact way of life. Also known as *millenarianism* or *messianism*.

Natural Area A distinctive geographical area set apart by physical or climatic conditions which tends to influence the cultural pattern of any community or society domiciled within its limits.

Natural Selection A process by which individuals and occasionally entire populations are selectively prevented from reproducing, proportionately to other members of the same or different species, thereby resulting in the progressive reduction of deleterious and less advantageous genes from the gene pool, and also in the promotion of gene combinations favorable to the survival of the species under the prevailing conditions.

Neanderthal A hominid variety known to have inhabited the West Asian, European, and North African area from around 250,000 B.P. down to the advent of Cro-Magnon man around

40,000 B.P., and also believed by some physical anthropologists to have interbred in certain areas with Cro-Magnon man. The term is also extended by most authorities to include other advanced hominids known to have inhabited Asia and Africa during the later Pleistocene who may likewise have made a genetic contribution to the living populations of these areas. Also known as *Neandertal.*

Neanthropic Referring to those various hominid varieties which present a modern appearance.

Necromancy Foretelling the future by magical means through communication with the spirits of the dead.

Negrito A relatively prognathous, curly-haired pygmy strain found in Southeast Asia, the Philippines, New Guinea, and parts of India.

Neolithic Age Originally designated the "New Stone Age" because of refinements in techniques for producing stone tools and the tendency to use stone that could be polished until it was smooth. More recently, however, the Neolithic has come to be associated with societies that have learned to cultivate plants and domesticate animals.

Neolocal Residence The custom by which newlyweds establish their own households in a new locality, separate from that of either parental kindred.

Neopallium Nonolfactory portion of the cerebral cortex which is largely concerned with consciousness and intelligence. The neopallium of living hominids ranges from three to six times the size of that found in gorillas and chimpanzees.

Neoteny The tendency, found in some organisms, for the adult to resemble an ancestral embryonic form because of the retention of fetal or infantile forms into adulthood. Thus man is in some ways a neotene ape, retaining in adulthood many characteristics of the primate young which are lost in adult apes.

Nomads A community of hunters and gatherers or pastoralists which moves its location at fairly regular intervals in pursuit of subsistence.

Norms The standards of value by which a group judges the conduct of its members.

Occipital Bun A ringlike protuberance circling the rear or occipital area of the skull.

Occiput The bone at the rear and lower portion of the cranium.

Oldowan An East African culture of the Lower Paleolithic.

Oligarchy The concentration of authoritative power in the hands of a small segment of society.

Oligocene A division of the geologic Tertiary period to which the first hominoid fossils belong.

Omnivorous The ability to consume both plant and animal foods.

Ontogeny The life history of an individual organism.

Opposable Thumb Primates are distinguished, among other features, by the ability to oppose the thumb to the finger in a prehensile grip, a biological trait which facilitated the use of tools among early hominids.

Oracle A person (or object) serving as a medium for communication with the spirit world.

Order A major taxonomic division (for example, Primata).

Orthograde Vertical stance as found in Australopithecines and their descendants.

Osteodontokeratic A hypothetical stage in the evolution of hominid technology in which extensive use would have been made of tools made from bones, teeth, and horn before stoneworking techniques were developed.

Pair-bonding The tendency in "family"-type mammalian societies for a permanent or semipermanent bond to form between a particular male and a particular female (or females). This bond involves sexual prerogatives, cooperation in the care of offspring, food sharing, and an elementary division of labor.

Paleoanthropology The study of extinct hominid life forms.

Paleocene A division of the geologic Tertiary period in which *Prosimii* were numerous.

Paleolithic Age The Old Stone Age, during which hominids were dependent entirely upon hunting and food gathering subsistence techniques. Commonly divided into a Lower, a Lower Evolved, a Middle, and an Upper Paleolithic level of technological evolution, each based upon particular improvements in stoneworking techniques.

Paleontology The study of the fossil remains of extinct life forms.

Paleozoic A major geological era dating from 575 to 225 million years ago in which the first chordates and vertebrates appeared.

Palynology The scientific study of pollen and spores especially in relation to paleontology.

Papyrus A type of paper made in ancient Egypt from the pith of sedge plants.

Parallel Cousins Cousins who are descended from two brothers or from two sisters. In many societies in which kinship is based upon a lineal clan system, such cousins would find themselves in the same clan, and thus be prohibited from marrying. In other societies, as among most Moslems, such marriages may actually be favored.

Paranthropus robustus An African hominid today regarded by most anthropologists as a species of Australopithecinae, and now known as *Australopithecus robustus*.

Pastoralism A pattern of culture based upon the herding of domesticated animals, commonly involving some degree of nomadism.

Patrilineal Descent Descent traced through the male line.

Patrilocal Residence with or near husband's parents.

Patrimony Property which properly belongs to the family in a patrilineal society, and cannot be alienated at the will of any individual member. It passes to the trusteeship of the eldest son or to the children generally, according to custom, following the death of the family head.

Peasant Society An agricultural society producing crops for personal subsistence rather than for an organized market economy.

Pebble Tools A Lower Paleolithic stone tool manufactured by knocking a large flake from a pebble to create a sharp cutting edge.

Period One of the major subdivisions of the Cenozoic, Mesozoic, and Paleozoic eras.

Personality, Basic Personality traits which are implanted by the prevailing cultural pattern of the group.

Phenotype The structure of any individual organism in so far as this is determined by biogenetic inheritance. The genetic characteristics that reveal themselves in an individual, as distinct from the total genetic code or *genotype*.

Phoneme The smallest units of sound that may be identified in any form of human speech.

Phonology The study of sounds in a language.

Phratry An exogamous unilineal subdivision of a tribe comprising two or more sibs or clans.

Phylogeny The evolutionary history of an organism.

Pictograph A picture intended to symbolize a particular concept or event; an early form of written communication.

Pit House A single structure, usually of wood and mud, raised over a shallow pit dug into the ground for protection against heat and cold.

Pithecanthropus erectus Java man, now placed in the general *Homo erectus* level of hominid evolution. Similar to modern man in body form, but with a less developed brain.

Platyrrhini New World monkeys with broad flat-bridged noses and nostrils that open to the side. Also known as Ceboidea.

Pleistocene A division of the geologic Quaternary period which began around 2.3 to 3 million years ago and is associated with rapid hominid evolution from Australopithecinae to *Homo sapiens sapiens*.

Pliocene A division of the Tertiary period in which the first hominids appear. The Pliocene followed the Miocene and preceded the Pleistocene.

Political System That part of the social structure related to the attainment of public goals, through which social order is enforced.

Polyandry A marriage system in which the female customarily takes more than one husband at the same time (for example, the Todas).

Polygamy A marriage system in which a member of either sex customarily takes more than one spouse at the same time.

Polygyny A marriage system in which the male may take more than one wife simultaneously (for example, Islamic society).

Polymorphism (genetic) Genotypic diversity; having two or more alleles at the same loci on matching chromosomes.

Polytheism The worship of more than one god.

Pongidae The taxonomic family of primates which includes the gorilla, chimpanzee, and orangutan.

Population Genetics The study of racial or genetic changes in Mendelian populations.

Potassium-Argon Dating A dating technique based upon the knowledge that living organisms absorb potassium 40, a radioactive substance which breaks down into argon 40 at a regular rate. By measuring the rate of conversion it is possible to determine the approximate age of fossil remains or even of carbon deposits derived from extinct life forms, as far back as the beginning of life, although this technique is not suitable for use in the case of fossil remains less than one million years of age, since the margin of error is too large.

Potlatch Northwest Coast Indian ceremonial in which property is given away or destroyed to enhance the owner's social status.

Potsherds Fragments of broken pottery uncovered by archeologists in excavation of Mesolithic and post-Mesolithic residential sites.

Prehensile The ability to grasp objects with hands, feet, or even tail.

Prehistory Any period of time prior to the existence of written records.

Priest A functionary who specializes in the propitiation of the god or gods of a society.

Primate A taxonomic order of placental mammals which includes the Anthropoidea (monkeys, apes, and men) and Prosimii (Lemuroidea and Tarsioidea). Characterized by stereoscopic vision, nails (rather than claws), a large cerebrum, and prehensile feet and/or hands.

Primatology The study of primates, usually with particular reference to the nonhuman primates.

Primogeniture The custom whereby the eldest son inherits all family titles, distinctions, and landed property.

Proconsul A Miocene hominid fossil found in East Africa and now classified as *Dryopithecus.*

Prognathism A condition in which the jaws protrude forward beyond the remainder of the face. *Alveolar prognathism,* characteristic of many early mammals, refers to a forward protrusion of the teeth.

Prosimii A suborder of the primate order including tree shrews, lemurs, and tarsiers.

Proterozoic The era of "former life," from 1.2 billion to 575 million years ago, characterized by the appearance of complex multicellular life forms.

Protista Unicellular plants and animals.

Proto- Used as a prefix, the term *proto* implies an early form of either a biological or a cultural organism, out of which later (usually more complex) varieties can be demonstrated to have evolved.

Protoplasm Organic living matter which constitutes the basic material in all living cells.

Prototheria A mammalian subclass, which today survives only in Australia, where they are represented by the duckbilled *platypus* and the spiny anteater (*echidna*). Prototheria have a furry or spiny covering, are warm-blooded, and the females have breastlike glands. Unlike other mammals, however, the females reproduce by laying eggs and the adults are toothless.

Protozoa A phylum which includes all unicellular animals.

Purdah A cloak or heavy veil, used in many Moslem societies to conceal women from the jealous gaze of nonkinsmen. Believed to be of Babylonian origin.

Quipu The Quechua name for a primitive counting and recording device comprising a number of knotted strings, common to various early civilizations.

Race A genetically distinct inbreeding division within a species. Often used interchangeably with the term *subspecies*.

Ramapithecus A species generally regarded as representing the earliest hominid fossils yet discovered. Found in western India and in Kenya and dated between 12 and 15 million years B.P.

Relatives, Collateral Relatives who are not in the direct line of descent, such as nephews, cousins, uncles.

Relatives, Lineal Relatives in the direct line of descent, such as, father, grandfather, son.

Religion, Comparative The comparative study of religion, emphasizing the historical development of religious thought in its variety of forms.

Religion, Ethnic A set of religious attitudes which is closely tied to the culture of a particular society. Ethnic religions usually serve to reinforce the sense of group identity and seldom seek or admit converts from other societies.

Religion, Missionary A religion which does not restrict its appeal to any one nation or society, and whose supporters actively seek converts from among members of other nations and societies.

Revitalism A movement which attempts to revive a former religious system by promising political, economic or supernatural rewards.

Rhodesian Man A fossil skull found at Broken Hill in Northern Rhodesia, classified as late *Homo erectus* or early Neanderthal and dated 40,000 B.P.

Ribonucleic Acid (RNA) A substance formed by nucleotides containing sugar ribose which transmits "coded" instructions from the nucleus of the cell to the surrounding cytoplasm.

Riss The third of the four major Alpine glaciations of the Pleistocene.

RNA *See* Ribonucleic Acid.

Rites of Passage A term applied to ritual ceremonies associated with birth, puberty, marriage, death, and similar crucial occasions when the individual passes from one status or life stage into another.

Semantics The study of the relative meaning of words as separate units.

Serology A science dealing with the properties of blood serum, useful in identifying genetic relationships between different species of animals.

Sexual Dichotomy Any division of structure or function between the sexes.

Shaman A term borrowed from certain Ural-Altaic societies and used by anthropologists in a generic sense to refer to any specialist in supernatural affairs who is not a member of a regular religious association or priestly hierarchy. Shamans are generally more concerned with magical than religious activities, but not all magicoreligious practitioners can be readily classed as either shamans or priests.

Shifting Cultivators Horticulturalists who are periodically obliged to transfer their operations to new land to escape the effects of soil exhaustion.

Shogun A Japanese feudal ruler with extensive military power.

Sib An extended kinship group larger than a family but fulfilling many functions of the family.

Siblings Children of the same mother.

Sinanthropus pekinensis Peking man, classified as *Homo erectus.*

Slash and Burn Cultivation A widespread form of horticulture whereby the cultivators slash down natural vegetation, burning off what remains, to uncover virgin soil for planting.

After a few years this soil is exhausted, and lacking any knowledge of crop rotation or of fertilizers, the cultivators then abandon the site and clear fresh land by the same method.

Slave A person who has no legal existence except as the possession of another legally recognized "free" person.

Social Anthropology A term, more widely used in Britain than America, which differs from the concept of cultural anthropology in that the emphasis is placed upon patterns of social organization rather than on material culture and methods of subsistence.

Social Distance A feeling of separation existing between individuals due to the recognition of cultural differences, sometimes but not always as a consequence of status or caste distinctions.

Social Heredity The transmission of culture to successive generations by a process of successful enculturation.

Socialization The process of communicating the culture of a group to newcomers.

Social Sanctions The enforcement power of a society aimed at obtaining conformity to its values.

Social Structure The forms and modes of social relationship as distinguished from their content or function.

Society The sum total of people occupying a specific territory who have fairly consistent intercommunication with each other and who share significant sections of culture in common.

Sociology The controlled observation and interpretation of differing patterns of human relationships, their sources, and consequences. Properly a branch of anthropology devoted primarily to the description and analysis of complex contemporary societies.

Sodality Any association or society limited to one or more objectives (for example, a religious order).

Solo Man A hominid transitional between *Homo erectus* and Neanderthal, whose fossil remains have been found at Ngandong in Java.

Solutrean A phase of the Upper Paleolithic culture in Europe.

Somatology The study of constitutional variations in man.

Sororate The custom whereby a widower is expected to marry one of his deceased wife's sisters.

Speciation The process of evolutionary divergence whereby two new populations or species arise from an originally common stock as a result of prolonged genetic isolation and differential selection.

Species A group of living organisms that share a marked degree of genetic homogeneity and consequently resemble each other closely. No comprehensive and universally satisfactory definition of a species exists, but geneticists frequently use the term to refer to distinct populations that are unable to reproduce except with their own kind. *Subspecies,* would thus be defined as subdivisions of species, whose members resemble each other in the possession of distinctive genetically controlled characteristics which set them apart from other members of the species with whom they seldom interbreed for psychic, geographical, or other reasons, even though they still retain the potential for fertile crossbreeding within the species. From the evolutionary point of view, subspecies that preserve their genetic isolation eventually become separate species. The hominid races may be regarded as subspecies.

Status The relative rank of an individual or group of individuals in the social hierarchy based upon the possession of characteristics highly valued in that culture.

Stratification, Social The process or condition whereby society is conceptually divided into several classes on the basis of wealth, power, influence, prestige, and any other determinants of status.

Stratigraphy The identification of archeological finds according to the relative strata in which they are found.

Structural-Functional The theory that all the cultural elements in an established cultural system will tend to become integrated into a harmoniously interdependent functioning whole rather similar to the interrelationship between the parts of a machine.

Subculture The distinctive meanings and values held by a subgroup in a society which distinguishes them from other members of the same society.

Subspecies *See* Species.

Supernatural That which cannot be explained by the laws of the natural world.

Swanscombe Man Ancestral to the Cro-Magnons. A fossil hominid today classified as *H. steinheimensis.*

Symbiosis An unplanned pattern of reciprocal relationships.

Syntax The study of the structure of sentences and of meaning as affected by the order of words in a phrase or sentence.

Taboo (*also* tabu) A term borrowed from the Polynesian languages to refer to any ritual prohibition, the infraction of which will cause the violator to suffer penalties of a magical or supernatural character.

Talisman An object believed to attract or exercise supernatural powers for the benefit of the wearer.

Taxonomy A system of classification of living organisms according to similarities of anatomy and physiology.

Technostasis A state of technological stagnation.

Teknonymy The custom of avoiding the use of direct names and instead referring to an individual by his or her relationship to some other individual (for example, "the father of Ana").

Teleology The belief common among primitive people that all events must be "willed" or preplanned and are therefore directed toward some preconceived end.

Tell An artificial mound resulting from an accumulation of ruins and debris from a town or village that has been continuously occupied for thousands of years. Characteristic of many Neolithic and post-Neolithic archeological sites in the Middle East.

Territorial Imperative The tendency common among more mobile animals to restrict their movements to a particular territory with which they are familiar, and also to a varying extent to defend this territory against intrusion by potential rivals for the same food resources.

Theocracy A society dominated by a religious priesthood.

Toponymy The analysis of place names, their origin, and anthropological significance.

Totemism A supernatural relationship between a clan or tribe and a particular type of plant or animal. Ritual ceremonials may be held in honor of the totemic image, the kinship group usually believing that the totemic plant or animal is a distant ancestor.

Tradition Meanings, values, or behavior patterns which have been commonly accepted and used in the past and which are passed on to newcomers as a part of the content of socialization.

Transhumance A seasonal migration based upon the need to maintain a pattern of nomadic herding and a measure of horticulture.

Tribal Initiation Rituals which are performed to commemorate the admission of individuals into full adult membership of the tribe. One of the *rites of passage.*

Tribe A poorly defined term used by different anthropologists in a variety of different ways. In the broadest sense the term *tribe* has been frequently applied to groups of exogamous bands whose members share a common genetic, cultural, and linguistic heritage. More strictly, however, the term *tribe* should be reserved for those inbreeding social groups which not only preserve a common cultural, genetic, and linguistic heritage but are united also by the possession of a coordinating political system, such as a tribal council and/or chieftain.

Trilobites Members of the class Trilobita of the phylum Arthropoda, now extinct, but formerly representing one of the earliest types of *Metazoa*.

Tropism A response to a stimulus such as light or gravity involving growth or locomotory movement (also called taxis) toward or away from the source of the stimulus.

Unilateral kinship Kinship recognized through one parent only. This will be either patrilineal or matrilineal, and usually gives rise to clan groupings.

Unscheduled Rites Magical or religious rituals which are performed in an emergency instead of on regular calendrical dates.

Untouchable The member of a subordinate caste (especially in India) who is considered to be ritually unclean and who literally may not be touched by the members of higher social castes for fear of ritual defilement.

Urban Referring to the type of social life generally found in densely populated areas, characterized by numerous segmentalized or secondary social contacts.

Vestigial Remains Organs which no longer serve a useful biological purpose.

Voodoo (*also* Vodun) A set of religious beliefs, still popular among many Caribbean Negro populations, which combines elements of West African (Dahomean) magicoreligious cults with the worship of a pantheon of supernatural beings largely borrowed from Catholicism.

Wergild A payment made by the relatives of an offender to the relatives of the party who has suffered an unjustifiable injury.

Wife Lending The custom whereby a man extends sexual privileges over his wife to another man as a gesture of friendship or brotherly affection.

Witch A supernatural specialist of either sex who uses inborn supernatural powers for antisocial purposes.

Witchcraft The technique of exercising magical control over other persons.

Witch Doctor A man who attempts to cure illnesses, believed to be of supernatural or magical origin, by the use of magic.

Würm The last of the four major Alpine glaciations of the Pleistocene.

Zadruga A historic type of village settlement which survived in the Balkans area of Europe from the Neolithic to the beginning of the present century. The village comprises a single patriarchal extended family sharing all property, labor, and agricultural produce. Each nuclear family, however, possesses its own house. The village activities are directed by a hereditary village headman who presides over an assembly comprising all adult male heads of families.

Ziggurat An earthen mound used as a basis for a temple or other public structure in ancient Sumeria.

Index

Protozoa, 21, 39, 40, 43
  colonial, 39
Psyche "soul," 244
Psychology, relationship to anthropology, 3
Puberty, 327
Puberty rituals, 264, 325, 336
Public contests, 209
Public law, 212
Pueblo Indians, 368
Pulque, 529
Pumas, as totemic animals, 506
Pumpkin, 371
Purda, 468
Pygmies, 85, 126, 127, 128, 142, 150, 155, 186, 207, 338–346 ff.
  and Negroes, 224
Pylos, 264
Pyramids, Central America, 263, 303, 496, 499, 503
  Egyptian, 471, 496
  Nuer, 404

Quechua language, 568, 570
Quipu, 466–508
Quito, 505, 511

Ra'atira, 453
Race, 98, 136 ff. (*see also* under individual races)
Racial cline, definition of, 30
Radcliffe-Brown, A. R., 201, 278, 313, 334
Ragnarok, 267
"Raiders," Masai, 407
Railways, 537
Rainmaking, Nuer, 402
Raj, 519
Rajah, Indian, 521
Rajanya, 235, 520
Rajasuya, 261
Ramadan, 271
Ramapithecus, 78 ff., 80, 83, 85, 175
Ramzan, 260 (*see also* Ramadan)
Rank society, 231, 233 ff.
Rasmussen, Knud, 250 ff.
Rats, Norwegian wild, 24
Reciprocity, 218 ff.
Red Crown of Egypt, 470
Redistribution, 220 ff.
Red ochre, 117
Religion, 256 ff., 309
  Aryan, 484
  Ethnic, 493
  Inca, 511
  Japanese, 493
  Sun-worshipping, 511
  Toda, 416
Religious bureaucracy, 517
  calendar, Aztec, 504
  ceremonies, Aztec, 503
  ethics, 417

systems, Masai, 409
Renaissance, 237, 277, 294
  Europe, 237
Rent, 515
Reproduction, 14, 45
  sexual, 17, 42
Reptiles, 42, 44, 47, 51–52
Respiration, 13
Rhine, 347
Rhinoceros, 483
Rhodesian man, 107, 109, 120, 149
  site, 108
Rh system, 131
Rhythm, 296
Rice, T. T., 425
Riss glaciation, 94, 105
Rites of passage, 264 ff., 407
Ritual, 263 ff., 279
  calendrical, 263 ff.
  circumcision, 265
  critical or unscheduled, 264
  funeral, 448, 455
  kina, 327
  marriage, 266
  Masai, 408
  metaphysical, 335
  mutilation, 329
  puberty, 325, 336
  sacrificial religious, 497
  secret, 407
  Semitic, 468
  snake dance, 373
  Sumerian, 468
  Toda, 416
Ritually stratified society, 184
Rivers, W. H. R., 410–411, 417
Rogers, Everett M., 518
Role obligations, social, 488
Romans, 204, 223, 252, 257, 264, 267–269, 274, 276, 284, 286, 293, 409, 440, 465, 479, 502, 549, 558
  Catholic Church, 511
  clan system, 508
Romantic language, 558
Romantic love, 196
Rome, 471
  ancient, 511
  Republican, 188, 206
Romer, A. S., 44
Roscoe, John, 442
Rosenthal, J. T., 209
Rostovtzeff, M. I., 426
Royal crown, 285
  sceptre, 285
Runes, 477
Runic stone, 262
Rust, Dr. Alfred, 259

Sabbath, Christian, 247
Sacrifice, 258 ff.